WITHDRAWN
UTSA LIBRARIES

Weapons
Proliferation
in the 1990s

A *WASHINGTON QUARTERLY* READER

Weapons Proliferation in the 1990s

edited by

BRAD ROBERTS

The MIT Press
Cambridge, Massachusetts
London, England

The contents of this book were first published in *The Washington Quarterly* (ISSN 0163–660X), a publication of The MIT Press under the sponsorship of The Center for Strategic and International Studies (CSIS). Except as otherwise noted, copyright in each article is owned jointly by the Massachusetts Institute of Technology and CSIS. No article may be reproduced in whole or in part except with the express written permission of The MIT Press.

Roger C. Molander and Peter A. Wilson, "On Dealing with the Prospect of Nuclear Chaos," *TWQ* 17, no. 3 (Summer 1994); Henry D. Sokolski, "Nonapocalyptic Proliferation: A New Strategic Threat?" *TWQ* 17, no. 2 (Spring 1994); Patrick J. Garrity, "Implications of the Persian Gulf War for Regional Powers," *TWQ* 16, no. 3 (Summer 1993); Aaron Karp, "The Arms Trade Revolution: The Major Impact of Small Arms," *TWQ* 17, no. 4 (Autumn 1994); Michael Moodie, "Beyond Proliferation: The Challenge of Technology Diffusion—A Research Survey," *TWQ* 18, no. 2 (Spring 1995); George Rathjens, "Rethinking Nuclear Proliferation," *TWQ* 18, no. 1 (Winter 1995); Mitchell Reiss, "The Last Nuclear Summit?" *TWQ* 17, no. 3 (Summer 1994); Gary K. Bertsch and Richard T. Cupitt, "Nonproliferation in the 1990s: Enhancing International Cooperation on Export Controls," *TWQ* 16, no. 4 (Autumn 1993); Harald Müller and Mitchell Reiss, "Counter-proliferation: Putting New Wine in Old Bottles," *TWQ* 18, no. 2 (Spring 1995); Lewis A. Dunn, "Rethinking the Nuclear Equation: The United States and the New Nuclear Powers," *TWQ* 17, no. 1 (Winter 1994); George H. Quester and Victor A. Utgoff, "Toward an International Nuclear Security Policy," *TWQ* 17, no. 4 (Autumn 1994); Gary L. Guertner, "Deterrence and Conventional Military Forces," *TWQ* 16, no. 1 (Winter 1993); Paul R. S. Gebhard, "Not by Diplomacy or Defense Alone: The Role of Regional Security Strategies in U.S. Proliferation Policy," *TWQ* 18, no. 1 (Winter 1995); Charles T. Allan, "Extended Conventional Deterrence: In from the Cold and Out of the Nuclear Fire?—A Research Survey," *TWQ* 17, no. 3 (Summer 1994); Brad Roberts, "Arms Control and the End of the Cold War," *TWQ* 15, no. 4 (Autumn 1992); Jonathan Dean, "The Final Stage of Nuclear Arms Control," *TWQ* 17, no. 4 (Autumn 1994); Graham S. Pearson, "Prospects for Chemical and Biological Arms Control: The Web of Deterrence," *TWQ* 16, no. 2 (Spring 1993). © British Crown Copyright 1992/MOD. Published with the permission of the Controller of Her Britannic Majesty's Stationery Office. David A. Kay, "Denial and Deception Practices of WMD Proliferators: Iraq and Beyond," *TWQ* 18, no. 1 (Winter 1995); Stephanie G. Neuman, "Controlling the Arms Trade: Idealistic Dream or Realpolitik?" *TWQ* 16, no. 3 (Summer 1993); Edward J. Laurance, "The UN Register of Conventional Arms: Rationales and Prospects for Compliance and Effectiveness," *TWQ* 16, no. 2 (Spring 1993); Avner Cohen and Marvin Miller, "How to Think About—and Implement—Nuclear Arms Control in the Middle East," *TWQ* 16, no. 2 (Spring 1993); John R. Redick, Julio C. Carasales, and Paulo S. Wrobel, "Nuclear Rapprochement: Argentina, Brazil, and the Nonproliferation Regime," *TWQ* 18, no. 1 (Winter 1995); Andrew Mack and Pauline Kerr, "The Evolving Security Discourse in the Asia–Pacific," *TWQ* 18, no. 1 (Winter 1995). Reprinted by permission of Westview Press from *Pacific Cooperation: Building Economic and Security Regimes in the Asia–Pacific Region*, edited by Andrew Mack and John Ravenhill. Copyright © 1995 Westview Press, Boulder, Colorado. Shahram Chubin, "The South and the New World Order," *TWQ* 16, no. 4 (Autumn 1993); Paul W. Schroeder, "The New World Order: A Historical Perspective," *TWQ* 17, no. 2 (Spring 1994); Brad Roberts, "1995 and the End of the Post–Cold War Era," *TWQ* 18, no. 1 (Winter 1995).

Selection and introduction, copyright © 1995 by the Center for Strategic and International Studies and the Massachusetts Institute of Technology.

All rights reserved. No part of this book may be reproduced in any form or by any means, electronic or mechanical, including photocopying, recording, or by any information storage and retrieval system, without permission in writing from The MIT Press. For information please address the Subsidiary Rights Manager, The MIT Press, Journals Department, 55 Hayward Street, Cambridge, MA 02142; e-mail: journals-rights@mit.edu.

Library of Congress Cataloging-in-Publication Data

Weapons proliferation in the 1990s / edited by Brad Roberts.
    p.   cm. — (A Washington quarterly reader)
    Includes bibliographical references.
    ISBN 0-262-68086-6 (pbk. : alk. paper)
    1. Arms race. 2. Arms control. 3. World politics—1989–
I. Roberts, Brad. II. Series.
UA10.W42 1995
327.1'74—dc20
                                                  95-12462
                                                CIP

Library
University of Texas
at San Antonio

Contents

vi

Introduction

WEAPONS PROLIFERATION HAS emerged as a preeminent issue of international security in the 1990s. Myriad events have attracted attention to the subject well beyond that of decades past, including the discovery of Iraq's advanced unconventional weapons programs; the collapse of the Soviet Union and the emergence of new nuclear states and the associated problems of uncontrolled weapons, materials, and expertise; and the crisis over North Korea's nuclear program. The new concern about proliferation has translated into increased interest in the analytical community in the subject, as well as renewed vigor among policymakers in the application of public policies aimed at preventing such proliferation.

The new prominence of the proliferation issue has also cast a harsh light on the conventional wisdoms that prevail in the analytical and policy communities. Traditional ways of thinking about the problem, as well as long-standing policy approaches, appear increasingly disconnected from the real nature of the problem as it exists in the 1990s. There is a risk not only of misunderstanding the problem but also of pursuing policies that are not merely wrongheaded but actually counterproductive.

But recognition of the limited utility of conventional wisdoms has stimulated a good deal of rethinking of the proliferation subject. The conceptual framework embodied in the traditional nuclear nonproliferation approach has been opened up to a much larger set of ideas and perspectives. This new thinking stands out as some of the best in the analytical community on the challenges of post–cold war international security.

The Washington Quarterly has been fortunate to serve as a venue for the publication of much of this new thinking. A journal of international public policy issues published by the MIT Press for the Center for Strategic and International Studies of Washington, D.C., *The Washington Quarterly* has a broad intellectual purview. Proliferation issues are but one cluster of themes given sustained attention by the journal as part of a broader effort to stimulate readers to think afresh about statecraft, international security, and, more broadly, the international engagement of the United States. Other compendiums of articles from the journal have appeared in recent years: *The New Democracies: Global Change and U.S. Policy* (Cambridge, Mass.: MIT Press, 1990); *U.S. Foreign Policy After the Cold War* (Cambridge, Mass.: MIT Press, 1992); and *U.S. Security in an Uncertain Era* (Cambridge, Mass.: MIT Press, 1993). Two more are forthcoming in 1995: *Order and Disorder After the Cold War* and *The New World Economic Order.*

The chapters included in this volume appeared in the journal between summer 1991 and spring 1995, spanning the period between the end of the Persian Gulf War and the extension conference of the Nuclear Non-Proliferation Treaty (NPT). Their organization here into chapters suggests an orderliness to the original editorial plan where none existed. We have simply set out over recent years to capture some of the best new thinking on the subject and we present it here in cumulative form. This means that our coverage of the issue is not comprehensive. It also means that for lack of space a large number of articles on closely related subjects are not republished in this volume. Readers with particular areas of interest are encouraged to use the index provided at the end of the autumn issue each year to uncover some of those other pieces.

Chapter I identifies the changing dimensions of the proliferation subject. The articles in it address a number of basic questions: Does the nuclear dimension remain paramount? What are the long-term implications of nuclear proliferation in a more multipolar world? What new proliferation risks have emerged in recent years? What political motivations drive the ambitions of states seeking to acquire new weapons capabilities? How is the arms trade changing and what is the impact of small arms? How should the ongoing diffusion of militarily significant technology change thinking about the proliferation subject?

These articles demonstrate the ways in which the inherited exclusive focus on nuclear weapons must give way to a broader understanding of the technical and political features of proliferation in the 1990s. Please note that Michael Moodie's article on technology diffusion was crafted as a research survey and thus has a character and style slightly different from the rest. [Each issue of *The Washington Quarterly* concludes with a survey of recent and ongoing research on an issue of emerging policy salience.]

Chapter II evaluates the role of nonproliferation policy in the 1990s. Basic questions include: What are the prospects for the NPT in the years and decades ahead? How important was the cold war strategic context to the past functioning of the NPT? How can strategies of technology denial be recrafted to cope with the emergence of new technology suppliers?

This chapter highlights the urgent need for significant policy innovations if nonproliferation policies are to continue to be effective in future years.

Chapter III describes the emerging debate about counterproliferation. Its component articles address two sets of questions. The first relates to the consequences of proliferation for U.S. security: What are the ambitions of the new nuclear powers? What are proliferation's implications for collective security and power projection strategies? The second relates to specific issues of U.S. security policy: Is counterproliferation a promising initiative or a dangerous departure in policy? Can the United States rely on conventional deterrence of new nuclear powers or are nuclear responses also a necessary part of the strategy? Can regional security approaches ameliorate the proliferation problem?

This chapter depicts the variety of ways in which people think about the counterproliferation issue in the United States and overseas. It reveals a deep, continuing debate about the implications of proliferation for U.S. defense policy. It also raises basic questions about the degree to which cold war–vintage thinking about deterrence is applicable to the post–cold war proliferation challenge. This chapter includes a second research survey, this one by Charles T. Allan on extended deterrence.

Chapter IV reveals the prominent new role of arms control in meeting the proliferation challenges of the 1990s. Basic questions include the following: Is the past distinction between arms control and nonproliferation still meaningful in the 1990s? How should the long-term goal of global nuclear control be reconceived? What are the prospects for the effective control of chemical and biological weapons? What are the mechanisms for stronger control of the trade in conventional weapons? What lessons arise from Iraq's denial and deception practices for future arms control?

This chapter underscores both the promise and limits of arms control in the post–cold war context. Special prominence is given to new initiatives on regional arms control and the often ignored experience of countries outside the East–West context in finding local solutions to proliferation problems.

Chapter V addresses the politics of proliferation in the post–cold war era. Shahram Chubin's article, "The South and the New World Order," explores ways of thinking about proliferation usually misunderstood by policymakers in the United States and other developed countries. Chubin emphasizes particularly the risks in a strategy that gives undue prominence to the proliferation concerns of the North. Paul W. Schroeder's article, "The New World Order: A Historical Perspective," offers a powerful critique of the new world *dis*order debate and the tendency to misuse the proliferation theme to create a false picture of a world adrift and headed toward chaos. He cautions that efforts to apply cold war–vintage solutions to post–cold war problems of conflict may create the very problem they are intended to prevent. My own article, "1995 and the End of the Post–Cold War Era," provides an essentially political description of the proliferation problem and describes the international political agenda playing out in the mid-1990s.

These three articles underscore the way in which the proliferation subject has become a vehicle for discussing larger issues of international security and the U.S. world role in the wake of the Cold War. They also cast significant doubt on the wisdom of traditional approaches that emphasize almost exclusively nuclear nonproliferation.

Please note that authors have not been given the opportunity to update their articles subsequent to their original publication. Although parts of some essays have necessarily been overtaken by events, each contribution makes arguments that remain relevant in any assessment of the new proliferation agenda. Please note further that all biographies are current to the time of original publication. The views expressed here are those of the authors alone and should not be attributed to any institutions with which they are affiliated or to the publishers, CSIS and MIT Press.

This volume reflects a great deal of patient inquiry and hard work by the authors whose articles are included here. It also reflects the skill and dedication of those talented individuals who have served in the editorial office of *The Washington Quarterly* during the period in which these articles were published, including particularly Yoma Ullman, James Rutherford, Denise Miller, and Lynn Northcutt de Vega. Translating good new ideas into a written product accessible to many is a challenging and often difficult task, and I wish to thank the authors and editors who have made it a successful and rewarding task as well.

Brad Roberts
Washington, D.C.
March 1, 1995

I. Proliferation's Changing Dimensions

On Dealing with the Prospect of Nuclear Chaos

Roger C. Molander and Peter A. Wilson

THE FOLLOWING ESSAY represents an attempt to stand back and take stock of the possible role of nuclear weapons in the international security environments that may unfold in the course of the next generation—say, the next 20 to 25 years.[1]

Although considerable rhetorical emphasis has of late been given to concern about the threat of nuclear weapons proliferation—and the Clinton administration has taken action in the case of North Korea and Ukraine in an effort to roll back two troubling new nuclear arsenals—it is not clear that President Bill Clinton and his senior advisers or the national security leadership in Congress have a strategic vision as to the ultimate objective of efforts in this critical post–cold war strategy and policy arena. Yet the United States faces a major, urgent challenge. It must foster and sustain a process leading to a new post–cold war strategy and associated policies regard-

ing nuclear weapons. This requires moving the post–cold war global nuclear security environment toward greater international integration by both declaratory policy and perceptible measures and by an accompanying deemphasis of nuclear weapons as a flagship element of national security. The initiatives called for to achieve such ends will almost certainly demand considerable political, economic, and military investment, if not sacrifice, in the face of powerful secular trends that appear to be moving the planet more toward conditions of chaos, especially in the political arena.

Overview

The first 50 years of the nuclear age were dominated by the Cold War. Its end, wrought by the spectacular, and by any historical measure dramatically fast collapse of the Soviet Union, created a *profound* discontinuity in the international security environment. The unexpectedly abrupt disappearance of the bipolar international security framework that had guided national security thinking in so many countries for so long caught nations and alliances by surprise—and wholly unprepared to consider the menu of security options that events now thrust before them. Nations once secure in the framework and discipline of a bipolar cold war standoff were abruptly

Roger C. Molander is a consultant on international nuclear security issues. He was a member of the U.S. National Security Council staff in the Nixon, Ford, and Carter administrations. Peter A. Wilson is a consultant on international security affairs. He served on the Policy Planning Staff in the U.S. Department of State in the Carter administration.

Copyright © 1994 by The Center for Strategic and International Studies and the Massachusetts Institute of Technology

forced, guided by the instinct of survival, not just to look at new alliances, but also to reassess self-reliance for security—and therefore to consider or reconsider obtaining some measure of nuclear weapons capability.

In its triggering events the end of the Cold War also unleashed centrifugal forces that not only immediately increased the number of states possessing nuclear weapons but also set in motion a virtually certain dispersion of nuclear weapons-related know-how and personnel. That dispersion—the telltale signs of which are starting to appear—will surge into a world that already had the character (thanks to the global spread of commercial nuclear power) of a nuclear supersaturated system—a virtual nuclear weapons cloud chamber where the entry of a small team (and plausibly even an individual) from the former Soviet nuclear weapons or ballistic missile development/production complex could dramatically alter a nation's nuclear weapons capability and thus its strategic position regionally or globally.[2]

Further complicating the challenge posed by this image of the future is what might be called the legacy of Rio—the inescapable global turning away from fossil fuels that is dictated by deteriorating global atmospheric conditions, punctuated politically by the United Nations (UN) Conference on Environment and Development held in Rio de Janeiro in 1992. This "why take the chance?" imperative to reduce dependence on fossil fuels occurs, unfortunately, in a context in which nuclear power is still the only universally available alternative with the potential to meet projected energy and energy security demands in many important parts of the developed and developing world.[3]

It seems clear that within the next two or three decades, maybe four at the very outside, we will move rapidly as a civilization through what might be called the middle years of the learning curve of the nuclear age. This will bring us to a state in which virtually any industrialized nation will have the scientific infrastructure and other wherewithal necessary to produce indigenously both nuclear weapons and associated modern delivery vehicles (probably, if deemed necessary, covertly by current inspection standards), and at an economically affordable cost.[4]

How many nations will maintain nuclear arsenals "at-the-ready"—available for use in minutes or a day or two at most—when the planet reaches that state? How many will openly maintain virtual nuclear arsenals—arsenals that by plan (prepositioning of materials, training of personnel, etc.) can be reliably built or assembled inside a nation's particular notional strategic warning time (that time, presumably a matter of weeks or months, for the appearance of dire political-military threats)? Which of these will be overt, and which covert? What military role or function will nations proclaim to themselves and others for their at-the-ready and/or consciously planned virtual nuclear arsenals? What uncertainty will there be—and what might be "acceptable" to national security planners or treaty monitors—about the degree to which a nation is nuclear-armed?

In thinking through these questions, we begin with a certain premise: For the future of conflict between human beings, the most important issue is *choosing* an asymptotic long-term goal (or plausibly achievable end state) for the nuclear weapons component of the nuclear age.[5] This choice must be squarely faced now.

By its nature the above premise demands that careful attention be given to the articulation and consideration of alternative nuclear asymptotes or end states *and* the ability of the United States to effect one or another of these possible futures. The body of this essay is directed to the framing of this alternative end states problem analytically and politically.

In the essay four illustrative alternative asymptotes are presented for consideration (and by implication for interpolation and extrapolation):

- *"High Entropy" Deterrence*—a highly proliferated world with few rules of the nuclear road, save possibly an enduring (if successful) cultural taboo on nuclear use that relies, inter alia, on an expanding web of bipolar or multipolar international deterrence relationships to keep the nuclear peace;
- *An Ever-Slowly-Expanding Nuclear Club*—acceptance of an inexorable slow growth in the number of nuclear-armed states, with new members of the club grudgingly (or sometimes willingly) integrated into the existing nuclear order and carefully educated to a set of nuclear norms of behavior and associated concepts of deterrence and balance;
- *A Two-Tiered Static "Have-a-Lot/ Have-None" International System*—a handful of "haves" maintain substantial (but limited by treaty) at-the-ready nuclear arsenals and commit themselves individually and/or collectively (most likely through the UN Security Council) as explicitly as necessary to maintaining the security of the "have-nots"; or
- *The "Virtual Abolition" of Nuclear Arsenals*—virtual elimination of existing at-the-ready nuclear arsenals (a handful of states maintain tens to hundreds of nuclear weapons at-the-ready) underwritten by an unprecedented comprehensive and

highly intrusive international inspection and collective enforcement regime.

In essence, the four asymptotic states, with their emphasis on the nuclear dimension of the international environment, are consistent with the broader view that each end state represents different levels of planetary political and economic integration or disintegration. Figure 1 displays a summary description of these four states. An elaboration of their major features follows.

Alternative Futures

"High Entropy" Deterrence

The "high entropy" deterrence state could well be the product of a post–cold war era during which the United States turns progressively inward and away from forceful involvement in an increasingly turbulent world that is slowly accelerating away from the order of the Cold War and into a period of increased international, political, economic, and military fragmentation. In such a world, many states could conclude that the possession of a nuclear arsenal is a reasonable answer to the real or imagined threat of regional or global predators. Although bilateral or multilateral nuclear arms-control agreements might seek to stabilize the size and character of at least at-the-ready nuclear arsenals, nations possessing such nuclear arsenals or substantial virtual nuclear arsenal capability would presumably go to great lengths to make such arsenals survivable against preemptive attack. In the worst case there might even be a number of small arsenals controlled by non-state entities, such as international criminal organizations and polit-

Figure 1
Alternative Nuclear End States

Plausible Nuclear Asymptotes (End States)	At-The-Ready Arsenals		Virtual Arsenals	Other Key Characteristics
1. *"High Entropy" Deterrence.* • Highly nuclear proliferated world • Many at-the-ready and virtual nuclear arsenals • Few "rules of the nuclear road" • Bilateral and multilateral deterrence relationships	U.S./Rus China/Ukr UK/France Israel/Ind/Pak Ten+ nations	5,000+ 1,000+ 100s 100+ 10s	Not relevant to major nuclear powers; state of many virtual arsenals unknown	• Weak international security system • Mixed national counterproliferation responses (defenses, counterforce, power projection adaptation, and/or neo-isolationism)
2. *An Ever-Slowly-Expanding Nuclear Club.* • Inexorable growth in no. of nuclear-armed states • New nuclear "club" members integrated and educated on "norms of behavior" • Little improvement in NPT inspection regime	U.S./Rus China UK/France Israel Ind/Pak Others	3,000 1,000 500+ 200 100+ 10s–100s	Not of concern to major nuclear powers; relevant to minor powers and others (e.g., Japan, Germany, Ukraine)	• No major change in current int'l security system • Little improvement in IAEA • Some counterproliferation responses constrained by arms control
3. *A Two-Tiered Static "Have-a-Lot/Have None" International System.* • "Idealized NPT": "Haves" (presumably UNSC PermFive) maintain substantial but treaty-limited arsenals	U.S./Rus China UK/France Others	2,000 600 400 0	300–1,000 in months 100–300 in months 100–300 in months 10s in weeks to months	• Strengthened int'l security system with new sec'y guarantees • Improved NPT regime (inspection & enforcement) • Counterproliferation deemphasized
4. *Virtual Abolition of Nuclear Arsenals.* • Deemphasis of military nuclear roles/missions • A few states maintain up to 100s of at-the-ready nuclear weapons (e.g., a global total of 1,000) to deter breakout	U.S./Rus China UK/France Others	300 200 100 0	200–400 in months 50–100 in months 50–100 in months 10s in months	• Robust int'l security system (great powers agree on "nuclear order") • Comprehensive/intrusive/relentless inspection and enforcement regime • Robust counterproliferation investment

ical or religious groups, that would take advantage of the increasingly challenging nuclear weapons control problem—or that might in a crisis (like the loss of central control in some nuclear-armed state) appear out of no-where. Defining international stability would be problematic.

The world of many nuclear-armed entities might emerge slowly over a transition period during which there is no use of nuclear weapons—in which case there could be growing confidence in the lasting viability, and the breadth of application, of nuclear weapons-based deterrence.[6]

Some variant of this end state might emerge from a dramatic demonstration of the military and political utility of nuclear weapons, for example, a war that leaves a clear victor *thanks to* use of nuclear weapons and no meaningful punitive response from the international community. In this situation nuclear weapons would be given a powerful legitimacy, especially if the use had not been catastrophic. Such an outcome would shatter any nuclear use taboo and could trigger a period of hyperproliferation as many states moved deliberately designed or inherent virtual arsenals much closer to operational status.

An Ever-*Slowly*-Expanding Nuclear Club

By definition the asymptote of an ever-*slowly*-expanding nuclear club is a slow growth curve along which the major powers of the international community *slowly* accept new nuclear-armed states. In essence, this end state is a description of the history of nuclear weapons proliferation during the first 50 years of the nuclear age and the current, late-twentieth-century circumstance. The fundamental assumption of this possible end state is that the process of nuclear proliferation can remain a slow-motion affair, with new entrants achieving acceptance in the nuclear club only after a protracted period.

In all cases, the security concerns of the new entrants to this choice of regime would take on broader legitimacy as the major powers (and, more important, the declared nuclear weapon states) tolerated and even helped ra-

tionalize the gradual appearance of a new nuclear-armed state or states.

To facilitate this process of gradual expansion, a variety of regional arms-control arrangements might well be negotiated by the new entrants to achieve new regional nuclear deterrence balances. The success of this strategy would be highly contingent upon the new entrants' accepting an internationally defined set of rules of the nuclear road and possibly some rationalized deterrence relationship(s). An underlying rationale for considering this kind of asymptote is the perspective that the United States may well be in the position of trying to make a virtue of necessity—that the process of the proliferation of nuclear-armed states is inevitable, and especially so in an environment or under conditions where the UN or a nuclear-armed power like the United States is not prepared to provide insecure states with credible extended deterrence guarantees. As with any two-tiered system, the international political legitimacy of this approach, in which "some will sit in judgment on others' needs," is somewhat shaky and viable only insofar as tested by time and experience.

The obvious first step under this asymptote would be to accept Pakistan, India, and Israel as official members of the nuclear club, legitimizing the Israeli and Pakistani arguments that a state without powerful and reliable allies should be able to compensate for its conventional military inferiority vis-à-vis some threat by deploying a nuclear arsenal. India would presumably find the rationale for its arsenal in classic bilateral nuclear deterrence concepts vis-à-vis Pakistan and/or China.[7]

Overt acceptance of Israel as a nuclear-armed state would undoubtedly further stimulate nuclear weapons programs among the Arab states and Iran so that a predictable sequel would be the eventual demand to grant legitimacy to, say, nuclear arsenals in Iraq and Iran. Crafting a three-party strategic nuclear balance among these three "greater Middle East" regional adversaries (which would rationalize the size of their at-the-ready arsenals) exemplifies the challenges that could be faced in the relative near term if the rate of expansion of the nuclear club remains slow.

A Two-Tiered *Static* "Have-a-Lot/ Have-None" System

A two-tiered, *static,* "have-a-lot/have-none" (hereinafter "have" and "have not") international system is still the implicit goal (and at times somewhat shakily proclaimed status quo) of the current international nonproliferation regime. One fundamental problem of this two-tiered system as currently constituted is the fading legitimacy of its basis: the five major powers on the winning side in World War II and the five Permanent Members of the UN Security Council are the five declared nuclear-armed states—the "haves" that this choice of preferred end state would presumably try to perpetuate.

One key to the viability of this kind of two-tiered system is thus the viability of the current composition of the Security Council. The difficulty of changing this arrangement, for instance, by adding Japan, Germany, and possibly India and Brazil as permanent members, will only be made more complex by the nuclear issue.[8]

In terms of the problems posed by India, Israel, and Pakistan, the existence of nuclear weapons in these nations is no longer questioned in public or private debate and discussion. Thus as a variant of the basic approach of

this alternative asymptote it might be possible to grandfather these three nations into the Nuclear Non-Proliferation Treaty (NPT) in a second tier of "haves" that agree, maybe in an NPT II, to accept severe limits on the size of their at-the-ready arsenals, greater transparency in their nuclear programs so as to limit their potential to mobilize a virtual nuclear arsenal, and a commitment to become a "have-not" in some long term. Whether the global community would insist on more explicit and restrictive limits on the size of the arsenals of the Permanent Five, or on greater transparency in their nuclear weapons programs, would remain to be seen.

Whether it would prove enforceable is another open question. It is important to acknowledge that the ongoing effort to eliminate Iraq's weapons of mass destruction capability is probably sui generis and may not amount to a real precedent. A posture among the Permanent Five that will permit their taking action in future regional crises of this character or on challenges of suspect violators cannot necessarily be guaranteed.

The "Virtual Abolition" of Nuclear Arsenals

The "virtual abolition" option reflects a view that in the post–cold war world the United States and other nuclear-armed nations could, and maybe in their own long-term interests should, abandon their current degree of dependence on nuclear weapons. In the U.S. military, for example, there appears to be a rising belief that a United States properly armed with conventional weapons may not need to rely on thousands of at-the-ready nuclear weapons to satisfy its future defense and deterrence needs (*assuming* continued improvement, however slow, in the U.S.–Russian political-military relationship); indeed, there appears to be a preference for this state of affairs. At the same time, looking to the future threat environment, there is a rapidly growing appreciation that a small nuclear arsenal in the hands of a regional predator (such as Iraq in 1991) would present any U.S. or U.S.-led military force with a daunting set of basic military problems. From this conjunction of factors there emerges an interest in exploring what it would take to deemphasize in a profound fashion the role of at-the-ready nuclear arsenals in international security.[9]

In such a context of nuclear deemphasis, one clear question is how far existing at-the-ready arsenals would need to be reduced to market the concept versus how far such arsenals can or should be reduced against an array of stability concerns. One possible approach along such lines would be to eliminate all nuclear weapons save for a handful of very small nuclear arsenals (e.g., a total of no more than a thousand weapons worldwide) in the hands of a carefully chosen set of nations, for example, the permanent members of the UN Security Council. Such an approach would require a body such as the Security Council to assume far-reaching, unprecedented, and highly intrusive responsibilities associated with early warning and the attendant enforcement measures as part of a new grand bargain on the nuclear weapons dimension of international security. Such roles might be extrapolated from the measures taken in Desert Shield/Desert Storm and the UN Special Commission (UNSCOM) created by Security Council resolution 687 in Iraq.

The constellation of very small (and highly survivable) nuclear arsenals would be designed to be the lid on the jar—a deterrent and hedge against any nuclear arsenal breakout. Accompanying this at-the-ready force would be careful, conscious thought and sustained attention to virtual nuclear arsenals. Two questions should stand out:

- What level of nuclear monitoring and thus intrusiveness and persuasiveness is necessary to ensure adequate early warning (e.g., months) of breakout efforts in any nation (including in those nations that possess small at-the-ready arsenals)?

- What virtual nuclear capability would be necessary to enable the United States, other nations with small at-the-ready arsenals, and possibly other selected nations (e.g., other UN Security Council members), faced with the necessity of responding to particularly heinous nuclear breakout scenarios, to be able to rebuild or build large nuclear arsenals (into the thousands if necessary) with full production beginning in a relatively short time (e.g., a matter of months)?

In providing very early warning of illegal nuclear weapons programs, the highly intrusive inspections would be designed to give the international community time for diplomatic action and to build consensus for emergency sanctions, and if necessary urgent (conventional) military actions, against newly discovered outlaw programs.

It is implicit in the level of nuclear order that would exist in this end state that substantial cooperation between the major powers—however armed—would be an imperative. The sturdy child of this common interest should be a sustaining major power interest in (and responsibility for) a broader range of global order and especially the *containment* of regional or even national crises in terms of the character, degree, geographical extent, and geographical impact of their violence. A nuclear civil war would likely be tragic for more than just the nation in turmoil.

The feasibility of this potential end state rests on the notion that potential proliferators can be convinced that at-the-ready nuclear weapons are in fact unnecessary to assure their national security—that under a virtual abolition regime, threats to national security, whether conventional or nuclear, would diminish sufficiently to render conventional defense and multifaceted security guarantees viable means of maintaining security and independence.

The Present Nuclear Vantage Point

In order to evaluate these alternatives, and to underscore the importance now of seeking to choose among them, a long-term perspective is necessary, one that starts at the very beginning of the nuclear age in order to reveal the potential role of nuclear weapons in the context of current challenges and opportunities. This will also help to define a strategy for getting from here to there.

Nuclear Weapons Production

In the immediate aftermath of the bombing of Hiroshima and Nagasaki, as the world confronted the implications of the development and use of atomic bombs to end World War II, it was poignantly clear to the Manhattan Project scientists that they stood on the cusp of an inescapable global nuclear weapons learning curve. Although there was considerable uncertainty as to when that curve would steepen and the number of nations with the indigenous wherewithal to

build nuclear weapons rapidly increase, there was little doubt in their minds that humanity would in time, be it over decades or generations, reach such a point. They clearly recognized that the biggest atomic secret of all—that weapons that harnessed the energy of the atomic nucleus could actually be built—was out of the box with Alamagordo and demonstrated for all to see at Hiroshima. They understandably wondered where it would end.

On the heels of the question of the rate of growth in indigenous capability came the companion question of just how many countries would exploit their newfound nuclear capability and build and maintain nuclear weapons for at-the-ready nuclear arsenals (see figure 2). A derivative concern was the question of how many nations might not appear nuclear-armed but might consciously and covertly lay plans to take a virtual nuclear arsenal to an at-the-ready state inside some notional strategic warning time.

As the United States considers where such learning curves stand today, it must recognize that the point may soon be reached at which a nation's virtual nuclear arsenal capability will be almost as important a metric as that nuclear arsenal it maintains at-the-ready. Figure 3 portrays the virtual arsenal concept as a function of the time required to bring nuclear forces to a ready-to-shoot status.

Figure 4 bears further testimony to this potential by highlighting the prospect that Japan's growing plutonium stockpile (and associated handling facilities), married to its substantial and growing satellite launch capability, could form the basis for an impressive virtual nuclear arsenal within the next 20 to 30 years (assuming that the Japanese would be prepared to accept the

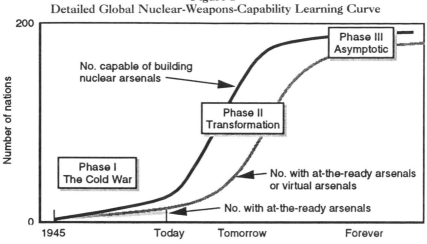

Figure 2
Detailed Global Nuclear-Weapons-Capability Learning Curve

Source: Molander and Wilson, *The Nuclear Asymptote*, p. 12.

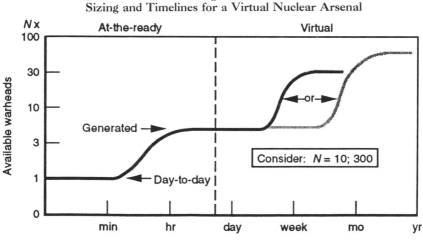

Figure 3
Sizing and Timelines for a Virtual Nuclear Arsenal

Source: Molander and Wilson, *The Nuclear Asymptote*, p. 13.

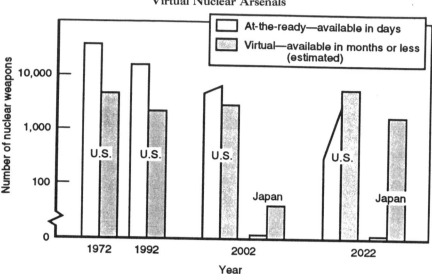

Figure 4
A Notional Comparison of U.S. and Japanese At-the-Ready and
Virtual Nuclear Arsenals

Source: Molander and Wilson, *The Nuclear Asymptote,* p. 13.

reduced yields of weapons made of reactor-grade plutonium).

The success of the Manhattan Project and of nuclear weapons in quickly ending the war with Japan drove home for everyone both the feasibility of developing nuclear weapons and their value. The United States immediately went to extraordinary ends—manifest in the 1947 Atomic Energy Act—to deny the acquisition of nuclear weapons know-how and capability by other nations for as long as possible. The Soviet nuclear test in 1949, however, and the British test in 1952 made it clear that there was going to be no U.S. monopoly on nuclear weapons, and U.S. efforts shifted to establishing and maintaining global superiority in this military realm.

In this same time frame the idea emerged in the United States that nations that might otherwise get on a nuclear weapons path could be enticed onto a more appealing commercial nuclear power path through the utopian reward of energy too cheap to meter. With the clarity of hindsight, pursuit of this idea—manifest in the mid-1950s in the U.S. Atoms for Peace plan—looks like one of the worst decisions of the nuclear age. Although the plan did draw many nations into the world of commercial nuclear power, the promised yellow brick road to cheap power (and peace) faded with the recognition of the complexity and cost of producing safe nuclear power plants and the challenge of disposing of nuclear waste—leaving in its wake a host of countries with a maturing nuclear infrastructure and unfortunately much of the basic nuclear know-how required to launch a serious nuclear weapons program. France unambiguously proved the dual-use value of this technology by exploding a nuclear weapon in 1960.

During this period, U.S. policymakers and military strategists were becoming increasingly concerned that the long-feared steepening of the at-the-ready or virtual nuclear arsenal curves of figure 2 was about to take place. It did not. President John F. Kennedy was not alone in his oft-cited estimate or admonition that there could be as many as 20 nuclear-armed states in 20 years, but the nations that might have launched nuclear weapons programs in this time frame were instead bought off or politically fenced off from such development by the U.S. deployment of theater nuclear weapons and the extended deterrence promise of shelter under the U.S. nuclear umbrella—or by the imposed nuclear umbrella of the Soviet-controlled Warsaw Pact. Nations that might otherwise have built nuclear weapons were persuaded not only to keep their nuclear efforts directed to nuclear power, but also to join in a global effort—eventually labeled the nuclear nonproliferation regime—to erect a comprehensive set of limitations (treaties, inspections, export constraints, etc.) that would deny or restrain access to key nuclear weapons-related technologies and materials.

The nuclear nonproliferation regime, anchored by the Nuclear Non-Proliferation Treaty completed in 1968, at least for a time did its job. Although China's explosion of a nuclear weapon in 1964 was not good news, it was no real surprise that the Chinese had made this political commitment and were able to mount the scientific and industrial effort to achieve nuclear club status. The fact that Israel in this same time frame was also achieving nuclear weapons capability—and that Sweden was planning a virtual nuclear arsenal—would have been more troubling and a clearer intimation of things to come if the Israeli and Swedish secrets had been less well kept.

India's explosion of a nuclear device in 1974, clearly with the aid of technology and materials procured under the guise of a peaceful nuclear power program, was a profoundly troubling development. It demonstrated that a nation with a sound scientific infrastructure and a nuclear power program, even if economically strapped, could covertly develop nuclear weapons. (Almost 20 years later Iraq, only in the middle tier of nations in terms of gross national product and also burdened by the cost of a long and difficult war with Iran, proved that point even more starkly with a highly advanced nuclear weapons program—and that achieved covertly in spite of being an NPT signatory.)

In this same period two other Asian nations—South Korea and Taiwan—also pursued serious nuclear weapons programs but in the mid-1970s they were leaned on heavily by the United States and the programs were halted, or at least went underground. The prospect that in spite of the NPT and safeguards imposed by the International Atomic Energy Agency (IAEA) nations other than Iraq might have advanced covert nuclear weapons programs, is one of the intangible but worrisome problems of the steep part of the growth curve in the global spread of the ability to build nuclear weapons. This capacity for clandestine development by a medium-sized power was also revealed by South Africa during 1993 with its confession that it had developed six nuclear weapons in a home-grown program in the face of severe international economic sanctions.

Contrary to this growth trend are the three nonproliferation success stories—Brazil, Argentina, and most recently South Africa. To all appearances, all three have now abandoned active nuclear weapons programs and appear ready to accept inspection programs that would provide substantial warning if they were to restart them. All three countries now presumably view their regional security circumstances as much improved compared to the period in which they launched their programs.

The shock of the extraordinarily advanced character of the covert Iraqi program has shattered confidence in the ability of the IAEA and other nuclear-intelligence collection capabilities to know just what is going on globally in this realm. This no-confidence condition can be rectified among political (and military) leaders only through repeated future detection successes—a daunting challenge.

In confronting the reality of the inexorable spread of nuclear weapons know-how, it is also critically important to recognize that the actual production of nuclear weapons is becoming monotonically easier. Largely as a consequence of improvements in technologies relating to commercial nuclear power, with every year it can be assumed that the size of the key facilities is getting smaller, as is the required number of scientists and technicians, the education level of this technical cohort, the amount of electrical power consumed, the release of telltale radio nuclides, and the time for each key step in the nuclear weapons development process. (A two-story centrifuge facility covering a single city block can annually produce enough highly enriched weapons-grade uranium for roughly 10 nuclear weapons—well within the size of facilities that could be hidden in existing mountain caves or readily constructed deep underground chambers.) The

South African nuclear weapons program carried on under international embargo stands out as the current most efficient effort in this nuclear olympiad; running about 10 years and involving roughly 400 key scientists and technicians, it cost an estimated $900 million in total expenditures (a minor fraction of South Africa's annual defense expenditures).[10]

Long-Range Bombardment

Long-range delivery systems have spread simultaneously with diffusion of nuclear weapons production capability. Another technology of 50 years ago, the ground mobile tactical ballistic missile, has now matured as the long-range bombardment means of choice for many regional powers. Although the U.S.-led coalition gained air supremacy during the 1991 Persian Gulf War, the allied forces were unable to neutralize Iraq's ground mobile tactical ballistic missile, the SCUD, a variant of the German V–2. SCUDs and their launchers were very hard to find even with the exploitation of advanced surveillance means, several thousand tactical air sorties, and special forces in suspected launch sites. Public reports indicate that the United States had no confirmed kills of a SCUD missile and launcher during the counterforce campaign in spite of aircraft sorties numbering in the thousands. Although the strategic psychological performance of the Patriot surface to air missile was impressive, after-action reports suggest that the number of SCUD warhead kills it achieved was abysmally low compared to what would be required for a serious strategic defense.[11]

Moreover, future proliferators should be able to take advantage of extant cruise missile technology to produce (possibly in very large numbers) a potent alternative to the long-range ballistic missile.

Through deployment of a large ground mobile missile force in concealed or heavily fortified sites (e.g., hardened, deep underground tunnels with multiple blind portals), a medium-sized regional power will be able to field a long-range strike force that would be difficult if not impossible to kill or neutralize by regional adversaries or possibly even by a major effort by a global power like the United States backed by coalition partners.[12]

The military performance of both ballistic and cruise missiles will also improve substantially with the full global exploitation of the Global Positioning Satellite (GPS) navigation aid. This constellation of navigation satellites, along with its competitors such as the Russian Federation's GLONASS, will provide missile accuracies measured in the tens of meters as against the near-kilometer miss distance of the SCUD.

Aside from the major powers that have the capacity to build intercontinental-range (>5,500 kilometer) ballistic missiles, for example, the Russian Federation, the United States, and China, there are a wide range of states that can produce theater-range (500 to 2,000 kilometer) missiles. Notable entrants into the long-range missile club include North Korea, India, Pakistan, Iran, Israel, and Egypt. The ongoing effort to restrict the flow of missile development and production-related technology through the Missile Technology Control Regime (MTCR) has made little difference here.[13]

A Bottom Line

It can be seen from the above assessment that a rapid maturing of inherent or readily obtainable national strategic nuclear capability is now taking place within a highly dynamic international security environment. This situation enables nations—or possibly peoples—that for hundreds if not thousands of years have sought a means of guaranteeing their security to see within their grasp a powerful means by which possibly to achieve strategic security—the chance of a millennium. An unusual historical moment such as this, a testimony to the common Chinese character for chaos and opportunity, could easily, for good luck or bad, be a quick path to the world of Frank Herbert's *Dune* where the tribes explored the galaxy with the "family atomics," in whatever real or virtual state, stored safely away.

Nuclear Weapon Use

In this post–cold war context of rapidly evolving weapons capabilities and international politics, it is important to examine the potential role of nuclear weapons in conflict—and especially how they might be used by new nuclear powers. The following sections assess the character and implications of an evolving spectrum of potential scenarios regarding post–cold war nuclear weapons use.

The Prospect of Nuclear Conflict: Generic Next Use Cases

With the end of the Cold War, there is now the real prospect that local or regional conflicts (some unleashed in part by the end of the bipolar standoff) will be the most likely route to nuclear war. Three generic circumstances would appear to capture the spectrum of such scenarios for the next use of nuclear weapons and supersede in all likelihood the classic superpower nuclear exchange scenarios of the Cold War:[14]

- the loss of central control, in which a national command authority fragments during the breakup of a heretofore unitary state, raising the prospect of a nuclear civil war;
- the emergence of a nuclear-armed regional predator, in which a major power (or a major power-led alliance) intervenes to thwart some nation's expansionist or hegemonistic efforts; and
- a regional war between two newly nuclear-armed states, the so-called Nth on Nth nuclear war problem.

Each of these cases represents a class of events characteristic of the post–cold war security environment. Note that this dynamic and uncertain international security context will most likely prevail through the first decade of the twenty-first century if not well beyond. Conventional wisdom suggests that future nuclear weapon use by a new regional nuclear state is unlikely unless that state is directed by a madman.[15] Contrary to this expectation, a wide range of use scenarios are plausible and may range from brandishing a nuclear arsenal, to a variety of crisis maneuvers, to outright use of one or more nuclear weapons to bring about a powerful regional strategic effect.

Over the course of the past three years RAND has been exploring the policy implications of future nuclear crises in a post–cold war context through a series of policy exercises. Several major insights have been gained from these exercises.

- Even a very small number of nuclear weapons in the hands of an adversary will affect the behavior of the United States and its coalition partners in future regional crises. Their impact is expected to be so strong as to call into question major

conclusions in the Department of Defense's 1993 *Bottom-Up Review,* which assumes that the U.S. military should prepare to fight two *nonnuclear* Major Regional Contingencies, and dictates major changes in the operational concept, organization, and equipment of future U.S. expeditionary forces.[16]

- A regional predator will find a small nuclear arsenal a powerful tool for collapsing regional military coalitions that the United States might craft to oppose such a future opponent.
- Design and deployment of military forces capable of destroying a small nuclear arsenal or even simply neutralizing that arsenal for a time represent a prodigious military-intelligence operational challenge. This problem is even further complicated by severe budgetary restraints.
- There are no apparent technological or operational silver bullets by which to defeat the "tyranny of small numbers" manifest in small regional strategic nuclear arsenals. A robust counterproliferation capability will require a large-scale investment in a new generation of sensors, active defenses, strike systems, and special operations capabilities.
- The conduct of a future counterproliferation campaign to neutralize a small nuclear force is likely to call for an all-service capability organized by a unified command that can conduct this high-performance mission with little operational warning and at a transoceanic distance.[17]

Non- and Counterproliferation

It seems clear at this writing that the Clinton administration's nonproliferation/counterproliferation strategy remains a work in progress, hampered to some degree by the lack of consensus (and a perpetuated and increasingly sterile debate) on the distinctions between nonproliferation and counterproliferation.[18] At the presidential level, the administration has so far emphasized somewhat traditional nonproliferation initiatives and in three main areas: (1) pressing for the indefinite and unchanged renewal of the NPT treaty document during the 1995 Review and Extension Conference; (2) negotiating a global comprehensive nuclear test ban; and (3) ending the global production of weapons-grade fissile material.

The counterproliferation concept has to date been manifest formally only in a speech made by then Secretary of Defense Les Aspin on December 7, 1993, in which he announced and described a Defense Counterproliferation Initiative (DCI).[19] Although he embraced traditional nonproliferation efforts and the ongoing antitactical ballistic missile program within counterproliferation, the major new elements in Aspin's speech were the call for improved counterforce capability against weapons of mass destruction and a charge to the military services and the regional commanders in chief to describe how they would propose to fight wars against adversaries who had weapons of mass destruction. At the same time traditional nonproliferation advocates within the Department of State and the Arms Control and Disarmament Agency (ACDA) question whether the concept of counterproliferation is appropriate and constructive in the face of current nonproliferation concerns.[20]

What seems needed at this stage is a vigorous and more disciplined White House-led, administration-wide effort to develop a new U.S. national security strategy that integrates and conforms the long-term objectives of (1) an evolving U.S. regional security strategy as articulated originally in the Bush administration and further embraced and emphasized in the 1993 *Bottom-Up Review;* (2) the more traditional U.S. strategic nuclear posture with respect to the Russians and China; and (3) the U.S. nonproliferation/counterproliferation strategy. If the United States does not decide where it is going, all roads lead there.

Alternative Pathways to an Uncertain Early Twenty-First Century

We turn now to the strategic road map from here to there. "Here" is the intellectual crashing together of the three strategy components cited above. "There" is, for example, one or another of the four exemplary asymptotic states.

From Here to High Entropy

There would appear to be two separable and still credible paths to a state of nuclear high entropy that are worthy of consideration. One is very rapid, the other is in slow motion. In both cases the pathway into a nuclear well-armed future for the planet would be cleared by a conscious national and international decision to step aside and *not* invest the energy and political leverage necessary to rein in the prevailing trends in the nuclear realm. Such a posture might credibly be adopted by default by an inward-turning United States.

The domino that is likely to decide the path that a world of relatively unfettered access to nuclear weapons will take—rapid or slow—is the ongoing struggle in Eurasia between the twin forces of integration and fragmentation. In this regard the appearance of an extreme nationalist and expansionist regime in Russia would be a disaster for the prospect of containing nuclear weapons proliferation.[21]

If the outcome on that supercontinent is a return to fragmentation and extreme nationalism, it is logical that many nations will be very quick to (re)consider nuclear weapons. It is not far from the view that "the best defense is self-defense" to that of "the best (and cheapest) means of self-defense is nuclear weapons"—on the grounds (probably correct) that nobody is likely to attack a nation that has a nuclear arsenal that is survivable and reliably deliverable—the iron logic of Charles de Gaulle.

Then we face a new dilemma. Once a nation has stepped over the line from nuclear weapons potential to nuclear weapons at-the-ready (or is about to do so), is it in the broader global interest to make that new nuclear-armed state a more competent club member—as experienced drivers would, for example, a novice at the Indianapolis 500? Should that nation get the latest safety equipment—safing, fusing, and firing mechanisms? Should it be educated in how best to hide its arsenal and be given the (almost?) latest in tactical warning systems as a means of helping ensure the survivability of its nuclear deterrent in the name of regional crisis stability?

If nuclear proliferation unfolds in this way then the United States might be much more inclined to ensure that those nations that choose to become nuclear-armed are safely so, a policy that itself might further accelerate an already rapid process. In any event, the world that would result would either be highly turbulent—one worthy of the label "nuclear anarchy" or "nuclear Hobbesian world"—or very quiescent, with the widespread deployment of nuclear weapons creating an interstitial nuclear force field that keeps adversary nations apart.

Even if the forces for global integration gain dominance in Eurasia, a world with a more laissez-faire attitude toward nuclear arsenals would still move unambiguously toward a state of high entropy, but presumably at a more deliberate pace, stimulated not by a continental trend but by region-specific security problems. For example, failure to resolve the security problems of the Middle East and Persian Gulf in the relatively near future is likely to see Iran convert its growing nuclear potential as a minimum to the brink of an at-the-ready nuclear arsenal and similar steps by Iraq once it is freed from the UN inspection and monitoring regime. Similarly, in South Asia, an unfettered India and Pakistan are likely to move over time to unambiguous deployment of small arsenals and a sustained debate over an appropriate nuclear asymptote for South Asia. In East Asia, failure to achieve peaceful Korean reunification in the near term is likely to lead to an unambiguously nuclear-armed North Korea, with South Korea hard on its heels. We can only speculate whether in this situation (or one in which a reunited Korea drags its feet in dismantling North Korea's nuclear weapons production capability) Japan would feel compelled to take its virtual nuclear weapons capability a few steps closer to an at-the-ready state. Of course, such a step may not be disclosed, much less rationalized.

The above assessment shows by credible examples already well known that the number of nuclear-armed nations could be at least 11 in 10 to 15 years, with more almost certain to follow—each generating policy questions such as those cited above.

Here Is There: An Ever-*Slowly*-Expanding Nuclear Club

If the United States and other key major powers were instead to adopt a more activist role in international affairs, a strong coalition could emerge that would seek to rein in—but not necessarily halt—the proliferation of at-the-ready nuclear arsenals. Such a coalition could conceivably include the United States, the major powers of Europe, Russia, India, Japan, and China.

As noted, the world is currently proceeding along the path of slow motion nuclear proliferation. With some additional effort it might be kept there.

A key early issue along this path—and the testing ground for getting down to cases on the policy questions regarding nuclear force safety and survivability cited above—would be how the undeclared nuclear-armed states, Israel, Pakistan, and India, are brought into this "slow-growing" nuclear club. This step of formally acknowledging these nations' existing (or imminent) status as nuclear weapon states might even be taken in the context of the 1995 NPT Review and Extension Conference.

From Here to a Tight "Five Haves" Two-Tiered System

To effect a future nuclear proliferation regime based on the logic of maintaining a small but finite number of nuclear-armed special nations—presumably (at least for now) the UN Security Council Permanent Five—would require convincing Israel, Pakistan, and India to give up their nuclear arsenals. This would presumably require both new and credible security commitments to and guarantees for all three parties *and* substantial progress on diminishing the sources of the conflicts

that stimulated these arsenals in the first place. In theory, this commitment could be made through the vehicle of a modified and reinforced UN Security Council framework supplemented by regional collective security guarantees.

If no such international commitment at present proves satisfactory, these states could in principle be grandfathered into the NPT on a one-time-only basis as temporary overt nuclear weapon states. Such temporary membership might be conditioned, for example, on agreement to limits or a freeze on arsenal size and nuclear infrastructure inspection procedures akin to the full-scope safeguards of the IAEA.

The maintenance of any such basically two-tiered system would require that all of the significant actors accept the international political status quo. Not surprisingly, a major war in which nuclear weapons came into play, either through brandishing or outright use, could rapidly collapse such a two-tiered system.

From Here to Virtual Abolition

Of those end states presented, the one that requires the greatest engagement and input of energy on the part of the major nations of the world is virtual abolition. This follows from two imperatives: (1) five major (and several other) nations must go through the wrenching experience of rethinking their own security situation without at-the-ready nuclear arsenals as a flagship element; and (2) unprecedented and far-reaching inspection and enforcement and other security guarantee elements in a new multifaceted security system based on the UN Security Council must be formulated and marketed.

A strategy of virtual abolition is

grounded in the concept that the threat to global peace posed by nuclear weapons proliferation is so great that the major powers will take heroic steps to make nuclear weapons illegitimate—to keep them off the list of weapons with which nations fight. These steps would include adding fundamental new elements to the existing international security system, including a highly intrusive global inspection regime and new and unambiguous security commitments to some nations as they need it. For the international community to head down this path, especially during this critical and difficult early phase of the post–cold war era, the United States in particular would have to become very active in promoting such a security structure to the major economic and military powers, in particular in Eurasia, possibly as a trial balloon as early as the run-up to the 1995 NPT Review and Extension Conference.

In further testing of the viability of such a concept, the United States and other like-minded nuclear-armed nations, by their own weapons procurement and posturing actions, might demonstrate their willingness to move away from large at-the-ready nuclear arsenals as a flagship element of a security posture and to expend the resources to develop the conventional forces wherewithal—whatever that might be—to play a lead role in extending deterrence to insecure nations and in the enforcement of a virtual abolition regime.[22]

From Here to the 1995 NPT Review and Extension Conference

In all four of the above road maps, the 1995 NPT Review and Extension Conference looms large as a forum that could reveal the direction that many

leading nations, and most notably the United States, will take on the nuclear proliferation problem.

If the 1995 conference is a repeat of 1990, 1985, and previous conferences—with the United States and other key nations basically paying homage to an unchanged NPT and engineering a political escape to a relatively short-term treaty extension—then one can infer that an implicit decision tantamount to global acquiescence to the force of nuclear entropy has essentially been made.

If the run-up to the conference is characterized by a strong effort to bring Israel, India, and Pakistan into the NPT as nuclear weapon states—or by no serious effort whatever to lobby these countries on NPT membership—then one can infer that the implicit choice is an ever-expanding nuclear club, with the first expansion beyond the core Permanent Five possibly tolerable as a separate category.

If the run-up to the conference is characterized by (1) a strong international effort to persuade India and Pakistan to rein in their nuclear arsenal building programs before it is too late to turn back and to join the NPT as non-nuclear weapon states in return for some new international security guarantees and/or change of international status (e.g., for India with respect to its concerns over China, the "payment" may be permanent membership in the UN Security Council); (2) a strong effort to forge a regional settlement in the Middle East within which Israel makes a commitment eventually to forgo at-the-ready nuclear weapons (although it may retain a significant, acknowledged, and well-planned virtual nuclear arsenal); and (3) attention to an improved IAEA inspection regime, then one can infer an effort at rollback and eventually holding the line on the Permanent Five (for now) as the only nations with at-the-ready nuclear weapons.

Finally, if the run-up to the conference is marked by seriously debated proposals among the Permanent Five for radical reductions in nuclear arsenals and the extending of new or reinforced security guarantees by that body—and the opening of their nations to the kind of intrusive inspection that would characterize a virtual nuclear arsenal regime—and if the 1995 conference sees the tabling of a new Permanent Five "interim" nuclear forces reduction package (say to 1,500 to 2,000 warheads apiece for the United States and Russia and 300 to 400 for the other three nations), then serious steps toward setting an asymptotic goal akin to virtual abolition will probably have been taken.

The Challenge

The successful constraint of the inherent entropy in the spread of nuclear weapons know-how and wherewithal will require a major sustained effort by the international community and especially leadership by key nations like the United States, Russia, China, France, and the United Kingdom, whose political leverage is essential if a far more effective regime of nuclear containment is to emerge. Without such a major input of energy now, the natural end state of the nuclear age asymptote is almost assuredly high entropy. Such a wide diffusion of nuclear weapons in the hands of many states and probably some non-state actors in a dynamic political soup would place before the international community the perpetual and ever more complex task of constructing multiple stable nuclear deterrence relationships and the strongest possible global cultural taboo on the use of nuclear weapons. Containing this tendency will require nothing less than an urgent commitment to the development of a broad international consensus on some asymptotic goal that reflects a concept of containment of such entropic forces and of an appropriate associated strategy.

With the end of the 50-year "national emergency" (December 1941–December 1991) the U.S. public and the political elites clearly would like to focus the nation's energies on long-neglected domestic concerns. This poses a special challenge for those concerned about the international security dynamic, because the burden of proof will be on those who argue for investing always precious presidential time and energy in an effort to build a strong and aggressive U.S. leadership posture in these crucial international matters, and in devising the necessary policies. Containing nuclear entropy in the long term will require nothing less.

The views expressed in this article are those of the authors and not necessarily those of RAND or any of its sponsoring organizations.

Notes

1. This essay summarizes a longer monograph, Roger C. Molander and Peter A. Wilson, *The Nuclear Asymptote: On Containing Nuclear Proliferation*, MR-214-CC (Santa Monica, Calif.: RAND, 1993). Its substance flows from three years of policy exercises and analyses conducted at RAND for various elements of the U.S. national security community during which Marc Dean Millot, the author of a companion essay in this issue, played a major role.

2. See Kathleen C. Bailey, *Strengthening Nuclear Non-Proliferation* (Boulder, Colo.: Westview Press, 1993), pp. 37–47, for a description of the likely diffusion of nu-

clear and missile expertise from the former Soviet Union.

3. The very success of the new economic "elephants"—the People's Republic of China, India, and Brazil—will place very heavy demands on the regional and global ecosystem as their consumption of fossil fuels for energy production and transportation rises. All three are short of domestic petroleum supplies and will rely heavily on the construction of a civilian nuclear power infrastructure. See William H. Overholt, *The Rise of China: How Economic Reform Is Creating a New Superpower* (New York, N.Y.: W. W. Norton, 1994) for an overview of China's explosive and therefore geostrategically significant economic growth.

4. See Peter D. Zimmerman, "Proliferation: Bronze Medal Technology Is Enough," *Orbis* 38 (Winter 1994), pp. 75–78, for a description of the South African nuclear weapons program.

5. The term *asymptote* is used in this paper in its mathematical sense of a limit—in this case, a steady state or a goal—that a curve or function approaches ever closer, but never quite reaches.

6. The contrarian view that nuclear proliferation is stabilizing was articulated by Pierre Gallois and André Beaufre, both leading French strategic theoreticians favoring Charles de Gaulle's decision to build an independent nuclear deterrent. More recent advocates of this thesis include Kenneth N. Waltz, "The Spread of Nuclear Weapons: More May Be Better," *Adelphi Papers* 171 (London: IISS, 1981); K. Subrahmanyan, ed., *Nuclear Myths and Realities* (New Delhi: ABC Publishing, 1981); and Martin van Creveld, *Nuclear Proliferation and the Future of Conflict* (New York, N.Y.: Free Press, 1993). Van Creveld's view is more subtle in that he believes that for state-to-state relations nuclear weapons have stabilized regional conflicts, while there remains the grave risk that nuclear weapons will fall into the hands of nonstate organizations that arise out of the disintegration of the nation-states.

7. For a sophisticated articulation of the case for an overt Indian minimum deterrent capable of reaching China's heartland see K. Sundarji, *Blind Men of Hindoostan* (New Delhi: USS Publishers' Distributors Ltd., 1993). Sundarji, a former Indian chief of staff, makes the case for an overt Indian nuclear weapons program and an appropriate political military planning mechanism, which does not exist at this time.

8. During the first few months of the Clinton administration, there was talk about adding Japan and Germany as new permanent members to the Security Council as part of a reform effort to revitalize the UN. Enthusiasm for such major changes has faded in the face of objections from France and the United Kingdom as well as other large states such as India.

9. One of the major findings of the RAND "The Day After" exercise series was the strong view held by many U.S. military participants that nuclear weapons no longer provide the United States with a net national security benefit. It was in this context that the early concept of virtual abolition was articulated. See Marc Dean Millot, Roger Molander, and Peter A. Wilson, *"The Day After . . ." Study: Nuclear Proliferation in the Post–Cold War World*, vol. 1, *Summary Report* (MR-266-AF); vol. 2, *Main Report* (MR-253-AF); vol. 3, *Exercise Materials* (MR-254-AF) (Santa Monica, Calif.: RAND, 1993).

10. Zimmerman, "Proliferation," pp. 77–78.

11. During the 1960s it became an article of faith within the U.S. strategic analytical community that small nuclear forces were dangerous and destabilizing due to their vulnerability to preemption. This was one of the central tenets of the nonproliferation argument that new nuclear-armed states could deploy only small and vulnerable forces. The SCUD campaign and the U.S. failure to identify the full range of installations associated with Iraq's nuclear weapons program suggest that a medium-sized power may have a wide range of options to deploy a small and survivable nuclear arsenal that cannot be easily neutralized by a counterforce attack. One can note the current debate within the U.S. national security community about the feasibility of "taking out" the North Korean nuclear weapons program and associated missile infrastructure.

12. See Thomas A. Keaney and Eliot A. Cohen, *Gulf War Air Power Survey* (Washington, D.C.: GPO, 1993), pp. 83–90, for an analysis of the anti-SCUD campaign. This study and others concluded that the allied air forces gained no confirmed kills

of a SCUD and its associated launcher after 1,000 attack sorties. Other reports suggest that some SCUD missiles and their launchers were destroyed by special operations forces in the Western Iraqi desert. See Christopher Bellamy, *Expert Witness: A Defence Correspondent's Gulf War 1990–91* (New York, N.Y.: Brassey's, 1993), pp. 107–108. The mobile missile challenge has a precedent; the lack of success of allied World War II air forces in destroying mobile German V–2 launchers. See David Irving, *The Mare's Nest: The German Secret Weapons Campaign and Allied Counter-measures* (Boston, Mass.: Little, Brown, 1964), pp. 304–313.

13. For an excellent survey of the status of the MTCR and the diffusion of ballistic missile development and production capability, see William C. Potter and Harlan W. Jencks, eds., *The International Missile Bazaar: The New Suppliers' Network* (Boulder, Colo.: Westview Press, 1994). Noteworthy is the description of long-standing cooperative relations between North Korea and Egypt and Iran.

14. See Millot, Molander, and Wilson, *"The Day After . . ."* Study, vols. 1 and 2, for a summary and analysis of the findings derived from the policy exercises conducted during 1991 and 1992. All of these exercises involved scenarios that led to the detonation of one or more nuclear weapons during a regional strategic crisis. During 1993 and 1994, the coauthors have been conducting a second generation of exercises that have explored a broader range of scenarios including direct nuclear threats to the United States.

15. As an example of the conventional wisdom that only a madman would use nuclear weapons see Bailey, *Strengthening Nuclear Non-proliferation*, p. 101.

16. Les Aspin, *The Bottom-Up Review: Forces for a New Era* (Washington, D.C.: Department of Defense, 1993).

17. For a further elaboration of these points see Millot, Molander, and Wilson, *"The Day After . . ."* Study, vol. 1.

18. See Marc Dean Millot, "Facing the Emerging Reality of Regional Nuclear Adversaries," in this issue for a detailed discussion of the first year evolution of the Clinton administration's non- and counter-proliferation policy. For a detailed critique of the strategic and budgetary planning assumptions of the *Bottom-Up Review*, see Andrew F. Krepinevich, *The Bottom-Up Review: An Assessment* (Washington, D.C.: Defense Budget Project, 1994).

19. See "Remarks by Defense Secretary Les Aspin to the National Academy of Sciences Committee on International Security and Arms Control," Federal News Service, December 7, 1993, LEXIS, for an outline of the DCI.

20. For a critique of giving too much emphasis to counterproliferation at the expense of a vigorous enforcement of the NPT regime, see Rupert Pengelley, "Betting Each Way on Proliferation," *International Defense Review*, 2/1994, p. 1.S.

21. Hopes to gain a consensus among the Permanent Five on far-reaching nuclear disarmament and arms-control initiatives will be shattered if the Russian Federation is headed by a regime that frightens many of its Eurasian neighbors, who in turn call for collective defense guarantees from the United States and/or the North Atlantic Treaty Organization. If these are not forthcoming, several might execute a nuclear weapons option, and others such as China might carry out a major expansion of their nuclear arsenals.

22. Even if Russia does not go sour, it will be a major diplomatic challenge for the United States to convince the Russian Federation, China, the United Kingdom, and France to consider a radical downgrading of their nuclear arsenals as part of a very ambitious post–1995 non- and counterproliferation regime of virtual abolition. The Russian Federation, for example, has announced a new military doctrine that renounces the Soviet no-first-use declaratory policy and highlights the need for nuclear forces. See Brigitte Sauerwein, "Russia Adopts New Military Doctrine," *International Defense Review*, 12/1993, p. 931. Furthermore, the French government is in the process of deciding whether to *expand* the deterrent role of its nuclear forces as a counterproliferation option. See Pierre Sparaco, "French Defense White Paper Paves Way for Six-Year Plan," *Aviation Week & Space Technology*, March 7, 1994, p. 39.

Nonapocalyptic Proliferation: A New Strategic Threat?

Henry D. Sokolski

WITH DESERT STORM and the efforts of the United Nations (UN) to dismantle chemical, missile, and nuclear facilities in Iraq, it is difficult to imagine any technology being of concern with regard to proliferation unless it involved weapons of mass destruction. Yet, reflection on both why weapons of mass destruction cause such concern and what other high-leverage military capabilities might inflict defeat on U.S. forces suggests several conventional military technologies for inclusion in the list of proliferation concerns. These conventional technologies and weapons might be termed nonapocalyptic because they are not weapons of mass destruction. They include submarines operating in confined waters, unmanned air vehicles (UAVs), and relatively advanced civilian command, control, communication, and intelligence (C^3I) capabilities. Like weapons of mass destruction, these technologies pose threats

against which the United States currently has little or no defense.

This new type of proliferation deserves attention for several reasons. First, if the United States continues to pay it inadequate attention, it could easily produce defeats like that suffered by U.S. forces in Lebanon in 1983. Indeed, nonapocalyptic military capabilities can accomplish some of the same missions as apocalyptic munitions. The key difference is that these nonapocalyptic military capabilities do not rely on indiscriminate destruction to accomplish these missions. Because of this, their employment is far less likely to run the risk of strategic retaliation and, thus, is more likely in the first place.

Second, unlike nuclear and biological weapons, nonapocalyptic military threats are much more susceptible to military countermeasures. Just how much of a problem nonapocalyptic proliferation is or will be, then, depends on what the most advanced military powers choose to do. If they recognize these threats now and develop adequate countermeasures before they are fully realized, nonapocalyptic proliferation may be manageable. If, however, they only try to delay the arrival of the threat with export or arms control, as they have with apocalyptic munitions, the threat will become quite real.

Third, with the exception of submarines, nonapocalyptic proliferation

Henry D. Sokolski worked in the Office of Net Assessment and as deputy for nonproliferation policy at the Defense Department and was military legislative aide to Senator Dan Quayle. He teaches at Washington's Institute of World Politics and is writing a book on proliferation as a National Institute of Public Policy fellow.

Copyright © 1994 by The Center for Strategic and International Studies and the Massachusetts Institute of Technology
The Washington Quarterly • 17:2

is more like biological and chemical weapons proliferation than the spread of nuclear weapons: It does not respond readily to export or arms control alone. The technologies involved are themselves easily available and are becoming increasingly popular for a growing number of legitimate civilian applications.

Finally, nonapocalyptic proliferation and how the United States chooses to address it will affect whether or not and how smaller nations might acquire and use weapons of mass destruction. Attempting to understand and manage the relationship between these two types of proliferation, then, will become more important as the United States increases its efforts to curb weapons of mass destruction and to plan its military requirements for the future.

Each of these points is discussed below, starting with a basic examination of what is of proliferation concern and why.

Proliferation: A Strategic Threat

In the late 1940s, when the usage of "proliferation" in connection with security was first coined, the West's first worry was Soviet acquisition of nuclear weapons. This concern, much like worries about smaller powers getting such weapons today, turned on three points:

- These weapons could inflict strategic, high-leverage harm. For far less expense than large modern fleets or armies, a potential adversary could threaten the United States with strategic—war-winning or victory-denying—harm simply by acquiring "the bomb."
- The United States had no effective defenses against these weapons, although it knew how to defend

against conventionally armed air strikes. Experience during World War II taught both sides that effective air defenses could generally disrupt a bomber strike and prevent it from accomplishing its overall mission. Against a nuclear bomber, however, such defenses seemed woefully inadequate, and the advent of nuclear ballistic missiles only compounded this vulnerability.
- The mere acquisition of these weapons by other nations could conceivably alter perceptions of who was the leading power. In 1946 the worry was that U.S. influence might wane or be challenged if the Soviets' nuclear weapons deterred those of the West.

Although a good deal has changed since 1946, what drives U.S. proliferation worries today is basically the same. U.S. planners still worry about the spread of weapons that can inflict high-leverage strategic harm. They are particularly worried if the United States lacks adequate defenses against such weapons. And they still worry that such proliferation will reduce U.S. ability to influence or control events in key regions of the world. This much is the same.

What has changed, and changed dramatically, however, is what major powers like the United States consider to be strategic. The word strategy is derived from the Greek word *strategos*—talk of the generals, talk about wars, about how they are won and lost. During most of the twentieth century and the Cold War the wars that U.S. generals worried about most were total or global in character. Even the smaller conflicts fought during the postwar period were cast in the context of the larger East–West struggle that threatened total conflict. In this context, strategic weapons took on a very specialized meaning: Only the longest-range and most destructive of weapons were considered strategic because only these, in and of themselves, could threaten war-winning or victory-denying results in the most feared of conflicts, World War III.

With the Cold War over and the Warsaw Pact defunct, however, the prospect of intentional U.S.–Russian intercontinental nuclear exchanges or global conventional conflicts seems remote. Now the most worrisome wars are regional, not global, more like Desert Storm than the fictitious portrayals of World War III in *Red Storm Rising* or *The Day After.*

Yet, more than merely war's dimensions has changed. In addition, the very aims of war and what their achievement requires have shifted. Instead of a rough symmetry of aims and means between two superpowers, in wars between smaller and larger powers, military aims and requirements are much more asymmetrical. Indeed, these aims and requirements are far more modest for smaller nations than for larger outside powers that might intervene against these nations.

Consider Iraq. After defeating his significantly weaker Kuwaiti neighbor, Saddam Hussein's requirements for maintaining his victory could be met by (1) keeping outside coalition forces from forming against him; (2) preventing them from staying in alliance against him; or, failing either of these two goals, (3) preventing these outside forces from executing a totally effective offensive against him. Saddam Hussein nearly succeeded in achieving the first aim, losing in the U.S. Senate on the question of the U.S. commitment to use force by only a handful of votes. He then tried to break up the coalition and caused a crisis by attacking Israel. But here he ultimately failed to undo the coalition, and in the

first round of military action against the coalition's massive military offensive he lost miserably. Saddam Hussein, however, has not yet been totally defeated and continues to have designs against Kuwait and the United States. Roughly speaking then, whereas Iraqi victory could be achieved in the councils of nations or the U.S. Congress, the coalition's success required inflicting decisive military defeat on the most powerful land power in the Persian Gulf and maintaining military vigilance even after this victory.

So far, smaller nations like Iraq have been able on occasion to subdue weaker neighbors. Until now, however, they have been unable to do this without risking military intervention by outside powers. This, among other reasons, is why several smaller nations have been so attracted to and determined to acquire weapons of mass destruction. Besides deterring the use of such weapons by neighbors, acquisition of these weapons may be the easiest way to scare off unwanted outside intervention.

It is unclear, of course, if mere possession of weapons of mass destruction by the smaller nations is sufficient to preclude unwanted outside intervention. This will depend on many variables. What is clear, however, is that in the coming decade there are likely to be other weapons capabilities besides weapons of mass destruction that may serve this strategic purpose.

The most prominent of these, ironically, were used by coalition forces against Iraq—accurate long-range, stand-off munitions, UAVs both lethal and nonlethal (some of which were launched from U.S. submarines), and robust civilian C^3I systems (including those afforded by civilian satellite services). Given Saddam Hussein's military weaknesses and inability to field any similar systems or to put up adequate defenses against them, these high-leverage military capabilities proved to be devastatingly effective against his forces.

This is what is likely to change. Not only are the defenses of smaller nations against these high-leverage systems likely to improve, but, far more important, these nations have begun to acquire and develop these capabilities in cruder forms for their own military purposes. Given the asymmetry of aims for aggressors in regional wars, even their crude imitations could have strategic consequences.

Nonapocalyptic Trends to Watch: Submarines, Accurate Missiles, and Satellite Services

When one speaks of weapons capabilities that can inflict high-leverage strategic harm, it is necessarily a very limited grouping. Weapons technologies that are only advanced (i.e., that incorporate high technology) frequently fail to make the grade: They are not necessarily high leverage and often fail to produce strategic consequences.

A good example here might be an advanced fighter plane. No one would dispute that it was high technology, but, lacking advanced stealth technology, the plane could be countered by existing air defenses. Moreover, in anything less than massive numbers that would take years and many billions of dollars to acquire (and as a practical matter would be nearly impossible to hide from other nations' notice), these planes would be unlikely to produce strategic results even in a regional conflict.

In contrast, the handful of nonapocalyptic technologies noted above could, if properly applied, make a significant difference for smaller nations not only against weaker neighbors, but

against outside expeditionary forces as well. Perhaps the clearest and easiest example here is the submarine operating in confined waters, which might not be high technology, but can nonetheless produce high-leverage strategic results that major powers still have difficulty preventing.

The reasons for the potential effectiveness of submarines for smaller nations are fairly immediate. First, major naval powers, including the United States, have only a very limited capability to detect or identify submarines (even old, noisy ones) in shallow or closed seas. The difficulty in detecting submarines in such waters is that there is already a great deal of background sound from other sources (e.g., surface ships and fish) propagating at fairly high levels. Also, because sounds reverberate much more intensely in shallow or closed waters, it is difficult to pinpoint precisely where any particular sound is coming from.

Compounding this problem is the trend toward significant levels of quieting in modern diesel-electric submarines. This quieting trend in the context of shallow and closed sea operations is quite likely to outstrip current antisubmarine warfare techniques for some time. And many of these quiet modern submarines are being sold to smaller nations (see figure 1). These sales are increasing and are likely to continue to do so (over the last decade submarine export deliveries rose by 29 percent and were the only category of major arms exports deliveries to grow).

Related to the detection problem, of course, is the identification problem. The sound signatures associated with Soviet nuclear submarines in open seas are of little value in trying to identify a particular diesel-electric boat in confined waters. Many of the smaller nations' current fleet of sub-

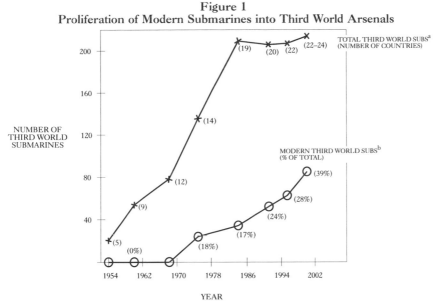

Figure 1
Proliferation of Modern Submarines into Third World Arsenals

Source: John Benedict, "Third World Submarines and ASW Implications" (Johns Hopkins University Applied Physics Laboratory, Baltimore, Md., January 9, 1992).
Notes: a. Mini-submarines/midgets excluded
b. Western supplied and less than 20 years old; Soviet Kilos or follow-ons.

marines, moreover, are of similar or identical types, having been made in only a handful of West European or Russian shipyards.

Second, the lethality of submarines against even the largest of capital surface ships is increasing. In 1971 an older Pakistani submarine of French origin managed to sink an Indian frigate with only three torpedo hits. A decade later in the Falklands campaign, the British, using 50-year-old Mark 8 torpedoes, managed to sink an Argentine cruiser with only two torpedo hits. These were not particularly heavy torpedoes. Heavier, more lethal ones are now available.

Submarines, of course, can also lay mines, and these nearly succeeded in sinking two U.S. Persian Gulf naval vessels. In addition to mines and tor-

pedoes, submarines can be fitted with torpedo tube-launched, sea-skimming, antiship missiles (e.g., the French Exocet SM–39, the U.S. Harpoon, and others) that have been marketed for export for some time.

Together, these considerations may make larger powers think twice about intervening in confined waters against a smaller power that has operating submarines. In fact, no major Western regional intervention has yet been attempted without employing capital surface ships early on. Indeed, it has always been assumed that these passive employments could be made with little controversy prior to overt hostilities and might themselves deter aggression. This may change. Although it is true that there are many things that are likely to prevent smaller nations from employing their submarines effectively (e.g., lack of adequate training and maintenance, inability to find surface ship targets in a timely fashion, etc.), it is frequently at least as difficult for advanced nations to conduct effective antisubmarine operations against such boats when operating in confined waters.

This in and of itself could produce chilling effects on the willingness of larger nations to enter confined seas. Instead of simply assuming that U.S. ships could be sent risk-free into the Persian Gulf, say to protect Saudi or Kuwaiti shipping against a hostile Iran, participating navies would first want to be sure that they knew where all of Iran's Kilo-class submarines were. More important, the admirals might deem it necessary to take overt action to neutralize these submarines before or simultaneously with the employment of surface combatants for escort duty.

Under these circumstances, the need to take overt action before being hit could prove fatal to public support for a democratic power that wants to conduct any naval operation. The smaller nations could exploit the disinclination of most large, liberal commercial powers to commit overt acts of war against any nation until they have themselves been hit.

The political leverage gained by smaller nations using submarines may, in fact, be even more substantial. Assuming these nations choose to use their submarines against foreign surface ships and actually hit one with a mine, torpedo, or missile, it is unclear what, if any, response a larger power could make. It would be difficult to find the submarine or to know that it delivered the mine, missile, or torpedo rather than some other ship, plane, or shore-battery unit. More-

over, even if a larger power could establish that the culprit was a submarine, it would be difficult, if not impossible, to identify the nationality of the submarine. In the Mediterranean, for example, Algeria, Egypt, Israel, Libya, and Syria all have operational submarines and are interested in buying more. Some of the submarine types they operate now, moreover, are quite similar to one another and to those operated by nations of the North Atlantic Treaty Organization (NATO) and Russia. And what is already true of the Mediterranean is likely to become true elsewhere (e.g., the Persian Gulf, where Iraq, Iran, and Saudi Arabia have all evinced an interest in ordering submarines of their own).

Considering these factors, the fear must be that eventually smaller nations' submarines might produce catastrophic events at sea that will be politically and militarily as embarrassing as the terror bombing of the U.S. Marine barracks in Beirut that prompted U.S. withdrawal of its forces from Lebanon.[1]

What smaller nations may be able to do at sea, newer, more accurate missiles aided by improved civilian C^3I capabilities are even more likely to do on land. This may at first seem improbable, given recent experience with SCUDs in Afghanistan, Iraq, and Iran, where such missiles missed their targets, frequently by one or two kilometers, and had lethal areas that were so small that their primary purpose was simply to scare city dwellers.

Several trends, however, are under way that are certain to change this. The first of these is the increasing availability of much more precise navigational and guidance aids. Shortly after the shooting incident involving Korean Airlines flight 007, the United

States decided to make highly precise navigational and guidance signals from its Global Positioning System (GPS) available to civilian users. The hope was that this would prevent future civil air tragedies associated with bad navigation. Shortly thereafter, the Russians announced their willingness to make their own similar GLONASS satellite systems available to civilian users as well.

These satellite systems were originally designed by the military to guide troops, ships, planes, and missiles. To help prevent misuse, the U.S. government decided to degrade the accuracy of the navigational signals for civilian users. Still, GPS will give civilians locational fixes that are accurate within 100 meters or less. The GLONASS system does not appear to be designed for such degradation. In unclassified tests conducted by Honeywell and Northwest Airlines, the GLONASS signals, in fact, were found to be accurate 95 percent of time to within 20 meters horizontally and 36 meters vertically. Greater accuracies are expected of the system once it is complete.

Instead of guidance errors of 1,000 or 2,000 meters, then, navigational and guidance errors can be measured in scores of meters. And there are means already available to reduce these errors to 5 meters or less. The simplest of these means is differential GPS (DGPS). This technique requires that a spot be surveyed to fix its location in altitude, longitude, and latitude. With sure knowledge of where this one spot is, a GPS or GLONASS reading is then taken. Once the difference between the survey information and the GPS/GLONASS readings is determined, a simple algorithm is used to eliminate most, if not all, errors from future GPS/GLONASS readings. From a single presurveyed site one can transmit differential corrections to other moving platforms up to 1,500 kilometers away.

There are, to be sure, limitations to all of this. Right now, one could probably jam differential GPS rebroadcasts locally without much difficulty. This may change, however, because there are already commercial firms that are willing to receive GPS signals, correct them, and rebroadcast the correction via satellite over large areas. This service is expensive but much harder to jam. So far, it is not widely available. Also, some of the most advanced GPS receivers (those that can operate above 600 feet and relay signals quickly to a ballistic missile flying several times the speed of sound), are expensive and are now controlled for export under U.S. export controls and those of the Missile Technology Control Regime. These controls, however, came into effect only after many ballistic-missile-capable GPS receivers had already been sold and such controls cannot be relied upon to prevent GPS receivers from being upgraded.

Allowing for these qualifications, then, the availability of GPS/GLONASS civilian signals is still producing a major revolution in missile guidance. Over the next decade, the aiming inaccuracies of proliferants are projected to tumble from their current level of 1,000 meters—e.g., SCUDs—to as little as 10 meters or less for unmanned air vehicles whose inertial guidance sets are updated with GPS or GLONASS differential signals. Keeping in mind that the probability of knocking out a specific point target is related exponentially to aiming inaccuracies, a 100-fold decrease in inaccuracies of this sort is equivalent to a 10,000-fold increase in the probability of destroying the target. Rather than having to use a biological, chemical, or nuclear weapon to threaten a point target, then, smaller nations could use UAVs and conventional munitions (see figure 2).[2]

Such lethality, of course, assumes that you can not only aim your weapon accurately, but that you know in advance at what to aim your missile. Until now, the best smaller nations could do for targets over the horizon was to use inaccurate maps and guess where to aim. For large targets like cities, this has generally proved to be good enough. But for military point targets, knowing precisely where you are firing from is not enough; you also need to know where your target is. To do this you must know that your target is present and map precisely where it is in longitude, latitude, and altitude. This is one of the reasons why the major powers have spent so much money on

developing precision maps based on overhead photography. Such imagery mapping used to be a supersecret operation and only the United States and the Soviet Union were capable of it.

Again, this is changing. With the increasing availability of civilian satellite imagery services such as Landsat and SPOT (which afford multispectral images of 10 to 30 meters resolution) and Russian marketing of archival imagery of 2 to 5 meters resolution, what were once supersecret capabilities limited to the superpowers are becoming publicly accessible at affordable subscription rates. To be sure, what is publicly available is not as good as what the best military spy satellites now produce, but for a smaller nation concerned about targeting relatively large, fixed targets, this may not matter.

In fact, in Desert Storm, coalition

Figure 2
System Accuracies with Satellite Navigation

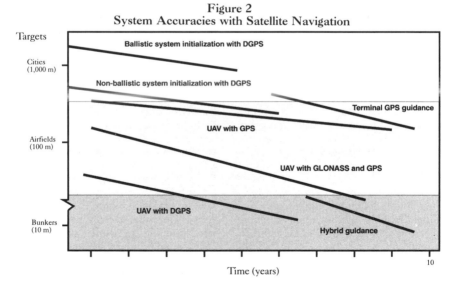

Source: Steve Wooley, "Proliferation of Precision Navigation Technologies and Security Implications for the U.S." (Institute for Defense Analyses, Alexandria, Va., December 9, 1991).

forces including the United States used Landsat and SPOT data extensively. Key applications included updating existing maps (the U.S. Defense Mapping Agency purchased $5.7 million worth of imagery from SPOT for this purpose), plotting major armored vehicle movements, doing bomb-damage assessment, and even air-strike mission simulation and planning.

The trend, moreover, is toward more types of civilian imagery services of this kind, made available in an ever more timely fashion. What now takes weeks to secure in the way of imagery will take only days, if not hours, by the end of the century, and the imagery will be of higher resolution and of a much broader spectrum (see figure 3).[3]

These trends have not gone unnoticed. On the one hand, several smaller nations, including Pakistan and Iran, are reported to be actively attempting to integrate GPS into missiles, particularly UAVs. Just as important, smaller nations, including an international Arab organization, India, Pakistan, Indonesia, and Thailand, have shown some interest in developing techniques to digitize imagery, such as that available from SPOT, and to insert GPS locational information to develop highly accurate three-dimensional maps using computer programs such as AutoCad. These maps have a multitude of legitimate commercial uses. They also are extremely useful for targeting.[4]

When we match these trends with the increased availability and development of UAVs, a potential cruise missile threat emerges. Whereas a decade ago very few smaller nations claimed they were developing such vehicles, today nearly a dozen claim they are working on over 100 such

projects. Even assuming that many of these claims are unsound, the trend toward serious indigenous UAV projects is up significantly.[5]

Certainly, one of the key difficulties associated with UAVs has been the difficulty of guiding them. Because they can fly for hours, and because the inertial guidance sets would drift significantly over such a period, there was no way for smaller nations to guide them except by radio signal. This was not only awkward, but vulnerable to jamming in war. GPS, GLONASS, differential GPS corrections, and the ability to integrate existing inertial guidance sets so GPS or GLONASS signals can update them eliminate many of these problems.

The result is a new kind of missile proliferation problem in the decade ahead—slow, low-flying UAVs that can be precisely targeted against fixed military assets. This, in conjunction with ballistic missiles, presents a genuine headache. First, it compounds the difficulties of the already stressed U.S. air defense systems. The current Patriot missile defense system worked at the margins against old SCUD ballistic missiles. The United States is now working on new defenses to cope with faster, staged ballistic missiles that will present a much smaller radar cross section than do Iraq's SCUDs. This will be difficult enough. To develop defenses to cope not just with such missiles and fast-flying airplanes, but also with slow, low-flying UAVs will stress U.S. defense efforts even further.

More important, there are likely to be critical targets worth defending. Such a target was nearly hit by accident in an Iraqi SCUD strike against Jubail, a key Saudi port, during Desert Storm. On February 11, 1991, a SCUD missile struck just 300 or so meters from a pier at which eight ships

Figure 3
Civil Space Systems Are Moving toward Higher Resolution
and More Timely Data Delivery

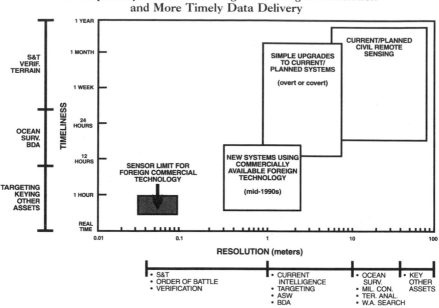

Source: Berner and Lamphier and Associates, "Proliferation of Space Technology" (Bethesda, Md., October 18, 1991).

Key: S & T   Science & Technology
       Verif.   Verification
       Ocean Surv.   Ocean Surveillance
       BDA   Battle Damage Assessment
       ASW   Antisubmarine Warfare
       Mil. Con.   Military Construction
       Ter. Anal.   Terrain Analysis
       W. A. Search   Wide Area Search

were berthed. Two of these ships contained virtually all the provisions for the U.S. Marine Air Forces. Another, the USS *Tarawa*, contained all the supplies and troops for the Marine Corps's quick deployment brigade. Others contained ammunition. Fortunately, none of ships and none of the 5,000 tons of 155-mm shells stacked on the pier that day were hit.[6]

With piers pretargeted in peacetime and agents spotting such targets on the ground (or timely civilian satellite imagery or UAVs doing the same), such targets could be aimed at and hit precisely with UAVs in the future. Other targets might include major gas and oil supplies, ammunition dumps, airports, command centers, desalination plants, or large truck parks. Hitting any of these targets even with a conventional munition could prove fatal to the timing and the ultimate success of a major land operation.

Again, detecting and identifying these attacks will be difficult. It is already very difficult to find mobile ballistic-missile launchers even when it is known from rocket plume detecting satellites that a missile has been launched. With UAVs the launchers will still be mobile but targeted forces will be less likely to know when or if any launch has taken place because there will be no rocket plume to detect. Also, unlike ballistic missiles, which have only so many ballistic trajectories, UAVs can take a far more varied number of flight paths. UAVs also have important nonlethal missions that they can perform (including suppression of air defense radars) as well as being able to deliver any and all kinds of munitions. Again, none of this will make developing an appropriate military response any easier.

Improvements in command, control, and communications (C^3) that are simply part of many smaller nations' efforts to upgrade their civilian communication and air traffic-control systems are also increasing the lethality of many of their military systems, including missiles. Advanced C^3, for example, makes coordinated, saturation missile strikes against defended fixed targets possible. This, in turn, can increase the lethality of a given strike 100 percent. Some of these new C^3 systems, moreover, can be far more difficult to target than Iraq's modern fiber-optic system. Specifically, microwave communication systems, which are highly desirable for civil applications, are small enough for both receivers and transmitters to be made mobile, and they emit their signals in a fashion that makes them quite difficult to locate.[7]

Finally, it should be noted that the imagery that will make UAVs more precise and lethal will also make covert insertion of major land forces against smaller nations difficult if not impossible. Anyone who had access to

SPOT images during the Persian Gulf War, for example, could have discerned the basic movement of coalition forces throughout January and February 1991. Deprived of surprise, it is unclear just how cheaply bought General Norman Schwartzkopf's success against Iraq would have been. Indeed, it is unclear if the general would have attempted the operation unless he had been confident of surprise.

What to Make of It?

As of yet, however, few of these various technologies have been crafted into meaningful military instruments by smaller powers. These threats may come later than projected. The major powers may, with great effort, significantly mitigate them by developing better defenses (both active and passive). Assuming, however, that insufficient efforts are made to defend against these nonapocalyptic threats, it is worth considering what they might mean more generally.

First, it ought not to be assumed that these nonapocalyptic capabilities will serve as substitutes for weapons of mass destruction. With or without nonapocalyptic capabilities, smaller nations will continue to desire weapons of mass destruction either to frighten neighbors who do not have these weapons or to deter them if they do.

On the other hand, what nonapocalyptic proliferation may change is the need or urgency smaller nations might otherwise have to threaten others with apocalyptic harm. It would seem that nonapocalyptic capabilities should reduce this need, at least with regard to preventing hostile interventions. Trying to control nonapocalyptic proliferation developments through explicit arms-control treaties, therefore, might be less than effective; such trea-

35

ties could prove to be counterproductive. Other efforts, including export controls interdictions, would probably make the most sense even though in many cases they would only delay acquisition of these nonapocalyptic capabilities.

This said, there may be a significant exception to this nonapocalyptically induced restraint. Although destructive, chemical weapons are nowhere near as indiscriminate as nuclear or biological weapons, which generally have a much larger lethal radius. More important, a key factor that makes chemical weapons indiscriminate is the inability to deliver them accurately enough (this is one of the reasons why it is necessary to deliver tons of agent to assure effectiveness against a given target). Precise UAVs might change this. If so, the current presumption that use of these weapons should be treated like the use of biological or nuclear weapons would encounter a major challenge, with numerous military and arms-control implications. Not the least of these might be to encourage the United States and its allies to prepare more carefully for chemical combat.

Second, nonapocalyptic proliferation should encourage the United States and its friends to reconsider how they might conduct their military affairs in the future. Certainly, the major powers will have to do more than figure out how to downsize existing forces. They will have to consider whether or not they can continue to take the sort of risks they have traditionally taken in expeditionary operations. Should they stay out of regions in which they have previously intervened? Should they plan (and even design) to have their ships take hits and persist? Are there some new, nonnaval ways in which they might project force? The same sort of considerations

need to be given to how they might conduct amphibious and land operations. Particular attention will need to be paid to potential logistical vulnerabilities and to how to train and game for future wars.

Finally, this new kind of proliferation will make operations against smaller proliferant powers much more complex and delicate than they have been to date. In Desert Storm the coalition was able to operate against Iraq and its weapons of mass destruction facilities from bases that were immune to attack. Future wars may require the United States to knock out and defend against weapon systems that can reach long distances and inflict both discriminate and massive destruction. To fight such wars may require herculean effort.

Indeed, what nonapocalyptic proliferation promises are wars that may stress U.S. capabilities in new ways the Cold War never did. That these wars may be smaller will not reduce the harm they may do, or their strategic significance.

Notes

1. For a thorough discussion of these points see Rear Admiral James Fitzgerald, USN, and John Benedict, "There Is a Sub Threat," *U.S. Naval Institute Proceedings*, August 1990, pp. 57–63, and John Benedict, "Third World Submarines and ASW Implications" (Johns Hopkins University Applied Physics Laboratory, Baltimore, Md., January 9, 1992).

2. These points are drawn from Steve Wooley, "Proliferation of Precision Navigation Technologies and Security Implications for the U.S." (Institute for Defense Analyses, Alexandria, Va., December 9, 1991).

3. These points are drawn from Berner and Lamphier and Associates, "Proliferation of Space Technology" (Bethesda, Md., October 18, 1991).

4. Wooley, "Proliferation of Precision Navigation Technologies."

5. Henry D. Sokolski, "The Military Implications of Proliferation in the Middle East," Testimony before the Senate Subcommittee on Technology and National Security of the Joint Economic Committee, March 13, 1992.

6. Joe Braddock, "Developing Lessons Learned from Desert Storm and Desert Shield," Draft Report of the Technology Transfer Panel of the Defense Science Board Task Force (U.S. Department of Defense, Washington, D.C., February 20, 1992), pp. 10–11.

7. Mat O'Brien, *C³I Upgrades for Developing Nations' Missile Operations* (Alexandria, Va.: Institute for Defense Analyses, 1992).

Implications of the Persian Gulf War for Regional Powers

Patrick J. Garrity

ON AUGUST 2, 1990, the very day that Iraq invaded Kuwait, President George Bush announced the outlines of a new U.S. defense strategy to an Aspen Institute Symposium.[1] The new strategy, prophetically, was based on the assumption that the challenge to U.S. (and international) security had shifted from the *global* competition between the United States and the Soviet Union to *regional* conflicts and instabilities. The Persian Gulf War was in an important sense the first example of this transformation. Saddam Hussein, of course, epitomized the danger of an aggressive regional despot. But in addition, the plight of the Iraqi Kurds and Shi'a in the war's aftermath symbolized the intrastate ethnic and religious struggles that are also likely to mark the post–cold war era.

In the United States, numerous official and unofficial groups have closely analyzed the lessons of Operation Desert Shield and Desert Storm for future U.S. foreign policy and military strategy.[2] But the leaders of other nations, too, have certainly gained in-

sights from the Gulf war. Some of the most important foreign reactions may come from key nations in regions where the potential for future conflict is quite high. For want of a better term, this article uses the expression "regional powers" to characterize this class of states. They include nations allied or hostile to, or having mixed relations with, the United States. The People's Republic of China (PRC) would be at the high end of the regional-power scale. Other examples of regional powers are India, Israel, Egypt, Saudi Arabia, Iran, Iraq, Libya, Syria, Cuba, North Korea, South Korea, Turkey, Serbia, and the states belonging to the Association of Southeast Asian Nations (ASEAN).

This article examines how this class of nations seems to be reacting to the Gulf war. Obviously, caution must be taken in utilizing such analysis. As with any summary, it necessarily relies on generalizations, which often lack nuance and neglect differences between the reactions of key states. Second, by focusing on the Gulf war, the analysis runs the risk of ignoring many other developments that may have been of equal or greater significance. The overarching events of international significance, obviously, were the end of the Cold War and the disintegration of the Soviet Union. Other key defining events will vary from nation to nation. Third, different entities within any specific regional power—

Patrick J. Garrity is a staff member with the Center for National Security Studies at Los Alamos National Laboratory. He is coeditor with Steven A. Maaranen of *Nuclear Weapons in the Changing World: Perspectives from Europe, Asia, and North America* (1992).

The Washington Quarterly

the government and the opposition, the foreign and defense ministries, and various military services—may draw very different conclusions from the war. Finally, and perhaps most important, foreign perceptions of the Gulf war have changed, and continue to change, over time. Developments such as the crises in Yugoslavia and the continuing struggle to enforce the resolutions of the United Nations (UN) against Iraq affect how regional powers look at the Gulf war in retrospect. Any assessment of foreign perspectives on the war can at best be a snapshot.[3]

With these caveats in mind, the article will focus on the three issues given prominence by the Gulf war that arguably had the largest impact on regional powers. The first concerns the necessity for regional powers to accommodate themselves to the surprisingly strong power position that the United States demonstrated during the Gulf crisis and war. The second deals with the importance of understanding and dealing with international coalitions that may be formed to intervene in future regional crises and conflicts. The third involves how regional powers may adapt their own military forces to account for the lessons of Operation Desert Shield and Desert Storm. The article concludes with an assessment of how these regional reactions to the Gulf war might affect U.S. foreign and defense policy in the future.

Regional Recognition of the Importance of the United States

For virtually every regional state, a central lesson of the Gulf war is that the United States is the only superpower. In summer 1990, by contrast, there were serious questions about whether U.S. power, and the U.S.

strategic relationships built up during the Cold War, would retain their relevance given the disappearance of the Soviet threat, the rise of the new economic superpowers in Germany and Japan, and the general diffusion of power in the international system. For some regional powers, notably in East Asia, the objective decline in the importance of the United States (as seen in mid-1990) suggested the emergence of a multipolar world. For others, notably in the Middle East, the questions about the relevance of the United States had less to do with uncertainties about its power than with its intentions and will to defend its interests.

The Gulf war thus represented something of a turning point, at least for the time being, in foreign perceptions of the United States. As of March 1991, the continued relevance—even dominance—of U.S. power, and of Washington's willingness to exercise that power, was essentially unquestioned.[4] The key to the U.S. power position was not simply the impressive military capability demonstrated in Operation Desert Storm but rather the ability to act as an integrator of nations and policies. One observer characterized the prevailing regional-power perspective on the United States as follows:

> The "super-power" of the U.S. clearly stemmed not simply from its size or its superior resources, but from its ability to harness its power and concentrate it effectively. . . . Above all it came from an ability to mount an integrated effort across a broad spectrum of capabilities and to marshal the resources—social and political—as well as economic and military in an integrated manner.[5]

By contrast, the Gulf war revealed to regional powers the essential irrelevance of the (then) Soviet Union, as well as the fact that Germany and Japan, despite their growing economic capabilities, still lack the full range of power resources to match or compete with those of the United States. This widespread assessment of a dominant U.S. position accordingly led regional powers to align themselves more closely with, balance against, or find autonomous means of influencing the United States, depending on their regional circumstances and ambitions.

Bandwagoning. For some governments, the perception of a dominant U.S international position led to overt steps toward an accommodation with the United States or making an existing pro-American alignment clearer. This was especially true in the Middle East. Egypt, for example, was confirmed in its long-standing judgment that the United States was the dominant global and regional power. Saudi Arabia clearly aligned itself more prominently with the United States and accepted Washington as the principal guarantor of security in the Gulf instead of building up an independent Saudi deterrent force or pursuing the Damascus Declaration idea of using Egyptian and Syrian troops in the Gulf.[6] The Syrians also used the Gulf crisis as an opportunity to improve their ties with the United States, implementing a policy decision that had actually been made prior to the war in light of the growing weakness of Syria's superpower patron, the USSR.

Balancing. But for other nations and other actors, the Gulf war pointed toward the necessity to find the means to balance an unexpectedly powerful United States. In fact, for many regional powers in the immediate aftermath of Desert Storm—and not just those hostile to the United States—there was considerable concern about

the possible emergence of a U.S.-dominated "unipolar world."[7] U.S. policy during the Gulf crisis and war suggested that Washington, freed of the constraints of the Cold War and in the wake of its overwhelming triumph in the Gulf, might enter into a new phase of international activism. This activism would be marked by Washington's efforts, using the political-military capabilities and strategy exhibited during the Gulf war, to impose its notions of democracy, human rights, and economic development on states with different values.

A number of regional powers believed themselves to be particularly out of step with the U.S. New World Order. The Gulf war demonstrated graphically that they could no longer rely on the implicit or explicit support of the former Soviet Union or use the Soviet card in some fashion to limit the range of U.S. action against them. In the aftermath of the Gulf war, these states—which included Iraq, North Korea, Iran, Cuba, and Libya—sought to find some means to offset U.S. power at a time when no obvious global or regional balancer was in sight. Essentially, these states seek to avoid short-term conflict with the United States (by means discussed in the following section) while waiting for Washington's inevitable decline.

From this perspective, the Gulf war represented the last hurrah of fading power. Deeply rooted trends in international relations toward multipolarity—trends that were evident long before the Gulf war—are expected to reassert themselves once the political afterglow of the U.S. performance in Operation Desert Storm wears off. The perspective of these regional powers, consciously or not, borrows heavily from the popular U.S. intellectual debate of the late 1980s about the longevity of U.S. power. Iraq's foreign minister Tariq Aziz, for instance, has argued that "the alleged American age lacks permanence, and is plagued by many factors of weakness and backwardness. . . . Any decline in the American power—which is at its peak and can grow no further—would mean relative progress for the Arab forces." Two serious problems—the budget and trade deficits—"constitute the gravest internal threat to American military power and superior political posture. The world has never seen an empire capable of maintaining military and political hegemony without a firm and stable financial base."[8]

By this line of thinking, the U.S. decline is not expected to manifest itself fully for another 5 to 10 years, so it has only limited operational value for day-to-day policy-making, even for those governments that claim to embrace this viewpoint. The long-term candidates for a great-power counter to the United States include the PRC (a popular choice in the Middle East), while some states hold out hope that a revived Russia or a united Europe might provide such a balance over time.

Autonomy. The most common response to the perceived rise in the value of U.S. power and commitment that emerged from the Gulf war and the end of the Cold War was neither simply to bandwagon with, nor balance against, the United States, but to seek some measure of autonomy or limited independence. The purpose of this autonomy is not necessarily to oppose Washington's policies but rather to acquire the political and strategic means to achieve minimum national objectives without reference to the United States, especially with respect to regional security issues. More important, some degree of autonomy provides nations with an ability to

influence the U.S. decision-making process in future regional crises. The search for autonomy vis-à-vis the United States is by no means new, but the Gulf war indicated that many states will have to find such autonomy through different means than obtained during the Cold War.

Israel's post–Gulf war policy provides an interesting example of the strategic reassessment that several important U.S. allies went through in 1991 and 1992.[9] The Gulf war held a mixed message for the Israelis: it demonstrated the importance of close ties with the United States, while at the same time it revealed that Washington, after the end of the Cold War, no longer placed the same value on Israel as a strategic ally. Given the fragility of the strategic relationship between the two countries, Israelis felt the need to reduce their dependence on Washington, especially in the military arena. Immediately after the Gulf war, Israeli policymakers felt a heightened awareness that Israel must develop an independent military force strong enough to enable it to cope alone with all foreseeable threats. This meant in particular dealing with the surface-to-surface missile (SSM) problem through the development of a wide range of countermeasures, including independent early warning systems as well as indigenous offensive and defensive counters to Arab SSMs. The Israelis felt that they paid a serious political and military price for their dependence on the United States for these capabilities during the Gulf war.

The Israeli case also points up the boundaries of the search for autonomy or limited independence, however. In the military arena, Israel is coming to the same realization faced by most U.S. allies: it is simply too expensive to pursue self-reliance in areas that would truly make a difference. Areas such as C³I (command, control, communications, and intelligence), ballistic-missile defense, and logistics require enormous investments that are difficult to justify in the current economic and security climate, especially when it is possible to "plug in" to the much more extensive U.S. capabilities (even if these capabilities come with an associated political price tag). There is evidence that Israel, upon reflection, may be inclined to work out a cooperative division of labor with the United States in some key sensitive areas, despite its initial post-Gulf impulse toward autonomy. The Israeli military feels that it can spend its limited dollars best if it can assume that U.S. capabilities will be available.

The Importance of International Intervention

The Gulf war set a critical precedent: in the future external military intervention in regional conflicts will probably occur under international, not national or bilateral, auspices. This precedent was set by Washington's choice. From the perspective of regional powers, the United States took this approach for several basic reasons that are likely to hold in future major crises. First, and most obvious, is the U.S. need for financial support. Second, it can be expected that the United States, or other major powers seeking to lead an international coalition, will use multinational arrangements to provide domestic and international legitimacy. Third, in many cases, intervention in some regional conflicts will be so demanding that these powers will require the support of many other states, which support is often most readily called upon through an international mechanism. This support—including bases, overflight rights, and logistical support—may be

necessary to apply *decisive* force (i.e., at a level that ensures a quick conflict with low casualties and low collateral damage). International support will be all the more necessary if another major power center besides the United States (e.g., Europe) takes the lead.

Various regional powers are responding to this implication of the Gulf war in different ways according to their particular national circumstances. Some states are eager to participate in such interventions as a means of gaining influence over the decision-making process of international coalitions and of advancing specific national interests. (Egypt clearly fell into this category during the Gulf war, although not all of its expectations were met in the end.) It is not inconceivable that some regional powers could configure their militaries largely for this purpose—to become the Swiss Guard of twenty-first-century international coalitions—as a means of gaining political and economic benefits.

Dissuading International Intervention. Another class of regional powers is concerned that its own actions or ambitions may trigger international military intervention and wishes to dissuade or deter such intervention. The general approach of such states is to rely on political measures designed to reassure external powers (or at least obfuscate the situation), coupled with measured increases in selected military capabilities to raise the price of intervention.

There is no indication that the Gulf war caused any regional power to alter its ambitions fundamentally over the longer term. The war, combined with the loss of the Soviet counterweight, nevertheless had a clear "chilling effect" on states potentially hostile to U.S. and Western interests (for example, North Korea, Iran, Libya, Cuba, and, of course, Iraq). As noted above, the Gulf war and the end of the Cold War led to fears among such states that U.S. activism would increase and that the United States would seek to impose a unipolar world. This has led to, or reinforced, a rule of thumb among them: Do not take actions that will provoke international intervention, especially those interventions that would serve as a cover for U.S. military action.

There is a problem with following such a rule of thumb: these regional powers are currently uncertain about the precise threshold for triggering international military action. For the moment, they tend to err on the side of caution while probing to determine where "red lines" exist. (Saddam Hussein has been quite active in this realm since the end of the Gulf war and seems to have developed a rather refined sense of where the tolerance level of the United States and the international community lies.) Again, states in this class have not abandoned their external ambitions, but they are seeking, or continue to seek, more subtle and long-term means of achieving them. These means include political "charm offensives" that break down the willingness of at least some key external powers to intervene against them.

From the perspective of Syria's Hafez al-Assad, for example, Saddam Hussein drew exactly the wrong lessons from the U.S. withdrawal from Beirut in 1983. By taking on the United States directly by invading Kuwait, Iraq courted disaster. (The Iranians, too, assume that if Saddam Hussein had approached the problem differently, subtly or by stages, for example by slicing off northern Kuwait or simply by the demonstrative use of force, Iraq could have avoided inter-

national intervention and gained all the benefits of its superior military power.) The Syrians believe that their approach to gaining greater regional power is more subtle and hence more effective—witness Damascus's gradual establishment of control over Lebanon, which eventually had de facto U.S. blessing. Saddam Hussein's style is to rob banks; al-Assad's style is to establish protection rackets. The latter style may become an increasingly preferred course for ambitious Middle Eastern states that have learned this lesson of the second Gulf war.[10]

The government of Serbia can hardly be accused of relying on subtle tactics. Nevertheless, there is strong evidence that the Serbian camp has been careful that its actions remain below the threshold of provoking unacceptable international pressure, particularly an armed intervention, based in part on its assessment of the Gulf war experience.[11] Belgrade assumes that the threshold for intervention is much higher in the case of Yugoslavia than was true in the Gulf, given the lack of overriding material interests (e.g., oil) in the Balkans. At those points in the crisis when international military action seemed most likely—for example, September 1991 or spring 1992—the Serbian camp made apparent concessions to the international community, however tactical in character.

The Serbians implicitly took from the Gulf war the lesson of the need to avoid international isolation; in the post–cold war environment, Serbia cannot necessarily hope to rely on "traditional" good relations with states like France but must make every effort to persuade potential members of an anti-Serbian alliance that it is not in their interest to back such a coalition. Serbian officials and media have accordingly suggested that any international intervention force would become bogged down in guerrilla war. Second, they have attempted to disguise Belgrade's military role and create the impression of a chaotic, uncontrollable ethnic war. The Serbians encourage the belief that an international intervention force would not only be bogged down militarily but would be caught in an incomprehensible political maelstrom. (This contention has the added benefit of being arguably true.)

Serbia's political strategy has required more effective use of the media than Saddam Hussein exercised in Kuwait or than the Serbians themselves were able to use during the Slovenian and Croatian phases of the war. The Serbian military's studies of the Gulf war pointed to the importance of developing good relations with a pool of suitably "informed" journalists. The leader of the Serbs in Bosnia (Radovan Karadzic) accordingly tried to seize the media initiative, giving frequent press briefings and interviews, sending letters to the *Times* in London, as well as allowing reporters access to the military units ostensibly under his control. Karadzic's key message for the Western press played down the image of a war between forces loyal to the Bosnian government and insurgents controlled by Belgrade and played up the image of a maelstrom of ethnic hostilities. The message was clear: international military intervention would be another Vietnam, not another Desert Storm.

Weapons of Mass Destruction. For the most part, the steps by regional powers noted above are political means designed to reduce the likelihood of external military intervention. They are *not* aimed at directly countering a future Operation Desert Storm. Some states are, however, contemplating means to raise the perceived costs of

action by the advanced military powers in hopes of deterring intervention even if political strategies are not successful. The military-technical counters to international military intervention are discussed in the following section, but one area is worthy of particular note in this section on international intervention: the potential utility of weapons of mass destruction and long-range means of delivery (especially ballistic missiles).

Some key states that fit the "aggressor" category—Iraq, Iran, North Korea, Libya, Syria—have placed increased priority on weapons of mass destruction and ballistic missiles after the Gulf war. The supposed remark of a retired Indian army chief of staff on the lesson of that war—"Don't fight the Americans without nuclear weapons"—has been widely cited as indicative of the thinking of regional powers on this issue. A more representative formulation might be stated as follows: If a state has nuclear weapons, it may not need to fight the Americans.

Some regional states have, in fact, a number of reasons to acquire weapons of mass destruction besides their effect on the United States and other external powers; one is prestige. From their perspective, international organizations and agreements (e.g., the United Nations and the Nuclear Non-Proliferation Treaty) are run by and for the great powers. Small countries must get around these agreements in order to buy themselves a place at the table of the great powers, and nuclear weapons, especially in light of the Gulf war, are seen as an important way to do this. But such programs are two-edged swords: nuclear weapons might conceivably deter international intervention, but they might also serve as a lightning rod for external military action designed to preempt such pro-

Patrick J. Garrity

grams or as an excuse for outside intervention in local or regional conflicts. The postwar fate of Iraq cannot have gone unnoticed. In short, calculating the costs and benefits of trying to obtain nuclear weapons is a complex exercise even for the most anti-Western states. The easy answer in all cases is not necessarily to acquire weapons of mass destruction, much less to use them.

Encouraging International Intervention. The Gulf war was a graphic demonstration to militarily less powerful regional states of their potential to become victims in the post–cold war era. For these states, the Iraqi invasion of Kuwait dispelled the notion that security could be maintained largely through non-military instruments or by local means.

Some regional powers, such as Saudi Arabia, have decided that because of their intrinsic importance they can rely on the military guarantee of the only superpower, the United States—although the Saudis still want the U.S. presence to stay over the horizon. But most other nations with the potential to become "victims" do not think that they can rely on Washington alone. Even a state like Singapore, which has sought to strengthen its ties with the United States since the Gulf war and which has no great-power alternative to U.S. protection, is dubious that the United States will intervene whenever or wherever a small state becomes the victim of aggression. It therefore favors strengthening UN security mechanisms that deal with the maintenance of international peace and security.[12]

But how confident can smaller states be of international mechanisms to maintain their security? The Gulf war initially created the belief that the international community might automat-

ically intervene to protect "innocent victims" of aggression—namely, that a New World Order existed in fact as well as rhetoric. In the early stages of the Yugoslav crisis in 1991, Croatia tried to adopt an "innocent victim" posture to prompt international armed intervention on its behalf, and official Croatian representatives made frequent public efforts to link Croatia's situation with that of Kuwait.[13] Serbian president Slobodan Milosevic was characterized as "the Saddam Hussein of the Balkans." The successful appeal for protection by the Kurds to the Security Council was seen as a precedent for Croatia's appeal to the international community.

The Croatian strategy was clearly not as successful. By contrast, official Slovenian assessments of the Gulf war in early 1991, which were part of a more comprehensive study by the international community, led to the conclusion that, unless there was an overriding material reason for international intervention, an "innocent victim" strategy would not suffice. Slovenia's defense preparations accordingly were consistent with the territorial defense doctrine of the old Yugoslavia (Doctrine of General People's Defense), that is, defend in order to mobilize international support.[14] The lesson for such states from the experience of Kuwait is that the lack of any effective defensive military capability invites aggression. The likelihood of successful international intervention, in turn, is thought to be increased if the "victim" can delay and complicate the actions of the aggressor.

The Importance of Modern Military Power

Operation Desert Storm demonstrated to most, although not all, regional powers the advent of a new type of modern warfare characterized by advanced military technologies, well-led and well-trained forces, and superior doctrine and operational concepts. This demonstration has forced a general reevaluation of regional military capabilities and competence.

Most foreign military assessments did not fail to note the unique or unusual circumstances of the Gulf war that favored the coalition; to some extent, this realization may qualify potential lessons learned. The Vietnamese leadership, although amazed by the relative ease with which the Americans destroyed the Soviet-built Iraqi air defense system, pointed out that the topography of the region was one of the major contributory factors in the U.S. success.[15] The Serbian military also noted the favorable desert terrain, the six months of uninterrupted time to build up forces in the theater, and the passivity of the Iraqi defenses. In the Serbians' view, the war was virtually won in the period of preparation.[16] But most foreign assessments tended not to dwell on the limitations on U.S. military power that these circumstances might have implied but rather on the inherent potential, capabilities, and advantages possessed by advanced military forces.

That said, most regional powers do not regard the U.S. style of war, as demonstrated in the Gulf, as something they will attempt to emulate. This fact limits somewhat the salience of Gulf war lessons learned for foreign militaries. To be sure, foreign militaries are actively pursuing certain technologies, capabilities, or concepts that were demonstrated in the Gulf, but Operation Desert Storm is regarded as a uniquely U.S. phenomenon. For the most part, foreign militaries believe that it is simply too expensive to try to duplicate U.S. technological capa-

bilities across the board. The decisive U.S. edge in the Gulf war was not merely one of superior quality but of quantity of quality. Also, the use of such technology requires an advanced social and educational infrastructure, which may not be well developed in many non-Western states.

General Reactions. Most foreign militaries found that the Gulf war tended to reinforce and accelerate existing trends and policies rather than set them off in a completely new direction. Most are thinking about selectively incorporating technologies or operational concepts demonstrated during Operation Desert Storm into their own national security objectives and military circumstances. The focus is on new technologies and capabilities that hold promise of being better able to achieve existing political-military goals rather than on striving for revolutionary changes on the battlefield.

One general point about regional military responses should be noted. The Gulf war clearly piqued the interest of foreign militaries in the high-technology systems displayed in Operation Desert Storm (many of which were known and sought after even before the war). This expressed interest, however, is not always matched by actual procurement. In most countries, budgets rather than military strategy are the dominant factor, and these budgets as a rule are flat or on the decline. A technical gap is therefore beginning to open between a relatively few regional powers who are moving ahead and their peers who are not. With a few notable exceptions such as the PRC and Iran, the former are pro-American and they are buying Western equipment.

Second, not surprisingly, most regional militaries have an increased appreciation of the value of air power and air defense. Nations such as the PRC and Iran see long-range aircraft, perhaps coupled with precision-guided munitions (PGMs), as providing a strategic power-projection force. But territory is still thought to matter. From Israel's perspective, for example, successful campaigns require proper air cover, but forces on the ground win wars. Under the right circumstances, air power might defeat invading forces, but it cannot occupy territory or force a change of regime.

Third, the war pointed to a few narrow technical areas on which regional militaries are now tending to concentrate. The most prominent among these are electronic warfare and electronic countermeasures, night combat capabilities, and PGMs. Other areas of interest include cheap means of surveillance (e.g., remotely piloted vehicles), C³I, and advanced SSMs. The second-tier states are tending to concentrate their resources in a few critical areas rather than revamp their military capabilities across the board, primarily because of the expense. These states also realize that to produce and operate advanced technologies is beyond the capacity of their societies.

Fourth, the Gulf war strongly reinforced the importance of professionalism over more politically oriented ("people's war") approaches to military affairs. As a consequence, regional powers are tending to move away from large standing armies toward smaller, more professional, and better-trained forces. In some cases, there may be an interest in moving toward two-tiered forces: a small, high-quality, high-tech, first-tier force and a larger, mass-oriented, second-tier force. Such developments may be driven as much by costs as by considerations of military strategy.

Fifth, Soviet hardware has not necessarily been devalued by regional powers simply because of its poor performance in the Gulf war. Iraqi misuse of Soviet equipment is generally understood. Systems like the MiG–29 and the T–72 are quite suitable for internal use and most regional conflicts, however inferior they might be to U.S. (or Israeli) hardware crewed by highly trained professionals. The concern of third world states about acquiring Soviet or Russian military hardware has more to do with uncertainty about long-term assurance of supplies and maintenance given the conditions in the former Soviet Union. Second-tier states that are committed to Soviet hardware can be expected to try to address specific problems revealed by the Gulf war through upgrades with Western subsystems. This process will not be cheap, however, and this may limit the extent to which such upgrades actually occur.

Sixth, SSMs look increasingly attractive in a regional military context, and they offer one of the few areas in which second- and third-tier states can compete with the major powers. Mobility for SSMs seems to provide real advantages over air operations designed to hunt and destroy mobile missiles. The effectiveness of Patriot against the Iraqi Scuds remains a controversial subject, but there is a sense among foreign militaries that more advanced SSMs will have an advantage over Patriot and its successors. Ideally SSMs would complement aircraft, but out of necessity they may have to be used for some missions that would normally be assigned to manned aircraft.

The Reaction of Potentially Hostile Regional Powers. There is a special class of states to which the Gulf war should logically have been of particular interest: regional powers whose ambitions could bring them, at least potentially, into military conflict with the United States and other advanced industrial nations. For these hostile states, the Gulf war represents a fertile laboratory from which to take military-technical lessons that might stand them in better stead in the event of a future clash with the Americans.[17]

Surprisingly, military lessons learned seem not to have been the focus of hostile powers as they reacted to Operation Desert Storm. This is not to say that the Gulf war was unimportant; quite the contrary. But rather than provide a blueprint for fighting the Americans, the war instead reinforced the importance of avoiding war with the United States and other major industrial powers. To the extent that Gulf war lessons learned are being applied at the military level, they are fundamentally conditioned by concerns other than those of fighting the United States. For most of the hostile powers, the dominant considerations are often as much internal control and prestige as traditional combat effectiveness. Military effectiveness itself is measured against potential regional adversaries much more than against the United States.

That said, hostile powers understand that circumstances beyond their control could bring about conflict with the United States and/or an international coalition. From the perspective of these powers, war is much more likely to occur as a result of what they regard as miscalculation or U.S. arrogance than because of deliberate provocation on their part. A few states, such as North Korea, are concerned with becoming directly involved against U.S. military power; a larger group of states fears the possibility of U.S. intervention in ongoing regional conflicts. In either circumstance, the limited evidence available suggests that the smaller powers would be in-

clined to adopt "asymmetrical counters" to the U.S. style of warfare and that the Gulf war represents a model (albeit imperfect) of how to prosecute such a war.[18]

The Outlines of an Asymmetrical Strategy. First, the essential goal of an asymmetrical strategy would be that regime's survival, not military victory over the United States or an international coalition. There is an almost universal expectation that U.S. military action would begin with a strategic air campaign, as it did during the Gulf war. A hostile regional power's asymmetrical strategy would thus depend first and foremost on avoiding the decapitation of the political and military leadership by that air campaign, especially at the outset of a conflict.

Second, a hostile regional power would try to prevent or dissuade the United States from "taking Baghdad" on the ground in later stages of the war. The hostile state may be unable to do this by military means; it must therefore be sensitive to providing the United States with incentives not to occupy the entire country. The Gulf war, in fact, may have shown that the United States is not inclined to force a regime change through a policy of conquest and occupation. The prolonged difficulties with Saddam Hussein after the end of the Gulf war might alter future U.S. war aims to include the replacement of the regime, but this has yet to be demonstrated. Still, hostile states must be aware of the need to stay below key U.S. thresholds—the threshold at which the United States would decide to intervene in the first place and the threshold of escalating the war to seek the overthrow of the regime. The threat of Secretary of State James A. Baker III to Tariq Aziz in January 1991 suggested a threshold of sufficient importance to trigger U.S. escalation—the use of weapons of mass destruction.

Third, an asymmetrical campaign by a hostile power would seek to seize or regain the initiative by striking at U.S. and coalition centers of political gravity. These centers of gravity are, first and foremost, the political system and public opinion of the United States, which are arguably sensitive to casualties, the length of the conflict, and civilian damage. These manifestations of the so-called Vietnam syndrome were not necessarily dispelled by the Gulf war; in fact, U.S. tolerance for the apparent costs of war may have actually declined because of the exceedingly high standards that were set by Operation Desert Storm. A future U.S.-led coalition would have the same sort of sensitivities, and there would be inherent differences of policy and interest among coalition members that would also be exploitable. Finally, coalition members would be concerned with any threats to their homelands that the hostile power might be able to pose.

In short, regional powers may regard Saddam Hussein's basic approach to the Gulf war as sound, even if his strategy was flawed and poorly executed. The challenge to future hostile powers that might find themselves at war with a U.S.-led international coalition is to devise better means to impose costs (casualties, time, collateral damage) on the coalition—without triggering escalation.

The Means to Execute an Asymmetrical Strategy. There is a strong sense that hostile regional powers confronting the United States in the future will try to optimize the low end of the technology spectrum, complemented with perhaps a few relatively high-tech systems. Cover, concealment, and deception are likely to rank high as elements of any aggressor's strategy against advanced military powers. This is widely recognized as the most effective Iraqi tactic during the Gulf war. For the Serbian military, for example, the Iraqi use of camouflage offered beneficial lessons which "for our armed forces are particularly significant." These lessons included not only the camouflaging of units, firing positions, and airfields, but also the creation of false targets using decorative and "sceniographic" methods. Among the specific successes mentioned by the Serbian military was the use of decoy Scud launchers.[19]

Cheap countermeasures are another potential means of delaying or disrupting operations by an advanced military power. Mobility seems to be the preferred low-tech counter to PGMs, but obscurants may also be employed to complicate their use. Relatively small and inexpensive lasers can blind sensors. Sea mines serve as effective barriers to amphibious operations. More ambitiously, hostile states might look to imaginative combinations of dual-use and proliferated technologies, possibly combined with new operational concepts. For example, as the *1992 U.S. Joint Military Net Assessment* noted:

The proliferation of high-technology equipment is giving more and smaller nations the ability to employ sophisticated countermeasures against US C⁴I systems. The rapidly growing use of computers and data networks in command and control applications presents adversaries with targets for exploitation at all levels of conflict. Potential threats are not limited to major military powers. The low cost and compact size of high-technology components make attempts at penetration of computer networks possible by "hackers," terrorists, drug traffickers, and hostile [states].[20]

Because collateral damage in the CNN era can be so politically troublesome, a hostile power might actually seek to "encourage" collateral damage. Rather than just park military aircraft next to historical monuments, a hostile power could structurally intermingle civilian and military infrastructures so that schools are part of nuclear research facilities. The United States might be tricked into attacking civilian targets that seemed to emanate military electronics traffic. Attacks on civilian installations can be faked. Along these lines, anything that can be done to confuse U.S. and coalition procedures to identify friend or foe and create friendly fire casualties would also be of interest.

Hostile powers may well seek means to strike directly at the territory of coalition partners or even the U.S. homeland. Given the Iraqi experience, mobile ballistic missiles are widely seen to have significant advantages over offensive counterforce and active and passive defenses and thus are very attractive instruments of power projection. Weapons of mass destruction could be a part of this power-projection package. Such a combination of SSMs and weapons of mass destruction could also conceivably have a serious military effect if they were, for instance, used to strike against high-value targets like air bases and ports or create nuclear effects. More accurate missiles and specialized conventional munitions for SSM warheads might even provide a credible nonnuclear alternative. And as the United States and its allies are likely to try to improve upon Patriot-type systems, potentially hostile states are likely to explore countermeasures, among them, warhead hardening, chaff and decoys, active jamming, stealth, and terminal maneuvers.

Terrorism remains another potential tool of taking the war to the enemy, along with ecological and economic warfare (which Saddam Hussein attempted by pumping oil into the Persian Gulf and destroying Kuwaiti oil fields). Potential examples of ecological or economic warfare include attacks or threatened attacks against nuclear power plants, civilian chemical production facilities, and electrical, financial, and telecommunication networks.

The advantages of trying to strike political centers of gravity in this fashion must be weighed against the possibility that such attacks would exceed U.S. or coalition thresholds and lead to an unwanted escalation of the war that would place the regime at risk. This suggests that such means may be thought of primarily as a deterrent— to deter U.S. intervention in the first place or preserve the regime if intervention does occur.

Evidence of Asymmetrical Thinking. The Brazilian military has been one of the few sources overtly to speculate, at least in a theoretical sense, on what would be required for a regional power to avoid being "Iraqed." The Brazilian hypothetical approach rests on two assumptions: first, no single tactic is likely to suffice against an advanced military power, and second, no regional power can afford the hardware to take on the advanced military powers as well as its regional opponents. These assumptions point toward the advantages of investing in a few carefully selected high-technology conventional weapons that could complicate the military operations of an advanced power and that might prove

51

decisive in a regional conflict. The Brazilians cite especially SSMs, space launch systems, PGMs, and nuclear-powered attack submarines. The lower-tech power should also exploit variants of irregular fighting, including terrorism and guerrilla warfare, depending on the local conditions. Finally, weapons of mass destruction can serve as a potent counter to the advanced military powers, with nuclear weapons being the clear preference.[21]

Implications for the United States

Much has obviously changed since the end of Operation Desert Storm in February 1991. The Gulf war, contrary to speculation at the time, did not lead to the creation of a New World Order. But the Gulf war remains the first real data point in the post–cold war era; foreign nations still judge trends—up or down—from this basic reference point. In addition, the Gulf war revealed, or confirmed, certain fundamental facts about international relations that continue to be relevant, although regional powers acknowledge the uniqueness of Operation Desert Shield and Desert Storm.

What do the reactions of regional powers to the Gulf war imply for U.S. policymakers? Some of the potential key issues are listed below.

First and foremost, it is essential to recognize the importance that regional powers continue to accord the United States as the organizing force in international relations. What is much less certain to foreign observers is whether, how, and for what purpose the United States will apply its power in the post–cold war, post–Gulf war world—especially given the electoral defeat of the architect of Desert Storm, George Bush.

The emerging short-term challenge for the Clinton administration is to demonstrate to foreign observers that U.S. power will continue to be applied purposefully and effectively to achieve U.S. and international objectives. This does not mean that President Bill Clinton need emulate his predecessor in the successful, large-scale use of military force, but it does mean that regional powers will be watching closely to determine whether, and how, U.S. interests and thresholds for diplomatic and military action might be changing. U.S. policymakers should be aware that their actions in the former Yugoslavia, Somalia, and elsewhere are becoming part of a pattern of international peacemaking and peacekeeping begun by the Gulf war. This pattern is being observed by foreign powers who wish the United States well, or ill, for clues about how they should behave in future crises closer to home.

Over the longer term, the United States will have to address three areas if it is to retain its central position in the international system. The first is economic and technological competitiveness. The fact that the United States had to seek major international funding for the Gulf war gave a serious, and negative, impression of U.S. economic weakness that must be addressed. The second concerns military power. Any sense that the United States could not perform a Desert Storm in 5 to 10 years due to military retrenchment would remove an essential pillar of U.S. diplomatic influence and encourage or impel other powers, major and lesser, to try to fill the vacuum. Finally, there is international legitimacy. As a legacy of its successful leadership during the Cold War, the United States enjoys a level of global prestige that goes beyond its economic and military strength and that allows it to guide the international community on issues Washington regards as vital. This prestige is not automatic; it ultimately depends on a sense that U.S. leadership is legitimate because it stands for something beyond the narrow national interest. Such legitimacy is essential in dealing with international fears about U.S. activism as well as speculation about potential U.S. decline.

Second, the Gulf war signaled the emergence of a potentially dangerous asymmetry of views concerning the future role and importance of nuclear weapons. The advanced military powers, notably the United States, Britain, and France, have made strong efforts to separate their nuclear capabilities from regional conflict contingencies. The Gulf war indicated that the advanced military powers believe that they enjoy such conventional superiority over regional rivals in high-intensity warfare that there is no need to play the nuclear card. These states indicated that if Saddam Hussein had used weapons of mass destruction (whether chemical or biological) during the Gulf war, their preferred method of retaliation would have been conventional in character.

On the other hand, for regional powers that are on the wrong side of the military-technical gap and that have reason to be concerned about a U.S.-led intervention, nuclear weapons appear to be an increasingly attractive means of offsetting that gap and deterring intervention. The preferred method for the advanced military powers to deal with this asymmetry will be primarily political in character and aimed at preventing proliferation through, for example, tightened export controls or reassurance of regional powers through measures such as a nuclear test ban, coupled with the threat of conventional preemption of nuclear facilities. But thought should also be given to circumstances in which a hostile regional power has obtained nuclear weapons. This hostile power may not share Western ideas of deterrence—which is not to say that it cannot be deterred, but that U.S. policymakers must understand the very different strategic dynamics that this situation could create.

In such a situation, Washington itself will obviously be concerned with the need to avoid being deterred by a nuclear-armed hostile regime from taking actions that otherwise would be in the vital interests of the United States. But there are other issues as well. For example, during a crisis or conflict, the nuclear command and control arrangements of the regional power may not be stable or secure. Internal conflicts may place the weapons in jeopardy. Other nations may inject themselves into the situation to protect their perceived interests, and so on.

Finally, the Gulf war did not necessarily signal a revolution in military affairs, but it will lead to, or reinforce, trends in national military thinking that could result in significant changes in future defense concepts, force structure, doctrine, and tactics. The United States now enjoys a unique global military capability that is unlikely to be challenged for perhaps the next 5 to 10 years. But that does not mean that the United States is omnipotent always and everywhere. The war with Iraq demonstrated that U.S. forces perform superbly in the desert—but can they do as well in mountains, jungles, or urban areas? At some point, a hostile regional power may intentionally or inadvertently test U.S. capabilities under these more difficult circumstances. If the United States performs less than adequately, this would offset much of the prestige that the U.S. military gained in Operation Desert Storm.

The Gulf war will in any case be a central reference point for any regional military that desires to move up to another level of technological capability and especially if it seeks to meet an advanced military power on more equal terms. Foreign militaries can thus be expected to continue the "lessons learning" process for some time, perhaps after a period of apparent lack of interest. This argues for the value of continuing to track foreign assessments of Operation Desert Storm. Looking into the first decade of the next century, U.S. policymakers should be aware of indications that regional powers, perhaps allied with more advanced states, might seek to develop high-technology, leading-edge forces with the aim of challenging U.S. interests across a range of contingencies.

In some cases, these highly capable units could supplement regular standing armies, perhaps as special operations strike forces. Like contemporary standoff weapons, however, such forces may become the symbols of a country's rapid-response ability to control strategic situations ("arriving first with the most"). These forces will be efficient not only as to budget and manpower but will conform to modern trends by emphasizing mobility and maneuver rather than overwhelming mass. The ability to produce and deliver nuclear, chemical, and biological weapons could become much more sophisticated and militarily effective. Hostile regional military powers can be expected eventually to go beyond low-technology countermeasures and attempt to devise means to strike directly at the U.S. military centers of gravity—command and control, logistics, and joint operations. Counter-societal tactics might also emerge, among them human and computer viruses, economic disruption through disabling key networks, and environmental warfare.

These speculations may seem far-fetched, but they are intended to reinforce one of the central theses of this article: regional powers learned a good deal from the Gulf war, but they do not expect or intend that the war will define their future. Regional powers are understandably working to accommodate or work around the Gulf war experience so that they will be in a better position to deal with future crises and conflicts. The U.S. performance in Operation Desert Shield and Desert Storm has played a major role in shaping the expectations of regional powers, but it must be borne in mind that the Gulf war afterglow will have a finite half-life.

This article does not necessarily represent the views of the Los Alamos National Laboratory or the U.S. Department of Energy.

Notes

1. This article is derived from Patrick J. Garrity, *Does the Gulf War Still Matter? Foreign Perspectives on the War and the Future of International Security*, CNSS Report no. 16 (Los Alamos, N.Mex.: Center for National Security Studies, Los Alamos National Laboratory, May 1993). Material and analysis for both documents were compiled during an 18-month CNSS project on lessons learned from the Gulf war by other countries that involved specially commissioned papers from country experts, a series of workshops on key regions, and extensive interviews with U.S. and foreign government officials and academic specialists. The assistance of Robert Swartz and James Thomas, CNSS graduate research associates, was critical in this effort. The substantive and editorial assistance of Gerrit Gong was also invaluable. The views

expressed in this article, however, are the author's alone and do not necessarily reflect those of any individual involved in the project.

2. See, for example, *Conduct of the Persian Gulf War: Final Report to Congress* (Washington, D.C.: U.S. Department of Defense, April 1992); Les Aspin and William Dickinson, *Defense for a New Era: Lessons of the Persian Gulf War* (Washington, D.C.: Brassey's, 1992); and James A. Blackwell, Jr., Michael J. Mazarr, and Don M. Snider, *The Gulf War: Military Lessons Learned—Interim Report of the CSIS Study Group on Lessons Learned from the Gulf War* (Washington, D.C.: CSIS, 1991).

3. Two other caveats should be made. Some nations may be careful to conceal—or at least not publicize—lessons that they may have drawn from the Persian Gulf crisis and war. Second, the most important factor in determining Gulf war lessons learned by many foreign states may well be their perception of what the United States learned. This is especially true at the military-technical level, where many nations simply lack the ability to understand what the United States did during the Gulf war.

4. Foreign observers noted certain U.S. weaknesses and certain constraints on U.S. action—most notably in finance, where the image of Uncle Sam going hat in hand for contributions for Operation Desert Shield and Desert Storm made a serious, and negative, impression. These weaknesses and problems tended to be washed out in the immediate afterglow of the war, however.

5. Shahram Chubin, "Iran and the Lessons of the Gulf War 1991" (Paper prepared for CNSS Foreign Gulf War Lessons Learned Study, November 1991), p. 1.

6. These Egyptian and Saudi alignments have not been made without important reservations that may have important implications for the future, however. See Garrity, *Does the Gulf War Still Matter?* chap. 1.

7. This does *not* mean that foreign elites rigorously apply definitions of "polarity" as defined by international relations theorists—merely that most are persuaded (or profess to be persuaded) that the United

States is the dominant power in the post–cold war world.

8. Baghdad Republic of Iraq Radio Network, May 20, 1992, in Foreign Broadcast Information Service–Near East and South Asia, May 21, 1992, pp. 19–20.

9. The following discussion is based on two papers written for the CNSS Foreign Gulf War Lessons Learned Study: Reuven Pedhatzur, "Gulf War Lessons Learned by Israel," January 1992, and Aharon Levran, "Gulf War Lessons—An Israeli Perspective," November 1991.

10. See Robert W. Swartz, "Lessons Learned from the Persian Gulf War: Middle East Perspectives," *CNSS Briefing* 8 (July 1992), p. 7. CNSS understanding of Middle Eastern lessons learned was greatly advanced by discussions with Ahmed Hashim, Michael Eisenstadt, Ken Pollack, Michael Dunn, and Seth Carus, among others.

11. The following discussion of Serbia is based on James Gow, "Yugoslavia and Lessons from the Gulf War" (Paper prepared for CNSS Foreign Gulf War Lessons Learned Study, October 1992). Gow emphasizes that the evidence for lessons learned by the various former Yugoslav republics is often inferential rather than direct.

12. Ishtiaq Hossain, "The Gulf War Lessons Learned by Foreign Nations: A Case Study of ASEAN States and Vietnam" (Paper prepared for CNSS Foreign Gulf War Lessons Learned Study, March 1992), pp. 6–9.

13. The following discussion is taken from Gow, "Yugoslavia and Lessons from the Gulf War," pp. 25–30.

14. The Gulf war also pointed to the importance of good media relations to Slovenia as well as Serbia—the Slovenians established a modern media center on the eve of their declaration of independence and provided efficient, regular briefings on events.

15. Written comments by Ishtiaq Hossain, National University of Singapore, September 16, 1992.

16. Gow, "Yugoslavia and Lessons from the Gulf War," p. 8.

17. As a U.S. defense official wrote after the war: "Potential adversaries of the United States will take note of Saddam Hussein's

shattering defeat and attempt to avoid a
similar fate, either by resorting to ambiguous, low-intensity violence or by acquiring their own high technology military capabilities, or by doing both." Alberto R.
Coll, "America as the Grand Facilitator,"
Foreign Policy, no. 87 (Summer 1992),
p. 51.

18. Much of what follows is admittedly speculative and is based on extensive discussions with regional experts to whom the
"what if war occurs" question was posed.
The most direct evidence of the attractiveness of an asymmetrical strategy actually comes from Soviet/Russian military
assessments of the war. See Notra Trulock
III, "The Soviet Military and the Gulf
War: A Preliminary Assessment" (Briefing,
CNSS, October 1991); and Jacob Kipp,
"The Gulf War, High Technology, and

Troop Control: The Nexus Between Mil-
itary-Political and Military-Technical Aspects of Future War" (U.S. Army Foreign
Military Studies Office, Fort Leaven-
worth, Kans., May 1992). Stephen Meyer
also provided helpful comments on this
subject.

19. Gow, "Yugoslavia and Lessons from the
Gulf War," pp. 10–11.

20. Joint Chiefs of Staff, *1992 Joint Military
Net Assessment* (Washington, D.C.: U.S.
Department of Defense, August 1992),
p. 11–8.

21. This assessment is taken from Domicio
Proenca, Jr., "Brazilian Perceptions of the
Persian Gulf War of 1991: An Impression-
istic View" (Paper prepared for CNSS For-
eign Gulf War Lessons Learned Study,
November 1991), pp. 21–22.

The Arms Trade Revolution: The Major Impact of Small Arms

Aaron Karp

DEPENDING ON ONE'S point of view, the international trade in military equipment has been going through a period of predictable adjustment or of radical transformation. The differences in perspective arise from basic concepts of what makes the arms trade important and about the objectives of arms transfer policy-making. Should that policy emphasize the most costly and advanced technologies, or those most likely to be used in warfare? Is the arms trade primarily about relations between sovereign governments and the health of key industries, or is it about the nature of conflict and the immediate danger to peace and prosperity?

Although it is only beginning to win the recognition it deserves, a revolution has hit the arms trade. Five years after the end of the Cold War, it is increasingly apparent that the role of that trade has changed dramatically. It

Aaron Karp is adjunct professor of international studies at Old Dominion University in Norfolk, Virginia. His publications include *Ballistic Missile Proliferation: The Politics and Technics* (1994) and *Arming Ethnic Conflict* (1994).

Copyright © 1994 by The Center for Strategic and International Studies and the Massachusetts Institute of Technology

The Washington Quarterly • 17:4

no longer serves primarily to influence the international balance of power. Instead it helps to regulate the emergence of new states. Its most important role is not arming the forces of allies and regional powers as in the past, but as a lever for controlling or promoting ethnic violence and the outbreak of war in the near future.

With this revolution in the nature of the arms trade's role has come an equally significant change in its tools. Although the trade in major weapon systems continues, it has lost most of its military and strategic importance. Instead it is the trade in small and light weapons that poses the most immediate threat to human well-being and international stability. No longer is the greatest challenge of arms trade policy the riddle of how to control the trade in major weapons between governments; rather it is the problem of addressing the flow of small and light arms to substate groups.

The Trade in Major Weapons: Transformation or Stasis?

How has the end of the Cold War affected perceptions of the arms trade? Reviewing recent books and articles in professional journals one gets the impression that those perceptions have not changed very much. Most studies continue to measure trends among suppliers and weaponry. A few evaluate the latest efforts at control. Others focus on the dilemma of how to minimize the trade's destabilizing international impact while preserving industrial capabilities at home. To the seasoned observer there is a sameness about these approaches that is at once reassuring and distressing. The unquestioned continuity of the work reaffirms the importance of long-standing issues. But the failure to react to the changing political environment is perplexing.

Although few dispute the extraordinary significance of the changes wrought by the end of the Cold War, arms trade policy and studies—more than most fields in international peace and security—have taken the changes in stride. Rather than reassessing the nature of the trade and stressing dramatic new possibilities, work on the arms trade continues to trudge along. Rather than seizing upon the sudden collapse of the post–cold war world order as an opportunity, long-standing approaches and priorities have been adapted. The net effect is to minimize, if not to deny, the transformation of the international system and the world order.

In other fields of competition between the major powers the end of the Cold War led to a breathtaking series of disclosures and agreements. It now seems all but inevitable that chemical weapons disarmament will be achieved for much of the world. Conventional forces in Europe are tightly regulated. In the nuclear field we have gone from the first Strategic Arms Reduction Treaty (START I) to START II, from South America's creation of a nuclear weapons free zone to South Africa's nuclear confessions. After decades in opposition, the United States has committed itself to negotiation of

a comprehensive nuclear test ban (CTB).[1] The most important barriers to outright nuclear disarmament are no longer raised by established nuclear powers. Rather it is the danger of proliferation that justifies the maintenance of residual nuclear forces. Perhaps the most important issue confronting nuclear strategists today is the question of minimum deterrence: How low can we go?

Arms trade policy-making and analysis, by comparison, continue pretty much as they did 10 or 20 years ago. A cold war Rip Van Winkle waking from a long nap would find the field completely familiar, dominated by the same policy questions and the same actors. Even the biggest changes have been met with minimal accommodation.

The disintegration of the Soviet Union has changed the hierarchy of arms exporters; the U.S. and German shares of the market have risen while most other exporters have seen their shares drop. With defense spending down around the world, the industry has gone through a round of shakeouts and consolidations. The list of recipients has seen some changes as well. After a buying binge in the wake of Desert Storm, Middle Eastern markets are declining, and East Asia has emerged instead as the world's only growing market for major weapon systems. These changes cannot be trivialized, but none challenges the basic rules of the game.

The stable rules of the major arms market are seen even more clearly in the political arena. Compared to the changes that have affected almost every other field in international security affairs, the arms trade is profoundly backward. Discussions among the five permanent members of the United Nations (UN) Security Council in 1991–92 resulted in promulgation of a set of vague standards, but nothing strong enough to affect major deals. The UN has established an arms register, but even its strongest defenders do not claim that this will change the nature of the trade. It is no overstatement to conclude that, compared to the opportunities for arms control and outright disarmament with regard to nuclear and chemical weapons, the trade in major conventional weapons is virtually unchanged.

Does the Trade in Major Weapons Matter?

Is there any reason to expect more ambitious responses to the changing political environment among students of the arms trade? One place to look for guidance is the theoretical literature on arms transfers. This is of little help, however, because it tends to stress the long-term continuities in the trade in major weapons. Recent and important additions to the field are illustrative. Each identifies a different factor as the basic engine of the arms trade: technology, power politics, or normative forces. But with their emphasis on the trade in major armaments none of these approaches explains anything about those weapons most likely to be used on contemporary battlefields.

The most innovative approach developed in recent years emphasizes the role of technological innovation and diffusion in shaping the trade in major weapons.[2] It suggests that every technological revolution brings with it a radical change in the arms trade, dominated every time by a handful of producers who are the first to master the new technology, which then is gradually disseminated throughout the world. The last wave began during the 1930s with the development of the turbojet engine, radar, battlefield electronics, and missiles and continues to this day. Over time more and more countries have acquired these technologies, but only a few, led by the United States, have remained their masters, allowing them to dominate much of the trade in major weapons.

This technological perspective offers great insight into the trade in major weapons, especially in explaining the patterns of the diffusion of technology and its consequences. But it also leads to the conclusion that the basic patterns of the trade in major weapons will continue much as they have throughout the post–cold war era. The end of the Cold War and the rising salience of ethnic warfare are simply not relevant.

Another, more orthodox approach stresses not technology but the role of the international system, that is, the distribution of power among states, as the basic force determining the rules of the game and who dominates the trade in arms.[3] From this perspective the changes in international politics—the disintegration of the Soviet Union and the rise of new exporters—are of greater importance. Without the rigid hierarchies and rules of the Cold War to guide it, the future trade in major weapons and advanced military technology will revert to the more confusing patterns of the 1930s.

Both the technological and systemic arguments are intellectually tantalizing, especially for understanding likely trends in the diffusion of major weapons. But there is little here that is relevant to technologically retarded phenomena like ethnic violence. Virtually all the weapons of ethnic warfare were designed decades ago. Today's battlefields look more like a museum than Silicon Valley. Indeed, one of the most perplexing problems of the trade in small and light arms is the near irrelevance of major powers and highly advanced states. This is a field in which small countries with archaic industries can directly affect global welfare.

A third, more nuanced approach to the arms trade emphasizes the role of international regimes, stressing the ways states buy and sell arms instead of the particular technology and countries involved. From this point of view the rules of the arms trade have changed repeatedly since 1945. Even so, the continuities outweigh the changes. The most sophisticated study to employ the regime approach maintains that the rules of the arms trade were fairly consistent throughout the years of greatest international transformation—1980 to 1992.[4] Profit all but replaced ideologically based aid as a motive for arms exports. Buyers became much more powerful in the market. Given greater freedom, it is no surprise that many buyers began to invest heavily in the proliferation of advanced weapons. But the basic processes and implications of the trade in major weapons remained the same.

By now it should be clear that no approach to the arms trade emphasizing the salience of major weapons can capture the substance of the recent revolution. It lies entirely beyond the reach of orthodox views of technology, the international system, and norms. It comes as no surprise that analyses of the arms trade have failed to confront the implications of the transformation even though we see evidence of it every day.

Much of the confusion also arises from the continuing role of the orthodox state-to-state trade in major military equipment. Traditional arms sales remain the preoccupation of government and industry officials, journalists, and activists, but their relevance is increasingly obscure. There is little danger that most of the major weapons

filling the world's arsenals will ever be used. They remain important in national economic and industrial policy, as symbols of national power and international commitments. But it is hard to imagine a recent international arms deal that has had an appreciable affect on regional stability, that has made war seem more likely or potentially more deadly.

As ethnic conflict has become the dominant form of warfare in the early 1990s, however, transfers of major weapons have lost much of their previous importance. It is light armaments that cause the greatest destruction today and that now deserve much greater attention. Rather than continuing to devote their efforts to the weapons of the Cold War, it behooves arms trade policy makers and analysts to concentrate on the weapons actually in use in the warfare of the new world order.

The Rising Salience of Smaller Weapons

The declining salience of major military systems reflects a broader transformation in the nature of warfare and international politics. Although there are countries like Iraq and North Korea that cause serious alarm, rulers bent on international conquest appear to be a dying breed. The danger of war breaking out is not the same scourge it was during most of the Westphalian era.

Among major powers warfare has long been unthinkable.[5] As the threat of major war recedes, so does the role of major weapons. Throughout the nuclear era, miscalculation or misperception, not deliberate choice, were always understood to pose the greatest risks. These risks proved to be manageable. The last serious confrontation between major powers came between the People's Republic of China and the Soviet Union in 1969, and that was easily contained.[6] The handful of confrontations that occurred subsequently carried slight risks of war by mistake, but not of war by choice. This was the case with the U.S.–Soviet confrontations over the Middle East in 1973 and over Poland in 1980.[7]

The logic that first prevailed among the major powers is increasingly dominant among regional governments as well. In regions as diverse as Latin and South America, Southern Africa, and Southeast Asia, there is little apparent risk of major war between states. Long-standing antagonists are able to agree on collective security arrangements. Even in areas where serious disputes remain and the threat of arms is ever present, the actual danger of warfare seems remote. India and Pakistan are still far apart on Kashmir, but far from ready to go to war. Even in the Middle East, all but a few governments are investing in the status quo. The few that still seek to change the geopolitical balance recognize that political—not military—processes offer the only sensible course to pursue. Iraq's invasion of Kuwait, far from starting a new trend, increasingly appears to have been an exception that taught obvious lessons.

If major war between states is increasingly seen as an anachronism, why do states still maintain large standing armies? Few states, it appears, are convinced that the changes in the international system are strong enough to justify breaking the habit. They are accustomed to standing forces; for over a century possession of a standing army was the physical proof of a nation's sovereignty. But the role of conventional forces is increasingly symbolic—to offer physical evidence of official seriousness, to command the respect of neighbors and rivals, and to

make the nation more visible and influential.[8] Although the risk that major weapons will be used in war remains, there are few regions where such a possibility seems even remotely realistic. As Martin Van Creveld has commented, "much present-day power is simply irrelevant as an instrument for extending or defending political interests over most of the globe."[9]

The dangers of regional conflict still compel the world community to minimize all arms transfers and to act aggressively against the most provocative arms deals. But the bulk of the trade in major weapons has become banal, posing no clear threat to security. Although all weapons may eventually be used in conflict, few if any major deals of recent years make war more likely. The controversies they generate inevitably have more to do with symbolism, business, or widespread distaste for the arms trade. The most serious contemporary arms disputes involve not major weapons but advanced technology and the growing risks of proliferation. Although opposition can still be mobilized against the most dangerous arms deals, is it any wonder that there is so little enthusiasm for broader control of the arms trade?

The best case for restraining the trade in major weapons is not to ease regional tensions or prevent war. Even diplomats and advisers involved in the creation of the new UN Arms Trade Register speak of more modest goals; building confidence, improving the general political climate, and supporting regional peace talks.[10] The most compelling rationale for controlling the trade in major weapons is not military or political, but social and economic. Rather than focusing on preventing war, efforts to control the arms trade may be more effective as an instrument for increasing regional

Aaron Karp

spending on health, education, and economic development.[11]

The major weapons of established states may not be benign, but the greater danger to international peace and security almost certainly comes from the weapons used in ethnic conflict. Over 75 percent of all warfare since 1945 has taken place within states. The fighting has not been between existing states, but over the emergence of new states. The end of the Cold War made this trend even more dominant. Ethnic strife is far and away the most common form of warfare today and it is almost certain to stay that way.[12]

Of all weapons, those suitable for internal warfare are the most likely to be used. When used, moreover, they are far more deadly than more sophisticated weapons. Although a fully armed fighter plane can obviously be much more destructive than a rifle, there are a lot more rifles in the world and they are used with much less discretion. The generous use of major weapons in Desert Storm led to less than 400 allied deaths (almost half from accidents). It is unlikely that the number of Iraqi dead in Desert Storm will ever be known exactly, but there is growing reason to believe that the losses were not nearly as great as initially feared. Whereas the first assessments guessed at 100,000 to 400,000 dead, more thorough studies place total Iraqi deaths—military and civilian—at 5,000 to 10,000.[13]

By comparison, every year since 1991 has seen at least 10 internal conflicts, each of which caused 10,000 deaths or more.[14] A few of these are well known, like Angola, Bosnia, Liberia, and Rwanda. Others have been virtually ignored by the outside world. Yet the fighting in Georgia, Southern Iraq, Sudan, Tajikistan, East Timor, or Southeast Turkey has easily surpassed the destructiveness of Desert Storm.

The reasons for this oversight are not hard to fathom. Western news agencies naturally focus on places where Western armed forces are engaged, be it Iraq, Bosnia, or Somalia. Without Western soldiers to attract notice, there has to be something especially spectacular to draw outside media attention to remote conflict, even when the scale is tremendous. Men carrying rifles are not enough. Major weapons fit the bill; they are more exciting in action, and they are easier for the human mind to track. Reporting of the fighting between Georgian forces and separatists in Abkhazia and South Ossetia, for example, was dominated by scattered incidents involving fighter aircraft and a handful of battles in which armored vehicles were deployed. The daily grind of a confusing infantry war is minor news by comparison.

Defining the Weapons of Ethnic Conflict

One of the analytical attractions of major weapons is their very size and value, which makes them relatively easy to identify and track. Although observers have long been aware of the dangers of other forms of the arms trade—especially the trade in manufacturing and dual-use technologies—these were not as easy to study. As the arms trade community shifts its focus to emphasize small and light armaments, observers face a much more difficult task.

The first and most obvious issue is especially problematic. What are the weapons we are discussing? Four definitions are especially relevant, none completely satisfying.

Defining Small Arms by Exclusion. First, one can define small and light arms by exclusion, as those weapons not covered in existing data collections on major weapons. Such a definition is unambiguously clear and easily applied. The best established system for monitoring the arms trade has been in place for over 25 years at the Stockholm International Peace Research Institute (SIPRI). The SIPRI system was developed to facilitate comprehensive coverage using publicly available sources of information, but this methodological emphasis leaves large gaps. It excludes not just small arms and ammunition, but most of the larger systems seen in ethnic fighting, some of surprising size and complexity. A 90 mm antitank gun, for example, will not fit in anyone's rucksack. Even a 30 mm antiaircraft gun system can be very sophisticated and costly. Moreover, the SIPRI definition includes no mortars or recoilless rifles and no tube artillery under 100 mm caliber. It also excludes most unguided rockets.

The UN arms register has even greater gaps because it was designed through political negotiations in which major exporters like China had an effective veto on what to include. As a result it covers only the largest weapon systems, those almost impossible to conceal. It excludes all the weapons missing from SIPRI coverage, as well as all surface-to-air missiles, all missiles under a range of 25 km, ships under 750 tons, all unarmed helicopters, and transport aircraft. In their 1993 reporting, a few exporters went ahead and included information on shipments of such equipment anyway, but enormous gaps remain.[15] The UN system is expected to be expanded in the near future to cover arms production and stockpiles, but the reporting categories are unlikely to be altered for some time to come. One is left with the conclusion that many of the categories excluded in these data sets are very major and that the clarity of such a definition obscures the real nature of ethnic fighting.

Small Arms Defined as Weapons Carried by Infantry. A second and more traditional approach is to define small and light arms as those weapons that can be carried by a normal infantry soldier. The list extends from pistols, grenades, and bayonets through squad-level machine guns, to include grenade launchers and light rocket weapons. It also includes some weapons usually defined as major, such as shoulder-fired surface-to-air missile systems and some antitank missiles. But it excludes an enormous range of weapons also excluded by the registers, such as all heavy machine guns and even the lightest antiaircraft artillery, weapons that may still have a major role to play.

Small Arms Defined as Those Transported by Animals and Light Vehicles. A third approach is to extend the concept of small and light arms to include those weapons that can be transported by pack animals and light vehicles (up to quarter-ton trucks). This standard permits extension of the definition to include heavy machine guns and some light artillery. It also permits inclusion of weapons like 107 mm recoilless rifles and 120 mm mortars, weapons that seem to fall between the cracks of every analytical system but that cause a huge amount of battlefield destruction. This standard overlaps the previous two definitions because it covers weapons above and below the SIPRI and UN thresholds. For those who want a clean break between major and light weapons it is not helpful, but it is far more useful from a military and political perspective.

The Empirical Definition of Small Arms.
A fourth and final method is to define
the weapons of ethnic war empirically,
listing all the weapons actually used in
internecine conflict. A review of the
history of many ethnic wars reveals
that small and light arms may carry the
burden of the fighting, but major
weapons are not entirely absent. In
most ethnic wars they are of marginal
importance. In others like Bosnia they
are militarily dubious—having little
effect on the shifting front lines—but
of great importance for civilian casualties. Sarajevo has been bombed by almost every form of projectile Serbian
forces can find, but it is the huge 152
mm howitzers that are most feared.[16]
Similarly, in Abkhazia and South Ossetia, small numbers of armored personnel carriers and artillery were critical to Georgia's defeat. Even aircraft
have been present, and although their
contribution is very questionable, they
cannot be ignored for definitional reasons alone. From a definitional perspective, it helps that the major weapons that matter most generally are the
oldest and least advanced.[17]

Major weapons tend to enter into
the forces of ethnic combatants late
and in small numbers. But their appearance can be especially decisive for
insurgents. Some 50 years ago J.F.C.
Fuller wrote that "weapons, if only the
right ones can be discovered, form 99
per cent of victory."[18] Allowing for a
certain amount of overstatement, his
quip explains much of the history of
contemporary ethnic conflict. In the
hands of ethnic insurgents, small arms
tend to prolong conflict, while major
weapons bring it to a close.

Small arms are enough to establish
an insurgency, to enable it to survive,
and to weaken the ruling government.
This was true of the Vietcong in the
mid-1960s and it is true today of the
Kurdish Workers' Party (PKK) in Turkey, the Shining Path in Peru, and the
Liberation Tigers of Tamil Eelam
(LTTE) in Sri Lanka. But most insurgents are not capable of coming to
power using small arms alone. Although the previously mentioned
groups are deadly, they seem unable
to reach a final victory. The infusion
of major weaponry, even in small
quantities, can be essential to defeat
an established government. Thus the
well-armed North Vietnamese Army
was able to defeat Saigon in 1975, and
the Palestine Liberation Organization
(PLO) established virtual sovereignty
over much of Lebanon in the late
1970s.

The definitional problem probably
cannot be resolved conclusively. Studies and policies must generalize, but
they must also cover exceptionally important cases. The role of small arms
in ethnic conflict is unquestioned, but
major weapons must also be subsumed
under the definition sometimes. The
tension between the need for consistency and the need for detail is irreconcilable and haunts social science
and government policymakers everywhere. The easiest alternative—
whether it is called realism or expediency—may be irresistible in this
case as in others. Clear definitions
should be a goal, but they must not
be allowed to become more important
than the reality we aspire to control.

Even using the most inclusive definition, the scale of the trade in arms
to ethnic conflict is small compared to
the orthodox government-to-government trade in major weapons. Even
though much reduced from its highs
of the mid-1980s, the orthodox trade
in major weapons was worth $18 bil-
lion in 1992.[19] Some speculate that
black market sales of small arms and
technology are worth another $5 to $10
billion, but these figures only make
sense if one includes large quantities

of illegally acquired advanced technology, mostly for use in weapons proliferation. A systematic review of ongoing ethnic strife shows that, at the highest feasible levels of consumption, the total value of the military hardware used annually by substate armed forces has been $2.5 to $3.5 billion in recent years. This includes small but often critical acquisitions of major weaponry, mostly artillery and armored vehicles.[20]

Can the Trade in Small and Light Arms Be Controlled?

Perhaps the greatest inhibition to attempting to control the trade in light weapons is the pessimism of experts. The world has seen how extremely difficult it is to control trade in the largest, most expensive, complex, and easily tracked weapon systems. It is only natural to suspect that it will be much harder to restrain the traffic in weapons that are small, cheap, simple, and easily concealed.

Although the trade in small and light arms will not be restrained quickly or completely, it may be easier to control than the trade in major weapons. Because these weapons are cheaper and simpler, governments do not have a strong interest in promoting their export. Domestic markets are almost always sufficient to ensure the health of domestic producers; exports are a pure luxury. The ease with which the United States established a moratorium on exports of land mines is a case in point. Exports can also be easier to deny because they lack the symbolic weight of major weapons.

The first step to dealing with the arms trade revolution is to treat small and light arms with the seriousness they deserve. Violence around the world is fed not by major arms but by small and light weapons. Chinese ex-

ports of automatic rifles, to cite an egregious example, fuel violence from Somalia to Kashmir to the streets of the United States. Only if governments take exports of such weapons as seriously as they already take exports of major systems will it be possible to restrain substate violence. Other channels must also be dealt with, especially illegal sales, and to a lesser degree home manufacture and captures made on the battlefield, but tighter export controls are the essential first step.

The regulatory systems of most arms-exporting countries were designed primarily to control exports of major weapons and secondarily to deal with the flow of advanced technology. Although most countries have regulations that can be applied to exports of small and light weapons, few governments apply those rules with the same zeal. For too long is has been assumed that small arms were inconsequential. It is becoming increasingly evident that in reality they are the most dangerous of all.

A second step is to coordinate export restrictions by reinstating the dialogue on arms transfer policy among major suppliers. Coordinating arms export policy has been difficult or impossible under the existing arms trade regime. The most prominent efforts—the Conventional Arms Trade Talks of 1977–78 and the dialogue among the five permanent members of the UN Security Council in 1991–92—were unable to agree on anything beyond platitudes. These failures reflected the special symbolic and economic politics of major weapons transfers. Yet the Permanent Five dialogue may be able to deal much more effectively with small and light arms because no major national interests are at stake. Revitalizing that dialogue, with emphasis on the weapons of ethnic warfare, could make a basic contribution toward formulation of common export criteria and oversight procedures.

Third, dealing with illegal exports of newly manufactured weapons is mostly a matter of domestic policy. It is in practice no different from controlling sales of any other sensitive technology. Tighter national laws and better enforcement, which have greatly reduced international trade in items related to the proliferation of weapons of mass destruction, can have the same effect on the trade in light weapons. The principal difference is that there are so many manufacturers of small and light arms. This creates special problems, but they are not insoluble.

It has been noted that the problem of controlling the illegal trade in light weapons is similar to efforts to control the illegal drug trade and just as unlikely to succeed. How can all shipments be searched, it has been asked, when the international trade is dominated by chartered aircraft and innumerable maritime containers? Today many of the world's ports process literally millions of these containers.[21] Obviously customs authorities cannot thoroughly examine more than a small proportion of them.

Such analogies exaggerate the scale of the problem. Unlike drugs, weapons are bulky. Whereas 100 kilos of heroin or cocaine might make a personal fortune, the same weight in guns will not win anyone's war. Armed conflicts are affected by large or sustained transfers. Controls do not have to stop every gun and bullet. Rather, it is enough to prevent the biggest transfers and to break up well-organized transfer routes. Tracking small arms shipments is also easier than tracking drugs because large-scale production is restricted to factories, almost all of which are well known. Shipping routes and storage areas are equally well known, narrowing the range of possibilities.

Catching major movements of small and light armaments does not require inspecting every aircraft and ship that crosses an international border. The trade in weapons is not random but highly patterned. The key is narrowing the search by identifying likely shipments and channels. This amounts to police work. With proper preliminary investigations to guide their work, customs authorities do not have to open every container coming through a port. Instead it may be sufficient for an investigation to examine a few dozen, certainly no more than a few hundred.[22]

The art of tracing even small shipments is well developed. As the intelligence expert Dino Brugioni relates in his history of intelligence collection during the Cuban missile crisis, aerial reconnaissance alone was able to pick out even small shipments of key items. Brugioni lists the following criteria distinguishing vessels for special scrutiny in summer 1962.

> To be of special interest, a ship had to meet one or more of the following criteria:
> a. It was a known arms carrier.
> b. It transited the Bosporus at night.
> c. It reported tonnage well below its capacity. . . .
> d. It made a false declaration of its port of destination.
> e. It carried suspicious cargo.
> f. It declared for Cuba.
> g. It was the subject of other pertinent information.[23]

Allowing for changes in shipping since 1962, especially the growth of the container trade, and substituting more relevant routes and destinations, this is a model for distinguishing dangerous cargoes today. Western police agencies and customs authority have demonstrated immense professionalism at this task. Although it has not been as successful in other fields, international collaboration has proven its effectiveness here.

The greatest hurdle to overcome in controlling the trade in light arms is not powerful lawbreakers but weak lawmakers. The experience of the UN embargo on ex-Yugoslavian states shows that the biggest problem is not illegal transfers. Interceptions of such shipments have not been inefficient; enough weaponry leaks through to seriously embarrass the UN, but not enough to affect the course of battle. The embargo has been most effective against highly isolated Bosnia; until an arms link was established through Croatia, so few shipments reached the Muslim state that it reportedly depended on buying black market weapons from the Serbs.[24] A far greater problem is the transfer of weaponry across the Bulgarian and Greek borders to Serbia and across the Hungarian border to Croatia, while government officials look the other way.[25] The problem stems from ambivalent policy-making and poor enforcement. Although the recent performance of many East European and ex-Soviet states has been disappointing, experience shows that the task is manageable given sufficient political will.

A fourth step that would help tighten law enforcement is radical extension of the UN arms register to bring much of the trade in small and light arms into the open. Instead of only tinkering with current reporting thresholds, the UN should be pressed to bring the thresholds down to the lowest levels feasible. It is technically little trouble to include all transactions of military equipment worth at least $100,000; almost all exporters already require formal licensing of such shipments. At this level the UN register would become a serious force inhibiting questionable transfers. The feasibility of such a change needs thorough investigation, but it should not pose excessive challenges. Verification, for example, can be adequate with minimal augmentation of existing customs authorities. The biggest hurdle may be nothing more than lack of interest.

Should the Trade in Light Arms Be Controlled?

Although controls on the trade in small and light arms could be much more effective than they are today, there is a need to be clear about the objective of such controls. Is it to end conflict? Or merely to minimize the responsibility of exporting countries, making it easier for them to avoid being drawn into regional wars?

Even the strongest controls are unlikely to do more than ameliorate the worst aspects of ethnic violence. Controlling the transmission of small and light weapons to areas of ethnic conflict will not deprive insurgents of their most important source of armaments— weapons captured from their adversaries. In some cases the best one can hope for is to reduce the direct responsibility of arms exporters and mitigate the violence.

Reducing access to armaments will not, however, reduce the scale of ethnic fighting in certain cases. All too often, these wars are not fought for political objectives that are amenable to outside diplomacy. Increasingly the world is plagued by wars fought for survival, wars in which the contestants feel—often justifiably—that everything is at stake. When the stakes are that high, lack of proper weapons is often not a force for compromise but an invitation to improvise.

Deprived of modern weapons, desperate forces adapt. Hopefully lack of arms will lead them to negotiate, but not always. The best example is probably Paraguay's War of the Triple Alliance in the 1860s. Launched by a would-be Napoleon, the dictator Francisco Solano López, and fed by rabid nationalism, this incomprehensible war of national suicide led Paraguay against the combined might of Argentina, Brazil, and Uruguay. An entire nation fought to the literal end, often armed with nothing more than razors tied to poles. Of its antebellum population of some 450,000 only 221,000 survived, including fewer than 28,000 men.[26]

The Paraguayan case cannot be dismissed as a pathological oddity. Rather it is an extreme example of a basic aspect of human determination. American troops fighting in the Pacific in 1942–45 often encountered similar resistance from Japanese soldiers and civilians, as did soldiers fighting in Vietnam 25 years later.

An especially relevant example occurred during the Iran–Iraq War. During this eight-year war, Iran faced an especially pressing point in 1984. Western controls on traditional arms exports to Iran were becoming very effective as a result of Washington's Operation Staunch, while Iraq still enjoyed considerable outside support. In 1985 Tehran developed relations with alternative suppliers. But during this desperate interval Tehran responded with extreme measures, trying to rely on human wave tactics that substituted poorly armed but fervent volunteers for major weaponry and made the war far more sanguinary.[27] Other groups, facing similar pressures may react to embargoes the same way.

Substate violence is part of the greater process of ethnic self-determination, a process that has con-

founded the best instincts of the international community throughout the twentieth century. By focusing its efforts on aspects of this process, like the trade in small and light weapons, the world community can hope to ameliorate some of the worst aspects of this long-standing problem. But if clumsily or lopsidedly imposed, even the best controls can become part of the problem.

Controlling the arms trade, like international sanctions or UN peacekeeping, is never going to be the total answer to warfare. Partial measures cannot achieve complete solutions. But even if not sufficient, such measures will be necessary to achieve greater progress. The final answers to ethnic violence will only be found in policies able to cope with the overall challenge that ethnic self-determination poses to international peace and stability. In the meantime it will be impossible to deal with the conflicts that torment the new world order without controlling the trade in small and light arms.

Notes

1. The U.S. commitment to a CTB treaty was reiterated by Ambassador Stephen Ledogar in a speech before the UN Conference on Disarmament, Geneva, on February 3, 1994. USIA Wireless File, February 3, 1994, pp. 21–22.

2. Keith Krause, *Arms and the State: Patterns of Military Production and Trade* (Cambridge: Cambridge University Press, 1992), pp. 9–10, 22, 206.

3. Robert E. Harkavy, "The Changing International System and the Arms Trade," *Annals of the American Academy of Political Science* (forthcoming September 1994); Stephanie G. Neuman, "Controlling the Arms Trade: Idealistic Dream or Realpolitik?" *The Washington Quarterly* 16 (Summer 1993), pp. 53–75; and Andrew L. Ross, "The International Arms Market: A Structural Analysis," *International Interactions* 18, no. 1 (1992), pp. 63–83.

4. Edward J. Laurance, *The International Arms Trade* (New York, N.Y.: Lexington-Macmillan, 1992).

5. John Mueller, *Retreat from Doomsday: The Obsolescence of Major War* (New York, N.Y.: Basic Books, 1989).

6. Henry Kissinger, *The White House Years* (Boston: Little, Brown, 1979), pp. 171–183.

7. McGeorge Bundy, *Danger and Survival: Choices about the Bomb in the First Fifty Years* (New York, N.Y.: Random House, 1988), pp. 518–527.

8. They are part of what Martin Van Creveld calls "make believe war." See his *Technology and War* (New York, N.Y.: Free Press, 1989), chap. 19.

9. Martin Van Creveld, *The Transformation of War* (New York, N.Y.: Free Press, 1991), p. 27. Bosnian Muslims also might be forgiven for wondering just what Western armed forces are supposed to do.

10. Edward J. Laurance, "The UN Register of Conventional Arms: Rationales and Prospects for Compliance and Effectiveness," *The Washington Quarterly* 16 (Spring 1993), pp. 163–173.

11. This perspective is closely associated with the work of Nicole Ball (*Security and Economy in the Third World* [Princeton, N.J.: Princeton University Press, 1989]) and Saadet Deger and Somnath Sen (*Military Expenditure: The Political Economy of International Security* [Oxford: Oxford University Press, 1990]).

12. Ken Jowitt, *New World Disorder: The Leninist Extinction* (Berkeley: University of California Press, 1992).

13. Eliot A. Cohen, "The Mystique of U.S. Air Power," *Foreign Affairs* 73 (January/February 1994), p. 122, and John G. Heidenrich, "The Gulf War: How Many Iraqis Died?" *Foreign Policy*, no. 90 (Spring 1993), pp. 108–125.

14. Ramses Amer et al., "Major Armed Conflict," *SIPRI Yearbook 1993* (Oxford: Oxford University Press, 1993), chap. 3.

15. *UN Register of Conventional Armaments*, A/48/344 (New York, N.Y.: United Nations, October 11, 1993). An invaluable commentary is Edward J. Laurance et al., *Arms Watch: SIPRI Report on the First Year of the UN Register of Conventional Arms* (Oxford: Oxford University Press and SIPRI, 1993).

16. Laura Silber, "Sarajevo Flame Dies under Serb Rain of Death," *Financial Times*, October 20, 1993, p. 3.

17. "Georgian Regional Capital under Aerial Attack," *New York Times*, September 21, 1993, p. A-7; "Shevardnadze, Reclaiming Job, Appeals to Rebels," *New York Times*, September 16, 1993, p. A-6.

18. J.F.C. Fuller, *Armament and History* (London: Eyre and Spottiswoode, 1946), p. 31.

19. Ian Anthony, "Current Trends and Developments in the Arms Trade," *Annals of the American Academy of Political Science* (forthcoming September 1994).

20. Aaron Karp, *Arming Ethnic Conflict* (Lanham, Md.: United Nations University Press, forthcoming), appendix II. These figures are only the value of weapons used. They do not reflect actual prices paid, which are much harder to determine. Much of this equipment is captured, moreover, and, in a sense, costs nothing.

21. Anthony, "Current Trends and Developments in the Arms Trade."

22. Having recently completed an international move of my entire household, though, I was very impressed—annoyed—by the thoroughness of customs authorities. The experience left no doubt that had my family's container held a rifle, they would have found it.

23. Dino A. Brugioni, *Eyeball to Eyeball: The Inside Story of the Cuban Missile Crisis* (New York, N.Y.: Random House, 1990), p. 73.

24. John Kifner, "With Little, Bosnians Sharpen Fighting Skills," *New York Times*, December 6, 1993, p. A-3.

25. Daniel N. Nelson, "Ancient Enmities, Modern Guns," *Bulletin of the Atomic Scientists* 49 (December 1993).

26. Charles J. Kolinski, *Independence or Death: The Story of the Paraguayan War* (Gainesville: University of Florida Press, 1965), pp. 7, 198.

27. Anthony H. Cordesman, *The Iran–Iraq War and Western Security* (London: Jane's, 1987), pp. 61–65, 68–69.

Beyond Proliferation: The Challenge of Technology Diffusion

Michael Moodie

THE COLLAPSE OF the Soviet Union, Iraq's challenge to the international community, and the rogue actions of North Korea have focused a spotlight on the dangerous and destabilizing impact of the spread of the instruments of war in the post–cold war environment. After the fall of the Berlin wall, nonproliferation became the international security community's "intellectual flavor of the month," and the Clinton administration entered office defining its national security agenda largely—some would say exclusively—in terms of the problem of proliferation.

In the post–cold war environment, however, national security, economic interests, and technology relate to one another in complex and crosscutting ways. The issue of the diffusion of militarily relevant technology in particular is introducing a new and contentious element into the international security arena. Disputes over export

controls and the sharing of technology, for example, have emerged as major stumbling blocks in several arms-control forums. At the same time, changing national priorities have resulted in declining defense spending in many developed nations, which in turn is fostering pressures to export arms and defense-related technology or convert defense industries to civilian purposes. In the face of these dynamics, the international community confronts a major challenge in managing global technology diffusion in a way that achieves international security goals while promoting commercial and other objectives. Although both the global process of developing and disseminating technology and the international security environment have altered radically in recent years, conceptual and policy thinking remain locked in modes more appropriate to an earlier time—whether the developed nations' Cold War or the nonaligned movement's anti-colonial struggle.

During the Cold War, for example, the challenge to the United States and its allies of preventing the acquisition of militarily relevant technology by the members of the Warsaw Pact overshadowed problems posed by the diffusion of such technology to other parts of the world. Although concerns

Michael Moodie is president of the Chemical and Biological Arms Control Institute. He is a former assistant director of the U.S. Arms Control and Disarmament Agency.

Copyright © 1995 by The Center for Strategic and International Studies and the Massachusetts Institute of Technology
The Washington Quarterly • 18:2

regarding the proliferation of weapons of mass destruction received some attention, Janne Nolan (1991) argues that in general the West seemed to operate on the assumption that it would maintain technological superiority over the industrializing world, and that this "technological stratification" would contribute to a stable security environment. These and similar assumptions must now be reexamined.

The domination of both academic research and policy formulation by the problem of the proliferation of nuclear weapons in particular must be scrutinized. In the final years of the 1990s, the scope of the problem extends well beyond nuclear weapons to encompass other weapons of mass destruction, conventional weapons, defense production, and, increasingly, technology development processes. The problem confronting the international community is not about weapon systems but about the diffusion of technology—some advanced, some simple, all potentially lethal. Dealing effectively with the full range of technology diffusion issues will be a critical test in determining whether the international community can promote regional and global security while it safeguards national economic interests and maintains a stable international trading system.

An example demonstrating the complexity of the challenge emerged after the Persian Gulf War. In light of the experience of some arms suppliers to Iraq who in that war confronted weapons they themselves had sold to Baghdad, expressions of concern intensified regarding the transfer of advanced conventional technologies to regions of tension and conflict. In the United States, the Bush administration felt a strong political need to "do something." The result was the initiative on

Arms Control to the Middle East (ACME). Natalie Goldring (1993) describes how over a period of several months, discussions among the top five weapon suppliers to the region—the United States, Russia, China, Britain, and France—produced guidelines regarding the types of arms transfers to the Middle East to be avoided in the future. The five also established guidelines addressing prenotification of sales and promised to consider the state of regional stability in future arms transfer decisions. They further agreed to apply their decisions not just to the Middle East but globally.

The ACME process made little real progress. The guidelines were generally perceived as not inhibiting any of the five suppliers from doing something they wanted to do—a perception reinforced by President George Bush's decision during the 1992 election campaign to sell advanced military aircraft to Saudi Arabia and Taiwan, a decision not opposed by candidate Bill Clinton. The Taiwan decision also served as a convenient excuse for China, which had been visibly unhappy with the process, to pull out. The talks have been in abeyance ever since.

The global diffusion of militarily related technology—especially below the nuclear level—has not received sustained attention from successive U.S. administrations at senior levels because it has often been seen to fall in the "too hard to do" category. In addressing the question of proliferation of weapons of mass destruction, "none" is the best objective, and one that is relatively easy to define operationally, if not to implement. In other realms, however, a complex dynamic is at work among a number of elements: the legitimate right of self-defense with the concomitant right to have weapons for that defense; pressures to sell arms in difficult economic times for defense industries; a growing demand for advanced technology; emerging norms against the acquisition of certain weapon systems; diplomatic and political reasons for and against transfers of technology; and concerns over introducing advanced technology with military utility into regions of tension. This dynamic does not lend itself to straightforward policy answers. Specific measures that achieve one objective but that do not injure another, equally valid interest are difficult to define.

The fundamental dilemma is balancing competing interests. This dilemma was captured in the Clinton administration's announcement promising a major review of U.S. arms transfer policy. The review, the White House noted (Office of the Press Secretary 1993), would take into account "national security, arms control, trade, budgetary and economic competitiveness considerations." Devising a policy that effectively meets all those interests is no mean feat. The basic dilemma is made more complicated by the fact that, in addressing the tradeoffs between short-term and long-term political, economic, and security benefits, not all states will make the same calculations.

The need to reexamine conceptual approaches and policy tools for dealing with post–cold war technology diffusion is generated by the combination of three sets of changes in (1) the way technology is developed, produced, and made available on a global level; (2) technology's impact on the battlefield; and (3) post–cold war security dynamics.

Changing Patterns of Technology Diffusion

The starting point is an appreciation of technology as something other than things. Harvey Brooks (1980, 66) has defined technology as "knowledge of how to fulfill certain human purposes in a specific and reproducible way." He goes on to argue that technology "does not consist of artifacts but of the . . . knowledge that underlies the artifacts and the way they can be used in society." As such, technology stands in contrast to science, which is the "knowledge of why things are as they are," and innovation, which is the process by which that knowledge is embodied and deployed in society (Keatley 1985; Skolnikoff 1993). Few, if any, aspects of international affairs have been untouched by science and technology (Skolnikoff 1993), and in the arena of security affairs, their impact has been immense.

The profound impact of science and technology on security affairs is, of course, not limited to the end of the twentieth century (McNeill 1982). History is replete with examples showing that military capabilities—traditionally a central ordering principle of international political power—have been decisive in relations among states. Some technologies have had more profound implications than others (Van Creveld 1989), permanently modifying the dynamics of military competition and altering traditional concepts of the purpose and use of military power. Eugene Skolnikoff (1993) points out that science and technology did not themselves make this happen, but that developments emerging from scientific and technological systems made such developments possible, confronting nations with new choices and greatly changed conditions and payoffs.

The impact of technology on society, then, including on its security affairs, must be understood not as the uncontrolled product of a machine or the outcome of some abstract process,

73

but of human choice. Technology may shape the context within which choices are made, create new paths open to the chooser, or change the calculations of costs and benefits associated with certain courses of action. The result, however, is determined by individuals. It is not the technology itself that is beneficial or harmful, but how it is used. This fundamental point is critical to those confronting the technology management challenge. It highlights the fact that their basic task should not be focused on the technology itself, but on channeling the choices of those to whom technology is available.

Although the impact of technology on security has been significant throughout history, today the scope and breadth of technological change are unprecedented. One important factor influencing the process of technology development and production in the twentieth century has been the institutionalization of technological change by Western societies in their universities and major businesses (Cooper and Hollick 1985). The incorporation of the process of technological change into social interaction by some nations has been an important element in their economic and security success. Now all nations want to share in the latest industrial revolution. As Simon Ramo (1985) points out,

> Every nation now perceives its economy, social stability, and national security to be highly dependent on its stature in technology. Each nation accordingly is avidly seeking to develop its technological resources. (p. 13)

What is true generally is also true in the military realm. The desire to be technologically capable is one of the

major propellants of the global diffusion of military technology.

Beyond these general considerations, some specific trends in the process of developing and producing technology have particular importance for the ability of policymakers to deal with the challenge of technology diffusion.

The Increasing Incorporation of Civilian Technology into the Military Sphere

During the 1950s and 1960s, and perhaps into the 1970s, defense research was viewed as an engine of economic growth, and there were significant spinoffs from the defense sector into the civilian arena. Steven Irwin (1993) points out that in the 1950s, 80 percent of the research and development in computing was defense related. The share of total U.S. research and development taken by the defense sector dropped from half in 1960 to one-third in 1990. Irwin argues that given this shift, a growing portion of defense research is focused today on requirements so uniquely military that their commercial application is negligible and that defense research efforts are yielding fewer commercial rewards. The result is growing isolation of military research activities from the commercial market.

Indeed, over the last two decades, the relationship between technology in the civilian and defense sectors has been reversed. It is not the defense community that is generating spinoffs for the civilian population, but the commercial arena that is producing an increasing amount of technology that is being incorporated into the design of weapons and other military equipment. As commercial technology develops further, it could greatly bolster military performance. Seth Carus

(1994) provides some recent examples of commercial technology with potentially significant military applications:

- modern strap-down inertial navigation systems can provide guidance using computer chips identical to those in commercial products;
- Motorola is developing a global cellular telephone network called Iridium that will allow direct communications anywhere in the world using cellular technology and that would not be difficult to adapt to provide over-the-horizon targeting updates for missiles;
- France and Russia are soon to offer satellites with 1 meter resolution; by comparison the resolution of the current commercially available French SPOT satellite, which was used during the Gulf war, is 10 meters; and
- biotechnology advances can provide for more cost-effective agriculture, better medicines, and disease control, but they can also be used to improve the development and production of offensive biological weapons.

In these and similar cases, denying technology to a potential recipient will be neither possible nor justifiable in light of the commercial utility of the technology in question.

Global Redistribution of Technology

The economic and technological performance of Taiwan, Israel, India, and South Korea demonstrates the increasing ability of industrializing countries to develop and exploit advanced technology, much of which is militarily relevant. Although some attention has been paid to the development of arms industries in developing countries, little research has been conducted from the security perspective on the diffusion of the scientific and technological foundation that has made the military technology advances of these states possible (Roberts 1993, 153). India, for example, has an enormous pool of computer expertise, and much of the software for the U.S. market is written there.

As more technology from the civilian sector is exploited in the military realm, the risks in not paying attention to the scientific and technological capability of such countries increase. If nothing else, the resulting lack of perspective narrows policymakers' appreciation of the dynamics at work and the problems they generate. Brad Roberts (1992) points out, for example, that the inherently discriminatory nature of traditional nonproliferation mechanisms and approaches is fundamentally incompatible with this trend of a globally spreading technological and industrial capability. Yet policymakers seem fixated on refining those mechanisms—such as export control regimes—rather than devising a whole new approach appropriate to the evolving situation.

The problem is not that these and other states will necessarily challenge the world's military technology leaders but that they can produce a limited number of highly capable systems—including weapons of mass destruction—that are especially dangerous in a third world context. When combined with the compulsion most third world technology producers feel to export their indigenously produced military hardware, the result will be the introduction of destabilizing technologies into regions of tension. A worrisome example in this regard is North Korea, particularly its missile sales to the Middle East. If Iran, for example, were to acquire Pyongyang's Nodong missile—and it is reportedly interested—Tehran would for the first time have the ability to strike Israel from its own territory.

Declining Share of the Market under Government Control

Before entering the Defense Department as its senior official responsible for nonproliferation, Ashton Carter argued that given the trend for defense to make up an ever smaller part of the global technology enterprise, "DOD will have far less leverage over the nature of the enterprise" (quoted in Nolan 1991, 7). Over the last 20 years, major advances in technology have been primarily the product of the private sector with little or no government involvement. Moreover, private industry is now building a greater number of linkages of greater complexity and sophistication across international borders. In the defense sphere, this trend has led some commentators (e.g., Anthony 1992, 37) to suggest that the major mechanism for transferring military technology in the future will be from one company to another or from one element of a multinational firm to another in a different country rather than through government-to-government transactions. Whether the process goes this far or not, these factors have diminished government's leverage in shaping global technology flows.

Economic Imperatives of Industrial States

The progressive constriction of the international arms market has intensified pressures on weapon suppliers to export their most advanced weapons and equipment and, in response to shrewd client demands, to develop more sophisticated technology-sharing arrangements with recipients. The pressure has been exacerbated in recent years by declining domestic defense budgets that have led to shrunken local markets and pressures to maintain jobs.

The economic pressures to transfer militarily useful technology are not limited to the Western industrial states. In the former Soviet Union, for example, the role of the state in supporting its arms industries—chiefly in Russia (in which 80 percent of the Soviet Union's defense industrial infrastructure was located) and Ukraine—has become part of the national debate between economic reformers and conservatives (Pierre 1993). David Tanks and his fellow authors (1993) note that some Russian officials have indicated that Moscow hopes to generate as much as $20 billion in foreign exchange through overseas weapon sales. Such hopes appear wildly optimistic in light of the fact that in 1992, Russian arms sales totaled only $1.3 billion. Nevertheless, the Russian government appears willing to sell virtually anything short of a weapon of mass destruction to anyone with the money to buy. The variety of weapons and military equipment that Moscow has exhibited at major international arms shows is staggering, including top-of-the-line equipment not yet in use with Russia's own forces (Markov 1994).

The Shifting Focus of Defense Technology

In addition to the changing patterns in technology development and economic realities, the challenge of technology diffusion is made more difficult by a number of developments related to defense procurement patterns.

The Shift toward Technology Rather Than Platforms as the Medium of Exchange in Defense-Related Transfers

In the 1950s and early 1960s, trade in military technology was basically the provision by the West—and the United States in particular—of obsolescent equipment to allies and friends. The late 1960s and early 1970s witnessed a shift as more sophisticated equipment began to be transferred and cooperative production ventures were initiated. By the late 1970s and early 1980s, arms producers were increasingly providing top-of-the-line equipment to their customers throughout the world, and a share of production became an essential part of any transaction (Pierre 1982). Today the transfer of finished systems and platforms is giving way to the diffusion of production processes and components (Laurance 1992). Tomorrow, the world is likely to witness increased emphasis on the transfer of development processes capable of generating enabling technologies needed to fight effectively on the twenty-first-century battlefield.

This shifting emphasis was captured by Egyptian analyst Abdel Monem Said Aly (1992), who argued that in terms of Arab future military requirements:

> Arab states do not need more expensive platforms, particularly aircraft, but rather less expensive and more effective delivery systems such as missiles. . . . These states do not need more arms—tanks, ships, and so on—but rather the technological devices that multiply existing forces, achieve greater accuracy, mobility, and effectiveness. (p. 69)

In the future, the performance of platforms—the aerodynamics of strike aircraft, for example—will be less important than the capabilities of the munitions they carry, the effectiveness of their integrated navigation and delivery systems, and the supporting command, control, communications, and intelligence capabilities that locate and deliver the ordinance on the target.

Expanding Defense Industrial Capability

A corollary of the trend for the recipients of military technology to increasingly demand a "piece of the action" in terms of production has been the internationalization of defense industrial capabilities. Luis Bitencourt (1994) points out that states have demonstrated a number of security, political, and economic reasons for pursuing indigenous defense production capabilities, and those that were most successful seemed to reflect some combination of a threat perception that drove domestic defense demand, access to capital, a diversified industrial base, and superpower support in a variety of forms.

Bitencourt argues that despite these internal characteristics, the high cost of producing advanced defense technology had several consequences for would-be producers. First, it forced these states to concentrate on low to medium technology as their major area of activity; the production of more sophisticated equipment came to be seen as a constant challenge. Second, it drove them to concentrate on capabilities with particular applications such as trainer aircraft and armored cars. Third, it required them to search for external markets. Virtually all of these industries became dependent on exports.

The result, according to Edward Laurance (1992), was the emergence of a group of "second tier" suppliers "who became firmly established as niche suppliers, being available in those circumstances where the major suppliers were unable or unwilling to participate fully in the market" (p. 138). Suppliers within this group, such as Brazil, were appealing as suppliers for a number of reasons: they offered good sales packages, dependable availability, and fewer political strings attached to any particular transaction.

The 1980s were the era of greatest success for these second tier suppliers. Because a number of them had carved out success in the Middle East in particular, the end of the Iran–Iraq War was the first blow to their continued growth. This was quickly followed by the global recession and the end of the Cold War, which ended or diminished superpower support or subsidies, made excess equipment that had been intended for Europe available for sale elsewhere, and promoted more aggressive export policies by countries whose own defense industries were declining and needed exports. This more competitive environment pushed some second tier suppliers into bankruptcy (Bitencourt 1994). The demonstration of the superiority of advanced technology in the Persian Gulf conflict further underscored the difficulty second tier supplier states have in moving beyond the niches they have come to occupy. Laurance (1992) argues that even these niches are not secure in the face of major suppliers who, for various reasons, may now want to enter these markets.

Despite these setbacks, second tier suppliers are not likely to disappear, and they will continue to provide militarily relevant technology that, while not necessarily at the cutting edge,

could have important consequences in particular conflict situations. Such states could also play a major role in the market for retrofitting and modernizing older equipment that has emerged in recent years in light of the high cost of replacing platforms currently in inventories. Israel's emergence as a leader in refurbishing Russian MiG aircraft is an example.

Moreover, the demand by many states for technology in addition to finished weapon systems will continue. David Mussington (1994) points out that the

> buyers market for arms has altered the terms of trade in the international defense sector. . . . Purchasers are no longer satisfied with marginal offset benefits but are now insisting on formal offset and technology transfer commitments *prior* to the conclusion of an arms transfer agreement. (p. 4)

The result could well be creation of new manufacturing capabilities and new sources for subsystems, components, and other items that might be incorporated into finished weapon systems. This development would reinforce the current trend that finds even systems that are ostensibly the product of one country really composed of elements assembled from all over the world. This trend is very established in the commercial sectors for major systems such as civilian aircraft, and it is increasingly the case in the defense sector as well.

Another aspect of the diffusion of militarily relevant industrial capability is the impact of global industrialization on the prospect for unconventional weapons development. The relative ease of production of biological weapons and the dual-use nature of their development and production technology is a case in point. As the biotechnology revolution proceeds, the interest in developing countries plagued by endemic disease in combatting serious global health problems will increase. As a result, biotechnology capabilities are likely to become more widespread, as will biological weapons capabilities, to which they are closely related. Similarly, the global expansion of petrochemical, fertilizer, and pharmaceutical enterprises has laid the potential industrial foundation for the production of chemical weapons. As the RAND Corporation has pointed out, there are now "virtual" nuclear weapon states with the technology to "go nuclear" should they make the political decision to do so (Millot 1994). A number of countries are also already "virtual" chemical or biological weapon states. Increasingly, the question will not be the capability to produce such systems, but the will and political choice to do so. Ensuring that the incentives and disincentives of the international system are structured to channel those choices in stabilizing and peaceful directions is a fundamental challenge of the post–cold war era.

Technology and the Twenty-First-Century Battlefield

Skolnikoff (1993, 50) points out that given the rewards that accrue to extending the limits of military capabilities, there is a constant pressure to stretch all the parameters of military performance whether they be size, speed, power, or capacity. The war in the Persian Gulf was the latest example of the benefits of such pressure. The Gulf war has sparked intense examination of whether the United States in particular is participating in a "military-technical revolution" that is reshaping the ways in which wars are fought (Bracken 1993; Gouré 1993; Mazarr 1993). Whether the United

States has already been through such a revolution, is in the midst of one, or could exploit one looming on the horizon, the Gulf war did show that technology, while perhaps not reshaping the nature of war, is significantly altering the battlefield.

The core of the technology that will define the twenty-first-century battlefield is information processing and systems integration. Carus (1994) summarized the augmented role of information in arguing that the military technical revolution "provides military forces with more information, which is better filtered and organized, and which is obtained and distributed more rapidly than was previously possible" (p. 168).

Systems integration will be critical. In some cases, the individual technology embedded in a particular piece of hardware is not intrinsically interesting—an advanced medium-range air-to-air missile, for example, uses an 80386 microprocessor—and what counts is the ability to put these technologies together. Similarly, as Carus (1994) argues, the Gulf war demonstrated the increasing importance of the ability to make independent elements—sometimes separated by considerable distances—work together. Surveillance and targeting capabilities, for example, are critically intertwined because precision munitions make it possible to exploit the new capabilities inherent in satellite-based information distribution systems.

One system reflecting the potential for integrated systems is missiles. During Operation Desert Storm, Iraqi SCUD missiles played cat and mouse with coalition air forces, both tying down important military assets and symbolizing to many a new capability in the developing world.

The proliferation of missiles is a relatively new concern on the arms-

---

control agenda, but one that is drawing significant attention (Carus 1991; Nolan 1991; Potter and Jencks 1994). Missiles are an attractive capability, at least in theory, especially when compared to the alternative of using manned aircraft. They are less complicated, and they require a less sophisticated infrastructure and less training to maintain and use them. Missiles are also less expensive; they are cheaper to procure and do not represent such a loss should they fail in their mission. Given expanding air defenses against manned aircraft around the world, missiles are also perceived as enhancing if not assuring successful delivery.

The military importance of missile systems—and ballistic missiles in particular—however, is uncertain. On the one hand, most missile technology diffusion has been based on the Soviet SCUD, which is essentially technology that is more than 30 years old and not capable of generating much more than marginal results against military targets. On the other hand, the Iran–Iraq War and Operation Desert Storm showed that missiles are not necessarily being used in traditional ways, or in the same way manned aircraft would be. Perhaps recognizing their military limitations, regimes are exploiting their missile inventories by using them against soft targets, including civilian population centers. If married to warheads of mass destruction, use of missiles in this way makes their military impact—in contrast to their strategic implications—a secondary concern.

A number of trends, particularly in the areas of inertial navigation and target acquisition such as the U.S. Global Positioning System (GPS) and the Russian GLONASS satellite system, are enhancing even older missile technologies (Sokolski 1994). In addition, attention is turning to missile capabilities other than ballistic missiles, par-

ticularly cruise missiles and unmanned aerial vehicles (Arnett 1992). Henry Sokolski, a former Defense Department official, points out that these kinds of capabilities, especially when combined with some ballistic missiles, will compound the problems for defense systems and pose enhanced dangers especially to fixed targets such as ports, airfields, and key logistics centers (Sokolski 1994).

Given that, like missiles, many of the military systems incorporating new technology are dispersed and many operate at ranges that are longer than those of earlier systems, the battlefield itself has been enlarged and become more fluid (Moodie 1990). This development has potentially destabilizing consequences in that controlling the forward edge of the battle area is likely to become less important than the ability to operate effectively throughout the entire battle space. Such a capability could expand the number of possible targets, including some traditionally considered off limits such as noncombatants. A further risk is that of drawing into a conflict other participants who could fall prey to the longer-range capabilities. Iraq's efforts to prompt an Israeli reaction to its SCUD attacks against Tel Aviv is one such example.

Other impacts of the military-technical revolution on the conduct of conflict are to increase the tempo of operations, shorten the decision loop within which critical choices must be made, and increase the attractiveness of moving toward an automated battlefield populated by expert systems (increasingly with artificial intelligence).

The importance of information in such an environment is obvious, but the dependence on information also creates a vulnerability. A critical impact of the new battlefield, therefore, has been to shift attention to what Geoffrey Kemp (1994) has described as "cyberwar," that is, an initial concentration on degrading the adversary's information and command and control capabilities. At the close of the twentieth century, winning the information war has become the equivalent of capturing the high ground in conflicts of earlier days.

From the perspective of technology diffusion, this shift has a number of potential implications. First, many of the critical technologies involved are identical to those in the commercial sector. In one sense, what is happening on the battlefield is another reflection of the emergence of the information age. The function of managing and distributing information is the same, only the environment is different. That difference may sometimes impose more rigorous performance standards, but not necessarily. As a result, digital computers, fiber optics, satellite imagery, and other widely available technologies have become the building blocks for the military-technical revolution.

Second, the availability of such technology will make it possible for most states to acquire some of these capabilities. The growing technological capabilities of states such as India, Singapore, or the Republic of Korea will allow them to produce this technology themselves, thereby creating potential new sources of supply. Some military technology, such as stealth, will remain beyond the grasp of all but a small number of states, but in most of the conflicts in which most states might be involved, the absence of such technology will not be decisive. Patrick Garrity (1993) argues also that in the event that a country finds itself confronting a major military power such as the United States, it is unlikely to think in terms of matching that

power's capabilities. Rather it will probably focus on how to counter its advanced technology by using "asymmetric strategies," a task often requiring less technological sophistication.

The availability of technology also does not necessarily translate into military capability. Many states, for example, are beginning from a very low base, having traditionally underinvested in such elements as command and control. Indeed, Paul Bracken (1994) has suggested that the performance of command and control systems in the developing world has been so low "that the question of which weapons are acquired is less important than whether *any* strategy can be implemented with them," and that the strategic benefits derived from such capabilities have been more a matter of luck than technological advantage (p. 157). The difficulties confronting developing countries in applying advanced military technology has also been emphasized by Stephen Biddle (1994) in his analysis of current trends in land warfare technology. Biddle argues convincingly that the new technology

offers new capability, higher mobility, higher operational tempos, and better protection—but it does so at a price. That price, moreover, is more than just the acquisition costs of the new hardware. New technology imposes systematically higher levels of complexity on unit commanders, operators, and maintainers. (p. 120)

It is questionable whether some, if not most, of the world's militaries can handle this greater complexity. Biddle contends that most states will not, with the net effect of making the "global distribution of conventional military power increasingly uneven" (p. 117).

This does not mean that they will not try, however, nor that they will not incorporate some of these systems into new ways of thinking about their military options and adapting their strategies and tactics to exploit them. In many regions of tension, state leaders do not have to be convinced that they can replicate the performance they saw on CNN during the Gulf war to believe that new conventional weapons acquisitions can be useful for specific national purposes.

The Gulf war also demonstrated that coalition forces—and those of the United States in particular—had the tactics, organization, and professionalism needed to maximize the impact of new technology. The contrast between the professionalism of U.S. forces against Iraq and the Iranian tactic of sending human waves to their martyrdom during the Iran–Iraq War was not lost on the leaders in Tehran (Garrity 1993; Kemp 1994).

Whether the full range of states can make the doctrinal and organizational adaptations necessary to exploit new technology remains to be seen. They will, however, try. The third implication for technology diffusion, therefore, will be increased pressure for the broader distribution of such technology. Given its dual purpose, however, attempting to curtail the development of potentially destabilizing military technology through denying the wherewithal to achieve it is likely to prove frustrating if not fruitless. Laurance (1992) points out the irony in a situation in which

just when some modicum of universal cooperation in conflict control is emerging, the methods that can now be used to acquire the military capability to wage unac-

ceptable armed conflict are much less susceptible to arms control measures. (p. 167)

Laurance may be overstating the propensity for cooperation, but not the difficulty inherent in the new situation.

Changing Global Security Dynamics

A further set of factors should also be addressed as contributing to the difficulty confronting policymakers in managing the diffusion of militarily relevant technology. This is the way in which the political dynamics have been altered in the post–cold war environment. These factors do not necessarily represent new issues, but the new situation enhances their salience. The most serious problem in this regard is, to oversimplify, North–South tension over arms control and nonproliferation. Differences over what to do with advanced technology, both civilian and military, stand at the heart of that confrontation.

W. Scott Thompson (1993, 3) argues that the notion that conflict has become unacceptable in the world is a peculiarly Western notion that has not spread to the Third World. As Shahram Chubin (1993) points out,

Many [states] have not had the means to assure their security unilaterally or through access to [conventional] arms or alliances. Nor have they been able to fashion a diplomatic compromise. Moreover, their security has not automatically been improved by the passing of the Cold War. (p. 99)

Belief persists in many parts of the world, therefore, in the military solution as the ultimate option of state leaders and their internal and external opponents. The result, according to John Chipman (1991), is that

> war has become politics by other means; government is the management of conflict; opposition has meant insurgency; and guerrilla activities have become a lifestyle. (p. 164)

Given this perception, it should not be surprising that third world security analysts have considered arms control alien and not a high priority. Chandram Jeshurun (1993) perhaps best summarized this view in describing attitudes toward arms control in Southeast Asia where

> governments are disinclined to embark on . . . measures that in any way touch upon issues relating to arms transfers, arms control and arms production in the current state of intra-regional and international strategic uncertainty. (p. 51)

Differences over nonproliferation—including the diffusion of technology—could prove especially troublesome in the future. From the South's perspective, the emphasis and approach of the U.S.-led industrialized states are hypocritical, selective, and discriminatory (Moodie 1994a). Regimes such as the Missile Technology Control Regime (MTCR) and the Australia Group (responsible for managing chemical- and biological-related technology transfers) are the objects of particularly intense Southern hostility. In the Southern view, these efforts to deny technology—especially because they deal with dual-use technologies—have discriminatory implications well beyond the military realm. MTCR guidelines are resented, for example, on the grounds that they deny nonaligned states the ability to pursue legitimate commercial ventures in the area of space launch vehicles. Regimes

such as the MTCR are seen as efforts to deny to the developing world the advanced technologies needed not only for legitimate commercial purposes but as the foundation for sustained development. This view is compounded by what C. W. Robinson (1985) has described as a "restitution ethic" in the South, reflecting its belief that the North, composed of former exploiters and colonizers, "owes restitution to the South for past transgressions" (p. 267).

An example of the competing perspectives was the 1994 session of the United Nations (UN) Disarmament Commission, which, after a multiyear effort, failed to secure consensus on a study of the role of science and technology in security and development. The sticking point was the report's language on nonproliferation (United Nations 1994, 8). Kemp (1993) summarizes the more general result of these intensely differing perspectives:

> a significant gap between the industrial powers and many regional states that see arms control initiatives as an attempt to interfere with their national security needs at a time when the old collective security umbrellas are being removed. (p. 127)

Given this situation, several points relating to technology diffusion are worth making.

First, the industrialized nations cannot have it both ways. They cannot extol the virtues of advanced military technologies for preserving their interests—the performance of advanced systems in the Gulf war, for example—and then attempt to deny those technologies to others. In the current environment, any sense that the developed nations are trying to preserve their dominant position in a technological hierarchy will be flatly condemned.

Second, continued reliance on denial strategies will undermine any progress on the technology diffusion problem because the political support of developing countries is crucial for the viability of any regime designed to restrict technology flows. Technology transfers are no longer conducive to restraint by suppliers alone (if they ever were).

Third, developing countries cannot continue to use arguments about non-discrimination, their right to a level playing field, and the obligations of former colonial masters to provide technological assistance to struggling, even failing, economies. Industrializing nations must acknowledge that the security problems associated with technology diffusion are as much a challenge for them as they are for developed states, and that they also have an obligation to contribute to a solution. It does little to advance any nation's security interests to score debating points by blaming the West, the superpowers, or the major arms producers for defining the ground rules and role of advanced weapons in the security perceptions of the developing world (Hussain 1992), nor do arguments that complain that export controls are racist and the product of an unsophisticated inability to distinguish between one country and another (Subrahmanyam 1993). Developing country representatives must engage positively on the issue if progress toward their objective of securing access to technology is to be made.

Beyond Export Controls: The Need for a Multifaceted Strategy

Under present circumstances, there are few incentives for the procurers of advanced technology to constrain their acquisitions. Proponents of constraint, then, focus on the providers of the technology, laying the responsibility for constraint entirely on their shoulders. The growing futility of this kind of supply-side arms control, however, arises not from the suppliers' economic or political incentives to continue to transfer weapon systems, but from the political unacceptability of such an approach *from the recipients' point of view.* Anything smacking of a hierarchy in which some states have the right to technology denied to others will be quickly and completely rejected. The international norms against weapons of mass destruction—as shaky as they might be—provide some basis for acceptance, at least in principle, by the entire international community of some kind of restraint in that area. In the absence of any such norm relating to advanced technology outside the realm of weapons of mass destruction, any restraint system is likely to be seen by those who would consider themselves the targets as illegitimate.

Given the trends complicating efforts to manage the process of technology diffusion, is the international community condemned to watch as the spread of advanced technology with military applications makes regional conflicts not only more deadly and destructive but more widespread and globally destabilizing? Is it to live with the paradox identified by Nolan (1991) of a policy that seeks to subsidize the costs of national security and sustain nations' economic competitiveness by enhancing the capabilities of smaller states not only to wage war with advanced weapons but to produce them? If policymakers think in terms of a single regime, legally enshrined, the answer is probably yes, especially if that regime is limited to technology denial.

On the other hand, if an approach is developed that emphasizes the coordination of multiple efforts, many involving cooperation among suppliers and recipients, chances for effective management of the technology diffusion challenge are enhanced. A number of measures have been suggested.

Technology-related Measures

The first is that group of measures that focuses on the management of technology itself. Although an exclusive or even primary emphasis on technology denial is an inadequate approach for dealing with the technological trends of the post–cold war world, export controls will still be needed. The free market should not be the only arbiter of technology transactions, especially in the security field. During the Cold War, export controls effectively delayed Soviet development of advanced, militarily critical, dual-use technology (McDaniel 1993). The operative word, however, is "delay," and as the Office of Technology Assessment (OTA 1994) points out, in the future the effectiveness of export controls in slowing proliferation will depend on many factors: the characteristics of the weapons concerned, the technological capabilities of target countries and programs, the controllability of the designated commodities or technology, the degree of international cooperation, and the quality of enforcement. The OTA argues further that in some cases, export controls may do little; in others, they may impose significant obstacles.

The problem is compounded by the perception that the cost of export controls is growing and that the task of designing a system that serves U.S. security interests while taking due account of U.S. economic interests and those of the business community pursuing exports is difficult (BENS 1993; OTA 1994). Douglas McDaniel (1993)

points out that in the initial postwar period, the cost of controls could be and largely was ignored. Today, that is not the case, although he argues that while some economic costs were associated with strategic export controls during the Cold War—with the burden falling particularly heavily on some industries—these costs were less than feared, at least in the short term. This stands in contrast to the anxiety expressed by the Business Executives for National Security (BENS 1993) who contend that, left unchanged, the current export control system will have a dramatic—and negative—effect on U.S. competitiveness. A study by the National Academy of Sciences (1988) estimated that in 1985 controls on high technology cost the U.S. economy $9 billion and close to 200,000 jobs.

There are, then, both security and economic reasons to adapt the current export control system. A number of ideas have been put forward regarding the proper direction. Nolan (1991) suggests, for example, that the first priority is to establish simpler guidelines that can win widespread support and be bureaucratically sustained. The problem in drawing up such guidelines, of course, is the selection of the technologies that warrant attention. The concept put forward by Roberts (1993) of "leveraging technologies" might be helpful in this regard. He defines these as

> technologies creating military capabilities of strategic consequence, which is to say capabilities that operate fundamentally on the perceptions of choice by the leaders of targeted nations. (pp. 148–149)

Focusing on those technologies that act as important force multipliers, not just on those related to traditional concerns about weapons of mass destruction, could produce a major impact on strategic capabilities.

The difficulties associated with such an approach should not be underestimated. In autumn 1993, for example, the Clinton administration modified its approach to export controls on certain items, loosening restrictions on some high technologies such as computers and space launch vehicles in order to promote the economic competitiveness of these industrial sectors. The move was immediately criticized for making it easier for potential proliferators to make a rapid transition to weapons programs because of the dual-use nature of the technology involved.

If it is increasingly difficult to draw distinctions between commercial technologies necessary for economic advancement and those for decisive military impact, however, then attempting to deny "leveraging technologies" will prove fruitless. The focus of restraint efforts, therefore, must shift away from attempts to deny technology itself to increasing the certainty about the uses to which that technology is put (Reinicke 1994), away from prohibiting technology exports to more emphasis on knowing what happens to them. In essence, what is needed is not a coordinated, but essentially unilateral, strategy of technology denial, but a multilateral strategy of technology management.

Such an approach requires close cooperation between suppliers and recipients, especially the latter, because the goal is to make it easy to see that the goods and services they are importing serve to support peaceful economic development or stabilizing military purposes. M. Granger Morgan and Mitchel Wallerstein (1992) suggest that a structure of both incentives and penalties be closely linked to the disclosure and transparency offered by these states. In essence, the more open a state is about the way it uses its technology imports, the more it is guaranteed access to international markets; the more unwilling a state is to operate openly, the greater the certainty it will be subjected to tighter controls.

Two other elements would also be critical to ensuring the success of such an approach. One is greater government-industry cooperation. The BENS report (1993) points out that the prevailing attitude in government has been to view industry as part of the proliferation problem and to underestimate its willingness to be a helpful participant in nonproliferation efforts. Nolan (1991) suggests that a model for cooperation between industry and government could be their experience during the negotiations of the Chemical Weapons Convention, when their close work together allowed Washington to put forward and ultimately incorporate into the final treaty positions that balanced national security and economic concerns. Given the trend mentioned earlier of greater company-to-company technology transfer below the government-to-government level, such cooperation would be critical to ensuring adequate information is available on the full scope on ongoing technology diffusion (Reinicke 1994).

A second vital element would be a long-term effort to diminish the dependence of the defense industry on exports. Because defense budgets are not likely to rise significantly (barring an international security catastrophe), thus keeping domestic demand dampened, heavy stress would have to be placed on defense-industrial conversion and cooperation.

A second set of technology-related measures reflects the fact that a supplier-only regime is likely to be doomed to failure. As long as any restraint efforts focus only on suppliers, the competing pressures that cancel out movement toward restraint are likely to prove too strong to resist. Rather than a supplier-only focus, therefore, the suggestion has been made for a supplier-recipient dialogue on a regional or subregional basis (Moodie 1994b). The goal of such a dialogue should be an understanding by all parties of what constitutes the critical military requirements of regional states and their implications for arms acquisitions. Such an understanding may foster, in turn, a willingness among regional states to forgo certain technologies or weapon systems that they—and not the suppliers—deem to be destabilizing.

Such an approach would have two beneficial results. First, it would avoid the resentment created by having decisions by outsiders imposed on regional actors. Second, it would promote the regional dialogue necessary to resolve the basic political disputes at the heart of regional tensions that spur the demand for military capabilities.

No one should be under any illusion that promoting such a regional or subregional dialogue, especially in areas of great tension, will be easy or yield quick results. Such a process of bringing technology suppliers and recipients together, however, may be the only way to overcome the reservations of nonaligned recipient countries toward policies of technology restraint.

Regional Arms Control

In the post–cold war environment, the regional conflict and instability generating demand for military technology must be addressed directly (Moodie 1994b). It is difficult to know, however, whether to be optimistic or pessimistic over regional arms-control prospects. The end of the Cold War has created opportunities that are, at least to some extent, being exploited. Examples include the Arms Control and Regional Security (ACRS) Working Group created as part of the Middle East peace process, the agreement on confidence-building measures between India and Pakistan, the decision of the Association of Southeast Asian Nations (ASEAN) to create the ASEAN Regional Forum (ARF) to address the security dimension of their dialogue, the agreement to create an African Nuclear Weapon Free Zone, and a number of developments in Latin America, including an unprecedented resolution adopted by the Organization of American States calling on its members to pursue arms control and disarmament more aggressively.

On the skeptical side, few if any of these efforts have yet to produce concrete results. Despite more than two years of discussion, for example, the ACRS process has produced no agreements. South Asia has done little to move from paper to practice. The ASEAN process has only just begun, among widespread anxiety as to where the process will lead.

Given the tentative nature of these efforts, considerable attention has been focused on building confidence among regional states as a necessary first step (United Nations 1992; 1993), particularly through increasing transparency as to military-related activities. The emphasis on transparency is based on the assumption that the more a state knows about the armed forces and military acquisitions of potential adversaries, the less likely it is to misperceive the actions of its rivals, thus becoming susceptible to making miscalculations that, in turn, escalate tensions and eventually erupt into conflict. In short, predictability breeds stability.

One small but important step has been taken in this regard with the creation by the United Nations of an arms transfer register. The register was a political response to a given situation—the experience with Iraq—at a particular point in time (Moodie 1992; Laurance 1993). The goal of the UN resolution creating the register was to focus attention on the problem of destabilizing weapons buildups. Gradually making information available on the nature of a state's military capabilities is intended to build confidence over time that the acquisition of new capabilities does not upset regional military balances. The initial experience with the register has been mixed. The large amount of data submitted and the number of countries participating in the first year was a pleasant surprise to many, even if the data were not all that some analysts would have liked. In the second year, participation in this voluntary measure dropped somewhat, and unresolved disputes plagued efforts to refine and bolster reporting requirements. Despite these shortcomings, the register has generally been considered a useful step, and it has prompted considerable discussion of regional registers whose details in terms of weapons categories and so on can be tailored to the specific concerns of particular areas. Whether the international community will be willing to go beyond this limited measure in the realm of constraining conventional arms, however, remains to be seen.

Conclusion

The package of measures examined here is neither neat nor simple. If technology diffusion is to be managed effectively, however, there may be no other workable choice. It must be remembered that technology itself is neutral, and that its impact derives from the choices that are made about it. The strategy for dealing with technology diffusion, then, must focus less on the technology itself and more on measures that can influence the direction of those choices. They are designed to shift the calculations of the costs and gains that might be associated with a use of technology that is inconsistent with international norms.

References

Aly, Abdel Monem Said. 1992. "Quality vs. Quantity: The Arab Perspective of the Arms Race in the Middle East." In Geoffrey Kemp and Shelley Stahl, eds., *Arms Control and Weapons Proliferation in the Middle East and South Asia.* New York, N.Y.: St. Martin's Press.

Anthony, Ian. 1992. "The Proliferation of Advanced Weapons: Current Trends and Implications for Arms Control." In W. Thomas Wander and Eric H. Arnett, eds., *The Proliferation of Advanced Weaponry: Technology, Motivations, and Responses.* Washington, D.C.: American Association for the Advancement of Science.

Arnett, Eric H. 1992. "The Most Serious Challenge of the 1990s? Cruise Missiles in the Third World." In W. Thomas Wander and Eric H. Arnett, eds., *The Proliferation of Advanced Weaponry: Technology, Motivations, and Responses.* Washington, D.C.: American Association for the Advancement of Science.

BENS (Business Executives for National Security). 1993. "Toward a Nonproliferation Partnership: Government-Industry Cooperation in Export Controls." Washington, D.C.: Business Executives for National Security. December.

Biddle, Stephen. 1994. "Recent Trends in Armor, Infantry, and Artillery Technology: Developments and Implications." In W. Thomas Wander, Eric H. Arnett, and Paul Bracken, eds., *The Diffusion of Advanced Weaponry: Trends, Regional Implications, and Responses.* Washington, D.C.: American Association for the Advancement of Science.

Bitencourt, Luis. 1994. "The Security and Economic Considerations of Arms and Technology Transfers among Exporting and Importing States." Presentation at a conference on "Arms and Technology Transfers: Security and Economic Considerations," organized by the UN

Institute for Disarmament Research and the Institute for Foreign Policy Analysis, Geneva, February 14–15.

Bracken, Paul. 1993. "The Military After Next." *The Washington Quarterly* 16 (Autumn).

———. 1994. "Command and Control Technologies in the Developing World." In W. Thomas Wander, Eric H. Arnett, and Paul Bracken, eds., *The Diffusion of Advanced Weaponry: Trends, Regional Implications, and Responses.* Washington, D.C.: American Association for the Advancement of Science.

Brooks, Harvey. 1980. "Technology: Evolution and Purpose." In *Modern Technology: Problems or Opportunity. Daedalus* 109 (Winter).

Carus, W. Seth. 1991. *Ballistic Missiles in Modern Conflict.* New York, N.Y.: Praeger.

———. 1994. "Military Technology and the Arms Trade: Changes and Their Impact." In Robert E. Harkavy and Stephanie G. Neuman, eds., *The Arms Trade: Problems and Prospects in the Post–Cold War World. Annals of the American Academy of Political and Social Science* 535 (September).

Chipman, John. 1991. "Third World Politics and Security in the 1990s: 'The World Forgetting, By the World Forgot?'" *The Washington Quarterly* 14 (Winter).

Chubin, Shahram. 1993. "The South and the New World Order." *The Washington Quarterly* 16 (Autumn).

Cooper, Richard N., and Ann L. Hollick. 1985. "International Relations in a Technologically Advanced Future." In Anne G. Keatley, ed., *Technological Frontiers and Foreign Relations.* Washington, D.C.: National Academy Press.

Garrity, Patrick J. 1993. "Implications of the Persian Gulf War for Regional Powers." *The Washington Quarterly* 16 (Summer).

Goldring, Natalie J. 1993. "Transfer of Advanced Technology and Sophisticated Weapons." In *Disarmament and National Security in an Interdependent World.* Disarmament Topical Papers 16. New York, N.Y.: United Nations.

Gouré, Dan. 1993. "Is There a Military-Technical Revolution in America's Future?" *The Washington Quarterly* 16 (Autumn).

Hussain, Mashashid. 1992. "The Role of Advanced Weaponry in Developing Countries." In W. Thomas Wander and Eric H. Arnett, eds., *The Proliferation of Advanced Weaponry: Technology, Motivations, and Responses.* Washington, D.C.: American Association for the Advancement of Science.

Irwin, Steven M. 1993. *Technology Policy and America's Future.* New York, N.Y.: St. Martin's Press.

Jeshurun, Chandram. 1993. "Southeast Asia." In Jayantha Dhanapala, ed., *Regional Approaches to Disarmament, Security, and Stability.* Aldershot, U.K.: Dartmouth for the UN Institute for Disarmament Research.

Keatley, Anne G., ed. 1985. *Technological Frontiers and Foreign Relations.* Washington, D.C.: National Academy Press.

Kemp, Geoffrey. 1993. "Regional Security, Arms Control, and the End of the Cold War." In Sheryl J. Brown and Kimber M. Schraub, eds., *Resolving Third World Conflict: Challenges for a New Era.* Washington, D.C.: U.S. Institute of Peace.

———. 1994. "The Impact of the Gulf War on States' Attitudes and Behavior Toward Advanced Technology." Presentation at a conference on "Arms and Technology Transfers: Security and Economic Considerations," organized by the UN Institute for Disarmament Research and the Institute for Foreign Policy Analysis, Geneva, February 14–15.

Laurance, Edward J. 1992. *The International Trade in Arms.* New York, N.Y.: Lexington Books.

———. 1993. "The UN Register of Conventional Arms: Rationales and Prospects for Compliance and Effectiveness." *The Washington Quarterly* 16 (Spring).

McDaniel, Douglas E. 1993. *United States Technology Export Controls: An Assessment.* Westport, Conn.: Praeger.

McNeill, William H. 1982. *The Pursuit of Power: Technology, Armed Force, and Society Since A.D. 1000.* Chicago, Ill.: University of Chicago Press.

Markov, David R. 1994. "Advanced Conventional Weapons Sales [Worldwide]." Presentation at a conference on "Arms and Technology Transfers: Security and Economic Considerations," organized by the UN Institute for Disarmament Research and the Institute for Foreign Policy Analysis, Geneva, February 14–15.

Mazarr, Michael, et al. 1993. *The Military-Technical Revolution: A Structural Framework.* Washington, D.C.: Center for Strategic and International Studies. March.

Millot, Marc Dean. 1994. "Facing the Emerging Reality of Regional Nuclear Adversaries." *The Washington Quarterly* 17 (Summer).

Moodie, Michael. 1990. "New Theater Conventional Technologies." In Kenneth B. Moss, ed., *Technology and the Future Strategic Environment.* Washington, D.C.: The Wilson Center Press.

Michael Moodie

———. 1992. "Transparency in Armaments: A New Item for the New Security Agenda." *The Washington Quarterly* 15 (Summer).

———. 1994a. "Constraining Conventional Arms Transfers." In Robert E. Harkavy and Stephanie G. Neuman, eds., *The Arms Trade: Problems and Prospects in the Post–Cold War World. Annals of the American Academy of Political and Social Science* 535 (September).

———. 1994b. "Regional Arms Control: Overlooked No Longer?" In James Brown, ed., *New Horizons and Challenges in Arms Control and Verification.* Amsterdam, The Netherlands: VU University Press.

Morgan, M. Granger, and Mitchel B. Wallerstein. 1992. "Controlling the High-Technology Militarization in the Developing World." In W. Thomas Wander and Eric H. Arnett, eds., *The Proliferation of Advanced Weaponry: Technology, Motivations, and Responses.* Washington, D.C.: American Association for the Advancement of Science.

Mussington, David. 1994. "Understanding Contemporary International Arms Transfers." *Adelphi Paper* 291. London: Brassey's for IISS.

National Academy of Sciences. 1988. *Balancing the National Interest: U.S. National Security Controls and Global Economic Competitiveness.* Washington, D.C.: National Academy Press.

Nolan, Janne E. 1991. *Trappings of Power: Ballistic Missiles in the Third World.* Washington, D.C.: The Brookings Institution.

Office of the Press Secretary. 1993. "Fact Sheet: Nonproliferation and Export Control Policy." Washington, D.C.: The White House. September 27.

OTA (Office of Technology Assessment). 1994. *Export Control and Nonproliferation Policy.* Washington, D.C.: GPO. May.

Pierre, Andrew J. 1982. *The Global Politics of Arms Sales.* Princeton, N.J.: Princeton University Press.

———. 1993. "Conventional Arms Proliferation Today: Changed Dimensions, New Responses." In Elizabeth J. Kirk, W. Thomas Wander, and Brian D. Smith, eds., *Trends and Implications for Arms Control, Proliferation and International Security in the Changing Global Environment.* Washington, D.C.: American Association for the Advancement of Science.

Potter, William C., and Harlan W. Jencks, eds. 1994. *The International Missile Bazaar: The New Suppliers' Network.* Boulder, Colo.: Westview.

Ramo, Simon. 1985. "The Foreign Dimension

of National Technological Policy." In Anne G. Keatley, ed., *Technological Frontiers and Foreign Relations.* Washington, D.C.: National Academy Press.

Reinicke, Wolfgang H. 1994. "Cooperative Security and the Political Economy of Nonproliferation." In Janne E. Nolan, ed., *Global Engagement: Cooperation and Security in the 21st Century.* Washington, D.C.: The Brookings Institution.

Roberts, Brad. 1992. "Arms Control and the End of the Cold War." *The Washington Quarterly* 15 (Autumn).

———. 1993. "From Nonproliferation to Antiproliferation." *International Security* 18 (Summer).

Robinson, C. W. 1985. "Technological Advances—Their Impact on U.S. Foreign Policy Relative to the Developing World." In Anne G. Keatley, ed., *Technological Frontiers and Foreign Relations.* Washington, D.C.: National Academy Press.

Skolnikoff, Eugene B. 1993. *The Elusive Transformation: Science, Technology, and the Evolution of International Politics.* Princeton, N.J.: Princeton University Press.

Sokolski, Henry D. 1994. "Nonapocalyptic Proliferation: A New Strategic Threat?" *The Washington Quarterly* 17 (Spring).

Subrahmanyam, K. 1993. "Export Controls and the North–South Controversy." In Brad Roberts, ed., *U.S. Security in an Uncertain Era.* Cambridge, Mass.: MIT Press.

Tanks, David, et al. 1993. *Defense Conversion and Arms Transfers: The Legacy of the Soviet-Era Arms Industry.* Washington, D.C.: Institute for Foreign Policy Analysis.

Thompson, W. Scott. 1993. "Where History Continues: Conflict Resolution in the Third World." In Sheryl J. Brown and Kimber M. Schraub, eds., *Resolving Third World Conflict: Challenges for a New Era.* Washington, D.C.: U.S. Institute of Peace.

United Nations. 1992. *Disarmament and Security in Africa.* Disarmament Topical Papers 12. New York, N.Y.: United Nations.

———. 1993. *Regional Approaches to Confidence- and Security-Building Measures.* Disarmament Topical Papers 17. New York, N.Y.: United Nations.

———. 1994. "Disarmament Commission Reports to General Assembly." *Disarmament* 12 (May–September).

Van Creveld, Martin. 1989. *Technology and War: From 2000 B.C. to the Present.* New York, N.Y.: Free Press.

II.
Nonproliferation in the 1990s

Rethinking Nuclear Proliferation

George Rathjens

SURPRISE THAT IRAQ had made as much progress toward acquiring nuclear weapons as it had before the Persian Gulf War and the more recent concerns about North Korea's nuclear program have meant that nuclear weapons proliferation is now getting attention in the U.S. government—and in others—to a degree unknown since the Carter years. The Clinton administration is supporting the policies developed during those earlier years to deny potential proliferators access to materials and technology relevant to weapons acquisition—and delivery—and it will try, with considerable international support, to get the Nuclear Non-Proliferation Treaty (NPT) of 1970 extended well beyond 1995, when it comes up for review. It is also developing, within the Department of Defense, new "counterproliferation" initiatives.

It is unlikely, however, that either the administration's commitment to

old policies or its new efforts will be very successful and they may, in some respects, be counterproductive. If one believes that the nuclear proliferation problem is serious, more will be required; in particular, a determined and sustained commitment to an international collective security regime, however distant its realization may now seem.

The Old Regime

Following the discovery of nuclear fission in 1938, scientists and the world's political leaders sought to prevent the spread of nuclear weapons through secrecy, through proposing that all of the world's nuclear activities be placed under the control of a single international agency, through attempting to ban all nuclear weapons tests, and through trying to limit access to critical materials and technologies by placing constraints on international trade and nuclear power facilities. In 1968, after 30 years of effort, the best hope seemed to lie in a treaty that would require:

- that the nuclear weapon states not assist others to acquire weapons;
- that the non-nuclear weapon states agree not to acquire them; and
- that facilities in the latter states capable of producing fissionable materials that might be used in weapons

George Rathjens is a professor of political science at MIT and is affiliated with its Center for International Studies. During the Carter administration he was deputy to Gerard Smith, the president's ambassador at large for nonproliferation matters.

Copyright © 1994 by The Center for Strategic and International Studies and the Massachusetts Institute of Technology
The Washington Quarterly • 18:1

be subject to surveillance by the International Atomic Energy Agency (IAEA) to assure that they were not being so used.

The result was the Nuclear Non-Proliferation Treaty of 1970. Its conclusion—and the fact that the vast majority of states, 164, acceded to it—has been widely hailed as a great arms-control achievement. Indeed, for many, it has been viewed as *the* cornerstone of the international nuclear weapons nonproliferation regime, and, as the treaty comes up for review and possible extension in 1995, it is still widely considered an indispensable element of the regime.

But the treaty has proved to be inadequate in important respects.

- Some of the states of greatest concern, notably Israel, India, Pakistan, Argentina, Brazil, South Africa, and North Korea, refused for many years to accede to the treaty. The first five still do; and at this writing, differences between the United States and the IAEA on the one hand and North Korea on the other regarding inspection of the latter's nuclear facilities remain unresolved.
- There is no provision in the treaty itself for sanctions. (In the event of discovery of a violation, the IAEA can bring the issue to the attention of the secretary general of the United Nations [UN], but the imposition of sanctions must be decided by the Security Council).
- Nothing in the treaty prohibits a state from developing indigenous capacities for the production of fissionable materials or producing and stockpiling such materials or other components that might be used in nuclear weapons. These lacunae are particularly troublesome because the development of facilities for uranium enrichment and

spent fuel processing and the acquisition of stockpiles of plutonium and enriched uranium can be rationalized, albeit with greatly varying degrees of credibility, as being consistent with non-military nuclear power aspirations.[1] Thus, there is the possibility that a non-nuclear weapon state, party to the treaty, might legitimately stockpile plutonium and/or enrich uranium, only to withdraw from it—as is permitted with three months' notice—to rather suddenly acquire a significant stockpile of nuclear weapons.

Appreciation of these inadequacies in the NPT has meant that increasingly there has been emphasis, particularly by the advanced industrial states, on preventing nuclear weapons acquisition through policies of denial extrinsic to the treaty. These have involved national and multinational controls on the export of critical technologies; economic and political pressure on many nations to forgo the development of indigenous uranium enrichment and spent fuel reprocessing facilities; and efforts, particularly by the United States, going back to the Ford and Carter administrations, to generally discourage the transport and stockpiling of plutonium and its use for power reactors.[2]

A fuller characterization of the nuclear nonproliferation regime of the 1970s and 1980s must also take account of two important features of the Cold War:

- In their worldwide competition for influence, support, and bases, the Soviet Union and the United States entered into alliances with other countries and, in some cases, intervened broadly in their politics and military policies, generally discouraging the independent acquisition of nuclear weapons by these states.

The quid pro quo was that the superpowers guaranteed, explicitly or implicitly, the security of these countries, some of which might otherwise have acquired nuclear weapons of their own for defense against a variety of real and imagined threats. The effect of the division of much of the world into the two great blocs was thus to greatly constrain the impetus to nuclear proliferation within them. Acquiring nuclear weapons seemed neither politically feasible nor militarily necessary in countries such as Italy and Poland.

- At the same time, the intensity of the U.S.–Soviet competition was so great that many other issues of concern in the two societies were treated with relatively low priority, and this included nuclear weapons proliferation. Thus, when the Soviet Union invaded Afghanistan the United States subordinated its efforts to dissuade Pakistan from going ahead with its nuclear weapons program to the higher priority of securing Pakistani support in thwarting Soviet advances in Afghanistan. At the same time, it backed off trying to induce India to accept IAEA inspection safeguards on all its nuclear facilities because of concern that if it did not back off, Soviet influence in India might increase.

Changes

Now though, the nuclear weapons proliferation problem must be considered in a new light.

Although the collapse of the Soviet empire brought freedom, relief, and hope to many of what had been its constituent peoples, concern is increasing about possible Russian efforts to reestablish influence and control. It is this fear that has underlain the interest of the Visegrad and the Baltic states in becoming members of the European Union and in getting the security guarantees of membership in the North Atlantic Treaty Organization (NATO). And this is the basis for Ukrainian pleas for guarantees of its security as a quid pro quo for giving up control over nuclear weapons on its soil that might serve as a deterrent to Russian irredentism. Although Russian economic pressure, coupled with Western economic carrots, might induce Ukraine to yield on the nuclear weapons question, their success is not clear at this writing. What is clear is that neither NATO collectively, nor the United States unilaterally, is soon going to extend security guarantees to any of the countries of Eastern Europe—or to any others—as it did to its NATO partners and to Japan and South Korea in the days of the Cold War. Moreover, in the light of recent experience in Bosnia, it is by no means clear that U.S. or NATO security guarantees would have much credibility, even if offered. Thus, the impetus to acquisition of nuclear weapons by states around the periphery of Russia is likely to be a potential problem for some years, and this may be true in other areas as well where states with hostile neighbors may no longer feel, as they could in the past, that they could rely with some confidence on U.S.—or Soviet—protection.

The demise of the Soviet Union has also brought to the fore questions of effective control of nuclear weapons and stocks of fissionable material, both in Russia and in what were the other Soviet republics. Moreover, it is now feared that skilled and experienced people who were formerly employed in the Soviet nuclear weapons program might sell their services to other states that have an interest in acquiring nuclear weapons.

Although the threat of war on a global scale, involving the use of many thousands of Soviet and U.S. nuclear weapons—along with perhaps hundreds from other countries—has certainly receded with the collapse of the Soviet Union and the end of the Cold War, these developments have also led, then, to the at least partially offsetting effect of an augmented impetus for diffusion of nuclear weapons to an ever greater number of states and possibly to an increase in the likelihood of their use in small numbers.

The other most significant development of recent years affecting perceptions about the proliferation problem has been the Gulf war. The reader may recall that persuading the U.S. Congress and public that the United States should use military force against Saddam Hussein was not easy. The Bush administration offered a series of rationales for such use: that it should be done to signal that deliberate aggression across frontiers would not be tolerated in the new world order; that the Iraqis had to be ejected from Kuwait, and control of the country had to be restored to its legitimate rulers; that the prospect that Iraq might acquire control over the bulk of Middle East oil was an intolerable threat; that Saddam Hussein was another Hitler; and even that U.S. jobs were at stake. Yet none of these appeals proved to be as effective as the contention that Iraq might soon acquire nuclear weapons. That possibility really did seem to trouble Americans, at least according to opinion polls.

With the allied military victory, it became clear that Western (including Israeli) intelligence had seriously underestimated the scope and scale of the Iraqi nuclear weapons program. Although Iraq had been a party to the NPT and had accepted IAEA inspection of its *declared* nuclear facilities, its very large nuclear weapons program had escaped IAEA notice. Moreover, after its military defeat, ascertaining the full scope of that program proved to be extraordinarily difficult, even with unprecedentedly intrusive searches and with information supplied by a defector. The lesson of this experience is that a nation determined to acquire nuclear weapons can go very far toward its goal without discovery, despite being a party to the NPT and accepting traditional IAEA surveillance. Even if, as expected, the IAEA will be more insistent on inspection of undeclared but suspect facilities in the future, and even if it has Security Council backing in doing so, there must be grave questions about the adequacy of the system and procedures. It is most unlikely that the Security Council would actually mandate the use of military force, and then, if necessary, that it would be used effectively to back up demands for unrestricted and unimpeded inspection, as the imbroglio over North Korea's nuclear program illustrates.

That problem prompts another observation about the "old regime." The existence of facilities in North Korea for the production of militarily significant quantities of plutonium, or its separation and stockpiling, will be accepted with great reluctance, if at all, by the United States and a number of other countries. Yet Japan has done the same things (and on a much larger scale), and although a number of governments have found this in some measure objectionable, it has not provoked anywhere near as vehement a response. This illustrates a major difficulty of trying to build a truly universalist nuclear nonproliferation regime or even one based on dividing the countries of the world into discrete classes, as in the case of the NPT, where the division is based solely on whether or not states had conducted an overt nuclear weapons test by the time the treaty entered into force.

In addition to these distinct events of recent years that bear so significantly on the proliferation problem—the demise of the Soviet Union, the end of the Cold War, and the Gulf war—important evolutionary changes should be noted.

The technical wherewithal for getting into the weapons business has become dramatically more accessible since the initiation by the United States of its "Atoms for Peace" program 40 years ago. That initiative led to the release of a great deal of previously classified information and the training of many students from third world countries in nuclear science and engineering.

Advancements in uranium enrichment technologies and the spread of those technologies is a particularly noteworthy development. At the beginning of the nuclear age, gaseous diffusion emerged as the enrichment technology of choice. It was, however, so difficult and so dependent on economies of scale that for some years the Soviet Union and the United States maintained an effective duopoly in the provision of enrichment services for commercial purposes. The prospect that other nations would pursue a weapons option based on highly enriched uranium was accordingly generally discounted. It seemed cheaper and easier for them to produce weapons-grade plutonium. But with the development of gas centrifuge and other technologies, including prospectively, laser-based enrichment, not to mention the Iraqi resurrection and improvement of the World War II calutron method, would-be proliferators have more enrichment options to consider.

Even more dramatic are the developments in computer capacity that make capabilities that are far beyond those available to the United States and the Soviet Union when they designed their first nuclear weapons available to virtually any state interested in weapons.

These and other technical developments are doubly troublesome from a nonproliferation perspective. It will be increasingly easy for would-be proliferators to design bombs and to acquire fissionable materials and other components for them; and it will be increasingly unlikely that the United States and other advanced countries will have positions in uranium enrichment and other weapons-usable technologies that are so dominant that they can be used effectively as leverage to induce other states to eschew weapons programs.

An additional point about uranium, albeit a relatively unimportant one because the amounts required for a modest weapons program are small: because prospects for nuclear power generation have sharply declined since the 1970s, and because there is essentially no demand in the nuclear weapon states for uranium for weapons, it has become a glut on the market. There is now a surfeit of potential suppliers, and the cost of uranium required to make a bomb has fallen drastically: from between roughly \$200,000 and \$400,000 15 years ago (and in 1979 dollars) to perhaps a tenth of that today.

It should be noted that, although it is not directly relevant to the acquisition of nuclear weapons, access to missiles capable of reliably delivering them can also be expected to increase.

One is left with the unsettling conclusion that trying to stem nuclear weapons proliferation mainly through policies of denial, that is, through the imposition of export controls on critical materials and the threat of sanctions against states that will not accede to and comply with the NPT, is not likely to be adequate and will be of diminishing utility. Yet, as the consequences of the end of the Cold War—chaos and the diminished willingness of the great powers to guarantee the security of other states—become more apparent, the interest of nations in acquiring nuclear weapons for deterrence may increase.

On New Approaches—or at Least Changes in Emphasis

Given the dramatic changes of the last few years, it is clearly time for some rethinking about national and international nuclear nonproliferation policies. This has begun, at least in the United States, where it has found its most notable expression in the Department of Defense. The new emphasis has its basis in three observations.

- Attempts to prevent the spread of nuclear weapons through export controls and other efforts at denial of critical materials and technology are likely to be of diminishing utility, as suggested here.
- With control over nuclear weapons spreading to increasing numbers of countries—and with possible erosion of control in the former states of the Soviet Union—the likelihood of their unauthorized or accidental launch is likely to increase.
- The spread may result in control being vested in the hands of some persons or regimes that cannot be deterred from using nuclear weapons by the threat of the use of force, nuclear or otherwise.

The result has been much talk about a new, or at least enhanced,

counterproliferation effort by the U.S. Department of Defense to complement nonproliferation efforts. Although the rhetoric includes references to such things as enhanced intelligence collection efforts and targeting and attack capabilities, the most—perhaps only—tangible commitment is to theater-based ballistic missile defense. The emphasis is perhaps understandable—or at least explainable. With the demise of the Soviet Union, the United States faces few direct military threats to either its territory or its forces abroad with which it cannot easily cope: the exception is those involving use of weapons of mass destruction. Putting aside for the moment the possibility of forcing a change in regime through military conquest, the U.S. military establishment has conceptually three options for dealing with threats of this last kind: deterrence, counterforce attack, and active defense. Having conceded that deterrence may not be effective in all cases, and recognizing the political difficulties of counterforce attacks, particularly of those involving preemption, the military must give active defense high priority. The alternative from the Department of Defense's perspective is to concede that this mission is beyond its reach—as it has been ever since the development of nuclear weapons. Making such a concession may be especially difficult considering that very strong claims—that were, as it turns out, wildly exaggerated—were made for the effectiveness of the U.S. Patriot air defense missile system against modified Soviet SCUD missiles in the Gulf war. But the concession must be made. Nuclear weapons are so powerful, and cities—and deployed troops—are so fragile, that a defense that is less than, say, 90 percent effective is not very interesting, and 90 percent success is probably just not in the cards, given the multiplicity of means of delivery of nuclear weapons, including particularly the possibility of the use of cheap, but effective, decoys in the case of delivery by ballistic missiles.

What is needed now is a broad reconsideration of the nuclear proliferation problem, one unencumbered by constraints of past thinking, particularly by the dichotomization of the world's nations, as exemplified in the NPT, into nuclear weapon and non-nuclear weapon states, and by the almost exclusive emphasis on denial as the means of preventing the spread of nuclear weapons.

As to the first point, instead of classifying states as either nuclear weapon states or non-nuclear weapon states, it might be useful to think in terms of the following classes:

1. those with no nuclear weapons and no apparent interest in them;
2. those holding such weapons who do not appear to have a real need for them;
3. those who might reasonably rationalize acquisition of nuclear weapons for deterrence of attack by others; and
4. those whose interest in nuclear weapons would seem to be mainly for coercive or aggressive use against others.

Most states clearly belong in the first category: the United States, Britain, and France, but probably no others, in the second. The third category might be usefully subdivided. There are states, such as Israel, that might have a perceived need for nuclear weapons to cope with conventional attack by an adversary. There are others, of which India might be an example, that might, in the event of a major

conventional war, reasonably want nuclear weapons to deter an opponent's use of them. Or, again in the event of a conventional war, a state might hope to deter intervention by third parties. With conventional war in Korea having been a real possibility for many years, and a continuing one, this could be an important motivation for North Korea's apparent nuclear weapons program, although probably not the only one. There are several states, such as China, Pakistan, Russia, and Ukraine, that might reasonably want nuclear weapons to hedge against both conventional and nuclear attacks. Libya and Iraq are examples of states that might belong in the fourth category, although the main motivation in the case of either or both could well be to deter third party intervention in conventional conflict initiated by them.

In exploring nonproliferation policy options, it would be wrong to simply dismiss the first class of states as of no concern. The world community ought to be sensitive to the possibility that attempts to impose universalist constraints on international trade in technology and materials that might be used for nuclear weapons programs can adversely affect the interests of these states even if it is other states' possible nuclear weapons aspirations that motivate such policy initiatives.

Turning to the second category, the United States, Britain, and France are not now directly threatened by any significant power, nor are they likely to be in the near term—or to be more precise, they are not likely to be subject to any direct threats to which nuclear weapons would be a remotely reasonable or even plausible response. Nor are nuclear weapons in the hands of these three Western powers likely to be either necessary or credible—much less both—for deterrence or actual use in dealing with likely threats to their interests abroad or to allies or friendly third parties. It is perhaps worth noting in this connection that none of the three, insofar as is known, seriously contemplated the use of nuclear weapons against Iraq in 1990–91 when Saddam Hussein clearly threatened their access to Gulf oil, even though it is hard to imagine a more serious threat to their interests, especially those of France, which, without any oil of its own, is more dependent than the others on imports from the Middle East. Western nuclear weapons are, therefore, essentially useless, and ought, accordingly, to be of little concern to anyone except their own citizenry, who are burdened with the cost of their maintenance.

Two slight caveats should perhaps be considered.

It is argued that nuclear weapons may have symbolic and even some diplomatic value. Certainly this perception was a factor in the British decision in the late 1940s to acquire them, when it was argued that having them would enable Britain to play a larger role in international affairs than it otherwise could. Now though, with a better appreciation of their limited military utility, their symbolic significance is much diminished. To the extent it is of residual importance, elimination of the U.S., British, and French weapons, or even just large reductions in their numbers, not to mention consummation of a comprehensive nuclear test ban treaty and agreements on the cessation of production of fissionable materials for weapons purposes, might have some salutary effect in inducing others to give up nuclear weapons or to forgo their acquisition. In the present environment, these last effects are probably more important to the United

States, Britain, and France than the symbolic effects of retention—and continued weapons testing.

There are also the possibilities of accidental or unauthorized use, or of some weapons falling into the hands of other nations or even terrorists. Although these risks can be easily reduced to almost arbitrarily low levels, given that there is no real need for maintaining Western nuclear weapons in any state of readiness, they cannot be totally dismissed.

For the above reasons, it would be good if the U.S., British, and French weapon stockpiles could be reduced or destroyed, but what might be done with them is really not of *first order* importance in consideration of nuclear weapons nonproliferation policies.

The real problems lie in the instances in which nuclear weapons may have perceived utility for either coercive or deterrent purposes. Whatever the rationale, questions will arise as to what might be done to prevent or dissuade would-be proliferators from pursuing weapons options, and how to neutralize capabilities should they be developed.

Efforts at denial have not been totally ineffective. Pakistan's acquisition of nuclear weapons was no doubt delayed as a result of the imposition of constraints by the United States and other industrial countries on exports to it. But it is not obvious that delay in this case has made much difference. In others, it may have. Where there were changes in domestic politics, motivations to acquire weapons may have dissipated before ambitions could be realized. Difficulties in access to technology may have had this effect in Argentina and Brazil. Although there are no obvious cases, there may also have been instances involving a close call where impediments to access, or the existence of the NPT and accession of neighbors to it, might have tipped the balance against a nation's going ahead with a weapons program. But with evidence that at least a half dozen states have made substantial progress toward acquiring nuclear weapons, notwithstanding efforts to impede their access to critical materials and technology, one cannot be very optimistic about the future of these approaches.

Counterproliferation efforts are not likely to be any more successful, assuming the focus is mainly on active defense. If, however, one includes the possibility of preemptive destruction of nuclear capabilities, at least short-term success cannot be dismissed on purely technical grounds. The world has seen two examples of such destruction—the Israeli attack on Iraq's Osirak reactor in 1981 and the allied attacks against a broader range of Iraqi nuclear facilities a decade later. But it is noteworthy that these have been the only successful attempts so far, that the Israeli attack was successful only in a tactical sense—its main effect may have been to reinforce Iraqi determination to acquire nuclear weapons, reflected in its subsequent efforts— and both these attacks were carried out when a state of war existed between Iraq and the attacking parties. The Israeli attack was noted with considerable opprobrium in many parts of the world, and the U.S.-led attacks were politically possible only in the context of much wider military operations sanctioned by the Security Council. It is most unlikely that such attacks would have been initiated had Iraq not invaded Kuwait, even as it now seems unlikely that the United States or another power will preemptively attack North Korea's nuclear facilities if it continues with its nuclear program, as

long as it does not also attack South Korea—or Japan.

We are left to conclude that continuing to try to deal with nuclear weapons proliferation through politically easy, supply-side options is likely to be of limited utility. There will undoubtedly be benefits in the extension of the NPT, in the selective use of constraints on the transfer of technology and critical materials, and maybe even in the Department of Defense's counterproliferation approaches, but such benefits must be weighed against the costs: in the case of active defense by the United States, the waste of many billions of dollars, with perhaps emulation to some degree by other countries, and possible undercutting of the Anti-Ballistic Missile Treaty; in extension of the NPT and in otherwise selectively constraining access to critical materials and technology through export controls, the political reaction to behavior that will be widely seen to be discriminatory. But the greater costs will arise from misleading people about the efficacy of such measures. The result is likely to be that people will discount the importance of reducing nations' motivations to acquire weapons. Thus, to continue nearly exclusive focus on policies of denial will be diversionary; quite possibly, critically so.

There are three possible options for reducing motivations: the resolution of basic differences between adversarial states, one or both of which may fear attack by the other; the provision of security guarantees to states that feel threatened; and military conquest of would-be proliferators, followed by occupation, most likely for a decade or more, to establish new regimes with no interest in nuclear weapons.

The United States has made serious efforts to catalyze the settlement of the Arab–Israeli conflict, and in the case of Egypt and Israel with some success, albeit at very considerable cost. The Camp David accords have meant that over 50 percent of U.S. foreign assistance has gone to those two countries. But other efforts, for example in trying to help in the resolution of Indo–Pakistani differences, have had little success. Realistically, in the world political environment of today, most of the impetus for the resolution of differences between adversarial states will almost certainly have to come from those states themselves. "Good offices" roles played by other states are likely to contribute only marginally, particularly if those other states are unwilling, as will generally be the case, to incur large political or economic costs.

Security guarantees have met with more success. It is indisputable that the U.S. guarantee of South Korea, exemplified by the stationing of 40,000 U.S. troops in that country for 40 years, has been an important factor in dissuading South Korea from proceeding with an overt nuclear weapons program or even with the construction of a spent fuel reprocessing plant for its commercial reactor fuel—a plant that could have facilitated its getting into the weapons business. But while South Korean restraint has been an important consequence, it was not the primary *reason* for the U.S. guarantee. The main motivation was rather the containment of communism. The same can be said of guarantees by the United States to its NATO allies and Japan. As noted earlier though, the world is now a very different place. It is now unbelievable that the United States would guarantee the security of, say, India or Pakistan, much less that of Ukraine, and beyond the wildest fantasy to believe that it would be willing to deploy large numbers of troops

for decades in any of these countries, even if they were wanted. And no other major powers are likely to be eager to play that role either.

As to conquest and occupation, the record of the United States has been mixed. After World War II, it nurtured the development of governments in Germany and Japan that could be trusted to use military power, if at all, only for purposes of which it would generally approve, but the U.S. record in the Caribbean and Central America has been quite the opposite. And it has to be noted that notwithstanding two attempts by Saddam Hussein to acquire nuclear weapons, the United States chose, after military victory in the Gulf, not to follow through with his removal and the establishment of conditions such that the possibility that Iraq would acquire nuclear weapons during, say, the next two decades could be safely dismissed.

Skepticism about the immediate prospects for reducing demand through a hegemonical approach would then seem to be warranted. Although Russia and China might conceivably play this role abroad—the former with respect to its "near abroad" and China in East Asia—for many years the United States would be the only conceivable candidate for such a role, and while it just might serve as a mediator, arbiter, or catalyst in the resolution of disputes underlying the interest of some states in acquiring nuclear weapons, and might even be able and willing to use force to cause the replacement of political authorities who aspire to get nuclear weapons by others clearly not interested in them, it is most doubtful that it could, within the next few decades, acquire the requisite strength, confidence of others, and support of its own people to meet the more fundamental objective of a truly effective nonproliferation regime:

guarantee of the security of all states that might otherwise feel a need for nuclear weapons for deterrence or self-defense.

Hope for the Future?

The best, albeit not very immediate, hope of meeting this last objective must lie in a collective approach to security. This was, of course, the great challenge for a fleeting moment at the time when the United Nations was organized and before the Cold War supervened. Now, the world has another chance: the possibility of restructuring the UN and related international institutions, and generating broad support for them and confidence in them, so that they can play the role—and more—envisaged for them when they were formed.

The challenges are different and in important respects more difficult than when the UN was being organized. Then, the main issues were to prevent the resurgence of the kinds of militarism demonstrated by Germany and Japan during the preceding decade and to cope with aggression across frontiers. Now there are, in addition, the more immediately troublesome problems of proliferation of weapons of mass destruction and of ethnic conflict, affronts to human rights, and chaos. These new challenges arise at a time when respect for the UN is low, and when, accordingly, there is great resistance to the surrender of sovereignty to it and little willingness to provide financial support for its operations; when, indeed, there appears to be widespread objection in nations throughout the world to incurring large costs, military or otherwise, to deal with threats that do not seem *immediately* serious to vital national interests.

Thus, the very idea of strengthening the UN so that it can be instrumental

in dealing with ethnic strife and civil conflict and in guaranteeing the security of states against external threats is understandably seen by many as little more than a will-o'-the-wisp or, at best, a very distant prospect. But the fact that there have been such dramatic—and not widely predicted—changes in the world as the demise of the Soviet empire, the sudden reunification of Germany, a so-far generally peaceful revolution in South Africa, and the glimmerings of hope for a resolution of Arab–Israeli differences and now between Catholics and Protestants in Ireland, all in the last several years, suggests that such cynicism may well be unwarranted. Surely in a time of such flux, it should be the part of statesmanship to approach the future with optimism about possibilities for changes in world governance and to resist both isolationism and go-it-alone approaches to security.

One's first impulse is to suggest that the lead in doing so will have to come largely from the United States; and for a brief instant, when Iraq threatened Kuwait in 1990, it seemed that President George Bush might commit himself—and, to the extent he could, the United States—to providing that lead. But it soon became clear that that was not to be the case. Notwithstanding glowing remarks about establishing a "new world order" and the impressive mobilization of broad international support for Desert Shield and Desert Storm, the administration displayed no initiative in trying to strengthen the UN so that it might deal more effectively with crises. On the contrary, it seemed more interested in using the UN than in strengthening it. Moreover, after its military victory over Iraq, it acceded to the protection of the Kurds in northern Iraq and to intervention in Somalia only after considerable pressure, it resisted making com-

mitments that might require the stationing or use of U.S. military forces
abroad, particularly if the commitments might be of extended duration,
and, in policy statements, it made it
clear that the United States would intervene militarily in areas of crises only
when it was in the U.S. national interest, very narrowly defined, and then,
only under severely circumscribed
conditions. It was not long before references to Bush's "new world order"
began to carry derisive connotations.

Coming to the presidency as Bill
Clinton did with only a minority of the
popular vote, with virtually no experience in foreign affairs and with no apparent sense of the need and opportunity for fundamental changes in world
order, it is hard to imagine a president
less well equipped than he to take up
the challenge with which Bush at least
flirted: namely, that of trying to change
the international system in fundamental ways from what Americans have
known since the United States
emerged as a world power almost a
century ago. Instead, Clinton's approach to international issues has been
essentially reactive, and such initiatives as his administration has attempted have been almost exclusively
in the domestic arena—or responsive
to domestic pressures. Although disappointing, it is hardly surprising that the
overall tenor of its May 1994 policy
statement on multilateral peace operations is one of constraint and retrogres-
sion, notwithstanding diplomatic obei-
sance in the document to collective
approaches to international security
and to hope for the UN.[3] The sad reality is, then, that we are not likely to
see, for at least the next two and a half
years, much, if any, presidentially inspired movement toward the development of a world order based on the
rule of law and on collective security
that seems needed if demands for nuclear weapons are to be largely eliminated.

Yet, if one looks to the next century,
the case for such development seems
overwhelming. The nuclear proliferation argument alone would seem
sufficient if one believes, as Albert
Einstein argued, that "the unleashed
power of the atom has changed everything save our modes of thinking, and
thus we drift toward unparalleled ca-
tastrophes."[4]

*This work was supported in part by the Carnegie
Corporation and benefited from discussions with
Carl Kaysen and James Walsh.*

Notes

1. Those not familiar with nuclear technol-
    ogy should understand that ordinary ura-
    nium cannot be used *directly* for fabricating
    nuclear weapons. For weapons purposes,
    the concentration of the isotope with a
    mass number of 235 must be greatly in-
    creased, typically from the natural concen-
    tration of 0.71 percent, to greater than 90
    percent, by a process called "enrichment."
    (Uranium enriched to this degree is also
    used to fuel most naval propulsion reactors
    and some research reactors. Most electric-
    ity generating reactors require fuel en-
    riched to about 3 percent U–235.)
    Alternatively, weapons can use plutonium
    as the fissionable material. It is produced
    in reactors from the much more abundant
    uranium isotope, 238. After removal from
    the reactor, it must be separated chemi-
    cally from the residual uranium and fission
    products in what is commonly referred to
    as spent fuel reprocessing. The Hiroshima
    bomb was made from highly enriched ura-
    nium; the Nagasaki weapon, and most oth-
    ers, from plutonium.

2. Some of these efforts can be, and have
    been, construed to be contrary to both the
    spirit and letter of the NPT. In addition to
    the features described above, the treaty
    specifies, as a concession to the interests
    of the non-nuclear weapon states, that
    nothing in it should be interpreted as "af-
    fecting the inalienable right of all the Par-
    ties to the Treaty to develop research,
    production and use of nuclear energy for
    peaceful purposes." Indeed, the treaty re-

quires that "parties in a position to do so shall cooperate in contributing to the further development of the applications of nuclear energy for peaceful purposes, especially in the territories of non-nuclear-weapon States Party to the Treaty." The conflict inherent in trying to both limit nuclear weapons proliferation *and* realize the benefits of the "peaceful atom" is also reflected in the dual mandate—and in the budget—of the IAEA.

3. "Executive Summary: The Clinton Administration's Policy on Reforming Multilateral Peace Operations," Presidential Decision Directive 25, unclassified document, Washington, D.C., May 3, 1994.

4. Quoted in Ralph E. Lapp, "The Einstein Letter that Started It All," *New York Times Magazine,* August 2, 1964.

The Last Nuclear Summit?

Mitchell Reiss

VISIONS OF POST–COLD WAR security structures, from President George Bush's "new world order" to national security adviser Anthony Lake's "democratic enlargement," place front and center the prevention of the spread of nuclear weapons (as well as other weapons of mass destruction and their means of delivery). Central to past success in the nuclear sphere has been the Nuclear Non-Proliferation Treaty (NPT) and the associated safeguards system applied by the International Atomic Energy Agency (IAEA). Multiplying political instabilities and the dissemination of advanced technologies make this global regime even more important in the post–cold war world.

In less than a year, on April 17, 1995, delegations from the NPT members will descend upon New York City to discuss the NPT and debate its extension. Unfortunately, the task of extending the NPT indefinitely, or even for another 25 years, may not be as easy or its success as inevitable as it once seemed. The Clinton administration's heavy concentration on do-

mestic matters has meant that the NPT Review Conference has received little high-level attention. Unhappily, the same warning signs that preceded the Bush administration's disastrous performance at the United Nations (UN) Conference on Environment and Development held in Rio de Janeiro in June 1992 are present here: no clear strategy, an inability to set the agenda, misapprehension of the politics, and division inside the administration.

The stakes for the United States, which seeks the treaty's indefinite extension, are enormous. Success in New York will reinforce the global norm against nuclear proliferation and make it easier to pressure recalcitrant states that remain outside the NPT to join the regime. Failure, on the other hand, will not only shatter a policy that Washington has promoted successfully for five decades, but will also seriously damage U.S. national security and foreign policy objectives.

Cause for Unease

A host of new developments has joined with old complaints about the NPT to challenge the future of the regime. The 1995 meeting will be the first review conference in which the superpower competition will not dominate nuclear questions. New security architecture to replace the previous bipolar international institutions remains inchoate or nonexistent, however. Meanwhile, events in the former So-

Mitchell Reiss is a guest scholar at the Woodrow Wilson International Center for Scholars in Washington, D.C., where he directs the Center's Nonproliferation Project and is completing *Bridled Ambition: Why Countries Curtail Their Nuclear Weapons Capabilities* (1995).

Copyright © 1994 by The Center for Strategic and International Studies and the Massachusetts Institute of Technology
The Washington Quarterly • 17:3

viet Union, Bosnia, Somalia, and elsewhere foreshadow a brutal and an often anarchic post–cold war society. In such an environment, trust in cooperative security arrangements such as the NPT increasingly seems misplaced, perhaps even foolhardy. As the disarray of the post–cold war international system becomes clearer, growing anxiety may compel more countries to reassess their previous decisions not to acquire nuclear weapons.

New York will also be the first review conference where the use of the "nuclear card" as a diplomatic gambit will be on display. The Review Conference presents Washington with an inherent asymmetry of interests. Because the United States is so closely identified with the NPT and global efforts to prevent the spread of nuclear weapons, it has a much greater stake in the Review Conference's outcome than any other single party. With Washington itself defining success as nothing short of the NPT's indefinite extension, other states gain substantial bargaining leverage to press their own agenda. By offering benefits to Ukraine, Kazakhstan, Belarus, and especially North Korea, in return for good nonproliferation behavior, the Clinton administration has encouraged this type of nuclear gamesmanship. Paradoxically, with the possibility that 1995 might be the last Review Conference if the NPT is extended indefinitely, many states are sure to view New York as their last, best chance to extract such concessions from the United States and the other nuclear powers.

Many NPT and non-NPT members as well have complained that the regime enshrines a discriminatory system of a few nuclear "haves" versus many nuclear "have-nots." New York promises to sound a refrain that has attended all previous review conferences, namely, that the nuclear weapon states have not adequately fulfilled their pledge under article VI of the treaty to seek "general and complete disarmament." To be sure, recent arms reductions by the United States and Russia have placed them in a much better position than before to credibly rebut such arguments. Yet even if the Strategic Arms Reduction (START) I and II agreements are ratified and fully implemented (which will not occur for many years), U.S. and Russian nuclear stockpiles will still be bigger than when the NPT was first signed in 1968. That New York will be the first conference attended by all five acknowledged nuclear powers (the United States, Russia, the People's Republic of China, France, and Britain) will ensure that this issue is heatedly debated.

Interestingly, much of the infighting is likely to be among the nuclear weapon states themselves. On issues ranging from a comprehensive test ban treaty (CTBT) to North Korea's nuclear program, opinions diverge widely. An obstacle to consensus among the nuclear weapon states will be the distinctive positions of first-time participants China and France. Moreover, the current troubled relationship between Washington and Moscow may imperil the continuation of previous U.S.–Soviet cooperation on nonproliferation issues.

The nuclear programs of Iraq and North Korea, both NPT members, have raised serious questions about the effectiveness of the NPT regime by severely testing, and breaking, its rules. The Iraqi case is the best documented. The extent of Baghdad's contempt for the NPT became evident only after its defeat in the Persian Gulf War. Only then did IAEA inspectors discover that Iraq had circumvented or simply ignored its NPT commitments during the 1980s as it aggressively pursued a nuclear weapons capability.

Doubts about the regime's effectiveness multiplied during 1993 and 1994 over North Korea's cat-and-mouse game with the IAEA. An NPT member since 1985, North Korea finally signed an IAEA safeguards agreement and allowed six inspections in 1992; but it refused access to two suspected nuclear waste sites. In early 1993, the IAEA's Board of Governors passed a resolution criticizing Pyongyang, which prompted a North Korean threat to withdraw from the NPT. Only after negotiations with Washington did Pyongyang "suspend" its withdrawal. Nonetheless, it continued to impede full access to its nuclear facilities. By the end of the year, the IAEA's ability to verify the "continuity of safeguards" was severely strained. At this point, speculation in the U.S. intelligence community hardened in its view that the North had acquired one or two nuclear weapons. It remains unclear if North Korea will permit full international inspections and become an NPT member in good standing. But what is clear is that the IAEA bent its own rules and undermined international confidence in its willingness to blow the whistle on those states that violate their legal obligations.

Finally, the Clinton administration appears to see the Review Conference with a mixture of trepidation and denial. Repeated assurances that nonproliferation is a top foreign policy priority have been betrayed by the administration's lackadaisical preparations. Despite commendable efforts by some individual officials, much time that should have been spent preparing for April 1995 has already been lost. In particular, the administration has taken an exasperatingly long time to fill key positions at the Arms Control and Disarmament Agency, which has lead responsibility for the Review Conference.

The Challenge in New York

There are only three possible outcomes at the Review Conference on the question of extending the NPT. As a purely legal matter, if the parties decide not to decide, article X(2) strongly suggests that the treaty will not lapse, but continue indefinitely. A second possibility is a decision affirming indefinite extension, which would make 1995 the last Review Conference ever. The third option is renewal for a fixed period of time. This possibility is receiving greater attention from U.S. experts than before, with many recommending extension for another 25 years. There is, however, no principled reason for extending the NPT for 25 years, versus 20, or 15. For that matter, why not only 1 year?

In the eyes of the NPT parties, extension will not be a legal or a technical matter, but a fundamentally political calculation. The politics of nonproliferation, both prior to and during the Review Conference, will determine how the treaty extension issue is resolved in New York.

The Clinton administration thus urgently needs to craft a *political* strategy to support the NPT's indefinite extension. In other words, the United States needs to filter its nonproliferation and foreign policies through the political prism of the Review Conference. A two-phase approach presents the greatest chance for success. First, Washington needs to address in advance possible criticisms that the non-nuclear weapon states are sure to raise in New York. Otherwise, the Review Conference risks becoming a global referendum on the nuclear policies of the United States, Russia, China, France, and Britain. As at previous review conferences, harsh criticism will be voiced at how far short of their article VI disarmament pledge the nuclear weapon states have fallen. Second, by preempting these objections, the Clinton administration can then set an agenda that focuses attention on strengthening the NPT regime. Most important, Washington will be able to make a persuasive case that the NPT deserves to be extended indefinitely.

Without such a strategic approach, the United States courts disaster in New York. The shorter the extension period, the more likely that NPT members will hedge their bets against the possibility of the regime's eventual demise. Hedging will take the form of countries increasing their nuclear competence; even if this takes place in accordance with applicable safeguards, it will erode confidence in the NPT regime and, by extension, will undermine regional stability. Efforts by some countries to acquire nuclear options will increase suspicion and mistrust among others, which in turn will feel compelled to undertake similar efforts. An element of self-fulfilling prophecy will be present, as countries that were initially motivated by caution will end up driven by fear. Unless the Clinton administration shapes the politics of nonproliferation to its objectives, the politics could distort a global regime that has well served both U.S. interests and the cause of international security.

Setting a U.S. Strategy: Phase I

The first phase of a U.S. strategy should aim at deflecting the international spotlight from the nuclear weapon states. Mere rhetoric will not suffice. A combination of symbolic and

substantive gestures is required. All of these initiatives should deemphasize the role and influence of nuclear weapons in international affairs.

At the top of the current nonproliferation agenda is broad support for a CTBT. A CTBT has been debated at every previous review conference and is certain to be discussed in New York. Although a testing ban will actually do little to slow the spread of nuclear weapons, it has assumed inordinate symbolic importance as a measure of the nuclear weapon states' commitment to nuclear disarmament. President Bill Clinton, in his speech before the UN in September 1993, endorsed a CTBT in principle, but he was only willing to commit the United States to a limited testing moratorium conditioned on similar restraint by other countries.

Expectations for a CTBT are so high that even a completed (if not widely ratified) treaty will not purchase the United States much credit in New York. After four decades of debate, a CTBT is now seen by many states as merely a "nuclear cover charge" that buys the nuclear weapon states little else than the opportunity to discuss the treaty's indefinite extension at the Review Conference.

Unfortunately, these great expectations have been formed with little or no regard to the very real technical difficulties involved in devising a verifiable CTBT regime. Drafting a meaningful definition of a nuclear explosion will be particularly nettlesome; it will have to capture very low-yield (less than one kiloton) tests that may not be verifiable even with wide-ranging and highly intrusive inspections.

One can thus envision three different types of CTBT. First, a CTBT could be a symbolic "declaration of intent" not to conduct nuclear tests, a sort of nuclear honor code. A second type would take the form of a traditional international agreement, subject to ratification, but without intrusive verification measures. All tests would be prohibited, but the treaty would not contain extensive, highly intrusive (and probably unacceptable) verification measures. Both these types of agreements could be formulated in relatively short order. A third type of CTBT would take much longer to draft. It would strive to eliminate any uncertainty that the parties were conducting even low-yield nuclear tests; by necessity, this treaty would contain elaborate and unprecedented verification provisions.

Irrespective of what the final CTBT looks like, there will be problems with the nuclear threshold states—India, Pakistan, and Israel—and two of the nuclear weapon states—China and France. If the language of a CTBT does not explicitly ban low-yield tests, certain nuclear activities prohibited to non-nuclear weapon states that are parties to the NPT could be legally sanctioned for non-NPT parties. For example, if India, Pakistan, and Israel, which are not NPT members, joined a CTBT, they might not be prohibited from conducting certain laboratory experiments and low-yield tests. To be sure, nothing prevents these countries from conducting such experiments and tests now. But an international treaty legitimizing such activities for non-NPT parties would be resented by those non-nuclear weapon states that are NPT parties. Further, this would create a special category of nuclear status for these countries—a step that India in particular has been urging for some time—and add a further discriminatory element to the NPT regime.

In addition, China and (perhaps) France are unlikely to join any CTBT

before conducting further tests to modernize their nuclear arsenals and ensure the reliability and safety of existing stockpiles. Although both countries have suggested privately that they may join a CTBT in 1996, this will come too late for the Review Conference.

Yet the best should not be the enemy of the good. The politics of the Review Conference demand that a CTBT, even if less than perfect, be in place before April 1995. For this reason alone, either of the two more symbolic approaches are preferable to the third, more complex one. The loophole for the threshold nuclear states can be narrowed (if not totally eliminated) by including language that expresses as strongly as possible that the spirit of a CTBT proscribes all nuclear testing. Washington should also reiterate to Israel, India, and Pakistan that it would strongly object to any nuclear testing. In addition, the United States should explain to Beijing and Paris the trade-offs involved with a CTBT. Most important, these objections to a CTBT should not be an excuse for further delay. If the United States had allowed the hesitation of other states to regulate its nonproliferation policy in 1968, there would be no NPT today.

President Clinton's initiative for ending the production of fissile material for nuclear explosive purposes or outside of safeguards, which he proposed in September 1993 at the UN, contains a number of problems similar to a CTBT. A cutoff convention risks creating a discriminatory system that perversely favors the threshold nuclear countries that are not NPT members at the expense of those countries that are. Under such a convention, nuclear material previously produced by the nuclear threshold states would not be subject to IAEA safeguards; in theory, this material could be used to make nuclear weapons. In contrast, all the nuclear material produced by NPT members would be under safeguards. As David Fischer, the former deputy director of the IAEA, has pointed out, the risk is that a cutoff convention would not only confer preferential treatment upon Israel, India, and Pakistan, but that it would also grant international treaty recognition to the three countries as de facto nuclear weapon states.[1]

Although capping fissile material stockpiles is a worthy goal, drafting an agreement that adequately addresses these potential pitfalls will be extraordinarily difficult. It is likely to take many years. Moreover, a cutoff convention has never been at the forefront of the debate at previous review conferences and does not really appeal today to the other NPT parties. One reason is that it is primarily aimed at capturing the nuclear programs in India, Pakistan, and Israel—none of which is an NPT member. With so many other items on the agenda, priorities must be set. The Clinton administration should consequently place this initiative on the back burner until after the Review Conference.

There are additional multilateral and unilateral steps Washington should take. The United States and the other nuclear powers should jointly declare that they will not be the first to use nuclear weapons. With the end of the Cold War and the Warsaw Pact's threat to Europe, many of Washington's previous objections to a no-first-use policy have disappeared or greatly diminished. Although Russia reversed the Soviet Union's no-first-use doctrine in fall 1993, this was primarily aimed at compelling Ukraine to return the strategic nuclear weapons based on its territory. With Kiev's ratification of the START I treaty,

Moscow may now be willing to adhere to its previous no-first-use stance; Washington needs to press this issue. China's long-standing policy states that it will not be the first country to use nuclear weapons. It is unlikely that Britain and France would hold out if the three major nuclear weapon states agreed. Further, given Washington's refusal to extend security guarantees (as opposed to security assurances) to other states beyond its traditional European and East Asian allies, a no-first-use declaration would go a long way toward reassuring the non-nuclear weapon states that they will not be subject to nuclear attack or nuclear blackmail.

Second, the United States should take the lead in coordinating a declaration by all nuclear powers that reiterates their article VI pledge to seek nuclear disarmament. No specific timetable need be set, but the aspiration should be clearly enunciated. Although some may dismiss this as a hollow gesture, it should more properly be seen as an important political symbol of the nuclear weapon states' vision of a world without nuclear weapons.

To provide tangible meaning to this goal, the United States and Russia should jointly reduce their nuclear stockpiles in accordance with the START I treaty limits and move quickly to ratify and implement START II. When the two sides ratified START I, they qualified their approval on prior fulfillment of certain conditions. The most important outstanding condition requires Ukraine to join the NPT. Consequently, arms reductions are being held hostage to the indecision of the Ukrainian parliament. Reductions under START II cannot proceed until START I comes into force.

START I and II are far too important for U.S. and Russian security interests for this kind of artificial linkage. Although the situation in Ukraine is still unclear, there are some signs that may make further delay unnecessary. In February 1994, Kiev effectively reaffirmed its non-nuclear stance by ratifying START I. Ukraine is obligated to return the strategic nuclear warheads stationed on its territory to Russia during the next three years. Further, recent public opinion polls show that the Ukrainian people have no desire to become a nuclear weapon state. Moreover, as Boris Yeltsin's future becomes cloudier and prospects for productive Russian–U.S. relations become more uncertain, there is a greater urgency to kick-start the START process so that it generates its own momentum, regardless of the day-to-day politics of the bilateral relationship.

To move ahead with START I and II will require the U.S. Senate and the Russian Duma to untie some of the previous conditions they attached to the START I treaty and then ratify the START II agreement. To make this politically acceptable to legislatures in both countries, language revoking the previous conditions could contain its own condition. This new condition would provide that the two sides retain their right to reconsider this accelerated arms reduction schedule annually in light of Ukraine's nuclear policy. (As an added bonus, rescinding the previous conditions will help reduce whatever bargaining leverage the Ukrainian parliament thinks it retains by withholding its assent to NPT membership.)

The United States should also agree to reciprocal monitoring with Russia of the dismantlement of nuclear warheads. According to testimony in September 1993 by Assistant Secretary of Defense Ashton Carter, the United States cannot verify that a single nuclear warhead in the former Soviet Union has actually been dismantled. Shared Russian–U.S. concerns over security should actually help in devising a joint supervisory system that would ensure greater transparency; the benefits of such a system would outweigh the liabilities. Although this arrangement might largely be a bilateral confidence-building measure, it would also be a useful indication of the seriousness with which Washington and Moscow view arms reductions.

Although Israel is not an NPT member, its nuclear program was on the agenda at the 1985 and 1990 Review Conferences and promises to be discussed in 1995. As with other issues likely to arise in New York, the United States should preempt this debate. Washington should urge Israel to shut down its Dimona reactor, which is nearing the end of its operating life. This will achieve the same objectives as the fissile material production cutoff without any of its liabilities. To be sure, this step will not satisfy all parties, but it will be a concrete indication of Israel's willingness to freeze its nuclear capabilities, as well as a step toward a broader arms-control regime, including a zone free of all weapons of mass destruction in the Middle East. Moreover, without some progress in this area, the concerns of Arab parties may dominate the Review Conference.

The United States can also pursue certain policies unilaterally. For example, the Clinton administration's "counterproliferation doctrine" is of increasing concern to NPT parties. Here especially, the United States needs to filter its policy through the political prism of the Review Conference. As articulated by the Department of Defense, counterproliferation covers a wide range of useful efforts to prevent the spread of nuclear weapons. Most critics have, however, focused on one aspect in particular, namely the endorsement of preemptive military strikes against the nuclear programs of other countries—a type of nuclear hunting license. Even countries that might welcome the elimination of potential nuclear threats object to having the United States act as self-appointed judge, jury, and executioner.

Counterproliferation promises to be a real liability for Washington at the Review Conference. At the very least, it will focus unwanted attention on the United States, instead of on other, more pressing issues. Most troubling for prospects in New York is that the current doctrine completely ignores whether potential target countries belong to the NPT or apply IAEA safeguards. A country's nonproliferation bona fides are immaterial, which undercuts the basic philosophy of the NPT regime. The United States could markedly advance its cause at the Review Conference if it explained counterproliferation's relationship to those countries that are NPT members and accept IAEA safeguards. In short, the Clinton administration needs to state clearly and loudly that this doctrine will not apply to any NPT party in good standing.

Finally, the United States should sign the three protocols to the Treaty of Rarotonga, which establishes a nuclear-weapons-free zone in the South Pacific. Washington has hesitated to take this step for fear of offending Paris, which would like to retain the option of conducting nuclear tests in the region. The Clinton administration's reluctance to sign the treaty stems from fear of losing French support for a CTBT. But this is logically inconsistent—France should not object to U.S. accession if Paris supports a testing ban. France will either endorse or oppose both agreements, as it chooses, but it should not be allowed to bluff the administration into refusing to support a nuclear-weapons-free zone in the South Pacific.

Many of these proposals are controversial. Many will undoubtedly be opposed by powerful institutions in the U.S. government, as well as by some U.S. allies. Significantly, however, few experts doubt that Washington will adopt many of these measures during the next few years. But when deciding these issues, Washington needs to factor in the costs of failure in New York versus the benefits of success. For the United States to reap the maximum political benefit—what might be termed the nonproliferation value added—the proposals need to be adopted and implemented before the 1995 Review Conference.

Finally, none of the proposed measures is irreversible. Should the international system become more malevolent during the next few years, the United States would retain the freedom to reverse course. But by seeing the Review Conference as an opportunity and seizing the initiative, the United States will be better able to mold a non-nuclear future consistent with its interests, thereby making such a reversal less necessary.

Setting a U.S. Strategy: Phase 2

By addressing some of the core concerns of the non-nuclear weapon states, Washington would be able to draw more attention to the actual sources of much current proliferation anxiety—unsettling developments in the former Soviet Union, Northeast Asia, and the Middle East. It would also be better equipped to promote measures designed to further energize the NPT and IAEA safeguards system, as well as the entire international nonproliferation regime.

During the past few years, a number of countries have curtailed or placed constraints on their nuclear ambitions—what some have termed nuclear rollback. South Africa is the most celebrated example; it voluntarily dismantled its nuclear stockpile and joined the NPT. Belarus and Kazakhstan also formalized their non-nuclear commitments and pledged to return to Russia the nuclear weapons stationed on their territories. Although virtue may be its own reward, the NPT regime needs to publicly encourage this behavior. The idea is to portray, as starkly as possible, the two choices confronting countries that are contemplating acquisition of nuclear weapons or development of a nuclear option. If they pursue a nuclear weapons capability, they may end up like Iraq, with a decimated nuclear program and years of effort and investment down the drain. On the other hand, if they become "repentant proliferants,"[2] they will be rewarded. The NPT regime already provides a few rewards, such as increased technical and nuclear assistance for countries that apply full-scope safeguards. In addition, Washington should enhance their prestige by finding a highly visible and influential role for these countries at the Review Conference.

But there is more that the United States can do. To punish countries that have developed nuclear weapons, Congress has frequently enacted domestic legislation that places restrictions on U.S. investment and bilateral cooperation. Unfortunately, even after these countries have reversed course and joined the NPT, these punitive laws have remained on the books. As a concrete reward to repentant nuclear states, Washington should announce that it will expeditiously lift domestic legal restrictions on bilateral trade and cooperation and will work to remove similar restrictions that may have been adopted by international lending institutions.

The United States also needs to forge a consensus on tightening the international safeguards system. The IAEA has the authority to request special inspections of suspicious facilities in a host country; it has invoked this right, unsuccessfully so far, with respect to North Korea. But it has received pledges from other countries, most notably Iran and South Africa, that its inspectors can "go anywhere, anytime." It is this broader inspection mandate that needs to become the rule, rather than the exception; it needs to become less special and more routine.

The NPT parties in New York will only be willing to accept more stringent safeguards as part of a deal that grants them greater access to nuclear assistance for peaceful uses of nuclear energy. The danger here is that such assistance may be diverted to military purposes. But as Iraq and other states show, nuclear weapons programs are more likely to be derived from dedicated, clandestine programs outside the safeguards system. Although this threat cannot be completely discounted, the United States should hold out the prospect of greater access to nuclear technology in return for more intrusive inspection methods.

This trade-off can only be justified if the IAEA's inspection capabilities are adequately staffed and fully funded. The IAEA has operated for the past 10 years with an essentially zero-growth budget. Unfortunately, this has coincided with additional demands on the Agency, especially from the newly independent states of the former Soviet Union. (These demands will increase further if a convention

115

ending the production of fissile material is ever negotiated.) Relatively small amounts of additional funding are required to maintain the integrity of the safeguards system. The United States should take the lead in winning added international financial support for the IAEA's safeguards budget.

Even after adopting this step, some non-nuclear weapon states will object that the safeguards system is one more discriminatory aspect of the NPT regime—safeguards are not required on the nuclear activities of the nuclear powers but must apply to all the nuclear activities of the non-nuclear weapon states. To remedy some of this imbalance, and to deemphasize Washington's reliance on nuclear weapons, the United States should place IAEA safeguards on its uranium enrichment and plutonium separation facilities at Hanford, Washington, Oak Ridge, Tennessee, and Savannah River, South Carolina. President Bush announced in July 1991 that these plants would not produce plutonium or enriched uranium, and this step would be consistent with President Clinton's September 1993 proposal to cut off the production of fissile material.

Implementation

In theory, the two phases of this U.S. strategy are mutually reinforcing; they can and should proceed in tandem. In practice, this will require setting priorities, negotiating trade-offs within the U.S. government, and tough bargaining with other NPT parties. Time is short; all of this must be done soon if New York is not to be the last nuclear summit. Managing the process will be difficult, complex, and time-consuming. To succeed, the Clinton administration needs to elevate the issue to

the highest levels of government and get senior officials closely involved. Most important, as April 1995 approaches, an increasing commitment of President Clinton's personal attention will be required.

Fortunately, the administration has already set an excellent precedent— its handling of the North American Free Trade Agreement (NAFTA). Many of the lessons learned from the White House's orchestration of NAFTA's passage are applicable to the NPT Review Conference: assigning a talented and experienced team to this single issue, developing a legislative strategy, authorizing key officials to take decisions, using the president's time to resolve disputes and lobby critical parties, and educating the public on the stakes involved.

The Clinton administration can also usefully borrow a page from the G–7 economic summits. In preparing for these meetings, each country assigns a "sherpa" to smooth disputes and seek agreement on major issues in advance. The United States should organize a group of key NPT countries to perform a similar function. Given the politics surrounding the NPT Review Conference, U.S. goals in New York may be better advanced in some circumstances if other countries take the lead. Such a group could include the five nuclear powers and Japan, Germany, Nigeria, Mexico, Australia, South Africa, Peru, Sri Lanka, Poland, Egypt, South Korea, and Argentina (if it joins the NPT before April 1995).

Finally, in preparing for New York, the United States would also do well to look beyond 1995. The Review Conference will reflect the importance of nuclear weapons and the role they play in international affairs. But it will also set a marker for the nature of international relations in the twenty-first century. Will the measure of international power and prestige be defined by military force or by other, more benign factors, such as economic prosperity and social harmony? In this sense, there are two paths to New York. One path leads back to a world perpetually governed by fear and insecurity. The other road is long, arduous, and uncertain. But it is the one most clearly in the interests of the United States.

The author would like to thank Kurt Campbell, Ronald Lehman, Joseph Pilat, and Zachary Davis for their help with this article. The views expressed here are solely those of the author, who assumes full responsibility for any errors of fact or interpretation.

Notes

1. David Fischer, correspondence with author, March 1994.

2. See Leonard Spector, "Repentant Nuclear Proliferants," *Foreign Policy*, no. 88 (Fall 1993), pp. 21–37.

Nonproliferation in the 1990s: Enhancing International Cooperation on Export Controls

Gary K. Bertsch and
Richard T. Cupitt

NONPROLIFERATION, NOT containment, is the dominant rationale for export control policy in the post–cold war era. Despite the emerging international consensus that export controls are an important supply-side tool for preventing the proliferation of weapons of mass destruction and their associated means of delivery, substantial debate persists in the United States and elsewhere on how to implement them. In particular, there is much disagreement on the future of the multilateral arrangements that supervise the export of military and dual-use (commercial and military) goods and technologies. These arrangements were created at different times, for different reasons, and by different states, and, consequently, the coordination of their activities has proved elusive.

On the basis of a recent study of the diverse export control policies of 10 countries, the authors of this essay argue for the development of a new typology of countries that goes beyond both the traditional East–West and North–South divisions.[1] Here they will present one such typology, which allows for the identification of the most pressing problems concerning proliferation the United States is likely to face and what it might do in response. For illustration the authors will examine how the newly independent states of the former Soviet Union (FSU) fit into the challenge to stem proliferation through export controls.

Multilateral Export Control Arrangements in the 1990s

Currently, there are four key multilateral arrangements to control the transfer of dual-use items. They are: the Coordinating Committee for Multilateral Export Controls (COCOM) for restrictions on a wide range of items that affect military capabilities; the Nuclear (or London) Suppliers Group (NSG) for nuclear items; the Australia Group (AG) for chemical and biological items; and the Missile Technology

Gary K. Bertsch and Richard T. Cupitt are codirector and assistant director, respectively, of the Center for East–West Trade Policy at The University of Georgia, and editors, with Steven Elliott-Gower, of *International Cooperation on Nonproliferation Export Controls* (Ann Arbor: University of Michigan Press, forthcoming).

Copyright © 1993 by The Center for Strategic and International Studies and the Massachusetts Institute of Technology

Control Regime (MTCR) for missile systems (see table 1 for summary information on each).[2]

The Coordinating Committee for Multilateral Export Controls (COCOM). Unlike the other export control arrangements, COCOM was created explicitly to restrict strategic exports to Communist countries. Throughout the cold war period, it maintained three lists of controlled items: the International Munitions List (IML), the International Atomic Energy List (IAEL), and the often controversial International Industrial List (IL) of dual-use items.

COCOM has undergone significant change in the post-Communist era. Controls on 350 of the 600 dual-use subitems on the old IL have been relaxed, and a new "core list" created on the basis of "higher fences, fewer goods."[3] COCOM has agreed on criteria for granting favorable consideration to certain countries, culminating in their removal from the list of proscribed destinations (e.g., Hungary).[4] Finally, COCOM members have created the COCOM Cooperation Forum (CCF), drawing the European neutrals and certain post-Communist states into discussions on export control issues.[5] Its original objective

> was to propose a new approach on COCOM export controls, which would contribute to the economic development of the reforming countries by providing wider access to higher technology while developing guarantees which ensure that sensitive goods and technologies are used solely for civil purposes in these countries.[6]

CCF members also agreed to discuss other export control matters but have not agreed on what the substance of those deliberations might be.

The Nuclear Suppliers Group (NSG). India's detonation of its "peaceful nuclear device" in 1974 led to the creation of the NSG. NSG members established guidelines for the transfer of nuclear materials, particularly to states that are not signatories to the Nuclear Non-Proliferation Treaty (NPT).

With some Communist states participating from its inception, the NSG appears well suited to make the transition to the post–cold war world. Beginning in the late 1980s, NSG members began to meet more frequently, agreeing to regulate 65 dual-use items and beginning to require full-scope safeguards for the transfer of nuclear items to non-member states. They also adopted a "no-undercut" rule on license denials. According to this rule, each member has final say on exports, but members will not license exports previously blocked by another member without prior consultation. Further, the NSG members created a permanent "point of contact" in Vienna staffed by the Japanese.

Australia Group (AG). Sparked by Iraq's use of chemical weapons, the AG was formed in 1985 to promote multilateral consultation, information sharing, and the coordination of export control efforts related to the development and spread of chemical weapons. With a predominantly Western membership, the AG identified a list of 9 chemical weapons precursors to be controlled and 41 others were placed on a warning list for monitoring.

More recently, members have expanded the list of controlled items to include 54 chemical weapons precursors, certain biological organisms, and processing equipment for both chemical and biological items. Members have also cooperated in the development of the Chemical Weapons Convention, agreeing to review controls on exports to any signatory state.

Although most member states have yet to change their national policies to conform with these controls, many have taken a more serious approach to implementation in recent years. After embarrassing revelations about exports to such countries as Iraq and Libya that resulted in the proliferation of chemical weapons capabilities, Germany tightened its chemical export controls considerably in 1990. Concern in Australia, Japan, Luxembourg, and the Netherlands also resulted in measures to strengthen their domestic chemical export controls. In its 1990 Enhanced Proliferation Control Initiative (EPCI), the United States pledged to implement controls for all AG chemical weapons precursors and to control 23 categories of chemical and biological processing equipment.[7]

The Missile Technology Control Regime (MTCR). Missile proliferation in the Middle East, Latin America, and Asia spurred the United Kingdom, the United States, France, Germany, and Italy to construct an interim agreement of guidelines for the transfer of missile technology in 1985. The original controls were on missile systems that could deliver a 500-kilogram warhead more than 300 kilometers, with an emphasis on nuclear weapons delivery. In addition to the guidelines, these states created a list of 18 technologies in two categories subject to control. Category I items, consisting mainly of complete missile systems and missile subsystems, had a presumption of denial, while Category II items, including computers and 15 other items, required end-use certification and other assurances.

After the Persian Gulf War of 1990–1991 and the experience with Iraqi Scuds, the MTCR took on considera-

ble salience and its membership expanded rapidly. Argentina and Hungary became members, while Israel, the People's Republic of China (PRC), Russia, and others have expressed either an interest in participating in the regime or a commitment to abide by its guidelines. This new membership would change the regime's exclusively Western and Northern composition.

Since the Gulf war, members have agreed on more specific export licensing requirements, and they are attempting to harmonize various national interpretations of controlled items. They now apply strict retransfer controls on list items as well. Most recently, members proscribed the shipment of any missile or unmanned air vehicle system or subsystem with a range of over 300 kilometers or any missile when there is evidence that it is intended for use with a weapon of mass destruction.[8]

Reforming Multilateral Export Controls in the 1990s

A number of proposals for reforming multilateral export controls have been put forward. Ashton Carter and his fellow authors argue that the nonproliferation and technology transfer regimes may erode without substantial fusion.[9] Other studies suggest the importance of integrating, unifying, and simplifying the existing export control regimes.[10] Peter Rudolf, for example, concludes that:

Cooperation within the framework of COCOM members would provide the best guarantee that varying national controls in North–South trade do not jeopardize the already advanced development of a license-free COCOM zone, in which intra-

Table 1
Control of Weapons Proliferation

	Nuclear Weapons	Biological and Chemical Components	Missiles	Strategic Goods
Multilateral Export Control Arrangement	Nuclear Suppliers Group (NSG)	Australia Group (AG)	Missile Technology Control Regime (MTCR)	Coordinating Committee for Multilateral Export Controls (COCOM)
Legal Status	Ad hoc	Ad hoc	Ad hoc	Ad hoc
Members of Arrangement	Australia, Austria, Belgium, Bulgaria, Canada, Czechoslovakia, Denmark, Finland, France, Germany, Greece, Hungary, Ireland, Italy, Japan, Luxembourg, Netherlands, Norway, Poland, Portugal, Romania, Russia, Spain, Sweden, Switzerland, U.K., U.S. (27) Other states applying some NSG standards: All NPT parties require IAEA safeguards on exports; Argentina, South Africa apply some additional NSG rules	Australia, Austria, Belgium, Canada, Denmark, Finland, France, Germany, Greece, Ireland, Italy, Japan, Luxembourg, Netherlands, New Zealand, Norway, Portugal, Spain, Sweden, Switzerland, U.K., U.S. (22)	Argentina, Australia, Austria, Belgium, Canada, Denmark, Finland, France, Germany, Hungary, Iceland, Italy, Japan, Luxembourg, Netherlands, Norway, Sweden, New Zealand, Spain, U.K., U.S. (21) Others applying standards: PRC, Israel, Russia	COCOM countries: Australia, Belgium, Canada, Denmark, France, Germany, Greece, Italy, Japan, Luxembourg, Netherlands, Norway, Portugal, Spain, Turkey, U.K., U.S. (17) Others fully cooperating: Austria, Finland, Ireland, Sweden, Switzerland, Hong Kong, New Zealand CCF countries[a]

Table 1 *continued*

	Nuclear Weapons	Biological and Chemical Components	Missiles	Strategic Goods
With Permanent Coordinator?	Partial (Japan in Vienna for NSG dual-use items)	Yes (Australia in Paris)	No, but officials in Paris serve as point of contact	Yes (U.S. in Paris)
Operating Rules	NSG: National discretion with "no undercut" rule (each member has final say on exports, but members will not license export previously blocked by another member without prior consultation); denial orders routinely circulated; agreed-upon criteria for exercising discretion	AG: National discretion; denial orders sometimes circulated; no agreed-upon criteria for exercising discretion; decision making based upon consensus and unanimity	MTCR: National discretion; denial orders sometimes circulated	COCOM: One-country veto/consensus review of license applications (members will not license export previously blocked by another member); periodic, systematic control list updating; some national discretion CCF: none as of 1993
Multilateral Sanctions	NSG to "consult" regarding possible sanctions in event of nuclear test by non-nuclear weapon states	Based upon national law	No multilateral sanctions mechanism	Ad hoc consultations, based on national law

Source: Adapted from Leonard S. Spector and Virginia Foran, *Preventing Weapons Proliferation* (A Report of the Thirty-Third Strategy for Peace, U.S. Foreign Policy Conference, Warrenton, Va., October 22–24, 1992).

Note:

[a] Countries attending the inaugural meeting of the CCF on November 23–24, 1992, were Albania, Armenia, Australia, Austria, Azerbaijan, Belgium, Bulgaria, Belarus, Canada, Czechoslovakia, Denmark, Estonia, Finland, France, Germany, Greece, Hungary, Ireland, Italy, Japan, Kazakhstan, Kyrgyzstan, Latvia, Lithuania, Luxembourg, Moldova, Mongolia, Netherlands, New Zealand, Norway, Poland, Portugal, Romania, Russia, Spain, Sweden, Switzerland, Turkey, Ukraine, U.K., U.S., and Uzbekistan.

western trade can develop freely.[11]

In their report *Preventing Weapons Proliferation: Should the Regimes Be Combined?* Leonard Spector and Virginia Foran examine three approaches for the possible integration of the various export control systems: unification into a single comprehensive export control monitoring scheme; keeping the regimes separate while incorporating the most effective practices of each into all; and keeping them separate while harmonizing to ensure consistency of approach and avoid undercutting.[12] Spector and Foran note that a unified membership, unified control list, and unified licensing rules "would be extremely difficult to realize."[13]

They recommend some combination of the last two options as more feasible and more effective. They suggest that the voting rules, list review process, and harmonization of CO-COM, the "access" rather than "denial" philosophy of the NSG, and other elements, where possible, be implemented in each of the arrangements. They also argue that, at a minimum, efforts similar to those adopted by the European Community to harmonize existing policies need to be undertaken on a multilateral basis to ensure consistency and avoid undercutting the controls in each arrangement. From their perspective, the disbanding of any arrangement or premature efforts to combine them all into one should be avoided during the current period of radical change in the proliferation community.

After 40 years of often taxing negotiations to harmonize policies among COCOM members, one should not be sanguine about the odds of enhancing cooperation even though this measure calls for relatively few changes in current policy. Although informative, the general debate often seems to ignore whether or not reforming the existing institutions will create a more effective export control system. Such an investigation requires that the views and preferences of a wide variety of states concerning these arrangements be considered. Only a few studies, however, go beyond an analysis of U.S. export control policy, and those focus on Western perspectives.[14] Technological diffusion, the evolution of global markets, the dissolution of Soviet communism, and the emergence of regional military powers, among other factors, suggest that such an exclusive view will not adequately explain the opportunities for and constraints on multilateral export controls. The authors of this article helped bring together studies of export control policies and preferences in Brazil, Bulgaria, the former Czech and Slovak Federal Republic, France, Germany, India, Poland, Russia, South Korea, and the United States in an attempt to bridge this gap.[15]

The Emerging Export Control Framework of the 1990s

From the 10 studies, it is clear that the export control policies of France, Germany, the United States, and arguably Bulgaria, the Czech Republic, Poland, Russia, and South Korea are converging around three shared beliefs:

- the acquisition and/or development of military or dual-use items by certain proscribed states and end-users poses a military threat to their common interests;
- multilateral export controls can be an effective and efficient means of limiting these threats; and
- export controls should not interfere

with legitimate commercial uses of dual-use items as long as the national security of the supplier state is maintained.[16]

Although the convergence of values intimates a substantial amount of congruence on foreign economic and national security policy among these states, can the analysis be extended to other states?

Patterns of membership in alliances and other international arrangements are good measures of the congruence of foreign policy interests among states. In essence, the pattern of a state's participation in international organizations, military alliances, and other multilateral arrangements reveals how it and others view its preferences. In this instance, examining the pattern of state adherence to CO-COM, the NSG, the MTCR, and the AG reveals a structure more complex than either the East–West division of the Cold War or the North–South split that dominates the development literature. Five groups emerge:

- Coordinating states. These states are members or affiliates of all four multilateral export control arrangements and include the members of COCOM (excluding Turkey), most European neutrals (e.g., Austria, Finland, Ireland, Sweden, and Switzerland), and New Zealand.
- Collaborating states. These states participate in some but not all four arrangements. They have, however, expressed their intention to join or work with all four in the future. At present, this group includes some of the post-Communist states of the former Warsaw Treaty Organization (WTO), including Russia, and Argentina, Hong Kong, Singapore, South Korea, and Turkey.
- Sensitive states. Some of these states (e.g., India) have the legal

and administrative basis for export controls, but most currently see limited military, economic, or political value in working within the existing export control arrangements. These states are engaged in producing, acquiring, or exporting items currently controlled under the arrangements, but their security policies do not, at this time, threaten the interests of the coordinating states directly. Countries like Algeria, Brazil, the PRC, India, Israel, Pakistan, Saudi Arabia, South Africa, Syria, Taiwan, and Vietnam fall into this category.[17]

- Threatening states. These states oppose the existing multilateral export control framework. They are acquiring, producing (and in some cases exporting) restricted items, and their actions directly threaten the interests of the coordinating states. This category in 1993 includes Iran, Iraq, Libya, and North Korea.
- Peripheral states. All other countries fall into this category. These states do not participate in the existing multilateral export control arrangements, and they have not developed projects of concern, either because of insufficient resources or a lack of intent.

States can change classes, although there is no example of a coordinating state being reclassified. It is important to realize that classification schemes cannot, by themselves, fully explain behavior nor will everyone agree with the exact disposition of states into these categories.

Classification schemes can, however, inform. The United States confronts different obstacles to enhancing cooperation on nonproliferation export controls for each group of states. It follows that the United States should

125

apply a different mix of export control strategies to each group of states (see table 2). Six sometimes complementary strategies are available for the nonproliferation export control policies of the coordinating states:

- harmonization—creating similar export control policies for each of the crucial supplier states;
- liberalization—reducing the barriers to trade among those states that cooperate on export controls and when export controls on some items are no longer effective;
- safeguards—requiring assurances for commercial end-use of exports and verification of that end-use;
- assistance—providing counsel, training, funding, or special intelligence on export licensing and enforcement matters;
- conditional aid—tying the supply of mutual defense assistance or devel-

opment assistance, or access to markets on a preferential basis to a state's export control policies and practices; and

- denial—restricting the export of dual-use goods and technologies to almost any end-user in a proscribed country.

These strategies are not independent. Liberalization without harmonization, for example, creates opportunities to exploit policy differences and undermine the impact of controls in a game of technology transfer arbitrage. At the same time, safeguard requirements without liberalization impose costs without rewards.

For the coordinating states like the United States, the issue is how to achieve a relatively free flow of trade among group members without undermining the effectiveness of controls on exports to non-group members. In

Table 2
Supply-Side Export Control Strategies

Strategy Toward	Major Problem	Primary Strategies
Coordinating states	Discretion	Harmonization Liberalization Assistance
Collaborating states	Adaptation	Safeguards Assistance Liberalization Harmonization Conditions on aid
Sensitive states	Participation	Conditions on aid Safeguards Assistance Denial
Threatening states	Containment	Denial Conditions on aid Safeguards
Peripheral states	Prevention	Conditions on aid Assistance Safeguards Liberalization

COCOM, for example, the United States sought (and still seeks) to harmonize the use of national discretion (i.e., national rather than COCOM decision-making) in licensing and enforcement, while it encourages less restrictive licensing procedures for items destined for other COCOM members. Many business executives argue that they can work with the existing control policies, as long as there is a level playing field that binds their major competitors by the same rules. This suggests that harmonization of export controls should be given slightly more emphasis than further liberalization among group members.

The collaborating states pose an altogether different question: how to couple their intentions to cooperate with action. Most of these states have little experience in implementing Western-style export control systems and clearly need technical and financial assistance in creating them. At least at first, these systems need not be exactly harmonious with those of the coordinating states but should establish the basis for future cooperation. In addition, they need access to the advanced dual-use technology of the coordinating states to demonstrate to the private sector in their state that the imposition of controls is, ultimately, a trade-enhancing measure. Current efforts to provide technical assistance to post-Communist states (e.g., Belarus and Russia) to set up safeguard and export control systems, along with the offer of "favorable consideration" status regarding high-technology imports from the coordinating states, are examples of this approach.

Sensitive states, such as India, may have an export control system, but they have yet to be persuaded to participate within the multilateral framework. Although the safeguard and assistance strategies of the coordinating states can influence the behavior of sensitive states, tying aid and trade liberalization to the adoption of multilateral nonproliferation norms (i.e., imposing conditions) is more significant. Nonetheless, access to Western technology and Western aid is not generally a powerful enough incentive to dissuade all sensitive states from developing and sometimes exporting their deadly arsenals. In these cases, concerted multilateral action of the coordinating states across the broad panoply of supply and demand measures is required, including security guarantees, confidence-building measures, and other military, economic, and political actions. In some cases, the coordinating states may resort to a strategy of denial.

In spite of variations in the exact export control strategies applied by the coordinating to the sensitive states, a supply-side strategy of conditional aid, safeguards, assistance, and a judicious use of denial may be used to try to induce some sensitive states to cooperate. The United States has threatened to deny the PRC access to the U.S. market on most favored nation (MFN) terms, for example, if the PRC violates multilateral norms on nonproliferation.

A containment approach may be the coordinating states' general response to the threatening states. While denying much that the threatening states desire, they can apply conditions and offer carrots when circumstances merit. They can also encourage the threatening states to adopt appropriate safeguards. Japan used its official development assistance to get North Korea to sign the NPT, but recent events suggest that the strategy did not remain compelling over the long term. Here a much wider range of political, economic, and security measures must be considered, from large-scale eco-

127

nomic incentives to military action in extreme cases.

Finally, the peripheral states may not be key to combating proliferation in the early 1990s, but some will become important in the longer term. The coordinating states can use conditions on aid and assistance to influence the behavior of many peripheral states. Most often, these states have insufficient economic resources for economic development or their development is skewed to depend on a single commodity, and aid should be used to promote balanced growth in sectors of the economy other than defense. Safeguarded access to dual-use technologies and assistance in creating a streamlined (and inexpensive) export control system can be used, although many of these states encounter problems with internal political and economic instability so severe as to make their access to advanced strategic technologies very risky in the long view. Liberalization does not offer promise for the many peripheral states that are among the poorest of the poor, although for others, like Thailand, it may prove valuable. The relative vulnerability of many of these states makes them prey to aggressive neighbors, which suggests that security assurances could be critical in achieving a commitment to nonproliferation.

The FSU and Export Controls

As the former target of COCOM, the most mature and extensive export control arrangement in existence, the FSU lags behind the West in the widespread application of many dual-use technologies, from avionics to telecommunications systems. At the same time, the states of the FSU are not without their technological achievements, especially in some critical mil-

itary and dual-use areas. With more than 1,000 defense enterprises spread throughout the FSU (although most are in Russia), and with political and economic instability in many of these states, the potential for proliferation in and out (i.e., via exports) of the FSU is high.

Most leaders in Russia and the other newly independent states of the FSU recognize the benefits of strategic accommodation and export control cooperation with the West, and there is little support for replaying the costly arms races of the Cold War. On that basis, most of the states of the FSU are no longer a military threat to the interests of the coordinating states. If this is so, which states are collaborating, which are sensitive, which are threatening, and which, if any, are peripheral?

Only three states of the FSU, Georgia, Tajikistan, and Turkmenistan, did not attend the inaugural 1992 meeting of the COCOM Cooperation Forum, and Tajikistan works with Russia to develop its own nonproliferation export control policies. Nonetheless, the export control policies of the states of the FSU vary considerably (see table 3).

At least two powerful factors drive the states of the FSU toward cooperation with the coordinating states. The first is access to the trade, technology, and economic assistance that the coordinating states can provide. The second involves the threats to their own security that arise from proliferation outside the FSU.

The coordinating states have made it clear to the states of the FSU that access to advanced technology, participation in normal trade and technological relations, and eligibility for economic assistance will not be provided to those who are party to or ignore the proliferation of weapons-related dual-

Table 3
Nonproliferation Export Control Policies of the Newly Independent States

Country	Legal Basis for Controls	Signatory to CIS Export Control Agreement[a]	CIS Export Control Arrangement[b]	CIS CW Agreement[c]	Member of CCF[d]
Armenia			Yes	Yes	Yes
Azerbaijan	Decree	Yes		Yes	Yes
Belarus	Decree	Yes	Yes	Yes	Yes
Estonia					Yes
Georgia		Yes			
Kazakhstan	Decree	Yes	Yes	Yes	Yes
Kyrgyzstan	Decree	Yes		Yes	Yes
Latvia	Decree				Yes
Lithuania	Decree				Yes
Moldova	Resolution	Yes		Yes	Yes
Russia	Decree	Yes	Yes	Yes	Yes
Tajikistan	Decree	Yes	Yes	Yes	
Turkmenistan					
Ukraine	Decree	Yes			Yes
Uzbekistan	Decree	Yes	Yes	Yes	Yes

Notes:

a Agreement of the members of the Commonwealth of Independent States (CIS) on June 26, 1992, binding them to develop coordinated national export control systems that will develop control lists modeled after multilateral export control agreements.

b An agreement to consult with one another on participation in nonproliferation export control arrangements. See ITAR-TASS, "Six States Join Forces to Enforce Export Control," February 9, 1993.

c The CIS Agreement on Chemical Weapons, in which article 5 requires the signatories to coordinate their policies to monitor the export of dual-purpose chemicals.

d COCOM Cooperation Forum; inaugural meeting in Paris on November 23–24, 1992.

use technologies or, worse, weapons of mass destruction. Where states have made substantial progress toward democratic and economic reform, however, for a coordinating state to adopt a strategy of denial will be counterproductive. Instead, phased liberalization of the coordinating states' export controls, with safeguards, will motivate FSU states to abide by international standards of nonproliferation. Moreover, they need specific assistance, from basic information on establishing nonproliferation export control systems to computer software and advanced training for customs agents.

The military security interests of Russia and the other newly independent states will not be served by allowing proliferation from their territories. Although the short-term economic benefits are tempting during the current period of economic hardship, the long-term security costs from proliferation are far greater. As the director of the Russian Foreign Intelligence Service notes:

> The problem of the proliferation of weapons of mass destruction (WMD) affects the immediate interests of Russia. A situation in which new states possessing WMD could appear on the perimeter of Russian borders looks unacceptable. This unacceptability is aggravated by the incompleteness of the process of state formation in many republics of the former USSR, some of which are enveloped by a fire of ethnic, national, and political conflicts. At the same time, an absolutely obvious tendency exists to draw neighboring states into these conflicts, some of which can be categorized as striving to possess WMD, or that already possess one or another type of mass destruction weapon.[18]

At the same time, reports of the transfer of strategic materials, technologies, and personnel from various states, including Armenia, Belarus, Kazakhstan, Russia, and Ukraine, and the reluctance of Kazakh and Ukrainian officials to reduce their respective nuclear arsenals as expected, continue to raise doubts about the commitment of some of these states to nonproliferation export controls.

As of this writing, Belarus and Russia are best classified as collaborating states. These two states have taken more steps to develop their domestic export control systems than the other states of the FSU. Russia has passed a series of decrees intended to establish the legal framework for its control of sensitive military-related technology and weapons exports. The most important is Decree No. 388 of April 11, 1992, outlining "Measures to Establish an Export Control System in Russia."[19] This executive order established an interagency Export Control Commission that must give approval before sensitive items can be exported. The commission includes deputy level officials from key ministries (e.g., Foreign Affairs, External Economic Relations, Economics, and Defense) and other relevant state bodies (e.g., the State Customs Committee).[20] The commission was first headed by Yegor Gaidar, who was later replaced by Georgii Khiza, who was more recently replaced by Oleg Soskovets.

The Russian Export Control Commission has the responsibility of implementing five control lists.[21] The first list deals with certain categories of materials, equipment, technologies, and scientific research that may be used for producing weapons. The selection of items was made with regard to their significance for weapons production and to the technical level of foreign models and their control. The second list contains dual-use equipment, materials, and technologies related to nuclear weapons production. The third covers chemical weapons precursors and their production technologies and reflects the items controlled by the Australia Group. The fourth list contains organisms, materials, and equipment that can be used for the production of bacteriological weapons, again intended to be in accordance with the Australia Group. The fifth controls materials, equipment, and technologies used for missile production and is intended to be in accordance with the MTCR list.

A Ministry of Foreign Affairs official, Nikolai Revenko, reported that the following questions are considered when making Russian licensing decisions based upon the five lists:

- Does the recipient country adhere to principles of nonproliferation and does it participate in the relevant multilateral nonproliferation export control arrangements?
- Is the recipient involved in clandestine or illegal purchases of items related to the production of weapons of mass production?
- Has the end-user ever previously been denied any authorized materials, equipment, or technologies or used such items for purposes inconsistent with its commitments and obligations?[22]

The Export Control Division of the Russian Ministry of Economics has been authorized to function as the central working organ of the Export Control Commission.[23] It prepares all documentation related to the operation of Russian export controls. It also issues opinions on the authorization or denial of exports based upon the questions and lists noted above.

In order to strengthen the legal framework of export controls, draft laws to be incorporated into the Russian Penal Code have been prepared.[24] These yet-to-be-adopted laws stipulate the penalties resulting from noncompliance. Although this and other important steps related to implementation and enforcement are unlikely to be adopted before 1994, most Russian leaders and officials are meanwhile attempting to establish a viable export control system for the Russian Federation.

Belarus has also taken important first steps in establishing a domestic export control system. Although no legislation has yet been adopted by the Belarus Supreme Soviet, it too has begun to implement controls based upon executive decrees.[25] Belarus has signed an agreement with the U.S. Department of Defense providing U.S. "assistance related to the establishment of export control systems to prevent the proliferation of weapons of mass destruction from the Republic of Belarus."

Both Belarus and Russia have begun to coordinate their export control efforts with other states. In June 1992, both states signed the Minsk Accord on export control coordination in the Commonwealth of Independent States (CIS). Signatories to the agreement were the republics of Azerbaijan, Armenia, Belarus, Georgia, Kazakhstan, Kyrgystan, Moldova, the Russia Federation, Tajikistan, Uzbekistan, and Ukraine. Reportedly, in February 1993, Belarus and Russia reached agreement with four other CIS states to cooperate in the control of exports of material, equipment, technologies, and services related to the production of weapons of mass destruction.[26] Although little has been done since the signing of these CIS agreements, they do represent steps in the right direction.

Belarus and Russia have also been willing to take steps toward coordinating their export controls in accordance with multilateral standards for nonproliferation control. Both have demonstrated their interest in joining or cooperating with the four multilateral export control arrangements discussed earlier. The Belarus Supreme Soviet approved accession to the NPT on February 4, 1993, and Belarus authorities have taken action to rid their country of all nuclear weapons. To demonstrate its approval of and support for these important first steps, the U.S. government has earmarked $2.26 million in export control assistance to Belarus.

Although both Belarus and Russia might currently be classified as collaborating states, one can easily imagine developments, particularly in the case of Russia, that might move them into the categories of sensitive or even threatening states. In part because it contains at least 1,300 defense enterprises, Russia may be reclassified as a sensitive state if it applies unique interpretations to the multilateral export control standards (such as arguing that the MTCR only concerns "offensive" missile systems) or if it cannot implement its export controls because of political instability, porous borders, or other reasons. Although the process of democratic reform in Russia is advancing (and democratic government is characteristic of a coordinating state), its underdeveloped economy may not offer sufficient means of earning hard currency in the next few years without the export of critical military and dual-use items to sensitive or threatening states (such as the recent sale of SU–27 jet fighters to the PRC). This sug-

gests the importance of political stability and economic progress in Russia. A politically stable, economically viable Russia can become a coordinating state (it is already so in the NSG). Political disintegration and economic deprivation, on the other hand, can move it to the sensitive, and perhaps, even to the threatening classification.

The Baltic states and Kyrgyzstan, although cooperative, appear to fall in the peripheral category. This is not to suggest that they should be ignored, but rather that assistance to these states should focus on transit and reexport controls, and that conditions on official development assistance could be very influential.

Armenia, Azerbaijan, Georgia, Kazakhstan, Moldova, Tajikistan, Turkmenistan, Ukraine, and Uzbekistan appear to fall into the category of sensitive states. Other than Kazakhstan and Ukraine, most of these states are racked by internal and external conflict and are not in a position to put export control systems in place, even if they intended to do so. Persistent reports that Kazakhstan has shipped nuclear materials to Iran, coupled with its reluctance to reduce its nuclear arsenal, raise questions about the commitment of Kazakhstan to very basic nonproliferation objectives.

The signals from Ukraine are also mixed, even beyond its efforts to receive more compensation for reducing its nuclear stockpile. Reports of Ukrainian officials stopping the shipment of a dual-use chemical precursor by a Moscow-based firm indicate that Ukraine may adhere to nonproliferation objectives. At the same time, allegations that all information on the import and export of arms, production equipment, and technologies is now classified, if true, will undermine efforts to evaluate Ukrainian behavior.

Conditions on all but humanitarian

aid and nonproliferation assistance should be considered for these states. Denying access to dual-use items, however, should be used only as a last resort or sanction, and then only implemented with great care more to foster a mutual interest in cooperation than to attempt to coerce these states into compliance. Supply-side strategies should be coordinated with the vigorous pursuit of other options to move these states to adopt nonproliferation as the basis for their export control policy.

Conclusion

As the United States and its allies revamp their export control policies to address the proliferation challenges of the post–cold war era, they must escape the simple divisions of the globe into East and West, North and South. The authors propose that national participation in multilateral export control arrangements will make a useful guide for policymakers and policy-making for the next decade. Applying this to the FSU, the criteria indicate that the United States should stress programs that will help Belarus, Russia, and others to adapt their export control systems to multilateral standards. U.S. policy should encourage other states of the FSU to establish national export control systems and participate in or at least support multilateral export control arrangements.

Experience in Central and Eastern Europe demonstrates that the first stages of liberalization (e.g., gaining "favorable consideration" status in COCOM) will be valuable to the states of the FSU. Although this argues for the coordinating states to press for evidence of an abiding commitment to nonproliferation in the early phases of liberalization, the economic plight of all new states in the

FSU will make full-scale implementation of a U.S.-style export control system impossible in the next few years. Moreover, the uneven distribution of relevant enterprises, irregular development patterns for new enterprises, and the extensive integration of mature enterprises in the command economy mean that these states should concentrate their limited resources on the export control problems most appropriate to their situation, be they organized crime and illicit exports, end-use diversion, reexport controls, transit controls, or licensing locally produced items. Getting a system in place, even an incomplete system, provides the foundation for wider implementation in the future while addressing some immediate concerns. It also gives the new governments a chance to become accustomed to export controls in line with multilateral efforts.

At the same time, the United States cannot rely on supply-side strategies alone. Export controls, for example, are only likely to delay the acquisition of critical dual-use technologies by a state determined to acquire them. Unless the United States and its coordinating allies address the demand for weapons of mass destruction and dual-use technologies, and pressures to supply those demands, nonproliferation policy will be incomplete. In some extreme cases, such as in Iraq, where United Nations coalition forces destroyed or dismantled Iraqi facilities, counterproliferation policy, more than supply-side controls, may be necessary.

Classifying states on the basis of their adherence to multilateral export control arrangements says little about why states act as they do. All coordinating states have a democratic form of government, for example, which suggests that continued democratization of the new states of the FSU may contribute to their support of nonproliferation goals. There are many reasons why democratic governments may be more supportive of multilateral export control efforts. Democratic states are less likely to use force in the settlement of disputes and, therefore, are not likely to make each other targets of controls. The possibility of debate and scandal in open and democratic societies also acts as a disincentive to proliferation.[27] In France, Germany, Japan, and the United States, revelations about illegal or indiscreet exports to threatening states brought about public debate and led to a reconsideration and tightening of export controls. In closed societies, such sales are less likely to be made public and often involve corrupt government officials.

The coordinating states are also characterized by high levels of economic development and economic interdependence. In their classic work on the North Atlantic security community, Karl Deutsch and his fellow authors noted that economic growth and interaction may promote the emergence of a security community among states.[28] Access to Western trade and technology will contribute to economic development and interaction within the FSU and Central and Eastern Europe. This in turn may enhance support for the norms of nonproliferation and export controls.

In the 1990s, the United States and other coordinating countries must take the lead in broadening their commitment to and participation in the multilateral export control arrangements. In its efforts to switch the basis of controls from containment to nonproliferation, the United States can do much to promote the norms and principles of nonproliferation. Making information on proliferation more accessible to other governments, to the business community, and to the general public will help make supply-side policies like export controls more understandable and acceptable worldwide. Until now, the informational activities of COCOM, the NSG, the AG, and the MTCR have focused on the coordinating states. In order to surmount some of the obstacles to cooperation in other countries, the principles of nonproliferation must be transmitted to a much wider audience.

In other global issue areas, including the environment, health, and population, conferences bringing together nongovernmental groups often parallel major multilateral governmental meetings. These settings allow for a swifter dissemination of ideas and a broader discussion of the issues. The authors believe that a similar effort for export controls would be useful in creating a culture of nonproliferation. This would be especially important for the business community, where the risk of being "soft on proliferation" can motivate appropriate control of military and dual-use exports without strangling trade or imposing a heavy regulatory burden on exporters.

COCOM, the NSG, the AG, and the MTCR may well evolve toward consolidation, but this must not impose an excessive cost on those collaborating, sensitive, or peripheral states whose leaders are considering if and how to comply with multilateral norms on export controls. States may find it convenient to join arrangements in some order of succession, or only join those that are most relevant to their immediate situation. If Kazakh officials, for example, believed they could comply with NSG guidelines but were unwilling or unable to comply with other controls, would a consolidated arrangement forfeit the obvious advantages to having Kazakhstan join the movement against nuclear nonproliferation? The authors believe that much can be accomplished within the existing setting of overlapping, mutually reinforcing export control arrangements. Strategies must be clarified and actions taken, however, before the current international momentum for nonproliferation is lost.

The authors would like to thank The University of Georgia and the Pew Charitable Trust for financial support for the Center for East–West Trade Policy's "Export Controls in the 1990s" project. They also thank the Robert Bosch Foundation, the Carnegie Corporation, the Japan Foundation Center for Global Partnership, the Japan–U.S. Friendship Commission, the W. Alton Jones Foundation, and the Ploughshares Fund for their support of the activities of the Center. The authors are grateful to Leonard S. Spector and Igor Khripunov for their thoughtful comments.

Notes

1. Gary K. Bertsch, Richard T. Cupitt, and Steven Elliott-Gower, eds., *International Cooperation on Nonproliferation Export Controls* (Ann Arbor: University of Michigan Press, forthcoming).

2. The supercomputer regime is a multilateral export control arrangement in the making. Although ongoing negotiations are likely to result in an arrangement that will include the European Community, as of this writing the supercomputer regime is a bilateral agreement between the United States and Japan, and the authors chose to limit the focus in this article to the four multilateral groupings.

3. Bill Root, "The Core List: Expectations vs. Reality," *Export Control News* 5, no. 7, (1991), p. 3.

4. In addition to Hungary, other countries (e.g., the Czech Republic and Poland) are in the process of being deproscribed.

5. Only those states undertaking significant military, economic, and political reform were asked to participate. By design, this excludes the PRC and North Korea, but includes Russia and the new states of the FSU. See table 1 for a complete list.

6. U.S. Department of State, *Press Guidelines* (Washington, D.C., 1992).

7. "Australia Group Considers Chemical Controls," *Export Control News* 5, no. 1 (1991), pp. 14–17.

8. "U.S., Allies Agree to Tighten Curbs on Missile-Related Goods and Technology," *International Trade Reporter*, January 13, 1993, in Nexis.

9. Ashton Carter, William Perry, and John Steinbruner, *A New Concept of Cooperative Security* (Washington, D.C.: The Brookings Institution, 1992), p. 37.

10. National Academy of Sciences, *Finding Common Ground: U.S. Export Controls in a Changed Global Environment* (Washington, D.C.: National Academy Press, 1991); National Academy of Sciences, *Balancing the National Interest: U.S. National Security Export Controls and Global Economic Competition* (Washington, D.C.: National Academy Press, 1987); John Heinz, *U.S. Strategic Trade: An Export Control System for the 1990s* (Boulder, Colo.: Westview, 1991).

11. Peter Rudolf, "Non-Proliferation and International Export Control," *Aussenpolitik* 42 (Summer 1991), p. 401.

12. Leonard S. Spector and Virginia Foran, *Preventing Weapons Proliferation: Should the Regimes be Combined?* (A Report of the Thirty-Third Strategy for Peace, U.S. Foreign Policy Conference, Warrenton, Va., October 22–24, 1992, sponsored by The Stanley Foundation).

13. *Ibid.*, p. 20.

14. See Harold Bauer, Owen Green, Vaughan Lowe, Nathalie Prouvez, and Marc Weller, *Arms and Dual-Use Exports from the EC: A Common Policy for Regulation and Control* (Bristol: Doveton Press for Saferworld, 1992); Kathleen Bailey and Robert Rudney, eds., *Proliferation and Export Controls* (New York, N.Y.: University Press of America, 1993); Gary K. Bertsch and Steven Elliott-Gower, eds., *Export Controls in Transition* (Durham, N.C.: Duke University Press, 1992); and Hendrik Roodbeen, *Trading the Jewel of Great Value* (The Hague: CIP-Gegevens Koninklijke Bibliotheek, 1992).

15. Bertsch et al., *International Cooperation.*

16. Richard T. Cupitt, "Synthesis and Impli-

cations:

Export Controls for the 1990s and Beyond," in Bertsch et al., *International Cooperation.* The policy of the former Czech and Slovak Federal Republic was also moving in this direction before the country split.

17. Although the central government of the PRC has indicated its willingness to adhere to the MTCR, there is sufficient evidence to question either its sincerity or its ability to control subnational decision makers regarding their commitment to nonproliferation export controls.

18. Yevgenii Primakov, director of the Russian Foreign Intelligence Service, reported in *A New Challenge After the Cold War: The Proliferation of Weapons of Mass Destruction* (Moscow, 1993), translated by U.S. Foreign Broadcast Information Service, February 1993.

19. *Rossiiskaya Gazeta,* April 16, 1992.

20. For a listing of other decrees and export control related information, see William C. Potter, *Nuclear Profiles of the Soviet Successor States* (Monterey, Calif.: Monterey Institute of International Studies, 1993), and

Michael Beck, Gary Bertsch, and Igor Khripunov, *Export Control Policy Development in Russia* (Athens, Ga.: Center for East–West Trade Policy, 1993).

21. Nikolai Revenko, Presentation at the International Seminar on Export Controls, Technology Transfer and Nonproliferation, Rynia, Poland, September 4–5, 1992, pp. 6–7.

22. *Ibid.,* p. 5.

23. *Ibid.,* pp. 5–6.

24. *Ibid.,* p. 8.

25. Potter, *Nuclear Profiles,* pp. 5–8.

26. ITAR-TASS, "Six CIS States Join Forces to Enforce Export Control," February 9, 1993. Also, see Foreign Broadcast Information Service–Central Eurasia, FBIS-SOV-93-026, February 10, 1993.

27. Cupitt, "Synthesis and Implications."

28. Karl W. Deutsch, Sidney A. Burrell, et al., *Political Community and the North Atlantic Area* (Princeton, N.J.: Princeton University Press, 1957).

136

III. The Counterproliferation Debate

Counterproliferation: Putting New Wine in Old Bottles

Harald Müller and Mitchell Reiss

COUNTERPROLIFERATION cata- pulted to national and international at- tention as the first major defense in- itiative of the Clinton administration when it was officially unveiled by Sec- retary of Defense Les Aspin in De- cember 1993.[1] Almost as soon as the concept entered the strategic lexicon, however, questions arose as to what it really meant. A cacophony of different voices from within the Clinton admini- stration not only confused those who wanted to understand the initiative's objectives and how they would be pur- sued, but also alarmed others who feared that the United States, as the world's lone superpower, was now de- vising the means to unilaterally and preemptively destroy the nuclear pro- grams of countries in the developing world.

Over a year later, it appears that most of the initial concern that the United States intended to establish it- self as global judge, jury, and execu- tioner against weapons of mass de- struction (WMD)—nuclear, chemical, and biological weapons, and the mis- siles that may carry them—has been misplaced. Although some Pentagon officials privately admit that counter- proliferation still envisions preemptive military strikes, more senior officials, especially Assistant Secretary of De- fense Ashton Carter, have explicitly and repeatedly disavowed any such role. This is also the approach adopted by the Western alliance, which has consistently ruled out any military ac- tion that is not sanctioned by the United Nations (UN) Security Coun- cil.

Although the debate over the con- tours and parameters of counterprolif- eration has continued (mostly intra-ad- ministration and even intra-Pentagon), it is fairly well settled that counter- proliferation is designed to prepare U.S. forces to deter, and if necessary defeat, an adversary's WMD on the battlefield. Pentagon officials now pri- vately concede that the selling of counterproliferation was a public re- lations nightmare, and they have la- bored mightily to assure countries

Harald Müller is director of research at the Peace Research Institute in Frankfurt, where he leads a multinational program on Euro- pean nonproliferation policy. Mitchell Reiss is a guest scholar at the Woodrow Wilson In- ternational Center for Scholars in Washing- ton, D.C., and is the author of *Bridled Ambition: Why Countries Curtail Their Nuclear Weapons Capabilities* (April 1995).

Copyright © 1995 by The Center for Strategic and International Studies and the Massachusetts Institute of Technology

what counterproliferation is (prudent military contingency planning), while at the same time explaining what it is not (preemptive military strikes).

Despite this rearguard action by the Pentagon, the confusion over counterproliferation has already damaged the international nonproliferation regime and further placed at risk chances for the indefinite and unconditional extension of the Nuclear Non-Proliferation Treaty (NPT) at the 1995 review conference. Such harm is not irreversible, however. Indeed, by linking counterproliferation efforts to the broader nonproliferation regime, the United States can strengthen both the regime and chances for success at the 1995 review conference.

What Is Counterproliferation?

In the brief history of counterproliferation, four definitions appear to have existed, three of which still possess some relevance. All derive from both the need to redefine the Pentagon's mission after the Cold War and the experiences of the Persian Gulf War.

In 1989, the Bush administration, led by Under Secretary of Defense Paul Wolfowitz, decided to change the orientation and mission of the Defense Department. To fight proliferation in all its aspects, by means ranging from the control of dual-use technology to the preventive destruction of WMD facilities, became a new priority for the U.S. military. This sweeping and ambitious program, entitled "counterproliferation," was not adequately implemented before it was handed off to the incoming Clinton administration in January 1993.

The second definition of counterproliferation is the one that has aroused the most attention, applause, and hostility: counterproliferation as offensive military actions to eliminate

the WMD capabilities, including the production facilities, of proliferators. It is true that today the Clinton administration is anxious to explain that this is not what counterproliferation means, very much to the dismay of enthusiastic supporters of exactly that option in some nongovernmental circles. Yet this concept remains alive, most particularly within the air force. The professional culture of this service has always been the strategic offensive—recall Strategic Air Commander Curtis LeMay's effort to pursue the active elimination of Soviet nuclear capabilities in the 1950s, a forerunner of this version of counterproliferation. In a scenario in which U.S. forces would confront a proliferator, it would fall to the air force to destroy the adversary's behind-the-lines capabilities. Such counterforce operations may be termed "neutralization" of WMD capabilities when the war has started, but the same weapons, tactics, and operations can just as easily be used for preventive or preemptive purposes before the onset of hostilities.

If counterforce is the name of the counterproliferation game for the air force, a curious and blurred bureaucratic compromise forged by the National Security Council in February 1994 is behind the third definition: counterproliferation is nonproliferation as performed by the Department of Defense. As so often with bureaucratic compromises fashioned by interagency disputes and rivalries, this one contains its own contradictions. Following its logic, a military officer in the U.S. delegation to the 1995 NPT review conference would do counterproliferation, while the U.S. Arms Control and Disarmament Agency representative in the next chair would be in the business of nonproliferation.

The absurdity is quite tangible if one looks at some of the Department of Defense activities that come under the heading of counterproliferation. For example, verification of a comprehensive nuclear test ban belongs to that category, as do steps taken as part of the Cooperative Threat Reduction (Nunn–Lugar) Program that are designed to ensure the safe and secure dismantlement and disposition of the nuclear weapons of the United States and Russia. Obviously, the first case clearly supports the existing nonproliferation regime, while the second helps prevent "loose nukes" from falling into the wrong hands. Both activities could be sensibly labeled "nonproliferation support programs." In no way do they involve "countering" a proliferator.

Finally, there is a definition that makes sense: counterproliferation involves preparing U.S. forces to fight and survive in a WMD environment. This delimits a specific set of activities, from intelligence collection to doctrine, procurement, and training, that is comprehensible and amounts to prudent contingency planning. Indeed, it is somewhat disconcerting that previous administrations have not undertaken serious preparations for such contingencies. Whatever its initial flaws in conceptual design and presentation, the Clinton administration deserves high marks for putting the time, energy, and resources into "counterproliferation."

Under this definition, preventive diplomacy remains the first, and by far the most important, line of defense against the spread of WMD. Neutralization operations against WMD stocks and programs during combat is a subordinate, if inevitable, option, while pride of place is accorded to protective rather than counterforce measures. As a sort of "buy one, get one free" benefit, the military capabilities for a neutralization campaign can also be

used for preemption. Regardless of the timing of such military measures, however, all responses will be conventional, because the Pentagon has ruled out employment of nuclear weapons for counterproliferation purposes.

This last definition, while comprehensible, moderate, and reasonable, reveals a considerable deemphasis compared with the early flamboyant rhetoric accompanying the term. Indeed, the reaction on Capitol Hill to counterproliferation has been a mixture of mild support and thinly veiled skepticism: support, because preparing U.S. soldiers against possible harm seems reasonable to all; skepticism, because members of Congress and their staffers see better than anyone else how much all services struggle to hang time-honored programs on the new counterproliferation Christmas tree, and how little that is really new is required by the much-heralded initiative. To be sure, if U.S. soldiers were sent on missions with a high probability of significant casualties from WMD, this attitude would quickly change. For the time being, though, Congress is approaching counterproliferation quite dispassionately. Taking a look at the various programs that are now labeled counterproliferation by the services, only a tiny part, approximately $30 million in fiscal year 1994 and $60 million in fiscal year 1995 appropriations,[2] are new categories for military spending.

The Foreign Reaction

As ambiguous signals about counterproliferation started to emerge from Washington in late 1993, those abroad trying to read these signals seized on their most audible and spectacular aspects: the apparent readiness of the United States to prepare for preemptive attacks on WMD facilities in hos-

141

tile countries. This aroused much anxiety, much of which has not yet been fully dispelled.

First, foreigners worried about the catalytic consequences such an action might engender. Preventing another country from acquiring WMD before its efforts bore fruit, or preempting the use of such weapons in a crisis, but before a conflict started—that is, military action during what would strictly be peacetime—could well provoke a war with devastating consequences. The Korean peninsula is a case in point, and the plea of North Korea's neighbors to the United States that it should refrain from actions that could precipitate armed conflict suggests the probable reactions of many countries should they find themselves in similar circumstances.

The only exception to this might be Israel, which itself conducted a successful "counterproliferation" operation and feels more acutely than any other state the threats that might emanate from a WMD-armed, aggressive regional power. Although the Israelis are today far less confident that the type of operation performed in their June 1981 raid against Iraq's Tammuz reactor could be successfully repeated,[3] they may believe that the alternative—to do nothing—would, under extreme circumstances, be worse than the attempt.

Second, and closely connected to the first point, foreigners experienced serious concern over the collateral consequences of a military attack on North Korea's Yongbyon nuclear complex. This reservation, in fact, found expression in many sober analyses by the U.S. military and intelligence community itself. If WMD or their production facilities can be found in North Korea and thoroughly destroyed (not always an easy task), the inventory may leak out, exposing vast numbers of people—both on the Korean peninsula and in the region—to lethal doses of radioactivity. A strike against an operating reactor or reprocessing plant could release radioactivity of an order of magnitude larger than the Chernobyl disaster. The political legitimacy and international lawfulness of such an action could be seriously in doubt, the distinction between military targets and innocent noncombatants could be blurred, and the proportionality of the response to the threat could be questioned.

Third, the international legitimacy of U.S. actions was itself an issue. Counterproliferation made it appear that the U.S. government alone would determine if a perceived security threat justified an offensive military operation. Attacking first in peacetime or during a crisis is a matter of gravest consequence, not only for the states involved, but for the world community. It is nowhere apparent in the Clinton administration's conception of counterproliferation that the UN Security Council might have a role to play in any decision to attack WMD.

This oversight was all the more unwelcome because the Security Council declaration of January 31, 1992, with the support of the United States, had declared that the proliferation of WMD constituted a threat to international peace and security. This opened the possibility of utilizing all the sanctions available under chapter VII of the UN Charter, including military measures, in response to such proliferation threats. That the United States would assume the role of nonproliferation policeman at the very moment when the Security Council had at long last recognized the role assigned to it under all three WMD nonproliferation instruments (the NPT, the Biological and Toxin Weapons Convention, and the Chemical Weapons Convention), in the eyes of many threatened to undermine the promising enhancement of the Council's role, and to replace the prospect of multilateral enforcement with U.S. unilateralism. That the United States could create a counterproliferation doctrine without reference to international procedures—for example, to the findings of the various agencies entrusted with verifying nonproliferation treaties, and to existing enforcement mechanisms, namely, the UN Security Council—was an alarming prospect for some, amounting to a sort of "nonproliferation imperialism."

For governments in the developing world, this perception immediately prompted another concern: that of U.S. selectivity in distinguishing between "friendly" and "unfriendly" proliferators. That U.S. nonproliferation policy had some selectivity to it has not been lost on developing countries, least of all those in the Arab and wider Islamic world. That such selectivity could extend into offensive military operations was seen as highly objectionable and threatening.

Fourth, again from the perspective of non-nuclear weapon states in the developing world, counterproliferation was a blow to enhanced efforts to obtain better and more credible negative security assurances from nuclear weapon states in the run-up to the 1995 NPT review conference. Negative security assurances are solemn declarations by nuclear weapon states not to threaten or attack non-nuclear weapon states with nuclear arms. So far, only China has given such an unconditional assurance. The United States, for example, has reserved the right to use nuclear weapons in defense against an attack by a non-nuclear weapon state allied to or associated with a nuclear weapon state. This is seen today by many, especially outside the United States, as a remnant of the Cold War that has little relevance to the current international security environment. It has, however, so far proved impossible to obtain uniform and legally binding security assurances by the five declared nuclear weapon states.

Counterproliferation, as it was perceived abroad, affected this discourse among and within the United States, France, and Britain in two ways. First, there was initially a lot of loose talk about developing new, small, highly accurate deep-penetrating nuclear weapons for counterproliferation operations. Second, there was a public debate—still not finalized—in the United States about the need to reserve the right of nuclear retaliation against the use of chemical and biological weapons. Together these possibilities would largely invalidate negative security assurances even in their present form, not to mention the chances of reaching consensus on more comprehensive assurances and guarantees.

Fifth, misgivings about illegitimacy, unilateralism, selectivity, and threat assessment cumulatively tend to widen the North-South gap, which continues to jeopardize the badly needed consensus in the global nonproliferation regimes. Justified or not, the nonaligned countries complain about inequality, discrimination, and "Northern" behavior that neglects their interests, views, and sensitivities. The United States, as leader of the industrialized world and the most powerful global actor, is the main target of such criticism. From the vantage point of the nonaligned, counterproliferation is seen as a logical corollary to the strengthening of international safeguards and the tightening of export controls, all directed against the developing world. Improvements in verification are seen as enhancing the ability of outsiders to collect intelligence in developing countries; that international verification agencies such as the International Atomic Energy Agency (IAEA) must rely on information from intelligence agencies of the "North," particularly the United States, only reinforces this perception. Export controls—indispensable as they are for any nonproliferation regime—are seen as proxies for controlling the speed and scope of economic development, and as a means to maintain and perpetuate the technological dominance of the industrialized West. Counterproliferation, then, completes the picture by adding a military dimension aimed at punishing those states that have successfully defied the spider's web of controls imposed by the industrialized world under U.S. leadership.

To be sure, much of this amounts to a paranoid interpretation of world politics, based on misinformation and misperception. Preventing the spread of WMD remains an objective that is shared by the overwhelming majority of states in the world, a goal that unites North and South. But it is nevertheless a worldview that must be taken seriously, precisely because it could impede the badly needed international consensus on which all successful nonproliferation regimes must rely.

This is all the more true because this consensus is necessary to give new life to the NPT. This indispensable instrument of the world nuclear order must be extended in spring 1995. The basic options before the April–May review conference are: indefinite extension; extension for a fixed period; or extension for an undefined number of fixed periods. The industrialized world has uniformly opted for indefinite extension. The developing countries are divided between a short fixed period and an indefinite number of fixed periods, with the chance for the parties to terminate the treaty at the end of each period. Only a minority of the developing world so far supports indefinite extension. Counterproliferation, if seen as an ominous, unilateral initiative undermining negative security assurances and defying decades-long attempts to outlaw attacks on nuclear facilities, could negatively influence developing countries' deliberations on which option to choose and erode their support for the nuclear nonproliferation regime after the review conference. Moreover, the counterproliferation initiative is cast in a dark light because it is being put forward just as the results of the U.S. Nuclear Posture Review are becoming known. The review advocates postponing consideration of further reductions of strategic nuclear weapons until after the first and second strategic arms reduction agreements (START I and II) are fully implemented, and retains the option of using nuclear weapons first, even when no credible enemy threatens the United States and its main allies. The world's most powerful nation is thus threatening to eradicate in others a sin that it has itself committed, and that it is willing to continue to commit. That the statement from the September 1994 Clinton–Yeltsin summit foresees talks on further nuclear reductions far sooner than the Pentagon's Nuclear Posture Review would suggest is a hopeful sign, but probably not enough to undo the combined effect of a badly sold counterproliferation initiative and stalling on further reductions in the U.S. nuclear arsenal.[4]

A seventh criticism, most openly expressed by U.S. allies in the North Atlantic Treaty Organization (NATO), but which has also been heard inside the Clinton administration, is that counterproliferation is meant as a substitute for traditional nonproliferation policy. This charge is based on reckless talk by some counterproliferation proponents to the effect that nonproliferation has failed and that now is the time for the serious people, rather than for the "nonproliferation regime wimps," to have their turn. There is concern that the traditional diplomatic means of nonproliferation that have, by and large, served the world well and succeeded beyond expectation, will be discarded in favor of a more aggressive, militant policy relying, first and foremost, on military instruments.

Few countries would be willing to support such a shift. The NPT is seen as a foundation for order and security in Europe and around the world. Much hope is placed in the Chemical Weapons Convention, which the United States has still to ratify. Greater transparency and confidence-building are expected from adding a verification protocol to the Biological and Toxin Weapons Convention. If the United States is deserting the difficult, but worthwhile, effort to reinvigorate these regimes, it is feared that such regimes will falter. This will, in turn, encourage potential proliferators to abandon or circumvent international legal constraints on WMD, and will confront good faith parties with the difficult choice of defecting as well or facing grave threats from their neighbors in the future.

The whole NATO debate on counterproliferation has been a lesson in damage limitation since the initiative was launched. Originally, the majority of European allies were shocked, although some invested time and resources in examining prevention options and certain procurement programs, such as theater defenses. Most sought assurances that the alliance's priority would continue to focus on nonproliferation and that any military

action would be subject to international law, namely, that it would be considered only on the basis of a UN mandate or an unambiguous case of self-defense. The German government went as far as to state this point openly in Foreign Minister Klaus Kinkel's nonproliferation initiative of December 1993.

The NATO allies were quite willing to do all that appeared reasonable—to consider how to protect those NATO allies that might be threatened by WMD and how to give NATO troops assigned to peacekeeping and related duties the capability to survive in a WMD environment. But even so, virtually all of the language in the NATO Council's June 1994 communiqué is devoted to strengthening time-honored nonproliferation policies; in its discussion of military efforts, the communiqué does not use the term counterproliferation once.[5] Nothing could better express NATO's cautious attitude toward the U.S. counterproliferation initiative.

Assessment

In assessing the merits and shortcomings of the counterproliferation initiative, the first step is to realize that several, divergent interpretations of it are still contending with one another. It is the most spectacular and frightening among them, that of unilateral, offensive military preemption in peacetime, that the Clinton administration has struggled most ardently to discard, and that has had the deepest impact on skeptics, adversaries, and supporters of the concept alike. That the administration has spoken with many, and sometimes contradictory, voices, has had a detrimental effect on the initiative as a whole.

This should not obscure the fact that the initiative is responding to a very real and serious problem: that some WMD proliferation has occurred, that chemical weapons and ballistic missiles have actually been used in combat recently, and that, despite best efforts, some proliferation is likely to occur in the future. U.S. and allied troops may be called upon to serve in environments where such weapons exist, and they have every right to be as well equipped and well prepared to survive in these environments as is possible. In other words, in its moderate, fourth interpretation as prudent contingency planning, "counterproliferation" is a sensible adjunct to both nonproliferation and traditional defense policy. As such, it is not a new concept, although the Clinton administration deserves high marks for starting to implement and operationalize its tenets. Still, the whole issue was not worth the fanfare with which it was first unveiled. The initial overemphasis on the "new" and the offensive mode of operation, although certain to attract sudden attention, was the worst possible strategy for winning support for the concept abroad.

The most disturbing aspect of the U.S. counterproliferation initiative was its unilateralism. The initial presentation was aimed exclusively at a U.S. public still impressed by the resounding military success of the Gulf war. The combination of a real problem with a huge military establishment looking for new missions complicated matters and impeded Washington's ability to exert international leadership. Little, if any, consideration was given to the effects the pronouncement would have abroad, even though this "abroad" contained both the target and the source of indispensable collaboration for both non- and counterproliferation. If the whole program had been defined as designed to improve U.S. national security and to im-

plement American alliance commitments, it would have largely been seen as inconsequential and unobjectionable. But with the label "counterproliferation," it was bound to evoke a reaction of legitimate global interest and concern: proliferation of WMD and the nonproliferation regimes are not a national U.S. matter, but belong to the world community. In a matter that goes to the heart of global international regimes, and consists of international legal obligations, political commitments, and national policies, the leader of the free world should have considered more carefully the international repercussions, and should have consulted with its allies and friends thoroughly and discreetly beforehand.

The relationship of the initiative to the nonproliferation regimes was not considered at all at the beginning and is still not well defined. The apparent intention of some advocates of counterproliferation to largely invalidate and replace traditional nonproliferation policy has been discarded. But the connection between a policy that is still strictly national or at best, confined to the Western alliance, and the global, legal-political systems that shape the nonproliferation regimes remains an odd one.

This present non-relationship with regard to the nuclear nonproliferation regimes is illustrated by the fact that counterproliferation has evoked even more interest in negative security assurances, a long-standing concern among the nonaligned countries. Yet there is no visible movement in this area on the U.S. side, and no one appears to have thought through how fears (even if unfounded) engendered by counterproliferation could be balanced by an appropriate new initiative for giving this kind of assurance.

Even more conspicuous is the absence of any reflection on what counterproliferation means in terms of positive security assurances. These are security guarantees given by the nuclear weapon states to NPT parties that are threatened or actually attacked by nuclear weapons. By developing the capabilities planned under the counterproliferation initiative, U.S. and potentially NATO forces will strengthen the very capabilities needed to give credible security assurances, to dissuade regional proliferators from acquiring WMD, and to deter them from exploiting any WMD advantages for political and military gain. Positive security assurances could thus be the bridge between a purely national counterproliferation policy and support for the global nonproliferation regimes.

But to achieve this outcome, careful analysis, political cooperation, and military planning must all be focused on the objective. The relations between national, alliance, and global decision making for contingencies where military means might be employed to preserve the nonproliferation regimes must be sorted out. Little attention has been devoted so far to these crucial questions.

Finally, one inevitable but fairly problematic risk needs sustained attention. The building of a structure to manage counterproliferation throughout the Pentagon creates vested interests. Civilian and military officers performing their respective roles may develop an inclination to discredit nonproliferation and put more currency (literally and figuratively) in hard-nosed "realistic" planning against the time when nonproliferation fails. Given the institutional weight of the Defense Department, this could lead very quickly to a shift of gears from preventive diplomacy to after-the-fact

military containment. Great care must be taken to prevent the emergence of a self-fulfilling prophecy that will enhance the military role at the cost of the diplomatic approach and stress unilateral action to the detriment of multilateral consensus-building. That the military establishments in some of the allied countries—although not the foreign ministries—have taken an interest in this issue and may emphasize aspects of counterproliferation that the Clinton administration is now abandoning, only adds to this concern.

In sum, activities under the label "counterproliferation" could serve as a useful adjunct to nonproliferation policies, which are among the most important elements of many countries' defense and security architecture. But they have not yet reached this point because their advocates in the United States have been guilty of poor public relations, weak and contradictory definitions, insufficient appreciation of foreign views, and a lack of strategic understanding as to how to connect counterproliferation to traditional, and prevailing, nonproliferation policies.

Recommendations

To shape the counterproliferation initiative to support the international nonproliferation regimes, especially the NPT as its future is decided in April–May 1995, is an immediate challenge for U.S. policymakers. Not only would such a revised understanding of counterproliferation provide a much-needed shot in the arm to prospects for the NPT's extension, but the Defense Department would also find a much better reception when it tries to advance its counterproliferation objectives.

The Clinton administration should therefore consider the following stylistic and substantive measures:

1. Eliminate the term "counterproliferation" and replace it with the phrase "nonproliferation support." Although this change may seem purely cosmetic, it would help enormously to clarify what the Clinton administration has in mind, would serve to calm those residual fears that exist abroad, and would contain the risk that a counterproliferation bureaucracy would supersede the traditional diplomatic approach to nonproliferation.

2. Develop clear definitions of what falls under nonproliferation support. Rather than marshaling everything that is dear to the Defense Department under the counterproliferation banner, each program assigned to nonproliferation support should clearly state how it is supposed to serve U.S. nonproliferation policy and, where applicable, the global nonproliferation regimes.

3. Continue to deemphasize preemption and emphasize protection. U.S. armed forces are far more likely to be called upon to afford protection to a country threatened by WMD than to strike a proliferator's WMD facilities. Planning, budgeting, and declaratory policy should clearly reflect this situation. The less the word "preemption" is used, the better. What is called "neutralization," that is, dealing with a proliferator's WMD assets in wartime, requires the same type of capabilities as preemption and such capabilities would inevitably be part of a military package that could be offered by the United States to parties threatened by proliferators. With developed neutralization capabilities, therefore, U.S. forces would be equally capable of responding to the order to preempt without undue and politically damaging emphasis.

4. Take visible steps to support the traditional nonproliferation regimes. The counterproliferation debate has confused some foreign audiences about whether U.S. support for existing nonproliferation regimes will be maintained or will weaken in favor of military solutions. To restore confidence, bold steps of support for the global regimes are in order. Such steps might include:

- support for an enhanced budget for the IAEA so that it can live up to its increasing challenges in the field of international safeguards;
- the prompt payment of U.S. dues at the beginning, rather than at the end, of the fiscal year;
- increases in the U.S. contribution to the IAEA's technical assistance fund;
- early ratification of the Chemical Weapons Convention and full support for the new Organization for the Prohibition of Chemical Weapons; and
- unambiguous U.S. support for current efforts to complement the Biological and Toxin Weapons Convention with legally binding verification and confidence-building measures.

5. Clarify the role of the UN Security Council in deliberating and deciding upon military measures in proliferation contingencies. Apart from clear and unambiguous cases of self-defense, which fall under article 51 of the UN Charter, it is the Security Council that acts as the bulwark for the nonproliferation regimes, as recognized in its declaration of January 31, 1992. A declaration by the United States that reaffirmed the leading role of the Council and related U.S. nonproliferation support contingency planning to the Council's duties in this area would allay fears about U.S. unilateralism and would solidify the new responsibility the Council has explicitly assumed in the nonproliferation regimes. As a practical matter, such a declaration

would not prevent the United States from acting, alone if necessary, to defend its vital national security interests.

6. Counter fears in the developing world about the perceived unilateralism of U.S. counterproliferation policy. A declaration by the United States that nonproliferation support aims at denying proliferators any political and military gains from their WMD programs and that regime members in good standing that have renounced the acquisition of WMD will be protected from attack would provide welcome reassurance.

7. Emphasize positive security assurances. How the security of countries that have renounced WMD can be guaranteed against those that have not is one of the issues most pertinent to shaping the coming world order and the fate of the nonproliferation regimes in the twenty-first century. Perhaps the most important contribution nonproliferation support could make to strengthening international regimes is in the field of positive security assurances. The United States should declare that nonproliferation support capabilities enable the United States to better implement its commitments under Security Council resolution 255—the pledge to assist NPT parties threatened by nuclear weapons (and by implication, to assist parties to the Chemical and Biological Weapons Conventions). The United States could invite other countries to explain what steps they were prepared to take to assist parties to these three agreements, thereby opening a debate on what positive assurances will mean in the future of these regimes. If the United States were ready to open this debate in this way, it could make an invaluable contribution to strengthening the nonproliferation regimes.

8. Offer joint training exercises and,

in emergencies, supply protective equipment to those countries threatened by WMD in their region. Such assistance measures are foreseen in the Chemical Weapons Convention, but they could be made a part of all nonproliferation regimes. Such assistance would be a tangible advantage of membership in a regime and could even be attractive to some countries that are still nonparticipants. This assistance would add to the multilateral dimension of U.S. nonproliferation support efforts and thus help to dispel concerns about unilateralism.

9. Integrate these policies into the preparations for the 1995 conference to extend the NPT. All the political risks connected with counterproliferation discussed above culminate in their potential impact on the extension of the NPT. These risks can be redressed by the timely preparation of the countermeasures discussed in this last section and their integration into the many consultations that will take place with representatives of leading nonaligned countries in preparation for the 1995 conference. Negative and positive security assurances will be an extremely important topic at the conference; such preparations could therefore make a great contribution to a successful outcome.

If the NPT is extended indefinitely and unconditionally, or even for an indefinite number of fixed periods, prospects for international peace and security will be significantly increased. A revised and expanded mission for counterproliferation would help to achieve this goal and win greater support for, as well as usefully reinforce, the international nonproliferation regime beyond 1995. The irony is that if the goal is, in fact, achieved, there will be far less need for the counterproliferation capabilities the Pentagon is currently acquiring.

This article benefited from the proceedings of an international seminar on counterproliferation sponsored in October 1994 by the Woodrow Wilson International Center for Scholars in Washington, D.C., and cochaired by the two authors and from briefings by officials from the Defense and State Departments, the Arms Control and Disarmament Agency, the National Security Council, and Congress, and subsequent discussions with the seminar's participants. The authors alone are responsible for the views expressed here.

Notes

1. Les Aspin, "The Defense Department's New Nuclear Counterproliferation Initiative" (Address to the National Academy of Sciences, Washington, D.C., December 7, 1993).

2. Department of Defense, "Counterproliferation Support Program: Program Overview, FY 1995" (Washington, D.C., December 10, 1994).

3. See Avner Cohen, "The Lessons of Osirak and the American Counterproliferation Debate," in Mitchell Reiss and Harald Müller, eds., *International Perspectives on Counterproliferation,* Wilson Center Working Paper (Washington, D.C.: Woodrow Wilson International Center for Scholars, December 1994).

4. Office of the Press Secretary, The White House, "Joint Statement on Strategic Stability and Nuclear Security by the Presidents of the United States and Russia" (Washington, D.C., September 28, 1994).

5. "Alliance Policy Framework on Proliferation of Weapons of Mass Destruction," *NATO Review,* June 1994, p. 28.

Rethinking the Nuclear Equation: The United States and the New Nuclear Powers

Lewis A. Dunn

THE PROLIFERATION OF nuclear, chemical, and biological weapons as well as missile delivery systems has ceased to be a policy backwater, quite frequently forgotten in the midst of cold war nuclear confrontation. Unprecedented attention is now rightly focused on what additional actions can be taken by the United States and other countries to prevent further proliferation or even in some instances roll it back. This must remain the top priority. At the same time, new-found interest among the U.S. civilian defense community and uniformed services has also triggered a long-overdue assessment of how to deal with or, in some instances, counter with military means, the consequences of proliferation for U.S. national security, regional stability, and global order. This is justified by the realities of ongoing proliferation across virtually all the regions of the world.

At the top of this latter agenda is the challenge posed by the new or emerging nuclear powers.[1] Nuclear weapons remain potentially the most destructive agents of mass destruction. Acquisition of nuclear weapons by hostile powers is the greatest threat to U.S. freedom of action to support long-standing friends and interests overseas. Although stable nuclear relationships may eventually emerge between rival newly nuclear powers, the transition could well be prolonged, unstable, and perhaps prone to escalation in the midst of conflict. Moreover, the breakup of the former Soviet Union and the weaknesses of controls on nuclear weapons and materials in its constituent territories have sharply increased the risk that a subnational terrorist group could gain access to a nuclear weapon or explosive device.

From the vantage point of U.S. defense planners, moreover, dealing with the consequences of possession of nuclear weaponry in the newly nuclear countries is all but certain to require new thinking and approaches. Traditional concepts of deterrence that guided the U.S. nuclear relationship with the former Soviet Union will at best need to be extensively adapted to changed circumstances; at worst,

Lewis A. Dunn is vice president and manager of the Weapons Proliferation and Strategic Planning Department of Science Applications International Corporation. He is a former assistant director of the U.S. Arms Control and Disarmament Agency and ambassador to the Nuclear Non-Proliferation Treaty negotiations.

Copyright © 1993 by The Center for Strategic and International Studies and the Massachusetts Institute of Technology
The Washington Quarterly • 17:1

Lewis A. Dunn

such concepts may need to be abandoned. Quite possibly, some heavily discounted or even once-discredited ideas may need to be revisited, not least thinking about how to conduct conventional military operations on a "nuclear battlefield" and to limit damage in the theater and at home should deterrence break down. In still other proliferation situations, crisis management, not deterrence, is likely to become the central theme of U.S. relations with some new nuclear powers.

The Newly Emerging Nuclear Powers

Significant differences exist among the newly emerging nuclear powers. At the political level, the direct threat posed to the United States and U.S. security interests by their acquisition of nuclear weapons varies greatly. A wide range of nuclear force–building outcomes also distinguishes these countries. Consider each element briefly.

Allies and Friends, Enemies and New Acquaintances

Looked at from the perspective of U.S. security interests and the risk of conflict involving American forces, differences between the new and emerging nuclear powers are clear. One of these countries—Israel—is a traditional friend and ally. In this instance, what must most concern U.S. policymakers are the indirect consequences throughout the Middle East and beyond, should Israel ever be forced to use nuclear weapons. The relationships with the United States of two others—India and Pakistan—have waxed and waned in recent years, but neither directly challenges core American security concerns and U.S. military intervention against either of them is difficult to envisage.

By contrast, hostility to the United States dominates the political outlook of several others, most especially North Korea, Iran, and Iraq. Moreover, U.S. forces continue to confront two of these countries on a daily basis, in one case at sea and in the air in backing up the terms of cease-fire, in the other on the ground across an unstable cease-fire line. In both Northeast Asia and the Persian Gulf, moreover, other countries depend on U.S. political and military support for their security.

Ukraine poses a still different problem. It seems ever more committed to an initial posture of nuclear ambiguity likely to be followed by an eventual decision to retain a considerable portion of what significant opinion in the country views as its nuclear inheritance from the former Soviet Union. Ukrainian and American leaders, however, want to establish a mutually beneficial and cooperative long-term political and economic relationship. Neither poses an intentional threat to the other's security. But in the event of an accidental or unauthorized launch of inherited Soviet systems, Ukraine alone among these countries could inflict massive destruction on the U.S. homeland.

Nuclear Force–Building

Similarly, no canonical new nuclear force exists. Instead, a wide range of outcomes is already emerging, reflecting these countries' technical capabilities; their geopolitical rivalries; and long-standing national approaches to the planning, organizing, and implementing of political decisions and military operations—what may be termed their strategic personalities for short.

Most basically, the size and sophistication of the newly emerging nuclear powers' arsenals already vary widely. Published reports suggest, for exam-

152

ple, a spectrum ranging today from possible North Korean diversion of sufficient nuclear weapons material to manufacture a single first generation fission device, through Pakistani and Indian possession of a handful of fission weapons, to potential Israeli clandestine deployment of upward of 50 to 100 more advanced nuclear weapons.

Readily available aircraft already provide all of the new nuclear powers with a proven and usable means of delivery. But over the coming decade, aircraft may increasingly give way to missiles as preferred delivery means. Missiles in particular offer concealment and mobility that could prove attractive to ensure survivability—not least as other countries learn the lesson of Iraq's successful dispersal of its mobile SCUD missiles during the Persian Gulf War. Deployments in tunnels, caves, and other forms of underground or silo basing are still other possibilities, reflecting the diversity of approaches open to these countries.

Important variations already exist, moreover, in terms of the range and sophistication of missiles operated by new nuclear powers. In that regard, a key threshold is whether a country's missiles can strike targets only in nearby neighbors or also in more distant countries (typified perhaps by the emerging North Korean missile threat to Japan). At least for this decade, however, none of the new nuclear powers (save Ukraine) seems likely to pose such a missile threat to the American homeland.

Nuclear decision making and command and control will all but certainly be shaped by existing patterns of civil-military relations in these countries. Two dominant approaches stand out: tight civilian control of military matters in countries such as India and Israel; military domination in Pakistan.

Particularly in personalistic dictatorships like North Korea and Iraq, centralized nuclear decision making from the top is likely to be emphasized as well.

The importance of the security of nuclear weapons is likely to be well understood in principle, especially but not exclusively in the more dictatorial new nuclear powers. Small numbers of nuclear warheads will also make it easier to ensure tight security. Basic safety principles for first generation nuclear weapons are also likely to be readily accessible. Effective implementation of basic security and safety principles, however, cannot simply be assumed. Overall readiness to pay a price to ensure effective security and safety may vary as well. In particular, safety measures have broken down in several of these countries (e.g., India's Bhopal chemical accident and the massive explosion of an ammunition storage dump in Pakistan). Very high rates of disability among workers were also apparently routinely accepted in the Iraqi chemical weapons program.

Uses and Usability of Nuclear Weapons

For U.S. defense planners, perhaps the most critical questions concern the purposes driving nuclear force–building in the newly nuclear countries and the conditions under which their leaders might contemplate the threat or use of nuclear weapons. At this stage, conclusive answers are likely to be difficult to obtain. Nuclear forces remain unacknowledged and public discussion is limited. Top decision makers may have only begun to focus seriously on such matters. Indeed, references to nuclear doctrine in the new nuclear powers should be used with care, lest a false impression result. Instead, what stands out now is a diversity of thinking about the uses and usability of nuclear weapons for deterring conventional, nuclear, chemical, or biological attack as well as a possibly greater readiness on the part of some new nuclear powers than their cold war predecessors to contemplate offensive uses of nuclear weaponry. Uncertainty and ambiguity about specific countries' thinking about the uses and usability of nuclear weapons also seem likely to persist for some time.

Deterring Regional Rivals. Considerable diversity appears to characterize thinking among the newly nuclear powers about the uses of nuclear weapons for deterrence of regional rivals. At one end of the spectrum, mere possession of nuclear weapons is sometimes seen as a political and security talisman, enhancing prestige and deterring attack by hostile neighbors. In turn, little if any thought may be given to theories of deterrence or to conditions for use of those weapons. For instance, some Pakistani officials suggest that as soon as Pakistan acquired a nuclear weapon, India could no longer contemplate invading and dismembering their country. Similarly, the most benign interpretation of North Korea's apparent pursuit of nuclear weaponry is that Kim Il Sung and his son and chosen successor Kim Jong Il view possession of nuclear weaponry as a political means to help ensure a successful transition of power, both by reinforcing the internal legitimacy of Kim Jong Il and making it less likely that South Korea will meddle in any power struggle or internal unrest that may ensue.

Signs of more explicit theories of deterrence, however, are also discernible. For some new nuclear powers, a readiness to threaten or actually use nuclear weapons offers a last resort deterrent to conventional military defeat, if not also possible national extinction.

Presumably, nuclear threat or use would lead the near-victorious opponent to cease military operations short of final victory—or perhaps to pursue more limited military objectives from the start. Such a last resort deterrence doctrine probably remains the dominant rationale behind Israel's nuclear weapons capability. It may also figure prominently in Pakistani nuclear calculations. How and when nuclear weapons might actually be threatened or used to implement this doctrine is a major uncertainty. Uses against advancing ground forces, more distant military targets, population centers, and remote unpopulated sites all are conceivable. With regard to timing, there could be considerable pressures not to wait too long.

Closely related, the threatened use or actual use of a nuclear device as a means to trigger intervention by outsiders on a new nuclear power's behalf comprises another doctrinal possibility. Senior South African nuclear decision makers, for instance, have publicly stated that such a theory of catalytic intervention—including, if needed, detonation of a nuclear device at South Africa's Kalahari nuclear test site to trigger U.S. and Western support against feared Soviet-backed Cuban invasion forces—was the driving motivation behind that country's nuclear weapons program. Given Pakistan's inability to prevail against India in a full-scale war (and its traditional reliance on outside support to "balance" India), this line of thinking may also be finding a receptive audience among Pakistani nuclear decision makers.

For some new nuclear powers, nuclear weapons may well be regarded as a means to deter use of chemical or biological weapons, either on the battlefield or against civilian targets. During the Gulf war, Israel took steps to signal that if Iraq used SCUD missiles armed with chemical warheads to attack Tel Aviv or Haifa, Israel might well retaliate with nuclear weapons. More broadly, Israel's nuclear arsenal also appears to be seen as a means to deter possible Syrian use of chemical weapons against Israeli air bases and mobilization centers in a new offensive.

At the other end of the deterrence spectrum, the threat of nuclear retaliation in response to nuclear use dominated the cold war confrontation. That threat could become a central doctrinal feature of some future regional nuclear confrontations. Planners among Israeli defense officials, as well as the wider elite, for instance, have already begun to debate the prospects for successful deterrence should it prove impossible to prevent the acquisition of nuclear weapons by an Arab government or by Iran. What to threaten in retaliation is an open question. Possibilities range from a Middle East variant on assured destruction to threats of retaliation against selected high-value targets. By contrast, occasional comments by Indian officials suggest that should Pakistan use nuclear weapons, India might not respond in kind but seek instead to use its overwhelming advantage on the ground to eliminate the Pakistani military threat in a subcontinental variant on the Gulf war cease-fire.

Nuclear Blackmail, Coercion, or Aggression. During the period of the U.S. nuclear monopoly from 1945 to 1949, some senior U.S. officials argued that the new weapon could and should be used to force political concessions from the Soviet Union. Nearly a decade later, Nikita Khrushchev consciously sought to foster the image of a significant Soviet advantage in deployments of nuclear-tipped intercon-

tinental ballistic missiles to back up his political efforts to force Western concessions on the status of Berlin. By the closing days of the Cold War, however, mainstream opinion in both Moscow and Washington had given up any lingering hopes that any perceived nuclear weaknesses could be turned into significant political advantages.

More offensive, less benign attitudes toward the uses and usability of nuclear weapons, reminiscent of early cold war attitudes, cannot be precluded on the part of certain new nuclear powers. From such a perspective, the purpose of nuclear weapons could well be viewed by some leaders as a means to blackmail neighbors and compel their political and economic support and to assert regional dominance. There is little reason to doubt, for example, that had Saddam Hussein obtained nuclear weapons, he would have regarded them as a means to enforce his will on neighboring countries. Despite their experience so far, the two Kims could yet view nuclear weapons not as something to bargain away for economic concessions but as a means to compel economic and political concessions from frightened neighbors, not least Japan.

Still another possibility, of particular concern to the United States and its friends abroad, is that some new nuclear powers will seek to use the implicit or explicit threat to use nuclear weapons to undermine U.S. readiness to deploy forces to protect critical interests and allies. Their goal would be to tip the balance of political debate, whether in Congress, the executive, or the military services, against running the risks of intervention. At the least, U.S. freedom of action could be severely constrained, for example, in a future confrontation with a nuclear-armed Iran or Iraq. At worst, a country might successfully use nuclear threats to hold the ring against U.S. involvement. Other countries might also be the target of nuclear blackmail, including U.S. allies in Europe and Japan, whose support would be critical for intervention in the Middle East, the Gulf, and Asia.

In turn, although Western thinking has long since grown skeptical of the battlefield use of nuclear weapons to achieve tactical advantage or defeat an adversary, such use against the forces of the United States and coalition supporters could well appeal to leaders in some newly emerging new nuclear powers. Early in a conflict, nuclear use could be regarded as a means to seize a decisive advantage; late in a conflict, it could become a desperate gamble. By way of example, use of even a few nuclear weapons by Saddam Hussein at the start of the U.S. military buildup for the Gulf war, for instance against the port of Jubail and the Dhahran air base, could have severely set back U.S. deployments. Assuming the worst motivations behind North Korean pursuit of nuclear weapons, similarly selective use of a limited number of nuclear weapons against ports and air bases in South Korea could greatly disrupt resupply and air operations should a second Korean war erupt out of the instabilities of transition in the North. At the least, North Korean leaders could contemplate last resort use of nuclear weapons against advancing South Korean or U.S. forces out of a "No More Inchons" psychology.

From the U.S. defense planner's perspective, the possibility of actual nuclear use by a hostile new nuclear power might at first glance appear low. It might simply be assumed that "they wouldn't dare." This would be a dangerous assumption. For an aggressive newly nuclear country, the potential payoffs of nuclear use would rightly be perceived to be high, from possibly shattering coalition solidarity and political will to severely disrupting military operations. Equally important, in that country's eyes the risks of using a few nuclear weapons to strike military targets could be seen as acceptable—or be miscalculated. Indeed, faced with such use, a U.S. president all but certainly would come under intense political pressures from at home and overseas not to respond in kind. Massive conventional air strikes, however, as witness the Gulf war, might prove a tolerable alternative.

One final, although admittedly extreme, possibility must be squarely faced. Actual use of nuclear weapons might be undertaken by some countries to fulfill a transcendent ideological, religious, or historical mission, regardless of the consequences for their societies. For the most likely target of such action, Israel, how much to fear this threat is already being debated in light of calls by Saddam Hussein and the Iranian ayatollahs for Israel's destruction. For outsiders, this would defy the logic of the cold war confrontation, with its emphasis on the balancing of tangible costs and benefits. For a leader following another logic, however, the costs and gains might be calculated quite differently. Commitment to serving a transcendent goal or pursuit of a place in history might override either moral restraints or concern about the costs of retaliation.

A New Intelligence Challenge
Across the newly emerging nuclear powers, as the preceding discussion illustrates, diverse doctrinal tendencies can be discerned or posited. Comparable diversity is frequently also evident within many of the specific countries in question. In large part, this reflects the impact of multiple threats on particular countries as well as the

fact that in some new nuclear powers doctrinal debate is just getting under way. Further, for certain new nuclear powers several very different doctrinal possibilities can be posited, given changed assumptions about their fundamental motivations to acquire the bomb.

A sound understanding of the nuclear force–building choices of the newly emerging nuclear powers—and of the purposes driving those choices—is absolutely essential for U.S. counterproliferation policy. It does not now exist. Instead, meeting this requirement will demand a partial reorientation of more traditional proliferation intelligence efforts. Until quite recently, analysis of proliferation problem countries, both within the U.S. government and on the outside, concentrated almost exclusively on tracking and assessing all of the steps taken by such countries in pursuit of their first nuclear device. Henceforth, tracking and understanding nuclear force–building and thinking "after the first bomb" must be an equally important priority.

Meeting this new intelligence requirement, moreover, will not be easy. Not only will nuclear force–building choices be subject to tight internal security, but lack of acknowledgment and open deployment will hinder efforts to track developments. Especially important in this regard, from initial reluctance to acknowledge possession of nuclear weapons to a possible desire to hide more aggressive intentions, virtually all of these newcomers have many reasons not to develop and articulate well-defined nuclear doctrines. Faced with this uncertainty, it will be critical neither to exaggerate nor underestimate the very real possibility that some new nuclear powers will think very differently about the uses and usability of nuclear

weapons than did either the United States or the Soviet Union even at the height of the cold war nuclear confrontation.

Deterrence and Reassurance

Deterrence and reassurance were at the heart of the U.S. nuclear relationship with the Soviet Union. From the early 1950s to the late 1980s, deterrence of Soviet aggression and reassurance of American allies provided the most critical requirements against which U.S. military forces were sized, postured, and deployed. Deterrence and reassurance must be a major component, as well, of any overall U.S. strategy to deal with or counter the consequences of proliferation. The concepts of cold war deterrence will need to be adapted, however, for changing circumstances. Greater attention will need to be paid, as well, to what to do if deterrence fails.

Rethinking Deterrence in a Proliferating World

Deterrence of nuclear blackmail or use offers a first line of response to the emergence of hostile new nuclear powers such as North Korea, Iran, and Iraq. Other approaches—whether attempts to destroy preemptively threatening nuclear forces, to detect and defend against them, or to conduct military operations despite their use— would all be less preferable and, should deterrence work, less effective. A credible deterrence posture would also be the best means of providing reassurance for neighboring countries. Retooling deterrence for these new situations, however, will entail crafting retaliatory threats tailored to a wider range of diverse countries. Serious consideration also needs to be given to a posture of deterrence based on the threat of "assured nonnuclear re-

157

taliation." This would rely on conventional and unconventional military means, as well as internationally implemented nonmilitary punishment in planning, threatening, and, if necessary, executing retaliatory responses to destroy what the leaders of an aggressive new nuclear power value most.

Tailored Retaliatory Threats. Deciding what consequences to threaten in response to use of nuclear weapons by a new nuclear power is the first step to crafting a deterrence posture. During the Cold War, there was considerable debate about how to answer this question of what to hold at risk, reflecting different appraisals of what the Soviet leadership most valued. At various times, it was suggested that the United States should hold at risk one or more of the following: Soviet population and industry, Soviet nuclear assets, Soviet conventional power projection capabilities, other Soviet military assets, Soviet economic recovery potential in the event of a nuclear conflict, Communist party control of Soviet life, and simply the lives of the central Soviet leadership.

Despite concluding that the Soviet political and military leadership most valued its own survival, U.S. cold war strategy steered clear of explicitly threatening to attack it. Instead, over the years, American declaratory policy stressed that U.S. retaliation would inflict assured destruction on the Soviet Union, deny any meaningful Soviet victory in a nuclear clash, and most simply, ensure that the costs far outweighed any putative gains. Concern about enhancing Soviet fears of a U.S. decapitating strike, with possibly destabilizing Soviet responses, may partly explain that reluctance. Nonetheless, for its part, U.S. targeting strategy continued to emphasize retaliatory strikes against this full range of assets.

Given the possibility that some hostile leaders could perceive high payoffs in using nuclear weapons, it will be especially important to tailor retaliatory threats to what the leaders of specific hostile new nuclear powers most value. The well-being of their populations is unlikely to be high in that ranking. Even preserving more basic military strength and economic/industrial infrastructure may be outweighed by other concerns. Rather, for some of the hostile newly emerging nuclear powers, like the two Kims or Saddam Hussein, the survival of the leader or the leadership could be what they value most highly; for others, including possibly the Iranian ayatollahs, survival of their basic regime may be their top concern.

Further, assuming that such leaders value their own lives or their regimes most, it could be more essential here than in the cold war confrontation to stress explicitly that any U.S. retaliation would be targeted on both. During the Cold War, the Soviet leadership must have seen the very prospect of all-out U.S. nuclear retaliation as a threat to themselves and their regime, regardless of their civil defense efforts to protect themselves. By contrast, leaders such as Saddam Hussein or Kim Jong Il could well believe that even though their society might be gravely damaged, they themselves might survive and emerge still in power. Saddam's Gulf war experience can only reinforce that view.

Reassessing In-Kind Nuclear Retaliation. Throughout the cold war confrontation, nuclear weapons—and the threat to use them in retaliation—were at the very core of the U.S. deterrent. There was little question that if nuclear weapons were used against U.S. forces overseas or the American homeland, the United States would respond in kind. Both the deployment of thousands of tactical nuclear weapons abroad and the very characteristics of the U.S. strategic nuclear forces posture enhanced the credibility of nuclear retaliation. The high probability that even limited nuclear use would escalate to an all-out exchange had a comparable effect.

It is likely to be much more difficult to make the threat to use nuclear weapons in response to nuclear use by a hostile new nuclear power sufficiently credible for high-confidence deterrence or reassurance. Particularly if nuclear use were against either U.S. forces deployed in a regional contingency or a U.S. ally before American deployments, a Saddam Hussein or a Kim Jong Il could believe that the U.S. president would not be prepared to respond with nuclear weapons. Any U.S. president's likely reluctance to go down in history as the second U.S. president to use nuclear weapons, domestic popular calls not to take an eye for an eye, all but certain pressures from allies and neighboring countries not to respond in kind, likely environmental impacts, and a perceived general American weakness of will could all be seen as greatly reducing the danger that a nuclear retaliatory threat would be carried out.

Even in the case of a use of a nuclear weapon against the American homeland, the cold war assumption of an automatic nuclear response might be doubted. All of the preceding reasons to doubt retaliation in kind would still be at work. In addition, much more than in the U.S.–Soviet confrontation, the president would have to choose to use nuclear weapons—absent the near automaticity intentionally built into U.S. cold war strategic forces and given far better appreciation of the potential effects of using nuclear weaponry.

In turn, under some conditions a hostile new nuclear power could be reluctant to rule out the possibility of U.S. nuclear retaliation, but still might not be deterred. A top presidential priority, should nuclear retaliation be authorized, is likely to be holding deaths among innocent civilians to an absolute minimum. The prospect of very limited and selective nuclear use, however, could prove too restrained to be an effective threat in the eyes of certain hostile leaders. Rather, given the potential benefits of use of even a few nuclear weapons, especially in a regional contingency, a proportional U.S. response could be thought a tolerable price to pay.

The United States could seek to enhance the credibility of nuclear retaliation against hostile new nuclear powers. For a number of reasons, however, this will be difficult in the post–cold war era. The withdrawal of ground-based and sea-based nuclear forces from overseas has eliminated a key symbol of U.S. nuclear power and commitment. Over time, a gradual loss of theater-level operational nuclear expertise except in the air force seems quite likely, thereby making it more difficult to redeploy nuclear weaponry abroad. As increasing efforts are made through formal and informal arms-control agreements as well as other unilateral steps to reduce the role of nuclear weaponry in U.S. strategy and global politics, this very ethos is also likely to undercut the perceived willingness of the United States to use nuclear weapons again.

More controversial perhaps, serious questions should be raised about whether it would best serve U.S. security interests in the post–cold war world to use nuclear weapons even in retaliation for nuclear use by a new nuclear power. Confronted by the first use of a nuclear weapon since Nagasaki, any U.S. response would need to serve several objectives. The United States, and for that matter the broader international community, would have a strong interest in punishing the user to demonstrate that the use of nuclear weapons does not pay. This would be important lest successful use stimulate a landslide of proliferation and encourage further uses of nuclear weapons by still other countries. Closely related, it would be important that any U.S. response help to restore the global taboo against nuclear use. In that regard, a second nuclear use in rapid succession, even if limited, could well have the opposite effect of further eroding that taboo, helping paradoxically to routinize nuclear weapons. Whatever the U.S. response, it should finally also contribute to resolving the original conflict on terms acceptable to the United States and any coalition partners. Here, too, however, further nuclear use could disrupt, not reinforce, political support for action in key countries both among the coalition and in the region.

Assured Nonnuclear Retaliation. From two perspectives, therefore, a U.S. strategy for deterring nuclear use by hostile new nuclear powers based on the threat of nuclear retaliation in kind must be challenged. Its credibility is questionable. Its implementation could adversely affect both near-term prosecution of any ongoing confrontation and the prospects for longer-term stability in a world of more nuclear powers. Instead, serious consideration should be given to adopting a fundamentally different deterrence strategy of assured nonnuclear retaliation.

At one level, such a strategy would emphasize enhanced conventional responses as well as recourse to other nonnuclear military means. Advanced conventional munitions technologies

and systems now on the horizon increasingly hold out the possibility of greatly increased nonnuclear lethality against such targets as leadership command bunkers, headquarters, and facilities; nuclear weapons production and storage sites; and other fixed military targets. Backed up by preconflict intelligence and intraconflict target acquisition, possession of such systems could afford the United States "near-nuclear" capabilities. Special operations units would have an important role to play, as well, in posing a credible threat first to locate and then destroy high-value assets.

At another level, however, putting in place a credible nonnuclear deterrence posture would require going beyond traditional military measures and responses. A key additional element, therefore, of this posture would be to create a strong presumption, by measures such as national policy statements and prior actions by the United Nations (UN) Security Council, that first use of nuclear weapons would lead to certain, swift, and all-encompassing international punishment. From traditional sanctions to a total air, land, and sea blockade, the purpose would be to isolate such a country, make it an international outlaw, and bring down its leaders. In effect, future U.S. efforts to deter use of nuclear weapons by hostile new nuclear powers cannot be separated from broader international efforts to stigmatize use of nuclear weaponry as outside the realm of acceptable international behavior.

Compared to the threat of nuclear retaliation, few if any questions are likely to arise about U.S. readiness to respond with advanced conventional weaponry and other nonnuclear military means. A properly crafted diplomatic strategy, building on recent acknowledgment by the Security

Council and other key international bodies that proliferation is a threat to the peace, should be able to muster declarations of support for international action to back up the global nuclear taboo. Public and political pressures to respond also are likely to be high, should use occur. More practically, reliance on advanced conventional weapons is likely to entail little if any loss of effectiveness for holding a wide range of high-value military and nuclear targets at risk. But considerable technological advances are still likely to be required to destroy certain other targets, including deep underground leadership bunkers. As for posing a credible threat to bring about a change of regime, the prospect of international isolation and outlawry, short of the no longer credible threat of massive nuclear response, could well pose the most concern for the leaders of a hostile new nuclear power.

The Reassurance Dimension
U.S. reassurance of threatened friends and allies was a defining feature of the cold war confrontation. The North Atlantic Treaty Organization (NATO) alliance, U.S. troop deployments overseas, repeated presidential statements and visits, and many other formal and informal links were all designed to reassure countries in Western Europe and Asia of American support if they had to resist Soviet blackmail or aggression. Similarly, reassurance already is and will remain a central part of any new U.S. strategy to deal with proliferation's consequences.

Close political, economic, and diplomatic linkages with threatened countries is one way to provide such reassurance. Declaratory policy and alliance ties can usefully reinforce such linkages. Capabilities to minimize the consequences of attempted or actual use of nuclear weapons against a re-

gional ally, discussed below, would also contribute to reassurance. Allies and friends will continue to want assurance that the United States (with others' support, as appropriate) will use military force to defend their vital interests. Perhaps most important, however, reassurance in the post–cold war world is likely to depend heavily but not exclusively on perceptions of the credibility of the U.S. deterrent posture. In particular, design and maintenance of credible deterrence of new nuclear powers is critical for reassuring American friends and allies now threatened by hostile newly nuclear neighbors. Whether in Japan and South Korea in Asia, Saudi Arabia in the Gulf, or Turkey in Central Asia, continued readiness to eschew pursuit of nuclear weapons will depend heavily on perceptions of the effectiveness of an American security umbrella. If such traditional American friends come to doubt either U.S. will to stand by them or whether in the final analysis the threat of U.S. retaliation would deter nuclear blackmail or attack by their regional enemies, pressures to seek nuclear weapons of their own will greatly increase.

If Deterrence Fails . . .
Regardless of which basic deterrent strategy is chosen—nuclear or nonnuclear retaliation—the prospects for successful deterrence are uncertain. Too little is known about the fundamental motivations and calculations of the leadership in such hostile newly emerging nuclear powers as North Korea, Iran, and even Iraq. Pessimistic assertions that such countries are "undeterrable" may prove wrong. But deterrence could fail whether due to calculation, miscalculation, ineptitude, accident, or command failure. Recognition of this stark possibility points in two divergent directions: back in time

to any intensified efforts that still might be taken in the immediate future to head off such countries' acquisition of nuclear weapons; forward to still other measures to deal with proliferation's consequences, in this case the consequences of a breakdown of deterrence and the use (or attempted use) of nuclear weapons against U.S. forces, friends, or the American homeland. Among those forward-looking measures are a heightened emphasis on damage limitation, defenses, and detection. U.S. planning for regional conflicts also needs to reflect explicitly the possibility that a nuclear weapon might be used by a new nuclear power against U.S. or coalition forces.

Revisiting Damage Limitation. Whether or not U.S. strategic offensive forces should be explicitly evaluated in terms of their capability to limit damage to U.S. society from a Soviet attack was hotly debated in the early 1960s. Since its rejection in the late 1960s, the idea of limiting damage in the event of a U.S.–Soviet nuclear conflict has more often than not found little favor among civilian defense decision makers. In part, skepticism about damage limitation reflected the loss of American strategic monopoly in the 1950s as well as the fact that soon thereafter U.S. preemption had vanished as a serious option—if it had ever existed. Mainstream civilian rejection of damage limitation also reflected the belief not only that little meaningful could be done to limit the catastrophic consequences of a nuclear war by military measures (as opposed to possible mutual acceptance of limits and restraint should war break out) but that pursuit of such measures would be destabilizing. By contrast, U.S. military planners and targeters continued throughout the cold war period to give highest

priority to targeting Soviet nuclear forces. For them, should a conflict erupt, one of the main purposes of U.S. strategic offensive nuclear forces would be prompt response to limit damage on the American homeland.

Confronting hostile new nuclear powers in third world contingencies, U.S. civilian defense planners need to revisit the objective of damage limitation in two related senses.

There are many obstacles to carrying out a successful U.S. disarming strike against a hostile new nuclear power on the verge of using nuclear weapons against U.S. forces or an American ally in the midst of a regional contingency. But past experience also indicates that such opponents make mistakes, their command systems break down, and their military planning and preparations can be flawed. The possibility cannot be precluded, therefore, that an opportunity could arise for the United States to carry out a disarming strike with very high confidence. Preparations are warranted to take advantage of such an opportunity should it arise in the midst of conflict with a new nuclear power and should there be warning that the latter was preparing for nuclear use. This would call for appropriate intelligence capabilities, command and control arrangements, and most important, for reasons already suggested, a nonnuclear, advanced conventional strike capability.

In turn, should a hostile new nuclear power actually use one or several nuclear weapons in the early stages of a conflict, limiting the potential damage of further nuclear use would be both an important and a potentially feasible objective. At the least, current counterproliferation planning needs to take this objective seriously to determine how much, at what price, and with what nonnuclear systems could be done to limit damage once deterrence had broken down. An ability to do so could be important not only to maintain coalition solidarity but also to prevail militarily in a larger ongoing regional conflict. Once again, possible nonnuclear strike capabilities for damage limitation warrant detailed identification and assessment.

Defenses. With the signing of the 1972 Anti-Ballistic Missile (ABM) Treaty, the United States set aside the goal of defending the American homeland from an all-out Soviet ballistic missile attack. This new consensus against defenses reflected concerns about the financial and opportunity costs, feasibility, and adverse implications for cold war security. The Reagan administration's pursuit of strategic defenses challenged but never successfully overturned the ABM treaty consensus.

For now, skepticism about U.S. deployment of homeland defenses, as opposed to continuing research and development (R&D) on future systems, still makes sense. Other, more pressing demands on scarce U.S. defense resources outweigh hedging against highly speculative scenarios involving an unauthorized launch of a few Russian or Chinese ballistic missiles against the United States. For the next decade or so, moreover, the most probable hostile new nuclear powers will lack ballistic missiles with ranges to threaten the American homeland. Further, successful pursuit of theater and regional missile defenses would shorten the lead times for deploying a limited homeland defense, should a hostile new nuclear power deploy intercontinental-range ballistic missiles more rapidly than currently anticipated.

By contrast, there is a growing, but not unquestioned, consensus in favor of development and deployment of theater and regional ballistic missile defenses. Iraqi SCUD attacks on Israel, Saudi Arabia, and Bahrain during the 1991 Gulf war boosted this interest in theater or regional ballistic missile defenses to help protect U.S. forces or allies. Programs are under way to upgrade existing capabilities and to test and evaluate new concepts and systems. Although uncertainty exists concerning the ultimate effectiveness of future theater missile defenses, accelerated R&D on defenses is essential. Should effective defenses prove attainable, their deployment would be a valuable hedge against a breakdown of deterrence. Equally important, a capability to deploy defenses rapidly to enhance reassurance and influence regional allies, as demonstrated in the Gulf war, could prove politically valuable in a future confrontation with a hostile new nuclear power.

Contrasted with continuing if controversial support for missile defenses within a significant part of the U.S. defense community, interest in civil defenses peaked in the 1950s and early 1960s and rapidly dwindled thereafter. This was a realistic response to the steady expansion of Soviet nuclear forces, which quickly made civil defenses a throwback to the prenuclear age.

For the next decade or so, the direct nuclear threat to the American homeland is likely to be very limited. A hostile new nuclear power might smuggle one or at most a few nuclear weapons into the United States and threaten an American city. Or a terrorist group might be able to pose a comparable threat, whether with a stolen, improvised, or otherwise obtained nuclear device or perhaps with a radiological weapon in which conventional explosives would be used to disperse radioactive materials. Motivations could range from blackmail of U.S. decision makers to simple terror and revenge.

At the least, more detailed assessment is demanded of what role reinvigorated civil defense planning could play in minimizing the consequences of an actual nuclear detonation in such situations. Without prejudging the results of such an assessment, possible contingency steps that could be identified and prepared for run from limited evacuations on warning to prompt provision of medical assistance. Further, planning would need to include preparations to evacuate the president and critical officials from Washington in the event of credible warning of an unconventional nuclear threat to the nation's capital. Although possibly viewed in some circles as itself an anachronistic throwback to cold war thinking, this type of planning could prove invaluable should an actual threat occur. Recent experiences with responses by the federal government to natural disasters suggest that absent such planning any response could be poorly coordinated, marginally effective, and result in an even greater loss of life and societal chaos.

Detection and Disablement. As the cold war nuclear confrontation began in the late 1940s, one of the possibilities considered but then discounted was Soviet smuggling of a nuclear weapon into the United States. For both hostile new nuclear powers and terrorist groups, however, unconventional delivery would be the most likely way of threatening American territory. Predeployment of a nuclear weapon into a neighboring country might also prove an attractive strategy for a regional aggressor.

The United States has long maintained an on-call emergency nuclear search capability. This existing capability for detecting clandestinely deployed nuclear weapons should be tested against the most plausible future scenarios. This approach might include, moreover, contingency planning for detection of a nuclear weapon smuggled into the capital of a close friend or U.S. ally. Timely and accurate intelligence will also be essential both to provide warning of possible smuggling efforts and to orchestrate tactical responses. Here, too, in-the-field exercises against posited future threats could help ensure maximum effectiveness of existing capabilities, including necessary linkages between intelligence collection and more operational responses.

Taking advantage of heightened emphasis on proliferation across the U.S. advanced technology and defense acquisition communities, it would be appropriate, as well, to take another look at what additional initiatives might be taken in this detection arena. New data processing and sensor technologies, for instance, could hold out the possibility of enhanced overall detection capabilities. Technology initiatives might also play an important part in ensuring a capability to disable and render safe recovered nuclear weapons or terrorist devices.

Regional Operations in a Nuclear Environment. Hedging against a breakdown of deterrence, finally, requires that U.S. defense planners explicitly plan for conducting regional operations against a hostile country armed with nuclear weapons. Secretary of Defense Les Aspin's "bottom-up" review of mid-1993, however, was based on the assumption that the U.S. opponent in neither of the two illustrative major regional conflict scenarios—respectively North Korea and a remilitarized Iraq—would possess nuclear weapons.[2] This assumption is open to serious question, particularly in light of the "bottom-up" review's own emphasis on the dangers of proliferation and its focus on a 10- to 20-year time horizon.

The decision not to assume that the U.S. opponent in at least one of these two major regional conflicts would possess nuclear weapons simplifies and eases the budget planning process. But it puts off asking and answering many tough questions. These concern the many ways that the threat or even possible use of one or a few nuclear weapons by a hostile new nuclear power will ultimately shape the sizing, posture, deployments, operations, and training of U.S. forces. It also makes it more difficult to ensure that needed defense planning and acquisition will take place in time to meet the augmented threat to U.S. forces overseas and regional partners of the United States posed by the emergence of hostile new nuclear powers.

Regional Nuclear Crisis Management

Deterrence and reassurance, adapted for the post–cold war environment and suitably hedged against a potential deterrence breakdown, provide a starting point for thinking about how to deal with proliferation's consequences. But some new or emerging nuclear powers pose no direct security threat to the United States or vital U.S. interests. In these proliferation situations, whether confrontations between India and Pakistan in South Asia, Israel and an Arab enemy in the Middle East, or Ukraine and Russia in Europe, nuclear crisis management will be the main challenge for U.S. policymakers.[3]

So viewed, the primary focus of nuclear crisis management in the post–

cold war world will differ from that of past decades. During the Cold War, crisis management virtually by definition meant joint efforts by the United States and the Soviet Union to manage direct confrontations and avoid open conflict that could have escalated to all-out nuclear war. In the future, "crises" may also arise in which the United States faces threats to friends and allies from hostile new nuclear powers. But from a U.S. defense planning perspective, those situations are better approached as challenges in deterring or responding effectively to nuclear blackmail or use rather than as exercises in mutual accommodation and restraint.

More specifically, during the next decade, one or more regional nuclear crises involving regional rivals but not the United States directly will all but certainly occur. Faced with the specter of the first use of nuclear weapons since Nagasaki, U.S. policymakers will need to strike the right balance between a desire to avoid major risks and the dangers of standing aside. Stepped-up pursuit of measures to prevent such regional nuclear crises in the first place may offer the least dangerous response; but contingency planning and preparations for last moment efforts to head off nuclear use also demand consideration.

Regional Nuclear Crises
South Asia remains the most likely region for a future nuclear confrontation between two newly nuclear powers. Indeed, during the winter and early spring of 1990, India and Pakistan appeared to be sliding toward military confrontation, driven by long-standing conflict over Kashmir, Indian charges of Pakistani support for the violence in the Punjab, domestic politics, deep mutual mistrust, and interacting deployments of conventional military

forces. Had open warfare erupted, the conflict could have escalated to use of nuclear weapons. For its part, U.S. diplomatic intervention and good offices played a valuable role in encouraging restraint and helping India and Pakistan to begin to stand down militarily.[4] The underlying roots of a future nuclear crisis still exist.

Elsewhere, the recent political breakthrough between Israel and the Palestine Liberation Organization (PLO) may lead to wider movement in the Middle East peace process, thereby changing the political and military dynamics of the region. Both Iraq and Iran, however, are outside the process. Many extremely complex problems remain, including between Israel and Syria. Political support is fragile in both Israel and among the Palestinian factions. A future nuclear crisis entailing unilateral Israeli nuclear threats or use in response to chemical or biological weapons attack in another Middle East conflict cannot therefore be ruled out, although it is considerably less likely today. Here, too, a partial precedent exists. As the outbreak of war in the Gulf came nearer in late 1990, the Israeli government apparently took pains to signal to Saddam Hussein that use of chemical weapons against Israeli cities might trigger nuclear retaliation.

Two very different types of regional nuclear crisis could occur in the former Soviet Union. At some point, Ukraine's continuing posture of nuclear ambiguity, combining refusal to make a legally binding commitment to give up all former Soviet nuclear weapons on its territory with incremental creep toward operational control over those weapons, could trigger Russian intervention. The latter could take the form of heightened economic and political pressures. Attempts might be made to disable and destroy

the weapons using covert or special operations units. Even large-scale military threats and action cannot be ruled out. Prospects for success are likely to be low and the risks to Russia high. But in the eyes of Russian civilian *and* military decision makers, Ukraine's prospective emergence as a nuclear power could well be their Cuban missile crisis.

A second type of crisis would be quite different. Russia could call for U.S. assistance to help respond to theft of nuclear materials or a nuclear weapon by a subnational group, domestic dissidents, or simply the Russian Mafia. Intelligence assistance in tracking down the thieves, logistics support in moving forces outside Russia for recovery, and active cooperation by U.S. nuclear search and recovery teams are all possible requests.

U.S. Interests and Risks

Depending on the specifics, American interests and the risks of involvement in nuclear crises between regional rivals will clearly vary. At one end of the spectrum, use of nuclear weapons in a war between India and Pakistan would not directly threaten the American homeland or its narrowly defined security interests. Nonetheless, first use since Nagasaki would shatter an emerging global taboo against nuclear use, which so far has proved a very valuable restraint and will be even more important for avoiding nuclear use if a world of more nuclear powers proves unavoidable. Humanitarian considerations, the wider impact of nuclear use on stability in Asia and on prospects for further proliferation, and perceptions elsewhere of American leadership would also argue against standing aside. The risks of measured diplomatic, intelligence, and political involvement, moreover, would probably be limited, especially since a U.S.

role might well again be found useful by both sides.

At the other end of the spectrum, Russian military threats or, in the worst case, intervention to block Ukrainian seizure of former Soviet missiles, would have strong direct and indirect consequences for U.S. security interests. Inadvertent launch could result in unprecedented damage to the American homeland. Even reliance on economic pressures and political threats would set back Russian relations with the United States and Western Europe, making it more difficult to reallocate resources to U.S. domestic needs. At least some neighboring countries could reassess the longer-term risks of remaining nonnuclear. Similarly, the risks of U.S. political if not necessarily military support to Ukraine in an actual Russia–Ukraine nuclear crisis would also be high.

Crisis Management Choices

At least four sets of regional nuclear crisis management actions warrant more detailed treatment and assessment as part of U.S. counterproliferation initiatives. These deal respectively with crisis prevention measures; precrisis steps to shape the nuclear force deployments of friendly new nuclear powers; use of intracrisis good offices; and broader efforts to buttress an emerging global nuclear taboo.[5]

Crisis Prevention Measures. Tailored explicitly to specific proliferation situations, prior crisis prevention measures are essential. Within South Asia, for instance, preventive diplomacy should include stepped-up efforts to damp down the Kashmir confrontation as well as to support a further confidence-building process. With regard to the latter, both countries should be urged to rigorously implement confidence-building measures agreed to since the 1990 crisis, among them mutual notifications of exercises. New measures might be proposed, including particularly enhanced military-to-military ties, exchanges on doctrine, and establishment of a crisis prevention center as a means to foster such exchanges.

Within the Middle East, successful pursuit of the peace process, building on the Israel–PLO breakthrough, would help excise the roots of some future crises. If successful, nonproliferation initiatives aimed at preventing the emergence of a Middle East of many nuclear powers would have a similar impact.

Continued efforts by the United States and others to establish a security network of informal and formal political, military, and economic linkages with Ukraine are essential. U.S. officials also could reiterate the political and economic downsides to Kiev of retaining nuclear weapons, including the likelihood that outsiders will stand aside if Ukraine keeps the weapons and Russia decides to act unilaterally. U.S.–Russian contingency planning and exercises for cooperative emergency responses to nuclear diversion are also in order to supplement other U.S. initiatives to help Russia strengthen security and controls over its nuclear arsenal. (Comparable initiatives, moreover, may be needed for the People's Republic of China.)

Shaping and Restraining Force Deployments. Precrisis actions to shape nuclear force deployments and thinking by these new nuclear powers may also sometimes prove a valuable crisis management measure. In particular, it remains a top priority to cap nuclear deployments in South Asia short of open integration into each side's military posture and the outbreak of a race to deploy nuclear-armed missiles. This would stretch out the time needed to use such weapons in a crisis, while helping to avoid possible technical force instabilities that could accidentally or inadvertently increase the risk of war. Global bans on the production of unsafeguarded fissile material as well as on nuclear testing, both supported by the Clinton administration, could be useful vehicles by which to pursue and facilitate comparable regional restraints not only in South Asia but also the Middle East.

With regard specifically to the Middle East, the time has long since come to begin a high-level, quiet dialogue with Israel on nuclear issues. Its purpose would be to avoid future surprises, signal U.S. concern, and to the extent possible influence Israeli thinking.

Proposals to provide friendly countries like India, Pakistan, and Israel with assistance to ensure that their nuclear arsenals are safe, secure, and tightly controlled are considerably more controversial.[6] Assistance could take many forms, from public release of unclassified information about the basic principles of safety and security to technology sharing. By lessening the risk of a nuclear accident or a command breakdown, such assistance would support nuclear crisis management and help contain the threat of nuclear use. Costs exist, particularly the danger of undermining basic nonproliferation norms and efforts. Space precludes, however, a detailed discussion of this issue. Suffice it to suggest, therefore, that the most critical next step for U.S. policymakers in thinking about how to strike a balance between the benefits and costs of assistance is to use U.S. experience to develop a detailed breakdown of the full spectrum of possibilities.

Intracrisis Good Offices. Particularly in South Asia, the United States should remain prepared, as well, to use its good offices diplomatically and politically to help to resolve future nuclear crises. This could involve serving as an intermediary between the parties, seeking to muster international support to encourage restraint, and, to the extent that doing so would help to clarify specific misunderstandings and misperceptions, providing intelligence information to both India and Pakistan. Prior discussions with China and Russia about actions that each country might take—or not take—to help defuse a future South Asian nuclear crisis could prove useful as well. In that regard, consideration might be given to establishing a Washington–Beijing hotline to facilitate rapid and reliable exchanges in crises.

By contrast, it is also important to acknowledge that in some nuclear crises, the potential scope of U.S. action may be very limited and the risks too high. This is likely to be so if a confrontation between Russia and Ukraine leads to open conflict. Beyond urging restraint, and hoping that Russian controls on inadvertent launch work, there may be little to do at the time.

Buttressing a Global Nuclear Taboo. Decisions by new nuclear powers to use nuclear weapons in a regional conflict with a neighboring country will depend on many considerations. Possible fear of nuclear use by a regional rival, goals being pursued, technical "use or lose" pressures, the ebb and flow of conventional conflict, concern about perceived resolve, and command dynamics will all play a part. In addition, the readiness of such countries—and for that matter, more hostile new nuclear powers—to use nuclear weapons will also be shaped in varying degrees by perceptions of the likely international repercussions of being the first country in nearly 50 years to do so, thereby breaking the global nuclear taboo.

As a final crisis management action, therefore, steps are needed to buttress that global nuclear taboo and expectation of swift international punishment for nuclear first use. Successful implementation of recent strategic arms cuts would serve that goal. So does the new U.S. readiness to negotiate a global nuclear testing ban. Pursuit of a cutoff of unsafeguarded production of nuclear weapons materials would have a comparable effect, while a global no first use of nuclear weapons agreement warrants consideration, too. Other desirable steps, as already suggested in the context of deterring hostile new nuclear powers, would seek to strengthen the presumption of action by the UN Security Council. In effect, now that the Cold War has ended and the threat to use nuclear weapons first is no longer needed to buttress deterrence in Europe, the United States would take the lead in attempting to create an international consensus that henceforth the only purpose of nuclear weapons should be to deter the use of other nuclear weapons.

Two objections are likely to be raised to this approach. In some quarters, renouncing first use of nuclear weapons will be criticized as overly constraining U.S. freedom of action, and in particular as precluding reliance on the threat to use nuclear weapons to deter use of biological weapons or actual first use of nuclear weapons preemptively in the midst of conflict with a hostile new nuclear power. Critics will argue, as well, that some new nuclear powers, including a U.S.

friend, Israel, want the option to use nuclear weapons first not for aggressive but for defensive purposes.

The actual extent to which biological weapons will ultimately prove attractive to third world countries is still uncertain. Backed up by enhanced stress on protective measures, a more credible and sustainable nonnuclear retaliatory strategy along the lines already proposed can be designed to deter use of biological weapons against U.S. forces or the American homeland.

Regarding Israel, it, too, has other options for deterring biological weapons threats should they emerge in practice. Perhaps more important, in a Middle East that may finally be making the transition toward political settlements among the central antagonists, the risks of nuclear restraint may appear considerably lower to Israeli officials. Most broadly, any such costs or limits to a conscious U.S. strategy of seeking to enhance the global nuclear taboo must be weighed against the potential payoffs not only for crisis management but also for deterrence and reassurance in the post–cold war world.

What Next?

In the proliferation arena, preventing the further spread of nuclear weapons should remain the top U.S. priority. For too long, however, U.S. policymakers and defense planners have neglected the need to focus seriously on how to deal with the consequences of proliferation for American security. Faced with the emergence of several undeclared nuclear powers, with others on the horizon, and with the loss of cold war missions, counterproliferation is now the vogue. The first steps are finally being taken to adjust U.S.

169

defense policies to deal with the proliferation threat to American allies, U.S. forces overseas, and perhaps even the American homeland. Detailed knowledge and tracking of nuclear force–building and thinking in real countries, not in abstract "proliferants," is vital. Initial discovery of proliferation needs to be matched by sustained attention to its implications throughout the defense policy and acquisition process, from long-term planning to execution of tactical operations. No simple solutions or generic approaches will work.

For some countries and regional proliferation situations, the primary objective will be to deter use of nuclear weapons against U.S. allies, forces, or the American homeland by hostile new nuclear powers. Successful deterrence will require discarding traditional cold war approaches to craft a nonnuclear assured retaliation deterrence strategy, buttressed by the presumption of swift and decisive international punishment in response to the first use of nuclear weapons. Greater attention must also be paid to responses should deterrence break down regardless. New thinking will again be needed, not least to ensure that U.S. and coalition forces can prevail in a future regional military conflict with a hostile new nuclear power.

Elsewhere, the primary challenge will be nuclear crisis management between regional rivals not directly threatening U.S. security. With the collaboration of other countries, the United States can play an important part in seeking to prevent and sometimes defuse such crises.

Most broadly, these two pillars—deterrence and crisis management—need to be strengthened by U.S. leadership in creating an international consensus behind an enforceable global nuclear taboo. This calls for U.S. readiness to renounce perhaps the central tenet of cold war military thinking—the option to use nuclear weapons first. The success of U.S. policies to deal with the consequences of proliferation cannot ultimately, however, be separated from a sustainable vision of the role of nuclear weapons—both old and new—in world affairs over the next decades of the nuclear age.

The views expressed in this paper are those of the author and not necessarily those of SAIC or any of its sponsoring organizations. I would like to thank my colleagues at SAIC, Gregory Giles, Jim Tomashoff, and John Sandrock, whose analyses of many of these issues and conversations with officials in key new nuclear powers have influenced my own thinking.

Notes

1. There is a growing appreciation that the proliferation of biological weaponry may now pose a greater threat than once was the case, particularly as a strategic terror weapon. This article purposefully limits itself, however, to the nuclear dimension of proliferation. On the biological weapons threat, see Brad Roberts, ed., *Biological Weapons: Weapons of the Future?* (Washington, D.C.: Center for Strategic and International Studies, 1993).

2. Les Aspin, *The Bottom-Up Review: Forces for a New Era* (Washington, D.C.: Department of Defense, September 1, 1993).

3. U.S. policy should also be concerned with capping, if not slowly rolling back, proliferation by these countries. Discussion of measures to pursue that goal, however, is outside the scope of this essay. Pending their success, moreover, crisis management will be essential.

4. Although Hersh apparently exaggerates how close to a nuclear war India and Pakistan came, see Seymour Hersh, "On the Nuclear Edge," *New Yorker*, March 29, 1993, pp. 56–73.

5. For a very useful discussion of regional nuclear crisis management, also see Raja Mohan, "Crisis Management and Confidence-Building in South Asia" (Draft paper presented at the Conference on Con-

fidence-Building Measures in South Asia, New Delhi and Islamabad, May 24–28, 1993).

6. See Gregory Giles, "Safeguarding the Undeclared Nuclear Arsenals," *The Washington Quarterly* 16 (Spring 1993), pp. 173–186.

Toward an International Nuclear Security Policy

George H. Quester and Victor A. Utgoff

OVER THE PAST few years, the long campaign against proliferation of nuclear weapons has had some major ups and downs. The more significant ups include: the disintegration of the Soviet Union now appears unlikely to create any new nuclear states; South Africa has dismantled the handful of nuclear bombs it had secretly created; Iraq's nuclear program has been suppressed; and the United States and Russia have dramatically reduced the numbers, types, alert rates, and widespread deployments of their nuclear forces.

In addition, international efforts to slow or stop nuclear proliferation are being strengthened. Substantial efforts are being made to win extension of the Nuclear Non-Proliferation Treaty (NPT) at the review conference in 1995. Efforts are also being made to strengthen a variety of inter-

national groups whose purpose is to control access to the materials, knowledge, and systems needed to create nuclear arsenals.

Still, serious challenges are being made to the nuclear nonproliferation campaign as North Korea continues its defiant pursuit of the bomb, and other states, including Iran and Libya, seek to build or buy nuclear weapons. Proliferation by North Korea or others would put enormous pressure on neighboring states to follow suit.

All things considered, one cannot be optimistic that nuclear proliferation will be stopped unless a stronger and more comprehensive effort is made. The growing technical and industrial capabilities of the developing world, expanding trade (particularly in materials and systems that have legitimate uses, but can also be used to create nuclear weapons), and the ambivalence or even opposition of some states to efforts to control nuclear proliferation, are all undermining the current strategy of limiting access to nuclear weapons. Thus, the United States is seeking new concepts and capabilities for halting or reversing the proliferation of nuclear, as well as chemical and biological, weapons.

The general objective of this broadened U.S. effort should be to raise the costs of pursuing and owning such weapons, and to minimize the value of owning them. If the aggregate of

George H. Quester is a professor in the Department of Government and Politics at the University of Maryland. His most recent book is *The Future of Nuclear Deterrence* (Lexington, Mass.: D. C. Heath, 1986). Victor A. Utgoff is deputy director of the Strategy, Forces, and Resources Division of the Institute for Defense Analyses. In 1990 he published *The Challenge of Chemical Weapons: An American Perspective* (New York, N.Y.: Macmillan).

Copyright © 1994 by The Center for Strategic and International Studies and the Massachusetts Institute of Technology
The Washington Quarterly • 17:4

their values can be reduced below the aggregate of their costs, proliferation can be halted.

The United States and like-minded countries have had success in keeping the costs of acquiring nuclear weapons high. Although the supply-side barriers imposed on the spread of sensitive technology can be overcome, they add a substantial economic price, and also a penalty, because states suspected of reaching for bombs are denied technology that might have been used quite legitimately for civilian purposes. States thought to be pursuing nuclear weapons have also been denied financial aid. The economic sanctions maintained on Iraq for not cooperating with efforts to eliminate its nuclear, biological, and chemical weapons programs are clearly very painful to that country. Sanctions against North Korea would impose similar accumulating pain. In sum, there should be little doubt that the strategy of raising costs has had some good effect in slowing proliferation, and that it will continue to be an important part of the larger solution to the problem.

It seems equally clear, however, that this cost-imposing strategy will not solve the entire proliferation problem. Some states appear to be willing to starve their people and to take enormous heat from the international community in order to obtain nuclear weapons. Thus, this article concentrates on the problem of reducing the aggregate value of owning nuclear weapons, a task for which military planning and preparations are especially relevant.

After short discussions of (1) why one should expect nuclear weapons to appear attractive to some states; (2) the character of the political-military threat posed by continuing prolifera-

tion; and (3) the types of counterproliferation actions needed, this paper argues that (4) the necessary actions will impose costly and risky burdens that the United States cannot and should not carry alone, and thus, (5) that the United States must initiate and lead an international counterproliferation effort.

Next the article expands in some detail on an idea for minimizing the potential for escalation to nuclear warfare through an agreement by all states that there be no-first-use of nuclear weapons without prior consultation with the United Nations (UN) Security Council. Finally, we propose that international discussions be started on the issue of how to create an international nuclear security policy, and we suggest some questions that might be on the agenda.

The main point of this article is that continued nuclear proliferation is going to change the nature of the world order in ways that will force the acceptance of strong and heretofore unpalatable countermeasures. Although the United States must take the initiative in defining and supporting the implementation of effective counters to proliferation, the definition and implementation of an effective policy must be an international undertaking.

Attractions of Nuclear Weapons

Although potential proliferators differ in the precise reasons why they seek nuclear weapons, it is clear that they do not share the sentiments of so many in the West that nuclear weapons have no value. In fact, given the substantial economic and political costs, and the real military risks of creating a nuclear arsenal, some states must find nuclear weapons extremely attractive.

The fundamental attraction of nuclear weapons is that unilateral proliferation promises a dramatic shift in the balance of power. Unilateral possession opens the door to direct threats against non-nuclear states. It also limits the risks for aggressively minded states of making conventional attacks on their neighbors because, in the event of a decisive reversal, the intended victim can be expected to be very reluctant to press for a total victory that would put the aggressor in a position of having nothing left to lose. Further, powers from outside the region might be expected to be more reluctant to come to the aid of a victim of aggression by a nuclear-armed regional state. An aggressively minded unilateral possessor can expect all these possibilities to be widely understood, so that, even without explicit threats or attacks on its neighbors, it can anticipate more careful international attention to its interests, and, among less well-armed neighbors at least, the kind of prestige that attends raw military power. Finally, an aggressively minded state might expect that, even when both sides to a regional dispute have nuclear weapons, outsiders will be dissuaded from entering, inclined to conclude that a nuclear-armed defender can take care of itself.

Even defensively minded states may seek unilateral possession of nuclear weapons within their regions. They may not have the population or wealth to match stronger conventional forces fielded by neighbors. Defensively minded states would be under great pressure to respond to nuclear proliferation by an aggressively minded neighbor. Perhaps most important, nuclear weapons can provide a strong guarantee that a state will not be put in a position of losing everything, even at the hands of an aggres-

sively minded state with nuclear weapons of its own.

If nuclear proliferation increases the power and influence of any state, it must be expected that this will also increase the attractiveness of nuclear weapons for others. Some threatened states will look for alliances with an existing nuclear power. But other states in the shadow of a proliferator will respond by seeking nuclear weapons of their own. As additional states continue to develop the capability to manufacture technologically sophisticated products, making nuclear weapons easier to obtain, threatened nations may feel less inclined to accept the uncertainties of protection by allies, and the number of independent nuclear forces could thus become very large.

In sum, it seems clear that nuclear weapons can be very attractive for states, and the most basic of attractions is the apparent guarantee they provide that their owners would never be put in a position of "nothing left to lose." Clearly, this is the most difficult to reduce of the attractions that can drive nuclear proliferation. Still, all of these attractions can be reduced, as we argue below.

Character of the Threat Posed by Nuclear Proliferation

The concerns that have been expressed for decades about the dangers of nuclear proliferation are obviously real; indeed they may have been understated. Thus, if raising the national costs of obtaining nuclear weapons is an insufficient barrier to proliferation, the United States cannot resign itself to the unimpeded spread of weapons of mass destruction. Rather, what is required, as outlined here, is an intensified effort to reduce any advantages a nation sees in proliferation.

In the absence of such an effort, the world is headed toward what could be characterized as a "six-gun" society. As in the old U.S. Wild West, too many of the globe's nation-state citizens would wear nuclear "big iron" on their hips. Even if such weapons were rarely used, unprecedented levels of violence would emerge when relations got completely out of hand.

The risk of catastrophic attacks on U.S. and other cities is only a part of the cost of widespread proliferation, however. The mere threat of such attacks would make the cooperative management of international problems generally more difficult. The states whose power is based primarily on population and productivity will be under constant pressure from those that have little more than frighteningly powerful weapons. The latter, dissatisfied with the distribution of global wealth and power, may periodically challenge the status quo in a most dangerous confrontation of will.

As individual cases of proliferation occur, additional risks may be run. Specifically, states acquiring nuclear weapons may be tempted to translate new-found military power into concrete geopolitical gains before their neighbors have acquired bombs of their own. More than a little good luck was involved in getting the existing nuclear powers through five decades with no nuclear detonations in anger. New proliferants will encounter new and unique problems, where a stable nuclear balance may not evolve.

As its concerns about the breakup of the Soviet Union have demonstrated, the United States also has even more reason now to worry about control over nuclear weapons by less reliable governments. The greater number of states that have such weapons, the greater the danger that political breakups, changes of government, or sloppy weapons custody will put nuclear weapons into irresponsible hands.

General Types of Actions Needed to Counter Proliferation

As argued above, the general objective of U.S. efforts to counter proliferation must be to reduce the attractions of owning nuclear weapons. Drawing on the discussion of these attractions presented earlier, five general types of action need to be taken.

First, the potential effectiveness of these weapons needs to be undermined with various kinds of defenses, as well as capabilities to destroy nuclear forces before they can be launched. Second, because defenses and prelaunch attack capabilities can surely not be perfect, the United States will also need to maintain nuclear deterrent forces to reinforce the perception that initiation of nuclear warfare against the United States, its allies, or their forces would be extremely dangerous.

Third, the United States needs to reshape its conventional forces so that states see them as capable of intervening against even nuclear-armed regional challengers without unacceptable levels of risk to themselves, and that interventions cannot be blocked or halted through the destruction of a few key ports, airfields, or forward supply centers. This will be a particularly expensive undertaking.

Fourth, sufficient protection needs to be offered to potential allies to enable them to provide support and participation in any confrontation with a nuclear-armed challenger. To the extent that regional leaders see their countries as completely exposed to nuclear attack, they will find it far more difficult to justify to themselves and their citizens that their countries should become engaged and to make timely decisions to support a multilateral intervention.

Finally, regional allies and friends must be assured that the United States, together with other responsible powers, will stand up to regional aggression that might threaten them, and thus, although they would be expected to make a reasonable contribution to their own defense in other ways, that they need not try to match the nuclear forces deployed by regional aggressors on their own. This is a tall order, as attested to by the complex, burdensome, and less than completely successful history of efforts to reassure the North Atlantic Treaty Organization (NATO) that the United States would defend Europe against the Soviet Union.

Nuclear weapons will seem substantially less valuable to potential proliferators if the above policies and programs are pursued. Each of these steps may be difficult and at times costly, but success in countering proliferation will require taking all of them to some degree.

Why the United States Should not or Cannot Take These General Actions Unilaterally

In addition to the high costs and risks involved, there are a variety of reasons why the United States should not try to take all these general counterproliferation actions single-handedly. First, and perhaps the most important, the United States cannot afford to let a counterproliferation campaign come to be seen as something it is bent on forcing the rest of the world to accept. It would be easy for the rest of the world to suspect that the primary U.S. motive in trying to suppress the value

of nuclear weapons is to maintain its current position as the world's preeminent conventional military power, able to intervene at will in the affairs of nearly any state it chooses.

This consideration implies that the United States must do all it can to develop a common international appreciation of the threats that continued proliferation will create to individual states, regions, and to a democratic world order. Equally important, the United States must find ways to convey that U.S. military preparations made to counter proliferation are driven by these threats and that they support the larger interests of the international community. No better means can be found for doing these things than to involve the international community in developing a common appreciation of what continued proliferation will bring, and in identifying and creating new means for countering it.

Indeed, efforts to control proliferation must ultimately fail if the larger international community is not willing to do the things that only it can. The many countries that could readily build nuclear weapons must continue to forgo them, and nonproliferation actions requiring international cooperation, such as application of economic sanctions when other means prove inadequate, must get strong international support. The likelihood of such support will be much improved if the international community plays an active role in developing the global counterproliferation strategy.

Second, it is clear that the kind of counterproliferation program needed will be complex, expensive, and hard to sell to the U.S. public. This is particularly true in the current political climate, in which U.S. military capabilities are being cut back and pressures on the government budget point to further cuts. Even more difficult,

177

the kinds of actions needed to confront a nuclear-armed regional challenger will be risky. Maintaining the internal political support needed to pay the costs of preparations, to accept the expectation, if not obligation, to intervene in overseas regional crises and wars that threaten to turn nuclear, and to act when there may not seem to be any immediate and direct threat to U.S. interests, will be extremely difficult if the U.S. public does not see the international community accepting a major share of the risks and burdens of solving this common problem.

Third, as we have argued at length elsewhere, extended nuclear deterrence will remain an essential element of any serious effort to undermine the attractions of nuclear weapons.[1] When it must be brought to bear to suppress the seeming advantages of first-use of nuclear weapons to a regional challenger, the states involved in confronting the challenger, those within reach of the challenger's weapons, and others, will all have a keen and legitimate interest in when and how the possibilities for nuclear retaliation are signaled, and, in the event that the need for retaliation arises, how it is carried out.

In fact, although the United States and other nuclear powers certainly will not surrender the final say on any such decisions to others, and although the independent decision-making capabilities of the involved nuclear powers can help to ensure that the coalition is not paralyzed when action is needed, consultations with allies are almost surely going to be one of the prices that must be paid to gain the necessary timely international support for the required military operations.

These nuclear demands the allies have on the United States are paral-leled by an additional set of demands that the United States should place on them. In particular, the United States should not let itself be placed in the position of being the coalition's "nuclear enforcer." To do so would make the United States a singular focus for the long-term resentment of the punished state, and would stigmatize the United States in the eyes of much of the world, casting long-term doubts on the United States as a fundamentally benign power.

Moreover, sharing the responsibility for nuclear deterrent actions should increase the efficacy of deterrence. International support would legitimize such actions. It would help to ensure that they are well coordinated across nations that might otherwise act independently. One heard very conflicting statements during the Persian Gulf War, from an RAF air marshal and others, about the circumstances under which nuclear weapons might be used. For discouraging nuclear first-use or nuclear proliferation, it is very desirable, for similar future situations, that the nuclear policies of the five permanent members of the UN Security Council be coordinated.

Perhaps most important, to the extent that the coalition takes coordinated actions and presents a united front, the challenger will be taking on an international community far better armed than itself, and vastly more survivable, and will tend to see itself taking on the world. Thus, if it becomes necessary to make explicit nuclear deterrent threats, and, worse, to launch nuclear retaliatory strikes against a nuclear renegade, the members of the coalition should make their support for these actions unequivocally clear to all. This requires that most, if not all, participate in making the required declarations, that they actively support selected preparatory actions, and that they participate in any required retaliation, in at least a supporting role.

More specifically, other nuclear members of the coalition should participate directly in making retaliatory strikes, although non-nuclear members might fly escort missions, consult on the selection of targets, or allow their air bases to be used to stage retaliatory missions. Exactly how these unhappy questions would be sorted out in any particular situation is not a concern here, but the principle of shared responsibility for any required nuclear deterrent activities is.

Finally, although the capabilities of the United States and its potential allies to intervene should not depend on access to a few ports or airfields that a nuclear-armed regional challenger might thus be tempted to destroy, the United States will need some access to the territory, airspace, or territorial waters of regional states. This factor also calls for international cooperation in developing and maintaining capabilities for regional interventions against nuclear-armed challengers. Although the United States has always sought to develop and maintain access to the regional bases and other facilities it might need, access requirements for interventions under the threat of nuclear attack are going to be different, and need to be thought through in advance, with the countries whose support could be needed.

Why the United States Must Take the Initiative in Countering Nuclear Proliferation

Even without getting into the specifics, there can be no doubt that countering proliferation successfully will be difficult and expensive. Preventing the launch of most of a potential re-

gional opponent's nuclear weapons is a daunting technical challenge that will be expensive to meet. Certainly the development and fielding of defenses against the variety of ways to deliver nuclear weapons will be very expensive. Restructuring U.S. intervention forces so that they can do their jobs without offering lucrative targets for nuclear attack will be even more so.

Mustering and sustaining the necessary political will to take these and the many other actions needed to minimize the attraction of nuclear weapons will not be easy. Given the limits on the resources available to the United States, an effective counterproliferation campaign will come at the cost of competing domestic priorities. The temptation to try to duck the problem and isolate ourselves from the dangers of regional nuclear proliferation will thus be substantial. Still, there are many good reasons why the United States cannot or should not do so, and why it must lead a global counterproliferation effort.

First, the proliferation of nuclear weapons risks the breakdown of the cooperative world order that the United States needs. The wealth available to the United States and to the rest of the world will be vastly greater if the world continues toward a single common market, and if Americans do not have to pursue expensive policies such as national energy independence. In addition, solutions to common problems, such as environmental pollution and management of perishable resources, such as fisheries and rain forests, are far easier to negotiate and implement in a cooperative world. Finally, the aggregate global burdens of national defense can be reduced to the extent that a more cooperative world poses fewer and less intense security challenges, and to the extent that cooperative solutions can be found to these security challenges. The shadow of continuing nuclear proliferation would upset each of these types of cooperation.

Second, the United States is the only nation that has any reasonable prospect of being able to lead the world to a solution to the problem of nuclear proliferation. It is recognized by most states as benign, if sometimes misguided, and as being committed to a democratic world order. Although U.S. military forces must be reshaped for interventions against nuclear-armed regional challengers, they remain the most capable intervention forces in the world. The United States also has a unique and lengthy history as the leader of many of the post–World War II period's most important international military, political, and economic institutions and activities.

Third, although most regional proliferators may seek nuclear weapons for reasons that have nothing to do with the United States, the United States can count on eventually having a vital and immediate interest challenged by a nuclear-armed regional state if proliferation continues.

Finally, the problem of proliferation is only going to get worse the longer the identification and implementation of an effective solution is put off. It is just a matter of time before nongovernmental organizations attempt to obtain and use weapons of mass destruction. Further, many states are already pursuing biological weapons, which may prove an even more difficult threat than that posed by nuclear weapons. Taking an even longer view, the history of mankind's development of ever more powerful weapons suggests that, unless something is done, the world is headed toward a situation in which the power to kill just about

everyone would be available to just about anyone. Clearly, this cannot be allowed to happen.

Fundamental Problems Encountered in Attempting to Reduce the Attractions of Nuclear Weapons

We have argued above that the dangers of nuclear proliferation require the international community to collectively identify and implement policies that substantially reduce the attractions of these weapons. We have also argued, here and elsewhere, that reducing these attractions substantially will require (1) a capability to threaten retaliation in kind for nuclear weapons use by regional challengers, and (2) reliable conventional and nuclear defense guarantees for regional allies, so that they see no need for their own nuclear insurance against total defeat. Still, although deterrence and defense guarantees appear essential to an international counterproliferation policy, they hardly constitute a policy that is complete and adequate. Moreover, they have some practical limitations, at least for the foreseeable future.

First, many states are deeply committed to first-use of nuclear weapons for their defense. Although the end of the Cold War dramatically reduced the prospects that the United States would ever have to initiate nuclear warfare, it has not eliminated it. The NATO allies have recently reaffirmed the need to retain first-use as a hedge against an uncertain future in Europe. It is easy to imagine that a North Korean attack could lead to a situation in which the choice would be the initiation of nuclear warfare or total loss of South Korea and the U.S. troops there. As we have argued repeatedly, so long as the allies of the United States see the option of first-use as a legitimate last resort defense option, the United States can either provide such an option or take the risk that they will provide it for themselves.

Moreover, other important states regard first-use as an important defense option. Russia has recently stepped back from the no-first-use declaration of the Soviet Union. Pakistan, India, and Israel seem to see nuclear weapons as insurance against conventional defeat by larger neighbors. Thus, nuclear first-use will be considered a legitimate option for last resort defense by countries whose cooperation is needed to counter proliferation. Still, in recognizing the legitimacy of nuclear first-use for defensive purposes, one is supporting what may be the strongest attraction of nuclear weapons.

Second, the international community may not be able to offer a timely and acceptable defense to all states in all circumstances. As Marc Dean Millot has suggested, states may not find satisfactory a defense guarantee that would liberate them after a long occupation while the international community mobilizes.[2] Moreover, the international community has historically found it difficult to come to the aid of unpopular or less important states, and this will not change quickly.

Third, policies of defense and deterrence are not easy to apply in some cases. A nuclear deterrent threat against a pariah state that is threatening important U.S. and allied interests is easy to imagine, as is protection for states that have close historical and cultural ties or control important resources. On the other hand, how would the international community apply deterrence and defense to a messy conflict over Kashmir that threatened to blow up into all-out war between India and Pakistan? Can it afford not to become involved?

The existence of these problems dictates that a sound and comprehensive international policy for substantially reducing the attractions of nuclear weapons will be a long time in coming. Still, the authors believe that continued proliferation will eventually come to be seen as having such painful consequences that these problems will be squarely faced and a way found to surmount them. In the meantime, there are useful steps that can be taken. At least one step that seems to move in the right direction was raised briefly in our last article in this journal.[3]

A Possible Step toward an International Nuclear Security Policy

Specifically, we propose that the United States consider announcing that it will not escalate any conflict to the nuclear level without first consulting with the UN Security Council, that it request other declared nuclear powers to agree to do the same, and, further, that all nations be asked to declare their support for such an agreement. Consultation of this kind would allow the world community, as represented by the Security Council, to offer an advance judgment on whether an escalation to the use of nuclear weapons was justified by the needs of the defense and by an absence of reasonable alternatives. Such a process should on balance reduce the attractions of nuclear weapons, and the reasoning is outlined below.

How No-First-Use-without-UN-Security-Council-Consultation Might Work

Further study and analysis of the specifics of such a consultative role for the

Security Council is required, and of how it would be implemented. The most basic element, however, would be developing an understood obligation by which the nuclear powers would give the Council at least a day or two's warning on any first-use of nuclear weapons, and would consult on the general nature of and specific justification for such use.

At least four kinds of response to such an instance of consultation could be envisaged. First, the Security Council might be able to offer an acceptable alternative, perhaps by negotiating a quick halt to the conflict, or by providing conventional military assistance to the defending side. The mere process of consulting and discussing alternatives might galvanize the rest of the world to rally conventional forces behind a threatened state, in a meaningful collective security, thus making use of nuclear weapons unnecessary. Second, the Council could reject the justifications advanced by the state wanting to use nuclear weapons, perhaps arguing that the intended use would be seen as a threat to the international community.

Third, the UN Security Council might agree that there are no reasonable alternatives, accept the fact that first-use might not be avoidable, and hope that reports of this judgment would have a sobering effect on the state attempting to defeat the prospective first-user, leading it to back off. Finally, the council consultation might prove inconclusive, allowing the warning time to run out and risking first-use.

Taken together, these four outcomes imply that this consultative process would raise the likelihood that nuclear first-use could be avoided, in that the first two outcomes avoid or

inhibit first-use, and the last two should not increase its likelihood. Thus, such an agreement would further one of the main objectives of a counterproliferation policy.

Additional Effects of a No-First-Use-without-Prior-Consultation Agreement

The agreement should have a variety of other useful effects that contribute to the suppression or avoidance of first-use and to the long-term effort to minimize the value of owning nuclear weapons. Four such effects are immediately evident.

First, development of such a commitment to consult before use of nuclear weapons will reinforce what has already become a major inhibition to nuclear surprise attack. States contemplating any such attacks now know that they would be flouting the will of the entire international community on a most vital matter. The commitment to Security Council consultation would stiffen the will of the international community to impose punishment for such an attack.

Second, by supporting such an agreement, the United States and the other nuclear powers would be accepting the narrowest possible role for their own nuclear weapons, consistent with the requirements of counterproliferation. Thus, the current politically chafing gulf between the nuclear opportunities of the haves and the have-nots would be reduced.[4]

Third, consultation in advance of nuclear first-use would provide an opportunity for the international community, with resources far larger than those available to almost any individual state, to propose alternatives to nuclear escalation that are not within the grasp of the prospective first-user. The community may be able to provide conventional forces that can defend the prospective first-user, or it may be able to get the attacker to back off.

Finally, the agreement would push the international community to focus more attention on heading off situations that might lead a nuclear state to consider first-use. It is hard to imagine a more distasteful or stressing task for the United Nations than to face a consultation of the kind called for here. The members would be under enormous pressure to find an acceptable alternative to justifiable defensive first-use, to threaten punishment for unjustified use, to form judgments on which are which, and to accept some degree of responsibility if the effort to head off first-use were to fail. Although the international community might prefer to duck such a task, there is no more vital task for which the UN Security Council is uniquely suited.

Effects on U.S. Freedom-of-Action and Historical Security Guarantees

This agreement would not significantly change the already constrained U.S. freedom to employ its nuclear weapons. The United States has long had plans to consult with its NATO and other allies before employing nuclear weapons. It has exhibited great reluctance to hint at nuclear use, even in circumstances where the immediate effect might have been to force an end to a conflict that was killing large numbers of Americans. Further, situations in which the U.S. leadership would not want to signal the possibility of first-use beforehand, or could not arrange to be able to afford to wait 48 hours before use, are hard to imagine,

particularly since the end of the Cold War.

More likely the future will bring situations in which the United States could find itself the intended target of a prospective first-use. To the extent that this agreement inhibits such use, the United States would be better off. Finally, if this agreement contributes to a reduction in the perceived value of nuclear weapons and helps to slow down or reverse proliferation, it will help to maintain U.S. conventional forces' freedom of action, which is essential to global stability.

Effects on Other States' Freedom of Action

Although only their political leadership can know how other countries might react to this proposal, the prospect seems remote of a threat to the currently *declared* nuclear powers serious enough to create a need for surprise or sudden first-use of nuclear weapons. In fact, their interests would seem to be much the same as those of the United States.

The *undeclared* nuclear powers or new proliferators could worry that their need to escalate to nuclear warfare could emerge suddenly, or even require surprise. They would also not want to agree to anything that implied their possession of nuclear weapons. The latter concern can be circumvented by formulating the agreement as a set of principles that all agree nuclear states must follow. Concerns with the requirement to consult a day or two in advance might lead those who chose to conform to the agreement to declare a potential first-use need on a precautionary basis.

The agreement is primarily aimed at constraining the freedom of action of states to make first-use of nuclear weapons for offensive purposes. States wanting to threaten or make such use should find their freedom of action to do so reduced.

Where Might a No-First-Use-without-Prior-Consultation Agreement Eventually Lead?

This agreement invites the evolution of a more general and rigorous international nuclear security regime over time. First, it focuses attention on the question of what means are legitimate for the self-defense of states and can be expected to lead to a narrowing of the range of situations in which the first-use of nuclear weapons could be seen as legitimate.

Second, although the power of nuclear weapons can never be concentrated in the hands of any single institution, the agreement will raise questions of how the UN Security Council can arrange for any required nuclear punishment of those who initiate the use of such weapons for clearly unjustifiable reasons. It is possible that the agreement could evolve in such a way as to cast some or all of the currently declared nuclear powers as "nuclear trustees" for the international community. The trustees could not be forced to employ their nuclear capabilities in the service of the international community, but expectations that they would do so could be reinforced.

Third, this agreement will highlight the need for a workable and more general international security system. As attested to by the apparent thinking of South Africa and Israel, states already recognize that possession of nuclear weapons can increase the will of the international community to help defend them. Still, this agreement may prompt a general strengthening of UN capabilities to provide to all

states the kind of urgent defense assistance they might have expected had they owned nuclear weapons. The international community should increasingly recognize that it cannot afford to refuse reasonable requests for assistance because to do so would strengthen the basis for proliferation.

Consultations on an International Nuclear Security Policy

This article obviously cannot hope to present answers to all the questions it raises. Indeed, we have argued that the formulation of an effective counterproliferation policy must be an international undertaking. Thus, there is little point in trying to identify and assess a full range of alternative policies by ourselves. At best, we can provide a few initial ideas for the needed international debate.

That debate could take many forms. Initially, it could take place informally within the growing flood of literature on the issue of counterproliferation. Alternatively, an international working group might be set up under the UN, or an unofficial outside organization might be created for the purpose. There are a wide range of questions that might be usefully addressed by such a group, including:

- How is continued proliferation of weapons of mass destruction likely to change the nature of the world order?
- Are there more effective institutional approaches or agreements for strengthening inhibitions against first-use or threats of first-use of nuclear weapons?
- Should the concept of justifiable defensive first-use of nuclear weapons be elaborated, and if so how, or should it be left undefined?

- Are the standard UN Security Council decision-making procedures suitable for addressing the questions raised by a consultation process of the kind envisioned here?

To these questions, one could add those that would need to be addressed in developing international concepts for providing nuclear deterrent cover for multilateral interventions against nuclear-armed challengers. This idea was developed at some length in an earlier article, which included a sampler of questions that might be considered in connection with it.[5]

We believe that these consultations should begin soon. The United States should obviously continue internal efforts to develop its conception of an effective counterproliferation policy, but it should not carry its own thinking very far without making a strong effort to involve the international community. Moreover, the international community should be involved in developing the fundamental appreciation of why its interests dictate that nuclear proliferation be halted. Unless the community participates in developing the counterproliferation policy, this policy will not get the strong international support it will need.

Summary and Conclusions

The main point of this paper is that continued nuclear proliferation is going to change the nature of the world order in ways that will force the acceptance of strong and heretofore unpalatable countermeasures. Although the United States must take the initiative in defining and supporting the implementation of effective counters to proliferation, the definition and implementation of an effective policy must be an international undertaking.

We have described one idea that might advance several immediate and derivative objectives of an international counterproliferation policy. Specifically, an agreement requiring prior consultation with the UN Security Council before any first-use of nuclear weapons could

- help to inhibit all but the most legitimate of last resort defensive first-uses of nuclear weapons;
- increase the likelihood that workable alternatives would be found in crises that threaten nuclear first-use;
- convey to the international community the acceptance by the current nuclear powers of the minimal role for their weapons that is consistent with the needs of counterproliferation; and
- serve as a good starting point for the international debate that must address the counterproliferation question.

Mechanisms of this kind, aimed at restricting first-use of nuclear weapons to the narrowest range of defensive situations in which reasonable alternatives cannot be made available, can help to reduce the attractions of owning nuclear weapons. These attractions must be reduced substantially if they are to be pushed below the costs of proliferation—a necessary condition for halting it.

Many in the United States will be skeptical about inviting an international debate on the future roles of nuclear weapons and counterproliferation policy. They may worry that U.S. sovereignty and freedom of action may be circumscribed. We see no need to compromise U.S. sovereignty in any way; U.S. freedom of action is far more likely to be seriously compromised by continued proliferation than by an international counterproliferation policy.

Others will be skeptical that the UN should be involved in any undertaking to define an international counterproliferation policy, or (even more stressful for the institution) an international nuclear security policy. We believe that these issues cannot be ducked by the international community, and that the UN is uniquely able to provide the needed legitimacy to define and implement the required policies and supporting regimes.

Finally, it is obvious that every effective approach to counterproliferation also seems to have serious drawbacks. As the problems of a highly proliferated world become more evident, however, the intolerable alternatives will appear less so. The question is whether effective controls on nuclear weapons can be developed and implemented before the next use of nuclear weapons in anger, or only after.

This paper reflects the views of the authors alone and is not necessarily endorsed by the Institute for Defense Analyses or the U.S. Department of Defense.

Notes

1. George H. Quester and Victor A. Utgoff, "U.S. Arms Reductions and Nuclear Proliferation: The Counterproductive Possibilities," *The Washington Quarterly* 16 (Winter 1993), pp. 129–140.

2. Marc Dean Millot, "Facing the Emerging Reality of Regional Nuclear Adversaries," *The Washington Quarterly* 17 (Summer 1994), pp. 41–71.

3. George H. Quester and Victor A. Utgoff, "No-First-Use and Nonproliferation: Redefining Extended Deterrence," *The Washington Quarterly* 17 (Spring 1994), pp. 103–114.

4. Brad Roberts argues the importance of reducing these gaps in Roberts, "Beyond Parochialism: Rethinking the Proliferation Agenda," in W. Thomas Wander, Eric H. Arnett, and Paul Bracken, eds., *The Diffusion of Advanced Weaponry: Technologies, Regional Implications, and Responses* (Washington, D.C.: American Association for the Advancement of Science, Program on Science and International Security, 1994), pp. 371–391.

5. Quester and Utgoff, "No-First-Use and Nonproliferation," p. 111.

Deterrence and Conventional Military Forces

Gary L. Guertner

THE SEARCH FOR a U.S. national security strategy periodically opens major policy debates that push policymakers in new, sometimes revolutionary directions. The collapse of the Soviet Union and the end of the Cold War have given rise to a national debate unmatched since the end of World War II. Dramatic changes in the international system have forced Americans to reevaluate old strategies and look for new focal points amidst the still unsettled debris of the bipolar world. At issue is the role of the United States in a new world order and its capabilities to defend and promote its national interests in a new environment where threats are both diffuse and uncertain and where conflict is inherent yet unpredictable.

The degree of uncertainty requires flexibility in U.S. military strategy and significant departures from cold war concepts of deterrence. This paper examines new options for deterrence. Its primary thesis is that new conditions in both the international and domestic environments require a dramatic shift from a nuclear dominant deterrent to one that is based on conventional forces. The paper identifies the theories and strategies of nuclear deter-

rence that can also be applied to modern conventional forces in a multipolar world.

One obstacle to analysis of that transfer is semantic. The simultaneous rise of the Cold War and the nuclear era produced a body of literature and a way of thinking in which deterrence became virtually synonymous with nuclear weapons. In fact, deterrence has always been pursued through a mix of nuclear and conventional forces. The force mix changed throughout the Cold War in response to new technology, anticipated threats, and fiscal constraints. There have been, for example, well-known cycles in both U.S. and Soviet strategies when their respective strategic concepts evolved from nuclear-dominant deterrence (the "massive retaliation" of Dwight D. Eisenhower and its short-lived counterpart under Nikita Khrushchev), to the more balanced deterrent (John F. Kennedy to Ronald Reagan) of flexible response, which linked conventional forces to a wide array of nuclear capabilities in a "seamless web" of deterrence that was "extended" to U.S. allies in the North Atlantic Treaty Organization (NATO).

Early proponents of nuclear weapons tended to view nuclear deterrence as a self-contained strategy, capable of deterring threats across a wide spectrum of threat. By contrast, the proponents of conventional forces have always argued that there are thresholds

Gary L. Guertner is director of research at the Strategic Studies Institute, U.S. Army War College. His latest book is *Deterrence and Defense in a Post-Nuclear World* (New York: St. Martin's Press, 1990).

Gary L. Guertner

below which conventional forces pose a more credible deterrent. Moreover, there will always be nondeterrable threats to U.S. interests that will require a response, and that response, if military, must be commensurate with the levels of provocation. A threat to use nuclear weapons against a third world country, for instance, would put political objectives at risk because of worldwide reactions and the threat of escalation beyond the theater of operations.

The end of the Cold War has dramatically altered the "seamless web" of deterrence and has decoupled nuclear and conventional forces. Nuclear weapons have a declining political-military utility below the threshold of deterring a direct nuclear attack against the territory of the United States. As a result, the post–cold war period is one in which stability and the deterrence of war are likely to be measured by the capabilities of conventional forces. Ironically, the downsizing of U.S. and allied forces is occurring simultaneously with shifts in the calculus of deterrence that call for conventional domination of the force mix.

Downsizing is being driven by legitimate domestic and economic issues, but it also needs strategic guidance and rationale. The political dynamics of defense cuts, whether motivated by the desire to disengage from foreign policy commitments or by the economic instinct to save the programs in the defense budget richest in jobs, threaten the development of a coherent post–cold war military strategy. This paper identifies strategic options for a credible deterrence against new threats to U.S. interests. Most can be executed by conventional forces, and present conditions make a coherent strategy of general, extended conventional deterrence feasible.

Critics of conventional deterrence argue that history has demonstrated its impotence. By contrast, nuclear deterrence of the Soviet threat arguably bought 45 years of peace in Europe. The response to this standard critique is threefold. First, conditions now exist (and were demonstrated in the Persian Gulf War) in which the technological advantages of U.S. conventional weapons and doctrine are so superior to the capabilities of all conceivable adversaries that their deterrence value against direct threats to U.S. interests is higher than at any period in American history.

Second, technological superiority and operational doctrine allow many capabilities previously monopolized by nuclear strategy to be readily transferred to conventional forces. For example, conventional forces now have a combination of range, accuracy, survivability, and lethality that allows them to execute strategic attacks, simultaneously or sequentially, across a wide spectrum of targets that include counterforce, command and control (including leadership), and economic elements.

Third, critics of conventional deterrence have traditionally set impossible standards for success. Over time, any form of deterrence may fail. The United States will always confront some form of nondeterrable threat. Moreover, deterrence is a perishable commodity. It wears out and must periodically be revived. Failures of deterrence provide the opportunity to demonstrate the price of aggression, rejuvenate the credibility of deterrence (collective or unilateral), and establish a new period of stability. In other words, conventional deterrence can produce long cycles of stability instead of the perennial or overlapping intervals of conflict that would be far more likely in the absence of a carefully constructed U.S. (and allied) conventional force capability.

How the United States responds to deterrence failures will determine both its credibility and the scope of international stability. Figure 1 summarizes reasonable standards for judging conventional deterrence.

Long periods of stability may or may not be attributable to the success of deterrence. In any case, no deterrence system or force mix can guarantee an "end to history." Paradoxically, stability is dynamic in the sense that forces are constantly at work to undermine the status quo. Those forces, also summarized in figure 1, mean that deterrence failures are, over time, inevitable. Readers may have difficulty associating the events in column 1 of the figure with periods of "stability." Regrettably, such is the nature of international politics.

The United States should, therefore, base its military strategy on weapons that can be used without fear of self-deterrence or of breaking up

coalition forces that provide political legitimacy and military capability. If the United States is serious about deterring regional threats on a global scale, this strategic logic will push it into a post–cold war deterrence regime dominated by conventional forces.

A Deterrent Based on Conventional Forces

Conventional deterrence has a future, but one very different from its past, in which it was subordinated to nuclear threats and strategic nuclear theory. The United States now faces a multipolar international political system that may be destabilized by a proliferation of armed conflict and advanced weaponry. To secure stability, security, and influence in this new world order, the United States can use the military prowess it demonstrated in the Persian Gulf War to good advantage. Using that force effectively, however, or threatening to use it, requires the formulation of a coherent

Figure 1
Conventional Deterrence and International Stability

Period of Stability →	Deterrence Failure →	Stability Restored	OR Instability Spreads
• Military technology advances	• Crisis or war	• Aggression is countered	• Aggression succeeds
• Weapons proliferate	– Collective security	• Conventional forces and doctrine demonstrate capabilities	• Deterrence fails
• Political and economic conflicts flare	– Collective defense	• Conventional deterrence revitalized	• Utility of aggression demonstrated
• Incentives for war increase	– Unilateral action	• New period of stability begins	• Period of instability extended in scope and duration
• Risk of miscalculation increases		• U.S. interests protected	• U.S. interests at risk
• Deterrence fails			

strategy of "general extended conventional deterrence" and the prudent planning of general purpose forces that are credible and capable of underwriting a new military strategy.

Neither proponents nor critics should judge this analysis in isolation. Conventional deterrence cannot succeed unless it is reinforced by supporting policies and concepts. The strategic concepts in the current National Military Strategy document that appear to have the greatest synergistic value in support of conventional deterrence are:

- technological superiority;
- collective security;
- forward presence;
- strategic agility; and
- theater defenses.[1]

Technological Superiority. Expected reductions in the overall force structure will make the force-multiplying effects of technological superiority more important than ever. Space-based sensors, defense-suppression systems, "brilliant weapons," and stealth technologies give true meaning to the concept of force multipliers. This broad mix of technologies can make conventional forces decisive provided they are planned and integrated into an effective doctrine and concept of operations.

The conflicts most likely to involve the United States will be confrontations with less capable states that have trouble employing their forces and their technology in effective combined arms operations. As Anthony Cordesman has concluded in his assessment of the Persian Gulf War,

the U.S. can cut its force structure and still maintain a decisive

military edge over most threats in the Third World. It can exploit the heritage of four decades of arming to fight a far more sophisticated and combat ready enemy so that it can fight under conditions where it is outnumbered or suffers from significant operational disadvantages.[2]

Exploiting technology to get economies of force will require investments where the payoff in battlefield lethality is greatest. Given the threats that U.S. forces are most likely to confront in regional contingencies, these technologies will include:

- battle management resources for real-time integration of sensors-command-control and weapon systems that make enemy forces transparent and easily targeted;
- mobility of conventional forces to fully exploit technological superiority and battlefield transparency;
- smart conventional weapons with range and lethality; and
- component upgrades for existing delivery platforms to avoid costly generational replacements. This means limited procurement of new tactical fighters, tanks, bombers, submarines, or other platforms that were originally conceived to counter a modernized Soviet threat.

Technology that leads to unaffordable procurement threatens the U.S. military with force multipliers of less than 1.0. Net decreases in combat-capable forces can best be avoided through combinations of selective upgrading and selective low-rate procurement.

Technological superiority will also depend on concurrent political strategies. Technology is a double-edged sword; it can act as a force multiplier, but the laws of science apply equally to potential U.S. adversaries. Multilateral support for the nonproliferation of both nuclear and critical conventional military technologies can be an equally effective means for preempting threats to U.S. interests and for underwriting conventional deterrence.

Collective Security. Collective security has become explicitly incorporated in the National Military Strategy. It is broadly defined to include both collective security (activities sanctioned by the United Nations [UN]) and collective defense arrangements (formal alliances such as NATO). These are linked informally in what could, if promoted by the United States, form transregional security linkages—a "seamless web" of collective action.[3]

The potential value of collective security to conventional deterrence is difficult to quantify because it requires the United States to link its security to the capabilities and political will of others. Its potential must always be balanced against the risk that collective action may require significant limitations on unilateral action. Nevertheless, there are three compelling reasons for the United States to embrace collective security.

- Allies or coalition partners are essential for basing or staging the range of capabilities required to fully exploit technologically superior forces against a regional hegemon.
- The American public shows little enthusiasm for an active role as the single, global superpower. Collective deterrence is politically essential for sharing not only the military burden, but also the increasingly salient political and fiscal responsibilities.
- Patterns of collective action, as demonstrated in the Persian Gulf War, give conventional deterrence

credibility and capabilities that the United States can no longer afford or achieve on its own. Even though collective action and shared capabilities may limit U.S. freedom of action, these limits are reassuring to others and may contribute more to stability than attempts by the world's only superpower to unilaterally impose deterrence—nuclear or conventional.

Forward Presence. The post–cold war shift in U.S. military strategy from large-scale forward deployments of military forces to limited or intermittent forward presence is linked to the credibility of both conventional deterrence and collective security.[4]

U.S. forces abroad will continue to be viewed as the most visible symbols of U.S. resolve and commitment to regional stability. They are vital components of both short- and long-range stability because they

- demonstrate U.S. leadership, commitment, and capabilities for collective security, collective defense, and peacekeeping operations;
- contribute to the preservation of regional power balances and provide disincentives for the nationalization of regional defense policies and of arms competitions; and
- contribute to the containment of security obstacles that, absent a U.S. presence, could disrupt regional economic integration and political union, both vital components of long-term regional stability.

The forward presence of U.S. military forces as part of collective security or collective defense regimes has a deterrent value in excess of its immediate military capabilities, provided that these symbols of U.S. commitment are backed by the strategic agility to bring credible military force to bear at decisive points and at decisive times in a crisis.

Strategic Agility. Strategic agility is a generic concept that reflects the dramatic changes in cold war forward deployment patterns that fixed U.S. forces on the most threatened frontiers in Germany and Korea. Old planning assumptions have given way to new requirements to meet diffuse regional contingencies. Simply stated, U.S. forces will be assembled by their rapid movement from wherever they are to wherever they are needed. Strategic agility requires mobile forces and adaptive planning for a diverse range of options. Many of these options signal U.S. commitment and demonstrate military capabilities short of war. Joint exercises, UN peacekeeping missions, and even humanitarian/disaster relief operations provide opportunities to display power projection capabilities and global reach despite reduced forward deployment of forces.

Theater Ballistic Missile Defenses. Nuclear and chemical weapons proliferation make theater air and antitactical ballistic missile defenses important components of conventional deterrence. The next states that are likely to acquire nuclear arms are under radical regimes that are openly hostile to U.S. interests (North Korea, Libya, Iran, and Iraq, if UN intervention fails).[5] The success of such regional powers in creating even a small nuclear umbrella under which they could commit aggression would represent a serious challenge to U.S. global strategy.

Theater defenses in support of conventional deterrence need not be a part of the grander objectives of the Strategic Defense Initiative or its most recent variant, Global Protection Against Limited Strikes (GPALS). The layered, space-based weapons architecture of these costly systems seems, at best, technologically remote and, at worst, a vestige of the Cold War.[6] What is needed in the near term is a global, space-based early warning, command and control network that is linked to modernized, mobile, land-based theater defense systems (Patriot follow-on or Theater High-Altitude Area Defense [THAAD] interceptors designed for greater defense of countervalue targets such as cities).

Theater Strategic Targeting with Conventional Forces

Uncertainties about nondeterrable nuclear threats make it all the more imperative that the United States also have credible warfighting options. Nuclear preemption prior to an attack is not plausible, and there are uncertainties as to whether any president or his coalition partners would authorize a response in kind, even if the enemy used nuclear weapons first. More plausible are the range of conventional options afforded by modern, high-tech weapons that have a theater strategic capability for both denial and punishment missions. The broad outline of a conventional deterrence strategy would include:

- conventional preemption of the nuclear/chemical infrastructure and key command and control nodes to deny or disrupt an attack (deterrence by denial);
- threats of conventional escalation to countervalue targets (economic) if nuclear weapons are used (deterrence by punishment);
- threats to seize enemy territory (deterrence by punishment);

- countervalue retaliation by conventional forces if deterrence and preemption fail (deterrence by punishment); and
- theater antitactical missile and air defenses (deterrence by denial).

The air war against Iraq demonstrated the limitations of counterforce targeting against missiles and nuclear/chemical infrastructures. Nevertheless, the impact of the coalition's technological superiority was felt throughout Iraq, particularly at the nerve center and heart of the Iraqi government and its war-making capability. The success of the stealth systems and precision bombing capabilities projected some of the same physical and psychological aspects as weapons of mass destruction without the liabilities of this type of weapon. Operations that could target Saddam Hussein and his war-making potential without causing widespread, indiscriminate destruction of the Iraqi people provided a counter to Saddam's attempts at influencing world opinion. Such precision prevented Saddam from successfully painting the coalition's actions as war on the Iraqi people.[7]

The imperfect capability of deterrence by denial (even with nuclear weapons) and the unknowable responses to threats of retaliation and punishment leave theater antitactical ballistic missile defenses as the last line of defense for U.S. and coalition forces. On balance, conventional deterrence that combines attempts to dissuade, capabilities to neutralize or capture, credible threats to retaliate, and the ability to defend is more credible against regional powers than nuclear threats. Together, these capabilities dramatically reduce the coercive potential of third world nuclear programs. This does not mean, however,

that nuclear forces have no role to play in the future of deterrence.

The Role of Nuclear Weapons in a Deterrent Dominated by Conventional Forces

The National Military Strategy 1992 states that the purpose of nuclear forces is "to deter the use of weapons of mass destruction and to serve as a hedge against the emergence of an overwhelming conventional threat."[8]

The dilemma confronting the United States is still the same classic problem that confronted strategists throughout the Cold War. Nuclear weapons fulfill their declared deterrence function only if they are never used. Yet, if everyone knows that they will never be used, they lack the credibility to deter. The most credible means to resolve this dilemma is through a combination of declaratory policies and military capability that emphasizes the warfighting capabilities of conventional forces with strategic reach.[9]

There is, however, a potential paradox of success if aggressive third world leaders believe that only weapons of mass destruction can offset U.S. advantages in conventional military power. Under such circumstances, theater nuclear weapons can have important signaling functions that communicate new risks and introduce greater costs for nuclear aggression that inflicts high casualties on U.S. forces or on allied countervalue targets.

Nuclear signaling can take the form of declarations by the president or the Department of Defense (DOD) that U.S. ships deploying to a hostile theater of operations have been refitted with nuclear weapons carried by dual-capable aircraft (DCA) and Tomahawk

Land Attack Missiles (TLAM).[10] Deployment options alone can play a critical role in the strategic calculus of aggressors who possess uncommitted nuclear capabilities.

The role of strategic nuclear forces is also directly related to the problems of reorienting the National Military Strategy from a global to a regional focus. The first problem is determining the force structure after the combined reductions of the Strategic Arms Reduction Treaty (START), unilateral initiatives, and the Bush–Yeltsin summit. The combined results will be dramatic cuts in U.S. strategic forces from some 12,000 warheads to 3,500 or less.[11] These cuts are prudent responses to the collapse of the Soviet Union and give the United States and its allies a long-sought opportunity to pull back from the nuclear brink where they so often found themselves during the Cold War. Moreover, these reductions are consistent with obligations under the Nuclear Non-Proliferation Treaty (NPT). They should be accompanied by strong U.S. endorsements of the treaty and support for the strengthening of the nonproliferation regime as a critical NPT review conference approaches in 1995.

The credibility of U.S. support for nonproliferation will also be affected by the declaratory policies and targeting strategy for a smaller strategic nuclear force structure. The most comprehensive review of the problem to date suggests that the United States could be moving in the right direction provided that the strategic role of conventional forces dominates future planning. A report by the Joint Strategic Target Planning Staff Advisory Group, chaired by former Secretary of the Air Force Thomas C. Reed, recommends major changes in the Single Integrated Operational Plan (SIOP).

The cold war SIOP contained carefully calibrated strike options against the former Soviet Union. In its place, the panel recommends an Integrated Strike Employment Plan (ISEP) with a "near real time" flexibility to cover a wider range of targets with a smaller force structure. The proposal identifies five categories of plans:

- *Plan Alpha* is a conventional force option against selected strategic targets of "every reasonable adversary."
- *Plan Echo* is a nuclear option for theater contingencies or "Nuclear Expeditionary Forces."
- *Plan Lima* is a set of limited SIOP-like nuclear options against Russian force projection assets.
- *Plan Mike* is a more robust version of *Plan Lima* with graduated attack options in the 10s, 100s, and 1,000s.
- *Plan Romeo* is a strategic nuclear reserve force (SRF) to deter escalation, support war termination, and preclude other nuclear powers not directly involved in an ongoing crisis from coercing the United States.[12]

In their current form, these recommendations are excessive and favor a nuclear force structure that is not well suited for credible deterrence in the new world order. If they were misinterpreted as official policy, the United States could be accused of a double standard in proclaiming the value of nuclear weapons at the same time that it was asking others to forswear them.

In the case of the former Soviet Union, U.S. targeting policy should be muted. Prudence dictates that advantage be taken of every opportunity for mutual reductions of force levels and confidence-building measures such as lower alert rates, improved command and control structures, and cooperative steps to improve the safety of nuclear storage, transportation, and destruction procedures.[13]

Russia will remain a nuclear power with a potential to threaten the United States and its allies. On the other hand, it is no longer the center of a hostile global movement or the leader of a powerful military alliance threatening Europe with overwhelming force deep in its own territory. Russian behavior is shaped more by its need for Western aid and technology than by U.S. military capabilities. It is difficult to conceive credible scenarios in which even the most reactionary Great Russian nationalist could find in nuclear weapons the tools that could be used against the West in preplanned ways to coerce concessions or that might tempt revisionist leaders to adopt reckless and inflexible positions. The United States will and should, along with its British and French allies, retain nuclear options, but it is premature in the extreme to plan robust nuclear attacks against the "force projection assets" of a state that is struggling for democracy and economic reforms.[14]

Even though the United States may be a benevolent superpower, the political impact of global nuclear targeting is more likely to stimulate rather than deter nuclear proliferation. An alternative set of declaratory policies that are consistent with nonproliferation includes commitments to deep cuts in nuclear forces coupled with a *defensive* strategy of direct retaliation against nuclear attacks on U.S. territory. Direct retaliation is one of the few credible missions for strategic nuclear forces in the post–cold war world. Extending deterrence should be a function of conventional forces (the option embodied in Plan Alpha above).

Global retargeting of nuclear forces is an unfortunate concept that is more likely to put U.S. interests at risk in the long run. Marshal Yevgenii I. Shaposhnikov, commander in chief of the Russian Armed Forces, struck a more positive image in his correct observation that retargeting frightens people. It is better, he said, to discuss "nontargeting," which lowers the level of alert to "zero flight assignments of missiles."[15]

The marshal's formulations are too vague to serve as the basis of national policy. Nevertheless, his point should not be dismissed. The objectives of national military strategy are more likely to be achieved through the *implicit* flexibility to respond to nuclear aggression from any source rather than *explicit* declarations of global nuclear targeting. Many regional crises may be precipitated by the proliferation of nuclear weapons and ballistic missiles. U.S. strategy will, therefore, require a delicate balance lest it give incentives to that very threat. A reassuring posture, in the eyes of regional actors and global partners, will require reexamination and "denuclearization" of deterrence in a new multipolar world.

Finally, and above all, this paper's primary purpose has been to recommend the option of using modern conventional forces for strategic purposes. A reliance on offensive nuclear weapons carries enormous risks that have already brought the United States and its allies to the brink of war during several cold war crises. The American public has every right to expect that the Cold War's principal legacy of danger not be deliberately extended into the new world order.

A conventional dominant deterrent will require full emancipation from cold war thinking. As Fred Iklé has wisely noted, strategic thought "remains locked into place . . . by dated nuclear arsenals," and these forces remain tied to imaginative scenarios that "persist, like a genetic defect."[16]

Freeing U.S. military strategy from its nuclear past will require deeper cuts in the existing strategic nuclear force structure and in strategic defense spending. The Bush–Yeltsin summit was a dramatic step, but one that when fully implemented will leave the United States with nearly as many strategic nuclear warheads as it deployed in 1970, the period when serious efforts were just beginning for negotiated limits on Soviet and U.S. nuclear forces.[17]

Deeper cuts will be required to win congressional support for a conventional force structure that is capable of meeting the regional contingencies in the new national military strategy. Failure to clearly address how and why the U.S. force structure must change will result in an impotent mix of nuclear and conventional forces that will neither deter nor be capable of meeting threats to U.S. interests.

The views expressed in this article are those of the author and do not necessarily reflect the official policy or position of the Department of the Army, the Department of Defense, or the U.S. government.

Notes

1. These strategic concepts are drawn from *The National Military Strategy 1992*, released by the chairman of the Joint Chiefs of Staff in January 1992. Some have been narrowed in scope for ease of analysis. For example, the NMS lists strategic deterrence and defense as one of the four foundations on which U.S. strategy is built. This paper narrows this strategic concept to conventional deterrence and theater defense.

2. Anthony H. Cordesman, "Compensating For Smaller Forces: Adjusting Ways and Means Through Technology" (Paper presented at the Third Annual Strategy Conference, U.S. Army War College, Strategic

Studies Institute, Carlisle Barracks, Pa., February 14, 1992), p. 2.

3. For a detailed assessment of collective security and U.S. strategy, see Inis Claude, Jr., Sheldon Simon, and Douglas Stuart, *Collective Security in Asia and Europe* (Carlisle Barracks, Pa.: U.S. Army War College, Strategic Studies Institute, March 2, 1992). Ironically, the administration's pledge to support growing UN peacekeeping activities is under attack by members of Congress because of a long-standing agreement that makes the United States responsible for 30 percent of the cost of every operation. Japan and the West Europeans could conceivably relieve part of the perceived inequity, but Congress should also examine these costs in the larger context of collective security and global stability. See Don Oberdorfer, "Lawmakers Balk at Peacekeeping's Cost," *Washington Post*, March 4, 1992, p. A–17.

4. *The National Military Strategy* describes forward presence operations to include forward stationed troops, forces afloat, periodic rotational deployments, access and storage agreements, military exercises, security and humanitarian assistance, port visits, and military-to-military contacts.

5. Leonard S. Spector, "Deterring Regional Threats from Nuclear Proliferation" (Paper presented at the Third Annual Strategy Conference, U.S. Army War College, Strategic Studies Institute, Carlisle Barracks, Pa., February 14, 1992), p. 31 and appendix A.

6. In his testimony before the House Armed Services Committee on December 10, 1991, CIA director Robert Gates stated that only missiles from Russia and the People's Republic of China (PRC) could threaten the territory of the United States. He did not expect direct risks from other countries for at least another decade. See *Statement of the Director of Central Intelligence*, pp. 16–17.

7. Colonel Douglas Craft, *An Operational Analysis of the Persian Gulf War* (Carlisle Barracks, Pa.: U.S. Army War College, Strategic Studies Institute, August 1992).

8. *The National Military Strategy 1992*, p. 13.

9. A major thesis of this paper is that conventional deterrence must occasionally give way to conflicts that demonstrate capabil-

ities, thereby strengthening deterrence for a new phase of stability. The bombing of Hiroshima and Nagasaki had much the same effect on nuclear deterrence.

10. President George Bush's unilateral initiatives in September 1991 eliminated ground-launched tactical nuclear weapons and withdrew them from surface ships and submarines. Some sea-based weapons are scheduled for destruction. Others are in storage whence they can be redeployed for the "signaling" purposes advocated here.

11. President Bush's January 1992 initiative pledged cuts in strategic nuclear warheads up to 50 percent below START-permitted ceilings of approximately 8,000 warheads. At the Bush–Yeltsin summit on June 17, 1992, dramatic breakthroughs were announced that included the agreement to reduce strategic nuclear warheads to a range of 3,000 to 3,500 by 2003, the lowest levels since 1969. The flexible ceiling reflects agreement to deploy asymmetrical force levels. More important, the Russians agreed to destroy all their land-based intercontinental ballistic missiles (ICBMs) with multiple independently targeted reentry capacity (MIRV), the core of their strategic force structure, and the most long-standing goal in U.S. arms negotiating strategy. The United States also agreed to reduce its deployed submarine-launched ballistic missiles (SLBM) forces by 50 percent. See R. Jeffrey Smith, "Arms Talks Devoid of Usual Anxieties," *Washington Post*, June 18, 1992, p. A–38, and Thomas L. Friedman, "Reducing the Russian Arms Threat," *New York Times*, June 17, 1992, p. A–11.

12. Thomas C. Reed and Michael O. Wheeler, "The Role of Nuclear Weapons in the New World Order," JSTPS/SAG Deterrence Study Group, Department of Defense, Washington, D.C., October 19, 1991, pp. 33–34. See also R. Jeffrey Smith, "U.S. Urged to Cut 50% of A-Arms," *Washington Post*, January 6, 1992, p. A–1.

13. These latter steps are well under way. Congress allocated $400 million to assist Russian efforts to transport, store, and destroy nuclear weapons, and on March 26, 1992, the State Department announced the appointment of Retired Maj. Gen. William F. Burns, former director of the U.S. Arms Control and Disarmament Agency, to head the U.S. delegation on Safety, Security, and Dismantlement of Nuclear Weapons (SSD Talks). Moscow has agreed to U.S. assistance in the production of containers for fissile material from dismantled nuclear weapons, conversion of rail cars for secure transport, construction of storage facilities, training in nuclear accident response, accounting procedures, and ultimate disposition of enriched uranium and plutonium. See Department of State Press Release, March 26, 1992.

14. Open discussions of nuclear targeting in the press were followed by equally controversial reporting of threat scenarios that were developed in the Office of the Chairman of the Joint Chiefs of Staff. These scenarios included a hypothetical NATO counterattack if Russia invaded Lithuania. There is virtually no support in NATO or in the U.S. Congress for such a course of action. The scenario does, however, raise the question of what the United States should do in the event of a Russian-initiated civil war to reunite the former Soviet Union. Russian nationalists could indeed threaten nuclear retaliation against Western intervention. History suggests, however, that Western response would be political and economic, but not military, thus making nuclear threats irrelevant. "Threat" scenarios are discussed by Barton Gellman, "Pentagon War Scenario Spotlights Russia," *Washington Post*, February 20, 1992, p. A–1.

15. Marshal Yevgenii I. Shaposhnikov, interview in *Red Star*, February 22, 1992, pp. 1–3. Quoted in Foreign Broadcast Information Service, *Central Eurasia*, February 24, 1992 (FBIS-SOV-92-036), p. 8.

16. Quoted in Michael J. Mazarr, "Nuclear Weapons After the Cold War," *The Washington Quarterly* 15 (Summer 1992), p. 198.

17. As noted in note 11, the Bush–Yeltsin summit agreement would reduce U.S. strategic nuclear warheads to 3,000–3,500 by 2003. In 1970, a period when the Soviets achieved strategic nuclear parity with the United States, U.S. strategic nuclear warheads numbered 3,780. Data compiled from *The Military Balance*, 1969–1972 editions (London: International Institute for Strategic Studies). Ironically, the Strategic Arms Limitation Talks (SALT I) initiated by President Richard M. Nixon in 1969 resulted, over time, in a fourfold increase in U.S. strategic nuclear warheads.

Not by Diplomacy or Defense Alone: The Role of Regional Security Strategies in U.S. Proliferation Policy

Paul R. S. Gebhard

IRAQI MISSILE ATTACKS during the Persian Gulf War on U.S. and coalition forces and the discovery of the advanced state of Iraqi nuclear, biological, and chemical warfare programs after the war, revealed the threats that the United States will likely face from hostile states in the future. To meet this challenge, the Department of Defense (DOD) has begun work to improve the capabilities of its forces to operate against aggressors armed with nuclear, biological, and chemical weapons and missiles (NBC/M). President Bill Clinton provided clear gui-

Paul R. S. Gebhard is director for Policy Planning and Regional Strategies in the Office of Counterproliferation Policy, Office of the Secretary of Defense. In previous assignments in the OSD, he worked on the NATO Strategic Concept and was part of the negotiating team for the CFE Treaty. A recent publication is "The United States and European Security," *Adelphi Paper* 286 (London: IISS, 1994).

Copyright © 1994 by The Center for Strategic and International Studies and the Massachusetts Institute of Technology
The Washington Quarterly • 18:1 pp.

dance to this effect when, in the public summary of his September 1993 directive on nonproliferation and export control policy, he stated:

> We will give proliferation a higher profile in . . . defense planning, and ensure that our own forces structure and military planning address the potential threat from weapons of mass destruction and missiles from around the world.[1]

These vitally important efforts by the DOD are, like the Nuclear Non-Proliferation Treaty (NPT), proliferation-specific responses to the threat posed by NBC/M. This article argues that the threat from hostile states with NBC/M capabilities is a larger issue for U.S. foreign and defense policy because of the implications for U.S. vital interests in the regions involved and for the U.S. ability to protect its interests. Because of this broader impact, the article argues that the United States needs to approach proliferation through its regional security strategies. The proliferation-specific efforts to date by Defense, State, and other agencies need to be integrated into regional security strategies and made part of a wider range of possible responses to meet the threat to regional stability and security posed by states with NBC/M capabilities. This presents a difficult challenge, especially for the DOD, which is charged with defending the United States and its security interests around the world.

Effective regional security strategies implicitly support efforts against proliferation. For example, during the Cold War the U.S. policy of extended deterrence to protect U.S. allies and interests—in Europe and Northeast Asia in particular—strongly supported its strategy to prevent the spread of nuclear weapons in these regions. More broadly, U.S. regional security strategies, if successful, make possible progress on important national and international goals such as stable economic development and political liberalization that themselves contribute to preventing proliferation and are necessary for the security of the United States and its allies over the long term. Although this article focuses on the role of regional security strategies in the proliferation problem, these larger linkages should be kept in mind.

Since the end of the Cold War, the likelihood that certain hostile states will be able to acquire NBC/M capabilities has increased due to a number of factors discussed below, such as greater availability of technical expertise and illicit supplies of previously controlled key technologies and materials. With these new capabilities, hostile states will be able to pose a stronger challenge to the security of their region and to the ability of the United States to carry out its regional security strategies, whether in Northeast Asia, the Persian Gulf/Middle East, or Europe. To meet this new

challenge, the key questions are: How can the United States supplement its regional security strategies to mold a security environment where states choose not to proliferate; ensure that the introduction of NBC/M does not impair the ability of the United States to protect its interests; and provide credible reassurances to allies so that they do not seek their security in arrangements with hostile states or by developing their own NBC/M capability?

Answers to these questions require an analysis of the impact of proliferation on the three defense elements at the heart of U.S. security strategies in regions where the United States has a vital interest and defense commitments.

- U.S.–allied regional security structure—multilateral, bilateral, or nascent;
- U.S. commitment of forces—to include issues of force size, composition, type of forward presence, exercises, and operational plans; and
- the ability of local and extra-regional allies to work with U.S. forces in joint operations—including inter alia issues of allied capabilities and joint U.S.–allied interoperability.

These three elements are different for Northeast Asia, the Persian Gulf/Middle East, and Europe, reflecting each region's distinct history and political topology. The three elements may not apply in regions, such as South Asia, where the United States has few direct security interests. The U.S. regional strategy there is focused almost exclusively on capping and rolling back Indian and Pakistani nuclear and missile capabilities.[2] Yet, in all cases where the United States has concrete vital interests, an increase in the possibility that certain states of concern may acquire—or are acquiring—NBC/M weapons will force the United States and its allies to respond by evaluating each of these three elements and determining how best to reestablish a sense of security and stability in the region.

The president's charge to respond to the threat posed by the proliferation of weapons of mass destruction (WMD) will require the United States to strengthen its ability to prevent states from acquiring NBC/M capabilities; assist in efforts to roll back NBC/M capabilities; and deter—and, if necessary, effectively defend against—attacks on U.S. forces, allies, and friends by aggressors possessing NBC/M capabilities. All of these goals must be accomplished in a manner that is not viewed in itself as threatening by U.S. allies and friends and that reassures them of the strength of U.S. security commitments. These are challenging, long-term goals, not all of which the DOD can accomplish alone. The security and arms-control bureaucracies of the federal government are already working on several approaches to meet the security challenges posed by proliferation.

The Department of State and the Arms Control and Disarmament Agency (ACDA) have devoted their attention to preventing and rolling back proliferation, including (inter alia) extension of the NPT in 1995 and other negotiated multilateral and bilateral approaches. U.S. initiatives include a proposed ban on fissile material production and stockpiling for nuclear explosive purposes or outside of international safeguards; reauthorizing the Export Administration Act in a revised form focusing on NBC/M proliferation; ratifying the Chemical Weapons Convention (CWC); and

seeking new transparency measures to improve the Biological and Toxin Weapons Convention (BWC). These initiatives are in addition to developing and implementing bilateral export control agreements and tracking dual-use exports. Multilateral regimes often have the legitimacy to set norms and standards globally, which is vitally important to discouraging the spread of NBC/M capabilities from region to region, and to act as a basis for policies against states that acquire these weapons in spite of the norms.

The DOD is pursuing two approaches to the security challenges of proliferation and has set clear priorities. According to the *Report on Nonproliferation and Counterproliferation Activities and Programs* by an interagency group chaired by Deputy Secretary of Defense John M. Deutch,

> The Department of Defense contributes to the full range of U.S. efforts to combat proliferation including diplomacy, arms control, export control, and intelligence collection and analysis, but places particular emphasis on assuring that U.S. forces and interests are protected should the United States confront an adversary armed with WMD.[3]

On the one hand, the DOD supports the negotiations and operation of multilateral restraint and inspection regimes and export control programs, where the Department of State and ACDA lead. On the other hand, the DOD is also seeking to ensure that U.S. forces are prepared to defend against NBC/M threats to U.S. interests. Toward this end, the DOD is undertaking a broad range of actions, beginning with a review by the Joint Staff of issues of operations against states with NBC/M capabilities in a missions and functions study. As part of the process of identifying shortfalls in need of correction, the interagency committee's report recommended additional funding for a series of priority objectives, including (inter alia) defeating hard underground targets where NBC/M facilities might be housed; improving capabilities to detect, locate, and disarm NBC/M weapons hidden outside the continental United States and chemical and biological weapons hidden by terrorists within the United States; producing vaccines more rapidly; improving detection and interception of cruise missiles; intercepting missiles in the boost phase; destroying mobile targets promptly; improving real time detection and characterization of biological and chemical agents; and detection and characterization of underground structures.

The key to using these improved military capabilities effectively is to incorporate them into U.S. regional security strategies whose goal is to protect the security of U.S. interests in a region, rather than narrowly to prevent, roll back, or defeat a proliferator's NBC/M capabilities.[4] U.S. regional security strategies should provide the defining context for U.S. policies on proliferation. They should incorporate the global themes of multilateral approaches to proliferation and improved U.S. military capabilities for NBC/M conflicts to ensure that both sets of tools can be applied as appropriate to specific U.S. policy goals in each region.

The magnitude of the undertaking, combined with the current budgetary resource limitations, requires the DOD in its regional security planning to address first those regions in which the spread of NBC/M weapons directly threatens vital U.S. interests, allies, and friends—Northeast Asia, the Persian Gulf/Middle East, and Europe.

How States with NBC/M Capabilities Threaten U.S. Interests

It is reasonable to ask why NBC/M weapons in the possession of regional powers pose a problem requiring new emphasis. Only a few years ago, during the Cold War, the United States and its European allies faced and deterred the huge arsenal of the Soviet Union. The new emphasis is required because particular states are trying to acquire NBC/M capabilities; the likelihood has increased that they will be successful in their pursuit of these weapons; and there is a new appreciation after the Persian Gulf War of the consequences of successful acquisition of NBC/M capabilities for regional security and of the impact of acquisition by potentially hostile states on future U.S. political and military options.

Many states anxious to acquire NBC/M capabilities—North Korea, Iran, Iraq, and Libya—are basically hostile to the United States and its interests, allies, and friends. Syria also, despite recent moderation, should be considered for this list. These states are led by undemocratic, unpredictable leaders whose motivations are largely opaque to outside observation and understanding. By comparison, the Soviet Union after Stalin, although it was an undemocratic, hostile state, was also in some senses conservative and stable, and provided a certain forced restraint against some regional conflicts, for example, in southeastern Europe. The collapse of the Soviet Union has largely removed this restraint.

These hostile states have possibilities for acquiring NBC/M capabilities that did not exist earlier. As Iraq's well-advanced NBC/M program illustrated, most of these states are developing an increasingly sophisticated technical infrastructure and the necessary personnel to support indigenous development of weapons with minimal outside assistance. The emergence of new suppliers of technology and materials, and especially the breakup of the Soviet Union, has made control over NBC/M-related technologies, know-how, matériel, and the weapons themselves extremely difficult, and thereby increased the possible sources of supply to interested states. The states of the former Soviet Union are working to establish effective export controls to stop illicit transfers but it is a huge task. This added availability of key technologies has come on top of the tide of broadly applicable technology—such as increasingly powerful computers—that is rising around the world.

Upsetting a region's security structure with the hope of improving its relative standing may be one of the prime motivators for states seeking NBC/M capabilities. With NBC/M weapons, these states can greatly increase the magnitude of their threats to others and expand war zones to include attacks on states or rear areas that were previously considered safe. Moreover, NBC/M weapons are also known collectively as "weapons of mass destruction," and as such are a great unknown that many states have not had to consider before. In Northeast Asia, North Korean NBC/M capabilities could upset a dangerous but stable pattern of security. In the Persian Gulf/Middle East, Iran or other states could seriously destabilize the fluid but relatively stable allocation of power among the larger states. In Europe, the threat from NBC/M capa-

bilities from outside the continent may complicate the formation of a new post–cold war pattern of transatlantic security. Compounding this problem is the possibility that in the near future NBC/M capabilities could be purchased from states like North Korea or smuggled out of the former Soviet Union and deployed anywhere virtually overnight. To illustrate these points, a brief discussion of the impact of NBC/M capabilities on the ability of the United States to defend its vital interests in each of the three key regions follows.

Northeast Asia

North Korea's programs to develop nuclear weapons and longer-range missiles, in addition to its chemical and likely biological weapons capabilities, allow Kim Jong Il to significantly increase his ability to threaten U.S. interests and allies throughout Northeast Asia and the Western Pacific directly. North Korea's significant export business in weapons also raises the specter of NBC/M exports to other regions of concern to the United States. The relatively opaque character of the North Korean leadership increases the difficulty of persuading the regime not to acquire NBC/M, to roll back its capabilities, or not to use them.

The new North Korean capabilities have the potential to increase the human and financial cost of a successful defense of South Korea and Japan—the top priority U.S. security commitment in Northeast Asia. If the North Koreans were to use chemical and biological weapons as part of an initial artillery and/or missile barrage against South Korea, they might cause enormous civilian and military casualties (Seoul lies within artillery range of the North Korean forces at the Demilitarized Zone [DMZ]), facilitate a breakthrough across the DMZ, and increase the speed of the North's initial advance. North Korean missiles, if fitted with nuclear, biological, or chemical warheads, could cause widespread panic and severe casualties in civilian population centers. North Korea could attack rear area targets, such as seaports and airfields, using missiles armed with chemical or biological weapons or special forces armed with biological agents. Depending on the persistence of the weapon used, these facilities likely would be shut down for a time or their operating tempo severely degraded.

The North Koreans could also use or threaten to use their newest technologies against Japan and pose new challenges for U.S. defense planners. Whereas previously North Korea threatened primarily South Korea, the range of one of its missiles in development, the No-Dong, allows it to target large portions of Japan.[5] The North might use its extended-range missiles to threaten Japan, hoping to deter it from allowing the United States to use facilities there for basing air power or staging reinforcements for Korea.

The North Korean ability to target Japan may help to remedy what has been a weakness in Northeast Asian security—the lack of a strong regional defense coalition. In Northeast Asia and the Pacific, the United States has strong defense relationships with South Korea, Japan, and Australia, but they are all bilateral ties. Among U.S. allies, there has been some wariness. The discussion of Japan in the South Korean Defense White Paper reveals this wariness in its over-careful formulations, such as "Japan seems to have refrained from excessive build up that could cause worries on the part of surrounding nations."[6] Only now, when faced with the increased threat posed

by NBC/M in North Korea (and sparked by U.S. leadership), is it possible that the region's states may develop a sense of common purpose that would permit closer security and defense planning. Also possible is further splintering of the security structure of the region as states seek to ensure their own security.

Beyond the immediate Northeast Asian region, North Korea has a wide export market for its conventional weapons and missiles that includes Iran, Iraq, and Libya. Moreover, the development of a North Korean nuclear capability could take on much wider significance. It is quite plausible that a cash-starved North Korean regime would turn to exports of a scarce commodity in much demand—nuclear weapons. Clearly, North Korean export of longer-range missiles that could reach Rome from Libya, or Tel Aviv from Iran, would gravely affect U.S. vital interests in Europe and the Persian Gulf/Middle East.

North Korean NBC/M capabilities might prolong the conflict on the peninsula and increase the cost to the United States but would not ultimately lead to North Korean victory, given U.S. military capabilities and a willingness to use them. The DOD is grappling with this challenge by (a) increasing U.S. and allied battlefield and active defense capabilities, (b) improving U.S. defense strategy for the region as a whole as the threat has expanded, and (c) determining how best to support U.S. diplomatic initiatives to roll back North Korean capabilities.

Persian Gulf/Middle East

The programs of Iraq and Iran to acquire NBC/M weapons pose grave risks to U.S. vital interests in a different region. The lack of long-established allies able to field significant, modern forces (with the exception of Israel) and newly minted, untried security structures makes regional defense in the Persian Gulf/Middle East theater a more difficult task. Deterring these new proliferators, especially the radical theocracy in Iran, will also be a challenge because the United States does not have a full understanding of the political factions and the specific internal motivations of the regimes in power that lead them to acquire and possibly use NBC/M. The potential impact of NBC/M weapons in the Iraqi inventory can be gauged by looking at Operation Desert Storm and the Gulf war. If Iraq had then had more fully developed and deployed NBC/M, it could have increased the complexity and scale of the conflict in the region significantly, even if it could not have changed the ultimate outcome. Saddam Hussein's "lessons learned" from the Gulf war must have said as much, but they may not predict eventual defeat in future contingencies with an Iraq robustly armed with WMD. Should long-term monitoring of Iraq fail, the potential threat to states in the region from a revived Iraqi NBC/M arsenal would be serious and could be immediate.

Iraq had a well-established missile capability that Saddam Hussein used to widen the geographic scope of the conflict in an effort to shake the fragile defense coalition. He was able to use missiles to attack (albeit ineffectively, from a military perspective) long-range targets that otherwise would have been safe rear areas, such as Riyadh and the port of Al Jubayl. Safe rear areas are important for supporting U.S. power projection into the theater; they serve to receive reinforcements, as staging areas for forming up units, and as logistical nodes for all types of supplies. Chemical or biological warheads

on the missiles might have degraded U.S. and allied operations, perhaps significantly. Chemical attacks on airfields might have slowed and impaired the use of ground-based air power. Biological attacks on crowded housing areas might have caused huge numbers of casualties.

Saddam Hussein also used his SCUD missiles to attack Israel in an attempt to provoke the Israelis into a counterattack. This could have had the effect of transforming the political character of the conflict into a war between Israel and its protector the United States on the one hand and the "Arab world" on the other, and of potentially fracturing the defense coalition. The use of NBC warheads might well have brought an Israeli response. With Israel in the war, Arab states in the coalition, such as Syria and Egypt, might have felt obligated to reconsider their participation and withdraw. This problem illustrates the fragility of the regional defense coalition during the Persian Gulf War and the political challenges confronting any subsequent regional defense structure for the Persian Gulf/Middle East.

Iraq's NBC/M programs have suffered a serious setback as a result of the war and the postwar United Nations (UN) dismantlement regime. Iran's programs, on the other hand, continue, although they lag behind Iraq's prewar capability. R. James Woolsey, director of the Central Intelligence Agency (CIA), has testified that Iran is at least 8 to 10 years away from a nuclear bomb.[7] Iran is reported to have chemical weapons and appears to be pursuing biological weapons. It has bought missiles.[8] Syria and Libya are generally reported as having undeclared chemical weapons capabilities and biological weapons programs, and both have ballistic missile inventories.[9]

As in Northeast Asia, the increased

threat may act as a catalyst for stronger regional defense cooperation. Although the period since 1990 has seen major enhancements in defense cooperation between the United States and its security partners in the Gulf, many obstacles remain to an effective regional collective defense structure. This is particularly true of cooperation among the regional states themselves. Complicating these security arrangements is a certain reluctance by regional states to host U.S. forces visibly in peacetime. Weak regional defense structures make it easier for hostile states to isolate their targets, while also making it more difficult for the United States and its allies and friends to coordinate and maintain a united front.

For the foreseeable future, the Iraqi, Iranian, and Libyan regimes are likely to remain hostile toward the United States and its allies in the region and to continue to seek to acquire or expand their capabilities for NBC/M warfare. Unfortunately, the United States knows comparatively little about what drives these regimes to act or, indeed, what deters them. For example, it does not know what deterred Saddam Hussein from using chemical weapons against Israel or the coalition forces (as he had against the Kurds and the Iranians).

Europe

The threat of NBC/M use against U.S. European allies, their territory, and/or their forces must be analyzed in terms of all aspects of U.S.–European security and the fundamental U.S. interests in the transatlantic alliance. NBC/M proliferation threatens U.S. interests in Europe, raises questions about the U.S.–European security tie, and threatens the ability of the United States to work with its European allies in protecting common interests be-

yond Europe. The United States and its allies need to be better prepared to defend against NBC/M use in Europe or anywhere that U.S. and allied forces might be engaged.

The states hostile to U.S. interests, friends, and allies in Northeast Asia and the Persian Gulf/Middle East are also among those of concern to U.S. European allies. Libya, Iran, and Iraq all have the ability to target missiles on European cities. As noted above, Iran has an ongoing NBC/M program; Iraq's program has been forcibly suspended for the time being but Saddam Hussein's desire to develop NBC/M capabilities may only have been sharpened by defeat. Although Europe may be out of its range for the moment, North Korea is a major supplier of missiles to Libya and Iraq and therefore is of concern to Europe's security. As noted above, if North Korea increases its catalogue of export items to include newer, longer-range weapons, the threat to Europe from North Korea's customers could increase dramatically almost overnight. Although the United States and its allies clearly have the ability to counterattack and thereby possibly deter attack at present, Europe has little or no ability to defend itself against incoming ballistic missiles.

Europe also must contend with the NBC/M legacy of the states of the former Soviet Union (FSU). Although most of these states are now committed to working bilaterally with the United States, Western Europe, and the North Atlantic Treaty Organization (NATO) on safety, security, and dismantlement of their weapons inventories, the fragile status of many of these governments should prompt prudent defense planning by NATO, especially in view of the sheer size of residual, Soviet-vintage inventories.

The issue of responding to the potential for proliferation has even been caught up and used in the debate within Europe on the European Union and the continued relevance of the United States and NATO to European security. European supporters of the European Union and its emerging defense arm, the Western European Union (WEU), have been casting about for a mission for a European-only defense institution to set the WEU apart from NATO. NATO was closely identified with meeting the Soviet threat as the institutional mechanism for U.S. extended deterrence to Europe and the basis for stationing large numbers of U.S. troops there. With the end of the Cold War and a two-thirds reduction in U.S. forces in Europe, WEU supporters began to question whether U.S. security guarantees were still relevant or would continue to apply to the remaining and emerging threats to Europe, especially to those threats that do not directly endanger the United States itself. Threats to Europe from Middle Eastern states armed with NBC/M capabilities could be seen in just this light and thus have been used by some WEU supporters in favor of the argument that Europe needs a defense organization without U.S. participation—and that the WEU should have a greater role in dealing with the proliferation problem. Since President Clinton at the January 1994 summit proposed that NATO address the defense dimensions of proliferation, the issue has been definitively NATO's, but also NATO's to lose if the Europeans do not find reassurance of U.S. guarantees for this new threat in the new work of the alliance.

At the same time, some Europeans also share the U.S. concern about their ability, with or without the United States, to deter the proliferators of greatest concern—North Korea, Iran, Iraq, Libya, and, should conditions change, Syria. The Europeans and the United States find it difficult to understand the strategic aims of these regimes. As noted above, unless the motivations of these states are understood, it could be much more difficult to deter them than it was to deter the Soviet Union during the Cold War.

Beyond the NBC/M threat to European territory is the impact of NBC/M on the ability of the European states to send capable forces outside the region, whether independently or as members of ad hoc coalitions with U.S. forces. The Gulf war demonstrated that the Europeans—the British and French in particular—are the allies best able to project their forces outside their region in any significant numbers. The United States has a strong interest in maintaining and increasing Europe's ability to project forces in the protection of common transatlantic interests. Moreover, of all U.S. allies, with the possible exception of Israel, the Europeans are the best prepared for NBC/M conflict because of preparations they had to make to defend against the cold war arsenal of the Soviet Union. In fact, during the Gulf war, the United States borrowed from Germany Fox NBC reconnaissance vehicles for contamination detection.[10] These preparations also apply to U.S. and European forces engaged in peacekeeping activities, where chemical weapons might be used by warring parties against each other. As the immediate cold war threat fades, the capability to deal with such weapons, like other capabilities in European and U.S. inventories, becomes vulnerable to budget cuts. The United States has an interest in maintaining European defense capabilities and encouraging the development of capabilities sufficient to meet new proliferation challenges. Without effective indigenous

European capabilities for NBC/M combat, the burden of defending common transatlantic interests, in Europe and elsewhere, will fall increasingly on the United States alone as aggressors field these new technologies.

Europe's greatest asset is the strength of its regional defense coalition, NATO. To a far greater degree than in Northeast Asia or the Persian Gulf/Middle East, the countries of Europe already have a common political commitment to defense that will prevent European states from becoming isolated and either providing for their own defense or coming under a hegemon's influence. A structure is also already in place to coordinate planning and defense responses across the region to any threat, including that from NBC/M-armed adversaries.

In closing this section, it must be said that the implications of success or failure of U.S. regional security strategies go well beyond any one region. Loss of confidence in U.S. security guarantees by states in one region may cause allies elsewhere to worry. Alternately, success in maintaining stability and security in one region such that proliferation does not occur, or in spite of proliferation, supports global norms against proliferation and thereby helps to maintain regional stability. In this way, the global norms and regional strategies are linked: the latter invoke the former in developing and implementing specific policies or actions in a region; the former build on the stability and security of states provided by the latter.

Regional Security Strategies: Issues for Investigation

U.S. regional security strategies must integrate the new threats from adversaries armed with NBC/M capabilities. A response is needed that will assure the security of the United States and its allies. Again, the basic questions are, how can the United States supplement or adapt its regional security strategies so as to convince states not to proliferate, prevent determined proliferators from acquiring these capabilities, and counter the impact of NBC/M weapons so that U.S. allies are assured of the credibility of U.S. commitments?

For each region, the U.S. security strategy will have to be examined and the three defense elements analyzed—U.S.–allied regional security structures, U.S. force commitments and operational plans, and U.S.–allied joint military capabilities. Should any of these elements for a region be changed? If so, how? Nor is this is a one-way process. The requirements of regional security strategies will also inform the development and direction of defense policies, tailoring them to meet the particular threats of each region of central concern to the United States.

U.S. regional strategies are not the exclusive domain of any one department or agency. State, ACDA, and others also will have to analyze the impact of proliferation on their policies. For the Department of Defense, in addition to improving military capabilities and plans for operations against NBC/M armed aggressors, there are a number of hard questions that need to be addressed as each of the three elements cited above is adjusted to meet the NBC/M threat.

Developing and Supplementing U.S.–Allied Regional Security Structures

Reassuring allies and friends who are threatened by the prospect of NBC/M adversaries will be an enormous challenge for the United States.

In Northeast Asia, it is reasonable today to consider whether the United States should seek to create a more multilateral regional security structure to form a more cohesive defense against North Korea and to better reassure frontline states. Should it support a larger U.S. presence or should it instead seek to obviate the need for a larger U.S. presence?

A similar question can be posed in the Persian Gulf region: Is the NBC/M threat sufficient to prompt the local states and the United States to seek to build a more multilateral security structure in the region? Would this structure act to form a more cohesive front against Iran and Iraq, among others, deter attack, and possibly build support in the region and in the United States for a more permanent and visible U.S. presence, should such a presence prove prudent or necessary?

Restructuring the U.S. Commitment of Forces and Operational Plans

U.S. regional security strategies must also rethink all elements of the U.S. commitment of forces overseas—e.g., the operational plan, the mix of types of forces, size of deployments, readiness, and length of deployments—to determine the right combination for U.S. goals in the region. For example, is it possible to reassure U.S. allies in Northeast Asia and deter North Korean attack by adding only a theater missile defense system to the current U.S. military posture, or should the United States consider increasing or raising the profile of the U.S. nuclear presence in the region? Alternatively, would the doubling of U.S. conventional forces in the region be the only credible reassurance possible?

Similarly, in the Persian Gulf the United States has allies, such as Saudi

Arabia, that are loath to host U.S. forces yet still seek assurance of U.S. commitment to their security. What would reassure the Saudis if they are faced with an increased threat to their security posed by Iranian nuclear and missile capabilities? A U.S. theater missile defense system not based in Saudi Arabia? U.S. forces based or frequently exercising in Saudi Arabia? Or U.S. nuclear forces in the region?

In the Persian Gulf/Middle East region, is it more reassuring and politically viable for the United States to station forces in the region rather than outside it, as the United States currently does for the most part?

If the NBC/M threat becomes acute, should the United States increase the peacetime presence of its forces in Europe and Northeast Asia, or alter how the presence of its forces in Europe is made manifest? For example, would increasing the number and/or size of field exercises provide greater reassurance to local allies?

The specific requirements for security and defense in each region will also influence the development of proliferation-specific measures. For example, are U.S. forces in Korea and the Far East capable of operating effectively as previously safe rear areas in South Korea and especially Japan become subject to attack? Further, how should U.S. forces plan to operate when subject not to attack by highly inaccurate, conventionally armed missiles but instead by sophisticated and NBC-armed weapons?

Improving U.S.–Allied Capability for Joint Operations

In this context, the important question is, should the United States push harder to ensure that South Korean and Persian Gulf allies have the ability to operate effectively with U.S. forces against an NBC/M-armed aggressor?

For example, in South Korea, U.S. forces are less than 6 percent of the total U.S./Republic of Korea defense force in peacetime.[11] No matter how well prepared and protected U.S. forces are against NBC/M attack, if their South Korean partners are not as well prepared, the combined force may be vulnerable, and a greater portion of the defense burden will fall to the United States. Burden sharing requires allied troops to have capabilities as effective as those of the United States.

As regards strengthening the European regional security structure to address the NBC/M threat better, work is already under way to increase the awareness of U.S. allies of the presence of an NBC/M threat to their region. The DOD is leading the U.S. initiative to improve the defense capabilities of NATO against threats from NBC/M-armed adversaries. In June 1994 NATO ministers approved a policy framework for the alliance's efforts, to include guidance for work on an examination of the NBC/M threat and its implications for current defense planning and future capabilities requirements. At the same meeting, NATO committed itself to consult with members of the North Atlantic Cooperation Council (NACC) and with states in the Partnership for Peace on fostering a common understanding and approach to the proliferation problem.[12]

Conclusion

This article has argued that proliferation of NBC/M is a larger issue for U.S. foreign and defense policy than previously thought because increasingly it carries serious security and defense implications regarding the ability of the United States to protect its interests if hostile states acquire these weapons. Because of this broader impact on U.S. regional security, U.S. policy needs to address the proliferation challenge through a new approach. It must attend to regional security strategies and the ability of the United States to protect its interests, allies, and friends, rather than define the problem narrowly as a question of responding to the acquisition of NBC/M weapons or technologies. Treating the issue as one of acquisition, U.S. proliferation policies are directed at persuading states to stop or roll back their efforts to attain NBC/M capabilities. Treating it as a regional security issue, U.S. policies are integrated into managing regional security to ensure that states choose not to acquire these weapons, or that states by acquiring these capabilities do not increase their ability to threaten U.S. interests.

The integration of the NBC/M threat posed by hostile states into U.S. regional security strategies should result in a powerful response to proliferation—it is above all a way to shape the security environment of potential proliferators. By shaping the regional security environment, U.S. policies may be able to influence the decisions of proliferators, either not to use or threaten to use what they may acquire, to give up what they have, or, best of all, not to acquire these weapons at all.

The views expressed here are those of the author and do not necessarily reflect those of the Department of Defense. He wishes to thank the following colleagues for their review and helpful comments on various drafts of this article: Lewis Dunn, Sherman Garnett, Robert Joseph, and Leonard Spector.

Notes

1. Office of the Press Secretary, The White House, "Fact Sheet on Non-Proliferation and Export Control Policy" (Washington, D.C., September 27, 1993).

2. *Ibid.*, and Department of State, "Update on Progress toward Regional Non-Proliferation in South Asia" (Washington, D.C., April 1994).

3. Office of the Deputy Secretary of Defense, "Report on Nonproliferation and Counterproliferation Activities and Programs" (Washington, D.C., May 1994), pp. 11, 22.

4. See discussion of regional nonproliferation initiatives in Office of the Press Secretary, "Fact Sheet on Non-Proliferation and Export Control Policy," p. 4.

5. Department of Defense North Korea Handbook, PC-2600-6421-94. Barbara Starr, "N. Korea Casts a Longer Shadow with TD-2," *Jane's Defence Weekly*, March 12, 1994, p. 1.

6. *Defense White Paper, 1993–1994* (Ministry of Defense, Republic of Korea, Seoul).

7. Testimony by Director of Central Intelligence R. James Woolsey to the House Foreign Affairs Committee, Subcommittee on International Security, International Organizations and Human Rights, July 28, 1993, p. 4.

8. U.S. Congress, Office of Technology Assessment, *Proliferation of Weapons of Mass Destruction: Assessing the Risks*, OTA-ISC-559 (Washington, D.C.: GPO, August 1993), pp. 64–66.

9. *Ibid.*

10. Department of Defense, "Conduct of the Persian Gulf War," Final Report to Congress (Washington, D.C., April 1992), appendix Q, p. 5.

11. *The Military Balance, 1993–1994* (London: Brassey's for IISS, 1994).

12. "Alliance Policy Framework on Proliferation of Weapons of Mass Destruction," North Atlantic Council, Istanbul, Turkey, June 9, 1994.

Extended Conventional Deterrence: In from the Cold and Out of the Nuclear Fire?

Charles T. Allan

GENERAL COLIN POWELL, former chairman of the Joint Chiefs of Staff, observed in 1992 that "Deterrence remains the primary and central motivating purpose underlying [U.S.] national military strategy" (1992, 6). The end of the Cold War, however, and the overwhelming U.S.-led victory in the Persian Gulf War have sparked a new discourse on the meaning, tools, and targets of U.S. deterrence strategy.

In 1993, then Secretary of Defense Les Aspin succinctly defined the changed national security environment in his *Bottom-Up Review.*

During the Cold War, our military planning was dominated by the need to confront numerically superior Soviet forces in Europe, the Far East, and Southwest Asia. Now, our focus is on the need to project power into regions important to our interest and to defeat potentially hostile regional powers such as North Korea and Iraq. (Aspin 1993a, 7)

Charles T. Allan is currently an Air Force National Defense Fellow at CSIS.

Copyright © 1994 by The Center for Strategic and International Studies and the Massachusetts Institute of Technology
The Washington Quarterly • 17:3

This statement has three major implications for deterrence strategy. First, the demise of the Soviet threat has significantly decreased the risk of war in Europe or direct attack on the United States. Thus, the central role of *nuclear* deterrence has declined. Second, deterrence strategy can no longer focus on a single adversary but must be tailored to a number of regional powers. And, third, as during the Cold War, the U.S. deterrent shield will be *extended* to interests far from the United States but very close to its potential adversaries (Arquilla and Davis 1992).

The overwhelming victory of the U.S.-led coalition forces over Iraq has also had major implications for deterrence. In analyzing the impact of Desert Storm, William Perry (1991) has observed that:

This new conventional military capability adds a powerful dimension to the ability of the United States to deter war. While it is certainly not as powerful as nuclear weapons, it is a more credible deterrent, particularly in regional conflicts vital to U.S. interests. . . . It should also strengthen the already high level of deterrence of a major war in Europe and Korea. The United States can now be confident that the defeat of a conventional armored assault in those regions could be achieved by conventional military forces, which could enable the United States to limit the role of its nuclear forces to the deterrence of nuclear attack. (p. 66)

In light of the increased lethality of conventional weapons and President George Bush's 1991 decision to eliminate ground- and sea-based tactical nuclear weapons, this analysis indicates that *conventional* weapons may form the basis of U.S. extended deterrence.

The purpose of this research survey is to determine the outline of U.S. post–cold war thinking on deterrence, while focusing on extended conventional deterrence. The survey does not attempt to parse the lengthy and complex cold war deterrence debate, which focused almost entirely on the North Atlantic Treaty Organization (NATO), the Soviet Union, and nuclear issues. To thoroughly address the issue of extended conventional deterrence, the survey falls into three sections:

Deterrence. The first section addresses the meaning of deterrence in the post–cold war era. It reviews recommendations to expand the meaning of deterrence to incorporate nonmilitary instruments of power and examines the debate over the types of military threats best suited to a post–cold war deterrence strategy. Here, the debate focuses on whether deterrence is purely punitive (i.e., incorporates only threats of countervalue punishment) or contains elements of both punishment and denial (i.e., defense). Finally, it asserts that a third form—dynamic deterrence—is emerging in the post–cold war, post–Desert Storm world.

Conventional Deterrence. The second section of the survey addresses current thinking on conventional deterrence. It delineates the rationale for conventional deterrence and its strengths and weaknesses. In addition, this section reviews the debate over the roles of conventional and nuclear weapons in extended deterrence.

Extended Conventional Deterrence. This section outlines the implications of the regional emphasis of U.S. national security policy on deterrence. It addresses the following issues:

- the necessity for clear commitments;
- the inadequacy of the classic "rational actor" model as a foundation for deterrence strategy;
- the role of coalitions in U.S. deterrence strategy;
- the role of reputation in supporting long-term U.S. deterrence stability; and
- potential counterstrategies to U.S. deterrence.

The survey concludes with a discussion of how the deterrence debate may affect U.S. national security policy and force structure and makes recommendations for future research.

What Does Deterrence Mean?

After 40 years at the center of the national security debate, deterrence is no longer frozen in its cold war constructs. Traditionally analysts have focused on deterrence as the use of threats of military retaliation to "prevent an adversary from using military force to achieve foreign policy objectives" (Huth 1988a, 15). The definition of deterrence is expanding to include more than military threats. In fact, the types of military threats that constitute deterrence are themselves the subject of debate. Ongoing deterrence studies focus on an expanded meaning of deterrence and its integration into overall national security strategy.

Expansionists believe the definition of deterrence should be modified to include all instruments of national security, not merely the threat of military force (Buchanan 1993; Blackwell, Mazarr, and Snider 1993). The new definitions are not limited to forms of coercion but incorporate positive inducements as part of deterrence strategy (K. Mueller 1991; J. Mueller 1992). This expansion of deterrence to include positive inducements would subsume a body of scholarship, represented primarily by the work of Janice Gross Stein (1991) and Richard Lebow (1985), that they refer to as "reassurance theory."

Paul Huth and Bruce Russett (1990) maintain that a key area for future deterrence study is how military threats, nonmilitary sanctions, and positive inducements may be integrated to prevent aggression. Robert Jervis (forthcoming) supports this line of inquiry, noting that the concepts of deterrence, reassurance, and positive inducements are essentially complementary. John Arquilla and Paul Davis (1992) and George Quester (1993) believe that the integration of military threats and other foreign policy instruments has synergistic effects that have not been adequately researched. Other writers feel that foreign policy initiatives, economic measures, and nonlethal forms of coercion will be essential deterrent tools in the post–cold war era (Buchanan 1993; Engstrom 1993; Starr 1993). The deterrent value of both nonlethal weapons and the growing field of information warfare are the subjects of intense study and wargaming. Although the purpose of this paper is to illuminate current thinking

on deterrence, it should not be construed as asserting that the relations between the United States and developing powers will be ones of confrontation and deterrence. On the contrary, most evidence indicates that cooperative engagement will be the primary mode of relations between the United States and the developing world. States will still compete militarily, however. The type of military forces and the modes of their application required to underpin national security remain the focus of the public debate on deterrence (Nitze 1994).

Punishment. The type of military threats that constitute deterrence will have a significant impact on military force posture and structure decisions (Jervis forthcoming; Cimbala 1991; Palmer 1992). The two prevailing schools of thought on these threats differ over whether deterrence should include only threats of punishment, commonly referred to as countervalue targeting, or both punishment and a defensive strategy known as denial. During the Cold War, deterrence was perceived as a primarily punitive strategy (Blackwell, Mazarr, and Snider 1993).

The cold war punitive definition of deterrence emphasized the devastating effects on the targeted society and regime. According to Stephen Cimbala (1991),

A deterrent threat is a threat to inflict unacceptable *punishment* to the society or government of the opponent, regardless of whether or not his forces prevail in battle. (p. xii)

Large-scale societal punishment, for many cold war strategists, was the sine qua non of a credible deterrent (Friedberg 1991; Cimbala 1991). This form of punishment rejects defensive forces and instead requires forces that are simultaneously irresistible in their application and instantaneously devastating in their effects. The cold war notion of punishment derived its strength from societal vulnerability to the incredible power of nuclear weapons (Cimbala 1991) and a lack of ballistic missile defenses (Davis 1993b). As Richard Harknett (1991) asserts, an aggressor faced with such a deterrent threat would theoretically have no way to contest the costs associated with challenging it. Because the outcome of war would not be determined on the battlefield, and the costs would be clearly perceived by the adversary as devastating to him and his society, resorting to force would be irrational. As long as the credibility of use remains perceptibly higher than zero, a devastating punitive deterrent should hold.

In fact, as David Abshire notes, the forceful component of NATO's deterrence of the Soviet Union was effective for precisely this reason (Abshire 1993). If societal destruction is the primary basis for a strategy of deterrence through punishment, then paradoxically it holds that the most destructive weapons will ensure the strongest and most enduring deterrent (Betts 1988; Jervis 1992; Harknett 1991; Cimbala 1991). Beyond deterrence based on societal devastation are strategies that incorporate threats of less devastating punishment.

Denial. Although massive retaliatory punishment was the underlying theme of cold war strategy, deterrence can also obtain through denial—the recognized ability to defeat the enemy's forces on the battlefield, thus denying him his military objectives and deterring aggression (Gray 1992; Quester 1992a; Jervis forthcoming).

Denial in its purest form, however, implies that the adversary is not punished for attempted aggression, only that his attempt to achieve his aims through force is denied. Thus, classical denial focuses on territorial defense (Jervis forthcoming). A deterrent based solely on denial eschews offensive capabilities in favor of concepts such as "non-offensive defense" (Nokkala 1991; Boeker 1990). A primarily defensive strategy would provide the type of deterrence described by John Mearsheimer (1983) and supported by Huth's analysis (1988a). Mearsheimer postulates that conventional deterrence is most likely to hold if it denies the aggressor a successful blitzkrieg option, thereby forcing a protracted conflict.

A New Approach. These forms of punishment and denial have constituted, and to some are still adequate as, the basis for developing deterrence strategy (Gray 1992). An emerging school of thought, however, advocates fundamental changes.

To the post–cold war advocates of conventional deterrence, the concepts of punishment and denial alone are insufficient to support deterrence in the new era. Two factors appear to mandate changes. First, in contrast to the cold war NATO scenario, enduring, significant U.S. ground forces will not be present at the beginning of future regional crises nor will these forces stay in a region once a crisis has ended (Haffa 1992; Arquilla and Davis 1992; Hooker and Waddell 1992). Second, precision guided munitions have demonstrated the capability to be discriminate in attacking a wide variety of targets. Consequently, a new, third deterrence modality is required. This new modality—here called *dynamic* deterrence—has three characteristics: (1) punishment need not be and no longer should be societal but tailored to the values of the targeted regime; (2) denial should not be a purely defensive concept but primarily offensive; and (3) the credible use of force should be viewed as essential to deterrence, not merely as a sign of its failure. For Robert Haffa (1992) this new modality means that

> A strategy of effective conventional deterrence must be . . . asymmetrical in threat and application, intense and overwhelming in its threat, offensive with a capability for punishment as well as denial, and extended globally through new technologies and weapons systems. (p. 19)

Paul Nitze (1994) and a Washington Strategy Seminar (WSS) study group (1993) have articulated almost identical views of conventional deterrence. The latest thinking postulates that punishment may be made more discriminating through targeting those things that a regime values most or possibly the leadership itself (Quester 1992a; Haffa 1992; WSS 1993). Even advocates of societal punishment cite precision strikes against a regime's leadership as an example of precision punishment (Harknett 1992). If punishment can be made more precise, then the moral and political dilemmas associated with the loss of innocent life can be avoided, thus making punishment more usable for U.S. deterrence strategy (Cropsey 1994).

Although punishment is to be more precise, denial will be more offensive in nature. Dynamic deterrence must include significant offensive counterforce capabilities because the long-term presence of large U.S. forces in a region will be problematic for both regional (Hess 1993; WSS 1993) and U.S. domestic (Sloan 1992) reasons. Cold war conventional deterrence concepts implied primarily the capability to deny an enemy a swift victory and were essentially defensive in nature (Mearsheimer 1983). To the current advocates of extended conventional deterrence, mere denial of a blitzkrieg is inadequate and antiquated (Haffa 1992). Because future deployments of powerful U.S. forces will be temporary (Hooker and Waddell 1992), as they were during the Persian Gulf War, U.S. decision makers will face the policy dilemma that forces either must be used to effectively eliminate the military threat that triggered their deployment or face pressures to leave with the threat still intact (George 1991; Record 1993; Garfinkle 1991). Defensive denial would require the long-term deployment of substantial U.S. forces. Dynamic deterrence would therefore reject exclusively "non-offensive defense." Of course, the advocates of dynamic deterrence are not proposing that the United States become an aggressive power. Just as NATO sought the capabilities to use offensive operations to strike deep against advancing Soviet forces in response to an initial act of aggression, so the advocates of dynamic deterrence would be prepared to strike deep in response to aggression. For the advocates of dynamic deterrence, however, U.S. forces must be projected from long range and force would be applied strategically to create the environment for long-term regional stability.

During the Cold War, war between the superpowers was an unacceptable outcome to deterrence. The advocates of dynamic deterrence believe the use of force may be necessary to demonstrate that the United States has the will, operational skill, and technical prowess required to defeat even the most powerful threats rapidly and at minimal cost (Haffa 1992). The consequence of overwhelming U.S.-led victories would be an extended period of deterrence stability while potential adversaries search for real or perceived weaknesses in U.S. strategy, operational art, or technology (Guertner 1993). Robert Art (1992–93) concurs that the periodic use of force may be essential for a broader, general deterrence to remain credible.

Conventional Deterrence

The advocates of *conventional* deterrence (conventionalists) propose that now is the time for deterrence to break its nuclear chains. Nitze (1994) has stated that:

> [T]he United States should consider . . . converting its principal strategic deterrent from nuclear weapons to a more credible deterrence based at least in part upon "smart" conventional weapons. It is a shift that could be justified as a coldly rational approach to a new security strategy and equally so as a morally correct foreign policy choice. (p. C–1)

In their extensive study of potential U.S. responses to nuclear proliferation and attack (Millot, Molander, and Wilson 1993), three RAND analysts note that participants in their "Day After . . ." series of war-games have provided supporting rationale to Nitze's arguments. Many participants, drawn from government, industry, and academe, offered two reasons for increased dependence on a conventionally based deterrent: as a result of Desert Storm U.S. conventional dominance would deter regional adversaries by non-nuclear means; and it is "counterproductive . . . to base extended deterrence on nuclear guarantees, even in the face of possible nuclear provocation by an opposing

regional power" (pp. x–xi). Other participants believed that "conventional weapons are or will soon enough be, nearly perfect substitutes for nuclear weapons in terms of military effectiveness, deterrent value, and reassurance" (p. 19). Thus, two arguments support the shift to a conventionally based deterrent: (1) conventional weapons have attained counterforce and countervalue capabilities previously achievable only with nuclear forces; and (2) nuclear threats are not credible in regional contingencies.

Improved Conventional Capabilities. Overwhelming conventional superiority is the key to increased reliance on conventionally based deterrence. The dynamic modality of conventional deterrence embodies the perceived characteristics of U.S. conventional dominance. Dynamic deterrence had its genesis in the drive to use technology to overcome the conventional imbalance in Europe and to delay resorting to nuclear weapons to counter Soviet aggression, thus making the active defense of Europe a more credible deterrent. This early effort to shift deterrence to a greater reliance on conventional weapons was the basis for *discriminate* deterrence as proposed in 1988 by the Commission on Integrated Long-term Strategy (CILS) headed by Fred Iklé and Albert Wohlstetter (Kaufman, Clark, and Sheehan 1991). The commission emphasized two concepts: stealth and precision guidance would allow conventional munitions to replace nuclear weapons for many missions; and new technologies and operational concepts would allow NATO strategy to be more offensive in nature.

The overwhelming success of Desert Storm and the post–cold war regional context of U.S. foreign policy provided the break between discriminate deterrence and dynamic deterrence. The advocates of discriminate deterrence could not foresee an era when the United States would have both conventional superiority over its primary adversaries and the ability to conduct a comprehensive counterforce and countervalue strategic conventional attack throughout the opponent's territory. The Soviet Union was too powerful and too vast to allow such possibilities. Perry (1991) emphasized the counterforce aspects of the new technologies in his assessment of the Gulf war. For him, Desert Storm provided a clear vindication of the advocates of discriminate deterrence by emphasizing how the new technologies had proven their ability to defeat armored forces. In this sense, Perry's thinking is transitional. The advocates of true dynamic deterrence would emphasize not only the destruction of battlefield targets but also the capability of conventional forces to strike strategically throughout the depth of an aggressor state (Nitze 1994; Haffa 1992; Drew 1993).

The proponents of dynamic deterrence believe that conventional weapons have not only become more effective in their counterforce roles but also incorporate significant countervalue capabilities. Conventionalists assert that current U.S. conventional capabilities are so overwhelming that they should intimidate any prospective regional adversary for the foreseeable future (Gray 1992; Guertner 1993). Haffa (1992) notes,

> For example, the development and deployment of survivable conventional delivery platforms and very precise munitions recently displayed in the Gulf War—the F–117s, with a probability of target destruction of .8,

approximated the requirements of the strategic nuclear-SIOP—suggest that conventional force has immediately become more punishing, more usable, and, therefore more credible. (p. 11)

Haffa and James Patton, writing together in 1991 and separately in 1992 and 1993, respectively, believe that the combination of stealthy platforms (i.e., F–117s, B–2s, and attack submarines) and precision munitions make conventional deterrence essentially uncontestable (no third world country will be able to challenge the survivability of these platforms) and devastating (hundreds of targets will be destroyed in a single day). Applying a similar rationale, Seth Cropsey (1994) proposes a deterrence strategy based on thousands of conventional cruise missiles. For the advocates of dynamic deterrence, conventional weapons can realistically replace nuclear weapons as the basis for deterrence because they have a devastating counterforce (denial) capability; precise munitions and stealthy platforms give conventional weapons a powerful countervalue (punishment) capability; and the low collateral damage associated with conventional munitions means the United States can and will use them effectively—making deterrence more credible (WSS 1993).

The advocates of conventional deterrence acknowledge, however, that conventional weapons will require improvements in two areas to convince U.S. adversaries and reassure U.S. allies that conventional deterrence can hold. First, as Haffa (1993) notes, weapons of mass destruction (WMDs) pose a serious challenge to the applicability of conventional deterrence. In the counterproliferation arena, former Secretary of Defense Aspin outlined three major requirements: improved capability to locate, identify, and attack mobile missile launchers; theater ballistic missile defense; and improved hard target kill capability (Aspin 1993b). Second, as noted in a RAND study of future force requirements, forces armed with current munitions may have been unable to establish an assured defense of key facilities in Saudi Arabia if Saddam Hussein's armored forces had continued south instead of stopping in Kuwait (Bowie 1993). Both of these deficiencies have been highlighted in Korea, where the exposed position of Seoul makes a conventional defense extremely problematic, and where North Korea's deeply buried nuclear facilities are inaccessible to U.S. conventional weapons (McPeak 1993). The RAND study (Bowie 1993) proposes possible solutions to the problem of defeating rapid armored advances while U.S. Air Force (Engstrom 1993) and Navy (Buchanan 1993) studies offer approaches to developing forces to support deterrence and counterproliferation. Even if the United States obtains the technological solutions to these problems, new, untried capabilities may have little deterrent impact (Lewis 1989). Despite the requisite U.S. capabilities to deter, an adversary may still choose war.

Critics point out that a conventionally based deterrent is prone to failure. They cite evidence that conventional deterrence has failed even when a defender has clear preponderance of forces (Wolf 1991; Stern et al. 1989; Lebow 1989). There are two salient explanations for these failures. First, it may be difficult to apprise a potential adversary of the elements of conventional war-fighting that would allow the United States to win decisively in a regional conflict, such as long-range aviation, strategic lift ca-

pability, and battlefield reconnaissance. Indeed, it is the capabilities that most contribute to U.S. conventional dominance that may be hardest to communicate (Harknett 1991; Arquilla and Davis 1992; Hooker and Waddell 1992). The skills required to employ and integrate new technologies as well as the technologies themselves are essential to U.S. dominance in conventional warfare (Perry 1991; Cohen 1994). Successful conventional war-fighting is a contest of skill and professionalism and requires an understanding of the operational art (Harknett 1992). An adversary may be unable to know, much less appreciate, these subtle but very real components of successfully waging conventional war (Cimbala 1991).

Second, conventional weapons may not be sufficiently destructive to deter the most risk prone and desperate of adversaries. Certain leaders will be unmoved by the magnitude of destruction that the United States is able to inflict through conventional means (Pape 1992). The destructive power of conventional weapons is after all finite and therefore contestable, and some aggressors may be inclined to believe that they will succeed despite evidence to the contrary (Harknett 1991; Cimbala 1991). Many critics of conventional deterrence believe that it will be unable to prevent a desperate adversary from using WMDs to avoid a decisive conventional defeat. Critics of conventionally based deterrence maintain that the inability to communicate both the quality of one's forces and the devastating power of new weapons is one of its key failings.

Conventionalists agree that adversaries will test conventional deterrence. Indeed, they argue the effective use of force is an essential element of conventional deterrence (Guertner 1992; Nitze 1994).

Deterrence failures [wars or crises] provide the opportunity to demonstrate the price of aggression, rejuvenate the credibility of deterrence (collective or unilateral), and establish a new period of stability. (Guertner 1992, 3)

Conflicts demonstrate new technologies and the skills to use them. Thus, both critics and advocates of dynamic deterrence agree that potential aggressors are very likely to assess improperly or totally ignore the value of technological and operational improvements without demonstrations of U.S. capabilities.

For the proponents of extended conventional deterrence, the character of war termination is a critical component of deterrence strategy. For some, U.S. responses to aggression must be disproportionate in order to convey the seriousness of challenging U.S. interests and preventing the United States from becoming involved in a protracted conflict (Buchanan 1993). Less than decisive outcomes may be interpreted either as a lack of capability or, possibly more seriously, a lack of U.S. will (Garrity 1993a).

The destruction of combat forces as well as the countervalue (punishment) targets of the regime should demonstrate the depth and breadth of U.S. conventional dominance. In the age of instant communications, all potential aggressors would observe the results (Haffa 1992). A new general deterrence environment would be established for the affected region and potentially globally. For the dynamic deterrence advocates, the more disproportionate the U.S. victory in breadth, depth, cost, and political implications, the broader and more persistent the new postwar deterrent will be. Because conventional force does not carry the global, national, or personal taboos that nuclear weapons do,

its use is far more likely and credible than the use of nuclear weapons in any crisis (Nitze 1994; Dunn 1994).

Credibility. The greater apparent willingness of U.S. leaders to use conventional weapons is the second underpinning of the conventional deterrence argument. Operationally, the United States retains a dramatic lead over any potential regional nuclear challenger. Other than the states of the former Soviet Union (FSU), none of the potential regional adversaries of the United States possesses a force capable of countering U.S. nuclear forces. In fact, except for vulnerability to unconventional entry— cargo ship, small civil aircraft, or advanced emplacement (Carnesale 1993; Levine 1993)—the United States is currently immune from nuclear attack by renegade states. Thus, the United States no longer faces the problem of self-deterrence resulting from the lack of credibility of trading "Boston for Bonn."

Yet concern over the adequacy of the "coupling" of U.S. strategic nuclear weapons to NATO has periodically undermined U.S. efforts to reassure its European allies about the reliability of its nuclear umbrella. Throughout the history of cold war deterrence, the United States sought to give its conventional and nuclear defense of Europe a greater war-fighting character. Until the end of the Cold War, however, the Europeans opposed most efforts to alter the fundamentally punitive and retaliatory characteristics of deterrence (Bitzinger 1989). Some believe, despite the profound asymmetry between U.S. nuclear forces and those of possible adversaries, a nuclear deterrent may not be credible in regional conflicts (Spector 1992; Flournoy 1993; Nitze 1994). This may be true even if the adversary uses nuclear weapons first (Guertner 1993; Odom 1993; Cropsey 1994). For the *antinuclear* conventionalists, nuclear threats are not credible in regional contexts in general because U.S. interests there will not be sufficiently vital, and it is in the U.S. interest to maintain a taboo against nuclear use, even when confronted by a nuclear attack against its forces or allies (Dunn 1994; Mazarr 1993; Cropsey 1994).

Despite efforts to give U.S. and NATO nuclear deterrence a war-fighting character, that form of deterrence succeeded in Europe precisely because of the devastating effects of failure (Quester 1992b). But for those who would delegitimize U.S. nuclear use (Kaysen et al. 1991; Cropsey 1994; Dunn 1994; Nitze 1994), nuclear weapons are nearly unusable as a policy tool because their employment would cause morally and politically unacceptable noncombatant casualties and environmental destruction. For example, although the CSIS Nuclear Strategy Study Group would retain the *threat* to use nuclear weapons in retaliation for nuclear attacks against U.S. forces and territory, it further states "in the actual event there may be good reasons for the U.S. leaders not to follow through on their threats" (Mazarr 1993, 52). Significantly, the group's report would provide no U.S. nuclear guarantees to support U.S. regional allies under the threat of WMD blackmail or to retaliate for WMD attack against those allies (p. 54). Consequently, conventional weapons should form the basis for future U.S. extended deterrence strategy (Cropsey 1994).

The credibility of U.S. nuclear use may be further degraded by both the asymmetries of stake in regional conflicts and the loss of the automaticity considered characteristic of the cold war environment. Lewis Dunn (1994) contends that the less vital interests involved in regional conflicts, the more relaxed time constraints placed on presidential decision making, and the intense U.S. aversion to innocent casualties combine to drastically reduce the credibility of a U.S. nuclear deterrent, even to an opponent's first use of WMDs.

Dunn makes a further argument against the continued credibility of U.S. extended nuclear deterrence. He contends that the withdrawal of theater nuclear weapons has eliminated the main symbol of U.S. nuclear commitment. Over time, he feels the ability to employ theater nuclear weapons will atrophy, seriously undercutting "the perceived willingness of the United States to use nuclear weapons again" (Dunn 1994, 13). Because Dunn believes that conventional weapons can replace nuclear weapons with little loss of capability and their use has far more credibility, he does not recommend rectifying this situation. The final argument against extended nuclear deterrence postulates that even if nuclear threats could be made credible, maintenance of a taboo against nuclear proliferation and use would be in the interest of the United States (Mazarr 1993; Nitze 1994).

If, as some analysts insist, U.S. conventional dominance is almost unassailable, then preventing the spread of WMDs and maintaining a taboo against their use is clearly in the U.S. interest. Unfortunately, half of this problem may already be beyond solution. North Korea may already possess a nuclear weapon and chemical and biological threats are spreading (Roberts 1993). Thus, the threat is present today (Aspin 1993b). With nonproliferation only slowing the expansion of nuclear possession, only the taboo against nuclear use remains salient, and then only if new nuclear powers accept it.

Aside from the substitution of extended conventional deterrence for extended nuclear deterrence and equipping forces for combat in a nuclear major regional contingency, the advocates of tightly constrained nuclear deterrence propose strong collective security measures by the international community as the best source of enforcement for a global ban on the use of nuclear weapons (Dunn 1994; Mazarr 1993; Levine 1993; Swiecicki 1992; Fetter 1991). The CSIS Nuclear Strategy Study Group concluded that

> A robust global agreement that provided for crippling political, economic, and military sanctions, in the event of nuclear use could in effect take the place of a credible nuclear retaliation in deterring nuclear war. (Mazarr 1993, 54)

The general components of this international regime are:

- an unequivocal U.S. renunciation of first use;
- universally enforced economic sanctions against the offending state;
- a strong presumption of action by the United Nations (UN) to include the ultimate military sanction of destroying the offending regime with conventional forces; and
- overall reduction in internationally perceived utility of force through expanded use of international forums for settling disputes.

Some supporters of reduced nuclear dependency add a fifth option for enforcing the nuclear taboo—preemption.

Normally, the definition of deterrence would not include the concept of preemption or preventive war. Gary Guertner (1993) includes preemption of a rogue state's WMD capabilities in his definition of conventional deterrence. For McGeorge Bundy (1991), one of the most important results of the Gulf war was the elimination of Iraq's WMD capabilities, which could not have occurred without the conflict. In addition, with the increased efficacy of conventional weapons in a counterproliferation role, Colin Gray (1992) postulates that if the United States does not wish to rely on nuclear deterrence, and conventional means for preemption are available, then there will be an increased temptation to preempt. Preemption is emerging as an essential element of current deterrence thinking (Davis 1993a; Buchanan 1993; Engstrom 1993; Strain 1993; Levine 1993). Without preemption of rogue WMD capabilities, the United States and its coalition partners might not have confidence that conventional deterrence would hold. Michele Flournoy (1993) and Philip Zelikow (1993) both recommend that preemption be considered against nuclear-armed adversaries or those striving for a nuclear capability. Zelikow believes an internationally supported declaratory policy of preemption might slow rogue state WMD proliferation. The inclusion of preemption, while somewhat inconsistent with the older modalities of deterrence, is essentially compatible with the concept of dynamic deterrence.

Thus, the arguments for conventionally based extended deterrence are mutually supporting. If conventional weapons can attain the strategic capabilities once held exclusively by nuclear weapons, and the use of nuclear weapons is politically and morally unacceptable, then the United States can and should shift the basis of its deterrence strategy from nuclear to conventional weapons. For the conventionalists, such as Guertner, "Direct retaliation is one of the few credible missions for strategic nuclear forces in the post–cold war world. Extending deterrence should be a function of conventional forces" (1993, 149).

It's Too Early. Despite significant support for a growing reliance on conventional deterrence even in the face of nuclear threats, extended nuclear deterrence still has advocates. According to Keith Payne (1992):

> Past U.S. policy has not been guided by the notion that nuclear weapons serve only to deter the use of other nuclear weapons, and it should not be so restricted in the future. Because deterring conflict is far superior to the actual use of force in most instances, we should continue to pursue nuclear policies that attempt to cast as long a deterrence shadow as is likely to be credible, including the deterrence of conventional, chemical, biological, or nuclear provocations. (p. 270)

The CILS report (Kaufman, Clark, and Sheehan 1991) on discriminate deterrence, despite advocating increased reliance on conventional capabilities, saw a continuing role for nuclear weapons in deterring the massing of forces necessary for launching a "no warning" conventional offensive (p. 112), as many believe is possible in Korea. Support for continued reliance on nuclear deterrence is based on essentially three arguments.

- The vast destructiveness of nuclear weapons and the inability to defend against them makes it easy to communicate their effect to even the most desperate opponents.
- The retrenchment of U.S. forces makes nuclear weapons essential to

maintaining an extended deterrence and discouraging WMD proliferation.
- Nuclear weapons are essential for reassuring regional allies faced by significant conventional or WMD threats.

The first of these arguments focuses on the punishment modality of deterrence. Its central theme is that the costs of challenging a nuclear deterrent are both uncontrollable and irrevocable for the aggressor. Robert Pape (1992) supports this position:

> In practice the vast gap in destructive power between nuclear and conventional weapons means that coercion in these two circumstances operates differently. Nuclear weapons can nearly always inflict more damage than any victim can withstand. Assuming the assailant's threat is credible, the resistance of even the most determined opponents can be overwhelmed. Conventional munitions can only inflict limited damage compared to the pain thresholds of modern nation states, so [conventional] punishment strategies are rarely effective. (p. 429)

For the supporters of continued reliance on some form of nuclear deterrence (nuclearists), this means nuclear deterrence may hold even in cases where the aggressor is irrational in Western political terms (Payne 1992; Harknett 1991). Conversely,

> Because the destructive potential of conventional weapons can be degraded significantly to the point that the challenger can perceive—correctly or incorrectly—that it is contestable, the costs associated with a conventional deterrent threat can be perceived as manageable [by the aggressor]. (Harknett 1991, 255)

Hence, nuclear weapons should disabuse a future adversary of an overly optimistic assessment of the outcome of conventional aggression or WMD use (Payne 1992). But deterring conventional aggression or WMD-based coercion may not be the most important use of U.S. nuclear weapons.

One of the key functions advocated for nuclear weapons in the post–cold war conflicts may be to provide intrawar dissuasion of the use of WMDs. A potential adversary faced with decisive conventional defeat or intolerable conventional punishment may choose to use WMDs in the absence of a credible U.S. nuclear deterrent (Payne 1992; Arquilla and Davis 1992). For nuclearists, there is the chance that a WMD-armed adversary will choose even a decisive conventional defeat rather than face the societal and personal devastation resulting from a U.S. nuclear attack.

To many analysts, the post–cold war retrenchment of U.S. forces makes nuclear weapons essential to maintaining extended deterrence and discouraging WMD proliferation among potential adversaries and friends. George Quester and Victor Utgoff (1993) argue that (1) the extreme concern over the proliferation of nuclear weapons demonstrated by the world community is itself a strong incentive for regional aggressors to proliferate; and (2) instead of letting the U.S. theater nuclear arsenal atrophy, the United States should maintain the quality of its theater nuclear forces to allow the United States to reverse the advantages of any aggressor's initial WMD use with finely tuned escalation designed to cause "minimum damage to innocent civilians" (p. 133). For Quester and Utgoff, maintaining a qualitatively superior U.S. theater nuclear capability in conjunction with highly capable conventional forces would re-

duce the significance of the rudimentary nuclear stockpiles acquired by rogue states and make proliferation unattractive. Others (Strain 1993; Dowler and Howard 1991) advocate that, although theater nuclear capabilities are required, they must be significantly improved to give them political and moral credibility for use. These improvements would include very low-yield warheads, nuclear earth-penetrating weapons (Dowler and Howard 1991), and the revival of neutron weapons (Strain 1993). Thomas Dowler and Joseph Howard (1991) and Frederick Strain (1993) assert that such improvements are essential to provide a credible nuclear deterrent to conventional regional aggression or WMD use.

The advocates of the continuing utility of nuclear weapons not only disagree with the *antinuclear* conventionalists over the types of nuclear weapons required for deterrence but also over the criteria for their use. The CSIS Nuclear Strategy Study Group report (Mazarr 1993) and Robert Levine (1993) advocate an unconditional no-first-use policy for the United States. Conversely, the nuclearists establish a variety of criteria for first use: deterrence of conventional attack on the United States and its allies (Payne 1992; Strain 1993; Dowler and Howard 1991); prevention of the destruction of a major U.S. military unit (Watman 1994; Dowler and Howard 1991); and retaliation for the use of biological weapons (Watman 1994; Quester and Utgoff 1994). Dowler and Howard (1991) are particularly concerned that the first U.S. forces to arrive in a theater during a crisis will be too light to stand up to the heavily armored units of local powers and must have some nuclear backup to prevent their conventional defeat. Quester and Utgoff (1993) assert that "no-first-use" would assure proliferators of the advantage of the first nuclear strike. They further state that, in conjunction with consultation with the UN Security Council,

> for the time being at least, the United States may also need to retain an option for exceptional first use of nuclear weapons in situations where allies and friends worry that they could be overwhelmed by hostile conventional forces. (1994, 112)

Payne (1992) and Quester and Utgoff (1993, 1994) are especially concerned that U.S. nuclear capabilities should reassure U.S. regional allies against coercion and keep them from seeking their own nuclear capabilities.

Ultimately, the U.S. nuclear umbrella has been an essential tool for preventing U.S. allies from seeking their own nuclear capabilities (Quester and Utgoff 1993, 1994). As Kathleen Bailey (1991) notes, in the absence of a nuclear umbrella the threat of conventional forces will become dominant, and U.S. allies may consider acquiring nuclear weapons as a deterrent against conventional attack. If, as is almost universally accepted, nuclear weapons can only be used to deter threats against vital U.S. interests, "the issues are, first, how to make an interest appear vital and, second, how to convince others that one's nuclear forces are adequate to the task" (Art 1992–93). Although Art believes that strategic nuclear forces can serve to extend deterrence to U.S. allies, for Quester and Utgoff (1993, 1994) the forward deployability of U.S. theater nuclear forces and their credibility for tactical application may provide the perception to allies and adversaries alike that defense of an interest is vital and under the protection of the U.S. extended nuclear deterrence.

Although there is a wide divergence in views over the dominance of conventional or nuclear weapons in deterrence, there is some convergence. Guertner (1993) states that:

> There is, however, a potential paradox of success [for extended conventional deterrence] if aggressive third world leaders believe that only weapons of mass destruction can offset U.S. advantages in conventional military power. Under such circumstances, theater nuclear weapons can have important signaling functions that communicate new risks and introduce greater costs for nuclear aggression that inflicts high casualties on U.S. forces or on allied countervalue targets. (p. 147)

Although they support continued reliance on extended nuclear deterrence, Quester and Utgoff (1993) believe that

> If the United States deploys a menu of conventional options comparable to that shown in Desert Storm, it enhances the impression that it can hold its own nuclear forces in reserve to retaliate for any use of nuclear forces by its adversaries, and that it can in the meantime punish and/or defeat such countries on the non-nuclear battlefield. (p. 139)

These views differ primarily over the character of nuclear forces. Guertner advocates a nuclear force adequate only for signaling, while Quester and Utgoff (1993) advocate nuclear forces whose deterrence value is enhanced by their quality, flexibility, and availability.

Implications. Whether conventional weapons or nuclear weapons will dominate U.S. extended deterrence strategy in the post–cold war era has significant implications for defense force structure. Given the capabilities of currently available conventional weapons, the United States would have difficulty providing an assured extended defense of regional allies against large-scale, rapid conventional invasions. Neither can the United States conventionally counter WMD-equipped ballistic missile attack with confidence. This situation poses three policy choices for U.S. decision makers:

- pursue the requirements of a purely conventional extended deterrence strategy while maintaining a near-term nuclear component for theater deterrence;
- take advantage of improved conventional and nuclear technologies to simultaneously reduce dependence on nuclear weapons and increase the credibility of their use; and finally
- improve the capability of conventional forces to defeat conventional invasion while ensuring the credibility of the existing nuclear forces to deter use of WMDs by adversaries.

This choice will determine the cost of U.S. force structure and its flexibility in meeting global U.S. commitments.

Extended Conventional Deterrence: Regional Implications

With the end of the Cold War, a world of relative order enforced by the bipolar superpower relationship has given way to one of global disorder in which regional powers pursue their own security arrangements. If deterrence is to play a role in this new world disorder, then it must apply in these regional contexts. No longer will 40 years of competition provide a modus vivendi between the United States and its potential adversaries (Pfaltzgraff 1993; Gray 1992). Determining

the efficacy of extended *conventional* deterrence in the regional context will require the examination of five questions:

1. Where must the United States apply deterrence strategy?
2. How will the adversary react to U.S. deterrent threats?
3. How will coalitions affect U.S. deterrence efforts?
4. What will be the role of U.S. reputation in developing a "dynamic," "general" deterrence environment?
5. What strategies will adversaries use to circumvent U.S. conventional deterrence?

In a post–cold war regional context, determining who should be deterred will be far more difficult than before.

1. Deterrence Strategy: Where to Apply It

Unlike during the Cold War, a U.S. decision to intervene in a particular regional conflict will depend on the assessment of U.S. interests in that conflict and not on any impact the U.S. intervention might have on a global competitor (Jervis forthcoming). In fact, because of the breakdown of the superpower relationship and its concomitant restraints on client state objectives, challenges to U.S. interests may become more frequent (Haass 1991; Nitze 1994). The outline of the debate over the locations of U.S. interests has been effectively delineated in a previous *Washington Quarterly* research survey by Don Snider and Gregory Grant (1992). As Art (1992–93) states, "Clarity about a nation's foreign policy goals is the fundamental prerequisite to the development of sound strategy" (p. 7). The outcome of this debate is crucial for the success of a U.S. strategy of extended conventional deterrence.

227

Regional powers will generally view their interests in a local conflict as more vital than those of the United States and, therefore, will tend to place less credence in U.S. deterrent threats (Jervis forthcoming; Palmer 1992; Flournoy 1993; Mahnken 1993; Gray 1992). The perception of weak U.S. commitment will be magnified where the United States has failed to explicitly identify or clearly communicate its interests. The muddled signals sent to Saddam Hussein prior to the Gulf war are a well-documented example of this failure (Stein 1992; Gray 1992; Blackwell, Mazarr, and Snider 1993). Deterrence threats are most effective when made before the attacker fixes his decision to move (Jervis forthcoming; Davis and Arquilla 1991). The lateness of U.S. decision making is a primary cause of confused signals of commitment.

Arquilla and Davis (1992) have noted that late expressions of commitment are endemic in U.S. efforts to deter and are a primary cause of deterrence failure. These late communications result from a failure of the U.S. foreign policy establishment to identify the commitment to itself. Only after a crisis has started does the United States assess its interests and decide to attempt deterrence. The lateness of these commitments attenuates their importance to an aggressor who has already decided to attack.

2. How Will the Adversary React?

More powerful states have failed to deter weaker states, even when their commitment was clearly expressed and the power imbalance between the deterrer and the attacker was obvious (Wolf 1991). Although U.S. will, commitment, and credibility may be readily apparent to all observers, ultimately the target of deterrence is a free actor who must decide to be deterred (Gray 1991; Cimbala 1992). Richard Hooker and Ricky Waddell feel that "The psychology of deterrence is . . . its most elemental feature" (1992, 81).

In deterrence theory, as opposed to deterrence practice, the opponent is assumed to be a "rational actor." Rational actors use an essentially economic "cost-benefit" analysis to determine whether or not to challenge a deterrent threat (Achen and Snidal 1989). Most post–cold war analysts of deterrence would argue that the archetypical rational actor model is unsatisfactory for developing deterrence strategy and must be tailored to a wide variety of behavioral characteristics (Payne 1992; Davis 1993b; Dunn 1994; Grier 1993). Deterrence analysts have proposed a variety of more complex models to replace the rational actor (Lebow and Stein 1989; Arquilla and Davis 1992; Metz 1993, 1994). Kenneth Watman (1994) has proposed that the ability to deter an actor should be evaluated on a continuum from "hardest-to-deter" to "easiest-to-deter." Steven Metz expands on the same paradigm, adding that an actor's susceptibility to deterrence will be determined by placement on eight continuums, each based on a given factor. Synthesizing Metz's analysis with those of other deterrence analysts, this survey addresses four such factors:

- quantity and quality of information available;
- cultural influences;
- assessment of the status quo; and
- psychological states.

One or more of these factors is likely to impede U.S. efforts to deter aggressors. At the high end of these continuums actors will be easy to deter. The low ends demonstrate a concept that permeates post–cold war deterrence literature, the "undeterrables."

Information. As we have seen, imperfect information about a defender's commitment may be present for both the defender and the attacker. Prior to the crisis, the "intended deterrees [themselves] will not know how much of a politically and technically credible threat it would take to deter them" (Gray 1991, 14). In addition, as Arquilla and Davis point out (Arquilla and Davis 1992; Davis and Arquilla 1991), adversaries have historically discounted key elements of U.S. power such as strategic mobility, precision weapons, maritime power, and airpower due to lack of familiarity with these systems. Without understanding these elements of U.S. military strength, the regional aggressor will view the absence of U.S. heavy ground forces as evidence of a lack of both capability and commitment. Moreover, Adam Garfinkle (1992) asserts that third world leaders are frequently misled into overly optimistic views of their own forces' capabilities. Without clear recognition of U.S. power, deterrence cannot hold.

Cultural Influences. Even in the presence of clear signals of commitment and unmistakable credibility, cultural differences between the United States and its potential opponents could sabotage a deterrence strategy (Jablonsky 1991). Thomas Mahnken (1991) places the impact of these cultural differences in the starkest light: "It is naive to expect cultures that place supreme value upon martyrdom, or regimes that slaughter their own citizens to embrace Western precepts of deterrence and stability" (p. 198). More subtly, cultural differences may make the format of a threat crucial. Garfinkle (1992) provides an example from the Arab world, where loud, public

deterrent threats are generally discounted as bluffs and a sign of weakness. Moreover, disrespect backs the attacker into a corner where his honor must be defended without regard to the apparent outcome. Understanding an adversary's thinking and reactions to threats may be as important as the will and credibility to back up those threats.

Assessment of the Status Quo. Yet an appropriately couched, credible threat may still not deter. An adversary's assessment of the status quo will determine how well an immediate deterrent threat will succeed. If in the estimate of attackers, the long-term status quo presents an intolerable condition, they may choose to go to war regardless of the current balance of power. The impetus to go to war may come from internal distress (Blackwell, Mazarr, and Snider 1993), or it may be the result of an assessment that the correlation of forces is shifting even more dramatically toward the defender and, therefore, opportunities for success will only decline (Arquilla and Davis 1992; Lebow 1989). Clearly, these circumstances are not the result of the opponent's irrationality, but of different perspectives on costs, benefits, and time.

Psychological States. Rejection of the rational actor model as a prescriptive tool does *not* imply that third world leaders are "crazy." As David Jablonsky (1991) correctly states, the "pure rationality model . . . is impossible to achieve since it presupposes omniscience and a capability for comprehensive analysis that time, cost and other factors do not permit" (p. 3). Arquilla and Davis (1992) refer to this condition as "limited" rationality.

Although none of the obstacles to rational decisions in a deterrence crisis listed above are truly irrational, "crazy" thinking can be present in crises. This apparently mad thinking is caused by three factors: cognitive dissonance; ideological, nationalistic, or religious values; and true psychopathology. Cognitive dissonance in a crisis results when decision makers are faced with unacceptable alternatives and filter out unpleasant information in order to increase the value of a chosen course of action (Wolf 1991; Jablonsky 1991; Lebow and Stein 1989). The dedication of adversaries to religious, nationalistic, or ideological forces may make them immune to threats that would be credible in U.S. eyes. Finally, Barry Wolf (1991) asserts that actual psychopathology among national leaders may be present at a relatively high rate. Such leaders may be willing to accept massive military or societal devastation to maintain themselves and their self-image (Record 1993). These leaders tend to be more common in the undemocratic or revolutionary states that will challenge the United States in regional contingencies (Jablonsky 1991).

The demise of the rational actor model has given rise to a replacement, the *strategic personality* (Engstrom 1993; Flournoy 1993). The strategic personality, which is a composite of the actor's position on the deterrability continuums, has significant implications for deterrence. The composition of a regional power's strategic personality will help to:

- establish the correct mix of reassurance and threat required to deter;
- assess the probability of successful deterrence; and
- determine the utility to deterrence of instruments that affect the opponent's situational perception.

If the strategic personality is to serve a prescriptive function, then the U.S. intelligence community must ac-

cept the task of determining its components on a case-by-case basis. Ultimately, strategic personality should reveal a regime's or nation's perceptions and values, allowing them to be manipulated or targeted. Utgoff (1993) asserts that developing research centers that focus on the strategic personality of regional powers may have extremely high leverage for U.S. deterrence strategy. If punishment is to be part of a U.S. strategy to deter, then the regime, its symbols, and possibly the leadership itself may be the only appropriate targets (Cohen 1994; WSS 1993). Understanding the regime's strategic personality will assist in precise target selection.

If a credible threat is not feasible, then exploitation of an adversary's strategic personality may offer an alternative. Some analysts (Cimbala 1993), U.S. Navy studies (Buchanan 1993), and Air Force studies (Engstrom 1993) propose that emerging information-based capabilities designed to modify an opponent's strategic personality may have the highest future deterrence leverage. Finally, if there is a reasonable probability, as Wolf (1991) and Payne (1992) indicate, that a future adversary might prove "undeterrable" even in the face of nuclear deterrence, active defenses and preemptive capabilities will be essential elements of U.S. force structure.

3. Multilateral versus Unilateral Deterrence

As Jervis (forthcoming) notes, "the question of whether policy is to be pursued multilaterally or unilaterally may be only slightly less important than the question of what interests are worthy of defense" (chap. 9). Advocates of a multilateral approach offer two reasons for depending more on international efforts and less on U.S. unilateral capabilities:

- U.S. power must be bound by international controls to assure other nations about its use and to prevent its abuse.
- The United States requires coalition bases and capabilities to conduct decisive, low-cost operations in a regional conflict.

For those who oppose reliance on coalitions:

- Collective security is a chimera: states will always act in their perceived best interests.
- Reliance on allies will be too constraining to U.S. policy in political, strategic, and tactical terms.
- The regional coalitions will be prone to fracture in the face of severe coercive threats.

The debate over the role of coalitions in deterrence is not one of absolutes, but of degrees.

Multilateralists. The advocates of multilateralism emphasize the value of coalitions as demonstrated in Desert Storm. They view Desert Storm as an extremely successful application of both the collective security powers of the UN and the power of the ad hoc Desert Storm coalition. It was also a harbinger of the future. "The United Nations, not the United States, will threaten a response to a North Korean attack south or an Iranian attack on Saudi Arabia" (Blackwell, Mazarr, and Snider 1993, 175). They see the UN role as vital in providing political legitimacy to U.S. actions in the Persian Gulf, creating an environment conducive to both international and domestic support for U.S. intervention. The leaders of regional powers viewed "the ability to act as an integrator of

nations and policies" as a key element of U.S. power (Garrity 1993b, 154).

Others would add that the predilection to act unilaterally is too destabilizing and might result in coalitions rising against the United States (Jervis forthcoming; Art 1992–93). Gary Guertner (1993) states,

Even though collective action and shared capabilities may limit U.S. freedom of action, these limits are reassuring to others and may contribute more to stability than attempts by the world's only superpower to unilaterally impose deterrence—nuclear or conventional. (p. 145)

Quester and Utgoff (1993) adopt a similar position, pointing out that the international community's fears of U.S. nuclear or conventional dominance "can be assuaged if the United States continues to develop confidence in its willingness to exercise power only on behalf of, and with, the world community" (p. 138). Although support from the world community may be politically useful, coalitions may be militarily indispensable.

In addition to political legitimacy, coalition partners provide two essential requirements for deterrence credibility: in-place forces with capabilities that complement those of the United States; and basing access (Guertner 1993). As noted in Huth (1988a) the local balance of forces has historically been a key to deterrence success in a crisis. In immediate deterrence crises, in-country coalition forces can complement U.S. capabilities (Odom 1993) and when combined with enhanced perceptions of U.S. long-range power may tip the balance in favor of deterrence. The Saudis, recognizing this fact, are currently modernizing and expanding their ground forces (Simon 1992; Atkenson 1992). Long-term force structure agreements with key coalition partners could enhance the complementarity of U.S. and coalition forces.

Without access to en route and in-theater logistical and basing support the United States could not have brought overwhelming power to bear in the Persian Gulf (Blackwell, Mazarr, and Snider 1993; Stein 1992). As Garrity (1993b) notes,

> in many cases, intervention in some regional conflicts will be so demanding that [the United States and its traditional allies] will require the support of many other states, which support is often most readily called upon through an international mechanism. This support—including bases, overflight rights, and logistical support—may be necessary to apply *decisive* force (i.e., at a level that ensures a quick conflict with low casualties and low collateral damage). (p. 157)

Although the Cold War has ended, the geostrategic quandary for the United States has not. U.S. interests in Eurasia are thousands of miles from the United States but within easy striking distance of regional powers. Michael Desch (1992) and William Odom (1993) assert, therefore, that overseas bases are vital for U.S. power projection capabilities.

Limits of Multilateralism. The opponents of extensive U.S. reliance on coalitions argue that the advocates of tying U.S. power to collective security are making a virtue out of necessity. First, they would argue that only the United States had the power to forge the Desert Storm coalition and that apart from U.S. capabilities only the availability of the Saudi bases was essential to U.S. success (Mahnken

1993; Garrity 1993a; Gray 1992). More generally, Josef Joffe (1992) and Gray (1992) argue that collective security has never really protected anyone and is doomed to failure because states will always act in their own self-interest. This has been true even in NATO, the most enduring of modern coalitions. The strength of the NATO alliance rested on the cohesion derived from confrontation with a central adversary, but NATO cohesion has sometimes failed when the alliance pursued problems of a peripheral or ambiguous nature (Kaufman, Clark, and Sheehan 1991; Mahnken 1993; Garrity 1993a). Policy differences with coalition partners may prove so constraining that the United States may be unable to deter aggression effectively or protect its vital interests.

The policies of its partners in a coalition may prove constraining to the United States in three ways: (1) their internal domestic policies may prevent deployment of U.S. forces prior to an immediate crisis; (2) coalition partners may honestly disagree with the U.S. assessment of the threat and the actions necessary to diffuse it; and (3) fear of the threat itself, particularly WMDs, may prevent the coalition partner from giving the United States access and cause threatened states to succumb to coercion. U.S. friends in Southwest Asia are particularly vulnerable to internal pressures to limit any permanent U.S. presence (Hess 1993; Simon 1992; WSS 1993). U.S. forward presence forces in the region could act as a lightning rod for social unrest. They could, for instance, undermine the legitimacy of the Saudi royal family (Hess 1993). Thus, U.S. forces must remain over the horizon (Garrity 1993b). A major goal of U.S. deterrence strategy must be to communicate the capability of its long-range forces to defeat aggression and cast the shadow of what Haffa (1992) calls their "virtual presence" as a replacement for forward-deployed forces.

Regardless of internal constraints, coalition partners may agree with U.S. objectives but disagree with U.S. tactics, making deterrence impossible. Prior to the Iraqi invasion of Kuwait, "The most persistent disbelievers in the possibility of an Iraqi invasion were other Arab leaders who continually cautioned President George Bush and others not to take any action that might provoke Saddam" (McCausland 1993, 7). A disagreement over tactics could also arise over counterproliferation efforts aimed at North Korea. Flournoy (1993) avers that efforts to gain collective approval could compromise preemption. There is little the United States can do except wait if its coalition partners prefer to take a passive or conciliatory position (Blackwell, Mazarr, and Snider 1993). Coalition partners may also restrain U.S. efforts to produce decisive victory by refusing to allow the destruction of the offending regime (Hess 1993). Thus, even if the possibility of attack is clear, the attacker's intentions are unmistakable, and decisive victory is possible, U.S. coalition partners may still balk at accepting U.S. forces or supporting en route U.S. deployment efforts and may limit the extent of the victory.

The contents of the threat itself may imply that a U.S. presence will provoke an attack. If waging war in alliance with the United States is too costly for the coalition partner compared to accepting the attacker's demands, then the partner may acquiesce even if the U.S. commitment is highly credible (Wu 1989). Most analysts, including some supporters of collective security, agree that the possession of WMDs by a regional aggressor will make forming coalitions extremely difficult if not impossible (Flournoy 1993; Garrity 1993a; Mahnken 1993; Zelikow 1993; Swiecicki 1992). Conversely, a powerful conventional threat, such as that posed by North Korea against the South, may provide a deterrent shield against preemption of the North's nuclear program (Spector 1992; Zelikow 1993). Consequently, despite credible U.S. commitment and capabilities, dependence on reluctant allies may allow a vital U.S. interest to be successfully challenged.

Although coalitions may offer the United States political advantages and in-place forces to provide assistance in immediate deterrence, reluctant coalition partners are likely to be an ingredient of regional conflict. This implies that the United States should retain a significant capability for unilateral intervention.

4. The Role of U.S. Reputation

Analysts of reputation since the Cold War have addressed three factors: the end of bipolar competition; the role of reputation in and out of crises; and the impact of war termination on reputation. Of these factors, the first has had the greatest impact on the current understanding of reputation.

For the United States, the strategic motivation for supporting or creating commitments in order to develop an image of U.S. credibility has disappeared with the end of the Cold War. Gains and losses in the developing world were important during the Cold War because of their impact on the perception of U.S. reputation by the central adversary and its allies (Desch 1992). The United States fought to defend areas of less than vital interest attempting to ensure its reputation in more vital regions (Gray 1991; Jervis forthcoming). U.S. decision makers viewed contests in peripheral areas as only parts of a larger conflict; a U.S. willingness to fight in these places, therefore, both supported containment and the reputation required for deterrence. But as Jervis (1989) observes, "it appears [other states] do not perceive commitments as so tightly linked and that the outcomes of confrontations are determined to a greater extent by each side's intrinsic interest in the issue at stake" (p. 192). Consequently, U.S. decision makers will not improve their reputation for acting decisively in regions of vital interest by creating and supporting commitments in peripheral areas.

If extended conventional deterrence is to protect vital interests, it must both effectively prevent and defuse crises. The most effective deterrence strategy will prevent threats from arising—an approach frequently called general deterrence (Wu 1989). For many analysts, the crushing defeat of Iraq by the U.S.-led coalition has created the reputation for U.S. will and capability that provides the basis for a long-term general deterrence environment (Guertner 1993; Perry 1991; Gray 1992). Yet failures to support commitments or effectively apply force may rapidly undermine this general reputation (Haffa 1993). Saddam Hussein has been broadly quoted as citing the failures of U.S. policy in Vietnam and the U.S. withdrawal from Beirut in the aftermath of the 1983 bombing of the Marine barracks as his rationale for discounting the U.S. commitment to liberate Kuwait (Stein 1992).

Because of its intense media coverage and lopsided outcome, the Gulf war may have had greater impact than past conflicts in establishing a general

U.S. reputation for the capacity and will to protect its interests (Haffa 1992). For reputation to be useful in an immediate extended deterrence crisis, it must be based on previous confrontations between the defender and the attacker (Huth 1988b; Wu 1989). But in an immediate crisis, a general reputation for will and capability to retaliate is apparently of questionable utility (Huth 1988a). Once an opponent has threatened to use force, the defender's general reputation has already been factored into the decision.

Finally, reputation depends upon the effective and decisive use of force. For deterrence to be effective, U.S. forces must be able to win decisively with low cost (Jervis forthcoming). Declines in U.S. defense spending will be closely followed by possible opponents and any perceived inability of the United States to conduct a Desert Storm–style operation will undermine deterrence (Garrity 1993a). In addition, U.S. decision makers must have a reputation for being willing to not merely reverse an adversary's aggression but to severely punish it as well (Haffa 1992; Buchanan 1993). Because of the propensity of conventional deterrence to fail, the character of the war that followed the last "deterrence failure" will affect how long deterrence credibility lasts after that war. To many analysts, the decision not to destroy the Republican Guards at the end of the Gulf war, whether emanating from humanitarian or strategic impulses, will affect the way potential aggressors will view the U.S. willingness to destroy regimes (Blackwell, Mazarr, and Snider 1993). To produce long periods of stability, conventionalists contend, dynamic deterrence must create a reputation for credibility, effectiveness, and decisiveness.

5. Counterstrategies

Although a powerful reputation may help sustain a strong general deterrence regime, a U.S. deterrence strategy must ultimately be effective against specific opponents. The targets of U.S. efforts to deter will seek strategies to counter the overwhelming U.S. military dominance displayed in the Persian Gulf. Eliot Cohen (1993) criticizes Secretary Aspin's "bottom-up review" for focusing on

> enemies who had learned nothing at all from Saddam's debacle. Nothing about playing on American sensitivity to casualties, nothing about using weapons of mass destruction to scare off America's allies, nothing about engaging in ambiguous aggression rather than Saddam's incompetent brutality. (p. 40)

The same general criticism applies to current thinking on extended deterrence. Advocates and critics of conventional deterrence have acknowledged that the victory in Desert Storm does not indicate any significant capability to combat guerrilla warfare, terrorism, or ambiguous challenges to U.S. interests.

Two studies have focused on regional counters to U.S. conventional dominance. Garrity (1993a) has integrated the thinking of numerous regional area experts to determine how U.S. enemies and friends are reassessing their national security strategies in light of the Gulf war. Mahnken (1993) has analyzed the strategies that a regional adversary might employ to deter U.S. intervention in a regional conflict. These studies and others suggest five broad categories of counterstrategies to U.S. conventional deterrence. An adversary could seek to (1) control the threshold of conflict; (2) control the spectrum of conflict; (3) exclude the United States from the region; (4) raise the costs of intervention; or (5) ensure the survival of its regime. Intelligent adversaries will not use these strategies in isolation but will seek an optimum mix to achieve their objectives. Because the bulk of U.S. power will be outside the area when a crisis starts, local powers will focus on strategies to keep the United States out of the region.

Control the Threshold. As most observers acknowledge, it is much easier for U.S. political leadership to develop the domestic political support to combat blatant adventurism than to deter ambiguous aggression (Blackwell, Mazarr, and Snider 1993). Future adversaries may seek to avoid the appearance of threatening U.S. interests in a region by employing limited aims strategies (Paul 1991; Stern et al. 1989), by incremental achievement of aims, and by obscuring the causes of conflict (Mahnken 1993). In a limited aims strategy, an adversary will use conventional means to take as much as possible of its objective without provoking U.S. intervention. An incremental approach is an expanded form of the limited aims strategy. Because the adversaries do not have a priori knowledge of the threshold for U.S. intervention, they will use limited probes to find it. Successes will be followed by periods of evaluation. U.S. threats will be honored with tactical retreats followed by attempts to find the limits of U.S. patience (Garrity 1993a). The probes would be calibrated never to exceed a newly established U.S. tolerance of the status quo.

Finally, by obscuring the source of the threat either through support of internal dissent or insurgency in the target state or assertions of self-defense, the aggressor may make the conflict sufficiently ambiguous to avoid triggering U.S. intervention. But because regional aggressors are unsure of the thresholds that may also trigger U.S. intervention, they will seek methods of negating U.S. conventional dominance.

Control the Spectrum of Conflict. Rogue states have two avenues by which to negate U.S. conventional dominance: control of the spectrum of conflict; and direct counters to U.S. capabilities. To control the spectrum of conflict the adversary will either concentrate on guerrilla warfare or threaten the use of WMDs. In Desert Storm the United States demonstrated the ability to roll an armored force back over territory it had taken. Even the most ardent supporters of the deterrent role of conventional weapons note that the forces and tactics that prevailed in Desert Storm are not readily adaptable to guerrilla warfare (Perry 1991). Metz (1993) believes that the utility of deterrence declines rapidly at levels of conflict below conventional warfare. Adversaries may also choose to leap over the conventional level of conflict by threatening to use WMDs (Cimbala 1993).

If faced with fighting the conventional forces of the United States, its rivals will also attempt to counter U.S. conventional dominance directly through technological and asymmetric means. Technological challenges will range from sea mines to disrupt U.S. logistics to improved air defenses and command and control. Advanced conventional weapons with improved accuracy may present new challenges to fixed U.S. bases and eventually to surface maritime power (Patton 1993). According to the CILS report, if the United States is to retain the technological edge needed to deter or defeat regional powers, it must assess future

adversaries' acquisition of advanced conventional capabilities (Kaufman, Clark, and Sheehan 1991). How readily regional powers will be able to absorb these advanced technologies remains the source of continued debate (Garfinkle 1992; Roberts 1993).

Adversaries will also seek passive and low-technology solutions to U.S. conventional supremacy. In the passive mode, the adversary will use mobility, hardening, foul weather, and dispersal to counter U.S. air supremacy and precision guided munitions. Finally, special operations forces may be the tool of choice to attack air bases and logistics facilities (Garrity 1993a).

Strategies of Exclusion. If an adversary believes that it will be unable to control the conflict spectrum it may be able to deny the United States access to the region. Regional powers have noted U.S. dependence on en route logistics support, transit rights, and in-theater bases to support Desert Storm. To keep U.S. power out of a region, two strategies could prove effective: capturing or destroying vital logistics nodes; or fracturing the coalition (Mahnken 1993; Dunn 1994). A fait accompli strategy could deny U.S. access to key facilities in the region (Paul 1991; Stern et al. 1989). This could be a high-risk strategy for the aggressor because it would threaten vital U.S. interests. If the United States chose to reverse the fait accompli through a long conventional war, then its war aims may not be limited. The regime itself would be threatened with destruction. To destroy ports of entry or render them useless through use of nuclear weapons or other WMDs would also be high risk because the United States maintains such overwhelming nuclear asymmetry with its potential regional opponents. *Threats* of terrorism and/or WMDs against coalition partners may be successful, however, in denying U.S. access to in-theater bases or en route facilities without activating a U.S. response. Finally, potential adversaries may attempt to extend their reach through coalitions with other rogue states (WSS 1993).

Raising the Costs. Even without the capability to deny the United States access to a region of vital interest, a local power may nonetheless prevent U.S. intervention by raising its perceived costs. If the United States perceives the costs in blood, national cohesion, and treasure as too high when compared to the value of the interests involved in a conflict then an aggressor may deter U.S. intervention. Perceived costs can be raised by the continued U.S. distaste for protracted, guerrilla warfare (Pfaltzgraff 1993; Blackwell, Mazarr, and Snider 1993) and military casualties (Safire 1993; Mahnken 1993) and a generally greater willingness on the part of potential adversaries to accept high casualties (Mahnken 1993). Part of this strategy may be threats of direct WMD attack against the United States either through ballistic missiles in the future (Mahnken 1991; WSS 1993) or terrorism (Dunn 1994). The specter of WMD use will also raise the perceived level of cost to U.S. forces. The U.S. aversion to casualties applies not only to its own and allied forces and civilians but also to the civilian society of the adversary (Cohen 1994; Glosson 1993). The decision to disperse military equipment to civilian neighborhoods or the actual use of civilians as human shields may further contribute to dissuading U.S. intervention (Garrity 1993b).

Finally, a belligerent may attempt to dissuade intervention by threatening critical economic disruptions or en-

vironmental destruction. Although there may have been tactical considerations to the Iraqi release of oil into the Persian Gulf (preventing an amphibious landing) and the igniting of the Kuwaiti oil wells (obscuring and hindering the allied land forces), these actions have been recognized as the first case of environmental "terrorism." In the future, a potential aggressor may threaten to cause environmental destruction as part of a strategy to dissuade U.S. intervention in a regional conflict.

Economic cartels and coalitions have generally proved ineffective at stopping intervention. In the future, belligerents may threaten or attempt new and different means of economic disruption. Robert Steele (1993) has done an extensive study of U.S. vulnerabilities to warfare in the information age. He points out that a belligerent may threaten to disrupt national or international trade, financial transactions, and communications through attacks on vital communications links and computer systems. Such attacks could take the form of overt destruction of critical rail links, air traffic control systems, communications links, electrical grids, and computer systems or could be more subtly affected by electronic infiltration and disruption (Steele 1993; Toffler and Toffler 1993).

Strategies of Regime Survival. Third world leaders consider the survival of their regime to be paramount (Dunn 1994; Garrity 1993a; Mahnken 1993). Regional aggressors will seek to prevent the United States from expanding its war aims to destruction of the regime and may view threats of WMD use as the ultimate guarantee of its survival (Payne 1992; Cimbala 1993; Arquilla and Davis 1992). With nuclear weapons ensuring the regime's

Charles T. Allan

survival, a rogue state may discount the risks of war and resort to force.

The recognition by regional powers of the strength of U.S. conventional capabilities is the central theme of the studies of counterstrategies to U.S. conventional dominance. This perception will effectively support deterrence of conventional conflict as long as the United States maintains the will to use the force, extreme technological asymmetry, and quantitative sufficiency demonstrated in Desert Storm. Other powers will continue to seek strategies that allow them to regain strategic independence by avoiding direct confrontations with the United States and will challenge U.S. deterrence through asymmetric means.

Conclusions and Implications

The end of the Cold War and the U.S.-led victory in the Persian Gulf have established a new security environment. Four characteristics of this new era will affect U.S. deterrence strategy. First, U.S. security policy will have a regional focus. Second, although the United States will be militarily dominant it will significantly reduce its in-place forces overseas. Third, and arguably, U.S. nuclear weapons will have little or no role in regional conflicts. Finally, just as in the Cold War, likely U.S. adversaries will enjoy the advantage of proximity to the theaters of potential conflict, while the United States must project power thousands of miles to protect its interests.

This new security environment has profound implications for the future of U.S. deterrence theory, strategy, and practice. This survey has approached the problem by addressing the meaning of deterrence, assessing the deterrent roles of conventional and nuclear weapons, and reviewing the ramifica-

tions of a regionally oriented security policy for U.S. deterrence strategy. Four issues have emerged from this analysis that will dominate the deterrence debate and establish the basis for further research:

- If deterrence is to be based on conventional weapons, what form of deterrence will overcome the twin U.S. dilemmas of distance from its vital security interests and retraction of U.S. forces from overseas? How will deterrence and the use of force interact? Is preemption of adversary WMD capabilities essential to the success of extended conventional deterrence?

- What will be the role of nuclear weapons in an era of U.S. conventional dominance, and how will that role be affected by the proliferation of weapons of mass destruction? If U.S. allies require a nuclear umbrella, are strategic nuclear forces adequate for the task or must the United States retain robust theater nuclear capabilities? Finally, will U.S. pledges of "no-first-use" or "negative security guarantees" promote or undermine nonproliferation?

- To what extent should or must U.S. deterrence strategy depend on multilateral or collective security? Can U.S. military supremacy be brought to bear without coalition support? Will the ability of the United States to act decisively unilaterally drive states to oppose it in order to retain some level of strategic independence? Can U.S. coalition partners withstand WMD coercion without U.S. nuclear guarantees?

- How will potential adversaries react to U.S. deterrence strategies? How will they attempt to circumvent the conventional dominance displayed in Desert Storm? How will a conventionally based deterrence strategy overcome strategies of exclusion, U.S. aversion to casualties, or ambiguous aggression?

This survey has illuminated contemporary thinking on these questions and identified areas of divergence and convergence. The issues of the role of nuclear weapons in extended deterrence and the level of multilateralism required in U.S. strategy generate the greatest divergence of thought in the policy analysis community. Conversely, there is more general agreement on the criteria for U.S. forces necessary to underwrite U.S. deterrence strategy.

Any U.S. deterrence strategy must rely on credible forces. Areas of convergence in the deterrence discourse imply several requirements for their structure. Credible U.S. forces must:

- promptly project sufficient firepower to reassure threatened allies against rapid conventional defeat;
- deter and defend against WMD attack in order to ensure coalition cohesion and protect forward-deployed U.S. forces;
- have the capability to fight a WMD-equipped adversary either through long-range attack or damage-limiting procedures;
- be discriminate in order to avoid civilian casualties while punishing a rogue regime and destroying its fielded forces and its war-making potential; and
- minimize dependence on overseas basing to circumvent strategies of exclusion.

The capabilities of the forces that meet these requirements must be clearly communicated to potential adversaries.

Neither current U.S. conventional nor nuclear capabilities satisfy all of these criteria. Although the military can design the necessary forces, the broader security policy community must establish the general signaling, dialogue, and posture required to make these forces an effective deterrent. The outcome of the deterrence debate will determine the configuration of U.S. force structure, the doctrine for its application, and the policies for its use.

Deterrence is no longer frozen in its cold war construct. Yet two factors may constrict its formerly preeminent role in U.S. strategy: the changing form of warfare itself, and increased cooperative international engagement. If for no other reason than the potential spread of weapons of mass destruction, however, it is not clear that deterrence is out of the nuclear fire. Ultimately, deterrence cannot be a stand-alone strategy in the post–cold war era and must be flexibly applied to meet the demands of the new security environment.

The views expressed here are those of the author and do not reflect the official policy or position of the U.S. Air Force, the U.S. Department of Defense, or the U.S. government. The author wishes to thank Mike Cantagallo for his assistance with this article.

References

Abshire, David. 1993. Interview by author. Washington, D.C., December 29.

Achen, Christopher H., and Duncan Snidal. 1989. "Rational Deterrence Theory and Comparative Case Studies." *World Politics* 41 (January), pp. 143–169.

Arquilla, John, and Paul K. Davis. 1992. *Extended Deterrence, Compellence and the "Old World Order."* Santa Monica, Calif.: RAND.

Art, Robert J. 1992–93. "A US Military Strategy for the 1990s: Reassurance Without Dominance." *Survival* 34 (Winter), pp. 3–23.

Aspin, Les. 1993a. *The Bottom-Up Review: Forces for a New Era.* Washington, D.C.: Department of Defense.

——. 1993b. "The Defense Department's

New Nuclear Counterproliferation Initiative." Address to the National Academy of Sciences, Washington, D.C., December 7.

Atkenson, Edward B. 1992. *A Military Assessment of the Middle East, 1991–1996.* Carlisle Barracks, Pa.: Strategic Studies Institute, U.S. Army War College.

Bailey, Kathleen C. 1991. *Doomsday Weapons in the Hands of Many: The Arms Control Challenge of the '90s.* Urbana: University of Illinois Press.

Betts, Richard K. 1988. "Nuclear Peace and Conventional War." *Journal of Strategic Studies* 11 (March), pp. 79–95.

Bitzinger, Richard A. 1989. *Reconstructing NATO Strategy for the 1990s: A Conference Report.* Santa Monica, Calif.: RAND.

Blackwell, James A., Michael J. Mazarr, and Don M. Snider. 1993. *Desert Storm: The Gulf War and What We Learned.* Boulder, Colo.: Westview Press.

Boeker, Egbert. 1990. "A Non-Provocative Conventional Posture in Europe With No First Use of Nuclear Weapons." In Elmer Schmaling, ed., *Life Beyond the Bomb: Global Stability Without Nuclear Deterrence.* New York, N.Y.: St. Martin's Press.

Bowie, Christopher, et al. 1993. *The New Calculus: Analyzing Airpower's Changing Role in Joint Theater Campaigns.* Santa Monica, Calif.: RAND.

Buchanan, Richard A. 1993. Presentation to CSIS Extended Conventional Deterrence Working Group, Washington, D.C., December 6.

Bundy, McGeorge. 1991. "Nuclear Weapons and the Gulf." *Foreign Affairs* 70 (Fall), pp. 83–110.

Carnesale, Albert. 1993. "Defenses Against New Nuclear Threats." In Robert D. Blackwill and Albert Carnesale, eds., *New Nuclear Nations: Consequences for U.S. Policy.* New York, N.Y.: Council on Foreign Relations.

Cimbala, Stephen J. 1991. *Strategy After Deterrence.* New York, N.Y.: Praeger.

———. 1992. *Force and Diplomacy in the Future.* New York, N.Y.: Praeger.

———. 1993. "Nuclear Weapons in the New World Order." *Journal of Strategic Studies* 16 (June), pp. 173–179.

Cohen, Eliot A. 1993. "Beyond Bottom Up." *National Review* 45, no. 22 (November 15), pp. 40–43.

———. 1994. "The Mystique of U.S. Air Power." *Foreign Affairs* 73 (January–February), pp. 109–124.

Cropsey, Seth. 1994. "The Only Credible Deterrent." *Foreign Affairs* 73 (March–April), pp. 14–20.

Davis, Jacquelyn. 1993a. *Deterrence Planning for Regional Conflict and Crisis Management: Setting Priorities for the 1990's,* Director's Workshop Report. Washington, D.C.: Institute for Foreign Policy Analysis.

———. 1993b. "Deterrence in the Twenty-first Century: Roles and Missions for Naval Forces." In Robert L. Pfaltzgraff and Richard H. Schultz, Jr., eds., *Naval Forward Presence and the National Military Strategy.* Annapolis, Md.: Naval Institute Press.

Davis, Paul K., and John Arquilla. 1991. *Deterring or Coercing Opponents in Crisis: Lessons from the War with Saddam Hussein.* Santa Monica, Calif.: RAND.

Desch, Michael C. 1992. "Conventional Deterrence and U.S. Post–Cold War Military Base Requirements in the Third World." Paper presented to the conference on "Conventional Deterrence in the Post–Cold War Era," U.S. Naval Postgraduate School, Monterey, Calif., August 13–14.

Dowler, Thomas W., and Joseph S. Howard III. 1991. "Countering the Threat of the Well Armed Tyrant: A Modest Proposal for Small Nuclear Weapons." *Strategic Review* 19 (Fall), pp. 34–40.

Drew, Dennis M. 1993. *Airpower in the New World Order.* Carlisle Barracks, Pa.: Strategic Studies Institute, U.S. Army War College.

Dunn, Lewis A. 1994. "Rethinking the Nuclear Equation: The United States and the New Nuclear Powers." *The Washington Quarterly* 17 (Winter), pp. 5–25.

Engstrom, Peter. 1993. Presentation to CSIS Extended Conventional Deterrence Working Group, Washington, D.C., December 6.

Fetter, Steve. 1991. "Ballistic Missiles and Weapons of Mass Destruction: What is the Threat? What Should be Done?" *International Security* 16 (Summer), pp. 5–42.

Flournoy, Michele A. 1993. "Implications for U.S. Military Strategy." In Robert D. Blackwill and Albert Carnesale, eds., *New Nuclear Nations: Consequences for U.S. Policy.* New York, N.Y.: Council on Foreign Relations.

Friedberg, Aaron L. 1991. "Is the United States Capable of Acting Strategically?" *The Washington Quarterly* 14 (Winter), pp. 5–23.

Garfinkle, Adam. 1991. "The Gulf War: Was It Worth It?" *World & I* 6 (October), pp. 70–79.

———. 1992. "Arab Political Culture and Deterrence." Paper presented to the conference on "Conventional Deterrence in the Post–Cold War Era," U.S. Naval Postgraduate School, Monterey, Calif., August 13–14.

Garrity, Patrick J. 1993a. *Does the Gulf War (Still) Matter? Foreign Perspectives on the War and the Future of International Security.* Los Alamos, N.M.: Center for National Security Studies.

———. 1993b. "Implications of the Persian Gulf War for Regional Powers." *The Washington Quarterly* 16 (Summer), pp. 153–170.

George, Alexander L. 1991. *Forceful Persuasion: Coercive Diplomacy as an Alternative to War.* Washington, D.C.: U.S. Institute of Peace.

Glosson, Buster C. 1993. "Impact of Precision Weapons on Air Combat Operations." *Airpower Journal* 7 (Summer), pp. 4–10.

Gray, Colin S. 1991. "Deterrence Resurrected: Revisiting Some Fundamentals." *Parameters* 21 (Summer), pp. 13–21.

———. 1992. "Deterrence in the New Strategic Environment." *Comparative Strategy* 11 (July–September), pp. 247–267.

Grier, Peter. 1993. "In Nukes Strategy Review, US Eyes 'Undeterrables.'" *Christian Science Monitor,* November 9, pp. 1, 4.

Guertner, Gary L. 1992. "Introduction." In Guertner, Robert P. Haffa, Jr., and George H. Quester, eds., *Conventional Forces and the Future of Deterrence.* Carlisle Barracks, Pa.: Strategic Studies Institute, U.S. Army War College.

———. 1993. "Deterrence and Conventional Military Forces." *The Washington Quarterly* 16 (Winter), pp. 141–151.

Haass, Richard N. 1991. "Regional Order in the 1990s: The Challenge of the Middle East." *The Washington Quarterly* 14 (Winter), pp. 181–188.

Haffa, Robert P., Jr. 1992. "The Future of Conventional Deterrence: Strategies and Forces to Underwrite a New World Order." In Gary L. Guertner, Robert P. Haffa, Jr., and George H. Quester, eds., *Conventional Forces and the Future of Deterrence.* Carlisle Barracks, Pa.: Strategic Studies Institute, U.S. Army War College.

———. 1993. Letter to author, November 21.

Haffa, Robert P., Jr., and James H. Patton. 1991. "Analogues of Stealth: Submarines and Aircraft." *Comparative Strategy* 10 (July–September), pp. 257–271.

Harknett, Richard J. 1991. "Conventional Deterrence and Strategic Change." Ph.D. diss., Johns Hopkins University, Baltimore, Md.

———. 1992. "Integrating Tomahawk into a Conventional Deterrence Strategy: Inherent Flaws, Blunt Solutions." Paper presented to the conference on "Conventional Deterrence in the Post–Cold War Era," U.S. Naval Postgraduate School, Monterey, Calif., August 13–14.

Hess, Andrew C. 1993. "Cultural and Political Limits on Forward Presence in Southwest Asia." In Robert L. Pfaltzgraff and Richard H. Schultz, Jr., eds., *Naval Forward Presence and the National Military Strategy.* Annapolis, Md.: Naval Institute Press.

Hooker, Richard D., Jr., and Ricky L. Waddell. 1992. "The Future of Conventional Deterrence." *Naval War College Review* 45 (Summer), pp. 78–87.

Huth, Paul K. 1988a. *Extended Deterrence and the Prevention of War.* New Haven, Conn.: Yale University Press.

———. 1988b. "Extended Deterrence and the Outbreak of War." *American Political Science Review* 82 (June), pp. 423–443.

Huth, Paul K., and Bruce Russett. 1990. "Testing Deterrence Theory: Rigor Makes a Difference." *World Politics* 42 (July), pp. 466–501.

Jablonsky, David. 1991. *Strategic Rationality Is Not Enough: Hitler and the Concept of Crazy States.* Carlisle Barracks, Pa.: Strategic Studies Institute, U.S. Army War College.

Jervis, Robert. 1989. "Rational Deterrence: Theory and Evidence." *World Politics* 41 (January), pp. 183–207.

———. 1992. "The Utility of Nuclear Deterrence." In Jervis and Robert J. Art, eds., *International Politics: Enduring Concepts and Contemporary Issues.* New York, N.Y.: HarperCollins.

———. Forthcoming. "What Do We Want to Deter, and How Do We Deter It?" In L. Benjamin Ederington and Michael J. Mazarr, eds., *Turning Point: The Gulf War and Future U.S. Military Strategy.* Boulder, Colo.: Westview Press.

Joffe, Josef. 1992. "Collective Security and the Future of Europe: Failed Dreams and Dead Ends." *Survival* 34 (Spring), pp. 36–49.

Kaufman, Daniel J., David S. Clark, and Kevin P. Sheehan, eds. 1991. *U.S. National Security Strategy for the 1990s.* Baltimore, Md.: Johns Hopkins University Press.

Kaysen, Carl, Robert S. McNamara, and George Rathjens. 1991. "Nuclear Weapons After the Cold War." *Foreign Affairs* 70 (Fall), pp. 95–110.

Lebow, Richard Ned. 1985. "The Deterrence Deadlock: Is There a Way Out?" In Robert Jervis, Richard Ned Lebow, and Janice Gross Stein, eds., *Psychology and Deterrence*. Baltimore, Md.: Johns Hopkins University Press.

———. 1989. "Deterrence: A Political and Psychological Critique." In Stern et al., *Perspectives on Deterrence*.

Lebow, Richard Ned, and Janice Gross Stein. 1989. "Rational Deterrence Theory: I Think, Therefore I Deter." *World Politics* 41 (January), pp. 208–223.

Levine, Robert A. 1993. *Uniform Deterrence of Nuclear First Use*. Santa Monica, Calif.: RAND.

Lewis, Kevin N. 1989. *Getting More Deterrence Out of Deliberate Capability Revelation*. Santa Monica, Calif.: RAND.

McCausland, Jeffrey. 1993. "The Gulf Conflict: A Military Analysis." *Adelphi Papers* 282 (November) (London: Brassey's for the IISS).

McPeak, Merrill A. 1993. Quoted in Barton Gellman, "Trepidation at Root of U.S. Korea Policy, Conventional War Seen Catastrophic for South." *Washington Post*, December 12, pp. A–1, A–49.

Mahnken, Thomas G. 1991. "The Arrow and the Shield: U.S. Responses to Ballistic Missile Proliferation." *The Washington Quarterly* 14 (Winter), pp. 189–203.

———. 1993. "America's Next War." *The Washington Quarterly* 16 (Summer), pp. 171–184.

Mazarr, Michael J. 1993. *Toward a Nuclear Peace: The Future of Nuclear Weapons in U.S. Foreign and Defense Policy*. Report of the CSIS Nuclear Strategy Study Group. Washington, D.C.: CSIS.

Mearsheimer, John. 1983. *Conventional Deterrence*. Ithaca, N.Y.: Cornell University Press.

Metz, Steven. 1993. Letter to author, December 14.

———. 1994. Letter to author, January 14.

Millot, Marc Dean, Roger Molander, and Peter A. Wilson. 1993. *"The Day After . . ." Study: Nuclear Proliferation in the Post–Cold War World*, vol. 1, *Summary Report*. MR-266-AF. Santa Monica, Calif.: RAND.

Mueller, John. 1992. "The Obsolescence of War in the Modern Industrialized World." In Robert Jervis and Robert J. Art, eds., *International Politics: Enduring Concepts and Contemporary Issues*. New York, N.Y.: Harper-Collins.

Mueller, Karl P. 1991. "Strategy, Asymmetric Deterrence and Accommodation: Middle Powers and Security in Modern Europe." Ph.D. diss., Princeton University, Princeton, N.J.

Nitze, Paul H. 1994. "Is It Time to Junk Our Nukes?" *Washington Post*, January 16, pp. C1–C2.

Nokkala, Arto. 1991. "Non-offensive Defense: A Criteria Model of Military Credibility." Helsinki: War College.

Odom, William E. 1993. *America's Military Revolution: Strategy and Structure after the Cold War*. Washington, D.C.: American University Press.

Palmer, Glenn. 1992. "Conventional Deterrence and Alliances: Three Models of U.S.–Allied Relations." Presentation at the conference on "Conventional Deterrence in the Post–Cold War Era," U.S. Naval Postgraduate School, Monterey, Calif., August 13–14.

Pape, Robert A., Jr. 1992. "Coercion and Military Strategy: Why Denial Works and Punishment Doesn't." *Journal of Strategic Studies* 15 (December), pp. 423–475.

Patton, James H. 1993. "The Impact of Weapons Proliferation on Naval Forces." In Robert L. Pfaltzgraff and Richard H. Schultz, Jr., eds., *Naval Forward Presence and the National Military Strategy*. Annapolis, Md.: Naval Institute Press.

Paul, T. V. 1991. "Asymmetric Conflicts: A Study of War Initiation by Lesser Powers." Ph.D. diss., University of California at Los Angeles, Los Angeles, Calif.

Payne, Keith B. 1992. "Deterrence and U.S. Strategic Force Requirements After the Cold War." *Comparative Strategy* 11 (July–September), pp. 269–282.

Perry, William J. 1991. "Desert Storm and Deterrence." *Foreign Affairs* 70 (Fall), pp. 66–82.

Pfaltzgraff, Robert L. 1993. "Change and Continuity in the 1990s." In Pfaltzgraff and Richard H. Schultz, Jr., eds., *Naval Forward Presence and the National Military Strategy*. Annapolis, Md.: Naval Institute Press.

Powell, Colin L. 1992. *The National Military Strategy—1992*. Washington, D.C.: GPO.

Quester, George H. 1992a. "Conventional Deterrence: The Past Is Prologue." In Gary L. Guertner, Robert P. Haffa, Jr., and George H. Quester, eds., *Conventional Forces and the Future of Deterrence*. Carlisle Barracks, Pa.: Strategic Studies Institute, U.S. Army War College.

———. 1992b. "The Future of Nuclear Deterrence." *Survival* 34 (Spring), pp. 74–88.

———. 1993. Interview by author. College Park, Md., December 9.

Quester, George H., and Victor A. Utgoff. 1993. "U.S. Arms Reductions and Nuclear Nonproliferation: The Counterproductive Possibilities." *The Washington Quarterly* 16 (Winter), pp. 129–140.

——. 1994. "No-First-Use and Nonproliferation." *The Washington Quarterly* 17 (Spring), pp. 103–114.

Record, Jeffrey. 1993. "Defeating Desert Storm (and Why Saddam Didn't)." *Comparative Strategy* 12 (April–June), pp. 125–140.

Roberts, Brad. 1993. "From Nonproliferation to Antiproliferation." *International Security* 18 (Summer), pp. 139–173.

Safire, William. 1993. "The Fault Dear Brutus, Is Not. . . ." *New York Times*, October 18, p. 17.

Simon, Steven. 1992. "U.S. Strategy in the Persian Gulf." *Survival* 34 (Autumn), pp. 81–97.

Sloan, Stanley R. 1992. *The U.S. Role in the Post–Cold War World: Issues for a New Great Debate.* Washington, D.C.: Congressional Research Service.

Snider, Don M., and Gregory Grant. 1992. "The Future of Conventional Warfare and U.S. Military Strategy." *The Washington Quarterly* 13 (Winter), pp. 203–226.

Spector, Leonard. 1992. *Deterring Regional Threats from Nuclear Proliferation.* Carlisle Barracks, Pa.: Strategic Studies Institute, U.S. Army War College.

Starr, Barbara. 1993. "The Jane's Interview: Rear Admiral Thomas Ryan." *Jane's Defence Weekly* 19 (May 29), p. 32.

Steele, Robert D. 1993. "War and Peace in the Age of Information." Presentation to the U.S. Naval Postgraduate School, Monterey, Calif., August 17.

Stein, Janice Gross. 1991. "Reassurance in International Conflict Management." *Political Science Quarterly* 106 (Fall), pp. 431–451.

——. 1992. "Deterrence and Compellence in the Gulf, 1990–91: A Failed or Impossible Task?" *International Security* 17 (Fall), pp. 147–179.

Stern, Paul C., Robert Axelrod, Robert Jervis, and Roy Radner, eds. 1989. *Perspectives on Deterrence.* New York, N.Y.: Oxford University Press.

Strain, Frederick R. 1993. "Nuclear Proliferation and Deterrence: A Policy Conundrum." *Parameters* 23 (Autumn), pp. 85–95.

Swiecicki, Juliet A. 1992. "Severing the Ties That Bind: Moving Beyond Deterrence." *Comparative Strategy* 11 (July–September), pp. 283–306.

Toffler, Alvin, and Heidi Toffler. 1993. *War and Anti-War: Survival at the Dawn of the 21st Century.* New York, N.Y.: Little, Brown, and Company.

Utgoff, Victor A. 1993. Interview by author. Alexandria, Va., November 22.

WSS (Washington Strategy Seminar). 1993. *Persian Gulf Working Group Report.* Washington, D.C.: Washington Strategy Seminar.

Watman, Kenneth. 1994. Presentation to the CSIS Extended Conventional Deterrence Working Group, Washington, D.C., January 27.

Wolf, Barry. 1991. *When the Weak Attack the Strong: Failures of Deterrence.* Santa Monica, Calif.: RAND.

Wu, Samuel S. 1989. *Extended Deterrence and the Onset of War.* Rochester, N.Y.: University of Rochester.

Zelikow, Philip. 1993. "Offensive Military Options." In Robert D. Blackwill and Albert Carnesale, eds., *New Nuclear Nations: Consequences for U.S. Policy.* New York, N.Y.: Council on Foreign Relations.

IV. Arms Control's New Nonproliferation Roles

Arms Control and the End of the Cold War

Brad Roberts

ARMS CONTROL WAS a stepchild of the Cold War. As the threat of nuclear confrontation between the United States and Soviet Union seemed to increase in the 1950s and 1960s, along with fears that such a war would lead to mutual annihilation, policymakers sought means to stabilize the competition between the two sides without resort to war. The result was both an arms-control process and an arms-control product. The process of arms control, that is, the negotiation of limits on military capabilities, became a significant—and at times the only—way to conduct a political dialogue between the two superpowers. It also served to reassure allies and the interested public that nuclear armageddon was not imminent. The product of arms control, in the shape of formal agreements, made the armaments competition between the two sides more manageable and contributed to some easing of the economic costs associated with maintaining defenses. Between 1959 and 1992, more than 30 arms-control agreements were signed by the United States, culminating in the deep cuts in nuclear and conventional forces of the early 1990s.[1] During the Cold War arms control was at the center of U.S. concerns and made all earlier experiences

with negotiated restraints on the use of force appear tangential, as in the case of the Geneva Protocol of 1925, or inconsequential, as in the naval agreements of the interwar period.

With the June 1992 summit of Presidents George Bush and Boris Yeltsin, the golden era of arms control has come to full fruition. The conclusion over the last five years of a very ambitious arms-control agenda between the two cold war adversaries raises a legitimate question about the future role and promise of arms control and its relative prominence in U.S. policy. The United States no longer lives at the brink of strategic conflict with an opponent threatening it with annihilation. The restructuring of the East–West relationship in ways well suited to the interests of the erstwhile Western pole has devalued arms-control talks as a way to manage conflictual relations. This has led to a review of the place of arms control in U.S. strategy, one manifestation of which is an incipient debate about the future of the U.S. Arms Control and Disarmament Agency (ACDA).[2]

The sense that arms control's day is over is reinforced by the widespread conviction that after the Cold War the security of the United States must be seen in new terms that emphasize economic, social, and environmental factors, among others. By this argument, arms control has been devalued as ir-

Brad Roberts is editor of *The Washington Quarterly* and a research fellow at CSIS.

relevant to a new international agenda for which military instruments themselves are not especially useful.

But the world has not changed this radically. Instead, it has grown even more complex. To be sure, there are problems of prosperity and well-being for which common international responses appear increasingly valuable. But the classic question of security in the interstate system has not disappeared with the passing of the Soviet empire. In a way, the pursuit of national and international security has grown more rather than less complex in the post-Soviet era as the study of security issues has been unleashed from cold war constraints that have for decades defined if not skewed the global debate about security.[3] Old problems of security and stability in Europe, Asia, and the Middle East have come into sharper focus after the Cold War. New problems have emerged, especially those related to the spread of unconventional weapons and advanced conventional capabilities in areas of military competition outside the East–West context. But new opportunities have appeared as well, both for the practice of statecraft free of the bipolar standoff and for the exploitation of common economic and political challenges to strengthen multilateralism as a principle of international affairs.

Does arms control have an important role to play in this new era? This article offers a speculative analysis. It reviews the three focal points of U.S. arms-control policy in the decade ahead: the continuing East–West agenda, the multilateral or global agenda, and regional measures. It then goes on to discuss the two principal determinants of the impact arms control will have on the management of international conflict: the ability to de-

sign and implement effective compliance mechanisms and the propensity to seek negotiated measures, what is termed here the sociology of arms control. It concludes that arms control will continue to be a prominent U.S. policy instrument, but not as before. Looking ahead, it is reasonable to expect that the number of arms-control products will grow as existing agreements are joined by new instruments, many of which will not involve direct U.S. participation. In particular, the regional agenda will require new U.S. attention and leadership. But arms control as process will also remain important. This is clearest in the relationship of the United States with the successor states of the Soviet Union, where the implementation of existing measures will require a degree of U.S. stewardship well beyond that of past practice in the arms-control field. But the arms-control process will also be valuable as a way to arrive at more cooperative international approaches to common problems of security.

The Continuing East–West Agenda

The East–West arms-control agenda has not disappeared with the end of the Cold War. Arms control will have a continuing impact in three areas.

The first is in the implementation of existing agreements. Confidence about the ability of the successor states of the Soviet Union to implement the major agreements of recent years—those on Intermediate-Range Nuclear Forces in Europe (INF), Conventional Forces in Europe (CFE), and Strategic Arms Reductions (START I and II)[4]—rises and falls with each new piece of news from that troubled region. The West, particularly the United States, has labored to ensure that these states assume the responsibilities accepted by the old Union government. It has also sought to use the arms-control process as a way to create incentives for the new states to centralize the command and control of the nuclear weapons of the erstwhile Soviet military. It may well be that the structures of zones and the allocation of weapon systems among them is simply too rigid for the new geostrategic realities in Europe. On the other hand, it is clear that many of the leaders and publics of the successor states see participation in binding arms-control agreements as an important sign of their acceptance and legitimacy as new states in the international system.

The demands of implementation will exceed previous experience. In the past, implementation of arms-control agreements entailed essentially monitoring and verification of compliance and attempts to resolve issues of noncompliance through committees established for that purpose or in the larger political environment. In the future, effective implementation will require not just a sharp eye on the actions of U.S. treaty partners but a willingness and ability to take certain stewardship responsibilities for the agreements themselves. Thus the verification tasks will be supplemented by those associated with brokering differences of view among states in a fluid international environment, amending measures as circumstances change and facilitating enactment of treaty commitments on the ground. One symptom of this broadening agenda is the growing role of the U.S. On-Site Inspection Agency in the implementation programs of the countries of the former USSR. Another symptom is the effort by Western states to stem the "brain drain" of Soviet weapons scientists to the devel-

oping world; although not precisely arms control, these efforts are important and useful adjuncts to U.S. arms-control policies.

Problems associated with the destruction of weapons have emerged as key unanticipated challenges to the implementation of existing agreements. Especially in the area of nuclear and chemical weapons, it appears that Russia does not have the fiscal means, the political will, or the technical ability to undertake the timely destruction of weapons in ways that will not damage the environment. If rapid progress cannot be made in destroying these weapons, it will sow doubts not just about the ability but also about the will of remnants of the old system to implement agreed measures.

The second arms-control topic remaining for the East–West agenda is the pursuit of follow-on agreements. In June 1992, there is a widespread sense in Washington and the media that the most ambitious possible East–West arms-control agenda has now been concluded, and that the future does not hold significant new agreements. With the rapid drift of international events and ever-changing thinking about the place of nuclear weapons in the post–cold war environment, this sentiment should not go unchallenged. Some interest remains in deeper cuts in the nuclear arsenal and, at some future time, in an arms-control agreement that also addresses the arsenals of the other advanced nuclear weapon states: Britain, France, and the People's Republic of China (PRC). Further unilateral arms-control measures by either Russia or the United States appear unlikely at this writing, given the apparent preference of both states for codifying restraints in formal measures so that they will have the benefits of verification and compliance mechanisms. Some arms-control steps, however, such as those related to the redeployment or elimination of short-range nuclear forces, are likely to remain informal in character.

The third 1990s remnant of the old East–West arms-control agenda is European security. The Conference on Security and Cooperation in Europe (CSCE) remains firmly in place and in spring 1992 gained a new forum for negotiating arms-control measures. Interest also remains strong among some Europeans in a follow-on CFE treaty (called CFE–1A), which would add manpower limitations to the armaments limits of the original agreement.

There is a sharp debate within the transatlantic community about whether these various negotiations should be used to deal with problems of possible future force reconstitution and peacekeeping or whether there should be some pause in the effort for negotiated measures and a shift of emphasis toward working with existing transparency and confidence-building measures. The United States has been undecided on this point, although it has rejected any effort to use the CSCE arms-control process as a way to negotiate constraints on forces in the continental United States.

The Global Agenda

The East–West arms-control agenda is only one element of the agenda of the 1990s. A second focus of arms-control energy will be the multilateral, global agenda. Such arms-control mechanisms are likely to grow in importance with the breakdown of the bipolar world order and with the industrialization of parts of the developing world and the proliferation of military

technology and capability, especially of unconventional weapons.

Efforts to strengthen the existing regime controlling the use of unconventional weapons will be the top priority. The Nuclear Non-Proliferation Treaty (NPT) is facing new trials in the early 1990s with the pull of events in the Middle East, South Asia, and the former Soviet Union. Following discovery of Iraq's sizable but secret nuclear weapons program going forward under the very nose of inspectors from the International Atomic Energy Agency (IAEA), measures associated with verification and compliance with the NPT are likely to enjoy growing support.[5] In 1995 states parties to the NPT will convene to consider the extension of the treaty either for another 25 years or for a shorter period. States opposed to the special rights of the pre-1967 nuclear weapon states may garner enough political support among the disaffected of the developing world to throw its extension in doubt. The status quo–oriented West tends to view this possibility as remote, arguing that most states of the world will see their security better served by an imperfect treaty than by the unrestrained acquisition of nuclear arms. Some other states believe strongly that unless a comprehensive nuclear test ban is implemented the established nuclear powers will have failed to make sufficient progress toward implementation of their commitments under the NPT. New issues are certain to crop up in the global debate about nuclear weapons in the years ahead, suggesting that it is too early to be confident about the outcome of the 1995 extension debate, especially given the many new demands upon the NPT regime to improve its performance as well as the uncertainties in regions where nuclear issues are of continuing or growing relevance.

The Biological and Toxin Weapons Convention (BTWC) of 1972 will also face growing scrutiny in the 1990s. Two decades after it was written, doubts are increasing about the seriousness with which some states take their commitment to the convention, with reports of between 10 and 15 countries possessing offensive biological warfare capabilities. These countries might see these capabilities as "the poor man's atom bomb."[6] The treaty lacks both verification and compliance provisions. The importance of a more effective regime has caught the attention of many policymakers impressed by the argument that the BTWC must keep pace with a changing technological environment: the biotechnology revolution may have created significant new risks of biological warfare, or may do so in the future, which has raised the stakes in the success or failure of the regime.[7] The means to strengthen the convention and to boost confidence in its effectiveness have been the subject of periodic review conferences, most recently in September 1991. Verification mechanisms developed for other global treaties will not easily be grafted onto the BTWC, given important features of the relevant technologies and production facilities, although work is ongoing to identify options to improve the monitoring of treaty commitments and to weigh those options in terms of the security benefits relative to their costs, either fiscal or in terms of lost proprietary information in the commercial sector. In the meantime, serious attention must be given to implementation of confidence-building measures and the equally important objective of getting all states parties to implement existing commitments.[8]

In the chemical area, negotiations appear in summer 1992 to be leading to the conclusion of a comprehensive disarmament treaty, the Chemical Weapons Convention (CWC). States parties to the convention would undertake to destroy existing arsenals and not to build or transfer chemical weapons to others. This agreement would represent a significant advance on the Geneva Protocol of 1925, which was an undertaking not to use these weapons and remains in force. Unlike the BTWC, the CWC would provide for some verification and compliance mechanisms. Unlike the NPT, it would require disarmament by states of both the developing and the developed worlds. The willingness of the United States to forgo chemical weapons appears consistent not with the disarmament ideology of the 1920s but with a prudent reading of national security interests in the 1990s. Under the CWC, the United States will trade away a military instrument last used in battle by the United States when Woodrow Wilson sat in the White House in exchange for a dampening of the pressures toward chemical weapons proliferation.

These global regimes are important not only for their effect in limiting the global spread of unconventional weapons; they also have the important benefit of generating norms of state conduct. Those who see the world in realpolitik terms decry the role of norms in politics, arguing correctly that norms are irrelevant to those determined to act with contempt for the standards of others. But policy realists too often miss the importance of norms in generating the political consensus necessary to punish behavior not consistent with those norms. Something of this mechanism was at work in the sharp international response to Iraq's annexation of Kuwait. Norms based on the selective rejection of categories of weapons deemed unacceptable create the foundation for sanctions, embargoes, and arguably more direct enforcement actions. Without the norms embodied in the global nuclear, biological, and chemical regimes, the international community would be far less ready to cope with the consequences of widespread access to the relevant technologies. The Outer Space Treaty of 1967, the Seabed Arms Control Treaty of 1971, and the Environmental Modification Convention of 1977 also embody norms likely to assume growing salience in the decades ahead as global industrial development puts the means to cause significant harm in each domain in the hands of an ever larger number of states.

A strengthening of these regimes will require concerted effort on the part of the United States and its allies. They must make astute use of periodic review conferences to gain consensus about problems and responses. As argued below, particular attention will be given to the inspection issue and to whether or how existing verification regimes can be improved to deal with new threats.

But effective multilateral arms control will require more than just some tightening of the existing legal framework. Complementary policies must be pursued as well. Policymakers should increase the diplomatic attention given proliferation issues. They must also cultivate those military capabilities that will shape the expectations of potential cheaters; this points to the continuing need for investment in technological superiority and defenses against specific types of weapons as well as the preservation of alliances and the political bases for collective security.

The 1990s will also witness the emergence of a new set of multilateral arms-control issues. The 1991 decision

of the United Nations (UN) to set up an annual registry of conventional weapons traded internationally suggests a growing global interest in arms-control transparency measures and in the use of negotiated measures to cope in new ways with the problems of competitive relations.[9] In a way, the registry idea represents a bit of old thinking about arms control—that it is weapons themselves that create security problems. But it also represents a new appreciation of the fact that the uneven flow of arms can and has produced not just competition but war, either by nourishing the ambitions of aggressors or deepening fear among the vulnerable. The UN initiative to police Iraq's compliance with the April 1991 cease-fire agreement points also to the possibility of a growing UN role in monitoring and verifying treaty compliance. The UN Special Commission's unique experience in the use of information provided by various national intelligence agencies has stirred interest in supporting new UN roles in this area.[10]

But because the global proliferation of military capability involves so many elements other than nuclear, biological, and chemical weapons, there is a widespread hope in Washington that arms control will take on a larger nonproliferation function in the years ahead. This hope is misplaced, because U.S. policymakers will find it impossible to employ traditional nonproliferation approaches as arms-control tools.

The weapons proliferation problem cannot be dealt with by placing a permanent barrier between the haves and have-nots, although this is exactly the focus of nonproliferation policy as it was pursued in the cold war era. The fact that the biological and chemical disarmament agreements impose equal burdens on the militaries of the developed and the developing world is one factor accounting for their future promise; the unequal burdens assumed under the NPT are a factor pointing to a very sharp future debate in the new century about the lingering rights of the pre-1967 nuclear states. The inherently discriminatory character of nonproliferation mechanisms is incompatible with an era in which technology, industrial capability, and expertise are slowly spreading throughout the world. Permanent firebreaks between the haves and have-nots will only fuel the ambitions of the have-nots to acquire what they have been denied. Such discriminatory mechanisms are necessarily stopgap measures, intended to buy policymakers time to arrive at more fruitful ways to address the will rather than the means to acquire weapons. This is not to deny their important interim value in constraining access to technologies that enable aggressive states to cross significant capability thresholds, that is, those related to the reach and essential military effectiveness of missiles or their warheads.

Thus, conspicuous by their absence so far from this review are the supplier regimes such as the Missile Technology Control Regime (MTCR), the Australia Group in the chemical area, and other collaborative export-control efforts designed to deny military-related technology to targeted countries. Export-control approaches will remain important in U.S. policy for many years to come, but they are a poor substitute for complementary and ultimately more durable approaches. Efforts to negotiate international limits on conventional arms transfers to regions in conflict are likely to be implemented in the years ahead, but their potential utility must be understood as limited in the same way as other supplier regimes. A complete

embargo of weapon sales by Western suppliers to regions in conflict may precipitate rather than ameliorate instability. This will compel suppliers finally to come to some agreement among themselves on what constitutes stabilizing and destabilizing transfers. Especially in the Middle East, limits on conventional arms transfers are likely to be supported by the supplier states only as an interim measure so long as they effectively contribute to achievement of a longer-term peace settlement in the region. This points to the essential linkage of such supplier regimes to future regional arms-control measures.

In sum, U.S. policy aimed at stimulating regional measures, strengthening global regimes, and integrating ad hoc supplier restraints could have a very powerful effect in stemming weapons proliferation or at least in coping with its most serious consequences, but only if pursued in this integrated way.

Regional Measures

Beyond the East–West and global arms-control measures, a new set is emerging in the early 1990s as a serious possibility—regional measures. Interest in regional arms control has been stimulated by the end of bipolarity and superpower preeminence, combined with the proliferation of advanced conventional and unconventional weapons in regions of chronic conflict. Latin America has advanced furthest in this new direction. For example, Argentina, Chile, and Brazil, building on the Treaty of Tlatelolco, agreed in September 1991 to create and police among themselves a zone free of nuclear, chemical, and biological weapons under the so-called Mendoza agreement.[11] In East Asia, elements of an informal arms-control

regime between the two Koreas over-
lap with North Korea's entry into the
multilateral NPT. In South Asia, the
nuclearization of both India and Pakistan has prompted fears of an arms
race and war, nudging them to begin
a dialogue about informal and formal
measures to limit the risks. And in the
Middle East, where some limited
arms-control measures have long been
implemented such as the demilitarization and international policing of the
Sinai, appeals in recent years by Presidents George Bush, Mikhail Gorbachev, and Hosni Mubarak have
helped to stimulate renewed interest
in regional arms-control measures.

In each of these regions, there is an
active exploration of the models of
arms control, including not just those
from the East–West experience but
also earlier efforts such as the various
measures of the years between World
Wars I and II. Such a historical review
shows arms control in three different
guises: disarmament (whether comprehensive or of selective systems),
arms control (meaning measures embodying choices by states to limit
weapons acquisitions or direct them in
ways not threatening to neighbors),
and confidence-building measures
(embodying undertakings related to
state behavior in the military domain
that reduce the risk of war through
misperception and miscalculation, that
increase transparency of military actions, and that may work over time to
change the political terms of reference
of conflict). Arms control qua disarmament and major force-structuring
agreements of the START and CFE
types appear today to be remote possibilities in the Middle East, South
Asia, and East Asia.[12] More fruitful en-
deavors may well be found in the areas
of confidence-building measures and
the codification of arms deployments

at existing thresholds of force levels or
capabilities.

A key issue with regard to regional
arms control is its fit with the global
agenda. If regional efforts succeed in
producing over time a series of diluted
agreements without the verification or
compliance mechanisms of the global
measures, their future efficacy will be
in some doubt. They may, in fact,
contribute to insecurity in time of crisis and near conflict because of their
failure to create real confidence about
the behavior and intentions of possible
adversaries. Such weak measures
would erode the global regimes. On
the other hand, regional measures that
match or exceed the standards of the
global regimes could prove valuable
complements to the latter.

New forms of arms control might
also burgeon from the creative talent
of newcomers to the arms-control process. The problem of dual-use technologies (i.e., technologies such as
those in the aerospace, chemical, biological, electronic, and systems integration fields that have both civil and
military applications) may stimulate
novel responses by states not members
of supplier cartels. It would not be
surprising, for example, to find like-
minded states in South America and
Africa agreeing to self-imposed restraints on military applications
backed by effective self-policing
mechanisms in exchange for access to
critical dual-use technologies.

The achievement of formal regional
negotiated measures will be difficult
for a number of reasons. Many of the
factors critical to arms control in the
East–West context are not characteristic of those conflicts, although there
is no reason to believe that sharp bipolarity and the presence of mutual
assured destruction are necessary conditions to arms control. There are im-

portant questions about the timing and scale of such undertakings and whether confidence-building measures really have anything to contribute to relations between historical enemies.[13] But if the East–West experience is any indication, arms control may contribute as much in the 1990s as a process of dialogue and signaling about political intent as it will in formal measures.

Compliance

How much or how little arms control occurs in the years ahead will be a direct function of how effective current and future regimes prove to be. Tending arms-control agreements has rarely attracted the same energy or public enthusiasm as creating them, but the success of their implementation will be critical in determining whether arms-control instruments will acquire such broad support as elements of national security strategy as they did in the West during the Cold War.[14]

The ability of arms-control measures to secure compliance by states parties is a function of two factors. One is the political context within which compliance is sought. Expectations of compliance will be shaped by the degree to which the general relations among states parties are peaceful rather than conflictual and by the level of interest shown by those with political, economic, or military leverage to secure compliance. Obviously, these dynamics differ markedly from region to region. The other factor is the compliance mechanisms designed into the treaty itself. Will parties to the treaty be able to detect cheating of a militarily significant character in a timely way through inspections specified in arms-control agree-ments backed by whatever separate intelligence resources are available to them? Will the inspection regime be perceived to be sufficiently rigorous to increase the costs of cheating or otherwise influence the calculations of risks and benefits by leaders contemplating noncompliant behavior?

The focal point for this debate in the early 1990s is how intrusive inspections must be to achieve the required results. The near brush with unconventional weapons in the Iraqi arsenal has led to widespread criticism of the limited mandate for inspections conducted by the IAEA and the absence of verification provisions under the BTWC. Iraq's ability to pursue research and development programs for nuclear (and biological) weapons despite periodic inspections in recent years has fueled international demands for a right under future or modified arms-control measures to highly intrusive inspections virtually anywhere and any time, without right of refusal.[15]

The intrusiveness issue has emerged as a sort of litmus test of one's commitment to effective compliance measures. The United States, for example, was widely criticized as abandoning the struggle for an effective CWC when in 1991 it backed away from its former rhetorical position of "anywhere, any time" inspections. But the Iraqi experience holds other lessons as well. It shows that finding the proverbial smoking gun will prove very difficult when inspectors are confronting a well-prepared adversary who has had time to bury, either literally or figuratively, proof of malfeasance, and that inspectors need not just a right to intrude in sensitive areas but also to conduct regular and indeed systematic inspections so that patterns of activity become known over time, leading to what are essentially political decisions about the level of confidence gained or not through the inspection process. This political context is often overlooked in the debate about inspections. It means that suspicions about individual sites will be weighed in the context of the larger relationship of that state to others. What is politically possible under a cease-fire order vis-à-vis the Iraqis is arguably not acceptable for states not at war.

Advocates of highly intrusive measures have also generally failed to account for the costs of such measures. Potential costs include not just the fiscal—including the substantial investment that would be necessary for the United States to maintain in readiness all facilities potentially subject to short-notice intrusive inspection—but also the loss of legitimately sensitive or proprietary information. Especially in Europe and the developing world, little attention has been paid to the costs and risks to industrial facilities of falling under the purview of intrusive treaties. In the United States, these issues have received some consideration. The U.S. chemical industry has shown interest in the stipulations of the CWC, much more so than the biotechnology industry in the BTWC or indeed industry in general that might be subject to "anywhere, any time" on-site inspections. Advocates of intrusiveness also generally have not weighed those costs against benefits. One of the emerging criticisms of START, for example, is that it will benefit the United States rather less than originally envisaged while costing a great deal for the quite elaborate verification provisions.

This is not to argue that intrusive measures are undesirable; rather, it points to the need to balance competing priorities. It points also to the fact that the debate about intrusiveness has become a substitute for a debate about compliance more broadly. Intrusive inspections are not a panacea for the problem of compliance; effective and comprehensive inspections are the foundation of a larger strategy relating to verifying whether or not a state is living up to its commitments and to enforcing compliance where that becomes necessary.

This compliance debate grew highly politicized during the Cold War. The dispute about whether or not the Soviet Union was complying with its arms-control treaty commitments became superheated in the United States in the 1970s and 1980s and led other states to shy away from the subject for fear of being co-opted by one side or the other. This was most evident in the debate about U.S. allegations concerning the use by Soviet or Soviet proxy forces of biological and toxin weapons in Afghanistan and Southeast Asia—the so-called Yellow Rain debate. No states, not even allies of the United States, wanted to take sides in the dispute for fear of the domestic and international political consequences. In retrospect, it has become clear that the Soviets were in fact cheating in the biological area by their continued programs in the offensive domain.[16] This episode also showed that in the absence of an obvious smoking gun, suspicions fall upon the accuser as well as the accused. Indeed, even given blatant proof of violations, as in the case of the Soviet radar facility at Krasnoyarsk, the political interest of some in sustaining an existing treaty seems to overwhelm the capacity to deal with noncompliance. The annual reports of the U.S. president to the Congress on Soviet arms-control compliance never produced the consensus necessary to deal with patterns of noncompliance as accepted political and military facts. This appears to have been less the case in the area of strategic arms, where the United States and Soviet Union were able to use the General Advisory Council to resolve problems of compliance with the Strategic Arms Limitation Treaty (SALT I) privately.

The end of the Cold War has created a widespread hope that the end of bipolarity will lead to a depoliticization of arms-control compliance issues and that existing compliance mechanisms will be able to operate to their full potential to deter and detect cheating and provide the foundations for enforcement. Will this hope be realized? Will it matter?

On the East–West agenda, issues of compliance seem to have receded. The widespread skepticism about Soviet compliance and the perceived high risks for the West of Soviet noncompliance have passed from the scene. The more pressing question today is not so much the will of the successor states to comply with existing arms-control commitments as their ability to do so given the other demands upon their resources and energy. The exposure of their weapons programs to international public opinion through existing verification mechanisms will weigh in their perceptions of their priorities, however, and effective compliance mechanisms are likely to prove quite central to any debate about future arms-control agreements between or among the successor states of the Union.

On the global agenda, there is a real possibility that arms-control negotiations long paralyzed by East–West division may now suffer the consequences of North–South division.[17] For some in the nonaligned movement, the debate about global agreements has become a vehicle for contesting the distribution of power and

influence in the post–cold war era. They abhor any agreement that preserves the long-term military or economic dominance of the developed world and may prefer to scuttle negotiated measures—or to sign them with the expectation of cheating—than to be seen to be acquiescing in the political agenda of the North. If they are to join regimes constraining their military choices, they are likely to do so only if the regimes give evidence of fairness and equity. This accounts for resistance to further have versus have-not regimes or to regimes that otherwise preserve special rights of enforcement or representation for specific categories of states. Hence the importance leading members of the developing world attach to global treaties that fully reflect their views and concerns.[18]

On the regional agenda, changing global politics may have some salutary effect on the ability of the UN to act as a guarantor of compliance. The UN's relative effectiveness to date in policing the cease-fire terms with Iraq and the evident coalescence of U.S. and Russian views on important regional security issues bodes well for the UN's functions in this area, although there is the risk that the PRC and perhaps future new members of the Security Council will exercise a veto in ways that frustrate UN engagement. In regions where the involvement of outside powers has a firm historical foundation and a certain level of legitimacy, such as the Middle East where the United States is concerned, the UN is unlikely to prove a substitute for that great power involvement. But the UN might become a facilitator of policing actions by regional organizations as yet not created or empowered to take on this task. Its effectiveness will also be determined by the specific rights accorded it by arms-control treaties. Its capacity to act to enforce arms-control commitments will be stronger in those instances where the UN itself has formal responsibility, as in postwar Iraq, and weaker where compliance findings are the responsibility of individual states.

Thus, there is no guarantee that the improved promise of the UN in strengthening the politics of compliance will translate into perfect compliance by all states to all new and future arms-control treaties. It is, therefore, also necessary to speculate about compliance by enforcement through military action in those instances where a state's broken commitments have led to war or appear to be doing so. Without some expectation that a renegade state will confront armed resistance, the leaders of such a state might care little even if inspections confirm noncompliant behavior. Much hope has been invested in the strengthened collective security operations of the UN, but there is also reason to doubt that it will always find the will and means to respond to aggression as it did in Kuwait. Efforts to strengthen the capacity of the UN to act in such circumstances may pay off by deterring potential cheaters from breaking with existing arms-control agreements. They would come to see that aggression employing those assets would prove futile.

Unilateral enforcement actions by any one party are likely always to be subject to at least some international criticism, just as people today reiterate their criticism of Israel for its 1981 bombing of the Osiraq nuclear plant in Iraq even after the existence of Iraq's nuclear programs became more widely known. Preemptive strikes in circumstances short of war will always have detractors and supporters arguing the implications of actions not taken. The UN as such will have limited po-

litical capacity to conduct such measures, except in circumstances such as those prevailing in Iraq today. Regional organizations may assume some growing role in this area, because regional consensus may be easier to achieve than global consensus in isolating and punishing renegade states because of the propinquity of the threat.

The United States appears to be attaching a growing priority to enforcement actions tied to and endorsed and legitimized by international entities, whether global or regional (such as the CSCE and the Organization of American States). Its ability to act in concert with others, or alone where deemed necessary, will be tied to military programs giving it the flexibility to do so. This suggests the relevance of a U.S. military instrument of sufficient strength, peacekeeping competence, and familiarity with other militaries to make its power projection credible.

In speculating about the future of arms-control compliance, it is important to bear in mind that a great deal of experience will be reaped in the 1990s. This experience will be as important in shaping the predispositions and abilities of states to deal with problems of noncompliance as was the cold war era.

The Sociology of Arms Control

As an institution of human and state behavior, arms control must be understood in relation to the broader political and intellectual environment of which it is a part. To exploit fully the opportunities listed above requires the setting aside of some old ways of thinking about arms control and problems of international security.

Among arms controllers in the United States (and also elsewhere in the West and perhaps in the erstwhile

East), thinking about arms control has been shaped by a number of factors that may not, in retrospect, be relevant to creative thinking about the arms-control tasks of today and tomorrow.

One factor is the era of strategic bombing that preceded the creation of the atom bomb and the resultant tendency to equate weapons of mass destruction with strategic weapons. This is not a good guide to understanding the important differences between nuclear, biological, and chemical (NBC) weapons, the different risks associated with each, and the motives driving their acquisition. The U.S. tendency to impute to NBC weapons programs in the developing world the same strategic purpose they have for the United States—deterrence—obscures other potential motives, whether military or symbolic, and the possible interaction of those motives with other national priorities. This makes it difficult to calculate the incentives states might have for agreeing to arms-control measures.

Another factor is the U.S. propensity to quantify military relationships and to view stability as inherent in specifically crafted and minutely measured force ratios—"bean counting" as it was decried in the 1970s. But regions where the number of competitors is relatively large or does not divide clearly into two sides and where the differences of geography, development, and military capability are sharp, stability may inhere not so much in exact parity but in equitable balances among military competencies, decreased reliance on specific use-or-lose weapons, and perceptions of the unwillingness of interested outsiders to acquiesce to aggression.

A third factor is the technological preeminence of the United States and the U.S. tendency to view compliance problems as amenable to technological fixes. The United States was able to begin the arms-control process with the Soviet Union because of its strengths in the national technical means of verification, strengths that states in the developing world do not enjoy.

A fourth factor is the East–West military buildup, which gave birth to a tendency to accept only the highest possible standards for arms-control measures because of their direct relationship to the immediate survival of the United States. It is not clear that all possible arms-control measures can or should live up to the exacting legal standards of the United States or that there are not also security benefits to be extracted from measures that are less than perfect. The United States will not join the CWC or agree to additional verification provisions for the BTWC unless it rethinks along these lines.[19]

U.S. attitudes toward regional arms control will also be shaped by cold war thinking about regional conflicts. For the last 40 years, senior U.S. policymakers have looked at the Third World through the filter of the containment strategy and too often have understood conflicts there only in their geostrategic context. Although it is weakening as the Cold War recedes, the legacy is a tendency to understand only the concerns of friends of the West in the Cold War rather than engaging in a broader rethinking of the dynamics at work in each region. In the future, there will be a much larger role than was possible during the Cold War for preventive diplomacy and peacebuilding in regions in conflict. Arms control is likely to feature as a significant element in such a recrafted strategy.

One measure of the continued primacy of these notions in U.S. arms-control thinking is the apparent failure of the United States to articulate the lessons of its arms-control experience in ways useful for interested observers in the Middle East and South Asia.[20] In June 1992 the United States, together with Russia, hosted a seminar on arms control for interested states in those regions as an adjunct to the Middle East peace process. Informal commentary from a number of regional participants reflected their frustration with Washington's need to tell the arms-control story as a kind of search for the holy grail and the inability of U.S. policymakers to transmit the benefits of their experience in weighing risks, calculating uncertainties, and coping with the politics of compliance.

Without active participation and leadership by the United States, progress on the three-part arms-control agenda under discussion here is doubtful.[21] The United States cannot do much to compel the adoption of regional arms-control measures. But given its political influence, sophisticated verification capabilities, and military strength, which enable it to cushion some of the risks for some of the states involved in the negotiations, the United States has the potential to serve as facilitator, monitor, and guarantor of some global and regional measures.

But it will do so only if it has a clear perception of the stakes. The success or failure of efforts to achieve meaningful arms control in regions in conflict will have tangible consequences for the security of the United States. In both Asia and the Middle East, it has a direct role as the guarantor of the security of one or more states, and the drift toward war in either region is likely to involve U.S. forces. Moreover, a general deterioration of the international security environment would make it much more difficult for the United States to reap the peace dividend at the end of the Cold War and would force upon it politically divisive choices about the kind of role it should play in maintaining peace in an anarchic world.

The critical U.S. policy choice is between a strategy emphasizing reliance on military means, for which funding and political support may not be forthcoming absent international legitimization, and one emphasizing pursuit of a more cooperative "order" that narrows military risks, isolates renegade states, and preserves options for diplomacy and force. Because no armed opponent now appears capable of or intent upon threatening U.S. survival, the United States may feel it not worth the effort to pursue the second strategy. Policymakers should recognize, however, that unless more effective responses are found to the problems of weapons proliferation and control, the risks to the United States may again escalate as more states acquire the ability to significantly increase the costs of U.S. power projection or directly to threaten the territory of the United States. A good beginning has been made in this direction in 1991 and 1992 with U.S. efforts to facilitate a peace process in the Middle East, promote a regional dialogue in South Asia, and broker the bilateral agreement between the Koreas. But good beginnings are valuable ultimately for what follows.

In the developing world as well as the developed, important aspects of old thinking continue to shape the way arms control is understood and evaluated. Salient factors include the following. The first factor is the long-term dominance of the North–South security agenda by a few states whose views are unrepresentative of the rest. The near-nuclear states such as India and others with major investments in weapons and military capability have co-opted many states of the developing world into a crusade for global equality and justice. But this crusade appears more oriented to the legitimization of their own national choices than to the fact that most states of the developing world have no interest in unconventional weapons or in military solutions to problems of national development and security. One indication of the gap between a few leading countries and the rest of the international community was India's decision after Iraq's invasion of Kuwait to sell to Iraq chemicals useful for making chemical weapons, surely one of the finest examples of pursuing principle (the right of any sovereign state to the weapons of its choice) to the point of folly.

Second, most diplomats of the developing world who are working today on regional and global arms-control issues received their training during postings at the Conference on Disarmament (CD) in Geneva, a UN-affiliated organization. The mantras of nonalignment have been particularly powerful there, and they include especially a pervasive anti-Americanism, the portrayal of disarmament in near-messianic terms, and the propensity to view interstate conflict in value-neutral terms unless it has clear Western involvement, when imperialism is decried. The easy resort to dogma at the CD has faded in recent years as the prospect of the successful conclusion of a CWC compelled states from the developing world to begin to grapple in a non-ideological way with their interests vis-à-vis the convention, but for decades the CD has served as a training ground for diplomats who seemed to see in arms control a political rather than a security instrument. The result has been a primarily ideo-

logical view of global and regional security issues.

A third factor is the rigid equation of military strength with national security and the symbolism of military power as national sovereignty. This is a manifestation of the weak relationship between civil and military officials in many developing countries. It leads some states to acquire weapons that create unintended fear among their neighbors, arousing unpredictable responses and rising insecurity.

A fourth factor is the fragile role of the non-governmental sector in developing countries. In the United States and the West generally, institutions and individuals outside government have usefully served to generate and test arms-control ideas and to weigh the arms-control record without the bureaucratic stake of governmental agencies or the vow of silence imposed upon those with access to classified information. In the Middle East and East Asia, a few such institutions and individuals are beginning to appear, but their continued ability to contribute to the arms-control debate is uncertain, as is the willingness of their governments to open that debate.

Finally, the publics in most developing countries have been fed for decades the state dogma on questions of international conflict and security through a compliant media and academe. A frequent private lament of diplomats from both the Middle East and South Asia is that decades of controlled debate and the resulting ideological blinkers widespread among elites have robbed policymakers of the room for maneuver they need in the new environment to take new risks and establish new international relations.

These factors will be important in shaping the ability of policymakers in developing countries to look to the consequences of their choices, to weigh the risks associated with alternatives, and to debate trade-offs in terms of national and international interests. This bodes ill for arms control, which necessarily entails the acceptance of risk, debates about competing priorities, and decisions to limit or relinquish military instruments otherwise available. These factors will not quickly pass from the scene. Nor should they all. The developing countries make a legitimate case—generally misunderstood or ignored by the United States—about the vulnerability of their own societies and the unequal distribution of power in the world.

There are reasons to believe that perceptions on questions of international security and arms control are changing and will continue to do so. Democratization in the developing world will have a profound effect on arms-control choices made by governments there. It facilitates a modernization of civil-military relations, a process that in Argentina, Chile, and Brazil helped to bring about a redefinition of national security and national priorities. Democratization also brings non-governmental organizations into the policy process, strengthens the role of the independent media, and stimulates public education on international issues—all of which permit a broader definition of national priorities and increase the susceptibility of leaders to international moral norms.

Economic factors are also important. Many states in regions in conflict are also struggling with problems of development, modernization, and debt. They will face increasing choices between weapons programs and other national priorities. Especially where budgetary claims are made for weapons development programs that would isolate the state from valued foreign relations, the international economy, and foreign investment—as when nuclear or other banned weapons are built—national decision makers will face even sharper choices about the allocation of resources. Unless those programs offer undisputed military advantages (and the military utility of chemical and biological weapons is hotly disputed) or the country faces the threat of imminent war, it is reasonable to expect some attenuation of funding commitments to such programs in all but the wealthiest of countries. In the developing world, only a few oil-rich countries like Iraq will be able to funnel millions of dollars into surreptitious weapons programs.

Military factors as well will contribute to some rethinking of arms-control options. As decision makers in regions in conflict increasingly anticipate the possibility of wars in which weapons of mass destruction and advanced conventional weapons are not just in their own hands but in those of others as well, their perception of the stakes in conflict must begin to change. This pattern of perceptual evolution is evident in East–West relations, and there are many reasons to expect that states in other regions will experience the same shift.[22] Leaders may come to believe that there is a threshold beyond which military instruments alone cannot provide security, and that they must look beyond national strategies emphasizing military preparation and symbolic military power to complementary measures that balance military options with more cooperative solutions.

The passage or refashioning of conventional wisdoms among elites in the developing world will not occur quickly. But the process can be accelerated by leaders committed to serious pursuit of negotiated restraints. As Anwar Sadat reminded the world in his trip to Jerusalem, leaders can redefine political reality. The rethinking of national strategies within governments and a willingness to look at arms control in new ways can be stimulated as well. A useful model for this purpose is ACDA. Established in 1961 as a separate agency within the U.S. government and charged with advocacy in the interagency process for policy approaches emphasizing negotiated restraints, ACDA proved instrumental in rethinking the U.S. approach to the Cold War and became a primary vehicle for the pursuit of U.S. strategy. Although its voice in the policy process has waxed and waned with the interest of senior policymakers, its record as a catalyst for more cooperative approaches to questions of international security suggests that it might be a useful model for other governments interested in improving their competence on arms-control matters.

Conclusion

The end of the Cold War has altered the place of arms control in U.S. policy but has not eliminated it. Arms control will remain a major focus of U.S. interest and energy in the decades ahead. But not as before.

In the narrowest sense, arms control as a body of legal treaties relating to the disposition of the military forces most threatening to the United States is likely to be of less salience in the 1990s with the demise of the Soviet Union. But plenty of work remains in the implementation of existing treaties and the strengthening of global regimes. Moreover, the United States has key roles to play as facilitator, monitor, and guarantor of future regional arms-control measures. In a broader sense, arms control as a set of formal and informal undertakings concerning the disposition of military ca-

pabilities—either local or global—will continue to have value as a way to shape the threats to regional and international security and to reduce the likelihood that U.S. forces will be called upon as a last resort. In regional conflicts, arms control is likely to become a principal element of preventive diplomacy and a way to diminish reliance on U.S. power projection.

Thus, from the perspective of U.S. policymakers in the 1990s, both an expansion and dilution of the arms-control agenda is in evidence. That agenda includes many more elements than in the cold war era, although they are of less direct short-term importance for the United States. They may nevertheless be critical tools in building a new order of international affairs that is more cooperative than anarchic and that channels the energies of the developing world away from military means of solving conflict and toward the building of stable, prosperous nations and regions.

Notes

1. *Arms Control and Disarmament Agreements, Texts and Histories of the Negotiations* (Washington, D.C.: U.S. ACDA, 1990).

2. In 1991 Congress requested a study of ACDA's performance of its mandated tasks together with recommendations for any reorganization of the executive branch that would strengthen the ability of the U.S. government to carry out arms-control functions. A report from the ACDA inspector general is due by December 1992.

3. John Chipman, "The Future of Strategic Studies," *Survival* (Spring 1992), pp. 109–131.

4. START II is being used unofficially at the time of this writing to describe the package of strategic nuclear measures agreed at the June 1992 Bush–Yeltsin summit.

5. Hans Blix, "Verification of Nuclear Nonproliferation: The Lesson of Iraq," *The Washington Quarterly* 15 (Autumn 1992), pp. 57–65.

6. For a review of these biological warfare allegations, see Elisa D. Harris, statement to the Defense, Foreign Policy, and Space Task Force of the Budget Committee of the U.S. House of Representatives, Hearings, May 22, 1991.

7. Erhard Geissler and Robert H. Haynes, eds., *Prevention of a Biological and Toxin Arms Race and the Responsibility of Scientists* (Berlin: Akademie Verlag, 1991).

8. Barend ter Haar, *The Future of Biological Weapons* (Washington, D.C.: Praeger for CSIS, 1991). See also Oliver Thraenert, ed., *The Verification of the Biological Weapons Convention: Problems and Perspectives* (Bonn: Friedrich Ebert Stiftung, 1992).

9. Michael Moodie, "Transparency in Armaments: A New Item for the New Security Agenda," *The Washington Quarterly* 15 (Summer 1992), pp. 75–82.

10. Rolf Ekéus, "The Iraqi Experience and the Future of Nuclear Nonproliferation," *The Washington Quarterly* 15 (Autumn 1992), pp. 67–73.

11. For full text see *Chemical Weapons Convention Bulletin* (Harvard-Sussex Program on CBW Armament and Arms Limitation), no. 14 (December 1991), p. 19.

12. Ivo Daalder, "The Future of Arms Control," *Survival* (Spring 1992), pp. 51–73. Daalder differentiates between approaches to arms control for states with essentially cooperative relations, such as those prevailing today in Europe, and those with basically competitive relations, and argues that measures beyond modest ones intended to build confidence and security are unlikely to be adopted in the latter case.

13. Geoffrey Kemp, *The Control of the Middle East Arms Race* (Washington, D.C.: Carnegie Endowment, 1992). See also Alan Platt, ed., *Arms Control in the Middle East* (Washington, D.C.: United States Institute of Peace, 1992).

14. Charles Flowerree, "On Tending Arms Control Agreements," *The Washington Quarterly* 13 (Winter 1990), pp. 199–218.

15. See Committee for National Security, *The Lessons of Iraq: Unconventional Weapons, Inspection and Verification, and the United Nations and Disarmament*. Briefing and discussion with Johan Molander, special adviser to the chairman, United Nations Special Commission on Iraq, November 13, 1991 (Washington, D.C.: Committee for National Security, 1991).

16. R. Jeffrey Smith, "Yeltsin Blames '79 Anthrax on Germ Warfare Efforts," *Washington Post*, June 16, 1992, p. A–1.

17. Joseph F. Pilat, "Yet Another Farewell to Arms Control?" in *The Future of Arms Control: New Opportunities*, report prepared by the Congressional Research Service for the Subcommittee on Arms Control, International Security, and Science of the House Committee on Foreign Affairs, April 1992 (Washington, D.C.: GPO, 1992).

18. Nabil Fahmy, "The Security of Developing Countries and Chemical Disarmament," in Brad Roberts, ed., *Chemical Disarmament and U.S. Security* (Boulder, Colo.: Westview Press, 1992), pp. 63–70.

19. Brad Roberts, "Framing The Ratification Debate," in Roberts, *Chemical Disarmament and U.S. Security*, pp. 119–149.

20. For a rethinking of the lessons of the interwar naval arms-control experience for future regional arms-control measures, see Caroline F. Ziemke, "Peace Without Strings? Interwar Naval Arms Control Revisited," *The Washington Quarterly* 15 (Autumn 1992), pp. 87–106.

21. Michael Moodie, "Multilateral Arms Control: Challenges and Opportunities" (Paper prepared for a conference on verification at the Southern Methodist University, April 25, 1992).

22. Kenneth Waltz, *The Spread of Nuclear Weapons: More May Be Better* (London: IISS, 1981).

The Final Stage of Nuclear Arms Control

Jonathan Dean

EVEN AFTER THE end of the cold war confrontation, nuclear weapons remain the chief danger to both the United States and other Western countries either through direct attack by a known or secret nuclear weapon state or through the deterioration of the international environment into one where a score of nuclear weapon states continually maneuver to maximize their own security.

These dangers do not have the immediacy of the global nuclear Armageddon that could have erupted within minutes during the Cold War. Nonetheless, they are serious. The United States or its allies could suffer immense nuclear devastation from direct attack from a nuclear weapon state like Russia or the People's Republic of China or from concealed weapons brought into their cities. And even with its status as the sole remaining superpower, the United States is not likely to be immune from attack in a future international system composed of numerous if less powerful states with nuclear weapons. Other countries less favored in location, size, and mil-

itary strength than the United States are even more exposed to these dangers.

Up to now, although there remain some very serious areas of difficulty, the administration of President Bill Clinton has done quite a good job in nuclear arms control. The administration has actively pursued proliferation dangers in Ukraine and North Korea, continued advance implementation of the Strategic Arms Reduction Treaty (START), pressed for a comprehensive ban on testing nuclear warheads, and proposed an international agreement on ending production of fissile material for weapons. It is energetically promoting indefinite extension of the Nuclear Non-Proliferation Treaty (NPT) at the 1995 review conference.

If it proves possible to carry out all these projects successfully, there would be a more effective nonproliferation regime, development of new weapons would be made more difficult, operationally deployed U.S. and Russian strategic-range nuclear weapons would have been cut back to their levels when the NPT entered into force in the early 1970s, and there would be an upper limit on the maximum size of the arsenals of the nuclear weapon states, both declared and undeclared.

These achievements would be very important. But in spite of them, the arsenals of the nuclear weapon states, especially that of Russia, where polit-

Jonathan Dean, a longtime State Department arms-control negotiator, is adviser for international security issues to the Union of Concerned Scientists.

Copyright © 1994 by The Center for Strategic and International Studies and the Massachusetts Institute of Technology

ical instability is likely to continue for decades, would remain dangerously large in terms of deployed weapons and reserve stocks of already-fabricated nuclear warheads and weapons-grade fissile materials. The big loophole in the administration's policy is that it has not yet put forward a long-term program of nuclear arms control that would comprehensively address the problems created by the Russian nuclear arsenal and then move on to include China, Britain, and France in an effective regime of nuclear arms control.

This shortcoming must be remedied, or nuclear dangers from Russia and possibly China will continue to threaten Western security, administration policy on controlling nuclear weapons will lack coherence, and the opportunity brought by the end of the Cold War for radical departure from nuclear confrontation may be lost. Time is not on the side of the United States in this matter: Russia is moving to the right politically, and its willingness to agree on far-reaching steps on nuclear weapons may already have decreased in the upsurge of national feeling reflected in the December 1993 election results.

What is needed is to articulate a nuclear arms-control program that can cope better with current dangers and, by defining a long-term goal, also infuse nuclear arms-control and nonproliferation activities with purpose and direction during the coming decade. One way of visualizing this long-term goal is what can be called the "neutralization" of nuclear weapons.

The neutralization of nuclear weapons would consist of action by all states with nuclear weapons to irreversibly reduce their arsenals to a minimum number and then to render this remnant unusable for surprise attack by separating warheads from delivery sys-

tems and placing both under international monitoring on the territory of the owner state. The first, most urgent step toward this goal is to begin now with reciprocal monitoring and an irreversible build-down of Russian and U.S. arsenals, using measures and techniques that can then be gradually applied to all nuclear weapon states.

Record of the Clinton Administration

The initial phase of the Clinton administration's policy in arms control was, as in other fields, marked by confusion and delay. Despite this, the administration's record on nuclear arms control is already quite extensive. Although these problems remain far from solution, the administration acted vigorously to meet the serious proliferation dangers from Ukraine's refusal to surrender the large nuclear arsenal it inherited from the Soviet Union as well as North Korea's possible development of nuclear weapons capability. If unresolved, these issues have the potential to undermine or even destroy the nonproliferation regime, encouraging wider development of nuclear weapons in both regions. Considerable effort by the administration paid off at the Moscow summit meeting of January 1994, when Ukraine (again) agreed to send warheads deployed on its territory to Russia for dismantlement and to sign the NPT and actually shipped a considerable number of warheads. North Korea, although it agreed to a limited number of International Atomic Energy Agency (IAEA) inspections after intensive negotiation with the administration, then called a halt to inspections, causing an acute international crisis. It may prove possible to resolve the Ukraine problem more rapidly than that of North Korea, which may continue until there is radical change in North Korea's political system. In the North Korean case, the administration has far less leverage with the national government than it has in Ukraine and it has to work with less cooperative coalition partners. Even as regards Ukraine, however, friction between Ukraine and Russia could at any time flare into armed conflict and cause Ukraine to decide to keep its remaining nuclear weapons.

After initially arguing that it should carry out a limited number of warhead tests before accepting a comprehensive test ban, the administration announced a moratorium on U.S. testing and pressed for a multilateral test ban, on which negotiations began in the Geneva-based United Nations (UN) Conference on Disarmament in January 1994. The administration maintained its moratorium on testing even though China conducted a nuclear test in October 1993 and was apparently ready to do so after a second Chinese test in June 1994. The reluctance of France and China to relinquish the possibility of testing makes it uncertain how rapidly a test ban treaty can be achieved, but if differences between national positions can be narrowed down, and the French or Chinese position stands as the sole evident obstacle to an otherwise workable agreement, international pressures on the holdout government to agree will be strong.

The administration has also proposed an international treaty to end the production of fissile material for weapons. If this goal is achieved, it would have the effect of placing a ceiling on the maximum size of arsenals both of the declared nuclear weapon states and, if they participate, of the undeclared nuclear weapon states—Israel, India, and Pakistan. The administration has been slow to formulate a

specific concept for these negotiations, and it has not attempted in this project to deal with the mounting stockpiles of plutonium for use in civilian power reactors that create a possibility for rapid breakout from the NPT regime and an opening for forcible seizure, theft, or illegal sale. A phased approach, however, starting with an effective ban on production of fissile material for weapons, and then moving toward increasing restriction on civilian production and use of plutonium, is reasonable. Attempts to achieve both goals at the outset would elicit opposition from precisely those governments—France, Britain, China, and Russia—whose support is needed for the ban on military production. The administration has also launched new approaches to regional nuclear issues, failing to make much progress on India and Pakistan, but contributing to progress on Near East issues.

The administration is energetically pursuing extension of the NPT for an unlimited period, to be determined at the review conference scheduled for April 1995. Given the initiatives just described and the important achievements of U.S.–Soviet and U.S.–Russian arms control, it is likely that the NPT will be extended either indefinitely or for a further considerable period. It will, however, take more than a simple majority of something over 80 votes among those states attending the review conference to produce a satisfactory result. The NPT cannot be effective over time if a sizable number of its participants are reluctant or grudging.

One area of the administration's policy on arms control has raised questions: the issue of defense against ballistic missiles. The administration intends to reach a new understanding with Russia on defining the dividing line between defenses against tactical missiles, which are permitted under the Anti-Ballistic Missile (ABM) Treaty, and defenses against strategic-range missiles, which are very strictly limited under the treaty. The administration's objective is to permit development of speedier defensive missiles to destroy tactical-range ballistic missiles. These new defensive missiles may possibly be developed in collaboration with Russia and other countries.

Even during the peak of the controversy over the Reagan-Bush program for a nationwide defense against strategic missiles, nongovernmental experts generally conceded the need for clarification of the definitions contained in the ABM treaty to cover technological advances only dimly glimpsed when the treaty was being negotiated in the early 1970s. There are, however, two main problems with the proposed changes to the treaty. The first is whether tactical missile defense, which is intended for overseas use and will not protect the territory of the United States at all and in any event does not protect effectively against aircraft or cruise missiles, is worth the large sum of $15 billion planned for its development over a decade. A sum this large might well be more effectively spent on positive ways to strengthen nonproliferation, like improving the capability of the cash-starved IAEA to verify adherence to the NPT or seeking a worldwide agreement to ban attack missiles above a minimum range.

Anti-tactical ballistic missiles (ATBMs) with greater speed and altitude will unavoidably also have some enhanced capability to destroy incoming strategic-range missiles.[1] Consequently, the second problem is whether reinterpreting the ABM treaty to permit tactical anti-missile defense of increasing capability, and

even U.S.–Russian cooperation in developing such systems, might not someday provide a resurgent Russia with an opening to deploy a nationwide missile defense system with considerable capability against strategic-range systems. If this happened, it could create pressures to expand U.S. holdings of offensive weapons to overcome these defenses and it could lead to a new U.S.–Russian arms race in offensive weapons. Moreover, looking ahead some decades, widespread deployment of high-capability tactical defensive systems in other nuclear weapon states could also create a competitive offense-defense relationship among them—for example, between Russia and China, Russia and France and Britain, India and Pakistan, or even Israel and its Arab neighbors—to the detriment of reducing the nuclear arsenals of those countries that already have them.

Dangers from Existing Arsenals

The big issue not covered in the administration's nuclear arms-control policy is the future of the large existing arsenals of the nuclear weapon states, especially Russia and the United States. These arsenals create two main problems: one is their significance for the long-term success of the nonproliferation regime. Without a sense that the world supply of nuclear weapons is steadily contracting and that the possibility of actual use of nuclear weapons is also steadily decreasing, it will not be possible over time to enlist the voluntary cooperation of scores of non-nuclear states necessary for effective operation of the nonproliferation regime.

The second, more immediate, problem is what to do about the dangers that already arise from the incomplete nature of the current U.S.–Russian nuclear arms-control regime and also from the failure so far to involve China—and Britain and France as well—in negotiated reductions of their nuclear arsenals.

The Clinton administration has moved to implement the Bush program of buying up to 500 tons of highly enriched uranium from Russian nuclear weapons to be made unusable for weapons and converted into fuel for nuclear reactors through blending with natural uranium. This is a valuable program for bringing about the enduring reduction of the Russian arsenal. Statements by the Russian minister of atomics Viktor Mikhailov, however, indicate that Russian stocks of enriched uranium for weapons and of already-fabricated warheads are much larger than originally estimated.[2] Moreover, the buyout program will take up to 20 years to complete. It also does not cover plutonium from Russian nuclear reactors.

The United States and Russia are continuing advance implementation of the START I Treaty, still not in force because of Russia's insistence that Ukraine first sign the NPT as a non-nuclear state. The two governments are dismounting warheads from missiles, withdrawing from field deployment missiles, aircraft, and warheads scheduled for reduction, and beginning the destruction of missile silos. The United States has taken operational delivery systems off alert and has agreed with Russia to retarget long-range missiles still aimed at their respective homelands, a desirable gesture but one that can be rapidly reversed. The two governments are also dismantling the warheads of tactical-range delivery systems withdrawn by informal agreement between the Bush and Gorbachev governments. But there is no explicit agreement on this subject between them, as yet no verification or monitoring of what is going on, and no monitoring of resulting stocks of fissile material. A U.S.–Russian agreement reached at the end of 1993 provides for phasing out three Russian plutonium production reactors that have produced heat and power for civilian use and plutonium for weapons. But completing alternative heating plants in order to close these reactors permanently will take several years—even if financing for this project can be found. In May 1994, the two governments agreed in principle that, in the interim, a system of bilateral U.S.–Russian safeguards should be installed to foreclose use for weapons purposes of the plutonium produced by these reactors. This is an important advance, but negotiation of a detailed agreement may not begin until 1995, and may well be time-consuming.

The United States has funded the design of two long-term storage facilities in Russia for fissile material from nuclear weapons and will also fund their construction. In return, the United States will be permitted some degree of access to reassure itself that stored materials, mainly plutonium "pits" from dismantled nuclear weapons, are not being removed from the facilities to construct new weapons. But construction of the first facility, scheduled to begin in mid-1994, has been repeatedly delayed and construction is likely to take considerably longer than the projected five years. Russia will pledge not to remove material once stored in order to construct weapons, but the Russian government has undertaken no obligation as to how much plutonium it will put in this repository.

In an important innovative proposal, the administration has said it would as a unilateral gesture place weapons-grade fissile material excess to its needs under international supervision. The extent of the stock of fissile material—both highly enriched uranium and plutonium—to be retained by the United States as a strategic reserve was not decided at the time of the proposal, but it is sure to be sizable. The administration intends that this program of handing over plutonium and highly enriched uranium to internationally supervised storage should be a demonstration to encourage similar action by other nuclear powers on a voluntary basis. A month before President Clinton proposed this action at the UN (September 1993), Russian delegates at the Geneva-based Conference on Disarmament made a similar suggestion. At the January 1994 Moscow Summit, President Boris Yeltsin indicated willingness to consider taking parallel action with the United States but did not then undertake a specific commitment. He did agree to the establishment of a U.S.–Russian working group to examine the possibility. But even if Russia decides to transfer some portion of its excess stocks to internationally monitored storage, this decision will not of itself give insight into or control over what Russia is retaining.

All of this U.S.–Russian activity, most of it initiated by the Clinton administration, is valuable, but it circles around the edges of the main problem—what to do now about Russia's huge stockpile of already-fabricated weapons and already-produced fissile material, perhaps more than 30,000 warheads, 1,000 tons of highly enriched uranium, and 100 tons of weapons-grade plutonium (see figures 1 and 2).

The main effect of the START nuclear arms-control agreements is to move a large portion of U.S. and Russian strategic nuclear forces from field deployment to stored, reserve status.

These agreements merit every support because they greatly reduce the short-term risk of nuclear war. But, with the exception of the 20-year project to purchase enriched uranium from Russia, the reductions they entail are not permanent or irreversible. There is no agreed limit on the number of already fabricated weapons or on the amount of weapons-grade fissile material that the two countries may retain in their stockpiles, as yet no ongoing exchange of data on these stockpiles or verification of these data (as there is under the START treaties on the number and location of warheads deployed in the field), and no arrangements for monitoring the stockpiles to help prevent unauthorized removal of warheads or fissile material.

Belarus, Kazakhstan, and Ukraine have agreed to send strategic nuclear warheads deployed on their territory to Russia for dismantling and these warheads are now being transported. Yet even if these agreements are implemented fully, Russia will hold the fissile material from these weapons. In addition, it holds two-thirds of the deployed warheads of the former Soviet Union and all of the Soviet Union's reserve warheads and unweaponized fissile material. In March 1994, U.S. Secretary of Energy Hazel O'Leary took the initiative of concluding a tentative understanding with the Russian minister of atomics to exchange observers of the process of dismantling warheads in the two countries on a trial basis.[3] This was a useful agreement in principle. Talks will continue during 1994 to identify the equipment that could be used to confirm that dismantling is going on, visits to dismantling sites will take place, and negotiation on details of an ongoing observation system will begin later. This concept, based on reciprocity, is valuable. But the question of which warheads will

Figure 1
Current Nuclear Weapon Stockpiles
(estimates as of December 1993)

United States:	10,500 active warheads, 400 warheads in the inactive reserve, 5,850 retired warheads (peaked at 32,500 warheads in 1967)
Russia:	15,000 active warheads, 17,000 inactive and retired warheads (peaked at 45,000 warheads in 1986)
United Kingdom:	200 warheads
France:	525 warheads
China:	435 warheads

Source: "Nuclear Notebook," *Bulletin of the Atomic Scientists* 49 (December 1993), p. 57.

Figure 2
Stockpiles of Highly Enriched Uranium (HEU)
and Plutonium (Pu) in the Nuclear Weapon States
(estimates as of 1990)

United States:	550 tons HEU in total stockpile, 285 tons of which are in weapons; 89 tons of weapons-grade Pu, 127.3 tons of Pu in spent fuel
Russia:	720 tons of HEU in total stockpile, 480 tons in actual weapons (assuming 32,000 warheads, 15 kilograms per weapon); 125 tons of weapons-grade Pu, 70.7 tons of Pu in spent fuel
United Kingdom:	10 tons of HEU in total stockpile, 3.0 to 4.5 tons in actual weapons (assuming 200 to 300 weapons, 15 kilograms per weapon); 11 tons of weapons-grade Pu, 26.1 tons of Pu in spent fuel
France:	15 tons of HEU in total stockpile, 7.5 to 9.0 tons in actual weapons (assuming 500 to 600 nuclear weapons, 15 kilograms per weapon); 6.0 tons of weapons-grade Pu, 67.2 tons of Pu in spent fuel
China:	15 tons of HEU in total stockpile, 6.0 tons in actual weapons (assuming 300 weapons, 20 kilograms per warhead); 2.5+/–1.5 tons of weapons-grade Pu
Israel:	330 kilograms of weapons-grade Pu
India:	290 kilograms of weapons-grade Pu
Pakistan:	130 to 220 kilograms of HEU

Source: Except as noted, figures are drawn from David Albright, Frans Berkhout, and William Walker, *World Inventory of Plutonium and Highly Enriched Uranium 1992* (New York, N.Y.: Oxford University Press for SIPRI, 1993). Figures are in metric tons, which weigh about 1,000 kilograms each, or 2,240 U.S. pounds. The 89-ton figure for the U.S. stockpile of weapons-grade Pu is from the U.S. Department of Energy.

be dismantled by both countries and how many is not yet up for discussion.

An administration mission to Moscow in May 1994 proposed reciprocal exchange of data on holdings of fissile material. That the proposal was made at all is useful progress. But the proposal did not cover already-fabricated warheads, on which the United States is not yet willing to exchange information. Definitive agreement on exchange of information on holdings of fissile material has not yet been reached and it is unclear when the exchange will actually take place, how comprehensive it can be, and to what extent it can be mutually verified. If the proposed multilateral treaty to end production of fissile material for weapons goes into effect—and this will not be for several years—it, too, would not close these gaps in knowledge of and control over present arsenals.

Launchers of reduced missiles will be destroyed under START I, including silos for intercontinental missiles and missile-equipped submarines. The United States has already destroyed some silos; Russia more. There is, however, no U.S.–Russian agreement—aside from the important agreement in START II requiring destruction of the Russian SS–18s—to destroy the actual missiles withdrawn from field deployment under reduction agreements or to restrict their production. Like warheads withdrawn from the field under reduction agreements, these missiles can be stored for later deployment. START I contains a verified upper limit on the number of mobile missiles that can be stored by Russia, but it is a generous one. Ukraine and Kazakhstan have insisted that missiles deployed on their soil be destroyed rather than returned to Russia for possible future use. By mid-1994, Russia had destroyed 300 older or withdrawn missiles from former Soviet holdings. But aside from the SS–18s, neither Russia nor the United States has undertaken bilateral commitments to destroy strategic-range missiles.

The underlying problem, to which the administration has not yet developed a coherent, comprehensive approach, is the uniquely dangerous combination of nuclear threat and proliferation risks arising from the Russian arsenal.

The Russian elections in December 1993 moved the country to the right and once again underlined the possibility that an authoritarian government could emerge in Russia, whether by parliamentary means or by coup. Such a government could use these reserves of warheads, missiles, and fissile material to organize rapid, large-scale expansion of Russian nuclear forces, recreating many aspects of the cold war standoff. As Richard Nixon commented after his last trip to Russia (March 1994), Russia is the only country in the world that could completely destroy the United States.[4] Moreover, although a decisive move to the right in Russia could come suddenly at any time, it will be many years before it becomes clear that functioning democratic institutions have taken root in Russia and have a real chance of surviving. This means that, unless there is decisive bad news sooner, the unstable political conditions of Russia and Ukraine will probably last for decades, and with them, Western concerns over the status of Russian nuclear weapons. This widely shared conclusion should have major impact on U.S. nuclear arms-control policy.

U.S. officials believe that Russia's armed forces have up to now provided reasonable security for warhead stocks. Problems of instability in Russia, however, are intensified by rising rates of crime and official corruption, including among the armed forces, not only as regards housing, but as regards rations and pay. In 1992, some 4,000 verdicts of corruption were brought against officers of the Russian armed forces. The Russian defense ministry reported 4,000 cases of theft of conventional weapons, some of them very large, from military depots in 1992 and nearly 6,500 cases in 1993.[5] Continuing ethnic clashes in Russia and its neighboring countries add significantly to the problem. In 1990, political extremists tried to take over a storage site for tactical nuclear warheads near the capital of Azerbaijan.

In these conditions, the risk of forcible seizure of Russian nuclear warheads or weapons-grade fissile materials by extremists and of theft and illegal sale of weapons or fissile material will remain unacceptably high, as will the possibility of leakage of nuclear knowledge or components through inefficient export controls or the hiring of Russian weapons experts, as North Korea has already sought to do in the field of missile construction. In presenting the National Academy of Sciences report on plutonium disposal released in January 1994, Chairman Wolfgang Panofsky said members of his panel were of the unanimous view that in present conditions, the Russian nuclear stockpile constituted a clear and present danger to United States security.[6] Russian officials insist that strict control has been maintained over warheads and that they have been able to frustrate some attempts to steal fissile material in order to sell it. But the U.S. administration has no direct knowledge of the situation. There is no monitoring, no data exchange, and no verification arrangement.

All of this means that the whole range of risks connected with Russian nuclear weapons may well be the West's most serious potential security problem today. Moreover, unless action is taken to meet this problem, it will remain serious for decades to come, a period in which continuing Western worry over this topic is likely to be repeatedly punctuated by dramatic, worrisome incidents. This situation is dangerous in its own right, potentially highly so. Beyond that, it will almost certainly sap and undermine Western willingness to continue the economic help and political support essential for long-term development of democracy in Russia, thus helping to perpetuate the underlying dangers. The logical answer to this entire problem is to get as many of these weapons and as much of the fissile material as possible out of Russia, or at least out of exclusive Russian control, at the necessary cost of reciprocal action by the United States. This is precisely what U.S. nuclear arms-control policy should seek to do.

The risks from the Russian nuclear arsenal described here do not reflect laggard cold war suspicions but the objective situation. At the outset, the Clinton administration rightly focused on breaking the logjam in Ukraine and on bringing about implementation of START I, with ratification of START II still to come. There is, however, as yet no administration project for comprehensively coping with the Russian nuclear problem. Nor is there any administration plan for bringing China, France, and Britain into negotiations on reducing and limiting their nuclear arsenals. The deployed Chinese arsenal is a small fraction of that of Russia and the United States, but no outsider knows how many warheads or how much fissile material China is storing. China is undergoing a generational succession crisis that could bring its nuclear weapons into the hands of extremist regional or national regimes or extremist political groups, creating dangers like those in Russia today. Moreover, the administration has as yet no plans for tighter controls over plutonium produced for power reactors, which can be used to make nuclear weapons. A recent study estimates that civilian reactors will have produced enough separated plutonium by the year 2000, most of it in France, Britain, Russia, and Japan, to fabricate roughly 40,000 warheads.[7]

The point is that there is probably considerably more danger to the United States and to its allies from already existing nuclear weapons and fissile materials than there is from the possibility of their covert development by third world countries. North Korea, bad as it is, may have two or three warheads; Russia has at least 30,000, with delivery systems to match.

These dangers should be clearly reflected in the priority the administration gives to dealing with the Russian nuclear stockpile, but they are not. Instead, both the Bush and Clinton administrations have taken a rather ambivalent position toward this problem. Privately, U.S. officials say that it is a serious and urgent one. But the leisurely tempo of their discussions with Russia on monitoring arsenals, exchanging information, and transferring plutonium to internally supervised storage does not reflect this assessment. U.S. officials justify this slow pace with the argument that the agenda of U.S.–Russian arms control is already full and that the United States does not want to overload an already burdened Russian political system. Public statements by U.S. officials are also muted by the understandable requirement to avoid public alarm in the United States and to maintain a cooperative relationship with the Russian government. But these considerations are not a sufficient reason for failure to respond adequately to the dangers of the Russian nuclear arsenal. The Russian political agenda will always be overloaded. Moreover, Russia itself has proposed many of the actions that are needed now.

Relevant to this issue, of course, is future U.S. nuclear strategy. What purposes will nuclear weapons serve in the future? The study of long-term nuclear weapons policy begun in fall 1993 under former Secretary of Defense Les Aspin might be a useful contribution to answering this question, although first indications are that it may be a fairly orthodox endorsement of a classic deterrence posture. Perhaps it can be agreed that the main justification for nuclear weapons now is to discourage war of any kind between the nuclear weapon states and to deter use of nuclear weapons by declared or clandestine nuclear weapon states through the capacity to retaliate. If so, nuclear weapons will probably be around for a long time to come. But at what level?

As long as the threat is one from rational governments concerned with the welfare of their own populations, the deterrence approach may hold. If the fear is, however, that unstable governments headed by political extremists or extremist groups outside government may gain control of nuclear weapons in Russia or China or that weapons and fissile material may be stolen or sold, then the traditional deterrence approach becomes less convincing, and measures directed at deep cuts and better control over remaining weapons become even more important. Moreover, if the deterrence approach is to be the main guide to dealing with potential dangers from Russia and China, it will inevitably call for maintaining a large U.S. nuclear arsenal indefinitely to cope with contingencies from these countries.

But if the main problems from Russian nuclear weapons are as described here, people will not want to live with them indefinitely in a perhaps somewhat scaled-down, but still highly dangerous version of the cold war nuclear confrontation. Maintaining a large contingency arsenal would be more dangerous, less effective, and in the long run both more costly and more difficult politically than moving toward irreversible reduction of the Russian arsenal and paying the necessary price of corresponding action by the United States.

A Possible Solution

One answer to this whole range of problems of existing nuclear weapons and fissile material, above all, those arising from Russia, is an approach with three stages: first, ensuring that the START reductions with Russia are irreversible; second, instituting a post-START arms-control program bringing in the remaining nuclear weapon states; and third, establishing what can be called the final stage of nuclear arms control. All three stages would share three features missing from the current administration program: (1) they would provide for bilateral or multilateral monitoring of storage of both warheads and fissile material; (2) instead of simply storing warheads reduced by agreement—or fissile material from these weapons—in the hands of the owner government, they would provide for dismantling all reduced warheads and transferring their fissile material to internationally monitored storage; and (3) they would provide for destruction of most reduced missiles and drastic restrictions on their future production. The three stages are described below in outline.

Stage I: Making START Irreversible

The measures included in this stage are:

1. Establishing a U.S.–Russian system of monitoring in both countries' stocks of warheads and fissile materials produced for weapons through a portal-perimeter system similar to that now in use under the Intermediate-Range Nuclear Force (INF) Treaty and applied to existing storage sites. The bilateral monitoring system would be superimposed on existing custody arrangements. Russian and U.S. personnel would continue to guard their own weapon storage sites. Monitoring would be designed solely to assure that warheads and fissile material were not withdrawn from storage without authorization previously agreed by the two governments. Access to details of weapons design would not be necessary.

Monitors can be overcome, but the act itself would give strategic warning. Their presence would help to inhibit the main proliferation dangers posed by Russian stocks: forcible seizure, theft, illegal sale, or use of stored fissile materials to make more weapons. The director of the Pantex plant in Amarillo, Texas, the United States' only weapons assembly (and disassembly) plant, has publicly stated that Russian monitoring of his plant is feasible without access to design information.[8] The priority recommendation of the National Academy panel is to set up a reciprocal U.S.–Russian regime for stockpile monitoring.

The administration has, as noted, been considering transparency measures to be applied at some future point to storage sites in Russia and the United States as well as some degree of monitoring of dismantling activity and storage of fissile material in each country. These are partial measures.

275

Why not go the whole way and monitor all warhead and fissile material storage in both countries, meeting the risks in Russia now, while they are at their peak, rather than later? These monitoring measures would also provide precedents and experience for monitoring storage of warheads and fissile material in other nuclear weapons countries.

2. Setting up a comprehensive data exchange between the United States and Russia on current holdings of warheads (deployed and stored) and fissile material for weapons, with mutual verification of the numbers. The "Biden Condition," agreed to by the U.S. Senate in ratifying START I for application to START II and subsequent agreements, requires reciprocal inspections, data exchanges, and other cooperative measures to monitor the number of nuclear weapons stockpiled on the territory of both countries and the location and inventory of facilities for producing or processing fissile materials. There have been repeated outside proposals over the years for data exchange, warhead tagging, and so on. The administration has proposed exchange of information on stored fissile material. As this is written, however, there is no operating system of reciprocal, comprehensive data exchange with Russia.

3. Reaching agreement between the United States and Russia to dismantle all strategic warheads reduced under the START treaties and subsequently, as well as tactical warheads withdrawn unilaterally; not to reuse their fissile material for weapons; and to transfer this material to storage monitored bilaterally or by the IAEA, or preferably, by a combination of bilateral and IAEA monitoring. "Monitoring" as used here means the continuous presence of on-site observers as well as the use of sensors.

The purpose of transferring fissile material to monitored storage is to signal that the owner country is definitively renouncing the right to use this material for weapons, although that country would maintain the right to downgrade highly enriched uranium to reactor fuel and then to use or sell it. Transfer of weapons-grade plutonium to monitored storage would be permanent, if this can be agreed. Monitored plutonium storage would last until long-term methods of plutonium disposal were agreed. To make the transfer measure effective, both governments would undertake not to produce further fissile material for weapons. Achieving this agreement should not be difficult because the United States has stopped production and Russia has announced its intention to do so. (As suggested by the administration, the output of Russia's three plutonium-producing reactors would have to be placed under safeguards.) A bilateral pledge in the near future to end production of fissile material would give an important boost to negotiation of a multilateral treaty ending production of fissile material for weapons.

The administration has stated that it is now dismantling tactical nuclear warheads withdrawn from Europe and from naval vessels at a rate of somewhat under 2,000 per year at the Pantex plant in Texas and that several more years will be needed to complete this task. Clearly, if the United States is to undertake the obligation of dismantling more weapons as suggested here, then extra teams of dismantling experts will have to be assembled to enable the Pantex facility to work longer hours or a barebones new facility will have to be established. Russia reports that it is dismantling tactical warheads at something over 2,000 a year, but it is believed to have additional facilities that could also be used for the task. Increasing dismantling activities could provide more work for jobless Russian weapons experts.

Verification of this scheme as it applies to strategic warheads need not be complicated. The number of deployed warheads and the number to be reduced have been computed for START. It should be possible to agree on the amount of fissile material contained in each type of warhead and to calculate the total amount to be turned over to monitored storage. Whether it would be feasible subsequently to move stored plutonium off the territory of the owner country to some internationally controlled storage site—a desirable move—is a question for later study.

4. At the same time, the two governments would agree to destroy all missiles withdrawn from field deployment, to comply with reduction agreements, and to end production of these missiles. In both cases, a limited exception would be made for missiles intended for space exploration and satellite-launching. All actual space launches would be inspected prior to launch and missile testing would end. Successful fulfillment of the INF treaty eliminating intermediate-range nuclear missiles has brought valuable experience for verifying such an agreement. A U.S.–Russian missile reduction agreement could serve as the basis for a worldwide treaty to ban production or deployment of missiles with ranges over 100 kilometers except for carefully verified space exploration or satellite launch. A U.S.–Russian agreement to this effect would at the least give added authority and effectiveness to multilateral efforts to restrict the sale of missile components.

5. In this next stage of U.S.–Russian nuclear arms control, the two governments could also move toward what

one expert calls "zero alert," a situation in which still-deployed warheads are dismounted from missiles as well as aircraft and separately stored, and missile launching submarines are delayed by verifiable agreed measures in possible preparations to fire their missiles. If a comprehensive system of U.S.–Russian nuclear monitoring has already been agreed, separate storage of warheads under zero alert could also be bilaterally monitored.[9]

These approaches imply a new concept of negotiated reduction of nuclear weapons, one that makes reductions irreversible by dismantling reduced weapons and disposing of the fissile material in a secure way, as well as by destroying missiles in a term laid aside during the Cold War and nearly forgotten, nuclear disarmament. The U.S. and Russian governments have both adopted the vocabulary of irreversible reductions. At the January 1994 Moscow Summit, the United States proposed to establish a working group "to consider steps to ensure the transparency and irreversibility" of nuclear reductions, and Russia agreed. What "irreversibility" should mean officially has yet to be established by the two governments. The first task of the working group, however, will be to review the administration's proposal, already described here, to place a portion of the weapons-grade plutonium holdings of the United States—and of Russia if it agrees—under international monitoring. This proposal is a potential first step in the direction of irreversible reduction of nuclear weapons. Yet, as noted, it will be voluntary, resting on unilateral decisions by Russia and the United States on how much fissile material each wants to transfer to international monitoring. This process should be made obligatory, perhaps by administrative agreement between the two governments,

277

while the Russian government is still in a position to agree to it. Halfway measures, such as further negotiated warhead reductions of the current type, perhaps with modest periodic increases in target goals for turning over fissile material to monitored storage on a voluntary basis, will not suffice here. An unstable Russia with 1,000 deployed warheads, but also with thousands of stored warheads and missiles in reserve, will present nearly as many dangers to the outside world as an unstable Russia with 6,000 (START I level) or 3,000 (START II) operationally deployed warheads.

It will not be easy to gain agreement to this concept of an irreversible build-down of nuclear arsenals. The Russian minister of atomics wants to use weapons-grade plutonium from nuclear weapons to fuel Russian energy reactors. Moreover, both U.S. and Russian military leaders strongly prefer to stockpile warheads and fissile material against future contingencies than to give them up for good. They want to do the same with strategic-range missiles. But that approach would perpetuate the dangers of the Russian arsenal.

The procedure suggested here is based on the idea that by assuring dismantling of existing Russian warheads and the transfer of their fissile material to monitored storage, the total Russian stockpile of nuclear weapons would be permanently reduced. It is also based on the assumption that these procedures—negotiated warhead reduction; obligatory dismantling of reduced warheads and obligatory transfer of their fissile material to international custody; plus destruction of missiles—could be taken up by the other nuclear weapon states at a later stage.

An alternate approach has been informally suggested by some representatives at the Geneva-based Conference on Disarmament. They have in mind a new multilateral treaty that would either follow the conclusion of a treaty on ending production of fissile material for weapons or complement it. The new treaty would obligate parties to turn over to international custody that portion of their overall holdings of weapons-grade fissile material, whether in deployed weapons, stockpiled warheads, or unweaponized fissile material, that is excess to a negotiated level. The level would be periodically lowered until the arsenals were very low or perhaps fully depleted. The obligation to transfer a portion of present stocks might also be applied at some point to stocks of weapons-usable separated plutonium for power reactors and highly enriched uranium from research or naval reactors.

This idea deserves consideration for later use. Rather than undertaking a cumbersome and time-consuming project for a new international treaty at this point, however, it seems simpler and more practical to begin with U.S.–Russian agreement to transfer to monitored storage the fissile material from dismantled reduced weapons and then to seek to extend this practice to other nuclear weapon states. In the case of the United States and Russia, as figures 1 and 2 show, already-fabricated weapons constitute over half of estimated stocks of highly enriched uranium and weapons-grade plutonium. Moreover, Russia has already declared its willingness to dismantle strategic warheads withdrawn from the other republics. If the process of irreversible build-down begins with dismantling warheads and transferring their content of fissile material to monitored storage, stocks of stored fissile material not yet fabricated into weapons could be dealt with at a later, more transparent stage. Nonetheless, if the fissile material stockpile approach to reducing stocks of warheads and fissile material proves more negotiable than obligatory dismantling of reduced warheads, it should be pursued earlier.

Stage 2: The Post-START Stage of Nuclear Arms Control

Circumstances argue for at least two more stages of nuclear arms control in coming years, a post-START stage and a final stage. The first should combine deep negotiated cuts in the arsenals of all five declared nuclear weapon states with moves to make these reductions irreversible. This stage is based on the assumption, despite all current uncertainties, that the Ukrainian and North Korean problems have been resolved; START II has been ratified and both START treaties are on their way to implementation; a comprehensive test ban treaty has been concluded; a treaty ending production of fissile material for weapons covering the five declared nuclear weapon states and also the three undeclared nuclear weapon states—Israel, India, and Pakistan—has also been concluded; and agreement has been achieved on extending the NPT either indefinitely or for a considerable period.

This sequence of actions may not take place. In particular, ratification of START II by the new Russian Duma appears uncertain. At best, the ratification process will be difficult and it may require renegotiation of some parts of the treaty, especially those that eliminate the Russian SS–18s while permitting a large preponderance of submarine-launched missiles for the United States. If START II is not ratified, the two governments might be willing to act to carry out some of its provisions by executive agreement, but if the Duma has failed

to ratify the treaty or has rejected it, it is likely that pressures from the Duma and also the U.S. Senate would place a limit on such actions. In such a situation, a bilateral U.S.–Russian agreement to monitor stocks of warheads and fissile material would be all the more needed. If renegotiation is required, the two governments should move directly to a still more advanced reduction agreement that prescribes even more drastic reductions—including deeper cuts in U.S. missile-equipped submarines—than START II's 3,000-warhead level and that also has the irreversible features of warhead and missile dismantlement described here. In the circumstances, such a new agreement might be more acceptable to the Duma than START II.

If START II is ratified or a replacement agreed, the post-START stage of nuclear arms control should consist first of agreement by the United States and Russia to continue with negotiated reduction of their own arsenals under agreed measures to make these reductions irreversible, followed by action to draw the three remaining nuclear weapon states into the reduction process. As suggested by General Andrew Goodpaster, the United States and Russia would first reduce to 1,000 warheads.[10] Then they would join the other three countries in a series of reduction steps.

At the outset, the other three countries would either freeze their warhead holdings or reduce them by a minimal figure, say 10 percent. They would agree to conditions similar to those of the U.S.–Russian program, that is, to establishing some reliable form of international monitoring of stored warheads and fissile material; exchanging data; dismantling reduced warheads and missiles; transferring fissile material to monitored custody; destroying missiles withdrawn from field deployment; and moving toward zero alert for still-deployed weapons. The five could also agree at this stage to decrease levels of stored fissile materials for weapons through transferring the excess over an agreed, periodically lowered level to internationally supervised storage. Fabrication of additional weapons would end; each country would be permitted only one monitored weapons fabrication plant for replacing still-deployed warheads on a one-for-one basis. At this stage, stockpiles of plutonium for civilian reactors could also be transferred to IAEA custody so that those countries that operate plutonium reactors for power would not have weapons-usable stocks of fissile material at their disposal; the material could be withdrawn on a supervised basis when needed for energy production.

Stage 3: The Final Stage of Nuclear Arms Control

In addition to the implementation of programs to cope with the immediate dangers posed by Russian nuclear arsenals and for post-START nuclear arms control, the last stage of nuclear arms control should be defined—the ultimate arms-control step short of abolition of nuclear weapons, a step that represents the ultimate concession that can realistically be made by the nuclear weapon states, a step that leaves only a minimum number of weapons in their hands and that makes it extremely difficult to use them, a program that in effect "neutralizes" nuclear weapons. The two earlier stages described here have already introduced three components of this final stage of nuclear arms control: bilateral or multilateral monitoring of warhead stocks; irrevocable transfer of fissile materials from weapons to in-

ternationally supervised custody for subsequent use as reactor fuel or indefinite storage; and destruction of reduced missiles.

Deep reductions are also necessary for a final stage of nuclear arms control. But reductions alone are only a part of the answer. Few of the more radical proposals, like those of Robert McNamara or Andrew Goodpaster urging reduction of U.S. and Russian warheads to 100 or 200 for each country, make detailed provision for monitoring reserve arsenals, for dismantling reduced warheads, and for progressively reducing the level of fissile material. Drastic reductions in deployed weapons can eliminate the danger of nuclear Armageddon or nuclear winter, but they cannot of themselves do more than somewhat reduce the danger of offensive use of nuclear weapons and they do not cope with the risk of rapid expansion of arsenals to a much larger size.

As regards still-deployed delivery systems, the Clinton arms-control program takes them off alert or retargets them. But these actions too can be rapidly reversed. A group of experts under the chairmanship of former Under Secretary of Defense Fred Iklé has gone further and has suggested that only a limited portion of U.S. and Russian strategic nuclear forces should remain operationally deployed.[11] In the remaining force, warheads would be separated from aircraft or missiles and placed in storage open to confirmation by the other side. There are no details in the proposal on how this confirmation might be carried out. Like the idea of zero alert, however, this approach has the virtue of adding to the concept of deep reductions the concept of separating warheads from delivery systems for a portion of the force. But the Iklé suggestion would leave deployed a large force with 300 warheads on each side untouched and rapidly usable, while the remaining warheads from an operational reserve could be rapidly redeployed. More far-reaching suggestions for zero alert calling for separation of the warheads from all deployed delivery systems and placing the warheads in monitored storage also lack detailed provision for monitoring that storage and for dealing with existing stocks of already fabricated warheads and fissile materials and the resulting potential for breakout.[12]

Consequently, for the final stage of nuclear arms control, all of these concepts should be combined: drastic further reductions; separation of warheads from delivery systems for the remaining deployed force; and the obligatory dismantling of reduced warheads, with transfer of their fissile materials to international monitoring. These procedures could form the basic elements of the final stage of nuclear arms control—a program for neutralizing nuclear weapons.

Neutralizing Nuclear Weapons

Even if some non-nuclear states and public groups throughout the world continue to advocate total elimination of nuclear weapons, it is very unlikely that the nuclear weapon states would agree to give up their weapons completely before there is a functioning system of world security with a proven record of achievement and a nonproliferation regime of recognized comprehensive effectiveness. These conditions are justifiable, but their fulfillment, if it can be achieved, is extremely distant. What is needed for the lengthy interim is an approach that defines an end point or goal for nuclear arms control and that is realistic enough to have some long-term prospects of practical implementation. It

should be an approach that would neutralize remaining arsenals of nuclear weapons both politically and militarily, and that would recognizably be the final stage of nuclear arms control prior to possible decisions to eliminate the weapons or to hand them over to a much-strengthened United Nations.

These prerequisites for a final stage could be met through an agreement among the five nuclear powers to reduce their total arsenals to no more than 200 warheads each, to separate these warheads from their delivery systems, and to place both the warheads and the delivery systems under multilateral control on the territory of the owner states.

The equal level of 200 warheads is selected for reasons of negotiability as slightly lower than the British nuclear arsenal and considerably lower than the French or Chinese level, thus requiring some reduction by all. The five governments would commit themselves to dismantle all the warheads that are reduced to reach the 200-warhead level and to place all weapons-grade fissile material from these warheads, as well as their remaining stocks of weapons-grade fissile material, under international monitoring as reductions are carried out.

Prerequisites for this final stage would be successful implementation of the two earlier stages. One further requirement is radical strengthening of the IAEA and its verification capabilities.[13] Another is conclusion of an international agreement ending the use of plutonium as fuel for energy reactors and replacing it with low-enriched uranium, which is in plentiful supply. Given the fact that plutonium for power reactors can be used to make effective nuclear weapons, it will not be possible to persuade the nuclear weapon states to reduce their weapons to very low levels while production of separated plutonium to fuel reactors continues. This affects especially the United States, which does not use plutonium for energy reactors.

In the final stage of reductions by the five nuclear powers, the undeclared nuclear states—Israel, India, and Pakistan—could also be given the choice between placing their warheads or explosive devices and fissile material in monitored storage or agreeing to their elimination. If the three retained their weapons and joined the monitoring scheme, it is unlikely that non-nuclear countries would object against such an arrangement as legitimizing possession of nuclear weapons by these three countries because the arrangement would place their weapons under international supervision and make it highly improbable that the weapons would ever be used, a great advance over the current status.

The owner countries would still have the right to withdraw their nuclear warheads from monitored storage in the event of acute national emergency or at the request of the UN Security Council. Monitors could also be overpowered, but removal of weapons under any circumstances would give notice of violations to all participants. Implementing this approach would mean elimination of the risk of large-scale nuclear attack without warning, elimination in practice of the possibility of threatening to use nuclear weapons, and relegation of nuclear weapons to a secondary, reserve status.

There are some risks in this concept; they would have to be met or nuclear weapon states would not be prepared to consider it. One possibility is that a nuclear weapon state might conceal some nuclear weapons or weapons-grade fissile material or that a non-nuclear weapon state might secretly develop weapons. A related problem is the potential vulnerability of a small number of known storage sites, missiles, and aircraft to attack by previously concealed weapons, although if only a few weapons have been concealed, they are perhaps more likely to be used for terror attacks against cities.

Dispersed deep storage sites, each of which would have to be attacked by many warheads, could be a partial answer to the potential problem of concealed weaponry. Moreover, at the outset, each nuclear weapons country could be permitted a handful of warheads on a few missile-equipped submarines at sea to deter such an attack, too few for decisive surprise attack, but enough to retaliate if need be. Later, if the scheme worked well, missile-equipped submarines could be prohibited completely. At that point, each nuclear weapon state might have the option of establishing a specified number of ground-based missile defenses to protect storage sites.

In later stages of the neutralization plan, the number of nuclear weapons still in the hands of nuclear weapon states would be further reduced until it became so small that, even if used, these weapons would not result in the total destruction of a major target state. Further, later refinements of the approach are also possible, like dismantling all warheads and leaving owner states only with their supervised fissile materials, which they would have to weaponize before seeking to use them.

Two Questions

First, how feasible is this scheme? If asked to sign on to it today, all five nuclear powers would very likely refuse outright. Indeed, one argument against the current proposal is that declaring it publicly could discourage governments of other nuclear weapon states from agreeing to essential early steps in the program. Each of these governments has, however, with whatever mental reservations, declared its willingness to move toward elimination of nuclear weapons. Articulation of a plan for achieving a final stage of nuclear arms control might increase their willingness to cooperate on the intervening steps. It would almost certainly elicit strong support from their publics. If the United States and Russia themselves made further deep cuts and themselves implemented the major components of the program—bilateral monitoring of stocks of warheads and fissile materials, obligatory dismantling of reduced warheads and handing over their fissile content to supervised storage, and destruction of reduced missiles—this example would have a positive impact on the other three nuclear powers. China would be attracted by the offer of equality with Russia and the United States.

Bilateral monitoring of the Russian and U.S. nuclear stockpiles is not a futuristic idea, but a present necessity in the U.S. national interest. U.S.–Russian agreement to dismantle all warheads reduced under the START treaties and to give up their right to reuse the fissile material in the warheads would be a very big step. Yet both countries are dismantling tactical nuclear weapons withdrawn from field deployment. Russia has agreed to dismantle warheads brought from Ukraine, Belarus, and Kazakhstan and to transfer a large amount of highly enriched uranium from dismantled weapons to the United States. The United States and Russia have agreed in principle to transfer some weapons-grade fissile material to international custody. Both governments are using at least the vocabulary of making nu-

clear reductions "irreversible." The prospects are fairly good for ultimate agreement on a multilateral treaty to cut off production of fissile material. Russia itself has in the past officially proposed reciprocal data exchange on U.S. and Russian stocks of both warheads and fissile materials.[14] In the negotiations on intermediate-range nuclear weapons, Mikhail Gorbachev proposed reciprocal destruction of the warheads as well as the missiles of this entire class of weapons. The United States did not pick up on these initiatives at the time. It should do so now.

The ratification of START II by the newly elected, more nationalistic Russian Duma is far from certain and may be the biggest stumbling block to the sequence of possible developments described here. If START II is ratified and both START treaties are implemented, however, there will probably be a START III, hopefully including agreement to dismantle warheads and transfer their fissile content to international custody. If START II becomes a casualty of the new Russian Duma, the two governments could move directly to a still more advanced reduction agreement that might have better chances of acceptance.

If there is a START III and an international fissile cutoff treaty, it is probable that these developments will lead to a five-power reduction agreement using as a model the contents of the U.S.–Russian reduction accords, including warhead dismantlement and transfer of fissile material to monitored custody if these concepts have been agreed between Russia and the United States. At some point thereafter, if all has gone well in the nonproliferation field, there will be mounting political pressure on the five nuclear weapon states from non-nuclear states to do still more to control their weapons. In these circumstances, it would not be a tremendous jump to move to the final stage of nuclear arms control described here. There are a lot of "ifs" in this sequence of events, but it is not an improbable one. Given the risks of the present situation, it is worth the effort to pursue this solution. Its realization would, of course, require presentation of an official U.S. program containing the elements described here.

A second question: If nuclear weapons, especially those in the hands of unstable or authoritarian governments like those of Russia and China, are the chief dangers facing the Western states, why not make this proposal go all the way to recommend abolition of nuclear weapons? My answer is that the purpose of this article is to present a program that the governments of the nuclear weapon states might at some point be willing to act on. Although the United States and Soviet Union/Russia—and China, France, and Britain as well—have at various times proposed or subscribed to abolition of nuclear weapons, and there is continuing widespread public support for the general idea, abolition of nuclear weapons is not a practical objective at this time. There is convincing evidence that the nuclear weapon states are not willing now to totally eliminate their nuclear weapons. States that have nuclear weapons regard them as the ultimate guarantee of their security in an uncertain world where there is no dependable central authority.

Moreover, under present circumstances, this unwillingness to relinquish weapons may serve a good purpose. It deters war, both nuclear and conventional, between the nuclear weapon states that are the world's major military powers, as well as policies and enterprises that could lead to conflict between them. It is also possible to imagine extreme circumstances in which multilateral use of nuclear weapons might be made at the request of the UN Security Council. On the other hand, total relinquishment of nuclear weapons under present conditions, which include the absence of effective global and regional peacekeeping mechanisms, would probably result not in decreasing the level of conflict in the world, but in increasing it. Among other developments, wars between the nuclear weapon states, now improbable, would become more plausible. Consequently, the most direct path toward eliminating all nuclear weapons may be to focus on measures for lowering the level and frequency of organized violence in the world. Nuclear weapons have not been used since Hiroshima and Nagasaki, but at least 20 million people have lost their lives in over 100 wars since 1945.[15]

It is difficult to imagine conditions under which the reluctance of the nuclear weapon states to relinquish their weapons completely would change. Two minimum preconditions are the existence of wholly dependable global and regional security institutions with a proven record of keeping the peace and of a nonproliferation system of utterly convincing effectiveness that reduces the possibility of clandestine development or concealment of weapons to a very low degree of probability. A third precondition, valid for the United States, Britain, and France at least, is the existence of functioning, enduring democratic government in Russia and in China. It is unclear whether these preconditions can be fulfilled and if so, when; only the future can give the answer here. In the interim, the "final stage" neutralization of nuclear weapons would provide a stable way of coping with the dangers of nuclear weapons that could last indefinitely.

One theoretical alternative, to hand over these weapons to a UN security force, raises essentially the same questions as proposals for abolition. In the present state of the UN, which operates by an uneasy consensus among the major powers that could be dispelled at any time, states with nuclear weapons will be unwilling to hand them over to an untried UN force over which control would be uncertain. The important thing now is to build a system of regional security institutions capped by the UN that would promote essential habits of cooperation among the nuclear weapon states and that could establish a record of lowering the incidence of armed conflict in the world.

To sum up, publicly defining the goal of neutralizing nuclear weapons as the final stage of nuclear arms control will create understanding and support for the many necessary intervening steps. Once nuclear weapons are actually neutralized as suggested here, they will cease to be a major factor in international security or international politics. Neutralizing the weapons will create conditions in which still further improvements in the nonproliferation regime can be pursued and the ultimate future of nuclear weapons can be dispassionately discussed.

This article draws on the author's new book, Ending Europe's Wars *(New York, N.Y.: Twentieth Century Fund Press, 1994).*

Notes

1. Lisbeth Gronlund et al., "Highly Capable Theater Missile Defenses and the ABM Treaty," *Arms Control Today* 24 (April 1994), pp. 3–8.

2. William J. Broad, "Russian Says Soviet Atom Arsenal Was Larger than West Estimated," *New York Times*, September 26, 1993.

3. Thomas Lippman, "Accord Set on Nuclear Inspections," *Washington Post*, March 16, 1994, and "Russia Set to Close Three Reactors," *Washington Post*, March 17, 1994.

4. Richard Nixon, "Moscow, March '94: Chaos and Hope," *New York Times*, March 25, 1994.

5. "The High Price of Freeing Markets," *Economist*, February 19, 1994.

6. National Academy of Sciences, *Management and Disposition of Excess Weapons Plutonium* (Washington, D.C.: National Academy Press, 1994), pp. 27–28.

7. Brian Chow and Kenneth Solomon, *Limiting the Spread of Weapons-Usable Fissile Materials* (Santa Monica, Calif.: RAND, 1993), pp. xiv, 15.

8. R. Jeffrey Smith, "Reporters Granted First Look at Texas Nuclear Weapons Facility," *Washington Post*, January 14, 1993.

9. Bruce G. Blair, "Global Zero Alert for Nuclear Forces" (The Brookings Institution, Washington, D.C., May 1994).

10. Andrew J. Goodpaster, *Further Reins on Nuclear Arms* (Washington, D.C.: Atlantic Council, August 1993). See also Jonathan Dean and Kurt Gottfried, *A Program for World Nuclear Security* (Washington, D.C.: Union of Concerned Scientists, February 1992).

11. Fred Iklé and Sergei Karaganov, *Harmonizing the Evolution of U.S. and Russian Defense Policies* (Washington, D.C.: Center for Strategic and International Studies, November 1993).

12. Arjun Mahkijani and Katherine Yih have made a farsighted proposal to separate warheads from delivery systems throughout the world and place the warheads under monitoring. The proposal does not, however, provide for ending the supply of fissile material for weapons or supervising undeployed stocks of weapons and fissile material. It also advocates immediate action to move to this goal without intervening stages of reduction or cooperation among the nuclear weapon states. This is unlikely to succeed. A recent study of the proliferation problem by the Council for a Livable World also recommends separation of delivery systems and warheads as a long-term goal. Arjun Mahkijani and Katherine Yih, "What to Do at Doomsday's End," *Washington Post*, March 29, 1992; Peter Gray, *Briefing Book on Non-Proliferation of*

Nuclear Weapons (Washington, D.C.: Council for a Livable World Education Fund, December 1993), p. 19.

13. These improvements might ultimately include: (1) a treaty requirement for supplier states to inform the IAEA of the sale or transfer of components involved in the production of nuclear weapons, including dual-use components (the present commitment is a voluntary one); (2) agreement of all NPT states to accept anywhere-anytime inspections of their nuclear and nuclear-related institutions, eliminating present requirements to justify special inspections and negotiate their conditions (only Iran and Libya have agreed to such arrangements); (3) a decision by the Security Council to require all UN member states to join the NPT or a regional organization with safeguards of equivalent stringency. The Security Council would point out that uncontrolled capacity to build nuclear weapons is a threat to international security and consequently that no UN member state should be without an adequate safeguards program. This measure, which would take effect near the end of the sequence of steps described here, would mean that the Security Council would be committed to take joint action, to include expulsion from the UN, against any state that refused to place its nuclear facilities under IAEA control or the equivalent, either by refusing to join the IAEA or a regional equivalent or by withdrawing from the NPT as North Korea has done or threatened to do.

14. Proposal by Foreign Minister Andrei Kozyrev at the Geneva Conference on Disarmament, February 12, 1992.

15. David Welsh, "Domestic Politics and Ethnic Conflict," *Survival* 35 (Spring 1993), pp. 63–80; Ruth Leger Sivard, *World Military and Social Expenditures 1993* (Washington, D.C.: World Priorities, 1993), p. 20.

Prospects for Chemical and Biological Arms Control: The Web of Deterrence

Graham S. Pearson

MAJOR CHANGES TO the world scene have taken place over the last three years with the dissolution of the former Soviet Union and the Warsaw Pact, the conflict between the Iraqi and coalition forces of 1990–1991, and the move away from bipolar tension toward regional conflicts and less stability. The same time frame has seen no sign of any reduction in the proliferation of chemical and biological (CB) weapons. Indeed some 10 nations are assessed as having biological weapons programs and almost twice that number have, or are aiming to acquire, chemical weapons.[1]

Following the Persian Gulf War, which saw a real threat of the use of CB weapons, the United Nations (UN) under Security Council Resolutions 687 and 715 established a Special Commission to oversee the elimination of Iraq's weapons of mass destruction and to carry out a monitoring regime to ensure that such a capability is not regained. The lessons being learned from the activities of the Special Commission are of immense importance for both CB arms control and

Graham S. Pearson is director general of the U.K.'s Chemical and Biological Defence Establishment at Porton Down. Since his appointment in June 1984 he has contributed actively to both CB defense and the CB arms-control debate.

for would-be proliferators; it is particularly important for the status of the UN, the deterrent effect of its resolutions, and the credibility of the CB arms-control regimes that the UN Special Commission should succeed in its activities and that Iraq should be deprived of its capability for weapons of mass destruction. In addition, negotiation has been completed for the Chemical Weapons Convention (CWC), which is due to be opened for signature in January 1993. Also, the Ad Hoc Group of Governmental Experts considering verification measures for the Biological and Toxin Weapons Convention (BTWC) from a scientific and technical viewpoint has met twice—in Geneva from March 30 to April 10, 1992, and from November 23 to December 4, 1992. The tasks for CB arms control have become more important. Success in these efforts appears increasingly possible. But the challenges have also come into sharper focus.

This essay starts by considering the nature of CB weapons. It sets this discussion in the context of the relative scale of effect of such weapons against a background of the current world scene and of the existing arms-control framework. Recent changes in the international arena influence perceptions about the promise for and limits of the arms-control agenda[2] and create new incentives and opportunities for states to work together to limit the proliferation of CB weapons. The aim is to achieve a web of deterrence to complement the imperfections of arms control with other measures so that a potential cheater finds obstacles to every possible avenue to cheating and is led to a judgment that the acquisition of chemical or biological weapons is expensive, of uncertain military value, and politically unacceptable.

The Nature of CB Warfare

The use of CB weapons involves the dissemination of materials that cause harm or death to the attacked population. In both the chemical and biological cases, the primary route of attack requires the material to be disseminated into the atmosphere so that it can reach and be inhaled by the target population. In the case of chemicals, the materials poison the person attacked; biological agents cause infection, with harm and death as the result of the ensuing disease. The potential chemical and biological warfare (CBW) threat spectrum ranges from the classical chemical warfare (CW) agents, such as mustard, nerve agents, and hydrogen cyanide, through toxic industrial, pharmaceutical, and agricultural chemicals, to bioregulators and toxins, and thus to both genetically manipulated biological warfare (BW) agents and the traditional BW agents such as bacteria, viruses, and rickettsia. The CBW spectrum is shown in figure 1: the materials in the four boxes to the left poison while those in the two on the right infect. The relative toxicity of CW and BW agents is shown in figure 2. As might be expected, the quantities required to infect are very much less than those needed to poison. Typically there is a

factor of about 1 million between the quantities of typical BW agents needed to kill a person and those of typical CW agents.

The greatly enhanced potency of BW agents means that the distances downwind over which such agents can have effect are significantly greater than those for CW agents. This is shown schematically in figure 3, which demonstrates that typically for CW agents a kilometer is a representative downwind hazard distance, while for bioregulators and toxins the distance is about 10 kilometers, and for BW agents it is a few hundred kilometers. All of these calculations assume comparable and favorable meteorological conditions. The other difference between CW and BW agents is that the former tend to be rapid acting, with nerve agents resulting in harm or death within minutes, whereas the latter are slower to act because of the need for the microorganisms to replicate themselves inside the host. Consequently, chemical weapons have potentially greater utility in a near-contact battle, while biological weapons are more appropriate for rear areas or for static situations. Biological warfare is essentially a strategic concept.

Comparisons of chemical, biological, and nuclear weapons have been published by both the secretary general of the United Nations, in 1969,[3] and by Steve Fetter of the University of Maryland, in 1991.[4] Both these comparisons (see tables 1 and 2 respectively) demonstrate clearly that chemical weapons have a significantly greater effect than conventional weapons, while biological weapons have comparable effects to nuclear weapons. Both chemical and biological weapons are unique in two respects:

- they produce no collateral damage; and

Figure 1
CBW Threat Spectrum

Mustard Nerve Agents Cyanide	Toxic Industrial Pharmaceutical Agricultural Chemicals Aerosols	Peptides	Saxitoxin Mycotoxin Ricin	Modified/ Tailored Bacteria Viruses	Bacteria Viruses Rickettsia
			Agents of biological origin ←————————————————→		
Agents not found in nature - designer drug modifications ←————————————————→					
Classical Chemical Weapons	Emerging Chemical Weapons	Bioregulators	Toxins	Genetically Manipulated Biological Weapons	Traditional Biological Weapons

- they require materials that can be acquired from legitimate peaceful facilities; there is no necessity for expensive nuclear facilities or for conventional military explosives.

Against that must be balanced several disadvantages, including, first, that of a delayed reaction over an area, second, dependence on the prevailing meteorology, and, third, the political reaction to a use or threat of use, which will be stronger than for any conventional method of warfare.

There can be little doubt about the utility of chemical or biological weapons. Chemical weapons were used in World War I, in Italian attacks on Abyssinia in the 1930s, and in the Iraq–Iran conflict of the 1980s. In all these cases, they were used against essentially unprotected personnel. Although the use of biological weapons in conflict has not been so unequivocally demonstrated, it is known that in conflicts involving conventional weapons more casualties result from disease than from the use of conventional weapons.[5] In addition, past offensive

biological programs have demonstrated the utility of such weapons by all means short of their actual use in war.

Divergent views are frequently expressed on the potential utility of chemical or biological weapons. It is frequently suggested that the meteorology is too uncertain, and that the user's troops may be at greater risk than those attacked. All such suggestions about the alleged disutility of chemical or biological weapons need to be carefully evaluated and investigated. Many are of doubtful validity. For example, despite meteorological conditions, an upwind chemical or biological weapons attack will be less sensitive to the accuracy of the delivery means than will a conventional weapons attack. As to the vulnerability of an aggressor's troops, it is important to remember that an aggressor knows what agents are available to it and can select the meteorology or other conditions to minimize the potential downwind hazard to its own forces.

Indeed, because of the uncertainty of the location of the precise hazard

Graham S. Pearson

Figure 2
Toxicity of CBW Agents

Chemical Warfare Agent   Estimated Lethal   Biological Warfare Agent
Dose in mg/man

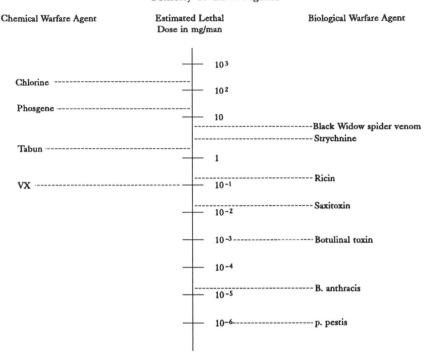

Source: SIPRI, *Problems of Chemical and Biological Warfare*, vol. II (Stockholm and New York, 1971).

area arising from a particular attack, it is necessary to adopt a greater hazard area—and consequently a useful force multiplier occurs in that protective measures have to be donned in a much larger area than the actual hazard area because the latter depends on local meteorological variations.

Finally, selection of chemical or biological weapons that result in incapacitation rather than in death can again act as a force multiplier because incapacitated personnel need to be looked after in a way that the dead do not. Although chemical and biological weapons require time to take effect, this is much less of a disadvantage for an aggressor because it can choose when to utilize the material and can thus select to do so at the optimum time—and this can indeed be an advantage, because it may be far from clear whether an attack has actually occurred and who carried it out.

CB Arms Control in a Changing World Scene

The first step in CB arms control was the Geneva Protocol of 1925, which essentially banned first use because several states retained the right to retaliate in kind should they be attacked with CB weapons. The next milestone was the Biological and Toxin Weapons Convention of 1972, which sought to

Figure 3
Downwind Hazard Distance for CBW Agents

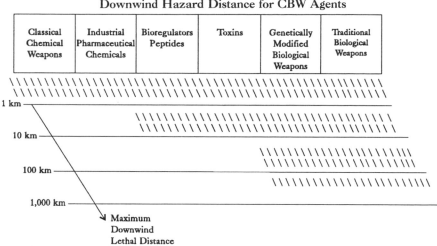

↘ Maximum
Downwind
Lethal Distance

ban a complete class of weapons. This had, as was usual at the time, no provisions for compliance and verification; nor did it address use. A further 20 years has brought agreement of a text for the Chemical Weapons Convention, which has provisions for ver-

ification and inspection as well as for investigations of use. These developments, coupled with the threat in the Gulf conflict of 1990–1991 that Iraq might use CB weapons and information about the former Soviet program, have reminded the international com-

Table 1
Comparative Estimates of Attacks on Unprotected Population Using a Nuclear, Chemical, or Biological Weapon

	Type of weapon		
Criteria for estimate	Nuclear (one megaton)	Chemical (15 tons)	Biological (10 tons)
Area affected	Up to 300 km^2	Up to 60 km^2	Up to 100,000 km^2
Time delay before effect	Seconds	Minutes	Days
Damage to structures	Destruction over an area of 100 km^2	None	None
Normal use after attack	3–6 months after attack	Limited during period of contamination	After end of incubation period or subsidence of epidemic

Source: UN, *Chemical and Bacteriological (Biological) Warfare and the Effects of Their Possible Use,* Report of the Secretary-General, A/7575/Rev.1, S/9292/Rev.1 (1969).

Table 2
Conventional/Chemical/Biological/Nuclear
Warhead Comparisons

Warhead Type	Dead	Injured
Conventional (1 ton of HE)	5	13
Chemical (300 kg of GB)	200–3,000	200–3,000
Biological (30 kg of anthrax)	20,000–80,000	
Nuclear (20 kiloton yield)	40,000	40,000

Source: Steve Fetter, "Ballistic Missiles and Weapons of Mass Destruction: What Is the Threat? What Should Be Done?" *International Security* 16 (Summer 1991), pp. 5–42.

Note: Missile with 1 tonne warhead against large city with average population density of 30 unprotected civilians per hectare

munity of the utility of such weapons and have focused greater attention on the need for effective and comprehensive regimes to ban them.

Against this background, the last three years have seen immense changes in the world scene that few would have predicted. The Soviet Union and the Warsaw Pact have been dissolved, and Iraq invaded Kuwait in August 1990 with Operation Desert Storm as the result. More recently, Yugoslavia has dissolved with bitter racial conflict and "ethnic cleansing." Few can predict with any confidence what developments may occur over the next three years, let alone the next decade, but the prospect of continuing regional conflicts must be high among them.

As noted, following the Gulf conflict the UN established a Special Commission to oversee the elimination of the Iraqi weapons of mass destruction. The UN's willingness to take on a more dominant role in the maintenance of international peace and security is welcome. It is, however, far from clear how far the UN is prepared to take such action against other states or in the event of lesser breaches of international security than the invasion of a neighbor. It is, however, clear that the world is no longer one of bipolar tensions but one in which re-

gional conflicts will dominate and unexpected alliances may be established to meet short-term goals.

In addition, it has been apparent throughout the past decade that the number of states possessing or seeking to acquire chemical or biological weapons has continued to increase. The United Kingdom Defence White Paper of July 1992 stated that a number of states are seeking chemical, biological, or nuclear weapons and the means to deliver them. About 10 countries are assessed as having biological weapons programs and almost twice that number have, or are aiming to acquire, chemical weapons. More than 20 countries outside the North Atlantic Treaty Organization (NATO) possess ballistic missiles.[6]

Although there have been significant developments and improvements in arms-control regimes, it has also become evident that no arms-control regime is guaranteed to be wholly effective. The recent changes in the world scene and increased awareness of the potential impact of CB weapons give a new urgency and incentive to devising a strategy that complements arms control with a range of other measures to form a web of deterrence such that an evader or potential evader will judge that acquisition of chemical or biological weapons would be prohibitively expensive, of doubtful military value, and carry substantial risk of detection that would make it politically unacceptable. The key elements of such a web are:

- comprehensive, verifiable, and global CB arms control to create a risk of detection and a climate of political unacceptability for CB weapons;
- broad CB export monitoring and controls to make it difficult and expensive for a proliferator to obtain necessary materials;
- effective CB defensive and protective measures to reduce the military utility of CB weapons; and
- a range of determined and effective national and international responses to CB acquisition and/or use.

The web of deterrence should lead a state to judge that acquisition of a CBW capability is not worthwhile. This aim of deterring many states can be achieved by a regime in which there is at least a finite possibility of detection of noncompliance; the risk of detection can be sufficient to deter without the discovery of a program being inevitable. The aim is to strike the right balance so that the resources required to achieve the degrees of deterrence and detection are commensurate with the security gains achieved.

CB Arms-Control Agreements

Although no arms-control agreement can be 100 percent effective—and this applies equally to CB arms control—it must be as effective and intrusive as possible because this greatly enhances both the chance of detection of noncompliance and the deterrent effect. The status of first chemical and then biological arms control is reviewed in the following sections.

Chemical Arms Control. The emergence of a final agreed text[7] of the Chemical Weapons Convention from Geneva in August 1992 is to be warmly welcomed because once the convention comes into force it will ensure that the possession of chemical weapons will be illegal and declared stocks of such weapons will be monitored and destroyed and their production facilities destroyed or converted. The scope of the CWC is such that it will include all chemicals misused for chemical warfare; it therefore covers past CW agents, known current CW agents, and possible future agents. The whole of the chemical weapons spectrum, including toxins, is included within the CWC's scope. In addition, provision is made for both routine and challenge inspection regimes so that activities that present a risk to the convention can be inspected and, should noncompliance be demonstrated, appropriate steps taken. Finally a section of the treaty addresses investigations of the allegations of use.

Although the Geneva Protocol signed on June 17, 1925, prohibits the use in war of asphyxiating, poisonous, and other gases and of all analogous liquids, materials, and devices and the use of bacteriological methods of warfare, there have been numerous allegations of the use of CW and BW over the years. Although the UN secretary general has carried out investigations of allegations of use, such investigations are wholly dependent on the accessibility of the site of the alleged attack to UN teams. Many CBW agents are non-persistent; in other words, the hazard is transient, borne on the wind and, as quickly as it comes, dispersed and diluted. The task of acquiring unequivocal evidence of the use of CW or BW agents is therefore a major challenge. The inclusion in the CWC of steps to address such allegations is a useful step forward.

For success, timely access to the location of the alleged attack is vital so that samples can be taken while traces of agent still persist and memories are still accurate as to the precise location in which the attack occurred. Samples need to be acquired at known locations that can be correlated with the collateral evidence that a CW or BW attack took place at that point. Samples have to be taken in such a way as to demonstrate that they have not been contaminated, and the sample trail from point of sampling to analysis needs to be rigorously validated. The analogy is to the acquisition and analysis of forensic evidence for the courts. The aim must be to obtain unequivocal evidence that can be presented to the UN without technical or political challenge.

Environmental samples are greatly preferable to biomedical samples although the latter are frequently more readily available. Biomedical samples are much more difficult to analyze effectively because CBW agents are by their toxic nature reactive with the body and in so reacting are metabolized. In addition, victims from such attacks will be given medication to treat the symptoms, and that medication will also be metabolized in the body. Subsequent analysis of a sample taken a few days after an attack presents a demanding technical challenge, especially if there is uncertainty about the nature of the agent used in the attack. It is hard enough to provide unequivocal evidence of an attack even when the nature of the agent is known.

The CWC offers the prospect of improved arrangements for investigations of allegations of use. This will require the training of teams of experts. They must be mentally and physically prepared to visit the site of alleged attacks to collect evidence by interviewing casualties and obtaining environmental samples for analysis. Such sample analysis will be futile if the teams of experts do not succeed in locating and visiting the actual scene of an attack. If they do succeed, then maps, the global positioning satellite location system, and video and still cameras are needed to provide incontrovertible evidence that the location is indeed correctly designated. Samples need to be collected, witnessed, and sealed. At each stage of the sample trail leading back to the analytical laboratory, any change of custody needs to be documented and witnessed. On arrival at the analytical laboratory, authenticated procedures need to be used to analyze the samples under conditions that can prove that the samples have not been adulterated or otherwise contaminated.

Investigations of allegations of use to date have concentrated on incidents relating to the use of chemicals, and such procedures tend to be focused on a search for the use of an unusual chemical if not for an actual CW agent. This emphasis needs to be broadened under the Geneva Protocol and as part of the secretary general's investigations to include analytical procedures that would detect if a BW agent or material had been used to cause disease. The analytical procedures for the investigation of allegations of use need to be reviewed to ensure that they are equally effective for chemical and biological attack and pose no hazard to the scientists at the analytical laboratory. This is particularly true where biomedical samples are concerned because these may be contaminated with naturally occurring endemic diseases such as AIDS. Laboratory procedures also need to ensure that there are no risks to the scientists carrying out the analysis to determine whether there is unequivocal evidence of a chemical or biological attack. For an investigation to be effective, timely access to the location of the alleged attack is vital. States need to agree to allow an investigating team access to an alleged attack on their territories within a matter of days after such an allegation. It is important to investigate allegations of the misuse of chemical or biological materials wherever these occur so as to confirm misuse, if any, and take appropriate action.

The CWC is due to open for signature in Paris in January 1993 and will enter into force not less than two years after that opening (i.e., January 1995 at the earliest) and 180 days after the 65th state has ratified the convention. Following signature, the Preparatory Commission (PrepCom) will meet at The Hague in the Netherlands to elect a chairman, appoint an executive secretary, and establish a provisional Technical Secretariat. The PrepCom will carry out a range of activities in preparation for the establishment, once the convention enters into force, of the Organization for the Prohibition of Chemical Weapons (OPCW), which will also be located at The Hague.

The PrepCom will be responsible for the recruitment and training of technical and support staff and for the purchase and standardization of equipment required by the OPCW. In respect of training, it will be important to determine an appropriate standard and to devise training courses that demonstrate that the required standard has been achieved. Modular courses leading to an academic qualification appear attractive. The PrepCom will also draw up a program of work and budget for the first year

of operation of the OPCW. In addition, the PrepCom will have a vital role in elaborating the provisions of the CWC through draft agreements, provisions, and guidelines. Examples of these are the following:

- detailed procedures for verification;
- detailed procedures for conduct of inspections;
- models for facility agreements;
- lists of approved equipment for use by inspectors; and
- guidelines for scheduled chemicals in low concentrations.

The elaboration of the detailed procedures for verification and for the conduct of inspections for the CWC will be greatly aided by the lessons learned by the UN Special Commission set up after the Gulf war to oversee the elimination of Iraq's weapons of mass destruction. The Special Commission itself was able to benefit from the considerable amount of work carried out by many states on trial inspections in preparing for and negotiating the CWC.

A crucial element of the Gulf ceasefire arrangements set out in Resolution 687 is the elimination under the supervision of the UN Special Commission and the International Atomic Energy Agency (IAEA) of Iraq's nuclear, biological, and chemical weapons, all ballistic missiles with a range over 150 kilometers, and the so-called Superguns and the means for their production, support, and maintenance. The United Kingdom rightly affords a very high priority to and plays a full part in the work of the Special Commission.

The inspection program has progressively disclosed a capability far greater than Iraq had originally declared, including an advanced program to produce nuclear weapons and a BW research program with offensive military applications. Arrangements for monitoring Iraq's long-term compliance with Resolution 687 have also been agreed in Resolution 715, which provides for a stringent and intrusive regime designed to ensure that Iraq never again possesses or uses these weapons.[8]

Among the valuable lessons learned from the inspections carried out by the UN Special Commission on Iraq are the following:

- intrusive on-site inspections are essential for the disclosure of the suspected capabilities;
- broad-based and sustained political commitment and pressure are essential to make the inspection program effective;
- all available information needs to be collated and continuity provided between inspections;
- the structure, timetable, and duration of inspections have to be flexible so that chief inspectors can achieve their objectives without being unduly constrained; and
- when inspectors are provided by a range of nations on an intermittent basis and with varying expertise, their training and organization require considerable attention.

Valuable studies are being carried out in various countries on the lessons learned from these Iraqi inspections; these lessons must be applied to the improvement of CB arms control.

In addition, it is vital that the regimes under UN Security Council Resolutions 687 and 715 succeed in removing from Iraq its capabilities for waging war with weapons of mass destruction. Should the Special Commission not be effective in eliminating Iraq's capability to produce and use such weapons, states contemplating regional aggression may learn a series of lessons about international resolve that would be extremely unpalatable to other states.

Another activity that will be addressed by the PrepCom is the training of inspectors to carry out the activities of the OPCW; such training will take place in a number of countries and the question of appropriate standards and appropriate expertise will need to be addressed. Inspectors will need to be trained to have appropriate skills—technical, personal, and perhaps linguistic—so that effective teams can be created.

The procedures for the analysis of samples taken by OPCW inspectors in the course of their inspections need to be developed. It seems probable that a system involving accredited national laboratories that will analyze samples distributed blind by the OPCW will be the way forward, with each sample being analyzed by one or more accredited laboratory. Attention needs to be given to an appropriate international standard of accreditation of any laboratory carrying out such analyses. Not only will the laboratories need to be accredited but certified reference materials will be required to ensure that analyses are unequivocal and can be relied upon to draw firm conclusions at the OPCW.

Equipment to be used by inspectors on-site will range from protective equipment to ensure that they are not at risk from any toxic or harmful chemicals that may be present during an inspection through equipment to aid them in carrying out their inspection. The latter equipment may well include some analytical capabilities, but it should be recognized that confirmatory analysis in an accredited laboratory will be required if there is to be confidence that the CWC is effective and is being firmly enforced.

Thus, with regard to chemical arms control, a significant step forward has been made with the agreement of the CWC, and it is now vital that the PrepCom draw on the experience gained by the UN Special Commission so as to elaborate as effective a regime as possible. There is a real opportunity to ban a further class of weapons and to seek to reverse the trend toward increased proliferation of chemical weapons.

Biological Weapons Convention. The Biological and Toxin Weapons Convention was opened for signature in April 1972 and prohibits the production, stockpiling, acquisition, and retention of microbial or other biological agents or toxins, "whatever their origin or method of production, of types and in quantities that have no justification for prophylactic, protective, or other peaceful purposes." Some 120 states have now signed and ratified the BTWC but there are others that have yet to sign or ratify it and initiatives to increase the numbers of signatories are to be encouraged. The BTWC was the first convention to prohibit an entire class of weapons but at the time that it was agreed it made no provision for monitoring compliance or verification. The past two decades have seen significant advances in the willingness of the international community to accept provisions for such monitoring. Intrusive inspections to confirm compliance and to verify that only permitted activities take place are now allowed by treaties such as the Conventional Forces in Europe (CFE) and Open Skies.

The BTWC has a review conference at five-yearly intervals. In the developing climate of arms control and confidence-building measures (CBMs), it is not surprising that at the Second Review Conference in 1986 four politically binding CBMs were agreed by states parties to improve transparency and confidence in the convention. These four CBMs require:

- declaration of all BL4 (maximum containment) laboratories and of all defense BL3 or BL4 laboratories;
- declaration of unusual outbreaks of disease;
- encouragement of publication of results; and
- encouragement of international contacts and conferences.

The Third Review Conference in 1991 resulted in a robust final declaration reaffirming the importance of the BTWC.[9] The CBM regime was improved and three new CBMs were added that are well focused on activities relevant to the convention. In addition, the conference mandated an Ad Hoc Group of Governmental Experts to examine potential verification measures from a scientific and technical viewpoint. In addition, the declaration encouraged measures to prevent BW technology transfer.

The politically binding CBMs agreed in 1991 require:

- declaration of all BL4 research centers and laboratories;
- declaration of national biological defense programs;
- declaration of unusual outbreaks of disease;
- encouragement of publication of results;
- encouragement of international contacts and conferences;
- declaration of legislation related to the BTWC;
- declaration of past activities in offensive and defensive biological research and development programs; and
- declaration of vaccine production facilities.

The responses to the 1986 CBMs were disappointingly slow because the number of states having made a declaration only climbed slowly; 13 at the end of 1987, 24 at the end of 1988, 28 at the end of 1989, 36 at the end of 1990, and 41 at the time of the Third Review Conference in September 1991. In contrast, by the end of September 1992 some 35 states had made responses to the CBMs agreed in September 1991. Although small in comparison to the total number of states parties (about 120), this figure is far more encouraging than that of 1987.

The mandate for the Ad Hoc Group of Governmental Experts to identify and examine potential verification measures from a scientific and technical standpoint requires the identification of measures to determine compliance with Article I, which reads:

Each State Party . . . undertakes never in any circumstances to develop, produce, stockpile or otherwise acquire or retain:

(1) Microbial or other biological agents, or toxins whatever their origin or method of production, of types and in quantities that have no justification for prophylactic, protective or other peaceful purposes.
(2) Weapons, equipment or means of delivery designed to use such agents or toxins for hostile purposes or in armed conflict.

The verification measures are to be considered singly or in combination and need to address the broad range of types and quantities of microbial and other biological agents and toxins, whether naturally occurring or altered, capable of use as means of warfare.

The measures once identified then have to be examined in terms of six criteria:

- strengths and weaknesses based on amount and quality of information provided;
- ability to differentiate between prohibited and permitted activities;
- ability to resolve compliance ambiguities;
- technology, material, manpower, and safety requirements;
- financial, legal, safety, and organizational implications; and
- impact on scientific research, cooperation, industrial development, and other permitted activities, and implications for confidentiality of commercial information.

The first meeting of the Ad Hoc Group of Experts (VEREX I) took place in Geneva on March 30 to April 10, 1992, when 53 states parties participated. Thirty-one working papers and 21 background papers were circulated. Background information was provided on the objectives for BTWC verification, the elements of the biological defense program, the lessons learned from other verification regimes, and information relevant to verification. The conference identified some 21 potential verification measures, which were grouped according to whether these were off-site or on-site measures.[10]

The off-site verification measures fall into four groups:

- information monitoring, including publication surveillance, legislation surveillance, data on transfers, and transfer requests and multilateral information sharing;
- data exchange, including declarations and notifications;
- remote sensing, whether from satellites, aircraft, or ground-based off-site; and

- inspection activities to be carried out off-site including sampling and identification, observation and auditing.

On-site verification measures include:

- exchange visits, which may be made under bilateral or multilateral arrangements;
- inspections, including interviewing, visual inspection, identification of key equipment, auditing, sampling and identification, and medical examination; and
- continuous monitoring on-site by instruments and/or personnel.

The second meeting of the Ad Hoc Group of Governmental Experts (VEREX II) was held in Geneva on November 23 to December 4, 1992, when 46 states parties participated. Over 100 papers were circulated. This meeting concentrated on examining each measure, defining the measure, and setting out its characteristics, capabilities, and limitations.[11] Evaluation of the measures against the criteria in the mandate will be carried out at further VEREX meetings in 1993, with the aim of completing the report of the Ad Hoc Group of Experts by the end of 1993 in accordance with the mandate from the Third Review Conference.

Following the first two meetings of the Ad Hoc Group of Experts, it became clear to many experts that an effective verification regime requires two key elements. The first is declarations of relevant activities within a state to provide a baseline of information. It is clear that any judgments of compliance must be made against an appreciation of what is the norm for the country concerned. That norm will be based on various sources of information but will depend primarily on declarations made by a state party. The second element is on-site inspections of the sites and facilities that present the greatest risk to the BTWC. The on-site inspection regime needs a considerable degree of flexibility so that an appropriate degree of intrusion can be made as necessary to confirm compliance.

Although some consider the BTWC to be unverifiable and that the VEREX process should not lead to a verification regime, such a wholly negative view is no longer tenable. The past decade has seen an increase in the number of states assessed to have or to be seeking to acquire biological weapons. The threat of biological weapons being used by Iraq against the coalition forces was real, and the UN Special Commission through its on-site inspections has revealed at least the existence of a biological weapons research program with offensive applications. It is evident that there are verification measures that have at least a finite possibility of detecting noncompliance, and such measures in combination have a very significant deterrent effect.

A spectrum of potential measures to detect and deter violation of the BTWC has been devised, ranging from political declarations through the CBMs agreed at the review conferences to declarations of patterns of national activity and inspections of high-risk sites to intrusive inspections. As we move across the spectrum we find increased confidence, increased deterrence, and an increased number of compliant countries. It will be necessary to strike the right balance so as to maximize the benefits to global and national security deriving from confidence that would-be possessors are effectively deterred.[12] It is important to recognize that the inspection regime will have a significant deterrent effect,

299

and the chance that a state will be deterred from acquisition of a BW capability will be very much greater than the chance that noncompliance will be detected. Nevertheless, there has to be a finite probability of detection of noncompliance to achieve a deterrent effect. For this reason, there must be planned uncertainty in the precise activities of a verification regime so that a potential proliferator remains uncertain as to whether his activities will be detected. Over a period of time, as more and more declarations are made by states and a better pattern of activity or norm for the state is built up, so the deterrent effect of the regime will increase.

CB Export Monitoring and Controls

With arms control as the anchor of the web of deterrence, other elements can be brought into play. A second essential element is export controls.

A state considering the acquisition of chemical or biological weapons capabilities will consider also whether the agents or the weapon systems are available from within the state using national resources or whether it must seek the agents or weapon systems from abroad. As both chemical and biological materials and related equipment have dual uses—that is, for permitted activities as well as for prohibited ones—the adoption of export monitoring and control measures is far from simple. Nevertheless it is important to ensure that materials and equipment are not freely available in order to prevent CBW capabilities from being easily acquired or rapidly exploited for a quick breakout from treaty commitments.

CB export controls need to be designed to avoid inhibiting permitted peaceful trade, yet they should be targeted so that a state seeking to acquire chemical or biological weapons does not find it easy to acquire the necessary skills, materials, and equipment. It should be appreciated that in the long run export controls will not prevent indigenous capabilities from being developed. Focused CB export controls on both materials and equipment add to the burden on the evader and aid deterrence, although alone they are insufficient.

The Chemical Weapons Convention in Article XI on Economic and Technological Development includes two specific requirements:

- That States Parties shall not maintain among themselves any restrictions, including those in any international agreements, incompatible with the obligations undertaken under this Convention, which would restrict or impede trade and the development and promotion of scientific and technological knowledge in the field of chemistry for industrial, agricultural, research, medical, pharmaceutical or other peaceful purposes;
- That States Parties shall undertake to review their existing national regulations in the field of trade in chemicals in order to render them consistent with the object and purpose of this Convention.

The aim of export controls is to impede the misuse of CB materials and equipment for prohibited purposes and is thus entirely compatible with and complementary to the objectives and aims of CB arms control. The Australia Group of countries has sought since 1985 to harmonize and agree export controls on dual-use equipment and materials and its work has been a useful deterrent to proliferation in the period when a CWC was still under negotiation. With agreement on the convention, it is entirely appropriate that the Australia Group's members should review their controls in the light of its implementation. The Group, however, is still likely to have a significant role in the period while the convention's provisions come into effect and in connection with biological materials and equipment that it does not cover.

CB Protective Measures

The third element of the web of deterrence is CB protective measures. These reduce the range of materials that are effective in use by an aggressor. They also reduce the range of materials that need to be the subject of an arms-control regime. In addition, they weaken the military utility of CBW because effective protective measures limit casualties and ultimately reduce the effectiveness of CBW. Furthermore, the provision of broadband protective measures effective against most of the CBW spectrum may force a user to acquire a larger capability, which is more likely to be detected.

A major concern in Operation Desert Storm was that Iraq might use chemical or biological weapons against the coalition forces. This had the effect of ensuring that the coalition forces improved the effectiveness of their protective measures against the threat of such weapons. Fortunately, neither chemical nor biological weapons were used in the conflict, and a contributing factor to their non-use must have been the perception that their use against well-protected and well-trained forces would not result in a significant military advantage.

Perceptions of the value of possession of chemical and biological weapons before and after Operation Desert Storm vary considerably. A number of important lessons were learned by both coalition forces and by CBW possessors. The coalition forces learned the importance of maintaining effective protective measures against both chemical and biological weapons so that the threat of their use will have only a limited impact on military capability. Future conflicts may well not have the long period of preparation that was possible in the Gulf conflict prior to the ground war.

The reactions to the Gulf conflict of governments in two states parties are instructive. The U.K. Defence White Paper of July 1992 stated that the expertise established at the Chemical and Biological Defence Establishment at Porton Down enabled the United Kingdom to make a timely response to a number of threats that emerged during the Gulf crisis.[13] Work will continue on evaluating the threat and hazard, particularly from biological agents, and on the research and development of detection equipment, physical protection, and medical countermeasures. In the United States, the Department of Defense's report to the Congress, entitled *The Conduct of the Persian Gulf War*, highlighted as a major deficiency the unpreparedness of the United States to face biological warfare.

Prior to the Gulf conflict, it was appreciated that chemical weapons had only been used against unprotected target personnel whether in World War I, Abyssinia, or against Iran and the Kurds. The availability of effective protective measures results in a marked decrease in the utility of chemical or biological weapons. The advantages from use of such weapons is reduced to the increased effectiveness of conventional weapons against an enemy handicapped by wearing full protection comprising masks and suits. Effective protective measures not only reduce the utility of a potential CB warfare attack, they also force the aggressor to acquire a sufficient quantity of agent to achieve benefits from the enhanced impact of conventional weapons and reduces the range of chemical or biological agents that can be used effectively. This reduction in the range of available agents is useful to both arms and export controls, which can consequently be better focused.

It is therefore evident that CB arms control must preserve the rights of states to maintain protective measures and indeed should encourage their maintenance in order to enhance both national and international security.[14] Proposals to prohibit defensive measures are unsound and destabilizing because they would decrease national and international security by allowing a wide range of chemical or biological materials to be used effectively against unprotected personnel. Equally, suggestions for pooled protective measures under international control are ill-founded because a defense that is available for a potential aggressor to examine, evaluate, and circumvent is no defense and would again decrease stability. Effective protective measures need to be maintained as a key element of the web of deterrence. CB defense programs are not a threat to arms-control conventions but complementary to them, provided that there is an adequate degree of openness—as indeed is provided for in both the BTWC's confidence-building measures agreed in 1991 and the provisions of Article X of the CWC.

A state seeking to acquire CB weapons has a wide range of available materials if the target nation has no CB defense. Continued improvements of CB protective measures will further reduce the available materials that an aggressor can use. It is important,

however, to recognize that arms and export controls may lead to the selection by a potential aggressor of novel materials that are not the subject of current control regimes. Such regimes need to have flexible amendment procedures that can add additional materials rapidly without encountering political arguments. Further, CB protective capabilities need to be improved so that the physiological burden is reduced, thereby reducing the force multiplier effect of that burden in respect of conventional weapons.

Determined and Effective Responses

Should a state be shown to have acquired CB weapons or used such weapons, there needs to be a range of determined and effective national and international responses—possibly including an armed response—that will result in clear political penalties. The exact nature of these responses needs to be uncertain so that a state considering acquisition of a CBW capability will find it difficult to judge whether the risks are politically acceptable. The prime requirement is that such a state should be in no doubt that there will be swift, painful, and determined international penalties.

Chemical weapons were used in the mid-1980s during the Iraq–Iran War. At that time, no concerted international penalties were imposed on Iraq. This inactivity sent the wrong signals to CBW proliferators and would-be possessors. The recent international changes and the willingness of the UN to become involved following the Iraqi invasion of Kuwait are much more encouraging signs. The serious view taken by the UN in investigating allegations of chemical weapons use in 1992 has also been a positive development. The CWC has a section on sanctions making it clear that noncompliance will be regarded very seriously and result in punitive sanctions. It should be equally clear that noncompliance with the BTWC will be regarded in the same light.

Key Arms-Control Issues

A new opportunity exists today to improve global security by further narrowing if not eliminating the instabilities, threats, and risks posed by chemical and biological weapons. But this is also a great challenge because it will require a sustained effort by states to integrate various policy approaches with the goal of a strong and seamless web of deterrence against the production, possession, and use of these weapons. To review, this requires the following actions:

- CB arms-control regimes need to be made as effective as possible so that a potential evader is far from certain as to whether his activities will not be detected—the agreement of the CWC and the work being carried out on the verification measures for the BTWC offer the prospect of arriving at a situation in which potential possessors of CB weapons will judge that the effort that would be required to conceal such capabilities and the penalties that result should such capabilities be detected are politically unacceptable;
- export of materials and equipment that may be used to acquire a CBW capability need to be monitored and controlled so that a potential proliferator finds the acquisition of such materials and equipment is hard and difficult to conceal;
- effective CB protective measures need to be acquired and maintained because such measures reduce markedly the range of CB materials

that may be used with effect and also reduce the utility of acquiring a CBW capability; and
- the penalties imposed by the world community should a state party be found to be in breach of its obligations should be such that a potential proliferator will be in no doubt that there will be a response by the international community and will judge that that response will be politically unacceptable.

To maximize the benefits for national and international security of this web, a number of activities must succeed. First, the UN Special Commission must be successful in its mission of overseeing the destruction of Iraq's weapons of mass destruction under Security Council Resolutions 687 and 715. The implications for the future of CB arms control if it is judged that Iraq has retained a capability for weapons of mass destruction will be greatly destabilizing. Second, the effectiveness of the Organization for the Prohibition of Chemical Weapons should be ensured. A considerable amount of work needs to be put into the PrepCom to ensure that the elaboration of the CWC enables the maximum benefits to be gained from the convention. Third, the effectiveness of the BTWC must be improved through the development of a cost-effective verification regime that will deter states parties from acquisition of BW capabilities.

Finally, a common political commitment is required. As we move toward the 21st century with the advances that are available to us from science and technology, we must concentrate on developing a cost-effective web based on experience and avoid the temptation to claim that commercial confidentiality or other sensitivities make elements of the web impracticable. The benefits to national and global security need to be weighed against the possible disadvantages, and in reaching such judgments we owe it to future generations to ensure that we make the best use possible of the scientific and technical means available to us. We have a unique window of opportunity to improve the web of deterrence by minimizing the perceived advantages of chemical and biological weapons and thus improving both national security and that of the world community. We must seize this opportunity.

© *British Crown Copyright 1992/MOD. Published with the permission of the Controller of Her Britannic Majesty's Stationery Office.*

I would particularly like to thank both David O. Arnold-Foster of the Ministry of Defence and Brad Roberts, editor of this journal, for their immensely helpful comments, which have helped to improve this essay greatly.

Notes

1. *Statement on the Defence Estimates 1992*, Cm. 1981 (July 1992), p. 7, para. 104.

2. Brad Roberts, "Arms Control and the End of the Cold War," *The Washington Quarterly* 15 (Autumn 1992), pp. 39–56.

3. United Nations, *Chemical and Bacteriological (Biological) Weapons and the Effects of Their Possible Use*, Report of the Secretary-General, A/7575/Rev.1, S/9292/Rev.1 (1969).

4. Steve Fetter, "Ballistic Missiles and Weapons of Mass Destruction: What Is the Threat? What Should Be Done?" *International Security* 16 (Summer 1991), pp. 5–42.

5. Various publications issued by the Medical Department, U.S. Army Office of the Surgeon General, Falls Church, Va., and the Center for Military History, Washington, D.C.

6. *Statement on the Defence Estimates 1992*, p. 74, para. 3.

7. Conference on Disarmament, *Report of the Ad Hoc Committee on CW to the Conference on Disarmament*, CD/1170, August 26, 1992.

8. United Nations, *Plan for future ongoing monitoring and verification of Iraq's compliance with relevant parts of Section C of Security Council Resolution 687 (1991)*, Report of the Secretary-General, Security Council S/22871/Rev.1, October 20, 1991.

9. The Third Review Conference of the Parties to the Convention on the Prohibition of the Development, Production and Stockpiling of Bacteriological (Biological) and Toxin Weapons and on Their Destruction, Geneva, September 9–27, 1991, *Final Document*, BWC/CONF.III/23, 1992 (Geneva: United Nations, GE.91–62715–Jan 1992–500).

10. *Summary of the Work of the Ad Hoc Group for the Period 30 March to 10 April 1992*, BWC/CONF.III/VEREX/2, April 13, 1992.

11. *Draft Summary of the Work of the Ad Hoc Group for the Period 23 November to 4 December 1992*, BWC/CONF.III/VEREX/CRP.25/Rev.2, December 4, 1992.

12. For a further discussion of the deterrent effect of verification regimes, see Graham S. Pearson, "Biological Weapons: The British View," in Brad Roberts, ed., *Biological Weapons: Weapons of the Future?* CSIS Significant Issues Series, vol. 15, no. 1 (Washington, D.C.: CSIS, 1993).

13. *Statement on the Defence Estimates 1992*, p. 74, para. 3.

14. For a further discussion of the continued need for CB defense even when the Chemical Weapons Convention enters into force, see Graham S. Pearson, "The Continuing Need for Chemical and Biological Defence Following a Chemical Weapons Convention," Proceedings of the 4th International Symposium on Protection against Chemical Warfare Agents, Stockholm, Sweden, June 8–12, 1992, pp. 353–358.

Denial and Deception Practices of WMD Proliferators: Iraq and Beyond

David A. Kay

WITH THE END of the Cold War and the Soviet threat, a broad consensus seems to be forming that U.S. foreign and defense policies and budgets can now be premised on the absence of any major threat to the United States or its allies and on such timely detection of any newly developing threat that defensive measures can be deferred until after a threat emerges. The case of Iraq should offer a warning against too much optimism.

The failed efforts of both the International Atomic Energy Agency (IAEA) safeguards inspectors and national intelligence authorities to detect prior to the Persian Gulf War a nuclear weapons program of the magnitude and advanced character of Iraq's

David A. Kay is assistant vice president of Science Applications International Corporation. He was chief inspector of the three early UN nuclear weapons inspections in post–Gulf war Iraq that uncovered the Iraqi nuclear weapons program.

Copyright © 1994 by The Center for Strategic and International Studies and the Massachusetts Institute of Technology
The Washington Quarterly • 18:1

should stand as a monument to the fallibility of on-site inspections and national intelligence when faced by a determined opponent. The Iraqi military buildup, as well as the multiple failures of its timely detection, is an experience rich in lessons that, if correctly understood, may help in detecting other covert weapons programs and, equally important, U.S. understanding of the limits of its ability to guarantee timely detection.

During the inspections in Iraq after the Gulf war, an immense military production establishment was found that was producing or striving to produce a broad range of chemical, biological, and nuclear weapons and missiles capable of delivering them. The nuclear program alone involved investments amounting to around $10 billion. Inspectors and those who monitor proliferation were surprised by the magnitude and advanced state of Iraq's efforts to obtain nuclear explosive devices.[1] At the time of the Gulf war Iraq was probably only 18 to 24 months away from its first crude nuclear device and no more than three to four years away from more advanced, deliverable weapons. Moreover, the amount of foreign assistance and technology that had fueled the Iraqi arms program was truly staggering.

On April 18, 1991, Iraq submitted to the United Nations (UN) Special Commission on Iraq (UNSCOM) and the IAEA details of the quantities and locations of its chemical, biological, ballistic missile, and nuclear materials stockpiles. This listing was required by the terms of Security Council resolution 687 and was designed to provide the baseline for the inspection activities that were to lead to the dismantling of Iraq's weapons of mass destruction (WMD). It was signed by none other than President Saddam Hussein and accompanied by a letter from Iraq's foreign minister, Ahmed Hussein. This declaration acknowledged nearly 10,000 nerve-gas warheads, 1,000 tons of nerve and mustard gas, 1,500 chemical weapon bombs and shells, and 52 SCUD missiles with 30 chemical and 23 conventional high explosive warheads. Iraq, however, denied that it had any nuclear materials that fell under the resolution or any biological weapons.

Although this declaration was eye-opening with regard to the Iraqi chemical weapons stockpile and its acknowledgment of chemical warheads for SCUDs, it was widely acknowledged at the time—and subsequently confirmed by on-site inspection—to be seriously misleading in the nuclear, biological, and missile fields. It also was soon discovered to be a serious misstatement of the size of the Iraqi chemical weapons arsenal as well. Rolf Ekéus, chairman of UNSCOM, informed the Security Council on July 31, 1991, that inspectors had already found four times more chemical weapons than Baghdad had declared (46,000 chemical shells as compared to 11,500, and 3,000 tons of chemical agents as compared to 650 tons declared). By October 1991, inspectors

had found 100,000 chemical shells and bombs—almost 10 times the number initially declared.

On the nuclear front, the scale of deception and denial was even greater. Iraq's initial declaration of April 19, 1991, avowed that it had no proscribed nuclear materials, but this was amended on April 27 to acknowledge that it did have what had been reported to the IAEA before the war, including 27.6 pounds of highly enriched uranium and 22 pounds of low enriched uranium and a peaceful research program centered on the Tuwaitha Nuclear Research Center. Subsequent inspections found an altogether different program. Iraq in fact had, beginning in 1981, embarked on a clandestine uranium enrichment program using three different methods: electromagnetic isotope separation, the so-called calutron method; chemical enrichment; and gaseous centrifuge enrichment. At the time of the invasion of Kuwait, it had begun the start-up for industrial-scale enrichment using calutrons and had acquired the material, designs, and much of the equipment for 20,000 modern centrifuges. Design, component testing, and construction of manufacturing facilities for actual bomb production were well advanced. Over 20,000 people were found to have been employed in this clandestine nuclear weapons program.

All of this is by way of prologue and scene setting to the main thread of Iraq's deception and denial activities, which were aimed at covering up its weapons programs. For purposes of analytical clarity, I have separated these activities into four separate, but overlapping, layers: political, procurement/acquisition, facilities and activities, and inspections. My conclusions are drawn largely from Iraq's nuclear program after 1981. I believe, however, that the deception and denial activities applied in the nuclear case are largely representative of those used in other weapon areas as well.

Political

According to Jaffar dhia Jaffar, the scientific leader of the Iraqi nuclear weapons efforts, in the wake of Israel's successful attack on the Osirak research reactor in June 1981 Iraq launched an internal review of the future course of its nuclear activities. This review concluded that a major effort should be made to develop a uranium enrichment capability, and that this program should be clandestine while Iraq maintained its status as a full member of the Nuclear Non-Proliferation Treaty (NPT). In these internal deliberations, as described by Jaffar, the deciding factor in the decision to stay in the NPT was the desire of the military and security services not to attract any undue attention to Iraq's developing nuclear program that would complicate procurement and development efforts. As he described it to UN inspectors, the argument ran, "Let Israel believe it destroyed our nuclear capacity, accept the sympathy being offered for this aggression and proceed in secret with the program."[2] If one accepts this account as broadly true of the internal Iraqi discussions in fall 1981 as to how to proceed with their nuclear activities, then by their own admission their program was rooted in a fundamental deception as to their NPT undertaking. Jaffar suggested in a July 1991 meeting to several inspectors that IAEA headquarters be told that he was thinking of traveling to Vienna for the 1991 IAEA General Conference to offer a seminar on "How to beat the NPT." He added, correctly, that this suggestion when reported to Vienna would not be welcomed.

Throughout the 1980s Iraq played an active role in the IAEA's various programs, welcomed agency staff and officials as visitors to its Tuwaitha Nuclear Research Center, sought and received equipment, expert assistance, and training from the IAEA's technical assistance program, and was a frequent member of the agency's Board of Governors. Iraq was a far from silent member of the IAEA, leading the demands for international condemnation of Israel's attack on its safeguarded reactor and pushing for international protection for peaceful nuclear facilities against military attack. Iraq repeatedly emphasized the peaceful and safeguarded nature of its nuclear facilities and contrasted its openness to inspection with Israel's refusal to sign the NPT.[3] In an irony that I am sure that I appreciate more than the Iraqi government, Iraq played a leading role in board meetings in 1985 in praising, and ensuring the continuance and eventual expansion of, a program I was leading to introduce more rigorous evaluation of IAEA programs. The praise was so extravagant that a member of the director general's staff asked me during the discussion whether I had an Iraqi relative. The ultimate irony is that Iraq's IAEA governor had in fact, as chairman of the Iraq Atomic Energy Commission (IAEC), presided over the initiation and large expansion of their nuclear weapons program in the early 1980s.

The strength of the Iraqi denial and deception program is that it was anchored in a real fact—*the Israeli destruction of the Osirak nuclear reactor.* This piece of reality was reinforced by the accompanying sympathy that this attack engendered in the West and the desire of those who carried out the Osirak attack, as well as those who

307

admired the technical skills it demonstrated, to believe that it had dealt a
decisive blow to the Iraqi nuclear program. The extent to which the rooting
of the Iraqi deception activities in the
reality of the destruction of their
Osirak reactor assisted the deception
effort can best be captured in a study
prepared in 1982 at the request of the
Senate Foreign Relations Committee
by the Congressional Research Service
(CRS) of the U.S. Library of Congress.
The CRS concluded that:

> At the time of writing, Iraq's long
> term potential had been reduced
> by Israel's bombing of Iraq's large
> research reactor. The assistance
> which that reactor might have
> provided now will not be avail-
> able until it is rebuilt. . . . Assum-
> ing that the research reactor were
> to be rebuilt and put into opera-
> tion by the late 1980s, it seems
> unlikely that Iraq's intellectual
> and industrial base can grow
> enough to materially reduce its
> dependence upon foreign imports
> and technical assistance during
> this time. It seems unlikely too
> that Iraq's own industries will be
> able to design and build a repro-
> cessing plant, an enrichment plant,
> or a nuclear power station for
> many years to come. . . . This as-
> sumes the undertaking could be
> kept secret for several years so
> that other countries would not
> have an opportunity to take coun-
> termeasures. While the success of
> such an undertaking cannot be
> ruled out as impossible, it none-
> theless appears to be improbable.
> In summary, Iraq's potential nu-
> clear weapons capability at the
> outset of the 1990s would still be
> small, assuming that it does not
> get access to engineers and tech-
> nicians experienced in the pro-
> duction of nuclear weapons
> materials.[4]

Outside the nuclear arena, Iraq

skillfully played throughout the 1980s
on the fear in the West and Persian
Gulf of Iranian fundamentalism. Iraq's
portrayal of itself as a secular bulwark
against the wild mullahs of Tehran
provided an effective rationale for its
large arms buildup. The fact that
much of this took place during the
course of Iraq's war with Iran, in which
most Western governments provided
assistance to Iraq despite their own
professed neutrality and often despite
domestic legislative prohibitions
against military assistance, provided
protection against too rigorous scrutiny
of Iraq's arms buildup.

Procurement/Acquisition

The physical scale of Iraq's arms program is what has astounded most observers. The facilities were large, over
scale even for Iraq; well designed; am-
ply furnished with the latest technologies; and often constructed with
foreign assistance. For the nuclear program alone it is easy to identify more
than 25 major facilities. What is less
clear, at least to most outside observers, is the multilayered deception
efforts that Iraq applied to avoid the
unmasking or accurate piecing together of this program by outsiders as
it was being assembled. These deception efforts consisted of, at least, nine
major thrusts. Each of these nine areas
is worthy of a much fuller treatment. I
hope that as pending criminal actions
are completed and some serious security concerns become less pressing, a
fuller treatment of these techniques
will be possible.

Compartmentalization and Multiple
Project Codes

The Iraqi nuclear weapons program
was heavily compartmentalized and
was managed through a complex sys-

tem of multiple and shifting project codes. Not only did various elements of the project teams generally not know of the total program, they often did not know of the real purpose of their own work. Firms—international as well as Iraqi manufacturing facilities—would be approached to manufacture components without being told the end use for these components. In the case of Iraqi manufacturing facilities, plans and material would be delivered by the IAEC with instructions to produce a set of components. After production, the items and all scrap or unutilized material would be taken back. With regard to international firms, again the end use would not be specified. As one example, many of the large pole magnets of the calutrons used to enrich uranium were produced in Austria by an Austrian state-owned firm that shipped the finished magnets to Iraq—half by trucks through Turkey and half by ship through Hamburg. The Austrians did not ask the purpose of these magnets and the Iraqis certainly did not volunteer this information. Much the same story applies to the high-quality copper that was used to wrap these magnets. It was produced in Finland to Iraqi specifications and went by ship to Iraq. In both these cases—and in many others—the Iraqis did not even have to go through the motions of creating a cover story, because the operating rule of the commercial world is "Don't ask, just sell."

Project codes, another example of simply good tradecraft, were an integral part of the Iraqi deception effort. PC-3 or Petrol Chemical Project 3, the overall project code for the Iraqi nuclear weapons program, became widely known after the Gulf war, but this misses the reality of the Iraqi use of project codes. Iraq used hundreds of multiple, constantly shifting, and overlapping codes for individual components of all of its arms program. It became clear during the course of the post–Gulf war inspections, where these codes were a constant source of confusion, that these codes had presented a real obstacle to various national intelligence services trying to track the Iraqi program. On more than one occasion, during the course of an on-site inspection, several of the governments that were providing intelligence support to the inspections would openly disagree on which element of the Iraqi weapons program a particular code related to. It is important to remember that the codes were used not only for the Iraqi nuclear program but for all of its most sensitive weapons programs. During the inspections, the project codes were a nightmare as inspectors tried to correlate documents, invoices, shipping crates, Iraqi declarations, and actual physical facilities. It is reasonable to assume that this relatively simple deception technique must have proved equally frustrating to analysts trying to decipher the Iraqi weapons program before the war.

Misdirection as to Purchaser and End Use

Most export control regimes do not attempt to block all exports to a given country, but rather to deny benefit from exports to specific institutions (e.g., the military), or to inhibit potentially harmful uses (e.g., chemical weapons programs). The guidelines of the London Suppliers Group identify items related to nuclear weapons that should not be exported to non-nuclear weapon states. In practice, however, nuclear export controls have proved to be vulnerable to deception. One major problem area is so-called dual-use exports. A high-speed, computer-numerically-controlled (CNC) machine tool may be used to produce truck engines for a civilian automotive industry or gas centrifuge rotors for a nuclear weapons program. The more modern and industrialized the economy the wider the possible permitted uses for almost any import. In a case that came to light during the inspections, Iraq ordered preforms for centrifuge endcaps from the Swiss firm Schmiedemeccanica SA, a metal forging company, and declared that the end use was for automotive part forgings. In 1992 the Swiss decided to drop prosecution after determining that these preforms so closely resembled the end use declared by the Iraqis that the Swiss firm could not be reasonably expected to know otherwise.

To further complicate matters, it is up to the importer to identify the user and uses for any imports and to a lesser extent to the exporting firm or its agents to confirm these facts.[5] Very seldom are on-site checks on such declarations made either before or after sales—all in all a system asking for abuse and deception. Iraq clearly understood the weakness of national export control regimes.

During the course of the UN inspections after the Gulf war it became clear that the University of Baghdad, the Ministry of Industry, petrochemical projects, and many other seemingly innocent purchasers had been nothing more than shells for the Iraqi nuclear weapons program. Falsified end uses were routinely declared, and in most cases the stories did not have to be terribly clever because—until Iraq lost the Gulf war—they never had to withstand any type of check after the item was received in Iraq. This stratagem worked particularly well for Iraq during the 1980s because parallel with a clandestine weapons program there

existed a very large conventional military program that, by and large, was not subject to Western export controls and also a booming civilian economy based on Iraq's oil revenues and loans from Gulf states.

Buy-in to Foreign Manufacturers

Iraq also used another deception strategy that is particularly hard to monitor in a world that places a high premium on international freedom to trade and invest, and indeed, a world where governments compete to attract foreign investment. Iraq invested in legitimate foreign firms that either manufactured equipment useful for the Iraqi clandestine weapons program or that could legitimately order such equipment purportedly for their own use. The most publicized case of this type was the Iraqi acquisition of the British firm, Matrix Churchill. Matrix Churchill was a small machine tool producer that in the mid-1980s was facing severe financial problems. When the Iraqi investors arrived on the scene, they were welcomed as financial rescuers. Over the years Matrix Churchill provided not only a valuable source for illegal exports of high-performance machine tools, but also a useful cover for ordering products from other firms for onward transshipment to Iraq.

Middlemen and Front Companies

Iraq benefited in building up its weapons program from its ability to use a complex network of middlemen and front companies. Some of these front companies and middlemen were purely creatures of the Iraqi weapons program, but others were associated with the shadowy world of smugglers, traders, and fast-buck artists that swarm to wherever there is money to be made. Modern electronic communications and the opening up of so many borders has made this a particularly powerful deception technique when money or material needs to move across borders without undue notice of its origin or destination. The Gulf region is particularly fertile ground for such operations because its new wealth reinforces its old cultural practices of smuggling and the predisposition to avoid too much attention from governments.

Multiple Purchases

The Iraqi weapons program is also striking in terms of the amount of money it spent—and seemed to overspend—in procuring foreign material. This "shop until you drop" mentality had several origins. As a deception strategy, it worked on a rather profound understanding of the way export controls are administered and how intelligence services interpret information. In seeking to purchase export control–sensitive items, the Iraqis would often place orders in quantities that were below the size that triggered controls. Their calculation was that this would avoid controls, and, even if detected, such small requests would signal that their program was in the early stages of development and not well thought through and hence not of great concern. Indeed, during much of the 1980s the threat estimate assigned to Iraq's nuclear program was downgraded because analysts could not find a pattern in Iraq's procurement that indicated a well-organized program moving toward early production of nuclear weapons. The Iraqis also seem to have understood that the discovery of one procurement channel would not trigger an intensive search for other pathways to obtain the same item. Iraq seems to have learned early that an

effective deception can be based on a defeat or loss—much faster than the victors learned that every victory contains the seeds for self-deception.

Multiple purchases of the same items were also central to the very nature of the Iraqi nuclear weapons program and if correctly understood could have raised serious alarm flags about that program well before the Gulf war. Iraq was engaged in a crash program to acquire nuclear weapons, roughly modeled on the U.S. Manhattan project. Research and development activities for uranium enrichment were paralleled by construction of large production facilities. For example, the large facility at Tarmiya designed to produce highly enriched uranium using the electromagnetic isotope separation (EMIS) process was constructed in parallel with Iraq's efforts to build their first small EMIS machines. Similarly, a very large facility to produce thousands of gas centrifuges at Al Furat was being constructed before Iraq had frozen the design on the type of centrifuge to be built. In such a crash program—particularly where the government rules by terror—any material bottlenecks would have very serious consequences. Iraqi officials attempted to insure against such bottlenecks by multiple purchases on the theory that even if several procurements failed for whatever reason the weapons program would go on unchecked. It was better, from the Iraqi perspective, to spend a lot of money for supplies, than to lack required supplies when needed and have a critical program grind to a halt.

System Integration in Iraq

Many of the equipment items required for the production of WMD and advanced conventional arms are legally exportable so long as they do not contain particular attachments (e.g., laser alignment systems or flow forming mandrels of the specific dimensions associated with gas centrifuge rotors). The principle involved is that without such attachments the equipment can only be used for less capable tasks either associated with permitted military applications or civilian uses. In addition, export controls operate on the assumption that even if states like Iraq manage to obtain the restricted attachments separately, they would be unable to successfully integrate them with the legally obtained parts to form the more capable equipment. This assumption reflects the view that countries like Iraq lack the system integration skills needed to merge research and development work on a process like calutrons or centrifuges with the civil construction of a production facility, the equipment installation, and the process engineering—all of which are critical steps in getting a uranium enrichment facility up and running.

Iraq successfully exploited the weakness of these assumptions. CNC machine tools that could not be exported legally from the United States with laser alignment systems were exported without them only to be mated later in Western Europe and Iraq with such systems. Iraq also demonstrated considerable experience with project management and system integration, particularly in their EMIS program.

Systems integration is a powerful deception technique. The focus of collection efforts inevitably has to be sharp enough to exclude most of the large trade and technology flows that go into even a mid-level industrializing economy, and yet most weapons programs are composed of a lot of very innocuous items that only take on their deadly character when combined

in very specific ways. If collection efforts are unable to detect the purpose of imports at their most vulnerable stage—when borders are being crossed—then a very heavy burden is placed on national technical means (NTM) and human intelligence (HUMINT) to detect the actual integration of these items into weapons production systems—and this occurs mostly inside buildings in secured areas.

"Simply Good Tradecraft"

Iraq applied a lot of what can best be described as "simply good tradecraft" to its efforts to disguise the clandestine weapons program. Invoices routinely had their supplier and banking transfer agent blacked out or completely cut out. Wooden shipping crates had the shipper and destination blacked out or physically chipped out as soon as they arrived in Iraq. Scientists who traveled abroad used false identity and travel documents. All of these techniques, and many similar ones, compounded well beyond the usual fog impeding analysis the problem of detecting the true purpose, size, and state of development of the Iraqi programs.

Competitive Commercial Negotiations

Iraq was able to use the strong desire of Western providers of technology to make sales both to conceal the true purposes of Iraqi efforts and to extract a considerable amount of proprietary information from Western companies without any compensation. A classic example of this ploy lay at the heart of Iraq's efforts to obtain technology for the chemical enrichment (Chemex) of uranium. There are two suppliers in the world of chemical enrichment technology, one is Japanese and the other is French. In the mid-1980s Iraq initiated preliminary discussions with both and indicated a desire to acquire a uranium enrichment capability using the Chemex technique. After preliminary exploration the Iraqis decided to concentrate on the French process. Inspectors learned during the course of the postwar inspections that a strong factor in motivating Iraq to abandon discussion concerning the Japanese process was that it requires a set of exotic resins that have few other uses and Iraq was worried that the large-scale importation of such resins would signal the scale of their uranium enrichment program.

Iraq engaged the French firm in negotiations stretching out over several years. The course of these soon took on a familiar pattern. Iraq would indicate it needed only a little more technical information on which to make a decision; the French would reveal more proprietary data and the cycle would begin again. The French firm was particularly anxious to make a sale as the process had yet to find its first customer. Finally, after the French firm had revealed essentially all of the technical details concerning its Chemex process, Iraq announced that it had concluded that the process was too expensive and was abandoning all interest in pursuing it. The French seem to have bought this story and went away believing that Iraq had given up on this process; Iraq went away and started clandestine development of Chemex.

Many of the natural forces of the commercial world—competition between suppliers, protection of proprietary customer information, reluctance to admit that a deal has been lost, and a lack of a basic counterintelligence perspective in most commercial enterprises—can actually help a proliferator's deception effort.

Large Industrial and Conventional Military Programs

The scale of the industrial and conventional military programs in Iraq in the 1980s—the conventional military program alone is estimated by Iraq to have cost $110 billion—must have made it almost impossible for any intelligence service to keep abreast of all the commercial discussions, imports of material and technology, and new construction that were under way and that might have had some relevance to clandestine weapons capability. Although it would be wrong to assert that the conventional military program and the large civil economy investments were part of an Iraqi deception effort, it would be equally wrong to dismiss the fact that they served that purpose. It is essential to recognize that in all but a few countries, such as isolated North Korea, the "noise" of normal commercial activities and conventional military programs may provide inherent deception for clandestine programs. This is particularly true for chemical, biological, and missile programs, which share many of the characteristics of innocent undertakings.

Facilities and Activities

The Iraqis paid as much attention to concealing the actual purposes of facilities and activities as they did to deception in their purchasing and acquisition efforts.

Facilities

Iraq well understood the deception advantage of hiding a clandestine program in plain sight. Their major declared nuclear research center at Al Tuwaitha was also the initial center of their clandestine nuclear program. Al Tuwaitha was visited every six months by IAEA safeguard inspectors who announced that there was no sign of diversion of nuclear material, thus giving a general clean bill of health to the facility. Two deputy directors general of the IAEA and many staff members visited Al Tuwaitha and reported no suspicious activity. Also selected Western scientists were invited to the facility to reinforce the impression that it was an open center of peaceful research.

This openness, however, was carefully controlled. The IAEA inspectors were only allowed to visit portions of three of the almost 100 buildings at Al Tuwaitha, and Iraqi escorts guided the IAEA staff and Western scientists through chosen laboratories and conducted meetings in the center's conference building. Although the restrictions on the movements of these visitors in retrospect seem like a warning sign, they were not recognized as such by most of the visitors at the time. The safeguard inspectors were used to such restrictions in every country they visited, and it is only since the experience in Iraq that this has begun to slowly change. The other visitors were controlled by "busy" schedules, generous hospitality, and cultural tourism. One of the IAEA deputy directors general, a former defense official of an Asian country, assured the UN inspectors before their inspection after the Gulf war that he had toured all of Al Tuwaitha and there was nothing at all there related to uranium enrichment or a weapons program. Although self-delusion was no doubt involved in some of the assessments of the peaceful nature of Al Tuwaitha, the Iraqis deserve credit for the skill with which they controlled visitors and the clever layout of the facility itself. The distribution of the buildings, the visual screening provided by trees, and the careful routing of the internal road system made it very difficult for any visi-

tor without access to overhead intelligence to accurately understand the size of the center and the relationship of the buildings to each other.

Understanding the Algorithms of the Photointerpreters/Analysts

The Iraqis demonstrated on numerous occasions that they had a rather accurate understanding of the limitations of U.S. technical collection systems and of how data gathered by such systems were interpreted.

The catalogue of techniques is long but includes construction of buildings within buildings (Tuwaitha); deliberately constructing buildings designed to the same plans and for the same purposes to look different (Ash Sharqat and Tarmiya); hiding power and water feeds to mislead as to facility use (Tarmiya); disguising operational state (Al Atheer); diminishing value of a facility by apparent low security and lack of defenses (Tarmiya); severely reducing off-site emissions (Tuwaitha and Tarmiya); moving critical pieces of equipment at night; and dispersing and placing facilities underground.

All of these techniques, and others, vastly complicated the job of understanding the nature of the Iraqi nuclear weapons program and provide at least a partial answer as to how a program so large could have been so incompletely understood by the world's intelligence communities.

Personnel

The Iraqi nuclear program involved at least 20,000 personnel, many of whom had training and contacts abroad. This was a potentially large source of leakage of information on the aims and direction of these activities. Iraq faced this problem and adopted a series of deception practices designed to limit any such loss.

First, Iraq managed its flow of personnel to ensure that students were not all sent to the same universities and countries. This had several advantages. Training in most scientific disciplines follows somewhat different approaches in different countries and provides access to multiple networks of information. This is particularly true in the various engineering and science disciplines that most concern a nuclear weapons program. For example, information concerning the ability and techniques involved in focusing X-rays was classified in the United States long after it was part of the general physics literature in Japan, Germany, and Britain. Also, by dispersing students, Iraq made it more difficult for any one country to fully appreciate the breadth of technical skills being built up in Iraq. And this dispersal of students certainly made it more difficult to track individual Iraqi scientists. Concerns with privacy and academic freedom as well as a low collection priority have meant that systematic data on foreign students are collected in few countries and seldom shared with other countries.[6]

Second, Iraq moved from an almost total dependence upon foreign training in the 1970s to almost totally indigenous undergraduate and master's level training, and even credible doctorate-level training in some fields, in the 1980s. This vastly complicated the task of accurately accessing the talent and direction of Iraq's scientific infrastructure. As we examined Iraq's weapons laboratories it became clear that the staff kept abreast of the latest scientific work in English, French, Russian, and German. On the other hand, few resources seem to have been devoted in the West to tracking the theses and other work coming out of Iraqi institutions.

Third, Iraq purposely followed strategies designed to ensure that the purposes of scientific visits would not be easily discerned. False names and passports were used, the purpose of visits and requests for training were misidentified to sound innocuous, and the employer was misidentified to avoid any connection with the IAEC or the military.

A final barrier to leakage of information from the staff of the nuclear program was a cleverly crafted set of fringe benefits and punishments that discouraged those who knew important details of the Iraqi program from divulging information. First, the staff of the IAEC received an automatic draft exemption from the Iraqi army—and this was at the time of the bloody Iran–Iraq War. Second, salaries were consistently kept above the announced government salary scale. Other benefits, including bonuses and access to travel and foreign goods, were also substantial. Although the benefits were good, the severance package was horrible in its brutality. Those who attempted to defect and were caught or who evidenced any sign of lack of loyalty to the regime—including not reporting on family members who were disloyal—were pitilessly executed, in many cases in front of their family.

Inspections—Prewar and Postwar

As a subscriber to the NPT, Iraq was subject prior to the Gulf war to routine—roughly once every six months—IAEA safeguard inspections of its declared nuclear material. These inspections took place only at the Tuwaitha Nuclear Research Center—the only site for which Iraq declared nuclear materials. As Tuwaitha was the initial center for Iraq's clandestine nuclear program, it was important both that these inspections not inadvertently stumble upon weapons activities and that Iraq appear to be fully cooperating with the IAEA and not trying to conceal some activities. Inspections were also the key to the post–Gulf war unraveling of Iraq's WMD program. In both the prewar and postwar phase, deception and denial activities played a key role in trying to limit the impact of inspections. The deception and denial activities can be separated into six major thrusts.

Fat and Happy Inspectors

Under the IAEA safeguard procedures, a country is allowed to designate the inspectors that it will accept to inspect its facilities. This provision, which had originally been insisted upon by some West European states to limit what they thought would be commercial espionage by inspectors from other states, has turned out to be a major brake on the integrity and efficiency of the safeguard system. Iraq consistently accepted only inspectors from the then Soviet Union, its allies in the Eastern bloc, and Africa. Not only were Soviet inspectors presumed to be more controllable, given their nation's close military arrangements with Iraq, but they were also the beneficiaries of a quirk in the way they were paid that made inspection missions highly profitable. Soviet inspectors had to turn over their salary to their government, which kept most of it to cover the cost of providing their housing in Vienna and "other expenses" and deposited the balance into a ruble account of no use to the inspectors while in the West. But there was one exception. Soviet inspectors were allowed to retain all of their per diem allowance received while on official travel. Thus the less a Soviet inspector spent on lodging and food while on inspection missions, the more

he had in hard currency to spend on goods unobtainable at home. Iraq was a particularly profitable mission for inspectors so inclined because the official conversion rate of the Iraqi pound before the Gulf war was artificially high and consequently the UN per diem rate was substantial.

Soviet and Eastern bloc inspectors and many from the developing world were widely known to seek out the cheapest available accommodations and to enjoy official entertainment as a money-saving strategy. The Iraqis exploited this desire by providing cheap accommodations, at a considerable distance from the nuclear research center at Tuwaitha, and by hosting late evening official dinners for inspectors. The result was that the inspectors were often weary, but happy at the money that they were saving and not inclined to do more than the limited and minimal official inspection tasks. To do more would have been to risk that Iraq would refuse to accept a particular inspector with the consequent loss for that inspector of valuable income.

During the first round of post–Gulf war inspections, the Iraqi authorities continued to try to delay and reduce the coverage of inspections by suggesting long and pleasant lunches, late dinners, and sightseeing visits to some of the interesting archeological sites several hours from Baghdad.

Threats and Intimidation

Iraq during the post–Gulf war inspections moved from positive inducements for easy inspections to physical and verbal threats and intimidation. Inspectors were awakened with telephoned threats; obscene and threatening notes were slipped under hotel doors; hotel rooms were ransacked; verbal abuse on the street and at inspection sites became common; on several occasions inspectors were physically attacked by outraged Iraqi "civilians"; UN vehicles were bombed and tires slashed; and shots were fired over the heads of inspectors as a team photographed Iraq's secret uranium enrichment equipment. The Iraqi authorities made it clear to UN and IAEA authorities which inspectors they found acceptable and which were not to be sent to Iraq again. Formal letters of censure were sent by Iraq to the UN and the IAEA concerning some inspectors, and the Iraqis demanded that no Americans be allowed to lead inspection missions. It would be easy to dismiss most of this except that it did have an impact. For a while Americans were not put in charge of missions, and some inspectors reported that the IAEA leadership sought to soften the tone of its inspection presence.

Study and Monitor Inspectors and Procedures

Iraq both before the war and during the postwar inspections carefully monitored inspection procedures and adapted its deception activities accordingly. During the course of the fourth postwar inspection the Iraqi national safeguard head—responsible for ensuring that national nuclear safeguards were applied—appeared and repeatedly bragged that he had applied everything he had learned from his earlier job as an IAEA safeguards inspector to ensure that his former IAEA colleagues would not detect the clandestine nuclear weapons program during their pre–Gulf war inspections. In great detail he described the dual books, limited access, and keep-the-inspectors-happy strategy that Iraq had used.

During the postwar inspections the

Iraqis engaged in active bugging of hotel rooms, meeting rooms, and office spaces used by the IAEA and the UN. Local Iraqi staff who were the drivers and maintenance personnel were often candid in their admission that the Iraqi security authorities required that they report daily on what they observed. Neither the UN nor the IAEA provided their staff with any training in counterintelligence or communications security. Although vigorous attempts were made to show how such lapses were seriously hindering effective inspections—and several embarrassing cases where IAEA "surprise" inspections became known in advance—this remained an uphill battle against an entrenched mind-set that still does not recognize the problem.

Misdirection

The postwar inspections began with the old IAEA cooperative inspection model of asking the Iraqi authorities to take the inspectors where they wanted to go. It should be no surprise to anyone that during the first inspection Iraq used this arrangement to carefully keep the inspectors away from sensitive sites. In the second inspection, when this same tactic was tried, the inspectors replied by producing handheld Global Positioning Satellites (GPS) instruments and current intelligence data, including very accurate line drawings of Iraqi weapon sites. This hindered but did not stop the Iraqi efforts to seek to misdirect the inspection effort at every stage.

Cover Stories

Another form of misdirection was the cover stories, some quite elaborate, that Iraq brought out in an attempt to shield its clandestine program. Tarmiya, one large site of Iraq's massive uranium enrichment effort, was said to be only a high voltage transformer testing facility; the Palm building where much of the testing for the Iraqi calutrons was done was said to be only an air force truck repair and radar testing facility; and the first calutrons seen by inspectors were described as only scientific mass spectrometers. Some cover stories were quite clever and required a great deal of scientific and inspection effort to penetrate, and some may never have been identified as false.

When cover stores were penetrated, Iraq would abandon them in a controlled fashion that tried to indicate that minimal disclosure was complete disclosure. The first admitted separation of plutonium was said to be the only separation—until another larger separation was uncovered by inspectors. Denial of any centrifuge activity was followed finally by an admission of a small centrifuge enrichment program that was said to be all there was—until a massive program was discovered by inspectors. Even a penetrated cover story served a useful purpose of allowing another opportunity for Iraq to claim that it had turned over a new leaf and was making a full and final disclosure of its secret activities. More than 10 such "full and complete" disclosures have been made, and yet the UN has remained unconvinced that the various clandestine programs have been fully disclosed.

Destroy/Shield

Before the first inspectors entered Iraq after the war and later when the inspectors began to close in on important elements of the Iraq nuclear program, Iraq began to systematically destroy facilities so that their true purpose and state of development could not be identified. At the Tuwaitha Nuclear

Research Center, the large calutron test facility (80 by 120 meters) had escaped all damage from the coalition bombing, but it was completely leveled by Iraq and covered with dirt before the first UN inspector entered the site. Laser and centrifuge test facilities also at Tuwaitha were similarly destroyed, leaving unresolvable uncertainty as to how much progress Iraq had made with these programs. In the North near Mosul at Al Jesira where UCl_4 and UF_6 were produced to feed the uranium enrichment program, two substantial buildings were leveled by Iraq and one was covered with thick layers of epoxy paint to make all sampling efforts impossible.

One reason why many of the early inspections in Iraq became confrontational is that Iraq made it impossible to obtain easy answers as to how far its program had proceeded. Faced with a massive denial effort and forceful deception, the inspectors had little choice but to adopt a search strategy that would take account of Iraq's moves. These counters required the inspectors to move to sites without prior notice, go after documents, make greater use of technical intelligence methods, and assert a healthy skepticism about all Iraqi claims.

Implications for Intelligence of Denial and Deception Activities beyond Iraq

In the wake of the discoveries of the extent of the Iraqi clandestine weapons programs and the role that organized denial and deception played in shielding these programs, the important question that remains is whether Iraq is only an exceptional case or whether it is the prologue to a period in which denial and deception activities gain even greater importance in shielding clandestine programs. Two major areas of concern that deserve greater attention are the implication of denial and deception for collection systems and for the intelligence analysis process itself.

Intelligence Collections Systems

Multilateral Information Sharing—the Downside. The UN inspection efforts in Iraq marked a watershed in the willingness of the U.S. intelligence community to share with an international inspectorate its high-quality intelligence product, including a broad range of NTM, HUMINT, and measurement intelligence (MASINT), and equally the willingness of the UN system openly to receive and act upon such information.[7] This was a marriage of immediate necessity, without a long courtship and a careful weighing of the long-run implications of the union. Once it became clear to U.S. policymakers that the Iraqi WMD program was much larger than estimated before the Gulf war and that much of it had survived—and the intelligence community was the first to perceive this—then the only instrument for eliminating Iraq's WMD capability became the UN inspectors. On the other hand, Iraq had demonstrated during the first IAEA inspection in May 1991 that if the inspectors did not have current intelligence Iraq would be able to continue to deceive the IAEA and to obtain a clean bill of health as to its nuclear program. The second IAEA inspection team that entered Iraq, in June 1991, was provided with a broad range of high-quality intelligence, both before and during its mission, and this directly led to the stunning revelation of the previously unknown Iraqi uranium enrichment program. This initial success in intelligence

sharing led to greater collaboration and was the essential element in the inspection successes in the second half of 1991 that led to the rapid unraveling of the Iraqi nuclear program.

Intelligence sharing between the United States and the UN that began in mid-1991 was not always a natural and riskless undertaking. The U.S. intelligence community was faced with a situation for which there were no parallels or rules. The UN system was riddled with cold war rivalries, nationals of many states had dubious records of being trustworthy, the UN and IAEA were totally unprepared at the basic mechanical level for handling confidential information,[8] and UN/IAEA personnel were not subjected to security clearances nor generally had they any real appreciation for the importance of protecting sources and methods. In the face of this, decisions had to be made about sharing the product of some of the very best collection methods available to the United States—and these were methods that would have to be continued to be relied on to monitor situations around the world. Even today—three years after the inspections began—the speed at which decisions were made to share intelligence information and the range of support provided to inspectors in the field is still amazing. In the clash of cultures represented by the open world of the UN/IAEA and the closed, secret world of the intelligence community, it needs to be recognized that the intelligence community took the first step toward sharing and ensuring that the UN system would have the information required to meet this first cold war challenge.

By the end of 1991, the lesson of Iraq that multilateral inspections can be made genuinely effective only if they are coupled with accurate and timely intelligence had been taken to heart by both the UN and the intelligence community. Although many problems remain in this relationship—and some of these deserve greater attention than they have been receiving—the sharing of U.S. intelligence with multilateral efforts is clearly now officially sanctioned.

The initial decisions to support the Iraq inspections with national intelligence represented a clear example of enlightened leadership. By 1993, however, other factors were also at play and beginning to lead to even greater efforts to share national intelligence information. With the disappearance of the Cold War, the scramble by intelligence community components to acquire customers and to appear useful began to lead to a fundamental shift in the philosophy of sharing sources and methods with multilateral organizations. Methods, including some of the best available MASINT, are now being shopped to multilateral institutions as vital enhancements to efforts to halt nuclear, chemical, and biological weapon proliferation as well as to thwart international crime, the drug trade, and money laundering.

In this rush to provide new tools for important missions—and to justify old programs in a new environment—probably too little attention is being paid to one of the most important lessons from Iraq. This lesson is that determined proliferators pay close attention to sources and methods with a view to countering them. Iraq's deception practices grew out of close scrutiny by Iraq and states that supported its efforts of U.S. collection methods. As the United States shares its collection methods more widely with the international community to support worthwhile international efforts, the underlying algorithms and weaknesses

of these methods will become much more widely understood. It is inevitable that these "best available" collection methods are not going to be as good five years from now as they were five years ago when they face a determined nation that wants to avoid detection of its activities.

New Investment Requirements. If existing U.S. intelligence sources and methods are being degraded by sharing—and there seems little doubt that they are—then new investments in upgraded technical means are necessary to maintain a qualitative edge.[9] These investment decisions should also pay considerable attention to developing technical systems that have pathways by which to release information that will not degrade core collection capabilities. During the Cold War little attention had to be given in assessing investment decisions on collection technologies as to whether the release of their product would degrade the underlying collection method. The rule was to limit the release and thereby protect the method. In the post–cold war world intelligence sharing will become the norm, and consequently technical selection criteria used in new investment decisions must reflect this choice.

Analysts and Deception

The front line in the struggle to penetrate denial and deception efforts will remain the intelligence analysts. The challenge they face is becoming much more difficult.

Virtual Proliferation and Virtual Deception. The scale of the Iraqi program—large and expensive, with a dedicated weapons cycle—may turn out to be a thing of the past and not representative of the character of future weapons programs. The industrial base of many middle-size, developing countries is such that a modest chemical and biological weapons program could be easily accommodated within their open civilian infrastructure, without the construction of significant dedicated facilities and with only trivial and short fused adjustments associated with final weaponization. The same peaceful petrochemical projects that make agricultural pesticides can make advanced nerve gases; a well-equipped university or hospital biochemical laboratory is quite adequate for the production of many biological warfare agents. Even in the nuclear arena, the civil and nuclear infrastructure of countries such as Taiwan and the Republic of Korea, and most of Western Europe, could easily and quickly produce a small number of simple nuclear weapons with little new construction and few warning signatures. In sum, the United States is entering a period of virtual proliferation in which capabilities are generally available and the real question becomes one of motivation and intentions. In such an environment the task of intelligence collection and analysis becomes harder as the requirements for denial and deception become easier. Discerning capabilities will become less significant than discerning intentions absent any detectable change in capabilities.

Spread of Deception Technology. Technologies that are capable of supporting robust deception efforts are now rapidly making their way into the civil economy, among them pollution control technology, data encryption, and electronic emission control. The most revolutionary advances are in the area of pollution control technology, which offers the capability to substantially reduce and even eliminate off-site emissions of particles, effluents, and

thermal and electromagnetic signatures. Such technologies are generally not subject to export controls or even tracking of foreign sales, and yet they strike at the heart of MASINT capabilities. Even newer technologies that, for example, are able to actively adjust their emissions to emulate various structures and processes, are emerging in the commercial entertainment market.

When the Standard of Success Becomes Not Conviction but Uncertainty OR Why "Shopping for Intelligence" Makes Deception Easier. A deception campaign that results in bureaucratic paralysis through uncertainty or disagreements as to capabilities and intentions will often be sufficient to obtain a state's objective—it will not need to reach the higher "gold" standard of widespread belief in the deception. Governmental authority, including the intelligence community, is becoming more fragmented both within states and between states. This fragmentation in authority very often gives an effective veto to the unconvinced. It is the rare policymaker who, if he or she desires, cannot find some element of the intelligence community that will either support his or her view with intelligence or question the foundation of the views of others. The objective of deception that seeks to delay or avoid action or to place a benign explanation in play has only to be to convince one and not the many—a far easier standard than in even the recent past.

In the case of WMD, the period of maximum vulnerability of a proliferator is precisely during the period of development of the first few weapons. Once, for example, one or two nuclear weapons are developed and hidden, the attraction of preemptive military actions or economic sanctions diminishes very rapidly. Yet perversely, deception during the development phase is the easiest. Analysts tend to look for reprocessing facilities, uranium enrichment facilities, biological warfare sites that look like those of the United States. The challenge to disguise such sites to look benign or to adopt an obsolete technology with which the analysts may be unfamiliar is not too difficult. This challenge becomes even easier when only one or two analysts need be convinced that the reprocessing site might be a rayon factory and they are able to shop this view to policymakers who will often be seeking to avoid or delay hard choices.

Countering Proliferation Deception

This article could easily appear to be a paralyzing depiction of the possibilities of denial and deception operations. This is not my intent. The outlook for the success of deception is depressing and the problem will become tougher, but there are actions and management steps that, if taken, can provide a far better chance of successfully defeating deception attempts.

Three "principles" should be borne in mind.

- Niches or the "it's not your account" type of thinking/management make successful deception more likely. Intelligence analysis is inherently a compartmentalized and specialized activity and this is never more so than when significant downsizing looms. On the other hand, successful detection of deception operations rests fundamentally on the ability to question the accuracy of observable facts and interpretations. Something does not "seem right," it "does not feel

right," it "fits together too well," or "can that sensor be spoofed by . . .?" These are all questions and surmises that can easily be rebuffed by organizational and turf barriers. Other damaging attitudes are, "you don't need to worry about my platform," "the PIs [photo interpreters] are the best in the business," or the ultimate put-off, "that's my job to worry about that, you just do yours."

- Detection of deception should not be ghettoized in the realm of counterintelligence or those who run collection systems. Obviously counterintelligence and managers and developers of collection systems have to worry about deception and can be a valuable resource in its detection. As deception technologies have improved, however, the detection of deception is less likely than in the past to result from a failure in the basic deception, that is, for example, a failure to mask all emissions. The keys in the future will more likely come from evidence of motivations and intentions or an unease about an overall pattern of activity rather than any specific, observable deception. If this is true, then all analysts need to be aware of deception possibilities and able to question all "facts."

- Believe deception can happen and study how it has and can happen. The message that needs to be at the forefront of every analytical activity is that *when the observable facts can be altered by deception measures, then reason is not a guarantee against deception.* This is a difficult message to get across in operations where the worth of the analytical product tends to be judged by the analyst's logical rigor, and it becomes even more difficult to communicate this message of caution at a time of generational change in a bureaucracy. Deception operations, such as Iraq's, and new deception possibilities need to be studied and not just by specialists. For example, it would be interesting to know how many analysts have participated in reviews of the impact of environmental control technologies on their ability to understand what is happening in their region of concern or how many analysts track the movement of such technologies into their regions. Analysts need to be given new tools to aid in the identification of deception activities.

Policy Nexus: What U.S. Interests Are Affected by Deceptions?

There is a tendency to view the growing likelihood of successful deceptions as only an intelligence problem. Surrounded by a fog of uncertainty, intelligence assessments have never been easy. Active deception has only increased the inevitable ambiguity that is associated with intelligence. Although this reasoning is no doubt soundly based, it misses the new context of the post–cold war world. Deception threatens two important aspects of U.S. national security policy for coping with emerging threats.

Ability to Build and Maintain Coalitions and Control Regimes

The proliferation of WMD and means to deliver them is now recognized as one of the highest-priority threats to the United States. Although there is no single answer as to how to meet this threat, it is clear that a major thrust will have to be to maintain effective technology control regimes that limit the further spread of such technologies. Technology control regimes (e.g.,

the IAEA, the Missile Technology Control Regime, the Australia Group, and the Chemical Weapons Convention [CWC]), to be effective, increasingly depend upon reliable, shareable intelligence. If deception activities make this intelligence appear to be less reliable or fear of deception makes it less shareable, then these regimes will lose their effectiveness. Even if the U.S. intelligence community is not deceived, but allied services are, then their willingness to support multilateral steps or even unilateral national controls will be lessened. Treaty compliance regimes such as the IAEA and CWC inevitably will operate with sources and methods that are less robust against deception than those of the United States. The willingness to share U.S. knowledge of deceptions with such regimes will have to struggle with the reluctance arising from loss of sources and methods. This means that such regimes will often (usually) operate with less than the best available intelligence and may not be able to detect or even confirm violations— even those that the United States may have a high confidence exist. The potential for such a process to unleash a corrosive type of relationship, both with the international control regimes and in bilateral relationships, has already been foreshadowed to some extent in efforts to keep WMD material out of the hands of Iraq and Iran.

Beyond multilateral technology controls are the issues of effective national export controls. General national export controls are rapidly disappearing and if replaced at all will only be replaced by limited controls on a few target states of notoriously bad character. Deception practices will at a minimum delay the targeting of such offenders and may in many cases make it impossible to build an effective case for controls until it is too late to check the proliferation.

Military Planning and Action

It is a military axiom that you cannot target what you cannot find, and that you only target what you find. Programs to develop WMD are most vulnerable to military and political actions before any weapons have ever been produced. At such times there are only limited concerns over collateral damage from preemptive military attacks and no concern that a state might be able to reply with a WMD. On the other hand, absent compelling evidence of such a weapons program, most Western governments will have considerable difficulty in embarking upon preventive military action. At this stage the role of deception is to raise doubt as to the true nature of activities of concern.

Although greater attention is now being given to the use of deception to actively shield a program, less attention has been given to deception that attempts to raise concern that a state may already have acquired such weapons. The most effective purpose of a small number of first generation nuclear weapons (a small number is probably any number more than 0 and less than 10) is intimidation and breaking up coalitions. U.S. military forces are rapidly changing from a forward deployed force to a power projection force that must depend upon forward bases and long logistical trains to operate. If those whose interest the United States is defending and those upon whose territory it relies for operational support believe that they are threatened by a nuclear adversary, they may well see political compromise and negotiations as superior to combat. Even the United States is likely to show less relish for military options that raise the

possibility that it may actually have to face a nuclear or biological attack. In such cases deception may be used effectively to raise the serious possibility either that a country has a nuclear weapon where no weapon at all may exist or that it is likely to use a WMD if forced into combat. If deception practices make it impossible for the intelligence community to give confident answers as to whether a country has a nuclear weapon or is likely to use one, and the location of such weapons cannot be given with confidence, then military and political action will become very unattractive. The intelligence community will then be the certain target of the charge that a "failure" of intelligence has left the policymakers with no choices except accommodation or unacceptable risks.

The views expressed in this article are solely those of the author.

Notes

1. "The point is not how wrong the United States was about Iraq's timetable for acquiring a bomb, but rather how greatly the United States underestimated the magnitude of the Iraqi covert effort. As it stands, such a massive miscalculation of a nation's capability, high or low, can surely happen again." John M. Deutch, "The New Nuclear Threat," *Foreign Affairs* 71 (Fall 1992), p. 128.

2. Conversation with the author, when the latter was serving as chief inspector on the Sixth UNSCOM/IAEA Nuclear Inspection Team in July 1991.

3. Mr. Al-Ashimi, Iraq's delegate to the IAEA's General Conference in 1981, declared that Iraq "had been one of the first countries to ratify the Treaty on the Non-Proliferation of Nuclear Weapons (NPT), despite the discrimination introduced by that Treaty . . . the Iraqi Government had always given its full support to the Agency's activities with respect to the peaceful uses of nuclear energy and the control of proliferation." IAEA, 24th Regular Session, GC (XXIV) OR.220, Vi-

enna, February 1981. Iraq was represented at the IAEA at the time the Gulf war began by a former chairman of the Iraq Atomic Energy Commission who had held that office when Iraq's program gained speed in the early 1980s.

4. Congressional Research Service, Library of Congress, "Analysis of Six Issues about Nuclear Capabilities of India, Iraq, Libya, and Pakistan" (Washington, D.C.: GPO, January 1982), pp. 37–39.

5. The newsletter *Nuclear Fuel* reports that several shipments of preformed tubes for scoops in gas centrifuges from the German metalworking firm Team GmbH were shipped to Pakistan after being declared as bodies for ballpoint pens. *Nuclear Fuel*, June 20, 1994, pp. 9–11.

6. I dealt for many months with a senior Iraqi scientist whose entire university training, from undergraduate to doctorate, had been in the United States and whose first job had been at a U.S. nuclear power plant, and yet basic data on or pictures of this key individual could not be found.

7. Although this was not the first time that intelligence information had been made available to the IAEA—intelligence-based briefings had been supplied earlier on several suspect nuclear programs—the breadth of information and the openness of the sharing during the Iraqi inspections has been so great as to mark a distinctly different approach.

8. The IAEA had not a single secure telephone or fax when the inspections began nor a single secure conference room.

9. It is striking that, at least in the unclassified testimony, U.S. national security officials have not shared with Congress this concern as they try to develop broader support for continued investment in technical collection methods.

Controlling the Arms Trade: Idealistic Dream or Realpolitik?

Stephanie G. Neuman

ARMS-CONTROL FEVER is in the air. Limiting the transfer of conventional weapons, once thought to be an idealistic dream, is now considered a viable policy option by policymakers and the media. The United States and the states comprising the former Soviet Union are reducing the number of strategic and conventional weapons in their arsenals. Two months after the Persian Gulf War cease-fire in February 1991, President George Bush announced his Middle East arms-control initiative for restraints on transfers of conventional arms to the region and a freeze on surface-to-surface missile (SSM) sales. In October 1991, the big five major exporters—the United States, the United Kingdom, France, the Soviet Union, and the People's Republic of China (PRC)[1]—agreed to exchange information and limit major weapons transfers to the Middle East. The following December, the General Assembly of the United Nations (UN) voted 150–0 in favor of an arms transfer register to collect and publish information on arms transfers in order to achieve transparency, promote restraint in the arms trade, and build confidence among states. Former President Bush,[2] Prime Minister Brian Mulroney of Canada, Prime Minister François Mitterrand of France, and other world leaders have proposed various schemes to further limit international arms sales. And on the national level, France and Germany have both tightened legislative loopholes regarding the export of weapons of mass destruction.[3] Several other states have initiated more restrictive domestic arms export regulations: Italy has frozen arms exports, and since 1989, Austria, Belgium, Finland, Norway, Sweden, and Switzerland have stiffened their export policies.[4]

A constellation of events has occurred that suggests the environment is ripe for conventional arms-control initiatives. Should we, then, be optimistic about the chances for limiting the spread of conventional weapons, or are there reasons for skepticism? What can we realistically expect?

Grounds for Optimism

A number of powerful factors support the case for optimism.

Stephanie G. Neuman teaches third world security issues at Columbia University where she is a senior research scholar and director of the Comparative Research Studies Program. She is the author of *Military Assistance in Recent Wars* (1987).

The Persian Gulf War: Moral Outrage and Enlightened Self-Interest. The Gulf war was a watershed, mobilizing world public opinion in favor of arms transfer restraints. Prompted by feelings of moral outrage at the behavior of Saddam Hussein, the war epitomized, particularly to the developed world, the dangers of weapons proliferation to areas of high tension and to aggressive countries such as Iraq. Prior to the invasion of Kuwait, the Middle East had been the leading importer of military equipment—$84 billion, or one-third of the world's total, between 1985 and 1989—much of it advanced technology. Iraq alone accounted for over one-quarter of the regional total.

For the militaries of the United States, the former Soviet Union (FSU), and the European allies, it was also a case of enlightened self-interest. The war alerted them to the potential threat their own troops now faced in theaters of conflict once considered peripheral to the central war zone. When it ended, the U.S. military voiced strong misgivings about the diffusion of advanced and intermediate conventional weapons—weapons that in its view increase U.S. vulnerability in regional warfare. Included were: submarines;[5] stealth low and very low observable technology (LO/VLO);[6] space-based reconnaissance systems;[7] high-speed computers;[8] and electronic warfare technology (EW).[9]

Compounding the general feeling of disquiet today is the spread of weapons of mass destruction along with their production facilities. The war that saw Saddam Hussein rain Scud missiles on the allies and Israel and threaten to use chemical weapons against them was a sobering experience. In the West, the outrage has been intensified by the knowledge that Iraq purchased Western arms and technologies illicitly, and that the Iraqi government lied regarding its nuclear production capabilities and intentions in spite of the West's assistance and support during the Iran–Iraq War.

This response to the behavior of Saddam Hussein has created a climate of opinion that is concerned about regional stability and is extraordinarily sympathetic to some kind of arms-control initiative.

Diminishing Soviet–U.S. Rivalry in the Third World. Other factors have also contributed to the growing enthusiasm for arms controls. The reduced tension between the United States and the former Soviet Union has prompted both governments to rethink their policies toward the Third World. During the Cold War, each tended to construe regional conflicts in terms of a zero-sum game, whereby each side considered the enlistment and support of proxies necessary to halt the political or territorial advancement of the other. A gain by one side's proxy was deemed a loss for the other superpower. Today, both the United States and the troubled newly independent republics of the FSU are more likely to perceive third world conflicts as internal or civil wars. Increasingly military or economic involvement is considered an unnecessary and insupportable expense as the 1991 U.S.–Soviet agreement to end arms sales to rival sides in the Afghan War portended.[10] Since the former Soviet Union's withdrawal from Afghanistan in February 1989, continued U.S. support for the Afghan insurgents, or for that matter other regional combatants, has become harder to defend in Congress and to the American people. For the independent republics of the former Soviet Union, removing irritants in their relations with the United States is seen as a way of earning vital economic assistance. They, too, are unlikely to risk unilateral intervention in distant regional conflicts. The fact that the world now looks to the UN to find solutions for the 48 ethnic wars still going on in 1993[11] demonstrates the extent to which East–West rivalry has receded in the Third World.

The Economic Dependency of the Newly Independent Republics. Closely associated with the diminished tension between the United States and the FSU is the economic and political disarray in the new republics. Seeking economic and technological assistance, and sorely in need of a tranquil international environment in order to stabilize their respective regimes, the republics of the FSU are eager to cooperate with the United States. They are unlikely, on this score alone, to challenge U.S. arms transfer initiatives. To date, control of the arms trade has been identified by the United States and both former Soviet president Mikhail Gorbachev and Russian president Boris Yeltsin as an issue of mutual concern.[12] According to Vladimir Shibaev, deputy minister of external economic relations, Russia is strictly adhering to the principles established at the October 1991 meeting of the five permanent members of the UN Security Council. He declared that Russia is observing embargoes on sales to Angola, Afghanistan, Cambodia, Iraq, Kuwait, South Africa, and the former Yugoslavia. He also indicated that Russia will no longer sell arms to Ethiopia or Libya,[13] and President Yeltsin declared Russia has stopped selling arms to North Korea, too.[14] As Julian Cooper concludes:

This commitment to the observance of international rules indicates the Russian administration's awareness of the importance of not allowing arms export activity to complicate relations with the West at a time when assistance and political support is needed.[15]

U.S. Primacy in the International System. The Gulf war also demonstrated incontrovertibly what past events in the former Soviet Union implied—that the United States is the predominant political and military power in the international system. In 1991, a U.S. official for the first time publicly declared the United States to be the sole world superpower. Itemizing measures of economic, political, military, and cultural power, Robert Gates, then deputy national security adviser, declared: "We have no challengers."[16] Once universally perceived as bipolar, the international system is now regarded as unipolar by a growing number of analysts.[17] Catherine Kelleher summarizes this view nicely:

The United States has the resources and universal culture that appeal to a broad faction of the global community; the system of alliances it leads and the informal coalitions it has built now constitute the most effective global management system. No other power or group of states will be able in the foreseeable future to command or co-opt this system.[18]

The significance of all this for arms control and arms transfers is far-reaching. As international tensions have diminished, tighter arms transfer restrictions have become more attractive to U.S. policymakers. Given its predominance in the system, U.S. preferences on this issue are likely to receive a favorable response from states now more dependent than ever on U.S. political and economic largess.[19]

Structural Arms Control. Economic factors are also enhancing the prospects for global arms transfer restraint. World recession combined with changes in the world political climate have created a situation in which the demand for military equipment is in decline. Falling demand has set into motion a cycle whereby shorter production runs raise the unit cost of military equipment,[20] which, in turn, places an additional burden on already shrinking budgetary resources, further decreasing the number of weapons the military can afford to buy. With orders dropping drastically, military industries everywhere are seeking financial relief through bankruptcy, production cutbacks, conversion, mergers, or a host of other economizing measures. As conditions continue to deteriorate, more countries may see it in their economic and political interest not only to curtail their own procurements but, through arms-control agreements, those of their enemies as well. Israel, for example, is now taking a new look at internationally organized controls. "This is a change in attitude," observed a Foreign Ministry official. "We preferred to stay out of international organs agreements because we felt they were politicized and stacked against us. We want to get involved now, if for no other reason than to see that others don't cheat."[21]

Declining Arms Imports
Worldwide

Many indicators demonstrate the presence of structural arms control. Worldwide arms imports have declined dramatically since the end of the Iran–Iraq War, dropping 28 percent from 1987 to 1989. Imports fell most precipitously, however, in the Third World (33 percent) and former Warsaw Pact countries (36 percent). In the Third World arms imports plunged; in the Middle East almost 50 percent, in Latin America 37 percent, and in Africa and East Asia 34 percent. Only

South Asia's military procurements increased in dollar value.[22]

Declining Arms Production
Worldwide

Worldwide military production, too, is expected to drop—some estimate as much as 20 to 30 percent in the 1990s.[23] For arms producers in general, falling defense budgets and contracted demand have had serious negative consequences for exports and military industrial infrastructure. In a reiterative downward spiral, the ability of small and medium-size states to produce sophisticated weapons is dwindling as their dependence upon the more advanced military production capabilities of others, particularly those of the United States, is growing.

Western Europe

In Western Europe not only is defense production declining for all the above reasons, but large numbers of domestic as well as collaborative programs are being cancelled, particularly for next generation platforms such as tanks and planes. As one analyst concludes, "It no longer seems possible to deny that in the short to medium term, aggregate defense production in Europe is declining rapidly and that a major restructuring is underway."[24]

Individual European states do not have the military market that allows for the economies of scale and the spreading out of research and development (R&D) costs enjoyed by U.S. industries. They depend to a great extent upon exports to make their defense industries economically viable. But European arms exports are down sharply. France's deliveries, for example, fell from approximately $7 billion in 1987 to $3.1 billion in 1991, a drop of 56 percent. Britain's decreased from $5.9 billion in 1987 to $3.6 billion in 1991, a 40 percent decline.[25]

The situation is exacerbated by the rapidly escalating cost of production and the speed of technological change. As Jean-Pierre Chevènement, former French defense minister, divulged in January 1991, France can no longer afford to manufacture 84 percent of its weapons.[26]

These economic realities suggest that European defense industries will remain dependent upon U.S. inputs of high technology into their defense industries and perhaps for off-the-shelf purchases of major weapon systems as well. If the past augurs the future, the arms export data support this view. Between 1985 and 1989, the United States exported (in current U.S. dollars) $22 billion in defense equipment to Europe and imported $6 billion, roughly a 4 to 1 trade advantage in favor of the United States.[27] Even France, which in the past made the greatest effort to maintain an independent military production capability, is now considering the purchase of foreign equipment.[28] France's former undersecretary of defense declared in May 1991:

There are some types of equipment that can be bought off-the-shelf without endangering our security. And if costs are attractive we could buy foreign equipment rather than launching French industry in complex and expensive development programs.[29]

But, if European states do increase their military purchases from the United States, many of their domestically produced military goods as well as their imported major systems will be subject to U.S. third party transfer prohibitions, providing the United States with an important means of controlling their spread.

The prospects for achieving econ-omies of scale and increased independence through integrated defense production is the wild card. Should Europe be successful in these efforts, as some predict, Europe's dependence upon the United States will diminish. In November 1990, 12 European Community (EC) states organized Euclid, a program to cooperate on R&D for defense to boost European technology and challenge U.S. leadership.[30]

But there is some doubt that Europe can compete independently with the United States in the defense sector. Thus far it has been unable to do so in major critical technologies. In a recent study comparing the production capabilities of various countries, the U.S. Defense Department found that North Atlantic Treaty Organization (NATO) European countries were on a par with the United States in 7 of the 22 critical technologies surveyed. Unlike Japan, however, NATO Europe was not ahead of the United States in any category.[31] Analyzing the strengths and weaknesses of Western Europe's military industrial capability, sector by sector, another study concludes:

Western Europe tends to be well established in older technologies—heavy mechanical engineering and hydrodynamics, for example—and fully on a par with America in these; but it occupies a weaker position in the newer and emerging technologies, especially in the vital field of electronics.[32]

Furthermore, Europe's experience to date has been that collaborative projects are inefficient and costly. With the huge gap in R&D expenditures (the United States spends four times more than all of Europe combined on military R&D), it would appear that even with cooperative efforts, unless Europe decides to invest significantly more resources in military R&D, it will not be competitive enough to either produce what it needs independently or to increase its exports substantially.[33]

Nationalism has been another obstacle to European collaboration in the past, and one that may persist in the future. Along with a general fear of loss of sovereignty, differences exist among European nations in perceptions of threat and doctrinal and defense requirements that make cooperation on military production and procurement difficult. European governments are also concerned about lost jobs and the response of the electorate to them. As a result, each country has tended to believe that it is financing other countries' programs and interests in cooperative ventures at the expense of its own. Other, more subtle, types of competition have also arisen, as exemplified by the Euclid program: after some dissension it was agreed to spell Euclid the English rather than French way.[34]

The best proof of the pudding is in the eating, and since 1957, when the first Franco–German cooperative agreement was initiated, Europe has taken part only sparingly in military industrial collaboration. Cooperative procurement ventures represent a fraction of European weapons programs: 15 percent for the United Kingdom and no more than 20 percent of conventional arms procurement in France.[35]

In sum, given depressed markets elsewhere, Europe is eager to maintain access to vital U.S. civilian and military markets[36] and is therefore sensitive to U.S. arms-control preferences and pressures. If the price of access is continued procurement from U.S. de-

fense industries and restrictions on arms transfers, then the likelihood of sustaining an independent European production capability and export policy becomes more remote. Some interpret Europe's support of Arab–Israeli negotiations and restrictions on arms transfers to the Middle East as denoting a more flexible and cooperative attitude.[37]

Russia and the New Republics

It is not necessary to detail the economic and political chaos unfolding in the former Soviet Union. Conditions in the military sector have been equally tumultuous in the Soviet Union before its disintegration and in the Russian Republic that inherited over 80 percent of the FSU's aerospace and defense industries and 90 percent of its military R&D.[38]

Drastic cuts in defense spending in the former Soviet Union caused severe production and research cutbacks throughout the industry.[39] Military orders to Soviet defense plants fell by 21 percent in 1991 from the previous year, and in January 1992 the Russian parliament approved a budget that slashed arms purchases to about one-seventh the 1991 level. Research and development funding is thought to have fallen by as much as 30 percent.[40] U.S. Defense Department 1991 figures show a critical drop in the FSU's major weapons production across the board (see table 1).

By 1992, factories were complaining that military contracts had been reduced to practically nothing.[41] Supplies, particularly those needed for civilian manufactures, had become increasingly difficult to obtain, and where production was still continuing, factories were drawing on existing stocks of material. Unless government policy shifts, some analysts believe

Table 1
Major Weapons Production in the Former Soviet Union

	1989	1990	1991
Main Battle Tanks	1,700	1,300	1,000
Infantry Fighting Weapons	4,800	3,600–3,900	2,100
Artillery	2,500	1,900	1,000
Bomber Aircraft	40	35	30
Fighters & Fighter Bombers	650	575	350
Attack Helicopters	100	70	15
Submarines & Major Surface Combatants	21	20	13
Strategic Ballistic Missiles	200–215	190–205	145–165

Source: U.S. Department of Defense figures cited in "Soviet Production Continues to Fall," *Jane's Defence Weekly*, September 26, 1992, p. 7.

that once these stockpiles are exhausted many of these factories will close.[42]

The hope of Russian arms industries is the Western market, particularly that of the United States. These companies are searching for joint ventures and collaborative projects that will help maintain or improve their technological base. According to Russian financial sources, U.S. companies are the primary participants in Russian joint ventures. As of mid-1992, U.S. investment reportedly constituted 60 percent of the funds involved in joint ventures.[43] But, as in the case of Europe, collaboration holds the risk of increased U.S. control over the sale of jointly produced military items by triggering U.S. third party transfer restrictions.

Arms exports from the former Soviet Union show similar declines, plummeting in recent years from $28.8 billion in 1987 to $7.7 billion in 1991, a drop of 73 percent in real terms.[44] According to official Russian sources, *actual* income from arms sales fell to $3.7 billion in 1991.[45] Dramatic declines were recorded in shipping tonnage as well.[46]

The defeat of Soviet military systems manned by Iraqis during the 1991 Gulf war has done little to encourage sales of Soviet-made equipment. Nor have falling production and the inability of Russia to provide adequate after-sales logistical support and spare parts helped the situation. Add to this the Russian government's policy of conducting all foreign trade in hard currency and pricing much of its military equipment commercially, and Russian sales promise to contract further in the future. In the short term, as Russia sells off its surplus equipment, there are still some bargains to be had.[47] But the comparative advantage of military equipment from the former Soviet Union—low cost at generous terms—will evaporate, making it even less attractive to its traditional market of disaffected, impoverished, and indebted third world and East European customers.[48] Unless the Russian Republic is able to resolve its internal problems and maintain a sophisticated R&D and industrial infrastructure over the long term, its role in the world's arms production and transfer system is likely to deteriorate further.

Eastern Europe
The situation in Eastern Europe is no better. Poland, Czechoslovakia, and other East European states have tried

without much success to raise cash by selling weapons. The end of the Iran–Iraq War and the collapse of the Soviet Union have sent weapon sales plummeting. Czechoslovakia, for example, once a major East European exporter of conventional weapons, went from approximately $700 million worth of exports in 1989 and 1990 to zero in 1991.[49] Competition for the few remaining hard currency contracts has turned fierce among the countries of Eastern Europe and the republics of the FSU. A Polish tank factory for example, which won Pakistan's order for more than 100 tanks, "beat out" Slovak and Russian competitors. Reportedly, Russian manufacturers had dropped their export prices to "fire sale" levels in an unsuccessful attempt to win.[50] Like Russia, these countries are now looking to Western Europe and the United States for joint ventures and collaboration in military production.[51]

The Third World
Similar conditions exist in the Third World. By 1989 imports of weapons had declined 31 percent from 1987 levels and exports had declined 29 percent.[52] For many third world producers whose defense industries depended upon the Iran–Iraq War for sales, reduced demand has spelled disaster. Brazil is a typical example. Its exports fell by 93 percent between 1987 and 1989.[53] The embargo on Iraq after it invaded Kuwait eliminated Brazil's major market for Astros II rocket launchers and missiles and Urutu armored vehicles. Because exports are vital to the health of Brazil's arms industries—until recently some 90 percent of production was exported[54]—many of these industries were thrown into bankruptcy or near bankruptcy.[55] For the foreseeable fu-

ture, then, the dearth of customers means that Brazil is unlikely to be a major arms supplier or manufacturer of finished end items.

Brazil's situation typifies that of other third world producers. As demand has fallen, so have prospects for viable defense industries, particularly for the production of major weapon systems. With few exceptions, third world military industries are in dire straits and are unable to compete in the world's arms market. Even the PRC faces severe constraints as its exports tumble. PRC arms deliveries have contracted from $4.2 billion in 1988 to $800 million in 1991.[56]

As the market has receded, third world military industries have turned to the West, but particularly to the United States, for possible sales. They, too, are searching for Western cooperative projects or other opportunities to facilitate market entry. Israeli defense companies, for example, are trying to expand into the U.S. defense market through acquisitions and joint ventures with U.S. companies.[57]

Economic exigencies are also affecting countries that do not produce arms. They, too, are dealing with the prospect of fewer military purchases. Not only have their domestic procurement budgets been slashed, but sources of military assistance are dissipating. Easy terms or gifts of equipment are no longer forthcoming from the FSU. Military grant aid from the United States—a major donor—is a declining asset.[58] The Gulf states, which in the past helped finance the military purchases of poorer Islamic countries, are also cutting back. Saudi Arabia, for example, has suspended financial aid to the Palestine Liberation Organization (PLO), Jordan, Sudan, Yemen, "and to some extent to Algeria and Tunisia," all countries that openly sympathized with Iraq in the Gulf crisis. Even aid to friendly countries and Arab allies, like Egypt, has been reduced.[59]

In sum, we are witnessing a structural form of conventional arms control caused by economic factors that makes arms-control initiatives potentially more attractive to recipients and suppliers. In response to the deflating arms trade, some supplier states have found it possible to initiate more restrictive arms export policies without paying a political price domestically. Many governments find themselves freer to respond to advocates for arms control in a situation in which military industries, weakened by falling orders and their own declining numbers, are able to fight less fiercely for permissive export legislation. Recipients, on the other hand, unable to afford large military procurements, look to arms export regulations to limit the procurement capability of their enemies as well. In general, the lower the level of arms transferred, the more feasible tighter arms-control legislation at the national and international levels becomes.

Reality versus Euphoria: Grounds for Skepticism

But how optimistic can we be about the success of future arms-control initiatives? How likely is it that suppliers and recipients will agree? How probable is it that they will conform to control regulations and not be tempted to cheat?

In spite of the favorable climate, expectations for conventional arms control must remain modest. Hopes for general and complete disarmament, or for the cessation of arms transfers, are bound to be frustrated by a variety of factors that conspire to make the effective implementation of stringent arms-control measures difficult.

Geopolitical Realities. Geopolitical realities in much of the Third World provide powerful incentives to evade arms-control restrictions. In the face of competing territorial claims, disputed borders, and unsettled ethnic and religious rivalries, many third world governments seek arms to maintain internal order, protect their countries from external threats, and ensure their own survival. From the perspective of third world leaders, arms controls are dangerous because they may or may not deprive their enemies of the wherewithal to attack, but they certainly deprive their own countries of the means of defense, particularly if they do not produce their own weapons. For these countries weapons, not arms controls, are the ultimate confidence builder, and arms imports the key to survival.

In the Middle East, for example, President Hafez al-Assad of Syria believes the U.S. policy on arms control in his region is designed "to strip the Arabs of their weapons" and "halt the import of arms by Arabs while allowing Israel to manufacture arms."[60] But from the Israeli perspective, domestic production is vital to survival in a hostile environment, and sophisticated arms exports to neighboring Arab states, such as the sale of F–15Es to Saudi Arabia, represent an escalated security threat and must, therefore, be controlled. One Israeli defense official has observed:

> Even if the Saudis did not initially become involved in a new Israeli–Arab confrontation, the deployment of F–15s at airbases such as Tabuk—only 6 minutes flying time from Israel—could tie down Israeli squadrons needed elsewhere.[61]

For major supplier states, such as the former Soviet Union and the

United States, tension has always existed between the desire to limit arms transfers to potential aggressors and the self-interested need to provide allies and friends with arms for their own defense. Fear of involvement in an unwanted, unsolicited war is a powerful inducement to help friends fight their own battles. Even today, the dilemma facing the United States is how to prevent larger, more aggressive states from preying on the weak without committing U.S. soldiers to protect them and how to initiate equitable arms controls that do not leave small states or non-producers at the mercy of their more militarily capable neighbors.

Policy debates regarding arms transfers and controls often revolve around this issue. In the Middle East, for example, smaller Gulf states, such as Kuwait, feel particularly vulnerable. A U.S. military attaché in the region observed: "In the next decade, Iran will become a regional superpower and Iraq will recover. If they will be aggressive or friendly, we don't know, but Kuwait will always have to live under threat."[62] The same holds true for the other Arab Gulf states. Their plan to build up their defense to prevent anything like the Iraqi invasion from happening again involves arms imports and military training. Responding to this security dilemma, the United States simultaneously called for restraint on arms transfers to the Gulf and, between June 1991 and January 1992, transferred $5 billion worth of weapons to the Gulf states.[63] And in spite of the U.S. arms embargo, in August 1991 the U.S. government approved the sale of equipment worth more than $300 million to Iran.[64]

A similar situation exists in South Asia. The United States, uncomfortable with Pakistan's human rights record and purported nuclear program, cut off U.S. military aid in October 1990. But India which, like Pakistan, refuses to sign the Nuclear Non-Proliferation Treaty (NPT) or to agree to international inspections and safeguards, has the material and infrastructure to produce more nuclear weapons than Pakistan and supports a much larger military-industrial establishment. To Pakistan, India constitutes a major security threat. Faced with this dilemma, the United States has permitted commercial sales of arms to Pakistan of about $400 million.[65] As one Indian analyst aptly puts it:

[U]nless the basic issue of the causes of insecurity and vulnerability in the developing world is adequately addressed, it would be overly optimistic to expect that the arms trade, which is a very minor aspect of the overall generation and stockpiling of arms, can be controlled.[66]

The conflict in the former Yugoslavia also illustrates the dilemma. By January 1993, a 1992 UN arms embargo on the former Yugoslavian republics was viewed by some as favoring the Serbs in Bosnia-Herzegovina, prompting calls to lift the embargo for Bosnia and send arms to the Bosnian Muslims. President Turgut Ozal of Turkey predicted failure for any peace talks until the Muslims were strengthened to fight the Serbs to a stalemate.[67] Some have even suggested that "had the Bosnians been armed a year ago, they might have deterred the Serbs."[68]

These thorny policy considerations will not evaporate in the future. Ironically, they make even peace treaties reliant on arms transfers for success. The precedent was set by U.S. actions in connection with the 1979 Israeli–Egyptian peace treaty. The United States promised and delivered to both signatories generous military assistance to allay their fear and mistrust of each other. Should current peace negotiations on the Middle East be successful, weapons transfers are bound to be a political outcome.

Economic Realities. Economic realities also conspire to undermine arms-control initiatives, motivating many suppliers and recipients to find ways around them. For most weapons producers, as discussed above, arms exports are a means of supporting their own arms industries, achieving economies of scale for equipment required by their armed forces, and earning needed foreign currency to shore up their economies. Traditionally only 5 to 15 percent of U.S. defense production has been exported,[69] but other countries have been more dependent on such exports and so the collapse of the arms market has hit them harder. Brazil, as already noted, sold 90 percent of its arms production abroad;[70] France exported an estimated 50 percent of the conventional weapon systems it manufactured;[71] and Czechoslovakia sold 70 percent of what it produced.[72] In Russia today, defense items are one of the few commodities left to vend on the world market.[73] Former Russian prime minister I. S. Silayev revealed in 1991 that 70 percent of the industrial enterprises on Russian territory belonged to the military-industrial sector and that civilian consumer goods accounted for only 26 percent of what Russian industries produced.[74]

Arms exports, therefore, represent an important input into struggling economies. Russia, for example, is attempting to sell a vast stock of surplus equipment created by its reduced defense budget, Conventional Forces in Europe (CFE) limitations, and the contracting size of its armed forces.[75]

Russian officials argue that arms exports are necessary in the short run to earn enough hard currency to fund defense industry conversion and social programs.[76] To compete, Russia is offering its excess inventory at cut-rate prices.[77] President Boris Yeltsin revealed that he had even suggested to President George Bush that Russia and the United States divide the world arms market. Reportedly, President Bush declined the offer.[78]

To date, the volume of Russian arms sales is low[79] and the uncontrolled flood of Soviet technology onto the market feared by the West has not occurred. Economic need nevertheless dictates that Russia and other East European arms producers cannot afford to halt sales entirely. These trends suggest that for Russia, and Eastern Europe as a whole, military sales will continue but at a significantly lower level.

Similar economic incentives motivate collaborative defense projects between other needy countries. In addition to the M–11 missile deal with Pakistan, the PRC entered into an agreement with Syria in 1988 to develop the M–9 missile. Both Pakistan and Syria are reported to have provided financing for the respective missiles.[80] These ventures furnish much needed foreign currency for the PRC's own military industries. Furthermore, the PRC has export obligations to these countries, and despite its November 1991 promise to abide by the Missile Technology Control Regime (MTCR), is expected to proceed with missile sales contracted before that date. Whether it sells the missile itself or, more likely, components and technical expertise,[81] the motive is economic and the result proliferation.

Inevitably, the need for defense exports influences how states respond to arms-control initiatives, and in many cases the economic incentives to cheat or find ways around them will be very compelling. For these reasons, agreement among supplier states on a unified arms-control policy will face serious difficulties. Within the EC, for example, restrictions on arms exports would inevitably have negative implications for the economies of scale of any EC collaborative production project, reducing its profits and increasing costs. Export controls would also raise questions about their differential impact on the economies of EC members. France and Britain, for instance, which are responsible for two-thirds of NATO Europe's arms exports, have been decidedly less enthusiastic about the prospect of a common export policy than Belgium or Holland, which together represent 6 percent.[82] Only in reference to the Persian Gulf has there been some unanimity among the 12 EC members. France, Germany, Italy, and Belgium have joined Luxembourg and the Netherlands in calls for tighter controls on arms exports to the region, although no specific measures have been agreed upon.[83]

Dissension over arms transfer restraints has strained relations among the five permanent members of the Security Council as well. The July 1991 agreement to limit arms exports to the Middle East, for example, began coming apart as early as September 1991, when the PRC withdrew citing U.S. sales of F–16 aircraft to Taiwan as the reason.

The imperative of technological diffusion presents yet another obstacle. The modernization needs of all militaries are a strong stimulus for activity in the arms trade and as technology improves vast amounts of obsolete equipment are made available, filtering out into successively less developed countries. States of the Third World are involved in this diffusion process as well, providing other states with old equipment they no longer need or want.[84]

Finally, there is some question as to whether all governments can equally and effectively regulate weapons transfers that originate from within their national borders. Clearly, the level of expertise and resources available to enforce export regulations varies from country to country.[85] There have been reports, for example, that undocumented Russian arms have found their way into the Caucasian republics and possibly into Iran, Algeria, Yugoslavia, and Western Europe,[86] and that uranium has been smuggled out of Belarus and possibly other FSU republics.[87] Chile's Carlos Cardoen, an arms manufacturer, has been accused of illegally exporting equipment to Iraq.[88] Even Japan,[89] Western Europe,[90] and the United States[91] have been unable to totally control unauthorized transactions, the magnitude of which is unknown.

The Changing Character of the Arms Trade. The changing character of the arms trade itself challenges the prospects for conventional arms control as what to control becomes a more baffling and complex question. Falling defense budgets are prompting states to upgrade existing inventories rather than purchase new and expensive end items. Whereas suppliers previously transferred complete weapon systems—tanks, ships, missiles, and aircraft—today the major trade is in components, spare parts, technical assistance, and production technologies. Many of these items are shipped in crates and containers, making verification problematic, subterfuge possible, and regulation more difficult.

A particularly nettlesome issue is

the increased transfer of production technology. Past and existing control regimes have focused on individual systems or components in the manufacturing process, while the export of turnkey factories that can be diverted to military usage is not prohibited. This comes at a time when automated production machinery is simplifying the task of sophisticated industrial production.[92]

More and more countries are acquiring the technical capability to upgrade weapons, if not to manufacture them. Iraq, for example, has extended the range of the Scud–B to produce its Al-Husayn and Al-Abbas missiles. Aiding and abetting this trend is the burgeoning world population of technically trained people—engineers, scientists, and technicians—who form an army of "intellectual mercenaries," able and willing to help other states acquire more sophisticated military-industrial capabilities. Largely educated in the West, many of them originating from the Third World, these men and women are returning in the thousands to their own countries or are selling their expertise to the highest bidder in others.[93] Their ranks are swelled by former Soviet defense scientists and technicians encouraged to flee their homeland by the economic chaos in the republics, the liberalization of travel restrictions, and continuing cutbacks on the former Soviet military laboratories.[94] These are developments that will be difficult to contain in the future.

The Blurring of Conventional and Unconventional Weaponry. Furthermore, the barrier between conventional and unconventional arms is rapidly eroding. Much attention has been given to the control of unconventional weapons— the so-called weapons of mass destruc-

tion, nuclear, biological, chemical (NBC) weapons and ballistic missiles—but new "conventional" systems such as sensor and communications technologies, advanced data-processing equipment mated with new delivery systems, low observable aircraft and missiles, long-range surveillance systems, and other technologies are expected to have a revolutionary impact on the future battlefield. The power and accuracy of these new weapons are blurring the distinction between tactical and strategic weapons and between the conventional and unconventional.[95] As one analyst claims: "If a full scale conventional war broke out in Europe, the battlefield two weeks later . . . would be, in visual terms, little different from an attack by Hiroshima class nuclear weapons."[96]

Many of these new technologies are also small, easily transportable, have dual-use functions, and may be available on the commercial market, making it possible for countries with meager manufacturing capabilities to dramatically increase the power, range, and lethality of older systems. According to some, these systems are of a sophistication that can radically change "the correlation of forces among nations used to depending on the generations of technology available on the fringes of the global arms bazaar."[97]

The concern is that the capabilities of these less glamorous systems will be ignored by adherents of arms control. Geoffrey Kemp, for example, points out that recent developments in long-range artillery rockets are beginning to erase the operational distinction between short-range ballistic missiles and unguided free-fall rockets.[98] In regions where distances are short and enemies close by, such as the Middle East, these weapons can serve as efficient delivery systems for chemical weapons.[99]

It has also been argued that

> any relatively modern strike aircraft or combat aircraft in regional [Middle East] service can carry in one sortie roughly four times more load than a single Soviet Scud ballistic missile. . . . It can be seen, then, that aircraft are by far the more significant and lethal platforms for mass destruction attacks.[100]

In some parts of the world, such as the Middle East, the conventional has become nonconventional, and arms-control regimes will have to take that into consideration.

Definitional and Regulatory Discrepancies. These ambiguities have complicated the task of control over the arms trade. Compounding the problem is the lack of accord over what should be controlled. There is no internationally agreed upon definition of an "arms transfer," and so export regulations vary widely from state to state. Some define "arms" narrowly to include lethal equipment only; others incorporate support equipment; fewer embrace defense production facilities, technical assistance, or training; and still fewer consider dual-use components in this category.[101] Disagreements arise even over the definition of weapon types. The Chinese, for instance, consider their M-11 missile, with a reported range of about 180 miles, as a short-range missile, although the United States considers it a medium-range missile covered by the MTCR agreement.[102] These definitional asymmetries have been a source of some acrimony, fueling the still unresolved dispute as to what should and should not be regulated.

Ambiguous and Conflicting Arms-Control Goals. Perhaps most intractable, however, are the ambiguous and conflicting goals of the arms-control proposals themselves, past and present. None directly addresses the questions: Who are arms controls designed to protect? Arms control for whose benefit? The classic arms-control goals—to reduce the probability of war or its destructiveness should war occur—are too vague to be useful policy guidelines and are open to wide interpretation. To be effective, policymakers must be clear about their priorities and focus the arms-control effort accordingly. They must decide whether the intent of arms-control accords is to safeguard third world countries from other aggressive third world countries, to shield the industrialized world from third world threats, or to protect industrialized countries from each other. Clearly goals determine the type of arms-control measures to be adopted. Weapons that are destabilizing in one regional context may not be in another. It is relatively easy to give lip service to the general concept of arms control—and apparently many states cynically do so—but unless the real purpose of arms control is articulated and agreed upon, it cannot be translated into implementable policy.

A Balance Sheet: Prospects for the Future

In view of these constraints, expectations for future arms-control measures must remain modest. As a practical matter, arms-control regimes do not augur the complete cessation of arms transfers. As in other foreign policy areas, an equilibrium will have to be sought between the self-defense requirements of recipients, the economic exigencies of the suppliers, and the desire of the public and politicians to restrict transfers that threaten to destabilize regional balances. The best to be hoped for are regional or global agreements to limit the export of specific types of weapons on a case-by-case basis and general accords to control the flow of arms to belligerents.

Ultimately, however, it will be U.S. interests, influence, and resolve that will determine the character and effectiveness of international arms-control measures, not the contents of multilateral agreements. In practice, restrictions on arms exports have been part of the arms transfer policies of the United States and other countries for some time. In yesterday's bipolar world, however, there were many incentives to cheat and much leeway to do so. But in the 1990s, U.S. leverage has grown and the leeway to cheat may have diminished. The end of the Cold War has catapulted the United States to a position of primacy. If the Clinton administration perceives arms control to be in the U.S. national interest, its policy preferences on this issue will carry great weight globally, and a more effective international arms-control regime may be possible. Success will depend upon the political and economic collateral the United States is willing to expend on its behalf.

Intelligence assets to verify supplier and recipient compliance will be critical. Monitoring the shipment of equipment through technical means—satellite photographs, message intercepts, and so on—is relatively straightforward and unambiguous. Tracking the development and production of weapons in regions of actual or potential conflict will be more difficult. The failure to gauge the magnitude of Iraq's nuclear, chemical, and conventional program, however, underscores this need.

More demanding still will be the requirement for broader, creative analysis to assess not only what is being produced and delivered, but how it will be used and what its strategic significance is over the long term. Grasping interrelationships among the diverse items being transferred by different sources to create a coherent picture of intention will not be easy and will require a major commitment of intelligence-gathering and analytical resources. This kind of surveillance will be necessary in most countries, but particularly in authoritarian states, where the government can compel civilian companies or individuals to provide services or dual-use technologies to the military sector.

Furthermore, if the United States, as the major producer of leading-edge technologies, hopes to contain the proliferation of advanced weaponry, it will have to keep better account of its own exported components and the use to which they are put by other countries. Third party transfer restrictions can work only if the United States has good knowledge of which significant components have been exported, the foreign weapon systems into which they have been integrated, and whether the buyer is exporting those weapons to third parties. This, too, is a task that requires good intelligence. In an age of increased international cooperation, joint ventures, mergers, acquisitions, and buy-ins, it will become increasingly difficult to define what legally constitutes a U.S. military product or, for that matter, a U.S. defense company. More attention needs to be given to this gray area.

Equally important and difficult to accomplish will be reaching consensus among suppliers and recipients on what to do when parties violate agreed upon arms limitation principles. Arms-control efforts in the past have been frustrated by lack of effective enforcement. Unless some penalties for violators are instituted and implemented, compliance for even minor conventional arms transfer restraints will be difficult to achieve. Similarly, compensation measures to mitigate the economic costs of acquiescence to arms control may have to be established in some cases.

Realpolitik and Arms Control: An Optimistic Conclusion

Based on the new global configuration of power, there is cause for guarded optimism if we do not expect too much. Given the military technological revolution, a world economic recession, and the changing political order, an international climate is evolving that may foster restraint on arms transfers among suppliers and recipients and encourage states to perceive some form of arms control as in their own national interest. We have arrived at a unique moment in history, when the configuration of political and economic forces makes possible reduced military transfers.

The United States is positioned to make a difference. The intractable problem, of course, is that arms controls, like arms transfers, are foreign policy instruments that are subject to conflicting political forces. Other perceived security interests conflict at times with the U.S. commitment to restrain arms transfers, producing an element of policy schizophrenia that confounds friend and foe alike. It will take time and patience on everyone's part, but the balance appears to be shifting in favor of further regulation of the conventional arms trade.

This article is a revised and expanded version of a paper delivered at the Conference on the Proliferation of Non-Conventional Weaponry in the Middle

East held at King's College, London, November 21–22, 1991. The views expressed in this paper are those of the author alone and not those of any institution with which she is affiliated.

Notes

1. The five major exporters accounted for 83 percent of the arms deliveries to the Middle East between 1988 and 1991. Richard F. Grimmett, "Conventional Arms Transfers to the Third World, 1984–1991," *CRS Report to Congress* (Congressional Research Service, Library of Congress, Washington, D.C., July 20, 1992).

2. The Bush administration articulated several foreign policy goals that entailed arms transfer restraint. In addition to limiting the level of armament in the Middle East, they include preventing the proliferation of nuclear, chemical, and biological weapons, and controls on the transfer of high technology. President Bill Clinton in his campaign speeches supported the idea of containing weapons proliferation, particularly nuclear weapons. "Statements on Foreign Policy from the Presidential Campaign, December 12, 1991–November 4, 1992," *Foreign Policy Bulletin*, November–December 1992.

3. In 1992, for example, embarrassed by disclosures that German companies had helped Iraq and Libya build chemical plants and had sent equipment to Iraq that could be used to build nuclear weapons, the German *Bundestag* created a new government agency to monitor exports. It also approved bills that will allow customs police to tap telephones and intercept mail to stop illegal shipments of arms. "Germany Acts to Curb Arms Exports," *New York Times*, January 24, 1992, p. A–3; "Germany to Allow Taps in Arms-Related Exports," *Washington Post*, January 24, 1992, p. A–18.

4. Aaron Karp, "A Farewell to the Arms Trade" (Unpublished paper, Stockholm, May 8, 1991), p. 24.

5. Some 41 countries collectively have 393 submarines and 19 countries are currently building them or have recently done so. Taiwan, South Korea, and possibly Chile and Canada are preparing to build submarines in the future. For a detailed analysis of the proliferation of submarine technology see Statement of Rear Admiral Thomas A. Brooks, USN, Director of Na-

val Intelligence before the Seapower, Strategic, and Critical Materials Subcommittee of the House Armed Services Committee on Intelligence Issues, March 7, 1991, pp. 59–64 (hereafter referred to as Brooks statement).

6. The fear is this technology will allow countries to modify their equipment to reduce signatures and vulnerability to attack. Brooks statement, p. 69.

7. During the 1990s, selected countries have embarked upon indigenous space-based reconnaissance development. The concern is that these countries will be able to achieve electro-optical imagery resolutions of less than one meter. France, India, Japan, the PRC, and the United States have imagery satellites. Countries that could have imagery satellites by 2000 include Canada, Germany, Israel, Italy, Pakistan, South Africa, South Korea, Spain, and Taiwan. Argentina and Brazil could have them sometime after 2000. Apart from the European Space Agency and the superpowers, four countries (India, Israel, Japan, and the PRC) now have the capability to launch satellites. Pakistan, South Africa, Taiwan, and others are developing the capability. Brooks statement, pp. 70–71.

8. "New Curbs on Exports Are Sought," *New York Times*, September 11, 1991, pp. D–1, D–28.

9. Many of these EW systems are already being exported. Problems in integrating various subsystems and components are delaying effective operational use of EW systems in most countries. As computers continue to be exported, however, these EW systems will become more user friendly. Brooks statement, p. 75.

10. "U.S. and Soviets to End Arms Sales to Afghan Rivals," *New York Times*, September 14, 1991, pp. A–1, A–4.

11. "As Ethnic Wars Multiply, U.S. Struggles to Meet the Challenge," *New York Times*, February 7, 1993, pp. A–1, A–12.

12. In the "Joint Statement on Non-Proliferation" signed in 1990 with the United States, the Soviet Union accepted the provisions of the Missile Technology Control Regime (MTCR) designed to halt the proliferation of missile technology. Eduard Shevardnadze, then foreign minister, suggested in a letter to the UN secretary general on April 15, 1990, that international

sales and supplies of conventional weapons should be limited as "a means of building a new model of security." *Izvestia*, August 15, 1990, cited in *SIPRI Yearbook 1991* (Stockholm, 1991), p. 220. Sergei Grigoryev, deputy to President Mikhail Gorbachev's chief spokesman, stated that developed nations should agree to limit arms sales to "dangerous" countries. (Summarized from wire copy, *Current News*, February 19, 1991.) In 1991 the Soviet Union welcomed a U.S. proposal to ban chemical weapons. (Summarized from wire copy, *Current News*, May 24, 1991.) President Boris Yeltsin, in a statement on January 27, 1992, to the UN secretary general declared that "Russia considers itself the successor to the USSR with regard to the responsibility for carrying out international obligations." He reaffirmed Russia's obligations under the treaty on the non-proliferation of nuclear weapons, its support for the arms trade guidelines approved in London in October 1991, for greater transparency in the military sphere, and for a global convention on the prohibition of chemical and biological weapons. United Nations, General Assembly, Security Council, A/47/77; S/23486, January 28, 1992.

13. *Rossiiski Vesti*, no. 2 (1992), p. 3; *Nezavisimaya Gazeta*, February 19, 1992; *Isvestiya*, June 12, 1992; all cited by Julian Cooper, "The Former Soviet Union and Conventional Arms Sales," draft chapter in Andrew J. Pierre, ed., *Cascade of Arms: Controlling Conventional Weapons Proliferation in the 1990s* (forthcoming).

14. "Russia to Halt Sub Production," *Defense News*, November 23–29, 1992, pp. 1, 21.

15. Cooper, "Former Soviet Union," p. 25.

16. "U.S. Declares Itself the Sole Superpower," *Washington Times*, May 8, 1991, p. 1.

17. See, for example, Charles Krauthammer, "The Unipolar Moment," *Foreign Affairs* 70, no. 1, *America and the World 1990/91* (1991), pp. 23–33; Lawrence Freedman, "The Gulf War and the New World Order," *Survival* 23 (May/June 1991), pp. 195–209.

18. Catherine McArdle Kelleher, "The Changing Currency of Power: Paper I," in "America's Role in a Changing World, Part

343

Stephanie G. Neuman

I," *Adelphi Papers* 256 (London: Brassey's for IISS, Winter 1990/91), pp. 28–29.

19. An interesting example is Eastern Europe. Reportedly U.S. concern over Russian arms sales prompted warnings to Moscow with suggestions that Western aid could be threatened (Cooper, "Former Soviet Union," p. 13). Similarly, when Poland, Czechoslovakia, and other East European states tried to earn hard currency by selling arms to countries considered inappropriate by the United States, they were stopped from doing so by strong U.S. pressure—in the case of Poland, three times. The Polish agreements were with Iran, Syria, and Myanmar. In addition, Poland honored the sanctions by the "U.S.-led UN," during the Persian Gulf War and thereby lost several hundreds of millions of dollars owed to it by Iraq. Andrzeh Karakoszka, "Models for Explaining the Global Spread of Weapons," in *The Global Diffusion of Military Technology* (Proceedings of a workshop held at the University of Wisconsin-Madison, December 6–8, 1991, sponsored by the Center for International Cooperation and Security Studies, University of Wisconsin-Madison), p. 14.

20. François Heisbourg found that the price indexes of arms, aerospace, and shipbuilding in comparison to other categories of manufactured goods were 26 to 90 percentage points higher. Heisbourg, "Public Policy and the Creation of a European Arms Market," in Pauline Creasey and Simon May, eds., *European Armaments Market and Procurement Cooperation*, pp. 60–88 (London: Macmillan, 1988), p. 61.

21. "Israel Battling Arms Sales to Foes," *Los Angeles Times*, January 2, 1992, p. 10.

22. U.S Arms Control and Disarmament Agency (ACDA), *World Military Expenditures and Arms Transfers, 1990* (Washington, D.C., 1990) (hereafter cited as WMEAT, 1990).

23. Keith Krause, "Trends in the Production and Trade of Conventional Weapons" (Paper prepared for the conference, "The Supply-Side Control of Weapons Proliferation," Canadian Institute for International Peace and Security, Ottawa, June 1991), pp. 6–7.

24. Edward J. Laurance, "A Model and Some Preliminary Indications" (Paper prepared for the annual meeting of the International

Studies Association, Vancouver, March 1991), p. 8.

25. Central Intelligence Agency world arms deliveries figures in billions of 1992 dollars cited in David Silverberg, "Amid Sales Flurry, Nations Pursue Arms Curbs," *Defense News*, October 5–11, 1992, p. 4.

26. Interview with Gerard Renon, "One on One," *Defense News*, May 27–April 2, 1991, p. 38.

27. WMEAT, 1990; U.S. Department of Defense Security Assistance (DSAA), *Foreign Military Sales, Foreign Military Construction, Sales, and Military Assistance Facts* (Washington, D.C.: Data Management Division, Comptroller, DSAA, September 30, 1990).

28. France imported from the United States $966 million between 1985 and 1989 or about 4 percent of Europe's total. DSAA, *Foreign Military Sales.*

29. Renon, "One on One."

30. "Europe Searches for Own Voice in Future International Conflicts," *Aviation Week and Space Technology*, December 24, 1990, pp. 37, 40. The European Cooperation for the Long Term in Defence (Euclid) program was organized on June 28, 1989. There is, apparently, no central budget. National governments finance the projects in which they are involved. Euclid members are Belgium, Germany, the Netherlands, Spain, Denmark, Greece, Norway, Turkey, France, Italy, Portugal, and the United Kingdom. The program operates under the jurisdiction of the Independent European Program Group (IEPG), which was founded in 1976 to facilitate closer European armament cooperation and to improve European competitiveness with the United States.

31. George Leopold, "US Faces Tough Competition in Critical Technologies," *Defense News*, July 16–22, 1990, p. 6.

32. Peter Bates, "Defence Technology in Western Europe," in Jane David Drown, Clifford Drown, and Kelly Campbell, eds., *A Single European Arms Industry? European Defence Industries in the 1990s* (London: Brassey's, 1990), p. 105.

33. For a discussion of the rising relative share of research and development in major weapons programs and the implications for Europe see Heisbourg, "Public Policy," pp. 62–66.

34. "Europe Searches for Own Voice in Future International Conflicts," pp. 37, 40.

35. Heisbourg, "Public Policy," p. 60. The percentage may be even lower for the United Kingdom. *Jane's* reports that 90 percent of the equipment the U.K. Ministry of Defense buys comes from the United Kingdom. *Jane's Defence Weekly,* December 7, 1991, p. 1081.

36. The U.S. economy and military market are the largest in the world. The U.S. GNP ($5.2 trillion) is almost twice that of its nearest competitor, Japan (WMEAT, 1990). In the military sector, even after budget cutting, the U.S. procurement allocation of $64.3 billion for fiscal year 1992 (down by 4 percent from 1991) is still the largest in the world. Department of Defense Appropriations Act, 1992, Public Law 102–172, November 26, 1991; Department of Defense Appropriations Act, 1991, Public Law 101–511, November 5, 1990.

37. Mark Kramer argues that Europe was less cooperative in the past, complicating past U.S. efforts in the region by providing alternate sources of arms, aid, and political support. He cites Iraq's missile and nuclear programs as only one example. Kramer, "Army Won't Be a Loose Cannon," *Los Angeles Times,* December 4, 1991, p. B–5.

38. Together, the Russian Republic and the Ukrainian Republic account for 90 percent of the FSU's end-product military industrial sector. Belarus and Kazakhstan are the only other successor states with significant military production capability. The defense industries of the latter three former Soviet republics, however, are heavily dependent on materials, systems, and components from Russia. "Industry Nears Independence," *Jane's Defence Weekly,* November 23, 1991, p. 995; "Drastic Cuts in Weapons Orders Under Way in Soviet Union," *Aviation Week and Space Technology,* January 27, 1992, p. 34; Cooper, "Former Soviet Union," pp. 10, 46–50.

39. Interview with Uri Ryzhov, chairman, Supreme Soviet Science Committee, in "One on One," *Defense News,* July 22–28, 1991, p. 62.

40. "Drastic Cuts in Weapons Orders Under Way"; "Wire News Highlights," *Current News,* January 24, 1992, p. 16; "Russia to Cut Arms Orders by 85 pc This Year," *Daily Telegraph,* January 16, 1992, p. 8.

41. "Arms Factory Can Make Bricks, But, Russia Asks, Is That Smart?" *New York Times,* February 24, 1992, pp. A–1, A–10.

42. "Drastic Cuts in Weapons Orders Under Way."

43. Steven Zaloga, "Russian Reports," *Armed Forces Journal International,* September 1992, p. 27.

44. Central Intelligence Agency world arms deliveries figures in billions of 1992 dollars cited in Silverberg, "Amid Sales Flurry, Nations Pursue Arms Curbs," p. 4.

45. Statement by Vladimir Gladyshev, vice president of the League of Russian Defence Enterprises, carried in "Russian Sales Fall by $9.8 bn," *Jane's Defence Weekly,* July 25, 1992, p. 20.

46. Brooks statement, p. 38.

47. Turkey, for example, has purchased $75 million worth of Russian equipment, but it will pay $60 million of the cost by taking over Russian debt owed to the Turkish export-import bank. Russia will, apparently, realize only $15 million in hard currency from the sale. "Turkey Buys Russian Arms," *DPA* wire service, November 9, 1992. The PRC, too, has negotiated part barter terms for its arms procurements from Russia.

48. Soviet deliveries to India, for example, declined in 1990 in comparison to previous years because of Indian budgetary constraints, stricter Soviet pricing policies, and contract completions. The hard currency policy is likely to further diminish future military deliveries to India because, in the past, India has paid in rupees. By 1992, Russian deliveries to India had slowed greatly, causing shortages in spare parts and ammunition. *Milavnews,* NL–354, April 1991; "Cash is Central Issue as India Prods Russia on Arms," *Defense News,* September 14–20, 1992, p. 46. Other third world countries are canceling contracts. Zimbabwe, for example, voided a $400 million order for MiG–29s, reportedly ordered as long ago as 1986, on the grounds that the aircraft were no longer needed because regional tension had diminished. "MiG Order Canceled," *Jane's Defence Weekly,* August 29, 1992, p. 12. For further discussion of third world–FSU arms trans-

fer relations, see Susan Kaufman Purcell, "The US and Regional Conflicts: Paper I," in "America's Role in a Changing World, Part I," *Adelphi Papers* 256 (London: Brassey's for IISS, Winter 1990/91), p. 75. East European countries, too, have expressed their desire to reduce arms purchases from the FSU. Regarding the unsuccessful attempt of Czechoslovakia and the former German Democratic Republic to cancel aircraft deliveries from the former Soviet Union, see *SIPRI Yearbook, 1991*, p. 213.

49. *SIPRI Yearbook, 1992* (Stockholm, 1992), p. 272.

50. "New Nation, Imperiled Economy," *New York Times*, February 12, 1993, p. D–1.

51. *SIPRI Yearbook, 1992*, p. 291.

52. WMEAT, 1990.

53. *Ibid.* According to the *SIPRI Yearbook, 1991*, Brazil's exports continued to drop in 1990, recording a 95 percent decline between 1987 and 1990 (p. 198).

54. Ron Matthews, "The Neutrals as Gunrunners," *Orbis* 35 (Winter 1991), p. 45.

55. Two of Brazil's three major arms producing industries faced bankruptcy in 1992. Testimony of Rear Admiral Edward D. Sheafer, Director of Naval Intelligence, to the Seapower, Strategic, and Critical Materials Subcommittee of the House Armed Services Committee, February 5, 1992, excerpted in *Arms Sales Monitor*, nos. 11–12 (January–February 1992), p. 5.

56. Central Intelligence Agency world arms deliveries figures in billions of 1992 dollars cited in Silverberg, "Amid Sales Flurry, Nations Pursue Arms Curbs," p. 4.

57. Elbit Computers Ltd. has purchased General Dynamics Corporation's Electronics Manufacturing Center in Forth Worth, Texas, in partnership with another U.S. company. The facility builds electronic equipment for the F–16 fighter. Elbit's president said: "We will continue to manufacture equipment for the F–16 . . . and hope to help [the company] expand its business base into new markets, both in the [United States] and around the world." "Israeli Firms Aggressively Try to Capture U.S. Market," *Defense News*, November 9–15, 1992, pp. 1, 29.

58. The total grant aid request for FY 1993 was $4.2 billion, down $500 million from 1992. About 70 percent of this is slated for Israel ($1.8 billion) and Egypt ($1.3 billion). *Arms Sales Monitor*, nos. 11–12 (January–February 1992), p. 5.

59. "Saudis Seek to Cut Funds for Militants," *New York Times*, March 1, 1992, p. A–8. Saudi Arabia's vast financial reserves of $40–$50 billion before the Gulf crisis reportedly were drained by the Gulf war, which cost Saudi Arabia alone $65 billion.

60. "Syrian Accuses the U.S. of Trying to Strip Arabs of Military Power," *New York Times*, March 13, 1992, p. A–10.

61. *Near East Report* 26 (March 9, 1992), p. 43.

62. "The Runaway Army is Back, but Standing at Ease," *New York Times*, January 14, 1992, p. A–4.

63. *Near East Report* 26 (March 9, 1992), p. 43. See also, *Arms Sales Monitor*, nos. 11–12 (January–February 1992), p. 2.

64. The equipment included oscilloscopes, computers, aircraft parts, radar, and navigational items. "Iran Builds Its Strength," *Jane's Defence Weekly*, February 1, 1992, p. 158.

65. "U.S. Expected to Pressure India on Nuclear Issue," *New York Times*, March 10, 1992, p. A–8.

66. Jasjit Singh, "Control of the Arms Trade as a Contribution to Conflict Prevention," in *Building Global Security Through Cooperation* (Proceedings of the Thirty-Ninth Pugwash Conference on Science and World Affairs, Cambridge, Mass., July 23–28, 1989), p. 351.

67. "Bosnia is 'Top Priority,'" *Washington Times*, January 28, 1993, p. 1.

68. "Clinton's World Disorder," *Wall Street Journal*, February 12, 1993, p. A–14.

69. *Defense and Economy World Report*, March 2, 1987, p. 5814.

70. Matthews, "Neutrals as Gunrunners."

71. Heisbourg, "Public Policy," p. 66.

72. Jiri Matousek, "Czechoslovakia," in Ian Anthony, ed., *Arms Export Regulations* (Oxford: Oxford University Press, 1991), p. 51.

73. In general the new republics, badly in need of revenues to shore up their economies, have little to export other than

weapons, advanced dual-use technologies, and parts of the space program.

74. Ivan Silayev, "We've Already Won Back the First Half," *Ogonek*, no. 24 (1991), p. 2, and "If There is a Strong Russia There Will Be a Strong Union," *Mezhdunarodnaya Zhizn'*, no. 6 (June 1991), p. 11, cited in Stephen R. Covington and John Lough, "Russia's Post-Revolution Challenge: Reform of the Soviet Superpower Paradigm," *The Washington Quarterly* 15 (Winter 1992), p. 17.

75. The Russians have 1,600 surplus military aircraft and 10,000 surplus tanks to sell. About one-sixth of the former Soviet navy is also for sale. "Get Yer Red Hot Bombers, Tanks, and Missiles," *Business Week*, September 21, 1992, p. 44.

76. Mikhail Malei, adviser on conversion to President Yeltsin, estimated it would cost about $150 billion to convert 70 percent of Russia's military-industrial complex to civilian use. "Russian Arms Official Wants to Continue Sales," *Washington Times*, October 14, 1992, p. 2.; also Cooper, "Former Soviet Union," pp. 14, 37, 41.

77. A second-hand T–72 tank is offered for $50,000 (compared to at least $2 million for a new Western model); a MiG–29 fighter aircraft is tendered for $5–$7 million in contrast to the $16–$20 million F–16C/D U.S. equivalent. An Ilyushin IL–76 TD transport aircraft can be bought for $40 million. (The price of the new McDonnell Douglas C–17 transport is approximately $350 million.) The Russian SA–10 missile is available for $75 million in contrast to the U.S. Patriot, which sells for $150 million. "For Sale: Weapons of the ex-Soviet Armed Forces," *International Defense Review*, August 1992, p. 736; "Get Yer Red Hot Bombers, Tanks, and Missiles," p. 44; "Taiwan Uses MiG, Mirage as Leverage to Buy F–16s," *Defense News*, August 17–23, 1992, p. 3; "Migs Anyone? T–72 Tanks?" *Forbes*, April 27, 1992, p. 18; "McDonnell, Lockheed Wrestle for Airlift Sales," *Defense News*, September 14–20, 1992, pp. 22, 24.

78. BBC, *Summary of World Markets*, SU/1219 B/3, November 2, 1991, cited by Cooper, "Former Soviet Union," p. 11.

79. Julian Cooper, at a workshop sponsored by the World Peace Foundation, estimated that Russia's arms exports in 1991 amounted to no more than 2 percent of total exports ("A World Peace Foundation Study: Conventional Arms Proliferation in the 1990s," Washington, D.C., November 12–13, 1992). Russian estimates for 1992 suggest that arms exports dropped significantly again. Russian foreign economic relations minister Petr Aven told the Congress of People's Deputies that Russian military exports would amount to only $3 billion in 1992 compared to the $7.8 billion in 1991. In his speech to the congress, then Prime Minister Yegor Gaidar identified the major recipients. Russia sold $600 million worth of arms to Iran, $1 billion to the PRC, and $650 million to India. Malaysia is reported to have agreed to make a $600 million purchase, too. Only part of these sales, however, represent hard currency payments. "Russia Relies on Arms to Solve Troubles," *Defense News*, December 7–13, 1992, p. 3; "Malaysia to Purchase 30 MiG–29s from Russia," *Defense News*, December 14–20, 1992, p. 23.

80. "U.S. to Press China To Halt Missile Sales," *Washington Post*, June 11, 1992, p. A–13.

81. "China Said to Sell Parts for Missiles," *New York Times*, January 31, 1992, p. A–1.

82. These export figures, in constant dollars, cover the 1979–1989 period. WMEAT, 1990. See also Laurance, "A Model and Some Preliminary Indications," pp. 30–31.

83. "EC Ministers to Examine Arms Export Restrictions to Gulf Region," *Defense News*, February 25–March 3, 1991.

84. Iraq, for example, exported captured Iranian equipment to Djibouti, Sudan, Mauritania, and Lebanon. Brooks statement, p. 47. Israel, too, is reported to have transferred vintage Soviet equipment captured from the Palestinians to other third world countries. And the end of the Lebanese war released artillery, rocket launchers, machine guns, and ammunition onto the arms market. See Frederick S. Pearson, Michael Brzoska, and Christer Crantz, "The Effects of Arms Transfers on War and Peace Negotiations," *SIPRI Yearbook, 1992*, pp. 399–415, for a description of the leakage of surplus and captured arms into the former Yugoslavia.

85. For a discussion of this problem as it related to the Coordinating Committee on Multilateral Export Controls (CoCom), see William Schneider, Jr., "The Emerging Patterns of Arms Export Controls Affecting Advanced Technology," *Contemporary Southeast Asia* 14 (June 1992), pp. 47–58.

86. Cooper, "Former Soviet Union," p. 40; Pearson, Brzoska, and Crantz, "Effects of Arms Transfers."

87. "Belarus Nuclear Smuggling Feared," *Washington Post*, November 26, 1992, p. A–55.

88. "Cardoen Accused Over Sales to Iraq," *Jane's Defence Weekly*, April 18, 1992, p. 638.

89. A Japanese company and four former officials were found guilty of illegally exporting missile parts to Iran. *Financial Times*, April 24, 1992, p. 4.

90. Major West European companies (in Austria, Finland, Spain, Sweden, and Switzerland), for example, evaded restrictions on arms exports by shipping arms to third world countries through the former East Germany during the 1980s. Weapons sold included hand grenades, ammunition, detonators, anti-tank weapons, and explosives. Former West German companies have been found guilty of similar activities, see n. 3, above. "Arms Dealers Evade Restrictions," *UPI*, January 16, 1992.

91. A U.S. rocket scientist was found guilty of selling classified Strategic Defense Initiative software to Japanese and South African concerns. In another case, U.S. companies were fined for illegally selling equipment to Libya. "Scientist Sells SDI Software," *Reuters*, April 21, 1992; "U.S. Imposes Fines for Libyan Tanks," *Financial Times*, March 9, 1992, p. 4.

92. On this point see Tom Clancy and Russell Seitz, "Five Minutes Past Midnight and Welcome to the Age of Proliferation," *National Interest* 26 (Winter 1991/92), pp. 8–10. The authors point out that "digitally controlled machine tools with optical sensors and air bearings" have revolutionized the quality of precision machining and substantially lowered the required proficiency and skill of their operators (p. 10).

93. According to Jacques Gaillard, the percentage of the world's scientists and engineers residing in developing countries rose from 7.6 percent to 10.2 percent between 1970 and 1980 and by 1990 exceeded 13 percent. Gaillard, *Scientists in the Third World* (Lexington: University Press of Kentucky, 1991), cited in Clancy and Seitz, "Five Minutes Past Midnight," p. 4.

94. Reportedly the PRC has hired 500 Russian weapon specialists to upgrade its military industries. As many as 2,000 Russian specialists have been employed to work in the fields of electronics, material science, and aircraft engineering. Many are working in the city of Xian, Shanxi province, where several aerospace companies are located. "China Hires Weapon Experts," *Defense News*, August 17–23, 1992, p. 2. Former Soviet nuclear scientists are also being employed by many third world countries, including 50 scientists working in Iraq. *Welt am Sonntag*, cited in an AP dispatch, September 28, 1992.

95. Paul W. Hoag, "Hi-Tech Armaments, Space Militarisation and the Third World," in Colin Creighton and Martin Shaw, eds., *The Sociology of War and Peace* (London: Macmillan Press, 1987), p. 79; Thomas J. Welch, "Technology Change and Security," *The Washington Quarterly* 13 (Spring 1990), pp. 114–115.

96. Quoted in Hoag, "Hi-Tech Armaments, Space Militarisation and the Third World," p. 79.

97. Clancy and Seitz, "Five Minutes Past Midnight," p. 8.

98. Geoffrey Kemp, *The Control of the Middle East Arms Race* (Washington, D.C.: Carnegie Endowment for International Peace, 1991), p. 197. Long-range artillery rockets in production or under development are: Egypt's Sakr 80, 80-km range; Iran's Oghab, 40-km range; and Israel's MAR–350, 90-km range.

99. The Iraqi 131-foot, long-range artillery piece—the so-called supergun—is a case in point. This enormous gun, with a 1,000 mm caliber gun tube that was shipped as oil piping, once operational, would have been able to fire conventional and unconventional munitions at ranges of approximately 1,600 km. As Kemp points out, the barrier between long-range artillery and

short-range tactical missiles is rapidly eroding. *Ibid.*

100. Uzi Rubin, "How Much Does Missile Proliferation Matter?" *Orbis* 35 (Winter 1991), p. 35.

101. For a country-by-country analysis of arms export regulations, see Anthony, *Arms Export Regulations*.

102. "China Said to Sell Parts for Missile," *New York Times*, January 31, 1992, p. A–1.

The UN Register of Conventional Arms: Rationales and Prospects for Compliance and Effectiveness

Edward J. Laurance

THE IRAQI INVASION of Kuwait and the allied response created an unprecedented international consensus that the accumulation of advanced weapon systems can be a major factor in the outbreak, conduct, and termination of armed conflict. It was a clear case of such accumulations being destabilizing in themselves and leading to negative consequences even for the major powers. Combined with the end of the Cold War and the decline of the military threat from the Soviet Union, the result has been a well-documented increase in the attention that the world now pays to the proliferation of destabilizing and dangerous accumulations of weapon systems as a major threat to international stability.

The response by the international community to this new threat of proliferation has varied according to the nature of the weapon systems. In the case of weapons of mass destruction,

the response has been a legalistic one based on a series of United Nations (UN) resolutions. The UN inspectors in Iraq are now a familiar sight as they search for and destroy nuclear and chemical weapons, their missile delivery systems, and the capability that Iraq had assembled for indigenous manufacture of such systems.

The question of what to do about destabilizing accumulations of conventional weapons, such as tanks, aircraft, and missiles not seen as directly associated with weapons of mass destruction, was more problematic. This trade is essentially a legal and legitimate means by which sovereign states provide for their national security. Debates on controlling the international arms trade have frequently surfaced since 1945 but have not led to anything approaching a consensus. In the wake of the Persian Gulf War once again there are calls for controlling the arms trade. Many suppliers tightened up their national export control systems. There were policy proposals from many quarters to develop multilateral and international control mechanisms designed to prevent a rerun of the Iraqi situation. The five permanent members of the UN Security Council began meeting in July 1991 to

Edward J. Laurance is professor of international policy studies and associate director of the Program for Nonproliferation Studies at the Monterey Institute for International Studies. His latest book is *The International Arms Trade* (Lexington, Mass.: Lexington Books, 1992).

develop some multilateral restraints on destabilizing arms transfers.

But these traditional arms trade control approaches soon fell victim to the realities that have always existed. Rarely can states agree prior to a transfer that it will indeed be destabilizing. Furthermore, with the end of the Cold War producing rapidly declining orders for domestic defense production, the pressure from the defense industries was clearly against any movement toward national or international arms export controls.

It was in this context that the United Nations began to seriously consider the idea of transparency as an alternative approach—the opening up of information on the arms trade so as to allow the affected states to dampen and eliminate the negative consequences that ensue. Much of the impetus for the idea came from the degree of transparency, albeit unintended, surrounding the Iraqi case, such as the unwanted publicity that Germany received as a result of transfers to Libya and Iraq. "Lists" of firms and the items exported that led to undesirable military capability in these two states provided thorough and public evidence regarding how a developing state can acquire the ability to produce ballistic missiles with warheads of mass destruction. In the spring of 1991, in the aftermath of the Persian Gulf War, country after country began to publish details of its arms exports, put forth proposals for transparency, and indicate support for the idea of an international arms trade register. The French, Germans, Bulgarians, Czechs, and Soviets all published heretofore unreleasable data on arms exports. In the summer of 1991 the European Community and Japan put forward formal proposals for an arms trade register as a first step in dealing

with this aspect of the proliferation problem. In December 1991 the UN General Assembly, by a vote of 150–0 (Iraq and Cuba abstained, Syria and the People's Republic of China [PRC] did not vote), approved the Transparency in Armaments resolution that established the Register of Conventional Arms, a process by which member states would incrementally make transparent the levels and types of conventional armaments exported, imported, and produced, eventually including weapons of mass destruction.

The UN has proceeded to implement the several provisions of the register called for in the resolution. The secretary general formally created the register on January 1, 1992, and the panel of governmental experts the resolution required met three times from January to July 1992, producing a consensus report on procedures for the operation of the register that was adopted by a consensus vote in the General Assembly on December 15, 1992.

Michael Moodie has posed three alternative futures for the register.[1] It could result in a new approach in coming to grips with the security problems of the post–cold war era. Or it might produce a sharpening of North–South cleavages. Or it might prove to be just another sterile exercise in disarmament and arms control. Although the first data on arms exports and imports for the year 1992 are not due to be submitted until April 30, 1993, the picture as to which states are likely to comply and why is already much clearer than it was upon passage of the original resolution in December 1991. Although the long-term prospect remains unclear, based on the evolution of the process to date it appears that the first and most optimistic of the three scenarios is now unfolding.

Basic Elements of the Register

Briefly reviewed, the basic elements of the register were contained in the original resolution and adjusted by the panel of experts. Member states of the UN are requested to submit data by April 30 each year on the number of items annually exported or imported in the previous year, by country, for seven major types of armaments: battle tanks, armored combat vehicles, large caliber artillery, combat aircraft, attack helicopters, warships with a displacement of 750 tons or above (and any size ship with missiles or torpedoes with a range of 25 kilometers or more), and missiles and their launchers with a range of at least 25 kilometers. (The missile category does not include ground-to-air missiles.) All categories include a description of what is covered, including types of accompanying armaments, ranges, and tonnage. The first five categories closely parallel the descriptions developed for the identical categories in the Conventional Forces in Europe (CFE) agreement. The register also requests states to submit background information on their military holdings, procurement through national production, and relevant policies.

The Work of the Panel

The charge of the 17-nation panel of experts was to make "adjustments to the annex to the present resolution necessary for the effective operation of the Register." It completed its work on July 17, 1992, submitting a consensus report to the secretary general.[2] The membership of the panel offers some relevant indicators of potential compliance in itself. It included an expert of ambassadorial rank from the Netherlands and from Japan, the same two men who had been instrumental in shaping the resolution so as to garner support from 150 countries. It also included the five permanent members of the UN Security Council (the top five arms suppliers), plus Egypt, India, Brazil, Argentina, Mexico, Malaysia, Canada, Italy, Czechoslovakia, and Ghana. Because it was a consensus report, support (or at least not vigorous opposition) was expected from these 17 countries in the steps that followed.

Moodie accurately depicts the opposition to the UN First Committee's version of the original resolution by countries such as Egypt, Pakistan, Brazil, and Argentina. This may, as he indicates, predict an upcoming North–South split in which developing countries will fail to submit data. It is just as likely, however, that having had their concerns incorporated into the resolution in the form of agenda items for an already approved 1994 panel, these states will submit data for the register during the first two years. They may feel the risk is worth it to see how serious the world is about dealing with their concerns, such as weapons of mass destruction and military technology. In addition, developing states may have drawn a lesson from the Iraqi case, namely, that there are limits to what the industrialized world will accept in the way of weapons accumulation, especially when such accumulations threaten major power interests. The work of the panel seemed to support this latter view because the developing states on the panel overwhelmingly supported maximum transparency.

It should not be forgotten that the panel produced a consensus report. Events since the 150–0 vote—support for the register in the declaration of January 31, 1992, by the first-ever Security Council summit, formal support for the register from states of the Conference on Security and Cooperation in Europe (CSCE) and the Organization of American States (OAS), and the enthusiastic support of the secretary general—have generated significant momentum.

It was also clear that the panel wanted no part of a hollow exercise. The study submitted on arms transfers by an expert group in September 1991[3] emphasized previous failures such as the arms trade data published in the *Statistical Yearbook of the League of Nations* from 1925 to 1938 and the practically defunct military expenditure reporting system in the UN. This seriousness was evident in the final reporting form, which contains a column designated "description of item" (i.e., designation, type, or model of equipment reported). This was a contentious issue because it went beyond the mere "number of items" language in the original resolution. The panel report has a caveat (paragraph 19), which allows that "such information might be affected by security and other relevant concerns" and "should be filled in at Member State's discretion." But in essence the panel produced a report and with it a reporting form that allows and in fact encourages states to submit data in the most transparent mode possible. Without such a form (i.e., without an explicit opportunity to provide information on equipment beyond the basic categories), the potential for transparency would have been diminished significantly. This flexibility does, however, set up a situation in which state reporting may be quite uneven in its level of transparency. Will the states that choose not to provide descriptions of the equipment look bad? This factor may both encourage and discourage states to be more open.

Resolution Adopting the Panel's Report

Once the panel had produced a consensus report, the prospects for adoption were almost certain. The chairman of the panel, Ambassador Hendrik Wagenmakers of the Netherlands, drafted both a summary of the report for presentation to the First Committee and a resolution, which he sent to all 17 panel members for comment. His actual presentation of the report to the First Committee and its adoption on October 13 thereby continued to reflect a consensus that ensured approval without opposition. As the draft General Assembly resolution that would adopt the report and finalize procedures for the operation of the register was gathering cosponsors, the secretary general delivered a major speech to the First Committee on disarmament. In that speech and in the report issued on the same day he emphasized that transparency in armaments and the register were assuming "even greater importance" than when the issue was debated in 1991. On December 15, the General Assembly adopted Resolution A/C.1/47/L.18 by consensus, endorsing the panel's report, calling upon all member states to provide the requested data and information, and declaring its determination to ensure the effective operation of the register.

Rationales and Prospects for Compliance

Up to this point it can be seen that significant momentum has been building in the direction of compliance. One editorial called the register idea "a noble one" and urged the Clinton administration to ensure that it was accurate, complete, and fair. "The creation of an arms registry is an important first step in laying the building blocks for future restraint of international arms trade."[4]

Yet some countries, especially the United States, appear skeptical and reluctant. Joseph Smaldone, chief of the Weapons and Technology Control Division of the U.S. Arms Control and Disarmament Agency (ACDA), expressed concern at a workshop on transparency held on October 28, 1992, that the United States would be providing most of the data and that "international cooperation on the register has been grudging and slow."[5] No one can know at this point who will report and at what level of transparency. Yet enough is known of the history behind the register to make a general assessment of the rationales for compliance.

The first reason why many states will submit data is basic inertia. As mentioned above, every step in the process has been carefully crafted so that the concerns of the maximum number of states are taken into account. Further steps are being planned, such as regional workshops prior to the submission date of April 30, 1993, to assist those states that desire to submit data. And this momentum has been rooted in realism and universality: all the states have refused to develop yet another sterile exercise so typical of the UN during the Cold War. A price has been paid for such support, namely a process that is very incremental. The first step, reporting arms transfers in seven categories of conventional weapons, is a small one. Yet the momentum is there. Having said yes at several stages in the process of developing the register, it is highly likely that a significant number of states will submit the requested data in its first year.

But there are more substantive rationales for compliance. Some states

in Europe (e.g., Italy) have domestic laws and policies that call for maximum transparency of arms data. These states will go far beyond the minimum transparency required, perhaps even including the financial arrangements of arms deals. In effect, actual submissions will begin to empirically define the concept of transparency. Much of the information to be reported has already been made public, if not by governments then by outside groups such as the International Institute for Strategic Studies and the Stockholm International Peace Research Institute. On the other hand, there are many states that not only do not practice such transparency at home but have laws that forbid such disclosure. This could be a barrier to reporting. Or, faced with the momentum and other advantages of international transparency, states may wish to change their domestic environment. The result would be a further increase in international transparency, beyond that achieved by the register. States that have long hoped for transparency on the part of their neighbors may go along with the register just to see if such a result may be forthcoming.

It should also be noted that reporting arms exports and imports, particularly for the first two years, presents minimal security risks for most states. Most of the data are public, and for the very sensitive transfers varying levels of transparency can be applied. The East–West dimension has disappeared and the international system is at a point where few conflicts are likely to be directly and immediately affected in a major way by arms transfers in the categories covered by the register. The next few years appear to provide a window of opportunity for such an experiment. It should also be remembered that for many states the register is not the first step forward toward controlling the arms trade but rather a step back from a degree of control envisioned by many. In the wake of the Iraqi invasion of Kuwait, the calls for arms trade control were many. States tightened up their export control systems, U.S. president George Bush called for control of arms exports to the Middle East, and the five largest arms exporting states began to discuss such control. When the rest of the world began to respond positively and indicate that this might be a good idea, the concept of the register began to take concrete shape. Recipients, traditionally worried about a northern conspiracy to deprive them of their right to national security, found the idea of a register a safer response to the Iraq situation. Suppliers, suddenly besieged by protests from their arms industries at the thought of arms export controls, also saw some comfort in the idea of the register as a first step. The above logic would seem to be that, rather than risk a failed register that might see more extreme control proposals resurface, many states will comply with this first incremental step.

Throughout the development of the register, the question arose as to how to deal with illegal arms transfers. The answer was always the same, that the register was about *legal* arms trade. In a very important way the register legitimizes the arms trade. It is not a *control* mechanism, and although the resolution expresses the hope that through transparency states may achieve security at the "lowest possible level of armaments," reduction of the arms trade is not the register's primary purpose. States submitting data are in effect saying that they do not view their exports and imports as destabilizing. Failure to report may have

the opposite connotation. In addition, there is no verification mechanism for the register, save the fact that the identical arms transfer has to be reported by both the importer and exporter states. This creates a situation in which a state hesitant to report an arms transfer may be faced with the state at the other end of the deal reporting, thereby creating further incentives to report. Ambassador Wagenmakers was asked at a press conference about the reports of Russian arms transfers to the PRC and whether the PRC would be offering information about these sales. His response indicated that Russia was a cosponsor of the resolution and would report any transactions with the PRC in the register.[6]

During the original debate many states complained that a register that reported only arms transfers would be discriminatory. Their concerns were taken into account by the provision of a formal agenda for a 1994 panel that would discuss expanding the register to request states to submit data on additional categories of equipment, procurement through national production, military inventories, weapons of mass destruction, and the transfer of military technology. In the second half of their report the panel made this agenda more specific. It now includes the possibility of expanding existing categories by modifying parameters or introducing new ones and introducing new categories. Items to be discussed for inclusion in the register in 1994 include aerial refueling, reconnaissance and electronic warfare aircraft, ground-to-air missiles, precision-guided munitions, cluster bombs, and fuel-air explosives. Assuming that these states were sincere in their desire to have universal and nondiscriminatory transparency, they would have a strong incentive to submit the requested data during the first two years of the register to see if the world is serious about taking their concerns into account. Lack of participation in the register by these states would provide powerful evidence for the naysayers who felt that the whole exercise was just more of the same rhetorical approach to international security problems.

Rationales for Noncompliance

Some states may be very reluctant to be completely transparent for security reasons. Political culture and attitudes toward secrecy in national security matters will be a very important obstacle for some states. As indicated above, the procedures developed for the register explicitly deal with this situation. Some states will have legal obstacles, in regard both to their domestic laws and the requirement to maintain confidentiality of commercial contracts. There are ways to deal with these questions. Russia, for example, has made it clear that it intends to query all of its client countries and seek permission to make public information on arms transfers covered by the register. A further reluctance may stem from the fact that if a country has once been transparent in submitting data, it will find it difficult to go in the opposite direction. This was a constant theme throughout the debate on whether a "description of item" column should be included as part of the declaration form. Without the column states would not have been in this dilemma. The consensus reached was that such a column is desirable, but it remains to be seen how states take advantage of the opportunity to increase the transparency of information on arms deals.

Some states may be waiting to see how others respond. If that is the case, the assessment of the participation and transparency levels actually achieved should cover the first two years in the aggregate, not just the first year. One can assume that the data from the first year will be well publicized and that many state-by-state assessments of compliance and transparency will quickly follow. Only when states have been given the opportunity to respond to such assessments can a valid picture emerge as to whether the register is producing the expected level of transparency.

The upheavals of the past few years have produced an additional obstacle for states reporting data on arms exports and imports. This is particularly true in the states of the former Soviet Union and Warsaw Pact. The national export control systems that would produce such data vary significantly in this part of the world. At the upper end of the scale are countries such as Poland and Hungary, which have taken major steps to control their arms industries and put export controls in place. Russia is experiencing serious problems because its central control system disappeared with the collapse of the Soviet Union and its replacement is only just taking shape. As a result, for the past year many arms deliveries have been made without the knowledge of the central national export control authorities who are responsible for reporting the data to the UN. In countries such as Ukraine, controls are practically nonexistent. At this point it would be literally impossible for Ukraine to comply with the register. It is ironic that just at that time in history when the Persian Gulf War has produced an international consensus that arms transfers can have negative consequences, a significant number of states with large arms exporting capabilities are having difficulty determining actual export levels.

Prognosis

The above discussion indicates that there are significant incentives for taking the first step in reporting arms transfer data to the register, despite some significant obstacles. And it should be noted that it will not be necessary for all states to submit data in order for the register to be a success. If most of the major suppliers and recipients report (perhaps 20 countries), a very high percentage of the world's arms transfers of major armaments will have become transparent.

Yet, as always, states will have to weigh the costs and benefits of participation in this new approach to dealing with international security. Given the lack of success of actions to control the arms trade, it would appear that transparency in armaments may be one of the few options left. The register codifies the fact that the international arms trade is not only legal but a legitimate tool of foreign policy and self-defense. In the resolution member states reaffirm the inherent right of states to individual or collective self-defense, "which implies that States also have the right to acquire arms with which to defend themselves." The register approach also confirms that there are no inherent norms that the international community has developed regarding the inherent destabilizing or otherwise negative qualities of conventional armaments. Many proponents of arms trade control and reduction may disagree and oppose the register on these grounds. But the transparency in armaments approach clearly states that conventional arms transfers can indeed have very serious and negative consequences, as seen in

the case of Iraq. The register approach is not only more incremental; it is also designed to build confidence and is more realistic.

A comparison with the talks on arms trade control among the five permanent members of the Security Council makes the point. Building on the international consensus that what happened in Iraq was wrong, secret talks started in summer 1991 to develop guidelines that would prevent arms exports from creating another Iraq situation. The focus was on notification prior to delivery. The approach was very similar to the U.S.–Soviet Conventional Arms Trade talks of 1978–1979, during which an attempt was made to develop a list of destabilizing weapons that could then be barred from specific regions. Those talks failed, as has the current effort. Although the PRC used the U.S. sales of F–16 aircraft to Taiwan as the reason for withdrawing from the talks, in fact they had stalled long before. The industrial pressures to export are too great for a state to say no to an arms export when a multilateral forum cannot agree that negative consequences will occur.

This is the current situation with Iran. The United States has been urging its G–7 partners to crack down on and control dual-use exports to Iran in the hope that this will prevent or at least slow down what the United States perceives as another Iraq—a movement toward the development of a capability to deliver weapons of mass destruction. But several G–7 countries objected, stating that such action was premature. Given the global recession and the fact that Iran is one of the few markets available for Japanese and European technologies, agreement is not imminent. A similar situation exists with advanced conventional armaments. Russia made it clear that it was selling modern submarines to Iran as a legal and legitimate transfer that Iran views as necessary for its legitimate self-defense. There is little hope that the United States can convince Russia to cease making such transfers based on a nonexistent a priori consensus that they are destabilizing, especially given the recent major sales by the United States to Taiwan and Saudi Arabia.

The register approach is different. It assumes that if data are available on levels of armaments delivered on an annual basis, even after the fact, the international community can discern the presence of a destabilizing accumulation. It will have early warning. Given the recent resurgence of the UN Security Council's role in peace-keeping and its identification of weapons proliferation as a major threat to international security, there is some optimism that this approach can work. This is not the ideal situation. The day may come when certain categories of conventional weapons may be universally condemned and allow a regime such as that which exists for nuclear nonproliferation to be more proactive in preventing the proliferation of conventional armaments. In the current international system such a consensus does not exist. The process that produced the register recognizes where the world is at this point in history and challenges the international community to respond.

U.S. Options

The United States would seem obligated to report exports and imports at a minimum level of transparency, as agreed to in the various stages of developing the register. This would ensure that the United States could not be blamed for the failure of the process should key suppliers and recipient states not report. It would also be a confirmation that the United States does not view its exports as destabilizing. Most of the information submitted is already public, because the United States releases more information on its arms exports than almost any other state. Failure to report exports at a level of transparency that already exists will result in a significant loss of U.S. credibility.

If the United States were to maximize the transparency of information submitted, especially information on the model, type, and capabilities of the equipment exported, it would set the standard for other states and could be used as leverage in succeeding years on those states of proliferation concern and their suppliers that may not have fully disclosed their transfers. The risks involved seem low, because during the first two years of reporting no major military threat to U.S. interests appears imminent.

If the United States chooses to actively promote the use of the register as a confidence-building and early warning mechanism, it could be viewed as setting the standard for a new approach to international security to *complement* multilateral and international export control regimes. President Bill Clinton could significantly increase the likelihood that states would submit data by announcing such a U.S. policy in his first speech to the UN. This would have the advantage of expressing concern about destabilizing accumulations of armaments while respecting the sovereignty of states. Additionally, it would not foreclose the chances for the process of transparency to expand to include weapons of mass destruction, as called for in the various resolutions that established the register. Such a strategy would send an immediate message that the United States was serious about an international effort to prevent those armed conflicts that result from destabilizing accumulations of armaments.

This policy should be pursued *in conjunction* with and not in lieu of other efforts at multilateral arms export control, so that the register is not seen as an end in itself. A U.S. policy that increases international transparency in armaments will provide the basis for keeping alive the possibility of controls.

Notes

1. Michael Moodie, "Transparency in Armaments: A New Item for the New Security Agenda," *The Washington Quarterly* 15 (Summer 1992), pp. 75–82.

2. United Nations, *Transparency in Armaments*, General Assembly Document A/47/342, August 14, 1992.

3. United Nations, *Study on Ways and Means of Promoting Transparency in International Transfers of Conventional Arms*, General Assembly Document A/46/301, September 9, 1991.

4. "Tracking Arms," *Defense News*, November 16–22, 1992, p. 28.

5. "UN Registry to Track Arms Trade Upsets U.S. Officials," *Defense News*, November 9–15, 1992, p. 13.

6. Press Conference on Conventional Arms Register, United Nations, New York, October 20, 1992.

How to Think About—and Implement—Nuclear Arms Control in the Middle East

Avner Cohen and Marvin Miller

THE PROSPECT OF a nuclear-armed Iraq and the reality of a nuclear-armed Israel cast an ominous shadow on the crisis and war in the Persian Gulf in 1990–1991 and focused attention on the danger of nuclear proliferation in the post–cold war era. More recently, suspicious nuclear activities in Iran and North Korea and the potential for the transfer of nuclear weapons materials, technology, and expertise from the former Soviet Union (FSU) have underscored both the global nature of the proliferation threat and the importance of agreements between the regional actors as a complement to the nonproliferation efforts of outside powers such as the United States.

In the Middle East, both the moderate Arab states and Israel now share a common concern about nuclear proliferation and also recognize the need to deal with it on a regional basis. It is one thing to recognize such a need, however, and another to come up with mutually acceptable ideas and modalities for meeting it. Achieving agreement on nuclear arms-control arrange-

Avner Cohen is a visiting scholar at the Center for International Studies at MIT. Marvin Miller is a senior research scientist with the Department of Nuclear Engineering and the Defense and Arms Control Studies Program at MIT.

ments in the Middle East involves three distinct problems: the linkage between the nuclear issue and the rest of the peace process; the linkage between the nuclear issue and the rest of the arms-control agenda, particularly with regard to chemical weapons and conventional arms limitations; and the difficulties intrinsic to the nuclear issue itself, namely, how to craft a realistic and effective arms-control agreement, given Israel's determination to retain its unacknowledged nuclear capability at least until there is *true* peace in the region and Arab demands for nonnuclear equality and symmetry.

These problems have already surfaced during the first two rounds of the ongoing multilateral talks on regional security and arms control in the Middle East. The Arab states want to put the nuclear issue at the top of the negotiating agenda, pushing "for a full accounting of Israel's nuclear arsenal and demanding the weapons' elimination" as early as possible,[1] but Israel maintains that the nuclear issue should be discussed only after all other arms-control issues are resolved. The problems of linkage are difficult, but hardly insurmountable. For example, the parties could agree to consider the nuclear, chemical/biological, and conventional weapons issues in separate parallel negotiations, with the proviso that the separate agreements would only be implemented as a single package. This essay focuses on the nuclear issue, specifically, on whether making Israel's unacknowledged weapons more transparent would aid or hinder efforts to reach a nuclear arms-control agreement.

The Post–Gulf War Context

Nuclear arms control in the Middle East must start from the implications of the Iraqi nuclear program. Major gaps remain in our knowledge of this program; indeed it is possible that significant activities remain unknown. From what we do know, however, it is credible that Iraq could have assembled its first nuclear weapons by now, or could have done so in the near future, with possibly catastrophic consequences. This realization is very chilling to many Arabs and Israelis alike. Fortunately, Saddam Hussein invaded Kuwait, refused to withdraw, was defeated in the Persian Gulf War, and had no choice but to agree to the draconian provisions of United Nations (UN) Resolution 687.[2] This led to the establishment of the UN Special Commission on Iraq, with its mandate to dismantle that nation's programs to develop weapons of mass destruction and ballistic missiles and to deny Iraq the possibility of resurrecting them. In the nuclear area, however, despite the well-publicized and sometimes heroic efforts by the inspection teams sent to Iraq to carry out this mandate, Iraq still refuses to provide a full accounting of its program or to agree to long-term surveillance of its territory.

The major lesson of Iraq for the nonproliferation community is that states with a limited industrial and technological base can obtain sufficient access to bomb-making technol-

ogies and know-how to initiate a large-scale nuclear weapons program and can largely conceal that program both from national technical means of gathering intelligence and the International Atomic Energy Agency (IAEA) safeguards regime. Further, although Iraq's nuclear ambitions were well known, virtually all concerned intelligence organizations had a flawed overview of the state of the Iraqi nuclear project prior to the war. This failure has led to much soul-searching and analysis in the United States and elsewhere to identify both its causes and possible remedial actions. It is plausible that the failure stems from a complex set of technical and political factors, including the tilt by Western governments toward Iraq during the Iran–Iraq War; Iraq's insights into and consequent ability to evade U.S. intelligence capabilities; the difficulty of finding what is not deemed credible, for example, the presence of electromagnetic isotope separation technology; and the lack of human intelligence on the spot until after the war. In response, new resources have been allocated to enhancing U.S. intelligence-gathering and analytical capabilities in the proliferation area. Similar efforts have probably also been made by other concerned governments, among them Israel, albeit on a smaller scale.

At the same time, there is now a much greater appreciation, both inside and outside of the IAEA, of the ability of states parties to the Nuclear Non-Proliferation Treaty (NPT) to conduct clandestine nuclear weapons programs behind the fig leaf of nominal adherence to their nonproliferation obligations. Over the last two years, the IAEA has taken several steps to deal with such clandestine programs. In particular, it has asserted its authority to conduct special inspections both at declared sites and at undeclared locations on the basis of all available information, including intelligence supplied by outside sources.[3]

Finally, the success of Iraq in obtaining the materials, technology, and expertise for a nuclear weapons program—often with the collusion of foreign suppliers and the knowledge of their governments—exposed major deficiencies in existing national and international regulations on nuclear export control. In response, embarrassed governments, for example Germany, have strengthened their laws on exports, and there is now an international agreement for controlling the export of dual-use, as well as specifically nuclear, materials and technology.[4]

In sum, the specter of a nuclear-armed Iraq, as well as similar concerns about the nuclear ambitions of other small countries with large grievances, has led to much rhetoric about the seriousness of the proliferation threat and some concrete actions designed to bolster the denial side of the nonproliferation regime. These words and deeds are laudable, but one can question whether the political will exists to thwart a state determined to acquire nuclear weapons, especially if military action is required. Nor is such action a panacea. As the Gulf war demonstrated, even overwhelming military power is ineffective in destroying clandestine nuclear facilities unless their location is known. Undoubtedly, intelligence capabilities will improve. But so will the ability to hide such facilities where we least expect to find them, whether underground, in urban areas, or in other countries. Determined states may even bypass the major barrier to possessing weapons by purchasing significant quantities of weapons-usable materials, if not actual weapons.

The end of the Cold War has undoubtedly changed the prospects for preventing further proliferation. The picture, however, is a mixed one. The good news is that nonproliferation is less likely to be traded against cold war interests and that nuclear arms reductions in the United States and the FSU support the devaluation of the idea that such weapons can be useful in fighting wars. The bad news is that nonproliferation is more likely to be traded off against economic interests in the FSU, the People's Republic of China (PRC), and other countries, just when the potential for post–cold war fragmentation of the international system exacerbates regional conflicts and heightens incentives for proliferation.

Thus, it is essential to strengthen policies of nuclear denial, but these must be complemented by greater efforts to reduce the incentives to acquire nuclear weapons. In the Middle East, this requires progress toward a political settlement of the Arab–Israeli conflict. Indeed, the prevailing view is that trying to reach agreement between the parties on arms control in general, and nuclear arms control in particular, before the peace process bears fruit would be futile, even counterproductive. But serious discussions about arms control can also *aid* the peace process by increasing each side's understanding of the other's basic security concerns. Moreover, on the long road toward a solution of the Arab–Israeli conflict, concrete arms-control confidence-building measures, both bilateral and unilateral, can help allay suspicions about the other side's true desire for peace.

The good news here is that the formation of a new government in Israel in summer 1992 has given impetus to the negotiations between Israel, the Palestinians, and Syria that began at the Madrid peace conference in October 1991. In addition, the Madrid conference framework provides a specific forum—the multilateral working group on regional security and arms control—for discussion of arms control and proliferation in a regional context. This group, together with four other multilateral forums on other regional problems, was created in January 1992 and has convened twice since. The first meeting, held in Washington in May 1992, was mostly an academic seminar, designed to acquaint the representatives from 12 Arab countries and Israel with the concepts and practices of arms control, with particular reference to the experience of the United States and the Soviet Union in this area. In the second meeting, held in Moscow in September 1992, there was the beginning of a dialogue between Arabs and Israelis about how to proceed with substantive discussions.

Unfortunately, three of the significant regional players are not at the table: Iraq is regarded as a pariah state so long as Saddam Hussein remains in power, while Syria and Iran, although invited, have declined to participate. This alone makes it highly unlikely that any substantive agreements can be negotiated anytime soon. Indeed, the group has not yet even agreed on what topics should be discussed and the priorities of such discussions. The very establishment of such a forum is itself significant, however. For the first time, delegates from Israel and the Arab states sit together, learning about arms control, and can talk to each other about their nations' threat perceptions and concepts of regional security.

Specifically, they can talk about nuclear weapons in the Middle East. In the past, the Arab states have raised the issue of Israel's nuclear capabilities as a threat to peace in such international forums as the UN and the General Conference of the IAEA. Israel has always resisted such pressure, insisting that the nuclear issue can be seriously addressed only in direct negotiations between the parties and in the context of agreement on other aspects of regional security. The Madrid conference has brought Arabs and Israelis together and given them the opportunity, at last, to concentrate on matters of substance, not just procedure.

Further, the events of the Gulf war have led to a rethinking of the nuclear issue by both Arabs and Israelis. On the Arab side, the human suffering, economic costs, and environmental havoc suffered by countries in the region because of the war, and the realization of how much worse the situation could have been if nuclear weapons had been used by Iraq and/or Israel, have caused the old Arab vision of establishing nuclear parity with Israel to lose much of its appeal. Moreover, even discounting the risk of actual nuclear use, possession of nuclear weapons by Iraq or Iran would cause a significant, and dangerous, shift in the balance of power in the Arab world between moderates and extremists, increase the latter's geopolitical ambitions, and lessen the appetite of outside powers such as the United States to intervene militarily to protect allies and oil supplies. In a peculiar way, the Gulf war has led to a shared concern on the part of Israel and most Arab states about the danger of nuclear proliferation in the Middle East, particularly in a resurgent Iraq or a fundamentalist Iran. Thus, below the surface of Arab public demands that Israel sign the NPT and place all its nuclear facilities under IAEA safeguards forthwith, lies a good deal of flexibility and realism about the virtues of reaching an interim nuclear bargain with Israel.

In Israel, too, the Gulf war has forced a quiet rethinking of the nuclear issue. It is now increasingly recognized that even if the twin pillars of Israeli nuclear policy for the past 30 years, that is, ambiguity about its own program and a parallel commitment to prevent Arab nuclearization, are still essential, the means to attain these ends need to be refurbished. In particular, Israel can no longer have confidence in its ability to detect and destroy a nascent Arab nuclear threat unilaterally, as it did in 1981.[5] Cooperation in this regard with other states, particularly the United States, has now become a necessity for Israel.

The concern about Arab and Iranian nuclearization is central to the political thinking of Israel's new prime minister, Yitzhak Rabin.[6] He believes that the Gulf war has given Israel a window of opportunity of perhaps 5 to 10 years to minimize this threat. During this period, Israel should contribute to a vigorous nuclear denial strategy via enhanced political and intelligence coordination with friendly states, and, more fundamentally, it should negotiate peace agreements with its neighbors to reduce incentives and support for nuclearization in the Arab world. In line with past Israeli policy, Rabin thus far has not mentioned Israel's own nuclear program, let alone hinted at a willingness to consider constraints on it. Instead, he is concentrating on achieving some measure of success in the negotiations with the Palestinians and Syria before engaging in serious talks on arms control. Such talks cannot be delayed indefinitely, however, and their chances of success depend crucially on the willingness of both sides to take calculated risks, with due appreciation of the complexities involved, especially with regard to the nuclear issue.

The Complexity of the Nuclear Arms-Control Problem in the Middle East

One long-standing idea for reducing the risk of nuclear weapons in the Middle East is to ban them by establishing a Nuclear Weapons Free Zone (NWFZ) in the region. Both Israel and the Arab states have endorsed this concept for years. This apparent consensus has, however, led to a blind alley because the formal preconditions that each side has stipulated in its proposals for such a zone have been patently unacceptable to the other. The Arab states have insisted on prior adherence to the NPT by all states in the region.[7] Israel, which has refused to sign the NPT, has insisted that the issue of an NWFZ in the Middle East can be addressed only through direct negotiations among all the regional parties and that a nuclear-free Middle East can become a reality only when there is true peace in the region.[8]

Thus in the past each side could claim the moral high ground of support for an NWFZ with the knowledge that it would not have to negotiate seriously about how and when such a zone could come into force. Although some of the formal sources of this impasse have now been removed—the multilateral arms-control talks provide a forum for direct negotiation on the whole array of arms-control issues in the Middle East—it remains highly unlikely that the apparent consensus on an NWFZ could be translated into action anytime soon. The substantive reason is known by all, but stated by none: until Israel feels truly secure, it will continue to regard its unacknowledged nuclear deterrent as an essential ingredient in guaranteeing its very existence and will not relinquish it.

In the interim, Israel might agree to constrain its nuclear capability as a step toward the eventual goal of a Middle East free of nuclear weapons. A basic difficulty remains, however: how to negotiate, or even talk about, eliminating, dismantling, or freezing an arsenal that is more than 25 years old, but does not officially exist.[9] Although Israel was the sixth nation to develop a dedicated nuclear weapons program, its behavior has been radically different from that of the five members of the de jure nuclear weapons club. Israel's policy has been to neither confirm nor deny its nuclear status, only pledging, since the mid-1960s, "not to be the first to introduce nuclear weapons to the Middle East." Although Israel has never explicitly defined what "to introduce" nuclear weapons means, this formulation is implicitly based on an understanding that such an introduction involves some kind of *public* act, for instance, making an official declaration of possession or conducting an acknowledged nuclear test. This Israel has steadfastly refused to do.

Israel's nuclear program was born and shaped many years ago. From the mid-1950s Israel's leaders, particularly its first prime minister, David Ben Gurion, regarded a nuclear deterrent as a necessity, the ultimate guarantee of the country's existence. At the same time, they feared nuclearization of the Arab–Israeli conflict, recognizing that any failure of the resulting "balance of terror" could be catastrophic for Israel. For this reason, Israel has never joined the official nuclear club. The taboo against public discussion of Israel's nuclear weapons in Israel is the natural outcome of this schizophrenic predicament.

In the United States too, since the Johnson administration, there has been a marked reluctance to discuss the nuclear reality in Israel. Even in periods of heightened concern about nuclear proliferation, for instance during the Carter administration, or at low points in U.S.–Israeli relations, the Israeli "bomb in the basement" has been treated by the U.S. government, particularly the Congress, as a special case. As recently as June 1991, Secretary of Defense Richard B. Cheney responded to a question at a news conference in Cairo by saying, "I don't know that Israel has any nuclear capability. They have certainly never announced it."[10]

Since the end of the Gulf war, however, there has been increasing criticism of the U.S. attitude as hypocritical and inimical to the fashioning of an effective global nonproliferation strategy. In particular, some security analysts have suggested that Israel's long-standing policy of ambiguity about its nuclear program is not compatible with arms-control agreements to prevent further nuclearization in the region. A representative view is that of Geoffrey Kemp:

> While Israel has good reasons for developing its nuclear weapons program, and has shown responsibility in not flaunting it, its existence has been a catalyst for other Middle East states to seek their own nuclear capability, particularly Iraq. But until there has been a long period of peace in the Middle East, Israel is unlikely to negotiate away its nuclear force. *In these circumstances, the best way to address the Israeli nuclear weapons program is to engage in a more open discussion of its existence and seek ways to limit its further growth, without, at this time, calling for its elimination.* Pushing Israel too hard on nuclear weapons while demanding that it be more flexi-

ble on giving up land for peace would be counterproductive. But to say nothing about this program, or engage in empty semantics, is equally counterproductive. (emphasis added)[11]

Interestingly, this argument for more nuclear openness or transparency has also been made by some Israeli and Arab analysts, albeit with opposite views about what the final outcome of the nuclear arms-control process should be. For the Israelis, nuclear arms control could provide a means for legitimizing Israel's nuclear monopoly. Even if Israel ultimately agreed to limitations on its nuclear arsenal, the quid pro quo would be Arab acceptance of this monopoly, at least for an agreed period of time.[12] On the other hand, some Arab analysts see more openness as the logical starting point for putting the Israeli nuclear program on the negotiating table explicitly as a weapons issue in order to first cap it and then to negotiate its elimination. If the Arabs are serious about dealing with Israel's nuclear capability, according to this view, they must first acknowledge reality in order to change it.[13]

There are persuasive reasons, however, for believing that open acknowledgment of Israel's nuclear program, at this point, would hinder rather than help the process of nuclear arms control both in the Middle East and globally. In Israel, the absence of any debate about the nuclear issue is more than a matter of imposed censorship; it reflects a genuine political, military, and societal taboo against considering nuclear weapons as real weapons. Official acknowledgment would run the risk of undermining this profound taboo. In particular, it could galvanize open public support for nuclear weapons, hence limiting the flexibility of the government in negotiating agreements involving nuclear limitations.

On the Arab side, open acknowledgment by Israel of its nuclear status would create demands for both more transparency, for example, declarations of how many weapons of what type existed and their means of delivery, as well as for a commitment by Israel to dismantle them verifiably at an early date. Absent such an unlikely commitment, there would be increased domestic pressure on Arab governments finally to end Israel's nuclear monopoly in the Middle East by whatever means necessary, including purchase of weapons. Globally, the sudden emergence of a new, declared, nuclear weapons state would provide support for similar actions by India and Pakistan and complicate efforts to extend the NPT in 1995. Some degree of transparency short of open acknowledgment might be helpful, but how much? As usual the devil is in the details, to which we now turn.

The Balance Between Transparency and Opacity

If open acknowledgment by Israel of its nuclear weapons program is not a good idea, what useful purpose would be served by, in Kemp's phrase, "a more open discussion of its existence"? In particular, would such a discussion enhance the acceptability to both Israel and the Arab states of "ways to limit its further growth, without, at this time, calling for its elimination"?

Since the sensational assertions about the size and scope of the Israeli nuclear program made by Mordecai Vanunu in 1986,[14] and more recently by Seymour Hersh,[15] there has been a growing sense of unease about the rationale for Israel's weapons and the genuineness of its declaratory commitment to get rid of them ultimately through an NWFZ. The principal concern with regard to the former issue for some Arab and non-Arab security analysts is that the assertions by Vanunu and Hersh imply a nuclear use doctrine that goes far beyond the traditional justification of "last resort." For example, according to Norman Moss:

> Deterrence for Israel would require a few nuclear bombs, and aircraft and possibly missiles able to deliver them as well as survive enemy air strikes. In October 1986, Vanunu told the London *Sunday Times* that Israel had assembled the material for 100–200 atomic bombs. Vanunu also said that Israel was well on the way to producing thermonuclear bombs. . . . This is far more than required for a last-resort nuclear strategy. It implies that Israel's purpose in possessing nuclear weapons goes beyond this and that it is ready to use or threaten to use nuclear weapons for several national objectives.

Moss also recognizes, however, that:

> Developing the Jericho missile and thermonuclear weapons does not necessarily mean that Israel has a strategy that requires them. On the basis of the U.S. experience, it would seem equally probable that once the initial decision was made, more and better weapons were built simply because of technological and bureaucratic momentum. The rationale, if any, followed.

Nevertheless, the existence of an advanced nuclear capability is worrisome:

> Future Israeli leaders may have less respect for the nuclear taboo than the superpowers have today and may refuse to see the nuclear bomb as a special kind of weapon to be used only *in extremis*. . . .

Nuclear proliferation means proliferation possibilities.[16]

These concerns have been echoed and expanded upon in a paper by Yezid Sayigh, the coordinator of the Palestinian team to the multilateral Middle East arms-control talks. According to Sayigh:

> More recently, Arab anxiety has grown that the Israeli "defensive shield" provided by nonconventional weapons can now be used assertively, as a strategic cover for conventional operations. The fear is that with its extensive first- and second-strike nuclear capability, long-range delivery systems and evolving reconnaissance assets . . . Israel is even in a position to wage an offensive nonconventional war, yet remain relatively immune from counterattack.[17]

These fears, Sayigh asserts, "are not far-fetched." Under opacity, there have been "subtle outward shifts in Israeli doctrine and policy" concerning its nuclear deterrent. In particular, Sayigh maintains that Israel has incorporated nonconventional capabilities in its "force structure and operational thinking"; there were demonstrative deployments of nuclear weapons by Israel during both the October 1973 and Gulf wars in order to convince the U.S. government of the risks of not attending to Israel's pressing security needs; and, finally, Israel has incorporated nuclear battlefield weapons, specifically, artillery shells and land mines, into its "war waging doctrines." Sayigh speculates that this capability, used in conjunction with "some elements in the Israeli space and [anti-tactical ballistic missile] programs, . . . lends itself to an evolving doctrine of controlled nonconventional applications," for instance, to "detonate a single [nuclear] weapon demonstratively, to halt an enemy offensive at an early stage and abort it before it poses a threat to national survival."

The statements by Moss and Sayigh raise two basic questions: to what extent are their assertions about a change in Israel's nuclear capability and doctrine credible and, to the extent that they are credible, is this change incompatible with a policy of last resort, that is, use of nuclear weapons as a means of avoiding the imminent destruction of the state? Israel has thus far not responded to these assertions. They cannot be ignored, however, particularly in the context of negotiations on interim confidence-building measures that would limit the further growth of Israel's nuclear capability. If Israel seeks to legitimize its interim need for *some* nuclear shield, it must convince others that their rationale is still last resort.

With regard to the credibility of these assertions, their primary sources are, as noted, Vanunu and Hersh. In general, the former is persuasive, and the latter a mixed bag. Primarily on the basis of the Vanunu evidence, it appears that Israel has indeed gone beyond the Nagasaki-type bomb to more advanced fission-only and fission-fusion devices. It also appears that *if* advanced low-yield weapons are part of the Israeli arsenal, the primary rationale for their development was, as in the U.S. case,[18] the desire to create options for nuclear use in a way that would minimize harm to both Arab and Israeli noncombatants, thereby obviating recourse to the morally repugnant—hence not credible—targeting of population centers and to permit use, in extremis, over Israeli territory.

Obviously, the perception that low-yield weapons can be militarily useful in war-fighting is dangerous because it weakens the essential taboo against *any* use of nuclear weapons. Unlike the situation in the United States, however, nuclear weapons have not been integrated into the military doctrine of the Israeli Defense Forces (IDF). And, in the event of a threat to the existence of the state that could not be countered by conventional means, for example, a massive enemy ground offensive or extensive use of chemical weapons against Israeli population centers, the selective use of small nuclear weapons, including the demonstrative use conjectured by Sayigh, is surely preferable to the destruction of Baghdad or Damascus.

In 1962, a decision was taken by Israel's political leadership that it would not integrate nuclear weapons into its armed forces.[19] The authors of this essay are convinced that Israeli nuclear weapons are still only a psychological insurance policy for last resort contingencies.[20] The military doctrine of the IDF remains conventional: as long as there are no Arab nuclear weapons, the Israeli army must plan its response to all military threats as if Israel had no nuclear weapons. The experience of the 1967 and 1973 Arab–Israeli wars—during both of which Israeli nuclear weapons were available—only strengthened the lesson that nuclear weapons have no military utility in almost any military situation in which Israel could find itself.

It is also reasonable to assume, with Moss, that technological and bureaucratic momentum has played a role in the development of the Israeli arsenal. Indeed, one would expect that its role in the highly secret, publicly unacknowledged Israeli nuclear program was even greater than in the United States.

In sum, like the declared nuclear weapon states, Israel has very likely developed an arsenal that, in theory at least, gives it more options than the destruction of enemy cities using Nagasaki-type bombs. But there has always been a high barrier against any use of nuclear weapons by Israel. It is important to convince the Arab states of this while avoiding an open discussion of what is in Israel's arsenal and why. Realistically, however, it can be anticipated that the Arab states will raise these matters in any negotiations on confidence-building initiatives in the nuclear area. Israel will surely refuse to participate in such discussions. As a result, initiatives whose purpose is to build confidence could instead raise suspicions of bad faith and would be likely to end in failure. How to proceed?

A Realistic Approach

It is useful to consider this dilemma in the context of specific proposals for nuclear confidence-building in the Middle East. Israel should cap its production of weapons-usable nuclear materials, while the Arab states and Iran should reinforce their declaratory commitment not to produce nuclear weapons by accepting the authority of the IAEA to make special inspections at both declared and suspect nuclear facilities.[21] The U.S. proposal for arms control in the Middle East of May 29, 1991, incorporated this idea but also went beyond it in calling for a verifiable ban on the production of enriched uranium and separated plutonium—not just nuclear weapons—by all states in the region. Indeed, the Arab states and Iran should signal their peaceful intent by not building or seeking to purchase nuclear facilities, including large research reactors, which have no clear relevance to their civil nuclear programs.

The reaction to the U.S. proposal in both Israel and the Arab states was not enthusiastic. For Israel, any change in a nuclear program born of

the trauma of the Holocaust and generally perceived to have reaped significant benefits is bound to be difficult. Although, after the Gulf war, there are now more Israelis who are willing to consider arms-control measures in order to prevent further nuclearization in the region, there is still significant opposition to such steps and even to more open discussion of the nuclear issue in Israel. Beyond this, Israelis also insist on the need to link nuclear constraints with other arms-control measures, particularly in the area of conventional arms. And, finally, although the proposal does not refer to existing weapons, but only to future production of weapons-usable materials, the negotiation of protocols to verify nonproduction in both Israel and the Arab states is certain to be a complex undertaking.

For example, even if the Arab states could be persuaded to accept, as an interim measure, a proposal that maintained a de facto Israeli nuclear monopoly, they are not likely to accept any asymmetry in verifying compliance. If Israel insists on stringent verification measures, for example, challenge inspections by teams including Israeli nationals, then it would have to accept similar measures to be carried out by other countries. Challenges to inspect the entire Dimona facility and other sites would be likely, but they would hardly be acceptable to Israel. As in the case of providing assurances to the Arabs about Israel's nuclear doctrine, any attempts to negotiate nuclear confidence-building agreements that create demands for a high degree of transparency are not realistic at this time.

A possible solution is for Israel to shut down the Dimona reactor, and hence cease its production of plutonium, as a unilateral undertaking[22] and to convey assurances about its nuclear doctrine in private discussions and through third parties, especially the United States. By this action, Israel would also join the growing global consensus on the wisdom of a ban on the production of weapons-usable material, contribute to efforts to minimize further proliferation in the Middle East, and lessen the opprobrium of remaining outside the NPT. Further steps toward denuclearization by Israel depend on the success of efforts to bring peace to the Middle East and to minimize the risk of further proliferation. It would be naive, however, to believe that Israel's perception of a threat to its existence and its consequent reliance on a nuclear deterrent would disappear overnight with the signing of a peace treaty. Indeed, Israel may feel less secure when it trades land for peace, and some will argue that nuclear weapons are the ultimate guarantee of a smaller Israel. Realistically, it will take many years of peaceful coexistence and major political changes in the Middle East involving, among the most important, the coming to power of liberal democratic regimes in the Arab states, before Israel will forgo its nuclear insurance.

Nor can this process be significantly accelerated by Israeli acceptance of U.S. security guarantees, possibly in the guise of a formal treaty.[23] Indeed, Ben Gurion himself sought a formal guarantee for Israel's territorial integrity from the United States during the late 1950s and the early 1960s, but he was turned down by Washington primarily because of concern that such a guarantee would increase Soviet influence in the Arab world and thus jeopardize U.S. interests. By mid-1963, however, when President John F. Kennedy was trying to abort the Israeli nuclear program, it appears that Ben Gurion was opposed to trading it for a U.S. security guarantee. Instead, Ben Gurion was interested in U.S. security guarantees *in addition* to Israel's own nuclear program, possibly as a way to keep the program undeclared.

It is highly unlikely that Israel would be ready to exchange its nuclear shield now for U.S. security guarantees. And the United States would also be reluctant to provide such guarantees in a post–cold war environment in which it seeks to reduce its overseas security commitments. However, the United States can—indeed it must— play a pivotal role in brokering a nuclear agreement in the Middle East. In fact, Israel is not likely to consider any constraints on its nuclear program without some prior understandings with the United States in this area. Thus, a willingness on the part of the United States to help Israel maintain a qualitative edge in the military area, including real-time access to satellite data, could reassure Israel about its ability to respond to regional threats. And the United States needs also to reassure the Arab side and thus orchestrate a positive Arab response to Israeli agreement on nuclear constraints.

Israel was not the first state to acquire nuclear weapons and, given its unique geopolitical security concerns, it should not be expected to lead the world into the nuclear-free age. Recognition that Israel's nuclear monopoly cannot, however, be maintained forever may be one of the strongest incentives for political progress and the ultimate meaning of "nuclear learning." In the meantime, emphasis must be on learning how to "lengthen the fuse" between political disputes and the nuclear powder keg.[24]

Notes

1. Ruth Sinai, "Mideast Arms Talks," *Associated Press*, May 11, 1992.

2. UN Security Council Resolution 687 was passed on April 3, 1991; two subsequent resolutions, 707, passed on August 15, 1991, and 715, passed on October 11, 1991, reaffirmed and extended the provisions of 687 by, e.g., demanding that Iraq halt all nuclear activities except for the production of isotopes for medical purposes and approving plans for long-term monitoring of Iraqi territory.

3. For an excellent discussion of the issue of challenge inspections and other measures to improve the ability of the IAEA to deal with clandestine nuclear programs, see Lawrence Scheinman, "Assuring the Nuclear Non-Proliferation System," Occasional Paper Series, Atlantic Council of the United States (Washington, D.C., October 1992).

4. The guidelines and the control list for the dual-use export control regime were published by the IAEA in July 1992 in INF-CIRC 254, part II.

5. Yitzhak Rabin, "Only the U.S. Can Prevent Proliferation," *Davar* (in Hebrew), January 17, 1992; Ze'ev Schiff, "Race Against Time," *Politika*, no. 44 (March 1992), pp. 14–17. This view was also expressed to the authors even more strongly in interviews with Israeli policymakers and politicians in summer 1992.

6. In his inaugural speech to the Israeli Knesset on July 13, 1992, Rabin stated: "Already in its initial stages—the government—possibly with the cooperation of other countries—will give its attention to the foiling of every possibility that any of Israel's enemies should get hold of nuclear weapons." See also his article, "Taking Advantage of the Time Out," *Politika*, no. 44 (March 1992), pp. 28–29.

7. For the history and details of the Arab, particularly Egyptian, position on an NWFZ, see Mahmoud Karem, *A Nuclear-Weapons-Free Zone in the Middle East: Problems and Prospects* (Westport, Conn.: Greenwood Press, 1988).

8. See Joshua Jortner, "A Nuclear-Weapon-Free Middle East," in Sadruddin Aga Khan, ed., *Nuclear War, Nuclear Proliferation, and Their Consequences* (Oxford: Clarendon Press, 1985), pp. 170–177.

9. See Avner Cohen and Benjamin Frankel, "Opaque Nuclear Proliferation," in Benjamin Frankel, ed., *Opaque Nuclear Proliferation: Methodological and Policy Implications* (London: Frank Cass, 1991), pp. 14–44.

10. Transcript of Secretary Cheney's Press Conference, Cairo, Egypt, June 1, 1991, Office of the Secretary of Defense, Washington, D.C.

11. Geoffrey Kemp, *The Control of the Middle East Arms Race* (Washington, D.C.: Carnegie Endowment for International Peace, 1991), p. 180.

12. Shai Feldman, "New Dilemmas," *Politika*, no. 44 (March 1992), pp. 56–59.

13. See Ze'ev Schiff, "Conditional Recognition," *Ha'aretz*, April 17, 1991.

14. "Revealed: The Secrets of Israel's Nuclear Arsenal," *Sunday Times* (London), October 5, 1986; Frank Barnaby, *The Invisible Bomb: The Nuclear Arms Race in the Middle East* (London: I. B. Tauris, 1989).

15. Seymour Hersh, *The Samson Option* (New York: Random House, 1991).

16. Norman Moss, "Vanunu, Israel's Bombs, and US Aid," *Bulletin of the Atomic Scientists* 43 (May 1988), pp. 7–8.

17. Yezid Sayigh, "Reversing the Middle East Nuclear Race," *Middle East Report*, no. 177, vol. 22, no. 4 (July–August 1992), pp. 16, 17.

18. See Matthew Evangelista, *Innovation and the Arms Race* (Ithaca, N.Y.: Cornell University Press, 1988).

19. See Yair Evron, "Opaque Proliferation: The Israeli Case," in Frankel, *Opaque Nuclear Proliferation*, pp. 46–47.

20. Even some of the strongest supporters of Israel's nuclear program subscribe to the view that an Israeli bomb has little military value. See, for example, Yuval Ne'eman, "Five Reasons Against Walking on the Edge," *Politika*, no. 44 (March 1992), pp. 30–32.

21. Avner Cohen and Marvin Miller, "Facing the Unavoidable: Israel's Nuclear Monopoly Revisited" (draft), Defense and Arms Control Study Program, Massachusetts Institute of Technology, Cambridge, Mass., June 1988; and in Frankel, *Opaque Nuclear Proliferation*, pp. 68–71.

22. This suggestion has been made informally by a senior Israeli nuclear analyst.

23. Charles William Maynes, "A Necessary War?" *Foreign Policy*, no. 82 (Spring 1991), pp. 171–172.

24. Joseph S. Nye, Jr., Albert Carnesale, and Graham Allison, eds., *Fateful Vision: Avoiding Nuclear Catastrophe* (Cambridge, Mass.: Ballinger, 1988), p. 7.

Nuclear Rapprochement: Argentina, Brazil, and the Nonproliferation Regime

John R. Redick, Julio C. Carasales, and Paulo S. Wrobel

THE APPROACHING 1995 Conference on the Review and Extension of the Nuclear Non-Proliferation Treaty (NPT) provides an opportunity to assess the prospects for successful consolidation of the nuclear nonproliferation regime. The conclusion of major strategic nuclear arms reduction treaties in the past, and growing prospects for agreements banning nuclear testing and production of fissionable material, broadly support a strengthened regime. So does the earlier acceptance of the NPT by China and France and, subsequently, its acceptance by the newly independent states of Belarus and Kazakhstan. Complete adherence by Ukraine to the Strategic Arms Re-

John R. Redick is an associate professor at the University of Virginia and a consultant to foundations on nuclear arms control issues. Julio C. Carasales is the former Argentine head delegate to the Conference on Disarmament, ambassador to the Organization of American States, and under secretary for foreign affairs. Paulo S. Wrobel is a professor at the Institute of International Relations in the Catholic University of Rio de Janeiro, Brazil, and editor of *Contexto Internacional*.

Copyright © 1994 by The Center for Strategic and International Studies and the Massachusetts Institute of Technology
The Washington Quarterly • 18:1

duction Treaty (START) I and the NPT, and the return of all its nuclear weapons to the Russian Federation, if accomplished, will be a particularly important nuclear nonproliferation accomplishment.

Other situations are far less promising. Three significant nations—Israel, India, and Pakistan—possess nuclear explosive devices and continue to reject the NPT. Perhaps more seriously, recent experiences with Iraq and North Korea have demonstrated that adherence to the NPT and to International Atomic Energy Agency (IAEA) safeguards is not necessarily an effective barrier to the development of nuclear weapons.

In the midst of this contradictory and cloudy picture, two regions stand in sharp and promising contrast, southern Africa and Latin America. South Africa is the first known example of a state that has unilaterally and voluntarily relinquished nuclear weapons. Between 1979 and 1989 the South African government constructed six nuclear weapons, partly assembled a seventh, and conducted research on thermonuclear weapons development. Subsequently, South Africa dismantled the nuclear weapons, joined the NPT, and implemented an agreement for full-scope safeguards. It is now actively participating in the negotiation of an African nuclear-weapon-free zone treaty.[1]

Latin America is the other region that has made significant progress in nonproliferation, first because it has nearly completed a nuclear-weapon-free zone and, second, because an extraordinary bilateral nuclear confidence-building process has developed between Argentina and Brazil. Latin America's two leading nations possess nuclear programs with military potential and they have traditionally opposed the nonproliferation regime. This article examines the process and the underlying factors that led them to make a dramatic reversal in their nuclear policy. The article also considers the implications of the successful Latin American nonproliferation experience, particularly the evolving Argentine–Brazilian nuclear relationship, for other regions and for the nonproliferation regime more generally.

Nuclear Suspicions and Restraint

Until the early 1990s, most surveys of nuclear proliferation put Argentina and Brazil on a short list of threshold nations that included India, Pakistan, Iraq, and North Korea.[2] The rationale appeared self-evident. Argentina and Brazil rejected the NPT as an inherently unequal and unacceptable treaty, and neither was a contracting party to the Treaty of Tlatelolco, which created a Latin American nuclear-weapon-free zone in 1967. Both nations had avoided full-scope IAEA safeguards and had certain unsafeguarded nuclear facilities with military potential. In Argentina these included a gas diffusion enrichment facility located at Pilcaniyeu in the Andean province of Rio Negro (developed in secret in the late 1970s and publicly announced in

1983), a small reprocessing plant and a fuel fabrication facility at Ezeiza near Buenos Aires, and an experimental pilot-scale heavy water facility situated near the Atucha 1 and 2 nuclear power stations in Buenos Aires Province. As part of a semi-secret "parallel program" under the leadership of elements of the military, Brazil commissioned a gas centrifuge unit at the navy-run Aramar facility near São Paulo in 1988 and a laboratory-scale reprocessing facility, also at São Paulo, and had plans under way for a military production graphite reactor at an army-run facility near Rio de Janeiro.

An additional issue of concern was a revelation in 1986 that elements of the Brazilian army had constructed a deep shaft on an air force facility in north central Brazil for the possible testing of a nuclear explosive device. Of similar concern was an Argentine air force project to produce a two-stage, solid fuel, nuclear capable missile (Condor II) with a range of 1,200 kilometers. Finally, both Argentina and Brazil strongly opposed efforts by the more advanced nations to use nuclear supplier guidelines to restrict their access to sensitive technology, and they actively engaged in cooperative relationships involving nuclear issues with Middle Eastern nations widely suspected of having nuclear weapons programs.

When considered in isolation, none of these positions or activities provided sufficient evidence to reach a conclusion regarding the nuclear weapons intentions of Argentina and Brazil. The composite picture, however, was persuasive to many observers: here were two competitive nations strongly opposed to basic tenets of the nonproliferation regime and possessing unsafeguarded and militarily significant nuclear facilities. Their inadequate internal accounting and control procedures for nuclear materials and lack of civilian/congressional oversight of their entire nuclear programs added to international suspicions.

In 1994 the situation is strikingly different: Argentina and Brazil have dramatically reversed long-held policies and initiated measures that, when fully implemented, will result in the total incorporation of the two countries into the nonproliferation regime. These new measures include a Bilateral Agreement, ratified by both nations in 1991, which established a joint nuclear materials accounting and inspection system administered by the Brazilian–Argentine Agency for Accounting and Control of Nuclear Materials (ABACC). Operating from headquarters in Rio de Janeiro, ABACC's 60 inspectors (30 from each country) are drawn from the two countries' respective nuclear energy commissions and report to the ABACC secretariat while undertaking inspections.[3] By mid-1994, considerable progress had been achieved by ABACC in finalizing procedures for accounting and control of all nuclear material and for determining the type and output frequency of all nuclear facilities in both nations (including the sensitive enrichment plants).

Argentina, Brazil, and ABACC have also negotiated an agreement with the IAEA (known as the Quadripartite Agreement) for the application of full-scope IAEA safeguards to all nuclear materials and equipment. In a ceremony witnessed in Vienna in December 1991 by then Brazilian president Fernando Collor de Mello and Argentine president Carlos Saúl Menem, this agreement links ABACC and IAEA accounting and inspection arrangements, thereby providing international confidence in the bilateral control system. The Argentine Congress gave its unanimous approval in 1992 and, after a considerable delay, the Brazilian Congress completed ratification in February 1994. The agreement entered into force on March 4, 1994.

A third important nonproliferation step was initiated by Presidents Collor de Mello and Menem on February 14, 1992, when they proposed a series of amendments designed to facilitate Argentine and Brazilian adherence to the Treaty of Tlatelolco. Both nations had chosen to remain outside the treaty, which had been ratified by all other Latin American nations except Chile and Cuba. The proposed amendments were adopted by the Tlatelolco parties in August 1992 and subsequently ratified by Chile and Argentina, which became full parties on January 18, 1994. The Brazilian Congress completed its approval on May 16, 1994, and Brazilian foreign minister Celso Amorim deposited the ratification instrument in a ceremony in Mexico City on May 30, 1994.

The Argentine–Brazilian joint disavowal in 1991 of their previous policy favoring so-called peaceful nuclear explosions (PNEs) was another highly significant nonproliferation measure. Although rejected by nearly all nations because of concerns about safety and proliferation, peaceful nuclear explosions remained an article of faith to elements of the Argentine and Brazilian military and nuclear establishments. Argentine–Brazilian acceptance of the view that there is no meaningful distinction between peaceful and military nuclear explosions had two important results. First, it eliminated any justification for a testing program as part of domestic policy and, second, it symbolically separated Argentina and Brazil from India's international posture as an advocate of PNEs.

Argentina and Brazil have also undertaken actions designed to bring them into conformity with international nuclear export control norms. Argentina has implemented far-reaching controls mandating that nuclear exports be made only to nations that accept full-scope IAEA safeguards, and that, as a general rule, enrichment and reprocessing technology will not be exported. Argentina also joined the Missile Technology Control Regime (MTCR) in 1993, and the Nuclear Suppliers Group (NSG) in 1994. The Brazilian Congress is expected to complete action in late 1994 on export legislation, enabling it to join both groups. Finally, both nations have joined in recent regional and international initiatives to ban chemical and biological weapons, and President Menem has announced his intent to complete Argentina's ratification of the NPT prior to the 1995 NPT Review and Extension Conference. In Brazil, although the ratification issue is under discussion, action prior to 1995 is highly unlikely.

From Competition to Confidence-Building

How has this remarkable change in Argentine and Brazilian nuclear policy occurred? For an answer it is necessary to begin with an understanding of the nature of the Argentine–Brazilian bilateral relationship.[4] Argentine–Brazilian relations have always been complex, beginning as early as the sixteenth century when their territories were part of the Spanish and Portuguese colonial empires. In the long period of colonial rule, Spain and Portugal inevitably clashed, and subsequent peace agreements failed to resolve territorial disputes in the area of the present Paraguay and the River Plate. Following independence in the early 1800s, Argentina and Brazil fought their last direct conflict in the River Plate region and the resulting peace treaty of 1828 established a new buffer state, Uruguay.

The rivalry persisted, however, with repeated border clashes in the Uruguayan area, leading in 1859 to a treaty by which Brazil gained portions of Uruguayan territory. In 1864 Argentine, Brazilian, and Uruguayan forces cooperated in a six-year war against Paraguay in which the latter lost 55,000 square miles and over half its population. In the bloody Chaco War (1932–35) between Paraguay and Bolivia, Argentina and Brazil were on opposite sides (Argentina supporting Paraguay; Brazil and Chile supporting Bolivia).

Throughout this period, and well into the twentieth century, competition for South American leadership and export markets—and an undertone of mistrust—were always present in the bilateral relationship. The possibility of armed conflict remained a very real element in the military planning of the two nations. Development in both nations in the 1960s of civil nuclear programs with military potential simply added a new dimension to the competition because each experienced heightened concern as to the other's intentions. The motivating factor for the nuclear programs was principally the drive toward development, modernization, and industrialization, with the military element as important but secondary.

Coordination of the nuclear nonproliferation policies of Argentina and Brazil was, however, growing parallel to their nuclear rivalry. This coordination was first evident in the negotiations between 1964 and 1967 that led to the Tlatelolco treaty. Although the treaty is often considered a triumph of Mexican diplomacy, it is notable that Brazil first proposed the concept of a Latin American nuclear-weapon-free zone in September 1962, prior to the Cuban missile crisis (which was the immediate catalyst to the treaty). During the treaty negotiations, Brazil initially supported a comprehensive nuclear-weapon-free zone agreement but shifted its position following the 1964 coup (which gave Brazil two decades of military dominated government). As the Tlatelolco negotiations continued after 1964, Argentina and Brazil increasingly found their positions in tandem and contrary to the views of the majority of Latin American nations. The shared objective of the two countries became the mitigation of the more restrictive elements of Tlatelolco and preservation of the independence of their nuclear programs from regional or international constraints.

This common approach represented the first step of an extended bilateral nuclear confidence-building process that, despite the traditional rivalry of the two nations, united them against the same enemy, the nonproliferation regime. Whether in regional forums, at the United Nations (UN), or at the Geneva Conference on Disarmament, the two Latin American nations increasingly opposed the dictates of the nonproliferation regime, which they saw as an imposition that threatened the independence of their nuclear programs and their development goals.

In 1975 West Germany agreed to supply Brazil with reprocessing and enrichment technology in the hope that the Brazilians would in response buy several German nuclear power reactors. In the United States this agreement was widely considered a nuclear proliferation wake-up call,[5] and it was an important catalyst for the Carter ad-

ministration's nonproliferation initiatives. The fallout from these events was important because, as U.S.–Brazilian relations worsened over nuclear issues, Argentine–Brazilian nuclear policy collaboration advanced. In early January 1977, Vice President Walter Mondale was sent to Germany to try to derail the projected sale to Brazil. This provoked a strong negative reaction by Brazil's military leadership. The Argentine leadership fully supported Brazil, and in late January the foreign ministers of the two nations issued a joint communiqué calling for cooperation in nuclear policy and technical exchanges between their nuclear energy commissions. It should be noted that this occurred during a period of military rule in both nations, and prior to resolution of the most serious Argentine–Brazilian energy and water disputes in the River Plate area. Despite suspicion of each other's nuclear progress, the two nations found it more compelling to assume a common posture of opposition to what they perceived as the infringements of the nonproliferation regime.[6]

The next step came in 1979 with an important agreement that established a framework for resolution of the problems in the River Plate area. This agreement opened the door for an across-the-board improvement in Argentine–Brazilian bilateral relations, particularly in the economic sphere, but also in the politically sensitive nuclear area. In 1980 the two nations signed a small, but symbolically important, agreement for nuclear fuel cycle cooperation, which included a clause calling for systematic coordination of nuclear policy in all international forums. The underlying motivation for this agreement was a shared view that modern technology, a powerful symbol of an advanced economy and prosperity, was unjustly dominated by a few highly developed nations. Consequently, Brazil and Argentina viewed collaboration in the nuclear field, rather than competition, as the best means to surmount the barriers presented by the inequitable nonproliferation regime.

A combination of domestic and international events significantly affected this bilateral nuclear relationship in the early 1980s. In Argentina the reaction to the loss of the Falkland/Malvinas war in 1982, public revulsion regarding the military's brutal actions against left-wing dissidents, and the woeful economic situation, all contributed to the return of civilian rule with the election in 1983 of President Raúl Alfonsín of the Radical Party. On the eve of Alfonsín's inauguration, the president of the Argentine nuclear energy commission, Carlos Castro Madero, announced the development of a gas diffusion enrichment facility (to the surprise of Western intelligence agencies, which had misinterpreted the nature of the installation). This was greeted in the United States as a second Latin American nuclear wake-up call and led to increased diplomatic and economic pressure on both Argentina and Brazil. Alfonsín wanted to end Argentina's diplomatic and economic isolation and assert civilian control over the nuclear energy program. He also wished to preserve Argentina's independent nuclear policy while reducing international pressure on his country to fall into line with the nonproliferation regime. Consequently, a new Argentine initiative to Brazil, which was then emerging from a two-decade twilight of military government, seemed opportune.[7]

President Alfonsín and the newly appointed Brazilian president José Sarney met in November 1985 and established a standing joint committee

on nuclear policy under the chairmanship of their foreign ministers with representation from their nuclear energy commissions. The purpose of the joint committee was to provide a regular channel for discussion of nuclear policy issues. In the following year, the two presidents signed a major trade pact committing their nations to creation of a Southern Cone Common Market (MERCOSUR) by 1995. Nuclear confidence-building and collaboration were now firmly integrated into a broader context of economic cooperation.

In September 1987 President Sarney announced that Brazil had independently developed a gas centrifuge enrichment plant at the navy-run Aramar facility in São Paulo. Argentina's response was extremely positive, owing in part to the fact that President Sarney had personally informed President Alfonsín prior to the public announcement. This confidence-building measure led to further discussions between the two presidents and their advisers, resulting in a remarkable series of reciprocal visits to previously restricted sensitive nuclear facilities. President Sarney visited the Argentine gas diffusion enrichment facility in July 1987, and in April 1988 President Alfonsín visited the Brazilian gas centrifuge plant. In November 1988 Sarney toured the Argentine pilot reprocessing facility. These visits had enormous symbolic importance and helped eliminate lingering suspicions. The growing nuclear collaboration was also used by the two presidents to exact greater control over their respective nuclear programs (Brazil's was still under the influence of sectors of the military). By the beginning of the 1990s, as both nations confronted a new period of political transition, it was still unclear whether they were prepared to institutionalize their nuclear relationship through a formal bilateral agreement or to integrate their nuclear programs into the nonproliferation regime through the full-scope IAEA safeguards.[8]

Political Change and Nuclear Cooperation

In 1989 the Peronist leader Carlos Menem was elected president of Argentina and immediately undertook dramatic new initiatives to reform the collapsed Argentine economy. To accomplish his development objectives and gain access to advanced technology, Menem and his pragmatic advisers concluded that Argentina's foreign policy needed to be coordinated with that of Western nations, especially the United States, and that continued rejection of the nuclear nonproliferation regime was counterproductive. Fortunately, with the election in 1990 of President Collor de Mello, Brazil was politically well positioned to reach new nuclear agreements. The new president shared Menem's view that continued rejection of the nonproliferation regime would result in unacceptable penalties because it would thwart ambitious development objectives. Consequently President Collor quickly appointed able civilian officials committed to civilian control of the nuclear program and, in a controversial move in September 1990, he flew to Pará State in the Amazon jungle to symbolically close a presumed nuclear test site, the "Cachimbo" shaft.

The actual nature of the Cachimbo shaft, constructed by one element of the army, remains the subject of much speculation.[9] Most Brazilian and other experts agree that at the time the hole was apparently constructed (1986), Brazil lacked sufficient material for a nuclear explosive device. Conse-

quently some have suggested that it was a facility to test the non-nuclear components of a nuclear explosive device. By most interpretations, it was intended to be a nuclear explosive test site and was constructed with the expectation that nuclear material would become available. Yet another view expressed by some Brazilian officials is that the shaft was constructed as a preliminary test site for eventual nuclear waste disposal, and was situated on a military base so as to avoid environmental challenges. Whatever the intent of the shaft, revelation of its existence, along with further revelations in 1987 and 1989 of secret European-based bank accounts used by the military government to fund importation of equipment for this parallel program, generated congressional concern regarding the whole nuclear program. The result was a provision of the new constitution (adopted in 1988) that limited all nuclear activities to peaceful purposes and subjected them to approval by the Congress. It also provided political support for Collor's subsequent efforts to gain control of, and reorient, the nation's nuclear program.

The internal political changes of 1989–90 in Argentina and Brazil provided the foundation for dramatic new bilateral and multilateral nuclear agreements signed by Presidents Menem and Collor on November 28, 1990. These agreements far exceeded the hopes of the most optimistic observers. The two leaders, meeting at Foz do Iguaçu, which forms a common border between Argentina and Brazil, agreed to renounce testing of nuclear explosive devices, create a mutual verification and inspection agreement with its own system of controls and machinery, establish a framework for implementation of full-scope IAEA safeguards, and adhere to the Latin American nuclear-weapon-free zone through an amended version of the Tlatelolco treaty.

The sweeping Foz do Iguaçu declaration, formally titled the Declaration on the Common Nuclear Policy of Brazil and Argentina, solidified and institutionalized the evolving nuclear relationship between the two nations. The bilateral agreement implementing the declaration was signed by the Argentine and Brazilian foreign ministers on July 18, 1991, in Guadalajara, Mexico, and entered into force on December 12, 1991, upon completion of the ratification process.[10] It established the Joint System for Accounting and Control of Nuclear Materials (SCCC) and the Brazilian–Argentine Agency for Accounting and Control of Nuclear Materials (ABACC). ABACC is composed of a governing commission of four members (the presidents of the respective nuclear energy commissions and the highest ranking Foreign Ministry officials with responsibility for nuclear issues), and a secretariat based in Rio de Janeiro whose secretary is one year a Brazilian national and the next an Argentine.

ABACC's principal responsibility is to administer the SCCC and verify that nuclear materials are not diverted to nuclear weapons or nuclear explosive devices. Under the SCCC's provisions, the Argentine and Brazilian national authorities provide ABACC with an initial inventory of all nuclear material present in each country and technical information on the design of all nuclear facilities. These are verified through inspections undertaken by 60 inspectors, who are selected by the commission and report to the ABACC secretariat. Periodic inspections, as determined by subsequent subsidiary arrangements, are carried out on all nuclear facilities. Any abnormalities detected as a result of inspections or assessment of national records are to be reported by the secretariat to the commission, which may call upon the offending party to correct the situation.[11] Serious noncompliance by either party enables the other party to abrogate the agreement and to notify the UN secretary general and the Organization of American States.

The Foz do Iguaçu declaration also transformed the relationship of Argentina and Brazil to the global nonproliferation regime. As envisioned in the declaration, Argentine and Brazilian representatives in Vienna began formal discussions in March 1991 with the IAEA for the conclusion of full-scope safeguards to cover the complete nuclear programs of both nations. These discussions were completed on November 21, 1991, and the Quadripartite Agreement between Argentina, Brazil, the IAEA, and ABACC was signed in Vienna on December 13, 1991. The agreement was concluded on the basis of IAEA statute article III, 5, which authorizes the IAEA "to establish and administer safeguards . . . and to apply safeguards at the request of the parties to any bilateral or multilateral arrangement." In a covering note of November 25, 1991, IAEA director Hans Blix described the agreement as comprehensive in nature, compatible with the Tlatelolco treaty, and covering "all nuclear materials in all nuclear activities within the territories of Argentina and Brazil under their jurisdiction or carried out under their control anywhere."[12] The Quadripartite Agreement has been signed and ratified by all parties and is now in force.

The conclusion and implementation of the Bilateral and Quadripartite Agreements also represented a highly significant evolution in Argentine and Brazilian perspectives on nuclear and nonproliferation policy. First, it signified an understanding on the part of important sectors of the leadership of both nations that the informal bilateral nuclear confidence-building process of the previous decade needed to be institutionalized into a formal accounting and inspection regime. Second, the Argentine and Brazilian leadership accepted the view that, although a bilateral inspection agreement could provide mutual confidence and security, this alone was insufficient to reassure the international community. Only an organic relationship between the bilateral (ABACC) and multilateral (IAEA) systems, including full-scope IAEA safeguards, would be acceptable to key nuclear supplier nations, especially the United States and Germany.

Entering the Nonproliferation Regime

Ratification of international conventions such as the Bilateral and Quadripartite Agreements requires the consent of the upper and lower houses of Congress in both Argentina and Brazil, followed by presidential proclamation. The Bilateral Agreement was ratified with relatively little difficulty by both nations in 1992 (with some opposition at committee level in the Brazilian Chamber of Deputies). The Quadripartite Agreement was approved unanimously by both houses of the Argentine Congress in July and August 1992. In Brazil the ratification process proved much more difficult, with the Chamber of Deputies providing approval only on September 22, 1993, and the Senate on February 9, 1994. President Itamar Franco formally promulgated the agreement on February 25, 1994.

The Brazilian ratification process was difficult, partly because of the protracted political divisions resulting from President Collor de Mello's resignation (in December 1992, following corruption charges), the inability of interim president Itamar Franco to provide effective political leadership, and a widening series of corruption scandals involving many members of Congress. There was also, however, vocal opposition to ratification in both houses by some members who argued that the agreement would compromise technological secrets and could lead to intrusive inspections and interference by the IAEA in the national nuclear program.

Several factors eventually contributed to Brazilian ratification, including a visit in August 1993 to Brasilia (just prior to the Chamber of Deputies vote) by IAEA director general Hans Blix. In meetings with congressional leaders, Blix was able to allay concerns regarding protection of proprietary information and facility attachments for Brazilian nuclear installations. On the former, he stressed that the IAEA had successfully developed processes for protecting proprietary information in arrangements with Japan and Germany. As regards submission of technical design information, he emphasized that compliance with this requirement would help minimize the intrusiveness of IAEA inspections by reducing their length and complexity.

A second factor contributing to Brazilian congressional approval was a visit in October 1993 by German foreign minister Klaus Kinkel, who reminded Brazilian officials that German law would require termination of all nuclear relations by 1995 if Brazil had not adopted full-scope safeguards by then. Ultimately, however, it was the combined effort of key Brazilian government officials and the scientific establishment that helped encourage favorable action by the Brazilian Congress. The Foreign Ministry and the respected head of the Strategic Affairs Secretariat, Admiral Mario Cesar

Flores, lobbied hard for the agreement's passage. Also arguing for approval was the president of the nuclear energy commission, Marcio Costa, and respected private scientists from leading state universities. The common denominator among arguments voiced in favor was that ratification was necessary if Brazil was to gain access to the advanced technology it needed for development.

In its approval, the Brazilian Senate included a statement, subsequently repeated by President Franco upon proclamation of the agreement, that any modifications in subsidiary arrangements between Brazil and the IAEA for application of safeguards would need to be resubmitted for congressional approval.[13] IAEA and other officials do not view this as compromising Brazil's responsibilities under the agreement.

With ratification of the Quadripartite Agreement complete, the critically important relationship between ABACC and the IAEA can develop. The agreement prescribes a relationship between the two bodies analogous to that developed between the European Atomic Energy Community (EURATOM) and the IAEA in 1977, after lengthy negotiations. That is, ABACC will serve as the principal safeguard authority, collecting and analyzing data and conducting inspections. IAEA inspectors will perform inspections at strategic points, working in tandem with ABACC to inspect sensitive facilities, especially the Brazilian gas centrifuge and Argentine gaseous diffusion enrichment units. Under the Bilateral Agreement, ABACC received initial inventory information from Argentine and Brazilian authorities in September 1992 and, in 1993, its inspectors completed initial inspections, focusing first on facilities not previously subject to IAEA inspections (i.e., the enrichment facilities). By early 1994 ABACC officials had initiated a bimonthly inspection process of the enrichment facilities that is expected to be incorporated into safeguard arrangements between the IAEA and ABACC as the Quadripartite Agreement is implemented.[14]

Another important linkage to the nonproliferation regime was Argentine–Brazilian action to adhere to the Tlatelolco treaty. The two nations, with the support of Chile, proposed amendments that in effect substituted the IAEA for Tlatelolco's own administrative body, the Agency for the Prohibition of Nuclear Weapons in Latin America (OPANAL), in undertaking verification and inspection responsibilities under the treaty.[15] The Argentine and Chilean Congresses completed ratification in late 1993, and the two nations became contracting parties in a special meeting of OPANAL held on January 18, 1994, in Mexico City. The Brazilian Chamber of Deputies approved the amendments on September 22, 1993, and the Senate gave its approval on May 16, 1994. In addition, on August 29, 1994, Cuba announced its intention to sign and ratify the Tlatelolco treaty. The decision was conveyed by Cuban president Fidel Castro in a letter to Brazilian president Itamar Franco, and simultaneously communicated to the Tlatelolco treaty depository government, Mexico. When final, Cuban ratification will remove a principal political barrier to completion of the Latin American nuclear-weapon-free zone prior to the 1995 NPT Review and Extension Conference.

Ratification of the NPT by Argentina and Brazil represents a final step of their complete linkage to the nonproliferation regime. The Menem administration now appears fully committed to Argentine ratification prior to the 1995 conference. Reasons cited by Argentine foreign minister Guido Di Tella include: (1) NPT ratification is a logical culmination of earlier decisions, including the decrees on export control of sensitive material, the Bilateral and Quadripartite Agreements, and adherence to Tlatelolco and the Nuclear Suppliers Group; (2) Argentina has already assumed requirements comparable, and possibly superior, to the NPT, but is not realizing the benefits of membership; (3) ratification will facilitate access to advanced technology in the nuclear and other fields; (4) Argentina will be able to participate in the 1995 conference and, thereby, actively promote disarmament progress; and (5) Argentina's participation in the NPT will provide balance to the nonproliferation regime, which is currently dominated by the nuclear weapon states and advanced nuclear supplier nations.[16]

Brazil's official posture continues to be opposition to signing the "discriminatory" NPT. Strong anti-NPT sentiment lingers in the Brazilian Congress. Although none of the leading presidential candidates for the 1994 national elections are likely to reverse Brazil's current nonproliferation commitments if elected, they are also unlikely to use political capital on the NPT. The Brazilian Foreign Ministry is somewhat concerned that Argentina is gaining certain international advantages from its strong nonproliferation stance, but it does not intend to actively lobby for ratification in the near term. In the longer term, following the national elections, many observers expect Brazil will ratify the NPT, thus symbolically completing its integration into the nonproliferation regime. As a party to the Quadripartite Agreement

and the Tlatelolco treaty, Brazil has already accepted the important requirements of the regime.

Factors Effecting Change

The remarkable evolution in the nonproliferation posture of Argentina and Brazil can be traced to a number of factors.

Mutual Security. The leadership in both nations came to appreciate the potential benefits of reducing tensions generated by their respective nuclear programs. Although military conflict was considered highly unlikely, a sustained military competition with a nuclear dimension could have been economically ruinous to their countries, which were already confronting severe economic challenges. In addition, military nuclear competition could have initiated a chain reaction in Latin America, exacerbating traditional rivalries and fueling regional tension.

Internal Political Change. The return of civilian leadership in both nations in the 1980s provided impetus to the ongoing nuclear rapprochement and to the evolution of their relationship to the nonproliferation regime. Presidential leadership and strong Foreign Ministry support were key to overcoming the resistance to the reversal of long-held policies among some in the military and nuclear energy commissions. A related factor was the civilian leadership's desire to restrain, in a nonconfrontational manner, some in their armed forces by incorporating national nuclear programs into a bilateral accounting and control regime.

Development Objectives. Pursuing an independent nuclear policy while rejecting the nonproliferation regime became increasingly at odds with the development objectives of both countries. As the Argentine and Brazilian leaderships moved to open their economies to foreign investment, the economic penalties of this rejection, including denial of access to advanced Western technology, stimulated increased internal challenges to the independent nuclear policies. Government leaders were joined by scientists and some business interests in promoting acceptance of regional and global nonproliferation agreements in order to facilitate access to advanced foreign technology and stimulate national development. The German decision in 1990 to require full-scope IAEA safeguards within five years by all nations with which it had a nuclear relationship also contributed to the internal pressure for change.

A Supportive International System. Evidence of international nuclear arms control progress provided important psychological support for Argentine–Brazilian nonproliferation initiatives. Nuclear arms control agreements among the superpowers, such as the Intermediate-Range Nuclear Force Treaty and START I, adherence to the NPT by France and China, and the dramatic reversal on nuclear weapons by South Africa, all contributed to a willingness by the Argentine and Brazilian leaderships to support a change in their policies.

Nevertheless, the Argentine–Brazilian decision to discard long-held policies and enter the nuclear nonproliferation regime was primarily a result of an indigenous bilateral process, rather than a direct response to external pressure. It grew out of a realization by the leadership of both nations that, whatever their differences, no rationale for possessing nuclear weapons existed, and that even the possession of so-

called peaceful nuclear explosives would disrupt bilateral relations and destabilize the peace and security of the entire region. Consequently, the two nations undertook a process of making their nuclear programs mutually transparent and of building confidence within the context of broader initiatives for bilateral and Southern Cone economic cooperation. External pressure exerted by nuclear supplier states and the IAEA influenced the process, but only at the margins; it was never the determining factor.

External pressure did contribute indirectly by fostering, at an early stage, the development of a common Argentine–Brazilian posture in opposition to the nonproliferation regime. This, in turn, evolved into an informal coordination of nuclear policies and, eventually, into the Bilateral Agreement and ABACC. External influence was also instrumental in helping encourage the opening of the Argentine and Brazilian economies to foreign investment. This stimulated pressure for change by domestic forces favoring modernization, who viewed the independent nuclear policies as impeding access to advanced foreign technology.

By the same token, continuation and consolidation of the nonproliferation process is a shared Argentine–Brazilian responsibility, with other nations and international organizations able to assume a supportive, but secondary, role. If Argentine and Brazilian policymakers do not continue to provide leadership, the nonproliferation process may falter. Necessary actions include: full implementation of the Quadripartite Agreement; provision of adequate resources and political support to ABACC; consolidation of nuclear export decrees into congressionally mandated laws; and development of effective congressional oversight responsibilities and independent regulatory mechanisms over the national nuclear programs.

Implications of the Argentina–Brazil Experience

Argentina and Brazil were suspicious competitors and rivals, but not enemies. This distinguishes the South American situation from more troubled regions such as southern Asia, the Middle East, or the Korean peninsula. With the caveat that a successful process in one region can rarely be transferred to another, the Argentina–Brazil experience does provide some useful precedents. At the most fundamental level it demonstrates that a rapprochement between rivals in the sensitive nuclear area is possible. It suggests an approach that others may follow, adopting those elements that are relevant to their particular situation.

The Argentina–Brazil experience also indicates that a nuclear rapprochement can best advance as part of, and may reinforce, a broader effort to improve relations encompassing political and economic factors. Efforts to foster mutual confidence based exclusively on the nuclear field, when other factors point to conflict and enmity, will prove difficult. The resolution of bilateral political problems in the River Plate area in 1979 opened the door to Argentine–Brazilian nuclear cooperation. Beginning in the mid-1980s, however, nuclear cooperation evolved quickly in tandem with efforts to reduce trade barriers and establish a Southern Cone Common Market. Committed presidential leadership in both nations cleverly used nuclear collaboration to deepen and extend the confidence-building process.

The Foreign Ministry can play a critical role in encouraging domestic political forces supportive of nonproliferation policy. This ministry is understandably more sensitive than other government units to the international costs of remaining outside the nonproliferation regime, as well as the political benefits of cooperation. The Argentine and Brazilian Foreign Ministries, with the cooperation of the economic ministries, lobbied hard and successfully for a shift in national nuclear policies over the opposition of some in Congress and the military.

External influence exerted by advanced nations is likely to be most effective in the form of incentives rather than penalties—carrots rather than sticks. The Argentine and Brazilian leaderships decided that an independent nuclear policy was contrary to their development interests in the context of a broader decision to open their economies to foreign investment. The United States, Germany, and other advanced nations reinforced this decision by presenting certain economic, political, and military benefits that could result from a cooperative posture regarding the nonproliferation regime. A more punitive approach on the part of the advanced nuclear nations would have undercut those elements in the Argentine and Brazilian leadership that favored progress.

The Argentine–Brazilian experience also suggests the importance of certain processes that significantly contributed to creating a climate of mutual confidence. These included the highly public reciprocal head-of-state visits to nuclear installations, advance notification of significant nuclear announcements, a long-standing pattern of technical exchanges producing considerable rapport between the nuclear energy commissions, and the creation of a standing committee to discuss nuclear policy issues. These actions preceded, and ultimately helped pave the way for, substantive bilateral, regional, and international nonproliferation agreements.

Finally, the Argentine–Brazilian nuclear rapprochement underscores the importance, both symbolically and substantively, of bilateral or regional machinery. Both nations strongly opposed the basic tenets of the nonproliferation regime, especially the NPT and full-scope IAEA safeguards. Condemnation of the regime as inequitable and discriminatory was an article of faith, widely accepted by nearly all political factions. An unambiguous reversal of these well-established positions, no matter how congruent with national interests, was politically unfeasible. In this regard the importance of a strong and independent ABACC needs to be underscored. The development of a bilateral nuclear accounting and control system, as administered by ABACC, assured the necessary political insulation for the overt policy reversal. ABACC provided political respectability to Argentine and Brazilian acceptance of the norms of the nonproliferation regime, including full-scope, NPT-equivalent IAEA safeguards.

ABACC, however, represents far more than political expediency. It fulfills a very real objective of providing mutual transparency to the nuclear programs of two highly competitive rivals. The initial approach developed by Argentina and Brazil of a bilateral accounting and inspection regime applicable to their sensitive, unsafeguarded nuclear installations, is a model that could prove acceptable elsewhere. It may prove particularly attractive to nations that, for whatever reason, distrust and resist IAEA safeguards. It provides a means to build mutual trust and security that may lead, at a later stage, to integration with the international nonproliferation regime.

The evolving relationship of ABACC with the IAEA system, as defined in the Quadripartite Agreement, is also rich with implications for other regional situations. That is, the relationship represents a careful balance between the prerogatives of the regional mechanism and the requirements of the international system. ABACC assumes primary responsibility for administering the control system and conducting inspections, but the IAEA retains carefully defined responsibilities including the right to undertake special inspections should it have reason to suspect the existence of undeclared nuclear facilities or materials.

Although Argentina and Brazil are now integrated into the nonproliferation regime, they do not accept an inequitable or discriminatory relationship on nuclear issues. To the contrary, both nations may be expected to use available nonproliferation forums to prod the nuclear weapon states for rapid progress in nuclear disarmament. Their views merit the respectful attention of the world community.

Research for this article was funded by the Rockefeller Foundation. The views expressed are solely those of the authors, and are not necessarily shared by any institution with which they are or have been affiliated.

Notes

1. The factors leading to the rollback of South Africa's nuclear weapons program are discussed in David Albright, "South Africa's Secret Nuclear Weapons," Institute for Science and International Security Report (Washington, D.C., May 1994), and by J. W. Villers, Rojar Jardine, and Mitchell Reiss, "Why South Africa Gave Up the Bomb," *Foreign Affairs* 72 (November/December 1993).

2. The standard survey book of this period is Leonard S. Spector and Jacqueline R. Smith, *Nuclear Ambitions, The Spread of Nuclear Weapons, 1989–90* (Boulder, Colo.: Westview Press, 1990).

3. ABACC, *Annual Report* (Rio de Janeiro, 1993).

4. Some of the better accounts of Argentine–Brazilian relations include Helio Jaguaribe, "Brasil–Argentina: Breve Análise das Relações de Conflito e Cooperação," in *O Novo Cenario Internacional* (Rio de Janeiro: Editora Guanabara, 1987), and Jack Child, *Geopolitics and Conflict in South America* (Stanford, Calif.: Praeger Special Studies, 1985).

5. The best example of this somewhat alarmist mind-set is Norman Gall, "Atoms for Brazil, Dangers for All," *Foreign Policy*, no. 23 (Summer 1976).

6. Support for the Brazilian position in its dispute with the United States over the German nuclear sale was widespread in Argentina. The more nationalist sectors of the Argentine military, while suspicious of Brazil's objectives, supported joint Argentine–Brazilian development in the nuclear field. See Juan Henrique Gugliameli, "The Brazilian–German Deal: A View from Argentina," *Survival* 18 (July–August 1976), and *Argentina, Brasil y la Bomba Atómica* (Buenos Aires: Ediciones Nueva Visión, 1978). The more moderate elements in the nuclear energy commission and foreign ministry supported Brazil's sovereignty and avoided suggestions of hidden motives. See Jorge A. Sabato, "El Plan Nuclear Brasileño y la Bomba Atómica," *Estudios Internacionales* (University of Chile, Santiago) 49 (January–March 1978).

7. The transition to civilian governments in both nations in the context of deep economic crisis and diplomatic isolation eventually became a principal impulse for the changing quality of the relationship. See Gerson Moura, "Brasil–Argentina: Com a Democracia o Fim das Hostilidades," *Ciência Hoje* (Rio de Janeiro) 8, no. 46 (September 1988).

8. The evolving perceptions of Argentine and Brazilian leaders regarding the non-proliferation regime at this point (1989) are documented in Paul Leventhal and Sharon Tanzer, eds., *Averting a Latin American Nuclear Arms Race* (New York, N.Y.: St. Martin's Press, 1992).

9. Brazilian studies focusing on the Cachimbo shaft include Frederico Fullgraf, *A Bomba Pacífica, O Brasil e Quatros Cénarios da Corrida Nuclear* (São Paulo: Editora Brasiliense, 1988); Luis Pinguelli Rosa, Fernando de Souza Barros, and Susana Ribeiro Barreiros, *A Política Nuclear no Brasil* (São Paulo: Greenpeace, 1991), and Tania Malheiros, *Brasil, a Bomba Oculta* (Rio de Janeiro: Gryphus, 1993).

10. The text of the joint nuclear accords establishing the SCCC and ABACC can be found in Foreign Broadcast Information Service, *Latin America*, September 12, 1991.

11. ABACC, *Annual Report* (Rio de Janeiro, 1993).

12. For the text of the Quadripartite Agreement, see IAEA Document Gov/2557 (Vienna, November 25, 1991).

13. The paragraph accompanying President Franco's promulgation, included at the request of the Brazilian Senate, states: "Any modifications to the subsidiary agreements and acts that may entail the revision of this agreement, as well as any acts that, according to the terms of Article no. 49, Clause 1 of the Federal Constitution, may entail demands or burdensome commitments on the national economy, will be subject to the approval of the national congress." Foreign Broadcast Information Service, *Proliferation Issues*, March 23, 1994. The relevant clause of the 1988 Brazilian constitution reads: "Any nuclear activities within the national territory will only be permitted if for peaceful purposes and if approved by the national congress." Foreign Broadcast Information Service, *Nuclear Developments*, April 28, 1988.

14. *ABACC News* (January/April 1994), and interview with ABACC officials at ABACC headquarters in Rio de Janeiro by John Redick and Paulo Wrobel, April 28, 1994.

15. For the text of the Tlatelolco treaty amendments, see IAEA Document INFCIRC 1411 (Vienna, July 12, 1993).

16. Foreign Broadcast Information Service, *Latin America*, March 1, 1994. Argentina fully accepted NSG guidelines and was

admitted to the NSG in 1994. Consequently, in certain respects, Argentina has accepted requirements that exceed NPT requirements. That is, under the NPT a party need not require a recipient of nuclear exports to adopt full-scope safe-guards, whereas members of the NSG must do so. For a thoughtful explanation of the NSG, see Tadeusz Strulak, "The Nuclear Suppliers Group," *Non-Proliferation Review* (Monterey Institute of International Studies) 1 (Fall 1993).

The Evolving Security Discourse in the Asia–Pacific

Andrew Mack and Pauline Kerr

SINCE THE END of the Cold War there has been a rapid and quite profound change in the Asia–Pacific security environment. In 1994, the region is probably more secure than at any time this century. This does not, however, mean there are no causes for concern. Territorial and sovereignty disputes remain unresolved, the continued commitment of the United States to the region is uncertain, and military budgets continue to rise. Rapid but uneven economic development causes concern about social dislocation and the concomitant risks of political instability.

This article traces the evolution of regional debates about security over the past decade. It argues that in late 1994 there is emerging consensus on a number of issues, but dissent on many others. It examines a number of potential causes of insecurity in the region including the regional arms buildup and the associated risk of "security dilemma" instabilities. It argues that the most appropriate strategy for dealing with security dilemma risks is "common security." It also examines the Association of Southeast Asian Nations (ASEAN) and Japanese concepts of "comprehensive security," which emphasize non-military means for achieving and maintaining security. It concludes by arguing that a combination of the military prescriptions of common security and the non-military approaches of comprehensive security will help reduce the risks of interstate conflict.

Background

The first postwar challenge to traditional superpower confrontationist policy in the region came from Moscow. In a major speech at Vladivostok in 1986, Soviet leader Mikhail Gorbachev argued that confidence-building measures (CBMs), including a "Pacific conference along the lines of the Helsinki conference," should be initiated to reduce the risks inherent in the superpower military confrontation in Northeast Asia.[1] The Soviet initiative, and the many that followed, undoubtedly

Andrew Mack holds the chair in International Relations at The Australian National University. Pauline Kerr is a doctoral student in the same department and is editor of the *Australian Foreign Policy Papers.*

This article is reprinted with the permission of Westview Press. It will appear in Andrew Mack and John Ravenhill, eds., *Pacific Cooperation: Building Economic and Security Regimes in the Asia–Pacific Region.* Copyright © 1995 Westview Press, Boulder, Colo.

The Washington Quarterly • 18:1

contained elements of propagandistic opportunism, but they were also very much in line with Gorbachev's emphasis on "new thinking" and "defensive sufficiency" that was beginning to revolutionize the security debate in Europe. Moscow's initiatives for confidence-building[2] were either rejected or ignored by Washington, where the official mindset remained committed to cold war policies of offensive deterrence.

Although it was easy enough for the United States to dismiss Soviet initiatives as designed simply to weaken the U.S. military position, it was less easy to accuse close allies of the same motive. In August 1987, the Australian foreign minister, Bill Hayden, warned of the risks inherent in the provocative strategies of the superpowers in the North Pacific. He urged measures that would dampen "the 'arms race' instability in military equations in the North Pacific"[3] and dismissed U.S. Navy arguments in support of some of the more provocative elements of U.S. maritime strategy as "unworldly armchair strategic reasoning."[4] Hayden went on to argue for a "superpower dialogue on security perceptions and concerns,"[5] for greater "transparency" on military issues, and for a variety of CBMs similar to those that had emerged in the Conference on Security and Cooperation in Europe (CSCE) negotiations in Europe.[6]

In June the following year, speaking to an American audience, Hayden argued that "we have to start a dialogue going among regional and other interested countries about specific problems in the security environment of the region."[7] The U.S. response was negative, if not hostile. Hayden's thinking and proposals were some five years ahead of their time.[8]

U.S. officials argued that CBMs risked undermining deterrence of the Soviet Union. Transparency measures, they suggested, did little to increase confidence while providing free military intelligence to the enemy. Limiting the scope of naval exercises and other "constraint" CBMs prevented the U.S. Navy from practicing its offensive maritime strategy effectively and thus reduced U.S. war-fighting efficacy. This, it was argued, would undermine deterrence and thus increase the risk of aggression. From this perspective CBMs could actually increase the risk of war. Adoption of even modest CBMs was risk prone because it could tip the United States down the slippery slope that led to constraint CBMs and naval arms control.

The End of the Cold War

As the Cold War wound down, the global bipolar security framework that had guided security thinking and planning for four decades appeared increasingly irrelevant.[9] By the mid-1990s, the focus of regional security has become the region itself. Russia has effectively ceased to be a major actor in the Asia–Pacific, while the long-term commitment of the United States to the region's security seems problematic, not least because the Soviet threat, which provided the central rationale for U.S. forward military deployment, has disappeared.

The end of the Cold War created opportunities for new ideas to be articulated—and listened to—and Australia and Canada were particularly active in advancing new security proposals. Although each is a close ally of the United States, both have been receptive to the strategic philosophy of common security that emerged from the liberal European tradition of security thinking and had little appeal for Washington.

The Australian and Canadian
Proposals

In 1990, undeterred by the evident
U.S. disapproval of the Hayden proposals some years earlier, Gareth
Evans, Hayden's successor as foreign
minister, made a series of major
speeches on regional security that endorsed both the concept of common
security and the idea of a "process and
institution" inspired by the CSCE.[10]
In July that year, Evans argued that
there was a need:

to be looking ahead to the kind of
wholly new or institutional processes that might be capable of
evolving in Asia, just as in
Europe, a framework for addressing and resolving security problems. . . .
Why should there not be developed a similar institutional framework—a "CSCA"—for addressing
the apparently intractable security issues which exist in Asia?[11]

In the same month, the Canadian
external affairs minister, Joe Clark, argued that the time had come "to develop institutions of [security] dialogue in the Pacific."[12] Like Australia's, Canada's approach was
strongly influenced by European security thinking. "We might consider,"
Clark suggested, "a Pacific adaptation
of the Conference on Security and Cooperation in Europe." But unlike the
Australian proposal, which embraced
the whole region, the Canadian initiative was to be limited to the North
Pacific.[13]
Both proposals were condemned by
the United States. Just two weeks after Senator Evans had argued the case
for a common security approach for the
Asia–Pacific before an American audience,[14] the assistant secretary of state
for East Asian and Pacific affairs, Richard Solomon, denounced

calls for a system of collective security in Asia . . . inspired by the
European experience of a region-
wide conference on security and
cooperation. . . . [T]he security
challenges . . . do not lend themselves to region-wide solutions. . . . [I]t is difficult to see
how a Helsinki-type institution
would be an appropriate forum for
enhancing security or promoting
conflict-resolution.[15]

U.S. policy, Solomon said, was based
on "forward deployed forces, overseas
bases, and bilateral security arrangements."[16]
The following month, the U.S. secretary of state, James A. Baker III, in
a classified letter to Evans, expressed
his disagreement with Australia's es-
pousal of a "regional security dialogue," or a Helsinki-type process for
Asia.[17] There was no need for change,
Baker argued, as traditional arrangements were more than adequate to
meet regional security needs. U.S.
officials subsequently argued against
change on the grounds that "if it ain't
broke don't fix it," and suggested that
CBM proposals were "solutions in
search of a problem."
The United States opposed an
"Asian Helsinki" because in the
CSCE process in Europe Moscow had
been treated as a partner. This was not
what the United States wanted in Asia,
because it would allow the Soviets a
forum in which to pursue, as Baker put
it, "their long-held goal of naval arms
control in the Pacific."[18] Although the
United States had a clear interest in
arms control in Europe, where Soviet
conventional forces had quantitative
superiority, it was opposed to arms
control in the Pacific theater, where
U.S. forces had unchallenged maritime
superiority.
The United States also preferred
dealing with regional states on a bilat-

eral basis, not simply because this was more familiar, but because Washington was unambiguously the dominant partner in each bilateral alliance relationship. In Europe, where the United States was locked into a multilateral security relationship, it was vulnerable to collective opposition from its allies on specific issues.

The ASEAN states also voiced strong opposition to the Australian and Canadian proposals—although on very different grounds to those of the United States. Arguing the case against the creation of a CSCE clone in the region, Singapore's foreign minister, Wong Kan Seng, claimed that "there has to be common ground before security issues can be discussed."[19] This was not the case in Asia, where, he said, "countries are so culturally, ethnically and politically diverse, that perceptions have to be harmonized."[20] Indonesia's foreign minister, Ali Alitas, made a similar point when he warned that "we have to be careful not to think that certain things that work in one region ought to be transplanted to another."[21] The prime minister of Japan, Toshiki Kaifu, reportedly described CSCE-type proposals as "premature."[22]

In criticizing the Canadian and Australian proposals the ASEAN states stressed the Asian preference for informal consensus-building and dialogue, which they contrasted to the more legalistic, rule-bound, institution-building approaches preferred by Western states. They also noted the different nature of alliance relations in the two regions, the fact that territorial disputes had been resolved in Europe but not in Asia, and the greater salience of maritime issues in the latter region. The fact that "inappropriate" European security concepts were being foisted on Asia by two Western countries only added to regional irritation.

In response to the near universal criticism of their proposals, both Australia and Canada backed off. By 1991, no Australian official was using the term "CSCA," and the two foreign ministers were in damage-limitation mode. In April 1991, Canada's Joe Clark was stressing that Canada was "not seeking to establish new institutions . . . nor [was it] advocating that we transplant mechanisms that have been successful elsewhere."[23]

Addressing the Trilateral Commission in Tokyo a few weeks later, Foreign Minister Evans expressed a similar view:

Nobody is naive enough to think that the CSCE process can be simply recreated in the Asia–Pacific environment. There are too many obvious differences for that.[24]

But he added that:

just because institutional processes can't be translated half a world away, that is not to say that the relevant habits of mind cannot be translated.[25]

In other words, Evans was arguing that although it made no sense to transplant CSCE institutions from Europe to Asia (which he had never proposed anyway), the security philosophy that underpinned the CSCE was indeed relevant to Asia.

By the middle of 1991, the Australians were more concerned to gain the support of regional states than that of the United States. And it was almost certainly in an effort to assuage Asian concerns that Evans now argued for a more modest regional security agenda. The emphasis, he suggested, "should simply be on dialogue, rather than on trying to force the pace in any institutional way."[26]

But while the Canadians and Australians were in full tactical retreat from their bold, original proposals, regional states were becoming more assertive. In July 1991, the ASEAN Post-Ministerial Conference (PMC) endorsed the proposition that the PMC was an "appropriate base" for discussion of regional security issues.[27] The decision was of major importance because the ASEAN states had, for a variety of reasons, long avoided multilateral security dialogues at the official level. ASEAN officials were concerned that narrow military conceptions of security would dominate the agenda of such a forum. They conceived security more broadly. As the Malaysian foreign minister, Datuk Abdulla Ahmed Badawi, put it, security had to be viewed "in a comprehensive manner."[28] ASEAN did not underestimate the importance of the military element, he said, but "focusing only on the narrowly defined military aspect of security" would distort national perceptions on relations between nations.[29]

Badawi went on to suggest that security would be enhanced by increasing "interdependence and confidence through economic cooperation and other regional endeavours, as well as through commitment to solve problems by peaceful means."[30] In other words it was more important to enhance security through non-military than military means.[31] This idea is central to ASEAN's conception of comprehensive security, which will be examined in more detail below.

At the same 1991 ASEAN PMC, Japan also endorsed multilateral security dialogue for the first time. The Japanese minister for foreign affairs, Taro Nakayama, stated that the annual PMC meetings should become a "forum for political dialogue" in the field of security as well as economic cooperation and diplomacy,[32] and proposed

that senior officials of ASEAN and its seven "dialogue partners" prepare a report on security matters as well as on Japan's foreign policy.[33]

Six months later, the ASEAN heads of state agreed to a more ambitious goal, namely, to "seek avenues to engage member states in new areas of cooperation in security matters."[34] ASEAN would also "intensify its external dialogues in political and security matters by using the ASEAN Post-Ministerial Conference."[35]

The United States, recognizing that its traditional security approach had grown increasingly out of step with regional thinking, did not offer any criticism. Indeed, some six months after the inauguration of the Clinton administration, U.S. policy was brought into line with the new regional realities. The assistant secretary of state for East Asia, Winston Lord, stated in May 1993 that the United States supported the dialogue on security within the PMC and that "the U.S. will fully participate."[36] The shift in U.S. thinking has helped quicken the pace and broaden the scope of regional security consultation, and in July 1993 the creation of a regionwide security forum came a step closer when ASEAN announced the establishment of the ASEAN Regional Forum (ARF).

The first meeting of the ARF was held in Bangkok on July 25, 1994. Foreign ministers from ASEAN, and ASEAN's dialogue partners, "consultative partners," and "observers" attended the meeting.[37] The foreign minister of Thailand, Prasong Soonsiri, who chaired the meeting, described it as a "historic event for the region," being the first time "the majority of states in the Asia–Pacific region came to specifically discuss political and security cooperation."[38] The meeting agreed that the ARF should be held annually and that the agenda of the follow-on ARF–Senior Officials Meetings (SOMs) and the 1995 ARF meeting (to be held in Brunei) should include comprehensive security, the issue of ARF state participation in the United Nations (UN) Conventional Arms Register, and preventive diplomacy. Notwithstanding consensus on many issues at the ARF, it is clear that there continues to be a tension between those, mostly from Western states, who wish to focus on more military confidence- and trust-building measures, and the ASEAN states for whom dialogue *at this stage* is more about building relationships than reaching specific agreements.

The Contemporary Track Two Dialogue Process

Parallel to and frequently influencing the evolution of the official security discourse has been the so-called Track Two dialogue process involving academics, "think tank" analysts, and officials who take part under the polite fiction that they are acting in their private capacity.[39]

In November 1992, representatives of a number of regional security "think tanks" met in Seoul to discuss the future direction of security dialogue activities. They concluded that the time was ripe to establish a regionwide coordinating council.[40] The Council for Security Cooperation in the Asia Pacific (CSCAP) was established in June 1993. It seeks to promote Track Two dialogue on regional security issues between all countries and territories of the Asia–Pacific region.

The main focus of CSCAP activity will be policy-oriented studies on specific regional political-security problems. These will be undertaken by working groups that will be open to countries that wish to participate. Current working group topics include:

- maritime cooperation in the Asia–Pacific region;
- enhancement of security cooperation in the North Pacific;
- concepts of cooperative and comprehensive security; and
- confidence- and security-building measures (CSBMs), and particularly transparency, with regard to the proliferation and control of weapons of mass destruction and new weapons technology.

The CSCAP proposal faces a number of practical and conceptual obstacles—including the inevitable problems of finance, organization, and membership.[41] If these problems are overcome, CSCAP may well play a valuable role in stimulating official thinking and policy. CSCAP studies will inform the deliberations of the ARF and its associated SOMs.

Late 1994: An Emerging Consensus

As of November 1994 broad consensus is emerging on a number of security issues:

- There is agreement that "multilateral dialogue" is security-enhancing because, as Winston Lord has suggested, it encourages states "to share information, convey intentions, ease tensions, resolve disputes and foster confidence."[42] In this sense it is a CBM, reflecting Winston Churchill's maxim that "jaw jaw is better than war war."
- There is general support for the principle of confidence- or trust-building, although what this entails in practice is often unclear. ASEAN conceptions of trust-building differ from the military-oriented, CSCE-derived confidence-building concepts of the West. In ASEAN greater emphasis is given to process

than to institution-building. As the former Indonesian defense minister Gen. L. B. Moerdani has put it, "processes are more important than structures."[43] The politically correct term for confidence-building in the region is now "trust-building." This term is preferred because traditional CBMs are seen as focusing too much on military issues. Trust-building is also supposed to connote the ASEAN view that dialogue is more important as a means of building relationships than as a means of achieving formal agreements.

● There is also consensus within the region that security needs to be comprehensive. This concept places great emphasis on non-military as well as military determinants of security. As will be argued later, however, comprehensive security means different things to different states in the region.

● There is almost total consensus that it is desirable for the United States to stay militarily engaged in the region.

● There is a widespread view among individual regional states that their military modernization programs build confidence and thus stability in the region. As Malaysia's defense minister, Datuk Seri Najib Tun Razak, has noted, "such modernisation should be seen as a positive step towards achieving regional stability."[44]

● Individual regional states believe that their military modernization programs should not be constrained by externally imposed limits on the number or types of weapons they acquire. With the exception of the U.S.-led campaign against Chinese and North Korean missile sales, controls on arms transfers have no support within the region and the Asia–Pacific is now one of the leading arms-importing regions in the world, absorbing around a third of total world arms transfers.[45]

● Finally, there is a fairly broad consensus within the region that the security environment of the Asia–Pacific is more benign now than it has been for decades, despite concerns about some long-term trends.

Causes for Concern

All of the above would seem to suggest that there is little cause to worry about the Asia–Pacific's security future. This is not the case. Notwithstanding the currently benign security environment, there are a number of reasons for concern:

● unresolved territorial and sovereignty conflicts, most obviously China and Taiwan and the two Koreas, but also many lesser disputes of which that over the Spratly Islands is simply the most visible;

● uncertainty about the long-term commitment of the United States to the region—and concern that if there is a major reduction in U.S. presence, aspiring regional hegemons will seek to fill the vacuum. China and Japan are the states most frequently mentioned in this context;

● rapid, but uneven, rates of economic growth throughout the region that risk generating political instabilities that could spill over into the security realm;

● proliferation of weapons of mass destruction in Northeast Asia—primarily nuclear, but also chemical and biological; and

● lack of any "habit of dialogue" in Northeast Asia to help mediate the hostilities between North and South Korea and the mutual suspicions that still exist between Japan and South Korea, Japan and Russia, and, to a lesser degree, Japan and China.

But for many analysts and commentators it is the rapid regional military buildup that is causing most concern.

The Regional Arms Buildup

In Europe, arms control was always a central element of the security discourse. Although the pan-European Mutual and Balanced Force Reduction (MBFR) talks and the subsequent Conventional Forces in Europe (CFE) and CSCE talks had only limited success, they were predicated on mutual East–West consensus that negotiated restraints on force structures, in particular on those that could "seize and hold territory," were desirable. No such consensus exists in the Asia–Pacific, where, in the name of force modernization and defense self-reliance, regional states are embarked on a far-reaching military buildup. According to Desmond Ball, some 1,500 new fighter and strike aircraft will be procured this decade in Northeast Asia; 300 in Southeast Asia.[46]

The buildup in air power, which also includes increased numbers of maritime patrol and surveillance aircraft and combat helicopters, is being paralleled, according to Ball, by naval modernization programs:

> Some 200 new major surface combatants are programmed for procurement through the 1990s, with several dozens (that is, about another 50) under serious consideration.[47]

In addition, "more than three dozen new submarines are planned for acquisition during the 1990s."[48]

Regional military capabilities are being further enhanced by the procurement of such force multipliers as Airborne Early Warning (AEW), in-flight refueling, enhanced signals intelligence and other surveillance capabilities, and modern over-the-horizon antishipping missiles like Harpoon and Exocet.

Although the above figures may well have to be revised (some are based on *probable* weapon system acquisitions that may not go ahead), there is no doubt about the general upward trend. Nor is there any doubt about where the buildup is concentrated. In 1991, the combined defense budgets of the Northeast Asian states were almost 600 percent greater than those of ASEAN, while between 1985 and 1991 the increase in defense spending was also some 600 percent greater in Northeast Asia than in the ASEAN states.[49] In the 1990s, with the important exception of Japan (which has by far the biggest military budget in the region), Northeast Asian states have increased their defense expenditures by around 10 percent or more a year.

The buildup has many causes. Corruption, prestige arms racing, and the political power exerted by the military in a number of Asian societies are among the critical domestic factors. It is also clear that one of the most powerful predictors of rises and declines in defense budgets is the rate of growth of gross national product (GNP). Rising GNP growth, which has been the norm throughout most of the region, enables absolute increases in defense budgets without any increase in the military share of national budgets.[50]

Among the more important strategic determinants of the buildup are the various unresolved territorial and sovereignty disputes noted above. Some of these disputes—that over the Spratlys is an obvious example—have been exacerbated by the creation of Exclusive Economic Zones (EEZs), which give the states that claim them the right to exploit undersea resources within them. The protection of EEZs has created new missions for the regional maritime forces that simply did not exist two decades ago.

But perhaps the single most important strategic cause of the buildup is the perception of strategic uncertainty in a region characterized by rapid and wrenching social and political change, and where the long-term commitment of the United States seems problematic. Confronting a highly uncertain strategic future regional states are, prudently in their view, planning for the worst. As Malaysian defense minister Najib noted in July 1993, the end of the Cold War has made the security environment in Asia "fluid and unpredictable," and countries should therefore "prepare for the worst scenario."[51] For most regional defense planners, preparing for the worst scenario means increasing defense outlays.

This said, and alarmist claims to the contrary, there is no arms race in the region at the moment. With the exception of the two Koreas, regional states are not arming competitively against each other, but rather against an uncertain security future. Moreover, no states within the region are seeking to acquire the numbers or types of weapons needed to mount invasions, or other major assaults, against their neighbors.[52]

Some regional security planners argue that for these and other reasons, there is no cause for concern. Indeed, as long as political relationships in the region remain generally benign, the arms buildup poses little threat to regional security. States do not generally worry when states they regard as friends increase their defense preparations.

But cause for concern remains, because no one can guarantee that politi-

cal relationships will not deteriorate in the future. It is in the context of escalating political conflict that the arms-acquisition process, which seems so necessary to military planners as a means of enhancing security, may actually undermine it.

What makes a military buildup destabilizing is not the buildup per se, but the balance between offensive and defensive forces.[53] The former are becoming increasingly significant in the region. As Desmond Ball points out:

Air power is at the forefront of the force modernization programs in the region, but it is also a principal means of projecting power in the region. Air power is inherently (although not only) offensive. The quantitative and qualitative enhancements of airpower are perhaps the most prone to triggering unanticipated and undesired arms acquisition programs.

Other acquisitions, such as submarines and long-range anti-ship missiles, are more disturbing in terms of their implications for crisis stability. The underwater environment is particularly opaque, and underwater operations are particularly subject to uncertainty, confusion, loss of control, and accidents. Similarly, over-the-horizon targeting of long-range anti-ship missiles raises the prospect of errors and miscalculation. Inadvertent escalation becomes increasingly likely.[54]

Military planners seek to acquire offensive weapons platforms because they are believed to enhance both deterrence and war-fighting capabilities. They may well do both. But offense-dominant force structures and strategies can also threaten strategic stability and it is important to weigh the alleged deterrence benefits against the strategic stability costs.

Because offensive arms can be used for aggression as well as defense, their very existence will inevitably raise suspicions about intentions in the minds of prudent adversaries who think in worst-case terms. When rival states each start adding offensive weapons to their inventories, following the ancient precept "If you want peace prepare for war," they are laying the basis for an arms race.

States usually engage in arms races to prevent war. They seek to achieve a military balance by matching the arms buildup of their adversary with a countervailing buildup of their own. In realist theory, this balancing process acts as a disincentive to war. But arms races generally do not achieve this desirable end. A study by Michael Wallace, a Canadian political scientist, found that 82 percent of arms races associated with serious international disputes culminated in war.[55] The reasons are not difficult to determine. Each new offensive platform that a state introduces into its force structure creates both a new threat to, and a new target for, its adversaries, creating an imperative for them to respond in kind.

Moreover, if striking first against an adversary's offensive weapon systems confers a clear strategic advantage, then preemption may seem a rational strategy in a crisis. The strategic logic, which applies to each side equally, is simple: destroy the adversary's offensive systems before your systems are destroyed. Neither side need harbor aggressive intentions toward the other for war, nevertheless, to result. This is a classic example of the so-called security dilemma, in which the defensive preparations—and actions—of each side conspire to undermine the security of both. Thus so-called inadvertent wars, that is, wars that none of the protagonists originally sought, are not the result of a revisionist impulse to old-fashioned aggression, but arise from a combination of uncertainty about intentions and the destabilizing dynamics of the security dilemma.

Common Security: An Appropriate Strategy for the Region?

Given the reality of the regional military buildup, given the fact that regional defense planners tend to see the world through the lenses of realist theory, and given that there are many possible causes for future political instability in the region, it might seem that addressing the risks that security dilemmas may generate should be high on the regional security agenda. This is not the case, despite much talk about confidence-building and cooperative security, that is, seeking security *with* other countries rather than against them. This interest is not yet reflected in regional defense planning—with one possible exception.

Common security strategies have been endorsed on a number of occasions by Australian foreign minister Evans and at least once by Malaysian defense minister Najib.[56] We believe that they are of particular relevance to the region and offer an escape from the destabilizing logic of the security dilemma.

Common security is predicated on the assumption that states share a common interest in avoiding war, that the security dilemma dynamic is a major cause of war, and that war avoidance is best pursued via strategies that emphasize cooperation and reassurance, and reduce the emphasis on confrontation and deterrence.

Common security does not mean the abandonment of military force. Military deterrence and defense will be necessary in the region for the foreseeable future because revisionist aggression, even if of declining importance among developed states,[57] remains a finite risk. But reassurance strategies are also needed to address the causes of instability inherent in the security dilemma. Political dialogue and trust-building, which have been very much part of the intra-ASEAN strategy of mutual reassurance, are clearly important here. But they do not address the force posture issue that is also critical if security dilemma risks are to be resolved.

To address both the risk of aggression and the destabilizing dynamics of the security dilemma, regional security policies must combine both deterrence and reassurance. Common security seeks to do both.

The problem for advocates of common security lies in finding an appropriate and stable balance between the requirements of deterrence and reassurance.[58] This is extraordinarily difficult—not least because they are often antithetical. One possible solution to the problem, a strategy that evolved in the context of the European security debate of the early and mid-1980s, is "non-provocative defense" (NPD).[59]

NPD has been defined as:

The buildup, training, logistics and doctrine of the armed forces . . . such that they are seen in their totality to be unsuitable for offense, but unambiguously sufficient for a credible defense.[60]

NPD strategies eschew offensive deterrent capabilities—"deterrence-by-punishment"—and rely rather on "deterrence-by-denial." The latter is predicated on the assumption that the anticipated cost of waging war *and not winning* constitutes a sufficient deterrent against aggression.

Critics of NPD argue that deterrence-by-denial is inadequate. Proponents counter by arguing that because security dilemmas are a far more probable cause of war than aggression, reassurance should take priority over deterrence in determining strategy and force structure—*even if war-fighting/deterrence capabilities are less powerful as a consequence.*

The strategic benefits of common security strategies tend to be rejected by realist proponents of peace through strength. Yet these benefits are considerable. Defense-dominant force postures signal to potential adversaries unambiguously defensive intentions, thus avoiding the exacerbation of suspicion, tension, and hostility that is characteristic of the security dilemma. NPD strategies remove *all* incentives for an opponent to resort to preemptive or preventive war—that is, they enhance both crisis avoidance and crisis stability. If adopted mutually, which is always the preferred option, they eliminate incentives for arms races. A state that has only defensive arms and adds more defensive capabilities increases its own military security without threatening that of other states, or requiring a countervailing response from them. In the Asia–Pacific, Japan's military posture fits closely with the precepts of NPD. Japan has deliberately eschewed the acquisition of long-range offensive weapons platforms—bombers, missiles, aircraft carriers, etc.—in part to reassure its neighbors. Japan has been able to do this, of course, because U.S. forces have provided the offensive sword to match the Japanese defensive shield. Many regional states worry that, should the U.S.–Japan alliance relationship unravel, Japan would seek to acquire the offensive systems it currently lacks—a move that could have grave consequences for regional security.

The key limitation of common security is that its focus is primarily military. Its proponents in Europe have had little to say about the non-military determinants or instruments of security, either at the national or international level. It remains, however, the one approach to security that offers a solution to the risks attendant in security dilemmas. And security dilemma risks cannot be ignored in a region that is characterized by both strategic uncertainty and a rapid military buildup.

Comprehensive Security

In sharp contrast to the strong military orientation of the Western-derived concept of common security, the concept of comprehensive security, which is widely endorsed in the region, emphasizes non-military means of achieving and maintaining security. Comprehensive security is not an idea that has been elaborated conceptually in the region to any degree—at least at the official level. But it does, in part at least, guide policy in a number of Asian states, particularly in Japan and the member states of ASEAN. There are important differences between the Japanese and ASEAN approaches, but both stress the importance of the non-military instruments of security policy.

In ASEAN, the concept of comprehensive security has been promoted most vigorously by Malaysia and Indonesia. In contrast to Western security concepts—and to that of Japan—the ASEAN concept of comprehensive security operates at three basic levels: intrastate, intra-ASEAN, and between ASEAN and the rest of the region.

The strong domestic focus in ASEAN's comprehensive security philosophy is not surprising. Both Malaysia and Indonesia are ethnically and culturally diverse societies and each

has endured years of civil strife. Comprehensive security policy at the national level seeks to promote "national resilience," nation-building, good governance, and thus political stability. The goal is not least to secure the state against dissident sectors of civil society. Although the military plays a role in this process, political, social, and economic policy is far more important.

This essentially non-military approach is similar in some ways to the core recommendations in UN Secretary General Boutros Boutros-Ghali's 1992 *Agenda for Peace*,[61] which called for more resources to be allocated to peace-building and to preventive diplomacy. Gareth Evans's 1993 *Cooperating for Peace* expanded on many of the ideas in Boutros-Ghali's 50-page report.[62] Evans argues that economic and social development, the protection of human rights, and promotion of good governance and democracy should be seen as security policies and receive a share of the security resources that now go overwhelmingly to the military.

Comprehensive security is also seen as having an important role to play in promoting intra-ASEAN security. Here the non-military approach becomes critically important because, although political relationships between member states are generally good, unresolved conflicts remain in intra-ASEAN relations that national defense planners must take into account. Many of these issues are so sensitive that it would be unthinkable to place them on any military security dialogue agenda. For example, prudent Singaporean defense planners have to take seriously the possibility that one day they could be involved in military hostilities with Malaysia—and vice versa. Their military contingency planning will necessarily reflect this fact.

Yet these are issues that, for obvious political as well as military reasons, security planners cannot openly discuss with each other.

It is, thus, somewhat ironic that, whereas defense planners in the North Atlantic Treaty Organization (NATO) could engage their adversaries in frank debate about fundamental security concerns, in ASEAN this is almost impossible—and is certainly avoided. Paradoxically, it may be easier to talk security with enemies than with countries that are ostensibly friends, but where underlying tensions in the security relationship remain. The need to avoid discussion of sensitive military issues suggests another reason why ASEAN's comprehensive security approach is so different from the military-oriented approaches of the West.[63]

Comprehensive security deliberately plays down the military dimension of security in intra-ASEAN relations while emphasizing such non-military factors as political dialogue, economic cooperation, interdependence, and good governance. This has been a remarkably successful strategy over the past three decades. Although many old tensions remain, they are now relatively marginal in comparison with the webs of cooperation and the bonds of common interest that have been built up over the years. Moreover, as cooperation and interdependence within the subregion increase, the costs of military conflict also increase—creating a further incentive to avoid it.

Promotion of national resilience is also directly related to intraregional security and to enhancing the security of ASEAN as a whole vis-à-vis the outside world. According to Jusuf Wanandi, one of Indonesia's leading strategic analysts:

if each [ASEAN] member nation can accomplish an overall national development and overcome internal threats, regional resilience can result, much in the same way as a chain derives its overall strength from the strength of its constituent parts.[64]

Regional resilience based on national resilience makes ASEAN a less tempting target for external intervention. Concern about the latter arises out of the historical experience of both countries and remains a sensitive issue.

Wanandi's suggestion of a link between national development and security also has some parallels with the argument that democracies do not go to war with each other. Throughout Asia there has been a move toward more pluralist and democratic political systems over the past decade. *If* the association between market-driven economic growth and political pluralism is what some claim it to be, then economic growth in the region may indirectly enhance regional security. Ironically, however, the same economic development that is seen as essential to comprehensive security is also a major factor driving the military buildup in the region. This, as argued above, could have a negative impact on regional security in the future.

In Japan, where the doctrine of comprehensive security emerged in the early 1980s, the focus of security policy is exclusively on the external environment. This, too, is unsurprising. Japan is, with some few exceptions, ethnically homogenous, developed, and politically stable. But Japan is also a society that has a relatively recent history of imperial war and that, as a consequence, is mistrusted by many of its neighbors. Reassurance of those neighbors is central to Japan's comprehensive security policy. In addition, because Japan is highly dependent on the outside world for key resources, security of access to such resources has also been a high priority for Japanese security planners.

Thus, unlike that of some of the ASEAN states, Japan's security policy is wholly outward in orientation. It seeks above all to maintain a benign regional environment. But because its "peace" constitution precludes the possibility of using military power as an instrument of statecraft, Japan can only pursue its security goals by political, diplomatic, and economic means. Hence Japan's trade and foreign direct investment policies—which create regional interdependency—and official development aid policy,[65] both have a security dimension. But Japan seeks above all to maintain the continued engagement of the United States in the region. The United States contributes to Japan's security directly via the commitment of U.S. forces to Japan's defense, and indirectly by "enmeshing" Japan and so providing political reassurance to other regional powers. As noted earlier, Japan's own military posture is closely in line with the precepts of common security and NPD—that is, it deliberately eschews offensive and power projection weapon systems. This has been an enormously important source of reassurance.

Conclusion

Comprehensive security and common security strategies are complementary in that each addresses security issues that tend to be ignored by the other.[66] The non-military instruments of comprehensive security can help prevent latent conflicts from becoming manifest and thus keep security dilemma risks at bay. Common security policies become relevant if the long-term

peace-building and shorter-term non-military conflict-prevention and management policies associated with comprehensive security fail. Comprehensive security emphasizes factors that lie outside the ambit of conventional security analysis and practice; the focus of common security lies primarily in the military realm. Both approaches, however, stress the need for cooperation. Within the region, comprehensive security exists as a fairly successful practice, but without a well-developed or articulated strategic theory underpinning it. Common security, on the other hand, does have a well-articulated strategic theory, albeit one that evolved in the very different strategic context of Europe, but common security principles are not reflected in regional defense practice—except possibly in the case of Japan. Indeed, regional states are currently arming themselves against the very neighbors with which they are seeking to cooperate and build trust.

In late 1994, the Asia–Pacific has reached the point where multilateral dialogue is accepted as a security-enhancing process and where, for the first time in the region's history, dialogue has been institutionalized—in the ASEAN Regional Forum and its associated Senior Officials Meetings. The 1990s have also seen a proliferation of new bilateral cooperative security arrangements between regional states—particularly in Southeast Asia. But whether the current enthusiasm for trust-building and cooperation in the region will move beyond the talking stage to affect the *practice* of regional defense planning—which remains wedded to the bleak assumptions of realism—remains to be seen.

Notes

1. See text of speech by Mikhail Gorbachev in Vladivostok, July 28, 1986, reprinted in

Ramesh Thakur and Carlyle Thayer, eds., *The Soviet Union as an Asian Pacific Power* (Boulder, Colo., and South Melbourne: Westview/Macmillan Australia, 1987), p. 223.

2. In subsequent proposals the Soviets suggested three-way talks between the Soviet Union, Japan, and the United States (see Daniel Sneider, "Soviets Wage Glasnost at Sea," *Christian Science Monitor*, August 4, 1989, p. 10); demilitarization of the Arctic; and U.S.–Soviet naval reductions and CBMs. In the 1990s they suggested multilateral naval arms limitations between the Soviet Union, China, Japan, and the two Koreas and an "open skies" agreement (see Trevor Findlay, "Asia–Pacific CSBMs: A Prospectus," Working Paper no. 90 [Peace Research Centre, The Australian National University, Canberra, 1990]).

3. Bill Hayden, "Security and Arms Control in the North Pacific," in Andrew Mack and Paul Keal, eds., *Arms Control in the North Pacific* (Sydney: Allen & Unwin, 1988), p. 4.

4. *Ibid.*, p. 5.

5. *Ibid.*

6. The first CSCE was held in Helsinki in 1975.

7. Bill Hayden, "Leadership in the Asia–Pacific Region" (speech at the East–West Center, Hawaii, June 6, 1988); and "Hayden Plan to Cut War Risks in Pacific," *Age* (Melbourne, Australia), June 30, 1988, p. 7.

8. At the non-official level, academic institutions, including the Peace Research Centre at The Australian National University, Stanford University in California, and the Institute of Strategic and International Studies (ISIS) in Malaysia, were all arguing for CBM regimes for U.S. and Soviet forces in the North Pacific. In 1987, ISIS Malaysia ran the first in a series of annual regional security roundtables in Kuala Lumpur. Many of the CBM proposals currently under consideration were first put forward at ISIS roundtables and are recorded in the roundtable proceedings published annually by ISIS Malaysia.

9. China's tendency to play balance of power politics between the two superpowers meant that bipolarity in Asia was never as simple as it had been in Europe.

10. Gareth Evans, address to the Committee for the Economic Development of Australia (CEDA), Melbourne, March 22, 1990.

11. Gareth Evans, "Australia's Asian Future" (lecture at Monash University, Melbourne, July 19, 1990), pp. 10–11.

12. Joe Clark, "Canada and Asia Pacific in the 1990s" (speech to the Victoria Chamber of Commerce, Victoria, British Columbia, July 17, 1990), p. 8.

13. The participants would be Canada, China, Russia, Japan, South and North Korea, and the United States. Both Canberra and Ottawa were quite cool to each other's proposals, even though they had much in common.

14. Gareth Evans, "Alliances and Change in the U.S. Relationship" (lecture given at the University of Texas, Austin, on October 9, 1990, printed in *Monthly Record* 61 [October 1990], p. 697). Evans, mindful of U.S. views, was careful to note that "the present framework of United States alliances in the region can and should remain, for the foreseeable future, as a solid base for that transition."

15. Richard Solomon, "Asian Security in the 1990s: Integration in Economics; Diversity in Defense" (lecture given at the University of California at San Diego, October 30, 1990).

16. *Ibid.*

17. *Australian Financial Review*, May 2, 1991. The letter was leaked to the *AFR* and printed in full.

18. *Ibid.*

19. "ASEAN Cool to Pacific Security Proposal," *New Straits Times*, and *Business Times*, October 8, 1990.

20. *Ibid.*

21. *Ibid.*

22. *Toronto Star*, July 25, 1990. Japanese Foreign Minister Taro Nakayama had a slightly different response, saying that Tokyo was interested in new security frameworks and envisaged a larger grouping of states than that in the Canadian proposal. See Edith Terry, "Canadian Proposal for Pacific Security Rejected by Tokyo," *Globe and Mail*, July 24, 1990, and "Japan Cuts

Loose from Old Isolation," *Globe and Mail,* July 25, 1990.

23. Joe Clark, speech to the North Pacific Security Dialogue in Victoria, British Columbia, April 6, 1991.

24. Gareth Evans, "The Asia Pacific and Global Change" (address to the Trilateral Commission, Tokyo, April 20, 1991).

25. *Ibid.*

26. Gareth Evans, "Australia's Regional Security Environment," in Desmond Ball and David Horner, eds., *Strategic Studies in a Changing World: Global, Regional and Australian Perspectives* (Canberra: Strategic and Defence Studies Centre, Research School of Pacific Studies, The Australian National University, 1992), p. 382.

27. Joint Communiqué of the Twenty-fourth ASEAN Post-Ministerial Meeting, Kuala Lumpur, July 19–20, 1991, p. 5.

28. Michael Richardson, "U.S. Wary of Japanese Plan," *International Herald Tribune,* July 23, 1991.

29. *Ibid.*

30. *Ibid.*

31. While the ASEAN countries were stressing the importance of economic and political cooperation as security measures, Australia was continuing to stress military measures. Among the CBMs proposed by Evans at the same 1991 July PMC were incidents-at-sea arrangements; greater transparency through exchange of data on military budgets and strategic doctrines; observers at exercises; and methods to prevent proliferation. See his address to the Twenty-fourth ASEAN Post-Ministerial Conference, 6 plus 7 Session, Kuala Lumpur, July 22, 1991, pp. 1–2. These types of CBMs reflected the military orientation of the European CBM agenda.

32. Taro Nakayama, "Statement to the General Session of the ASEAN Post-Ministerial Conference" (Kuala Lumpur, July 22, 1991), pp. 12–13; also "U.S. Looks to New Ties with ASEAN Allies," *Canberra Times,* July 24, 1991.

33. At the time, the ASEAN states rejected Nakayama's proposal for a senior officials meeting. Later, in February 1993, ASEAN agreed to the idea. The first meeting was held in Singapore in May 1993. See Yoshihide Soeya, "The Evolution of Japanese Thinking and Policies on Cooperative Security in the 1980s and 1990s," *Australian Journal of International Affairs* 48 (May 1994).

34. *Singapore Declaration of 1992,* press release by ASEAN Heads of Government Meeting, Singapore, January 27–28, 1992, pp. 1–8.

35. *Ibid.*

36. United States Information Service, "Lord Lays Out 10 Goals for U.S. Policy in Asia," Canberra, April 5, 1993, p. 10. In July 1993, President Bill Clinton said in an address to the Korean National Assembly, "[s]ome in the U.S. have been reluctant to enter into regional dialogues with Asia [because] they fear it would seem a pretext for American withdrawal from the area," but he saw such dialogues as the PMC "as a way to supplement [U.S.] alliances and forward military presence, not to supplant them." See Bill Clinton, "The Remarks by the President in Address to the National Assembly" (speech to the National Assembly, Seoul, July 13, 1993).

37. ASEAN consists of Brunei Darussalam, Indonesia, Malaysia, Philippines, Singapore, and Thailand. ASEAN's dialogue partners are Australia, Canada, the European Union, Japan, New Zealand, the Republic of Korea, and the United States. Its consultative partners are China and Russia, and its observers are Laos, Papua New Guinea, and Vietnam.

38. *Chairman's Statement, the First Meeting of the ASEAN Regional Forum (ARF) 25 July 1994, Bangkok,* ASEAN Regional Forum Press Release, July 25, 1994, issued at the ASEAN Regional Forum.

39. See Paul M. Evans, ed., *Studying Asia Pacific Security* (North York: University of Toronto–York University, 1994), pp. 309–316, for an inventory of dialogue channels.

40. The founding institutes are: the Strategic and Defence Studies Centre (SDSC) at The Australian National University, Australia; the University of Toronto–York University Joint Center for Asia Pacific Studies, Canada; the Centre for Strategic and International Studies (CSIS), Indonesia; the Japan Institute of International Affairs (JIIA), Japan; the Seoul Forum for International Affairs, Republic of Korea; the Institute of Strategic and International Studies (ISIS), Malaysia; the Institute for

Strategic and Development Studies, Philippines; the Singapore Institute of International Affairs (SIIA), Singapore; the Institute for Security and International Studies (ISIS), Thailand; and the Pacific Forum/CSIS in the United States.

41. See Desmond Ball, "CSCAP: Its Future in the Regional Security Architecture" (paper presented at the Eighth Asia–Pacific Roundtable, organized by ASEAN–ISIS, Kuala Lumpur, June 5–8, 1994).

42. USIS, "Lord Lays Out 10 Goals," p. 10.

43. L.B. Moerdani, dinner address at a conference on "The Future of Asia Pacific Security Studies and Exchange Activities," co-organized in Bali by the Centre for Strategic and International Studies, Jakarta, and the University of Toronto–York University Joint Centre for Asia Pacific Studies, December 12–15, 1993, p. 5.

44. "Najib: Asean Needs Arms Registry to Instil Confidence," *New Straits Times,* June 10, 1993, p. 3.

45. In 1991, the Asia–Pacific accounted for 35 percent of all imports of major weapons, more than any other region including Europe. See Gerald Segal, "Managing New Arms Races in the Asia/Pacific," *The Washington Quarterly* 15 (Summer 1992), p. 83. Segal bases his figure on statistics taken from the U.S. Arms Control and Disarmament Agency, *World Military Expenditures and Arms Transfers, 1990* (Washington, D.C., 1991), and *SIPRI Yearbook 1992* (Oxford: Oxford University Press for SIPRI, 1992).

46. See Desmond Ball, "Trends in Military Acquisitions in the Region: Implications for Security and Prospects for Constraints and Controls" (paper prepared for the Seventh Asia–Pacific Roundtable organized by ASEAN–ISIS, Kuala Lumpur, June 6–9, 1993), pp. 17–19.

47. *Ibid.,* p. 18.

48. *Ibid.,* p. 19. There are approximately 100 submarines already in the region, but many are obsolete and out of operational service.

49. See *The Military Balance, 1992–1993* (London: Brassey's for International Institute for Strategic Studies, 1992), pp. 220–221. There are no reliable data for the Indochinese states, but there is general consensus that their defense outlays have been falling in the 1990s largely as a consequence of the domestic economic crises that all are suffering.

50. Indeed when GNP growth rates are high, defense budgets can decline as a percentage of GNP while still rising in absolute terms. The absolute figure is a far more important indicator of military capability than the percentage of GNP figure.

51. *Age* (Melbourne, Australia), July 13, 1993, p. 9.

52. North Korea already has such a force and, given the size of its armed forces, China inevitably has some ability to seize and hold the territory of its neighbors, as does Russia. However, neither the current procurement plans nor exercise patterns of China and Russia suggest any intent to invade neighbors.

53. It is often argued that there is no such thing as a defensive weapon because defensive systems can act as force multipliers for the offense. This is both true and irrelevant. The issue is not particular weapons, but total *force postures*. It is possible to categorize a force posture as more or less offensive. Japan, an island state that has eschewed long-range offensive systems, provides one such example.

54. Ball, "Trends in Military Acquisitions in the Region," pp. 22–23.

55. See Michael Wallace, "Arms Races and Escalation: Some New Evidence," in J. D. Singer, ed., *Explaining War: Selected Papers from the Correlates of War Project* (Beverly Hills, Calif.: Sage, 1979).

56. Datuk Seri Najib Tun Razak, "Regional Security: Towards Cooperative Security and Regional Stability" (paper prepared for the Army Land Warfare Conference, Darwin, February 1992). Neither Evans, Najib, nor any other official has spelled out in detail what they mean by the concept.

57. The following factors combine to reduce the utility of aggression as an instrument of statecraft: the growing global norm against the use of force in international affairs; the increasing costs and declining benefits of war; the increased salience of economic over military power in international relations; and the declining utility of coercion as a tool of governance.

58. If reassurance were the sole goal of common security, then unilateral disarmament

would be the most obvious means to achieve it.

59. The idea of non-provocative defense had earlier antecedents—and many different names.

60. F. Barnaby and M. Ter Borg, *Emerging Technologies and Military Doctrine: A Political Assessment* (London: Macmillan, 1986), p. 276.

61. Boutros Boutros-Ghali, *An Agenda for Peace* (New York, N.Y.: United Nations, 1992).

62. Gareth Evans, *Cooperating for Peace: The Global Agenda for the 1990s and Beyond* (Sydney: Allen and Unwin, 1993).

63. *Non*-sensitive military issues can, of course, be discussed and military cooperation can take place to a certain level. What cannot be dealt with are such issues as the military contingency plans of ASEAN states.

64. Jusuf Wanandi, "Security Issues in the ASEAN Region," in Karl Jackson and M. Hadi Soesatro, eds., *ASEAN Security and Economic Development* (Berkeley: Institute of East Asian Studies, University of California at Berkeley, 1984).

65. Japan is now the world's largest aid donor.

66. One should also note that the evolving security discourse in the region contains several notable silences. Collective security is frequently used in the region but in many different ways. Little attention is paid to collective security in the classic sense of the term. Nor have peace-building or preventive diplomacy been much discussed.

V. Proliferation and World Order

The South and the New World Order

Shahram Chubin

THE INTERNATIONAL SYSTEM of the last 50 years, one dominated and framed by the bipolar superpower rivalry, has been replaced by something more regionally fragmented and multifaceted, more plural and varied. Within this new system, the perspectives, interests, and security needs of the states of the South play an increasingly significant role. For lack of a better term, the "South" is used here to describe that diverse collection of countries in varying degrees developing, nonaligned, and heretofore peripheral to the centers of world politics. Whether they will contribute toward the emergence of a new order, or reinforce the drift toward anarchy, remains to be seen. The developed world is ill-prepared for this fact, both conceptually and as a matter of policy.

This article surveys the perspectives and attitudes of leaders in states of the South concerning the emerging international agenda. It is an explication, not a defense, and a partial one at best. There is no such thing as a coherent worldview of the South. But the failure to understand the South and to translate such understanding into effective diplomatic, economic,

political, and military strategies will have profound consequences. Partnership between North and South remains a possibility, although arguably an improbable one. Antipathy and confrontation are also possible, and made more likely by Northern complacency.

The article begins with a review of the state of the South in the 1990s, evaluating the problems of security and development faced by these countries and the changing international context in which leaders of these states make choices. The analysis then turns to the key issues of world order on the North–South agenda, namely proliferation, arms control, and collective security. The aim of the paper is not to justify proliferation in the South or the repressive domestic policies of some of these states, but to argue that a U.S. policy style more sensitive to a broader consensus will be more effective in achieving its proper ends than a peremptory style that Americans might find congenial in an era of limited attention to and patience with the South.

The State of the South

Most scholars in the North appreciate that the South faces large challenges of economic development. But this is hardly enough. In writing about "the end of history," Francis Fukuyama has helped to broaden common under-

Shahram Chubin is a specialist in Middle East politics and security studies who is based in Geneva, Switzerland.

Copyright © 1993 by The Center for Strategic and International Studies and the Massachusetts Institute of Technology

standing of the South by describing it as pre-historical and still embroiled in "struggle, war, injustice and poverty" even while the North moves on to a new level of historical development.[1] Even this fails to capture the enormity of the challenge. The South faces, in fact, a daunting set of interconnected problems in the economic, political, social, and security domains. Many Southern countries are also corrupt, unrepresentative, and repressive. Because these problems coexist with rapidly rising expectations, these countries cannot develop at the more leisurely pace enjoyed by the now developed world, where progress toward the current level of development is measured in centuries, not decades. Thus, in some fundamental sense, the circumstances of the South are without precedent. Moreover, the South is under siege—from an international community impatient to meddle in its affairs. States of the South are losing their sovereignty, which in many cases was only recently or tentatively acquired.

The problems of development confronting the South do not require recitation here. The large gap in living standards between South and North is well known. Less well known is the fact that in many parts of the South population pressures, chronic misgovernment, political insecurity, and conceptual poverty combine to drive countries backward, not forward—so the gap widens. The revolution of expectations, both political and economic, is putting governments under new stresses to perform and to direct the myriad processes of change.

Northerners are now engaged in a debate about whether the essence of power is military or political, but for most Southern states this debate is immaterial—they are unable to achieve either. The rentier states of the Per-

sian Gulf after two decades of respectable oil revenues have been unable to achieve sustained development, transform their economies to guarantee results without oil, cooperate meaningfully on regional security, or move toward democracy, which some of them deny to be compatible with their traditions. As for military power, the accumulation of arms has been an empty and futile policy gesture except as a means of buying into Western security by recycling oil money to the West—a modern form of subvention.

Even where the economy is growing, as in Indonesia, there is no respite from concern for security. There, as elsewhere in the South, this is mainly defined in terms of internal security and unity. This implies controlling government institutions and securing the people's loyalty, which in turn implies cultivating the "values" of the country as well as developing its national resources. In areas where national polities are fragile, state institutions new, weak, or under attack, ethnic balances unstable or poorly structured, the tendency to emphasize the center, and to hope that it will "hold," is commonplace and understandable. People concerned about keeping the country together find intrepid researchers looking for clues of civil society or embryonic pluralism a nuisance. In many places, the state is under pressure from corrupt oligarchies (whether traditional, governmental, or business) and international institutions dispensing advice about structural adjustment. No wonder, then, that there are countries in which the state has simply broken down, unable to deal with demands and stresses.

In an era of growing global interdependence states of the South remain more vulnerable than their counterparts in the North and more sensitive to forces beyond their borders. Consider the sliding commodity prices over the past decade, or even the much weakened position of oil producers, a relatively privileged group. Consider, too, the issue of the environment, where Southern states are being asked to meet standards and to consider the question cooperatively and in terms of interdependence. Yet as Maurice Strong, former director general of the United Nations (UN) Environment Program, has said: "The absorptive capacity of the eco-system is being preempted by the North," which should accept the responsibility of "making space" for the others.[2]

Furthermore, in much of the South, states and frontiers are relatively artificial, and the forces keeping them intact have weakened. The end of the Cold War and bipolarity undermined a framework that had favored the territorial status quo and made international intervention difficult. The end of the Communist empire has set off fissiparous tendencies long latent in the multinational composite bloc and simultaneously sapped and delegitimized authoritarianism everywhere.[3]

Moreover, the developing states are undergoing change at a time of maximum exposure to political pressures: "A crucial difference between the nation building of Western Europe and that of Africa and much of Asia," we are reminded, "was that the processes in Europe occurred well before the rise of popular demands for democratic rights: nations already existed as relatively cohesive citizenries."[4] It is no comfort to these countries that sovereignty has been, or is being, redefined in the home of the nation-state, with a turn toward smaller communities and intermediate institutions between government (the market) and the individual.

All of this has undermined tradi-tional notions of state sovereignty in the South. As one scholar has put it, international law now protects "the people's sovereignty rather than the sovereign's sovereignty." Sovereignty can no longer be considered an exclusively domestic issue, or "used as an all-purpose excuse or wall by states to exclude external interest" or intervention. States like the People's Republic of China (PRC), which continue to try to emphasize noninterference in the internal affairs of others, are thus considered "wholly anachronistic."[5] In the words of the secretary general of the UN, "the time of absolute and exclusive sovereignty . . . has passed; its theory was never matched by reality." He called for "a balance between the needs of good internal governance and the requirements of an ever more interdependent world."[6]

The North's weakening commitment to the sovereignty of states of the South is evident in the increased concern about human rights as an international rather than strictly domestic concern, and the concomitant increased willingness to intervene in a state's internal affairs in defense of ostensibly international standards. This has made leaders of states of the South fearful. Their fear grows even more sharp when well-meaning analysts argue that as an antidote to the excesses and disintegrative tendencies of self-determination, minority (communitarian) or individual human rights should be stressed.

It is, of course, one thing to observe the drift toward weakening sovereignty, and entirely another to encourage it as an unmitigated good in itself, castigating the backsliders who resist. The PRC is a favorite whipping boy here: "Many states, especially China in recent years, have sought to hide behind 'sovereignty' to shield themselves from international criticism of their abysmal human rights records."[7] Western policy appears to have exacerbated the problems of sovereignty facing the South with little consideration of ultimate objectives. Chester Crocker has it right: "We in the post-industrial north are encouraging an across-the-board challenge to the political and territorial status quo."[8]

To be sure, the human community appears to have reached a stage "in the ethical and psychological evolution of Western civilization in which the massive and deliberate violation of human rights will no longer be tolerated."[9] Criteria have been defined whereby intervention will occur only if human rights violations constitute a threat to international security. Nonetheless, it is easy to see that a right to intervention is an implicit challenge to states if not a direct threat, especially if broadened as an excuse for intervention to unravel and make over states. What the Islamic Republic of Iran disarmingly calls "international arrogance" can be precisely that. On these issues its views are not far from those of India, the PRC, and many other states of the South. Few are sufficiently homogenous or confident of their policies toward their minorities to be unaffected by the cultivation of the right or duty to intervene that has been promulgated in recent years.

Advocates of the right of intervention would do well to note that despite all the global forces promoting cultural convergence or standardization, homogenization has not (yet) been achieved. Regrettably or not, nations remain different and determined to pursue their own ideas about politics, the role of the state, religion, independence, equality, and cultural liberation.

Cultural differences among states influence their perceptions of international relations. Many states of the South believe that existing international legal rules were not only made by the European or Western powers but "were also substantially made *for* them" (emphasis in the original).[10] Within the non-Western world, international relations are shaped by forces not evident in Europe today. As one expert has written: "One of the main shared themes in the non-Western realms . . . is the reaffirmation of traditional religious beliefs as ultimate norm-setting principles of identity in politics and culture."[11] The resurgence of religiosity is stronger in Islam than in any other religious tradition, although it is hardly confined to it. In the Middle East this has been given an additional twist by the proximity of Christianity, with which it has battled for some 14 centuries.

By and large, Western values have been imposed on societies that have ritualistically admired or accepted them. But as one observer has written: "the alien laws, not being rooted in deep convictions and old customs, were simply not accepted by the people as the necessary regulative principles of society." Rather the central issue for them was "how to preserve the community and make it strong by generating dynamism and common will."[12] As Adda Bozeman notes, religion and identity gravitate toward the past,

> And since the glory of the past is forever associated with Islam, it is the road back to the Koran that is being fervently sought not only in the Near East but throughout the commonwealth of *c.* 600 million believers. This means, *mutatis mutandis*, a near total refutation of the West's Promethean civilization which earlier generations had accepted as the most promising source of guidelines for

the recovery of success in history.[13]

Among other things, the concept of "state" does not have the legitimacy or currency in Islam as elsewhere, especially as it applies to the idea of a "community of states" as opposed to traditional Islamic concepts. Ayatollah Ruhollah Khomeini used to say that he had not promised democracy but Islam, which is what his followers had clamored for. In Algeria in 1993 the same issue is raised—Islam or democracy—for the two are not identical, nor, given the latter's emphasis on pluralism, necessarily compatible.

In a multicultural world, life may be richer but disputes harder to resolve. Combined with inequalities and political resentments, cultural differences and incomprehension can exacerbate North–South relations in a profoundly negative way.

During the Cold War, the states of the South were able to partially compensate for their weaknesses by banding together under the rubric of nonalignment. But this political device is now lost to them. Nonalignment died with the Cold War. More than that, the way the East–West rivalry ended, with the values and systems of the West vindicated and triumphant, undermined the very basis of the nonaligned movement, which had adopted as its foundation a moral neutrality between the two blocs.

For the erstwhile nonaligned, the end of the Cold War has had cataclysmic results. The old uncertainties of the cold war structure, which tended to nurture the status quo and play to the strengths of authoritarian regimes, have given way to a more fluid world in which the assets of the South, whether individually or collectively, are transformed. No longer proxies, clients, and strategic bases, these states are judged by their adherence to standards, values, and procedures that are now generally and unabashedly seen as full international responsibilities. These states now face strong pressures to adhere to various norms (human rights and democratic procedures) and policies (adherence to nonproliferation of nuclear and other mass destruction weapons and limitations on military spending), which some may find difficult or undesirable.

On the other hand, the end of the Cold War has freed the North to indulge its basic antipathy toward the poorer South, to dictate to it without delicacy or dialogue, and to dispense with the appearance of soliciting its views or the pretense of equality. Given today's domestic preoccupations of the North, it may be difficult to generate sympathy for a South that seems mired in problems attributable to bad governance, corrupt elites, and docile and work-shy populaces more eager to resort to rhetoric, excuses, and feuds than to build the foundations for a better future. Indeed it is not clear that the South or the developing countries generally merit sympathy. They exploited the Cold War, used it as an excuse, pampered bloated armed forces, and in some cases acted as clandestine proliferators and shameless regional predators.

However much the postindustrial world may wish it, insulation from this other, more populous and turbulent, world is simply not possible. These worlds intersect most obviously in the former USSR, where the fate of Russia and its neighbors could weigh heavily in the balance between North and South. In other respects, too, the fate of the South inexorably impinges on that of the North. Due to the globalization of economies and the growth of interdependence (including the rise of transnational issues) areas cannot simply be insulated from the rest of the world. This is most evident with respect to political instabilities, in the presence of which uncertainty, repression, or persecution can give rise to large-scale migration into adjacent areas, perhaps disturbing the ethnic or national balance in the host country. It is even more clear when "domestic" issues like ethnic balance or policy toward minorities may give rise to civil wars spilling over into neighboring states and increasing the risks of "interstate war" and "outside" power intervention. (The very categories appear archaic and forced.) In the most obvious case, interstate conflicts spur migration and damage the economic prospects of belligerent states.

There are still other reasons to pay attention to the South. At the most obvious level, population pressures compel attention. Moreover, many of the new security issues such as environment and migration directly concern the South, and its fate and policies in this respect will inevitably affect those of the North. In much of the South the wave of democratization, however dimly sensed or remote from traditional culture, is welcomed by the populace and provides hope for their future. Furthermore, any world order, whether it is underpinned by balance of power, collective security, or unilateral or ad hoc interventions, must, if it is to become durable, eventually be seen to be legitimate. For this it must solicit the support of the widest number of states possible.

The United States will be a principal determinant of the character of North–South relations on these issues in the new international system. This fact alone has generated concern in the South. Especially after the Iraqi crisis, the United States appears to feel not only that its capabilities have been tested but also that its judgment has

been validated. From a distance at least a whiff of uncharacteristic hubris and querulousness is discernible. This translates into "no apologies" take-it-or-leave-it attitudes, especially evident in relations toward the South, which is either ignored or subjected to the Marines—Somalia being a vivid case. The South is often depicted as the "new threat," and some of its members characterized as "rogue" states.

Li Peng, the PRC's prime minister, in a visit to India at the end of 1991 referred to the "emerging international oligarchy," hinting that no one country should be allowed to be in a position to dictate to others. Feeling "excluded from the new world order," the two Asian powers found solace in a convergence and criticism of U.S. "hegemonism." Each was and remains concerned about the degree to which Soviet disintegration has left the United States unchecked and in some senses unbalanced.[14]

The United States has translated its episodic interest in the external world and in the South into new pressure on those states to adhere not just to existing standards of international politics but to higher ones. It has enshrined human rights as a centerpiece of its global engagement, and in postwar Iraq it has used military force to partially dismember a state that failed to meet the new norm.

It has also enshrined nonproliferation. States of the South are now expected to exercise restraint in arms expenditures, to imitate the North (Europe and the superpowers) in arms control and disarmament, cultivate transparency, and practice "cooperative security." Whether or not they feel their security has been enhanced by the end of Cold War, they are being told to get into step with the North or else risk a cutback in development as-

sistance. In emphasizing weapons proliferation as a new priority the United
States appears to be targeting an issue
that it feels can generate domestic
concern and consensus; but it is arguably a false or exaggerated issue,
and a crusading policy style that tends
to unilateralism is the exact reverse of
what is called for if the aim is to establish meaningful restraints rather
than temporary obstacles to the spread
of these weapons.

Thus, the South struggles not only
with its own problems of political and
economic development, domestic stability, and regional antagonisms, but
also with a changing international system that promises it little in the way
of assistance or relief. On the contrary,
the South faces many international
pressures well beyond its control, not
least the actions of some leading actors
in the international system to define
and enforce new standards of behavior
for which a common basis of international understanding does not exist.
Unless North and South are able to
arrive jointly at ordering concepts for
the new international system, the possibility of conflict between them grows
more likely. This is a shame, because
it is avoidable and unnecessary.

World Order: A View from the South

Whatever else the new world order
portends, it does not mean the end of
international hierarchies or a new age
of equality. Nor is it clear, whatever
its shape, how—or whether—it will incorporate the needs and demands of
the South into its priorities or agenda.
What is the new order? From the
South, it looks like a new form of
Western dominance, only more explicit and interventionist than in the
past. In some Western states a shrill-
ness is detectable when the South is
discussed, as if the enemy has shifted
there. Consider the following:

- New rationales for intervention appear to be minted daily—human
rights, democracy, drugs, environment, and weapons proliferation
(while unilateral application of laws
extraterritorial and seizures of foreign citizens are upheld by U.S.
courts);[15]
- Armed forces structures and sizes
are being configured and geared to
contingencies in the South;
- The North Atlantic Treaty Organization (NATO) has designated a
rapid-reaction force for "out-of-
area" contingencies;
- An antitactical ballistic missile
(ATBM) system against limited
strikes—GPALS, or Global Protection Against Limited Strikes—has
an explicitly Southern orientation
and it is on these terms that it has
been offered to and considered by
Russia;
- Even nuclear targeting is being
reassessed, justified, and recali-
brated for contingencies involving
Southern states;
- The Coordinating Committee for
Multilateral Export Controls
(COCOM) is being reconfigured for
use and application against the
South;
- A host of regimes to control and restrain suppliers are in place or soon
will be, all designed to deny certain
technologies to Southern states (the
London Club or Nuclear Suppliers
Group, the Australia Group in
chemicals, the Permanent Five [P–
5] of the UN Security Council on
conventional arms transfer registers,
the Missile Technology Control Regime [MTCR] on missile technology); and
- Arms-control initiatives, whether
nuclear, chemical, biological or con-

417

ventional, strategic or tactical/theater, are now planned and assessed for their impact on the South. Consideration of a total nuclear test ban (CTB), verification mechanisms, reduced reliance on nuclear weapons, elimination of missiles of a certain range, and possible missile test bans, are now all considered in terms of their impact on the South. The Strategic Arms Reduction Treaty (START) is now presented as an important nonproliferation tool.

The North makes no apologies about being more demanding and is not timid about asserting its values since their vindication by the outcome of the Cold War. Illustrative is the North's increasing tendency to insist that there is a definite positive connection between democracy and economic development and democracy and international stability.

Economic assistance is being tied to reduced expenditure on arms. Barber Conable (president of the World Bank 1986–1991) argues that when military expenditures are above 5 percent or in excess of health and education combined "it is hard to see the good sense of lending to such countries."[16] Robert McNamara argues that the West should link economic aid to the former Soviet republics with progress in shifting priorities from military to economic development.[17] The recipient states (the G–24) have been reluctant to accept conditions imposed by the International Monetary Fund and World Bank that would establish a certain ceiling for military expenditures above which no aid would be forthcoming.[18]

Such proposals appear to the South as earnest cant. Money is of course fungible. It is also arguable whether defense is the business of the Bretton

Woods institutions. Military spending is simply another excuse, after human rights and the environment, not to transfer resources to poorer countries, to avoid a candid admission that the poorer countries are no longer of strategic interest.[19]

Military spending in the South appears especially wasteful to Americans and Europeans now destroying, transferring, or converting arms. The costliness and futility of the past arms race appears to them all too apparent. Yet it is significant that there is no consensus on the role of arms and especially nuclear weapons in the Cold War: Did they deter a Soviet conventional attack? Were they instrumental in keeping the peace on the Continent? Would deterrence have been as effective at much lower levels of nuclear weapons? Were nuclear weapons essential? Without serious evaluation of the past role of nuclear weapons in the North it seems premature to deride their utility elsewhere. Also it may be noted by the states of the South that even in this phase of enthusiasm for arms control in the North, although some suggest a minimum deterrent posture, scarcely anyone suggests complete nuclear disarmament. Even nuclear weapons still retain a role in the security of the North, however residual. Why, it may be asked, can they not play a similar role in the South?[20]

The fluidity of the current period has not made predictions any easier, yet it is evident that the hierarchy of power has been blurred as other forms of power have become more relevant. Although this blurring may have led to the "obsolescence of major war" in the North, as some suggest, this is less evidently the case elsewhere. Even in an interdependent world competition and rivalry will drive an interest in relative as opposed to absolute standing. States will still be concerned about their relative power positions. Traditionally war has been the means by which power and status have been defined and change has occurred. Choices about war and peace will depend on the alternatives and these choices are not always the same in the South as in the North. The South lacks a security community as a nucleus for order that is present in the North. The mechanisms for peaceful change in the South are not yet designed or constructed.

Weapons Transfers and Proliferation

Since the end of the Cold War the United States has been free to define arms transfers as an arms-control rather than foreign policy problem. This is logical for purely selfish reasons, for as the superpowers reduce their nuclear inventories, the salience of others' nuclear weapons increases. Indeed, at a certain point (not yet reached) the incentives for cheating or breaking-out may increase considerably.[21]

The encounter with Iraq's arsenal provided an additional incentive. The "lessons" of the Persian Gulf War will provide grist for many varied mills for the foreseeable future. Iraq gave reality to a looming apprehension: a regional predator with a whole panoply of advanced arms—possibly soon to include nuclear weapons—that had shown itself unready to be bound by restrictions on their use and has shown a parallel reluctance to be limited in its employment of chemical weapons (CW) by using them in a war with its neighbor. Western concern, of course, was stimulated only when the risk was seen to affect Westerners, for the silence was deafening when Iranians were the victims.

The Iraqi "lesson" unleashed American activism. There was much talk of

"coercive disarmament" or what Rolf Ekéus refers to as "arms control by imposition." Some argued that one lesson was that prevention is easier than cure. The new world order could scarcely be jeopardized by a few bad eggs like Iraq. The United States, some implied, might simply have to decide for others what was permissible and define their legitimate defense needs.

As the risks of proliferation of new arms have become more apparent, Northern states have begun to consider ways of limiting arms and technology transfers to the South. As the developing countries now account for some 75 percent of arms traded, their military expenditures have grown at three times the pace of that of the North and now account for between two to three times their expenditures on health, education, and welfare. Apart from the distortion to their societies, such spending constitutes a potential threat to neighbors as well as the more distant North.

This Northern concern is, however, selective. Where states are poor and unable to pay for arms, Northern states advocate reduced military spending. Where there is a large market for arms, Northern suppliers compete to get orders for their shrinking defense industries (as in the Persian Gulf and East Asia). Little systematic consideration has been given to the types of arms that are particularly destructive, whether stabilizing or destabilizing; often this distinction corresponds to what you are selling as opposed to what your competitor is selling. The issue is difficult enough without commercial competition and hypocrisy, because all too often such definitions depend as much on the recipient's military doctrine as on the intrinsic characteristics of the weapon systems.

Equally little thought has been given to the relationships among various categories of arms and the reasons for proliferation. Focusing on particular weapon systems like missiles makes little sense out of context. In terms of destructive power and practical military effectiveness missiles do not (yet?) compare to advanced strike aircraft. Nor does an attempt to ban missiles treat the question of motivation in its context. Iran's quest for missiles, for example, came as a result of an inability to acquire parts for its air force (due to the embargo) and its need to counter the much larger and more varied stock of missiles of its adversary (Iraq).[22] For Syria and others, missiles are a psychological comfort or equalizer, guaranteeing some penetration against a foe with a much superior air force.

Nonetheless, in the fight against weapons proliferation the United States in particular has singled out missiles and weapons of mass destruction. Concern about them seems to focus on the following: Under certain conditions they could increase incentives for preemption. Given their relative inaccuracy, population centers may be targeted; moreover, low accuracy may lead to a preference for mass destruction weapons over conventional ones. Some categories of unconventional weapon systems, like chemical weapons, that may be intended to deter an opponent's nuclear arms may complicate deterrence and blur thresholds. Missiles also to some extent decouple a capacity to damage or destroy an opponent from underlying industrial and societal sources of military power.

These concerns are too simplistic. Mating unconventional warheads to ballistic missiles is not easy. The effects of biological warheads are difficult to predict. An international treaty banning chemical weapons should make the deployment and use of these particular weapons more difficult. In any case, the effort to ban only missiles with specified range and weight (300 km and 500 kilograms) tends to obscure the problem of improving accuracies. Even missiles with ranges shorter than 300 km, if forward-deployed and capable of delivering a strike against an opponent's military arsenal, increase the incentive to strike preemptively. As accuracies increase, more missiles may be used for counterforce strikes, and as ranges increase, they could pull into conflict a wider circle of states.

The direct military threat of these and other weapons to the North is as yet remote. But the potential threat is significant as delivery ranges increase. By one report, by the end of this decade, eight states of the South will have the ability to produce nuclear weapons, while six will have an intercontinental ballistic missile (ICBM) capability, presumably capable of reaching the United States.[23] A larger number of countries will have the ability to build or acquire chemical and biological weapons and other missiles—perhaps as many as 50 states. Of course, the North faces a more immediate although more remote threat in terms of its access to certain regions or the possibility that regional conflicts will erupt under the nuclear umbrella it extends to a few allies in the South.

In a world where distances are shrinking while the capacity to wreak devastation is dispersing, it is not surprising that the Northern states should be inclined to do something. This impulse has translated into energetic efforts to restrict the trade and transfer of technologies that might increase these military capabilities. But this approach runs counter to much of the liberal and open exchange of information and the spread of technology that is part of the modern world. It also risks seeking to restrict dual-use technology for which Southern states may have legitimate commercial or developmental needs.[24]

Are there alternatives to these strategies of technology denial? The control regimes could be improved by expanding membership beyond the Western club, adopting a more comprehensive approach that tries not to segregate technologies, and working toward universal, not discriminatory, standards. But arms control based on denial alone tends only to delay programs and will ultimately contribute to security only if the time gained is used to reduce the motivations for acquisitions. This requires active, constructive diplomacy in regions of endemic rivalry and conflict, notably the Middle East, the Korean peninsula, and South Asia. Moreover, reducing the rhetoric and volume on the subject of missiles would also be useful; their military importance has been overstated and has doubtless stimulated and misguided some Southern policymakers into acquiring them.[25]

Nuclear Proliferation

After the end of the Cold War no issue appears to threaten global stability more or evokes as immediate a response as the prospect of nuclear proliferation. It conjures up images of direct attacks on the homeland of states of the North as well as a kind of global anarchy. Nuclear nonproliferation has been rediscovered with an intensity and vigor that suggest either blind neglect in the past or frenzied displacement of energy at present, for it cannot be justified by any evidence that more states are energetically looking toward nuclear weapons. It is also an issue around which the inchoate fears

of the threat from the South can coalesce.

"Nuclear Saturday night specials" are a growing preoccupation in the United States, where there is a perceived need to "spur a new coalition for . . . elimination [of] the existing or would-be arsenals of South Africa, Syria, Israel, China, India, Pakistan, Argentina, Brazil, the two Koreas and Iran as well as Iraq."[26] Even relatively civilized voices talk tough: "If you can't beat them the gentlemanly way, biff them. That should be the motto for the bomb-busters from the International Atomic Energy Agency (IAEA)."[27] Others refer to nuclear inspections, arguing that it is "time for hardball."[28] The inference is that the United States should no longer be "Mr. Nice-guy." The experience with Iraq has seemingly resulted in putting the onus on states to show that they are not even thinking about "going nuclear." As one senior official monitoring North Korea put it: "We don't even believe our eyes—especially when it looks like nothing is there."[29]

In the United States, this combative "show me" attitude is particularly strong. Americans appear on the brink of unilaterally redefining the bargain entailed in the Nuclear Non-Proliferation Treaty (NPT). As one journal put it:

> The nuclear have's promise to work toward disarmament. The have-not's promise not to acquire weapons and in return are given help with their civilian nuclear industries. Both sides can gain more if they persist with this bargain than if they abandon it.[30]

The price they may well pay for attempting a redefinition of this bargain is its unraveling. There is justifiable concern that much of the expertise and training that can be attained in a "peaceful" program is in fact indistinguishable from that needed for a weapons program. But the United States now seeks (with some success) to stop the transfer of any nuclear technology to countries like Iran whether or not they have ratified the NPT, negotiated safeguards agreements, and accepted special inspections. The United States may demand much more stringent conditions about that country's intentions, but precisely what it would take to reassure Washington is not yet clear apart, perhaps, from a change in regime.

This position frankly discriminates between friendly and unfriendly states, focusing on signatories (and possible cheats) like Iran but ignoring actual proliferators like Israel. It is perforce more intelligible in the North than in the South. The discrimination is especially unpalatable for countries that accept special IAEA inspections, knowing that these are "targeted inspections" relying on U.S. intelligence sources. As the IAEA has noted: "Intrusive inspections make some countries nervous: We need to maintain political support."[31]

This is not an argument for nuclear weapons proliferation. The North also fears that its own experience, in which nuclear weapons and deterrence stabilized the East–West confrontation, is unlikely to be replicated elsewhere. The geostrategic circumstances of the East–West nuclear standoff may prove in retrospect to have been highly unusual. In other areas, the political, situational, and technical prerequisites for establishing stable deterrence might not be present.[32] Politically, stable deterrence requires established lines of authority, civil peace, and clear criteria for use. Most developing countries are prey to civil strife, coups, and struggles for power, making un-

authorized use more likely. Outside of Europe, multiple axes of conflict (consider India, Pakistan, and the PRC) are likely to shape the propensity for conflict rather than a bimodal context. This makes doctrine, targeting, and so on more problematic. In addition the superpowers were not neighbors, had no bilateral territorial disputes, were not traditional adversaries, and above all had time to develop, or let evolve, their deterrent relationship. The superpowers' technical situation will also be difficult for others to match. Its most important aspect is the need for secure second-strike forces, the foundation of a stable system of deterrence. Without this the incentives for preemption or early use will be great, inviting crisis instability. Technical deficiencies will make possible unauthorized use, accidents, theft, leakage, and deterioration. In sum, nuclear deterrence is neither automatic nor universal and there are grounds for suspecting that it will not have the same robust qualities as it did in the East–West context.

There are other considerations. The new nuclear weapon states are not likely to be as satisfied with the international order as the two superpowers, nor will they act as status quo powers.[33] There is also the potential impact that proliferation in the South might have on the North. Japan or Germany might come to see such proliferation as detrimental to their own security and requiring the acquisition of their own nuclear weapons. Another serious consequence could come from the use of nuclear weapons; the global taboo, the "tradition of non-use," has created a threshold for nuclear weapons that separates them from other weapons. If the threshold were to be (frequently) broken, so too would the taboo. A buildup of nuclear weapons in the South would also probably halt or reverse the ongoing nuclear arms reductions in the North.[34]

Although there are many good reasons to suspect that more nuclear weapon states would contribute to global insecurity, these and other arguments do not fully satisfy skeptics, largely in the South. The recently revived crusade against proliferation suggests to some not a new threat, but a new need to focus on a threat—any threat—preferably one in the guise of an Islamic foe. In general, the poorer states find it difficult to stomach the patronizing, rueful air surrounding the subject of nuclear weapons. Despite McGeorge Bundy's conclusion that "in the long run, possessing nuclear weapons is hard work and in the absence of a threat, these weapons have little or no day-to-day value,"[35] the original nuclear powers are fated, it seems, to keep theirs because "they can't be disinvented." So the nuclear states of the North modernize their nuclear forces, even as the threats for which they were constructed have disappeared, while also pressing the South on the nuclear nonproliferation agenda.

The Southern skeptic asks why the argument of France and Britain that nuclear weapons are important for the "seat at the table" they ensure is not equally valid and just for nuclear-capable states of the developing world. They also ask why the North pursues a policy of "selective" proliferation rather than nonproliferation. Some Southerners find it difficult to understand why their major security threats cannot be met by nuclear weapons when they have little capacity to provide for a sophisticated conventional defense or deterrent.

Skeptics also take issue with the argument that stable deterrence cannot emerge outside of the "civilized" North. Their views echo those of one Western scholar, who a dozen years ago argued that the nuclear military revolution itself, because of the destructive power of such weapons, compels a refashioning of political relations.[36] He has gone on to ask more recently whether the fact that the nuclear weapon states have been less involved in conflicts than was traditionally the case with the great powers has something to do with the nuclear weapons they possess.[37]

Concern about possible nuclear weapons use in the South is also difficult to understand for those who have endured many years of war on their territory. If conventional deterrence is less effective than nuclear deterrence, and the threat of nuclear war can deter conventional attacks, then, it is argued, perhaps nuclear deterrence might rid the South of repeated wars. As for irresponsibility, it is difficult to imagine a more dangerous policy than the "extended deterrence" that was the cornerstone of the Western alliance; prudent states would be reluctant to seek to widen the utility of nuclear weapons in this fashion.

None of this means that countries of the South are queuing up for nuclear weapons, or that the benefits of nuclear status are uppermost in their minds. Wars, conflict, and instability regrettably have been the lot of many of these states. Many have not had the means to assure their security unilaterally or through access to arms or alliances. Nor have they been able to fashion a diplomatic compromise.

Moreover, their security has not automatically been improved by the passing of the Cold War. Regional concerns persist. Yet these states are usually only noticed, or taken seriously, if they look as if they are interested in nuclear weapons. Otherwise they are ignored or marginalized.

Those states that *are* interested in nuclear weapons have, for the most part, specific motivations. It is difficult to define the prestige, status, or self-image dimension of India's motivation, which might have led it toward the bomb anyway, but its national security motivation vis-à-vis the PRC and Pakistan cannot be denied. In the Middle East there is little question that Israel's understandable quest for a "last resort" device as insurance against the superior numbers of its foes has created an asymmetry that has stimulated the development of chemical, and possibly biological, weapons and missiles by Syria, Iraq, and possibly Egypt. Attempts to contain one without the other are unrealistic, yet given the short distances and the number of parties that could be involved (among them Saudi Arabia and Iran), any attempt to deal with proliferation here becomes an exercise in managing, if not actually settling, a host of problems from the Persian Gulf through to North Africa.

Iraq's experience in the Persian Gulf War will have an impact on nuclear weapons proliferation. No doubt states of the North hope that potential proliferators will appreciate the risks Saddam Hussein ran with his ambitions and the fear that galvanized the coalition into coercive action. Equally certain is the fact that states of the South will find other lessons as well, not least in Saddam Hussein's mistake in moving before he had nuclear weapons, and the fearsomeness of the North's conventional weapons, suggesting that states wishing to avoid such interventions may find it prudent to acquire other means to deter them.

Nuclear weapons will continue to hold a fascination for states in an insecure and fluid world. Whether as shortcuts, equalizers, status symbols, or simply as "options" to be kept against the possibility of need at a future date, they will be sought by states anxious about their security and/or keen to play a role in international affairs. States poor in resources or technical manpower will find it hard to acquire nuclear weapons and may not even consider them. Those states in a security environment that does not dictate their consideration, such as Latin America, may pass them by. Still others may find the original motivation for them reduced (e.g., South Africa). This will leave a number of states of some wealth, incentive, or capability that, whether from ambition, security, status incentives, or considerations of prudence, will want either to develop nuclear weapons or maintain the option of developing them quickly later.

If arms-control responses are to be found to this strategic reality, they must strive for universal, equal obligations. The extension of positive security guarantees for those states renouncing nuclear weapons that might come under nuclear threat should be considered. With the revival of the UN Security Council as an instrument for peace and security, and given its interest in proliferation issues, perhaps it might take such an initiative. Other measures, such as renunciation of use of nuclear weapons against nonnuclear states, a comprehensive test ban treaty, further cuts in nuclear arsenals, and the like, will all be helpful in giving the appearance of greater equality of treatment. These political incentives for nuclear weapons seem to be given shorter shrift these days when the focus is on denial of technology.

Technology- and weapons-denial strategies are not only morally unsustainable—they can scarcely be counted upon as a long-term solution. The nature of the world—technologically, scientifically, and economically—is such as to make diffusion inevitable. The real question is whether the time bought by such measures is well used to erect more effective barriers against the use of weapons of concern. A good way to do this might be to involve a large number of states in the enterprise that today are treated merely as objects of the control regime. As in other arms-control agreements, there is a trade-off between the rigor of the instrument and the need for the widest possible adherence; in this case surely a wide membership should be consciously sought in order to build a global norm. Technology-denial regimes such as the MTCR are one-way arrangements in which the South has to like it or lump it. This is hardly the stuff of a consensual world order.

The case of North Korea is illustrative. Here is a state with few resources, no allies, and a dim future. Neither the threat of sanctions nor a military strike is an adequate or plausible response. It may be too late for technology denial as well. A policy that combines engagement, dialogue, and positive inducements stands a greater chance of success.

Ukraine is another case. A state concerned about maintaining its new-found independence and deterring a nuclear neighbor—Russia—that seems erratic and unpredictable cannot be said to lack cogent reasons for delaying its renunciation of nuclear weapons. Ukraine needs reassurances and security guarantees if the military incentives for the retention of these weapons are to be weakened.

Iran is analogous to North Korea. It may or may not be moving toward nuclear weapons. If it is, this is due less to pressing or identifiable security concerns than to status considerations and possible bargaining leverage. Margin-

alizing Iran, denying it access to dual technology, and depicting its conventional military programs as a regional threat will do little to deal with the problem. It is simply not feasible in today's world to attempt to deny a country the size, weight, and location of Iran access to the fruits of modern technology for very long. Weak in other areas, Tehran may only redouble its efforts at depicting U.S. and Western hostility as the cause of its economic problems. Ultimately a U.S. policy of "sanctions only" can buy time and impose costs. But unless the time is used for diplomacy, it is wasted. Furthermore, this U.S. policy vis-à-vis Iran's alleged nuclear program risks unraveling, for it may well be seen as politically motivated.[38] To build global norms the United States will have to eschew favoritism, selective applications of norms, and build the broadest possible consensus.

States do not generally seek nuclear weapons, or seek to leave open the option to do so, for frivolous reasons. It would be helpful if the United States in particular attempted to consider the motivations in a balanced way. In seeking to address the motivations of potential proliferators, it would find that there is some relationship among the regional security context, the presence or absence of reliable sources of conventional arms, the availability or lack of allies, and the means for self-expression internationally. The reason why states like North Korea or Iran should not be cornered incessantly in every forum and on every front is precisely because it leaves so little room for dialogue. South Africa shows the way in which a change in political perceptions and regional politics can change incentives to acquire nuclear weapons. With the ebb and flow of time even rogue states can become responsible. Trying to get even the most recalcitrant states on board is worth the effort.

The issues raised by the quest for equality and the needs of order are not susceptible to easy solution. As Hedley Bull wrote of nuclear proliferation: "This is one area in which the goals of international order and of international justice or equal treatment are in conflict with one another."[39] It may be precisely for that reason that the foundations of international order need to be broadened to include more states, giving them a feeling of participation and a sense that their interests are also being accommodated.

Collective Security

If one primary element of the new world order agenda relates to the proliferation of advanced military capability, another relates to the rules and norms governing the use of force in international affairs. The term collective security has been used over most of the last half century to encompass the state of thinking about these matters that emerged at the end of World War II. Today, much hope is being placed by the North in a reinvigorated UN system, released from the fetters of the Cold War, to achieve the benefits of concerted international responses to aggression.

Unfortunately, the renovation of the UN system and of collective security is taking place in a haphazard and ill-defined way. Improvisation has perforce been the dominant motif. The risks of mistakes, incompetence, overload, and disappointment are real. Little effort has been made to clarify the criteria for UN intervention, whether to make, keep, or enforce the peace. This issue is especially salient for the states of the South—the likely target, after all, of such intervention. On the face of it, such matters are by definition under the jurisdiction of the Security Council, where the South has little or no say. The capacity of the Council to act coherently and forcefully has of course changed with the end of the Cold War, and today, in principle at least, threats to the peace, breaches of the peace, or acts of aggression that may constitute threats to international peace and security can be the basis for action by air, land, or sea forces. But the capacity to act is not exactly as UN advocates might envisage. The weakening and impoverishment of Russia and the agile diplomacy of a PRC that seeks to use its membership (votes and vetoes) for unilateral advantage has undermined the value of the Council as the locus of great power authority and will.

Ambiguity is the stuff of international politics, and it is far from clear how ambiguous circumstances in the South will be evaluated by the great powers of the North. Within the South, there is considerable skepticism that its interests will be taken into account. An obvious example is the fate of Bosnia's Muslims. In the former Yugoslavia, the complexities of peacekeeping are great, the parallels with Kuwait few, and the potential for spillover of conflict into Western Europe quite real, but it is nonetheless striking how many Islamic states have felt it necessary to suggest that UN reluctance to act stems from a double standard concerning the fate of Muslims. This accusation of a double standard emanates not just from Iran but also from Western friends such as Turkey, Saudi Arabia, and Egypt, whose leaders evidently share a view that Muslims are marginalized and treated differently, if not in fact actively discriminated against.[40]

A related concern of states of the South is that the Security Council today disproportionately reflects U.S.

power. One need not agree with Mu'ammar Qadhafi that the UN Security Council risks becoming an extension of NATO to note that, with Russia in its present condition, the United States and its allies dominate the Security Council to an extraordinary degree. Moreover, talk among these countries of reforming the membership of the Council tends to focus on adding membership for Germany or Japan, and not any Southern state, except as a bogey or argument against reform.

It is true that the United States has much to contribute to the effective functioning of the UN system. It is the only great power with a global view of issues that is not mired in regionalism and parochialism. And when it comes to major or distant military operations, the United States and its NATO allies are the only entities able to provide the requisite logistics and airpower. But even U.S. allies cannot avoid the thought that this is too much of a good thing. How might such U.S. dominance be replaced? How might U.S. engagement be sustained in a way that promotes global stability without it assuming an impossible role as "guarantor of the globe's existing borders"?[41]

Talk of revitalizing the UN Security Council assumes a degree of consensus about the role of the United States that may not be present in today's still culturally diverse world. Collective security will continue to be defined selectively and unequally, reflecting limited resources among the great powers, different priorities among nations generally, and uneven commitment to underlying international norms. The Security Council will be only one of several possible candidates for involvement in crisis areas. The broadest possible consensus on and involvement in collective security is important for practical and moral reasons. It will protect the reputation of the UN when it decides *not* to act, where it acts unsuccessfully, and where it acts controversially. Situations in which the UN will need such support will surely occur in the future, if the cases of Bosnia and Cambodia are any indication. A broad and diverse constituency can thus act to undergird the UN's collective security effort; to act as proof against its trivialization (e.g., the assertion of the UN Security Council that the situation in Haiti constitutes a threat to international peace and security under chapter 7 of the charter); to enable it to retain its authority and legitimacy even in contingencies when it acts and is bogged down; and to protect it from the charge of selectivity or political bias. Collective security operationally may be a preserve of the great powers and cannot prudently be undertaken in the teeth of their opposition, but without broader involvement, it risks being more exposed and brittle politically than it need be.

Regional organizations might be one alternative. Responsibility might be devolved to them for the development of structures for conflict reduction and prevention, confidence-building, and the elaboration of regional norms. Of course, there are obvious difficulties where the region is riven by conflict, regional organizations resemble regional alliances not security communities, and transparency by definition is in short supply. But in some regional conflicts an outside power is essential as a catalyst, so long as it remains evenhanded. It may spark something that can then become self-sustaining or orchestrate harmony where local parties left to themselves would be stymied—witness the U.S. role in the Middle East peace negotiations.

The promise of regional organiza-

427

Shahram Chubin

tions is limited, however. The Middle East case is an exceptional one unlikely to be replicated elsewhere. In the South generally disputes and instabilities are more likely to have to play themselves out unless local initiatives and self-restraint emerge. Regional organizations are generally weak and as polarized as the parties to the conflict—witness the absence of the Organization of African Unity in the tragedy in Somalia. Nonetheless, their efforts to elaborate norms dealing with border disputes, intervention in civil wars, treatment of refugees, and the like should be encouraged.

Some of the most promising responses are local. Because many parts of the South will continue to be neglected in the new world order, it will be better to count on local resources rather than to wait for others to bail them out. Perhaps the new wave of more representative governments will be more responsible than their authoritarian predecessors in struggling with these issues.

The theme for states of the South must be self-help. Southern states must devise their own organizations to replace those like the irrelevant nonaligned group to deal with their own affairs. In an era of compassion fatigue, domestic concerns, and competing demands, help from the North will only be forthcoming if the South is seen to be helping itself.

But even with Southern activism, there is no guarantee that the North will be able to engage the South in a coherent and progressive program to deal with questions of international security. With the sharp domestic economic concerns of the North and the turmoil in Eastern Europe and Russia, the North appears unable to look beyond short-term issues such as weapons proliferation.

This would be a tragic mistake. The gap between rich and poor is increasing. Problems of migration, which involve political stability and peace as much as economic motives, need to be tackled as a common security issue. If such questions are not dealt with constructively, if other cultures are not treated with respect, and if the populous weaker nations are not given a larger platform and coopted into the system of security management that purports to be global, the present happy juncture of hope and opportunity will be shattered by a deteriorating international security environment.

Conclusion

The issues dividing North from South today are numerous, ranging from the proliferation of nuclear, chemical, and biological weapons and missiles, to technology transfer, population growth, developmental inequality, migration, and environmental issues. None of them will be dealt with productively if conceived of, and treated as, North–South security issues. They are more accurately global security issues, requiring dialogue, compromise, and grand bargains.

The system of global order centered on the UN Security Council was based on the premise of great power collaboration. It languished for 45 years and now is being revived. That revival must go very far indeed—well beyond what the existing great powers now envisage—if it is to have a meaningful impact on the security agenda of the future.

As Hedley Bull observed, no international order sustained by the great powers can provide equal justice for all states, but much can be done to alleviate this perhaps necessary and inevitable inequality.[42] To provide "central direction in international affairs,"

428

the major powers need to "explain, prepare, negotiate, coordinate and create a consensus with other states . . . to involve [them] directly in the defence of the existing distribution of power." Bull argued that the fact that great power management of the international order may not "afford equal justice" to all did not necessarily make it intolerable, because the great powers might have a greater stake in that international order of which they became guardians. But these same powers "do, however, have a permanent problem of securing and preserving the consent of other states to the special role they play in the system."

This managerial role, Bull believed, is only possible "if these functions are accepted clearly enough by a large enough proportion of the society of states to command legitimacy." Inter alia, great powers should "seek to satisfy some of the demands for just change being expressed in the world," which include economic justice and nuclear justice among others. Where the demand cannot be met, great powers need to go through the motions of considering them: "A great power hoping to be accepted as a legitimate managerial power cannot ignore these demands or adopt a contrary position."

The states of the North, with only one-fifth of the world's population and a dynamic two-thirds of the global economy, have a long-term interest in framing a new order that is acceptable to the majority of the world's populace. A world of diffuse discontent surely cannot be an orderly one. In a world where nuclear proliferation cannot be frozen permanently and where science and technology spread quickly, it is important to involve all states in elaborating norms and to give them a stake in the more plural world order that is at once desirable and inevitable.

The views in this article are the author's alone and not those of any institution with which he is associated.

Notes

1. Francis Fukuyama, *The End of History and the Last Man* (New York, N.Y.: Free Press, 1992), p. 318.

2. David Lascelles, "Life, the Universe and Everything," *Financial Times*, March 21, 1992.

3. See Robert Cooper and Mats Berdal, "Outside Intervention in Ethnic Conflicts," *Survival* 35 (Spring 1993), pp. 119–120.

4. David Welsh, "Domestic Politics and Ethnic Conflict," *Survival* 35 (Spring 1993), p. 64.

5. John Chipman, "The Future of Strategic Studies: Beyond Even Grand Strategy," *Survival* 34 (Spring 1992), pp. 117–118.

6. Quoted in Gerald B. Helman and Steven R. Ratner, "Saving Failed States," *Foreign Policy*, no. 89 (Winter 1992–93), p. 10.

7. *Ibid.*

8. Chester Crocker, "Ad Hoc Salvage Work Won't Make for World Law and Order," *International Herald Tribune*, December 22, 1992.

9. The quote is from Pérez de Cuéllar cited by Steven S. Rosenfeld, "When There's Good Cause to Meddle," *International Herald Tribune*, October 12–13, 1991. See also Lionel Barber, "UN Takes First Hesitant Moves to Armed Intervention," *Financial Times*, September 27, 1991.

10. Hedley Bull, "The Revolt Against the West," in Bull and Adam Watson, eds., *The Expansion of International Society* (Oxford: Oxford University Press, 1984), pp. 217–220. See also editors' introduction, p. 9.

11. Adda Bozeman, "The International Order in a Multicultural World," in Bull and Watson, *Expansion of International Society*, p. 400.

12. Paraphrase of Albert Hourani, *A Vision of History* (Beirut, 1961), pp. 151ff., in *ibid.*, p. 402.

13. Bozeman, "International Order in a Multicultural World," p. 401.

14. See "China and India Reject US Primacy," *International Herald Tribune*, December 13, 1991; "New Delhi et Pékin critiquent la domination des Etats Unis dans les affaires mondiales," *Le Monde*, December 15–16, 1991; and Edward Gargan, "India and China: Much Said, Little Done," *International Herald Tribune*, December 14–15, 1991.

15. See Abraham Lowenthal, "Latin America: Ready for Partnership?" *Foreign Affairs* 72, *America and the World, 1992/93* (1993), p. 85, and Marc Weller, "The Invasion of the Bodysnatchers," *Independent*, March 13, 1992.

16. Barber B. Conable, Jr., "What the Third World Needs is Growth, Not More Weapons," *International Herald Tribune*, December 26, 1991.

17. Nicole Ball and Robert S. McNamara, "Make Aid Conditional on Demilitarization," *International Herald Tribune*, January 13, 1992.

18. See Stephen Fiddler and Peter Norman, "Survey of the World Economy," *Financial Times*, October 14, 1991.

19. See "Let Them Eat Guns," *Economist*, November 2, 1991, p. 67.

20. On this topic see Edward Mortimer, "Superpowers Move the Winning Post," *Financial Times*, February 2, 1992.

21. As Hans Blix has argued in these pages, this will increase the need for confidence in arms-control agreements and require correspondingly tighter safeguards. Blix, "Verification and Iraq," *The Washington Quarterly* 15 (Autumn 1992), p. 65.

22. This falls very much into the category of motivations noted by John Harvey in his thoughtful analysis "Regional Ballistic Missiles and Advanced Strike Aircraft: Comparing Military Effectiveness," *International Security* 17 (Fall 1992), especially p. 78.

    Because ballistic missiles confer status on their owners, acquisition by one state may compel its adversary to do likewise, regardless of their military utility. The inability or unwillingness of a state to "maintain missile parity" may convey a perception of inferiority, or a lack of will, to defend itself. This dynamic can stimulate regional arms races.

23. Quoted by Thomas L. Friedman from a "recent administration study." *International Herald Tribune*, February 8–9, 1992.

24. For a discussion of the need for technology transfer from a different perspective, see Kenneth Keller, "Science and Technology," *Foreign Affairs* 69 (Fall 1990), pp. 123–138. See also Janne E. Nolan, *Trappings of Power* (Washington, D.C.: Brookings, 1991).

25. Some of these suggestions are found in Harvey, "Regional Ballistic Missiles," especially pp. 81–82. See also Steven Fetter, "Ballistic Missiles and Weapons of Mass Destruction: What Is the Threat? What Should Be Done?" *International Security* 16 (Summer 1991), pp. 5–42, especially pp. 34, 41–42.

26. Roger Morris, "For a New Foreign Policy That Forgets the Cold War," *International Herald Tribune*, February 6, 1992.

27. "Getting Tough with North Korea," *Economist*, February 27, 1993, pp. 16–17.

28. Stephanie Cook, "Nuclear Inspections: Time for Hardball," *International Herald Tribune*, July 30, 1992.

29. The "senior official" quoted was in the Pentagon. See *International Herald Tribune*, January 6, 1992.

30. "Bombs for All," *Economist*, March 14, 1992, p. 15.

31. IAEA spokesman David Kyd, quoted by Paul Lewis in "UN Nuclear Inquiry Exposes Treaties' Flaws," *New York Times*, November 10, 1991.

32. See Lewis Dunn, "Containing Nuclear Proliferation," *Adelphi Paper* 263 (London: Brassey's for IISS, Winter 1991).

33. Robert Jervis, *The Meaning of the Nuclear Revolution* (Ithaca, N.Y.: Cornell University Press, 1989), p. 26, n. 73.

34. Dunn, "Containing Nuclear Proliferation," p. 67.

35. McGeorge Bundy, *Danger and Survival: Choices about the Bomb in the First Fifty Years* (New York, N.Y.: Random House, 1988), p. 516.

36. Kenneth Waltz, "The Spread of Nuclear Weapons: More May Be Better," *Adelphi Paper* 171 (London: IISS, 1981).

37. Kenneth Waltz, "Nuclear Myths and Po-

litical Realities," *American Political Science Review* 84 (September 1990).

38. International Institute of Strategic Studies, *Strategic Survey 1992–1993* (London: Brassey's for IISS, 1993), p. 124.

39. Hedley Bull, *The Anarchical Society: A Study of Order in World Politics* (London: Macmillan, 1977), p. 243. For arguments along the same lines refer to Brad Roberts, "Arms Control and the End of the Cold War," *The Washington Quarterly* 15 (Autumn 1992), especially pp. 43–50, and Christophe Carle, "Proliferation and the New World Order" (Paper presented to the European Strategy Group–Aspen Strategy Group Annual Conference, Rome, Italy, October 28–30, 1992).

40. For a discussion of these views see Gassan Salame, "Islam and the West," *Foreign Policy*, no. 90 (Spring 1993), pp. 22–37.

41. James C. Clad, "Old World Disorders," *The Washington Quarterly* 15 (Autumn 1992), p. 148.

42. Bull, *Anarchical Society*, pp. 227–229.

The New World Order: A Historical Perspective

Paul W. Schroeder

THE NEW WORLD order (NWO) is a term that burst onto the scene with the outrage accompanying Iraq's annexation of Kuwait and seems to have passed as rapidly from the scene as its creator, George Bush. As a rallying cry it certainly has fallen from favor, but as a kind of conceptual shorthand it continues to engage anyone interested in the character of the post–cold war world.

Most of the writing about the NWO has been done by policy specialists, but the rest of us should not allow them to coopt entirely the discussion of post–cold war order. After all, they are usually preoccupied with the present, looking little beyond the immediate task of defending or criticizing specific policy initiatives by the United States on the world scene. Questions of order and disorder in the international system cannot be brought into focus in this fashion. Here the historian has something unique to offer, not narrowly in the

Paul W. Schroeder is professor of history and political science at the University of Illinois and specializes in the history of international politics. His most recent book is *The Transformation of European Politics, 1763–1848* (Oxford: Clarendon Press, 1994).

Copyright © 1994 by The Center for Strategic and International Studies and the Massachusetts Institute of Technology

sense of useful analogies that shed light on specific decisions, but more broadly on how to think about larger questions, issues, and trends.

This historian's perspective on the NWO debate is that the policy pundits have it wrong. A new disorder has not replaced the new world order. The historic moment has not passed. Something important remains in the discussion of the NWO, something that will help the United States and the international community to get their bearings in this period of uncertainty, to chart a course away from the anarchic tendencies of the moment and toward a world more orderly in its affairs.

The most basic questions about the NWO—does one exist? how substantial is it?—cannot in fact be answered without a fairly long historical perspective. Such a perspective is essential for understanding the nature of the contemporary international system by revealing how it developed and how it differs from previous counterparts—and thus for understanding where and how to invest the intellectual and political energies of the United States, to say nothing of national blood and treasure.

This article offers one such historical perspective. Admittedly, my task is to paint a big, complex picture inside a very small frame—the short page length of a journal article. By necessity, this means omitting and oversimplifying a great deal and making a few assertions that a lengthier format would permit me to explain and defend. But the point here is to craft a cogent, albeit sketchy line of argument that makes possible some of these other tasks.

The Current Definition

The phrase "new world order" is commonly used without explicit definition and ideas on it doubtless vary. Yet one can elicit a working definition from the kinds of measures carried out or called for in its name since the end of the Cold War, most of which involve peacemaking actions of various kinds in different world trouble spots—actions intended to preserve or restore law and order; deter, stop, and punish war, aggression, and oppression; relieve civilian suffering; and promote civil and human rights. One therefore could define the NWO as an international system in which the United States and like-minded friends and allies act together, preferably under the aegis of the United Nations (UN), to preserve or establish peace by upholding international law and order against aggressors, lawbreakers, and oppressors. The definition, if the NWO is to survive and work, implies that the international community in some cases will have to proceed beyond persuasion, mediation, and conciliation to deterrence and compellence, that is, the use of force, to make certain actors stop certain actions and perform others. Again, this fits common usage. According to many, including former President Bush, the NWO was founded by the Persian Gulf War, a UN-sanctioned collective war against Iraqi aggression. Actions taken since by the United States and other states

in Iraq and Somalia, like those often proposed in regard to Bosnia, involve the use of armed force. Coercive actions against other supposed aggressors and lawbreakers are often urged in the name of the NWO, and the humanitarian and prudential arguments used in favor of such measures assume that there is an NWO that mandates such peacemaking actions by the international community.

Few Americans condemn the idea of such an NWO on principle or oppose all U.S. participation in international efforts to promote peace and humanitarian causes. Disagreement arises, however, over using force (especially U.S. force) to uphold the NWO, namely, to bring supposed aggressors and lawbreakers into line with some law or code of international conduct supposedly set by the international community through compellence and deterrence. Often the concerns are practical (the operation's sustainability, limits, chances of success, costs, risks, precedents, unintended consequences, etc.). But other challenges go to issues of principle. Who is to decide who is right among the parties in conflict, and by what right or principle? What gives UN resolutions the sanctity and force of law? Why should some resolutions be rigorously enforced and others not, some international crimes punished and others ignored?

Thus Americans may agree tacitly on the definition of the NWO, but sharply disagree over its reality, practicability, and desirability. The split can be seen as one between "idealists" and "realists" (by which I do not mean the two schools in international relations theory, but simply those who believe that certain norms, rules, and laws can and should be enforced in international relations, as opposed to those who believe that conflicting state interests and balance of power politics still prevail). Idealists, noting the spread of civil, ethnic, and interstate conflict in the world since the end of the Cold War, argue that a failure now to uphold the rule of law in critical areas will encourage lawlessness and aggression, undermine the NWO, ruin a historic opportunity to promote peace and justice, and promote new violence and conflict throughout the world. Realists, recognizing the same world trends, stress different problems and dangers—the difficulties, risks, and unpredictable consequences of intervention, the limited resources of the United States and its allies and their frequent divergences of views and interest, the shaky juridical basis and controversial nature of claims about international law and justice, and so on. This leads them to an opposite conclusion about the NWO: that it is a mirage, that historical patterns of power politics, national conflict, and great-power rivalry still govern world politics, and that the goals of limiting war and preserving general world peace are better served if U.S. force is used solely for clearly defined and strictly limited U.S. national interests.

Frequently in debates like this, key assumptions are shared by both sides without their being fully aware of it. These assumptions, left unarticulated and unchallenged, distort and stultify the debate. This essay contends that this holds true here, with paradoxical effects. Where the two sides openly disagree, on the likely consequences of acting or failing to act according to the NWO's supposed mandates and requirements, they are both correct; but where they tacitly agree, in how they define and conceive of the NWO, they are both wrong.

How Both Sides Are Right about the NWO

To start with the idealists: they are right to insist that a genuinely new and effective NWO has emerged in the last 50 years, especially the last decade, and further right in believing that this NWO, if not sustained and developed, may break down at great cost and risk to the United States and the whole international community. One need not be an international historian to see that a new era in international relations has emerged since World War II. In fact, the evidence of it is by now so familiar that Americans take it for granted and fail to see how startling it is in historical perspective. The signs include:

- the conversion of Germany and Japan in one generation from militarist, imperialist aggressors to stable, democratic industrial giants ambitious for trade and prosperity rather than military or political power;
- the economic and political integration and permanent pacification of Western Europe;
- the dismantling of the great European colonial empires, largely peacefully and voluntarily;
- the expansion of the UN to worldwide scope, the recognition of official juridical equality among its members, and its growth in reach and effectiveness for practical peacekeeping;
- the preservation of general peace (i.e., no system-wide wars and no all-out wars between major powers) through four decades of intense ideological and political competition between rival blocs, even while new powers were emerging and dangerous regional conflicts and rivalries constantly flared up;
- the gradual development of re-

435

straints on the arms race and the cooling of ideological rivalry even while this competition went on;[1]
- the admission of a host of new or transformed states into the world community; and, finally,
- the end of the Cold War and the (until now, at least) generally peaceful dismantling and transformation of the Soviet empire.

The point is not that this has yielded a brave new world free of war and upheaval. No one claims that; few if any think that such a world will ever come about. The point is rather that accomplishments such as this were unheard of and impossible in previous eras of history. When one adds to these developments others perhaps less spectacular or more disputable but nonetheless hopeful and progressive (e.g., democratization in Spain and Portugal, the end of apartheid in South Africa, progress toward Arab–Israeli peace, the astonishing economic and political development of the western Pacific Rim, and the decline of dictatorships and rise of democracies in Latin America and elsewhere), the case for the existence of the NWO, that is, a genuine new order of international politics, becomes overwhelming.

The historian's contribution to understanding this remarkable change is not to try to show that the more things have changed, the more they have stayed the same. This is the line some so-called realists take, insisting on the unchanging dominance of power politics and the primacy of the balance of power. The historian should know better. Granted that grave international problems and dangers still exist or will arise, what sensible person would exchange the current problems for those of 10, 50, or 100 years ago, or insist that they are really still the

same? The international historian can indeed identify certain roots and antecedents of the NWO in history, can even (in my view) show that it is not solely the product of the last 20 or 50 years, but the climax of a long historical development stretching back to the sixteenth and seventeenth centuries. Yet the very historical insight that sees the NWO as the fruit of a long evolution highlights the contrast between this era and the past, emphasizing how the NWO now enables statesmen to manage problems and maintain a stable international order in ways that statesmen of previous eras could only dream of. Denying the fundamental differences between the world orders of previous centuries and that of today is like denying the changes in the capitalist system over the same period.[2]

Yet, on the other side, the realist critics are right to claim that current ways of using and sustaining the NWO are not working well, and if pursued much longer may harm both the NWO and world peace. Once again special historical knowledge is not required to see this or understand the reasons; in fact, political and social science, international relations theory, practical experience in international politics, and plain common sense work as well or better. The special contribution of historians is first to point out that the idea of preserving peace and establishing a new international order through collectively enforcing international law against violators or imposing certain norms of international conduct on all actors—an old idea that goes back at least to the high Middle Ages and figures in most peace plans developed in the centuries since[3]—has regularly failed in history, proving ineffective and utopian at best and productive of even greater violence and wider war at worst. Second, historians then help show why the reasons for this persistent failure still prevail under the NWO today. The central reason, familiar to all scholars, is that making international politics into a confrontation between alleged lawbreakers and supposed enforcers of the law runs counter to the core of the international system that originated in Europe between the fifteenth and the seventeenth centuries and now embraces the whole world. That system, as the term "international politics" implies, presupposes the coexistence of independent states in juridically coordinate rather than superordinate and subordinate relations with each other, each claiming sovereignty, that is, the sole right to proclaim and enforce the law within its own domains, and demanding recognition of that sovereignty from the others. Carried to its logical conclusion, the concept of the NWO as the collective enforcement of international law against transgressors fundamentally challenges and undermines this order, still the only one available, and therefore must tend to provoke resistance and heighten conflict.

This shows up in international affairs in various ways, obvious and commonplace yet often overlooked. Tactically, this concept of "law enforcement" makes international confrontations and conflicts into something like a gunfight between the sheriff and the outlaws in a movie Western. Yet for purposes of limiting conflict and promoting peace in international affairs, force, if it is unavoidable, should be used as in judo rather than as in a gunfight. The object in judo, to use an aggressor's own force combined with a minimum effort of one's own to overbalance and disarm rather than destroy him, is better not only because it results in less violence and destruction, but also because a key assumption in an international system is that all essential actors should be preserved, because even an aggressive opponent, once curbed, has a necessary role to play. Psychologically, when sanctions imposed by the international community are portrayed as enforcing the law against violators, the honor as well as the interests of the accused party are impugned, giving it additional incentives to resist (for a government that cannot defend its honor often quickly loses its power) and effective propaganda to rally domestic support against outsiders. (Precisely this has happened in the former Yugoslavia and Somalia.) Strategically, this outlook pulls the international community into pursuit of a vague, almost undefinable goal (when is the law sufficiently enforced, the lawbreaker adequately punished?). This raises the stakes for the international coalition in terms of its prestige and credibility, while leaving its means of enforcement limited and the concrete interests of its various members in the quarrel divergent—a sure prescription for disunity and defections. Juridically, it encourages challenges to the legitimacy of the action that an aggressor can easily exploit. Practically, it engenders disputes over meeting and sharing the costs and burdens of enforcement, and fears that enforcing the law will result in more suffering and damage than did the original alleged violation.

All this, added to the fundamental reluctance of states to acknowledge an authority higher than themselves and thereby implicitly surrender their right to judge and defend their own cause, makes it clear that the NWO, so long as it is conceived as a collective effort to enforce compliance with international law or the will of the international community, faces grave obstacles.

The conclusion seems to represent an impasse. The NWO is real and vitally important, as its defenders insist; yet the measures it apparently requires are unworkable, counterproductive, and dangerous, as its critics claim. The way out calls for rethinking the NWO.

The NWO: Not Compellence-Deterrence, but Association-Exclusion

This rethinking begins with seeing that the NWO did not basically arise from successful compellence and deterrence, and does not mainly require these means to survive and work today. The account offered here of how the NWO was actually born and has worked is, like the whole essay, brief, oversimplified, and doubtless controversial, but it rests on well-known historical facts. The NWO as it emerged after World War II was principally the product of a durable consensus among a sizable number of major states and smaller powers, mostly West European and well developed politically and economically, that certain kinds of international conduct (direct military aggression and threats, the undermining of foreign governments by subversion, economic practices considered tantamount to economic warfare, and even some forms of civil war or internal oppression) had to be ruled out as incompatible with their general security and welfare. They formed various associations based on this consensus, designed both to deter external actions or threats of this kind and to promote a different kind of international conduct among themselves, namely, to encourage political and economic cooperation and integration, expand trade and communication, resolve conflicts peacefully, and promote broad political participation, civil and human rights, and the economic and social welfare of the member states. The various associations and institutions created for these purposes (the Western European Union, Benelux, the North Atlantic Treaty Organization [NATO], the European Coal and Steel Community, the European Community [EC], the European Free Trade Area, and others) proved over time not only durable, able to withstand external challenges and internal disintegration, but also successful in promoting prosperity, political stability, and democratic freedoms among the members themselves. As a result, these kinds of association promoting these patterns of conduct became a leading model for international politics in the developed world and much of the developing world, tending to pull other states toward it and to undermine associations and practices hostile to it.

The story is familiar; the historian's contribution is again to emphasize how new and unprecedented this development was and remains. A rough rule of thumb on alliances and associations in European international history is this: in the seventeenth century, all alliances worked almost purely as instruments of power politics (i.e., self-defense, war, and territorial expansion), even when ostensibly created for other purposes (e.g., religion or dynastic unions), and all were highly unreliable, no matter how solemnly sworn and guaranteed or expensively purchased with subsidies and bribes— so much so that it was impossible to calculate when or under what circumstances an ally was likely to defect. By the eighteenth century, alliances and associations, although still oriented almost exclusively to power politics, had grown more reliable, but not much more durable. They lasted only so long as they served the special interests of the contracting parties and so long as other more profitable alliances were not available. Thus eighteenth-century statesmen, in concluding alliances, had to try to calculate roughly when and under what circumstances an ally would defect. Nineteenth- and earlier twentieth-century alliances became much more durable, but still normally served the power-political ends of defense against enemies and acquisition of special advantages. Because they primarily served these purposes, their very durability and reliability, and the resultant rigidity of alliance systems, became a prime cause of war, especially World War I. With certain exceptions, it proved impossible in these earlier eras to erect and sustain durable, effective associations to promote the common good and general peace.[4] Only the late twentieth century has seen durable international alliances and associations of a new kind, directed not simply against common dangers, but also for common constructive purposes. These associations control the international conduct of the members themselves and make overt war among them unthinkable. They are also valuable enough that members hardly think any longer of abandoning them, and that outsiders want to join them rather than weaken or break them up. More than anything else, it is this startling change in the structure, purposes, and uses of international alliances and associations that makes the NWO new.

In contrast, the collective action that supposedly gave birth to the NWO, the Persian Gulf War, was not new at all. One can give the Bush administration full marks for skillful diplomacy in forming and sustaining the coalition. Nonetheless, this was normal, old-fashioned power politics, basically no different from other military coalitions against, for example, Louis XIV, Hitler, or Napoleon. Nor was it unique in its success. On Na-

poleon's return from Elba in 1815, in an era of much slower communications and inferior military technology, the allies formed an even wider coalition still more quickly and won a quicker, more brilliant, more complete, and more durable military success against a more serious foe.

To be sure, compellence and deterrence were not absent from the emergence and the operation of the NWO; some have claimed they were decisive in its creation. According to this view,

- united military action by a huge allied coalition destroyed Nazi and Japanese imperialism in World War II;
- military defeat and occupation plus forced democratization and economic liberalization transformed Germany and Japan;
- the threat of Soviet expansion and subversion compelled Western Europe to integrate, and U.S. leadership, economic aid, and military protection made that integration possible;
- the Western system of political and economic freedom was able to demonstrate its superiority over communism only because NATO held the West together and kept Soviet imperialism at bay; and, finally,
- it was U.S. military and economic superiority that defeated the USSR in the Cold War, causing its internal change of course, the collapse of its empire, and the downfall of communism itself in rapid succession.

The case looks plausible, but it rests on turning a contributing factor or, at most, a necessary but not sufficient condition in the rise of the NWO into the main cause. Compellence and deterrence may have been indispensable at certain points in the process, but their role was still ancillary. Force cleared away obstacles to positive changes; it did not produce the changes themselves, and carried too far, it could obstruct them. In exaggerating the role played by coercive force in building the NWO, this view obscures the real creative power behind it, which was a broad process of political and cultural learning. This process of collective learning shows most clearly in the defeated enemies of World War II, but it also worked profoundly throughout the Western community, and spread eventually far beyond it.

The process involved absorbing and internalizing two lessons. The first was a widespread recognition of failure, a realization that traditional ways of pursuing vital national and societal goals would not work, had intolerable consequences, and must be abandoned. The second involved devising other kinds of processes and institutions to achieve national goals that went beyond normal power politics, and deciding to try them. In a word, the NWO emerged when a critical mass of the international system's member states and peoples learned to repudiate the old power-political methods of achieving security and welfare and worked out new and different means for doing so.

This formula, although oversimplified, fits all the major post–World War II achievements that prove the NWO a reality—both those changes now permanent and irreversible (in Germany, Japan, Britain, France, other former colonial powers, Western Europe in general, and the western Pacific Rim), those changes under way in Eastern Europe, and those apparently starting in the Middle East, Africa, the People's Republic of China, India and Pakistan, and Central and South America. In every case of such collective learning, even where compellence and deterrence—coercive force—may

have played a role, it was never decisive. Germany and Japan were not really forced by armed coercion to become democratic members of a liberal capitalist world system; rather they were brought by the hard experience of disastrous failure, including military defeat and occupation, to recognize that their former strategies of imperialism, militarism, and autarky could not make them secure, prosperous, and great. Presented with the chance to try an alternative route to security and prosperity, they chose to earn their way back into the international community by it. Many of the forcible measures originally proposed to transform Germany and Japan into safe members of the world community were, fortunately, never carried out— a sweeping partition and total demilitarization of Germany, its permanent deindustrialization, long-term control of German and Japanese education by outsiders, permanent controls on trade, abolition of the imperial office in Japan, abolition of Shintoism as a state religion, and so on.

The same point, that armed force, although needed to defeat their imperialist aggression, was not the main source of their collective learning, holds elsewhere. Great Britain was not compelled by outside force to give up its empire, not even in India. France was not forced out of Algeria—not by the Algerian rebels. France won the military war, and then abandoned the political one. The Soviet Union was not driven by force out of Afghanistan, and still less out of Eastern Europe or the various parts of its former empire, now independent. The United States was not really forced to abandon Vietnam or its military campaigns against Nicaragua and Cuba; not forced to recognize China or end the war in Korea. Change always reflected the same two-sided process of learning (even where it remained incomplete or dangerously reversible): the recognition that an old method, primarily resting on force, would not work or would cost too much or was too dangerous, and that another way was conceivable—and worth a try.

This will sound "soft" to any realist—idealistic in the bad sense, wet, sentimental, willfully ignorant of the realities of power and the need for coercion in international politics. Two comments: first, no one should allow so-called realists to define what is real and genuine in international politics, for nothing is more likely to make one miss what is deeply involved in it, and above all what is changing in it, than their kind of reductionism. Second, the coercion and pressure clearly connected with the NWO from its beginnings and still involved in its operation are essentially different in kind and operation from power-political compellence and deterrence.

No one claims that these vast changes since World War II came about because governments, leaders, or peoples simply said to themselves, "What we are doing is not working. We need to try another way. Look at what the Americans or the West Europeans or the Japanese are doing; let's try that." Pressure and coercion were needed and frequently exerted, especially at critical points. What counts is the kind of pressure; it did not mean the use or threat of force to compel states to obey international law or deter them from breaking it. Instead, the pressure exerted consisted primarily of the members of the various associations discussed earlier combining the carrot of actual or potential membership with its attendant benefits with the stick of exclusion from the association with the attendant penalties and denial of benefits. The carrot and stick, group association

with a promised payoff and exclusion with threatened denial, became the dominant form of sanctions in the development and operation of the NWO.

The psychological and political superiority of this approach over compellence-deterrence is easy to see. The association-exclusion model assumes that states will more readily perform certain desired actions or conform to a desired rule if they are either already members, or have the prospect of becoming members, of an association in which the performance and rules are jointly decided upon and upheld by the group and all share in the group benefits, and in which the main sanction is exclusion from the group and its benefits. There is a major difference between in effect saying to an opponent, or an ally threatening to defect and become an opponent, "Stop what you are doing or threatening to do, and do what we tell you instead, or we will punish you as a lawbreaker," and saying, "What you are now doing or threatening to do is against our group norms; it will eventually fail and hurt you and all of us. If you continue to try it, you will be barred from our group and excluded from its benefits; if you change your policy you can remain in the group, or keep your chance of joining it and promoting your interests within it." It is just as easy to see the tactical, strategic, and economic advantages of this approach.

Clearly this kind of pressure was most effective in promoting the NWO in the past. Germany and Japan were taught to become liberal and democratic not by force (a contradiction in terms in any case), but by the knowledge that this was the price of association with the West and its markets, military security, and respectability. Britain and France were not forced to decolonize by the United States; they were only taught, sometimes with brutal clarity as in the Suez Crisis of 1956, that they would lose the economic and political benefits of association with the United States if they did not. The United Kingdom was not forced into the European Common Market; it was merely compelled to recognize that opposing it was futile and costly, and that it could enter only on Europe's terms, not its own. Superior Western military power did not force the Soviet Union and its former satellites first to revise and then to abandon their social and economic systems. Exclusion from Western technology, markets, and other desirable goods and the knowledge that they were losing the peaceful competition with the West without them was what mainly did it. Examples could be multiplied.

This mode of international sanctions (association with benefits versus exclusion and denial) is not new in the sense of being unthought or untried earlier. The peace plans and dreams conceived in the sixteenth to eighteenth centuries regularly summoned states, rulers, and peoples (at least all the right, qualified states, rulers, and peoples) to unite in a permanent association for peace and share its benefits. The concept is therefore not new; what is new is its present effectiveness, its far greater power to reward and penalize without the overt use of force. Formerly the idea always foundered on the problem of sanctions, among other things: how to maintain the association, enforce its rules, and discipline wayward members or outlaws. Mere exclusion from the association was not enough, but the joint use of armed force against the offender (i.e., war) was impracticable and as harmful as the offense or worse. Only one previous international association, the post-1815 European Concert, succeeded for a time in keeping its great-power members and

lesser states in line, not primarily by military force and threats, but by the prospect of exclusion from the Concert and the European family of states with its benefits and privileges. But this too broke down in time, because some states, like Austria and Russia, ruined the Concert's attractiveness by tying it to their rigid and repressive purposes, while others, like France, Sardinia-Piedmont, and Prussia, developed aims in violation of the association's rules and therefore set out to wreck it, and the leaders of still others, especially Britain's Lord Palmerston, preferred balance of power confrontational tactics to the Concert strategy of grouping and joint pressure for conformity with group norms.[5]

Obviously the NWO today faces analogous dangers of ruin or repudiation. At the same time, the improved effectiveness, broader applicability, and greater durability of these nonforcible mechanisms of association and exclusion make it no longer utopian to hope and work for their indefinite duration and extension. In any case, in one sense the United States can really no longer choose in many instances to use this form of pressure or forcible compellence and deterrence instead. The very success these mechanisms have had, not only in the so-called free world among U.S. friends and allies, but also now in Eastern Europe, the former Soviet Union, the Middle East, South Africa, Latin America, and other areas, has effectively deprived Americans of that choice. The fact that one country after another has opted to abandon rivalry with the so-called free world in favor of association with it makes it impossible to revert to cold war methods, even if the United States wanted to; Americans can only try to help make that choice work for them and themselves. This is really what "the end of the Cold War" means. Even where a confrontation in some form still persists, with Cuba, China, North Korea, and elsewhere, the best hopes for change and means to promote it are those of association-benefits/exclusion-denial. Although the new methods cannot work quickly to end fighting already begun or control parties already locked in mortal combat over irreconcilable positions, as in the former Yugoslavia and parts of the former Soviet Union, even here they are not useless. Ultimately the only kind of pressure and coercion helpful in producing a durable settlement is one that induces all parties to recognize that violent solutions do not work in the long run, and that another way is open. (Witness the recent signs of a break in the Israeli–Palestinian and Israeli–Arab impasse.) This is what the NWO sanctions of association and exclusion are designed to do; the NWO not only enables the United States to use them, but almost compels it to do so.

Some Implications for Policy

Changing the way Americans think about the NWO and its operation affects their goals, priorities, and expectations in its regard. If the NWO is developed and works, not by enforcing international law and punishing violators, but by forming and maintaining associations that reward those who conform to group norms and exclude those who do not, then the main goal of policy under the NWO should be sustaining this process of association and exclusion. This sounds like a mere truism, but it has specific, important implications. It means that the prime concern in regard to the NWO should not be how it can be used in particular problem areas to advance

particular ends, values, and interests, even vital ones like peace, democracy, and human rights, but rather to make sure that the NWO itself is preserved and developed, for its own sake. The NWO, in other words, must finally be seen as an end in itself, the necessary means and condition for other vital ends and values. Americans accept this logic in other contexts. They understand, for example, that even in the hurly-burly of domestic politics they must be concerned to uphold the Constitution and the democratic process, so that politics can remain free. They know that agreements and institutions like the General Agreement on Tariffs and Trade (GATT), the International Monetary Fund (IMF), the World Bank, the Group of Seven, and others are needed not just to promote economic stability and prosperity for themselves and their friends, but to maintain a viable world economic system generally. The same principle applies to international relations. If the NWO's working principle of association-exclusion enables the international community to accomplish important tasks better and more safely than can be done without it, then that system itself deserves support as something of intrinsic and not mere instrumental value. The descriptive analysis must have prescriptive implications.

This applies a fortiori to the associations that produced the NWO and make it effective. The UN, which once could be dismissed as merely a useful talking shop or meeting place handy for certain purposes, has become valuable in its own right as an integral part of the NWO. This is even more true of the narrower associations that in recent decades have succeeded in keeping their members in line and making others wish to join them. The end of the Cold War has made them not less but more important in a practical, immediate way, at the same time presenting them with major challenges of reorientation, consolidation, and expansion. The most vital task in the NWO today is not stamping out conflict and enforcing international law everywhere in the world, but preserving and consolidating gains already made and in danger of being lost—not putting out brush fires in remote areas, but securing and expanding the homestead and the corral as a place of refuge from them. This means keeping the EC cohesive and attractive, NATO intact and functioning as a vehicle of integration and cooperation, the Japanese–American economic and political relationship stable, the progress of the Pacific Rim going, the world system of relatively free world trade working, and the road to freedom and prosperity in eastern Europe and Russia open in the long run.

If one recognizes that the NWO, thus understood, has intrinsic value and is best maintained by preserving and developing the associations and mechanisms that support it, this suggests in turn a simple, practical rule of thumb for policy. Each proposal that the UN, the EC, the United States and its allies, or some other international group should carry out some mission or measure in the name of the NWO must face an initial question: Is this action compatible with the special nature, mission, and methods of the NWO, primarily those of association and exclusion? If so, and if the action is also desirable and practical per se, then it is worth considering; if not, then not. In other words, Americans must stop expecting and demanding that the NWO perform tasks it was not designed to do, which would wreck it if seriously tried, and then denouncing it or despairing of it when these mis-

sions are not undertaken or the effort fails.[6]

This happens repeatedly—whenever, in fact, the UN and/or some other international community or authority is called on to intervene in civil wars and ethnic conflicts, restore civil order, alleviate starvation, break illegal blockades, settle territorial disputes, impose armistices, stop governmental oppression and violations of civil rights, establish war-crimes tribunals and judge war criminals, punish countries for defying UN resolutions or supporting terrorism, and so on—all without asking whether the way the NWO actually works makes these tasks necessary or possible. Name any international evil or problem, and it is a safe bet that someone has called on the world community to solve it, and denounced it or proclaimed the demise of the NWO for its failure to do so. Much of the current cynicism and despair about the NWO derives from the inevitable disappointment of unrealistic expectations. Although, as already noted, such proposals are frequently opposed on practical grounds, little attention is given to the danger of ruining the NWO by burdening it with assignments unsuited to its mission and methods.

This perspective also calls for some faith in the NWO, patience with the process of association and exclusion by which it works, and allowing it sufficient time and steady application to work. It is unreasonable to argue, for example, that if there were a real NWO the international community would long since have acted to bring the fighting in Bosnia to an end, stop "ethnic cleansing" and other atrocities, relieve the suffering of civilians, settle the territorial and other disputes there, and establish a viable Bosnian state. Whether one believes that more could have been done earlier to achieve these ends through diplomacy or other means, or believes (as I do) that these goals were largely unattainable from the outset given the circumstances and the attitudes and aims of the various parties involved, and regardless of the inherent desirability or undesirability, feasibility or unfeasibility of these ends, achieving them is not now and never was the kind of task the NWO is designed or suited to carry out, and they must not be made the test of its existence and worth.

This does not mean that the NWO is useless or irrelevant in situations like Bosnia. It rather means that the real task of the NWO in Bosnia and the Balkans as a whole, and the real test of the efficacy of its principle of association-exclusion, still lie ahead of it, after the current conflict, which Serbia and Croatia have already effectively won, is over. The vital question, once the fighting is ended and some sort of "peace settlement" is patched up, will be whether the international community decides to forget the manner in which the newly independent states of Serbia and Croatia were founded and the integral-nationalist ideologies on which they are based, and receives them back into Europe and the world as full, normal partners. Should this happen, it would constitute weighty evidence that there is no real NWO; for this would represent the old politics pure and simple, even if it were defended as a way to forget the past and promote peace and reconciliation among former enemies. It was characteristic of previous eras that successful aggression usually paid. States could generally expect, once they had made their gains and got them sanctioned in some sort of treaty, to be treated once more as a normal member of the family of states; this is

exactly what Serb and Croat nationalist leaders are counting on now. If, however (as could relatively easily be done), the international community chooses to exclude Serbia and Croatia after the "peace settlement," that is, to ban them from full membership and participation in the UN and its constituent agencies and above all from the EC, until and unless these two states give concrete evidence of change in their fundamental outlook toward other states and people, especially Muslims, Albanians, and Macedonians, this would be evidence of the NWO in operation. Moreover, this kind of isolation and confrontation would have every chance of success, given the sorry state of the Croatian economy and the still worse condition of Serbia's—success of course being defined not as the destruction of either state but a realization in both, by leaders and peoples, of what their victory and the policies of aggression and ethnic cleansing used to achieve it has cost them in terms of European and international recognition and status, commerce, technology, academic and cultural exchanges, tourism, foreign investment, international sports, and more. Such long-term pressures of exclusion-denial would have a far better chance of bringing about the needed changes in attitude and political culture in Serbia and Croatia (above all, the realization that prosperity and security in today's Europe and the world cannot be based on aggression, ethnic cleansing, and authoritarian nationalist programs) that using external force for deterrence and compellence could not produce, even in the unlikely case that force was successful in a military sense. This is said merely to illustrate how the NWO could work. Rather than prescribe a policy, it suggests an idea for one, as part of an argument that the NWO makes strategies and outcomes possible now that were futile and utopian even a few decades ago.

Some Objections

There are some likely objections to this view that deserve brief discussion, less to refute them (the answers have mostly already been indicated) than to avoid misunderstandings and correct wrong impressions.

One is that this view of international politics is soft and sentimental, ignores its harsh realities, and relies on reason and moral suasion for peace and stability. Surely, however, a view that gives the maintenance of an impersonal system and process in international politics priority over all other goals, including the promotion of justice, civil and human rights, international law, the relief of innocent suffering, and even the prevention of local wars, is not sentimental. Nor is it soft to call for excluding successful aggressor states from the international community, and making their peoples pay the heavy political and economic price for that exclusion.

Another objection is that this proposal reflects too academic a concept of how human beings learn and the world works. It expects history to teach peoples and states their errors and induce them to change, when in fact people generally learn what they want to from history, mostly the wrong things or nothing at all, and many leaders are totally indifferent to "lessons of history" and the costs of their failures so long as they can keep their state machines and essential followers under control, make the masses pay, and deceive them into blaming the outside world for their sufferings. This is largely true, but irrelevant.

This view of the NWO *does not propose to let* history teach Saddam Hussein or Slobodan Milosevic, or their peoples, that aggression does not pay. True, history left to itself can and does "teach" almost any lessons one wants it to, including the lesson that aggression does pay. This is instead an argument that the NWO enables the current generation, unlike past generations, to control the "lessons" of history in some measure, by affording it means other than external armed force, and better than armed force, to make governments and peoples recognize that certain courses fail and have negative results and that others are unavoidable and more profitable. Certainly peoples often resist learning from history, clinging stubbornly to a familiar version of the past that validates their collective image and self-view and justifies their actions. The historian Lewis B. Namier's comment that Freud's definition of neurosis, to be "dominated by unconscious memory, fixated upon the past, and unable to overcome it," is the regular condition of historical communities,[7] points exactly to a big part of the current problem, especially in the Balkans. But the strategy of exclusion and denial is a good way of helping states and peoples to get over their history, to break out of it. Repeated, long-term experience of failure is a powerful teacher, especially in teaching that one must break with one's past to have a tolerable future.

The most important criticism, however, is the charge of ineffectiveness: that the incentives and sanctions of association-benefits and exclusion-denial are too weak to produce a stable world order. They will be ineffective with dictators like Saddam Hussein or against dedicated or desperate peoples, groups, and organizations of all kinds, and will fail to stop civil wars, settle serious territorial disputes, or curb terrorism. They also act too slowly, and therefore cannot prevent or quickly stop developments too dangerous or horrible to be tolerated—aggressions like the invasion of Kuwait, the acquisition of weapons of mass destruction by rogue governments or terrorist organizations, the spread of aggression, conflict, and ethnic cleansing from one region to another, or genocide and mass starvation. In other words, even if the so-called NWO and its methods may work with reasonably mature, developed, peaceful states, they cannot handle the real problems of a world still violent, hostile, and chaotic. These problems call for either the old instruments of individual state action and power politics, or newer ones in the form of effective forcible sanctions imposed by the international community through the UN, or a combination of the two.

Much of this is true, and has already been admitted; this essay has emphasized that there are tasks the NWO cannot do, and should not be expected or asked to. One can go further: forcible sanctions are still needed in cases where a particular evil or danger so clearly and directly threatens the general peace and the continued existence and operation of the whole international system that it must be averted promptly at almost any cost. But this does not annul the case for the NWO as presented here, or even weaken it. To believe in the reality and efficacy of the NWO does not mean to suppose that everything in international politics is new, that coercive force, including military force, need no longer ever be used, or anything of that sort. Any "new order" in history (even where this much-abused term is legitimate) is never wholly new; the term means only that a corner has been turned, a trend set, a new way of doing things

become dominant, and an old one recessive. So, here, the claim made about the NWO means only (but this is a great deal) that the principal hopes and chances for durable, general, relative peace in the world (all the adjectives are important) rest now on a world order operating primarily by association-exclusion rather than deterrence-compellence. This certainly implies that the rewards and sanctions of association-benefits and exclusion-denial must be in general more effective for more of the required purposes of general world order and peace than deterrence-compellence. That claim, however, can be sustained despite exceptions.

To be sure, NWO-style rewards and sanctions will not achieve some desired ends in international politics—but neither will armed force. The question of which is more useful under more circumstances for more important goals, moreover, must include an analysis of costs. A historic trend in international politics, rapidly accelerating in this century, has been the steep rise in costs attached to the use of armed force, both absolutely and in ratio to the benefits achieved, and a corresponding diminution in what it can usefully accomplish. To the old familiar escalating costs—possible failure and defeat, blood, lost treasure, diverted resources, ancillary destruction, lasting alienation and bitterness—the emergence of the NWO has added an important opportunity cost: that ends conceivably attainable by association-exclusion become impossible once force is used. Using armed force against an international transgressor like Serbia or Iraq is not a more quick and effective way of teaching it the same lessons about international association and cooperation as are intended by the tactics of association-benefits and exclusion-denial. Instead, trying to "teach" these lessons by armed force obstructs teaching or learning them by the other route at all, as current U.S. experiences in Iraq, Bosnia, and Somalia indicate and many historical examples attest. The more the lesson desired is inflicted by external armed force, the less the experience of defeat and failure is likely to be internalized in a useful way and lead to the kind of durable change desired. Furthermore, every resort to armed force willy-nilly teaches both the participants and the bystanders the retrograde lesson that the NWO and its methods cannot be trusted in critical cases to get the job done—which becomes a self-fulfilling prophecy.

Another major element in the cost-benefit analysis is the consideration that many of the proposed aims in international politics for which NWO methods are admittedly ineffective— enforcing international law, reversing historic wrongs, stopping civil wars, imposing territorial settlements in hotly disputed cases, punishing international crimes and criminals and compensating their victims—are unattainable by any means and incompatible with any working international system. The truth is that many evils and injustices in the world are too deeply rooted to be undone; that, as the nineteenth-century publicist Friedrich von Gentz said, "All historic rights are wrongs, sanctioned by time"; and that the only sane response to historic wrongs is often, as Prince Metternich of Austria argued, to "outlive the evil." Recognizing and accepting the NWO means, among other things, coming to terms with these commonplace truths, accepting that some goals possibly desirable in themselves cannot be pursued under it and are not worth pursuing at the cost of the system as a whole. At the same time, association and exclusion are not in-

effective in achieving the goals most central and important to the NWO, namely, rewarding international cooperation and inducing aggressors and troublemakers to recognize failure and change course. To see this, one need only look at the long list of states that since 1945 have been excluded, or have excluded themselves, from the mainstream of international commerce, industry, technology, communications, travel and tourism, exchange of information, international capital, and so forth. None of these states has found peace and prosperity; most have tried or are trying to escape from that exclusion, often changing the policies the international community objects to in the attempt.

Naturally this learning process required to bring states and peoples into the NWO takes time. Important, durable changes in collective mentality and political culture cannot happen overnight—which means (to reiterate) that some threats may require a different, speedier response, despite the strictures and reservations discussed above. Yet one of the important things making the NWO new is the fact that now such changes can develop much faster and be more predictable, even controllable, than in the past. International history used ironically to illustrate the Old Testament saying that the sins of the fathers are visited upon the children to the third and fourth generation. Generations usually passed before leaders and peoples became aware of the real consequences of past policies, or even recognized past follies and crimes as such. Prussians tasted the full fruits of Frederick the Great's militarism and aggression only in Napoleon's time; only in 1919 and 1945 did the full consequences of Bismarck's founding of the Second Reich in 1871 become clear. This still is often the case, of course; but much speedier learning has now become possible. Germans and East Europeans, for example, have judged and decided between two competing systems in one generation. In the NWO, with history accelerated and the speed and ease of communication enormously increased, it is no longer unreasonable to expect children to see and repudiate the sins of the fathers while the fathers are still around.

There is a further objection to this view of how the NWO works and should be used that, if true, cannot be answered by rational argument. It is that this way of conceiving and managing the NWO does not fit the U.S. character and political system. It requires patience, steady attention to the long view, a willingness to wait for results, and the ability to adjust to changed reality and to accept blurred, complex, uncertain outcomes and live with them if they are the best attainable—all virtues that the U.S. public does not possess and the U.S. political system, focused on domestic concerns, immediate issues, simple solutions, and clear-cut moral dichotomies, neither teaches to citizens nor rewards in politicians.

It is not clear to me that so sweeping an indictment of the U.S. political culture and its effects on international politics is justified. Americans, both leaders and the public, have over the last 50 years or so shown in some instances a striking ability to learn, adjust, stay the course, and adapt to change in the international arena—witness their support of Israel, commitment to NATO, general maintenance of free trade, and acceptance of relative failure and the limits to U.S. power in Korea, Vietnam, and elsewhere. Yet it may be that calling on Americans to accept this version of the NWO and lead it (for who else can?) means calling for a United States dif-

ferent from the existing one—less prone to violence at home and abroad, less shortsighted about its own interests and those of other states, less provincial and ignorant about the rest of the world, and less insistent that in dealing with any crisis it call the shots and that, if it decides to get in, other states must help it get the job done quickly and get out. Clearly the NWO cannot work under this kind of leadership or these conditions. Even more important, this attitude on the part of many Americans is incompatible with the ongoing transformation of international politics through a collective learning process, a change in collective mentalities and political cultures involving whole nations and peoples, enabling them to adjust to each other successfully in a new order. Americans need to be part of this learning process as much as other people, perhaps in some respects more. Americans deny this cardinal need and responsibility whenever they say in effect, "The United States cannot follow this or that policy in international affairs, even though it is necessary and legitimate, because the American people will not support it and the American political system makes it impossible to sell it to them." What they really say by this is that they want to run the NWO and enjoy its benefits, but not belong to it, or change and grow with it—that they are stupid and inconsistent, and prefer to stay that way. A nation that uses that excuse for very long must sooner or later excuse itself into disaster.

The author first wrote this essay as a Jennings Randolph Peace Fellow at the United States Institute of Peace, whose support he gratefully acknowledges. He also wishes to thank Jack Snyder of Columbia University's Institute of War and Peace Studies for his comments. The views expressed in this article are the author's own and do not necessarily reflect the views

Paul W. Schroeder

either of the University of Illinois, or of the United States Institute of Peace.

Notes

1. Roger Kanet and Edward A. Kolodziej, eds., *The Cold War as Cooperation* (Baltimore, Md.: Johns Hopkins University Press, 1991).

2. In a forthcoming book, *The Transformation of European Politics, 1763–1848* (Oxford: Clarendon Press, 1994), I argue that the Congress of Vienna transformed international politics in 1814–1815, producing a new international system much more peaceful and stable than any previous one, resembling the current NWO in certain respects. I would argue just as strongly, however, for the superiority of the current NWO over the Vienna system in providing solutions to various problems that the Vienna system only dimly foreshadowed.

3. See, for example, Jacob van Meulen, *Der Gedanke der Internationalen Organisation in seiner Entwicklung 1300–1800* (The idea of international organization in its development 1300–1800) (1917; The Hague: M. Nijhoff, 1968), or F. H. Hinsley, *Power and the Pursuit of Peace* (Cambridge: Cambridge University Press, 1963).

4. Even the two most important exceptions really prove the rule. The German Confederation of 1815–1866 was originally founded both to provide for the common defense of its members, the various independent German states, and to promote their joint welfare in various ways. Yet its leaders, especially Austria, quickly stultified its potential for advancing the general welfare, for particular Austrian reasons, and after 1848 it could no longer even serve for common defense and for reconciling power-political differences between its members, especially Prussia and Austria. Similarly, the European Concert worked well from 1815 to 1853 to preserve international peace, but mostly failed as a way of promoting a common approach to more general European political and social problems.

5. See Norman Rich, *Why the Crimean War? A Cautionary Tale* (Hanover, N.H.: University Press of New England, 1985); Anselm Doering-Manteuffel, *Vom Wiener Kongress zur Pariser Konferenz* (From the Congress of Vienna to the Conference of Paris) (Göttingen: Vandenhoeck and Ru-

precht, 1991); Winfried Baumgart, *Der Friede von Paris* (The Peace of Paris) (Munich: R. Oldenbourg, 1972); and my own *Austria, Great Britain and the Crimean War* (Ithaca, N.Y.: Cornell University Press, 1972).

6. This view rejects, to be sure, the widespread condemnation of the international community for not stopping the current fighting and atrocities in Bosnia. István Deák, a renowned historian at Columbia University, for example, concluded a series of review articles on recent works on the Holocaust in the *New York Review of Books* by remarking that the undertaking had left him with "a sense of hopelessness" at the refusal of states and peoples to learn from the Holocaust—a refusal that the "international failure to act" in the face of ethnic cleansing and other horrors in Bosnia demonstrates. "Holocaust Heroes," *New York Review of Books*, November 5, 1992, p. 26.

Deák and others are entirely right to remind us that human beings are still capable of bestial conduct, and that many individuals and groups have refused to learn from the Holocaust and other acts of genocide, or learned the wrong things. To ascribe the ongoing tragedy in Bosnia simply to an "international failure to act," however, is a mistake. It misunderstands the nature of the NWO and its methods, as already argued; it underestimates the real, formidable obstacles to any kind of international action capable of preventing or ending this kind of warfare in this region as in many others; and above all it ignores the huge difference between the international response to these particular Balkan horrors and the historic responses to all earlier ones. Central to all previous international responses to internecine Balkan conflicts has been the primary concern of the great powers to safeguard their individual great-power interests, spheres of influence, and positions of power within the region. Even where, as often happened, the great powers did not mainly try to exploit the conflicts for selfish ends but cooperated to regulate and end them, they were always concerned to preserve a favorable balance of power.

The most obvious feature of the current international response is that this long-dominant motive has almost totally disappeared. States that formerly would never have allowed the Balkan balance to shift fundamentally against them—Britain,

450

France, Italy, Germany, Austria, Russia—now would prefer to ignore the struggle entirely and intervene, if at all, primarily for peacekeeping and humanitarian reasons. A frequent argument for forcible intervention in Bosnia is that the conflict should be stopped to prevent it from spreading into a wider Balkan conflict that could trigger another wider war like World War I, touched off precisely in this area. The danger of a Balkan ripple effect is no doubt serious and important; the danger of another 1914 has virtually disappeared, because the general outlook prevalent in 1914 among all the powers, great and small, that the Balkans were vital to the general European and world balances has disappeared. It is one thing to emphasize the tragedy of the current situation for Bosnians and many others on all sides; another to claim that unless the international community under the NWO does something immediately effective to fix it, the NWO is useless and the world has learned nothing. This very situation, for all its horrors, proves that the international community, especially in Europe, has learned something, changed for the better.

7. Lewis B. Namier, "History," in Fritz R. Stern, ed., *Varieties of History: From Voltaire to the Present* (Cleveland, Ohio: World Publishing Co., 1956), p. 375.

1995 and the End of the Post–Cold War Era

Brad Roberts

MAKING SENSE OF the new currents and dynamics of international security after the Cold War is no small challenge. Analysts and pundits have made a fetish first of the new world order and more recently of the new world disorder. Especially in the United States, people seem to have been lulled by a sense that the nation's status as "the sole remaining superpower" cushions it from disruptions from abroad. Widespread throughout the Western community of international security specialists is a sense that the post–cold war era will linger in its current shape for years if not decades to come. This may prove a dangerous complacency.

The coming year, 1995, promises to be a significant turning point in the post–cold war international security dynamic. The reason is simple: during that year, a tier of states newly capable of making their own high-leverage weapons will reach basic decisions about their participation in a broad array of global treaty regimes. The decisions of these technically empowered states will be made in part based on answers they find to questions they pose about the United States—about its desire to tie its power to common purposes, its capacity to formulate a broad vision of global affairs, and its ability to lead. Many Americans will perhaps be uncomfortable with these questions at this juncture in the national history when domestic preoccupation and vacillating leadership have cast the U.S. world role in a particularly unfavorable light. They may be even more unhappy with the answers these states come to and the possibility of major departures from U.S. preferences by states throughout the world in the coming year.

This article begins with an effort to shift the focus of thinking away from the foreign policy crises of the moment that have gripped public and intellectual debate to the deeper currents of international security politics in the 1990s. Special emphasis is given to the proliferation problem. This problem has been paid a great deal of lip service in recent years but a basic misreading of its fundamental attributes impairs the policies being pursued in response to it. The article then defines the agenda that will play out in 1995 and the mistakes of apathy or old thinking in U.S. policy that have set the stage for a volatile year. It concludes with recommendations for an international security strategy that of-

Brad Roberts is editor of *The Washington Quarterly* and a research fellow at the Center for Strategic and International Studies.

Copyright © 1994 by The Center for Strategic and International Studies and the Massachusetts Institute of Technology

fers some promise of buttressing the sources of order in the new era. It also attempts to define the necessary and appropriate role of the United States in pursuing such a strategy as an alternative to simply muddling through.

Understanding the Post–Cold War Dynamic

In trying to understand the fundamental reorientation and restructuring of world affairs today, analysts have turned to historical examples. Some look at the era of drift and uncertainty that followed World War I and the war that broke out two decades later, and see an unwelcome parallel in the inconsistency of Western and U.S. leadership on problems of international security in the 1990s. Others look at the years after World War II and emphasize the need to restore a similarly dominant U.S. role encompassing a broad international strategy oriented toward containment of aggression and a liberal international economic and political order. These and other analogies offer insights into the unfolding events of the 1990s, but they tend to discount the unique features of the international system at the moment the Cold War ended. Moreover, because the features of most importance for the emerging global order are not the same as the features that were of central importance during the Cold War, they tend to be slighted or misunderstood today.

In addition, analysts labor with an intellectual inheritance often ill-suited to the problems of the present: common wisdom about the way states behave, problems of war and peace, and strategic weapons, arms control, and stability all derive from the highly distinctive cold war era. Government officials tinker with policy instruments designed for the problems of a differ-

ent time. It is not surprising that the rapid and dramatic changes in international affairs of the last decade should have outpaced the understanding of an academic, policy, and intellectual community whose stance has been largely reactive.

Weapons proliferation is widely recognized as a major post–cold war issue. It never fails to appear on lists of post–cold war U.S. foreign policy priorities. But scratch beneath the surface and one finds that people invoke an understanding of the problem rooted firmly in the 1960s and 1970s. There is an almost exclusive focus on nuclear weapons. All proliferation is decried as dangerous and destabilizing. Nonproliferation is prescribed as the antidote.

One of the best symptoms of this way of thinking is the national decision memorandum on proliferation issued by the Clinton administration in 1993, which reportedly contained hundreds of paragraphs on nuclear weapons and nonproliferation and but one or two on all other types of proliferation. That memorandum and the policies it generated rightly emphasize the critical importance of stemming any proliferation threat associated with the breakup of the Soviet Union. Efforts toward this end are an essential building block in the nonproliferation effort; failure to get it right here would render all other attempts to halt proliferation moot. But it is only one building block.

Looking afresh at the proliferation problem, what are its essential features in the post–cold war era? Two stand out.

First, nuclear weapons have been joined by other weapons as topics of concern. This is true of biological and to a lesser extent chemical weapons. In places like the Middle East and East Asia these weapons may be seen by decision makers to offer high political leverage or decisive military advantage in time of conflict. Today, the 5 or 8 or 9 nuclear states have been joined by another dozen or so states with programs aimed at waging war with biological weapons and 20 or so that have an offensive chemical warfare capability.[1] Furthermore, some conventional weapons that upset stable balances or significantly increase the strategic reach of nations fall into this category of high-leverage weaponry, such as the Russian-built submarines now in Iran's navy or the ballistic and cruise missiles that are now found in many regions of the world.

Second, the ability to produce weapons of all kinds has diffused even more widely than the weapons themselves. This is particularly true as regards conventional weapons. The defense industrial base associated with the production of military hardware is spreading. In 1945 only 4 countries outside the developed world produced military equipment (Argentina, Brazil, India, and South Africa); today, about 40 do so, with over one-quarter of those having significant defense industrial infrastructure.[2] Nearly 100 major conventional weapon systems are licensed for production in the developing world.[3] Seven countries have achieved the ability to produce weapons in each of the major combat categories (land, sea, air, and missile): Argentina, Brazil, China, Egypt, Israel, South Africa, and Taiwan.[4] These states have enjoyed only mixed success in overcoming thresholds related to the range, accuracy, or lethality of domestically produced weapons. But they have emerged as important niche market suppliers amid a pattern of deepening cooperation at the commercial and military level.

And this is also true as regards unconventional weapons—chemical and biological as well as nuclear. The Iklé–

Wohlstetter Commission on Integrated Long-Term Strategy predicted that by the year 2000 40 countries will have the ability to produce nuclear weapons.[5] The emergence of a new tier of suppliers of nuclear technology, numbering 15 new entrants over the last decade, seems to support this conclusion.[6] So too does the diffusion of expertise in the nuclear domain: to cite but one illustration, between 1954 and 1979, approximately 13,000 foreign nationals received nuclear training in the United States, one-quarter of them from states not party to the Nuclear Non-Proliferation Treaty (NPT).[7] The number of states capable of making large quantities of chemical warfare agent quickly easily numbers 100 or more. The number of those capable of doing the same in the biological area may be somewhat smaller; but this is only a matter of relative preparedness, because the science and technology of chemical and biological warfare fall within the reach of virtually any nation with even minimal industrial competence.

There is, moreover, a huge international flow in those "dual-use" technologies with both civil and military applications in the nuclear, biological, and chemical domains; in 1989 in the United States alone, approximately 120,000 licenses were issued for dual-use exports. Factoring in the likely scale of exports of these technologies from other industrialized countries as well as those newly industrializing, one begins to appreciate the diffusion of the means to make unconventional weapons. A recent RAND study of nuclear proliferation coins a term that usefully captures the new drift of proliferation: it cites a growing number of "virtual" arsenals and "virtual" weapon states that possess the capability to rapidly arm while also adhering strictly to non-weapon status.[8]

This is not to argue that the nuclear proliferation problem is somehow less relevant today. The nuclear dimension remains of course paramount, for there is no gainsaying the significant implications associated with nuclear proliferation. But other types of proliferation are of increasing salience and they must be integrated into the concept of the problem—but without trying to force them into the nuclear paradigm.

What does this imply for the old assumption that all proliferation is destabilizing? Little thinking has been done about the implications for stability of weapons capabilities as opposed to weapons themselves or about high-leverage systems that are not also nuclear.[9] As the diffusion of conventional weapons emerges as a topic of international concern, the norm against proliferation is brought into starker contrast with the norm of self-defense. For purposes of this analysis, it is useful to speculate about several different possible outcomes of the current proliferation dynamic. One is an evolutionary accretion of military capability: the piecemeal accumulation of military competence and hardware does little to change regional balances, the security of major states, or the functioning of existing international institutions. A second potential outcome is revolutionary: accumulation leads to instability if not war, erodes existing alliances, thereby encouraging states to pursue national self-reliance, and fosters an abandonment of reliance on collective security principles. A third outcome is transformational: states, finding themselves unable to achieve security through a weapons-based strategy of national self-reliance, seek new patterns of relations with potential adversaries based on cooperation and arms control.

In fact, in the 1990s, all three patterns are in evidence: the first in Southeast Asia, the second in the Middle East, although the pattern that has prevailed historically may be giving way, and the third in South America. This points to another weakness in the old nuclear nonproliferation model— its focus on proliferation as a global phenomenon, when it is of course something that occurs within individual countries, with implications that extend throughout specific regions. Today, proliferation must be seen in three dimensions: global, regional, and national.

For many in the security policy community, the proliferation threat succeeds the Soviet threat as the key organizing principle for formulating military strategies and regional and global security strategies. These are entirely legitimate and necessary tasks. But this threat-based view of the world dangerously skews thinking about the world order challenges that have emerged in the 1990s. The proliferation of weapons and military infrastructure leads many to the false conclusion that the problem of the twenty-first century will be the problem of deterring the use of all new high-leverage arsenals, by threatening not just denial of war gains but also punishment through retaliation with overwhelming military power, and perhaps retaliation with nuclear weapons for nuclear use by new nuclear powers. Seen in this light, neither an effective Security Council, strong alliances, nor a global policeman might credibly be expected to fight the tide of proliferation.

This is simply wrong-headed. Objectively, the threat of war among the great powers is extremely low and receding. Wars of conquest are virtually unknown. Interstate wars are receding dramatically as a problem of global affairs; within an overall declining number of conflicts, civil wars have become much more prevalent.[10] Moreover, economic interests among states are not only linked but enmeshed within an expanding trading system just as political interests are increasingly connected on a global basis. Somalia, Haiti, and to a lesser extent North Korea are essentially problems at the margins of the international agenda, despite their prominence in the media. Many attributes of order are to be found today, mostly derived from the benefits of economic and political association. They are by no means durable, but neither are they irrelevant, and tending to their foundations is a top priority in the 1990s.[11]

A threat-derived assessment of the proliferation dynamic blinds people to the simple fact that the primary implication of proliferation is not military but political. The primary immediate effect of the ongoing diffusion of the ability to make high-leverage weapons is the creation of a technically empowered tier of states that can, if they choose, build and use high-leverage military instruments. If the Iklé–Wohlstetter estimate is correct, it numbers about three dozen states beyond the established nuclear powers. If one factors in those possessing long-range delivery systems such as missiles, the number is smaller. If one factors in those capable of producing militarily significant quantities of chemical and biological weapons, the number is considerably larger.

The emergence of a tier of states technically capable of producing high-leverage weapons is unprecedented in international affairs. Its emergence is coterminous with the end of the Cold War. The intersection of these two processes constitutes the unique moment in world affairs today. How this tier of technically empowered states responds to the new circumstances

created by the end of the Cold War will be a critical determinant of the future character of the interstate system. Will they opt to exploit their weapons potential to buttress themselves in an uncertain world, thereby undermining global institutions and weakening regional security? Will they look upon proliferation as an incentive to move toward more cooperative relations with other states, thereby strengthening global norms and collective action? In short, their attitudes toward their weapons potential has a significance generally underappreciated in the West. And they should constitute the target of efforts to strengthen and expand the cooperative mechanisms of international order.

This tier of states is hardly a unified group; it is not the "South" envisaged by those who anticipate a future dominated by North–South conflict. It includes states as diverse as Germany and Egypt, Kazakhstan and India, Japan and Indonesia, Cuba and Argentina. Many if not most are secure and currently face few or no regional pressures to build new weapons capabilities—Germany and Argentina, for example. Some are in areas of insecurity but enjoy alliances that, so long as their guarantees remain credible, will dampen proliferation pressures—Turkey and Japan, for example. Some are in areas of instability but see no security in the long-term nuclearization of their regions—Belarus and South Africa, for example. Some see no alternative to nuclearization—Pakistan and North Korea, for example—or to acquisition of chemical and biological weapons—Syria and Iraq, for example. In many, growing economic ties with their neighbors and with the global trading systems provide new possibilities for avoiding arms races and their destabilizing aspects; on the other hand, the record suggests that

457

states with growing economies tend to spend more on arms, not just in gross but also in relative terms.[12] Many also enjoy the benefits of more open and stable systems of governance that have helped to dampen proliferation pressures, whether by permitting broader political contact with the international community, as in South Africa, or by changing the domestic political debate about the ingredients of national security and the proper balance of power among civil and military authorities. On the other hand, few developing countries also enjoy strong political institutions and domestic social harmony and thus their leaders may perceive themselves to be immersed in insecurity, thus generating pressures for strong military instruments—whatever their relevance, or lack thereof, for civil wars.

The New Tier in the New World Order

The course chosen by these states will be a basic determinant of the drift toward order and disorder in the world system. If they can be kept firmly involved in the international effort to prevent the militarization of conflicts, to control armaments, and to promote the cooperative resolution of common problems, the international community will have gone a very long way toward putting in place essential ingredients of a durable world order.

But if they drift away from these efforts, the consequences could be profound. At the very least, the effective functioning of inherited mechanisms of world order, such as the special responsibility of the "great powers" in the management of the interstate system, especially problems of armed aggression, under the aegis of collective security, could be significantly impaired. Armed with the

ability to defeat an intervention, or impose substantial costs in blood or money on an intervening force or on the populaces of the nations marshaling that force, the newly empowered tier could bring an end to collective security operations, undermine the credibility of alliance commitments by the great powers, extend alliances of their own, and perhaps make wars of aggression on their neighbors or their own peoples.

Of course, changes to the inherited mechanisms of world order may not necessarily bring disorder. Indeed, it is conceivable that the compulsion to respond to new forces of international politics and new security problems will generate new institutions, processes, or mechanisms that better serve the security agenda of the twenty-first century. But so far, at least, there is no indication of an awareness in the traditional nonproliferation community—and indeed in the foreign policy community in the West as a whole—of the agenda ahead or of the possibilities that may be opening up in future years.

Given the great variety among states in this tier, no single factor will determine whether individual states build or use high-leverage weapons. If the past proliferation behavior of threshold states is any guide, a multiplicity of military, political, and economic factors will be relevant to their decisions. But two broad factors will have a significant impact on all of these states.

One factor is the end of the Cold War. Historically, the Cold War provided a certain structure to their choices: the credibility of security guarantees extended by the superpowers prevented allies from moving to build their own weapons, while superpower fear of catalytic war arising in regions where interests conflicted generated strong incentives to limit regional wars to the conventional level. Within this rigid structure, implementation of a nonproliferation regime proved quite effective.

The passing of the Cold War has had repercussions in most regions of the world, leading to the resolution of some conflicts, as in Central Europe; the passing of old constellations of interest that underpinned particular regional orders, as in the Middle East; and the unleashing of new tensions and conflicts, as in Central Asia. We can no longer be so confident that the systemic disincentives to proliferation are as strong as they were or that nonproliferation tools will continue to enjoy their past efficacy as instruments of international security.

The second cross-cutting factor is the perceived utility of alternatives to national self-reliance in meeting the challenges of an uncertain era. For some, alliances with stronger states may well dampen proliferation incentives; but for how long and with what degree of certainty about their credibility? For others without alliances with strong powers or regional collective defense organizations, collective security principles will be important; but they too face questions of credibility. Yet others may question more broadly whether participation in a broad range of international institutions, such as the United Nations (UN) and the World Trade Organization (WTO), actually advances national interests in any sense; the international community does, after all, include states holding fundamentally different worldviews.

The management of the proliferation dynamic thus emerges as one of the central tasks of world order construction in the post–cold war era. If the process is managed in ways that enhance the security of key states, promote cooperation, and strengthen the

norms that shape the way nations decide to act, order will have been strengthened. But if it is managed in such a way that major international institutions are weakened and regions are destabilized, greater disorder will prevail, with consequences not just for international security but also for the broader transnational agenda related to the global trading system and the environment that now features so prominently in the international dialogue.

Among governments committed to preventing further proliferation, much of what has been done over recent decades has been productive. But because of the changing nature of the proliferation subject and the international political dynamic, business as usual will not suffice. In fact, the extension forward of past practice has already begun to be not only unhelpful but in some instances actually counterproductive. This is especially true of U.S. policy, where the outdated proliferation concept described above combines with a foreign policy that is reactive, crisis-oriented, and backed by only scant investments of political capital to work at cross-purposes with the need to meet the new proliferation challenge in a creative and forceful way.

Three missteps stand out in recent U.S. policy—missteps insofar as they affect the perceptions of this newly empowered tier. The first was the effort to reinvigorate strategies of technology and weapons denial that gripped policymakers during the late 1980s and early 1990s. Born of the belief that barriers to the flow of technology can effectively be constructed between industrial and developing or undeveloped countries, initiatives to expand and strengthen export controls and the associated coordinating mechanisms (such as the Australia Group for chemical and biological materials and the Missile Technology Control Regime for missiles) were combined with proposals to broaden the global nonproliferation regime beyond the nuclear domain into the chemical, biological, and missile areas.

But the broad diffusion of technology combined with the changing nature of high-leverage systems and the spread of the defense industrial base conspired to diminish the leverage of the industrial powers. And the basic political bargain embodied in the NPT, whereby some states enjoy formal recognition as weapon states while others do not, proved not to be replicable in other issue areas at the global level. Thus, after years of trying to strengthen these regimes, there is today a broader understanding that strategies of denial have only a limited, albeit important, role to play in the nonproliferation project. In general, only diminishing returns can be reaped for every new investment of political capital or bureaucratic energy in export controls.

Among the technically empowered tier are some states that participate in the effort to control dual-use technology exports. But many do not. Pakistan and Indonesia are representative of many states that believe that to put strategies of denial center stage in the global response to proliferation reflects a Western desire to keep the developing world both insecure and poor. They naturally criticize anything that suggests that the rich are willing to trade off the development aspirations of the poor in order to protect their own security and wealth. They also decry unilateral pronouncement by the rich of ostensibly global norms, arrived at without participation by the larger international community (as in the case of "norms" against missile proliferation).

In the negotiation of the Chemical Weapons Convention (CWC) in particular, these states sought to extract commitments from members of the Australia Group to abandon the suppliers' cartel approach and instead to work within the framework of the emerging disarmament treaty regime to manage the problem of states that misuse dual-use exports. (They succeeded in extracting a commitment by Australia Group members to review the group's activities after an unspecified period of treaty operation, with the presumption that it will cease to exist if the treaty is functioning well.) More fundamentally, these states tend to see these treaties as being about the security interests of the "North" and the development aspirations of the "South." States like Pakistan and Indonesia were willing to make concessions in the military domain deemed important by the West (such as forswearing chemical weapons and opening facilities to inspection) in exchange for expectations of enhanced commercial trade. These critics of the Western strategies of denial are numerous among the states of the new tier and are vigilant to prevent greater reliance on export controls and discriminatory measures in the years ahead.

The second misstep was encompassed in the counterproliferation strategy of the U.S. military. The problem is not with the strategy per se, which was born of the entirely reasonable beliefs that appropriate military planning for a proliferating world is an urgent priority and that such preparations by the United States will pay dividends in reassuring friends and allies overseas while deterring potential military adversaries.[13] Instead, the problem is with the political context—or lack thereof—within which the strategy was promulgated.

Originally, counterproliferation was

defined by some as an alternative to nonproliferation, or as the successor policy when nonproliferation had failed. This suggested that the United States was abandoning the nonproliferation effort in the wake of the unsettling discoveries about the weakness of the existing regime in safeguarding nuclear materials. To many in the developing world, the counterproliferation strategy suggests that the United States intends to make war on them, perhaps for the very purpose of denuding these states of weapons deemed unacceptable by the United States. It suggests to them a United States moving in its "unipolar moment" to aggressively police rules of its own making. Among the friends and allies of the United States are many who are unsure of its actual willingness or ability to perform such a role, given its history as a fickle great power, uncertain of its interests overseas and unwilling to consistently use its power even for stated purposes, as in Vietnam or Lebanon. Among potential adversaries, the fear of an overarmed and aggressive United States may well have accelerated the search for "asymmetric strategies." Such strategies seek to pit the strengths of the weak against the vulnerabilities of the strong; they threaten to inflict huge casualties on U.S. power projection forces and/or the U.S. populace through unconventional attack with unconventional weapons.[14]

Thus, the second misstep in U.S. policy was not counterproliferation per se but the failure to create a political and diplomatic context that made the necessary military preparations supportive of security policy generally. The initiative of the Department of Defense in this area thrust into the spotlight the paucity of thinking elsewhere in the U.S. government about the post–cold war security agenda. Un-

less the United States can begin to define security as a means to some larger end, and not just an end in itself that keeps America safe, it is unlikely to find broad support for its international security agenda among states other than its traditional allies.

The third misstep was to allow arms-control policy to fall into disarray. The new administration arrived in Washington with a notion to shrink the Arms Control and Disarmament Agency and end its tenure as an independent agency reporting directly to the president (in fact, just such a notion had been quietly debated by some in the previous administration). The resulting debate took many months to resolve and certainly reinforced the perception that arms control has little priority for the new administration, except in terms of its relevance for managing the consequences of Soviet collapse. Arms-control diplomacy has been pursued largely on an ad hoc basis, often by a corps of talented professionals working without meaningful political support from their superiors, who appear not even to understand the changing nature of the global arms-control agenda. The energy invested in securing extension of the NPT in April 1995 or to getting the new Chemical Weapons Convention entered into force is a mere pittance in comparison to the energy expended in managing the crisis in North Korea. Yet that crisis fully illustrates the relevance of global norms and mechanisms for successfully managing specific crises. Furthermore, ad hocism has reinforced the view, widespread among U.S. experts today, that proliferation is a problem separate and distinct from arms control. It is still common to hear policymakers define arms control as an instrument for managing East–West relations and nonproliferation as an instrument for managing North–South relations—but the only place in which they are meaningfully separable appears to be in Washington bureaucratic politics.

The ad hoc nature of U.S. arms-control diplomacy has combined with the seeming inability of senior political leadership in the administration to articulate the issues involved in preventing proliferation. Nonproliferation is praised as a civic virtue but its value as an instrument of national security for nations other than the United States is rarely noted. This has nurtured a concern among both friends and potential adversaries among the new tier that the United States is simply going through the motions, unaware of the stakes, unconcerned about the breakdown of existing treaties, unmindful of the insecurities that might be generated and that themselves might drive some states to consider acquiring these weapons.

The reactive character of U.S. policy has also given a great deal of leverage to states that seek to exploit their nascent weapons capabilities for political or economic gain. No one can dispute the importance of managing the crises in East Asia and in Central and Southwest Asia; but most would deplore a diplomacy seemingly driven by crisis, reactive to the initiatives of those who do not share U.S. interests, and devoid of a sense of where the international security dynamic needs to be in a decade or two and how the United States can help lead it there.

In relations with this newly empowered tier, a singling out of the proliferation problem as the major or sole theme only accentuates the problem. This gives states of the South reason to believe that the North little understands or cares about their security problems and also reason to fear punitive Northern attack. In response the South resorts to armaments and rheto-

ric that induce the North to sustain large and modernized nuclear weapon stockpiles for possible North–South conflict.[15] Ironically, if overaccentuating the theme has these effects, too little attention might well convey lack of interest, with the result that newly emboldened states might seek to acquire or use arms to test the limits of the North's will.[16]

None of this is to argue that the United States and other states interested in halting weapons proliferation should not have sought to strengthen export controls, improve the capacity of the U.S. military to prevail on battlefields where unconventional weapons might be present, or rethink arms-control approaches after the Cold War. These are all necessary ingredients of a successful strategy to contain proliferation and its consequences. But they are only a few of the building blocks necessary for success. If pursued in the absence of a larger strategy that integrates policy elements in coherent fashion and that is informed by the political context within which the proliferation dynamic is unfolding, their actual contributions to the intended goal will be disappointing, when not actually counterproductive.

The 1995 Agenda

Getting beyond these missteps of policy does not require formulation of a grand, new, comprehensive global political agenda. In fact, just such an agenda is being forced upon the United States and the international community in 1995. By simple coincidence, the year brings with it a series of major decisions about most of the significant elements of the global "system"—the major institutions of disarmament and arms control, collective security, and the trading system. Analysts tend to view the forthcoming events as disconnected and unrelated; one of the central theses of this article is that the reverse is true, because of the political connections among these events as perceived by the newly empowered tier. The year will prove a genuine turning point. Basic international institutions will end the year either much strengthened or much weakened. And as argued above, the outcome will depend critically on decisions states in the new tier make about the United States in the interim.

The year 1995 will be the critical year for the global treaty regime for the control of nuclear, chemical, and biological weapons. During the year, the NPT will be considered for review and extension; at this writing in autumn 1994, the proponents of indefinite and unconditional extension face an uphill battle, although the consequences of anything less for the credibility of the regime could be considerable. Also in 1995, the new CWC will either enter into force or give way rapidly to inertia and ennui; in autumn 1994, the latter tendency prevails. In late 1995 or early 1996, a review conference of the Biological and Toxin Weapons Convention (BWC) will be convened to consider the addition of a compliance protocol, not included in the disarmament agreement negotiated in the early 1970s; here, good progress has been made in 1994 under the VEREX exercise,[17] but the successful addition of meaningful new provisions will depend fundamentally on what happens first to the NPT and CWC.

The importance of this global treaty regime to management of the proliferation problem may seem obvious, but its basic purpose is often misconceived by Western speakers. The regime is more accurately characterized as a control and disarmament regime than as a nonproliferation regime. Two of its three primary elements—the CWC and BWC—entail equal obligations for all signatories; developed and developing alike forswear all such weapons. The third—the NPT—is interpreted by many non-nuclear weapon states as establishing equal disarmament obligations as a long-term goal. If the NPT is given only weak endorsement in April, the CWC languishes, and the BWC remains devoid of compliance mechanisms, the next decade may well witness a broad diffusion of these weapons, a redistribution of military power away from the advanced industrial countries highly interested in stability, and outbreaks of the regional instabilities associated with conventional and unconventional arms races. But if they are well tended and strengthened, the international community will have the essential tools for beginning to work more productively on the proliferation problem (there being, of course, no guarantee that it will also use these tools well).

Governmental and nongovernmental experts have generated a raft of ideas for strengthening the nuclear nonproliferation regime, building up an effective chemical disarmament regime, and strengthening the BWC compliance mechanism. Talented individuals with strong commitment to each regime are laboring to succeed in these tasks. But their various "fixes" are by and large a poor substitute for a strategy that puts this global treaty regime center stage in the effort to stem proliferation. The NPT and BWC have been weak in the past not just or even primarily because they lacked certain provisions; rather, they were not invested with the fiscal resources, intelligence support, and above all political will of states parties, minor and major alike. There is a widespread tendency to treat them as legal instrumentalities rather than political bargains codified in treaty form. But it is

463

their political content and character that gives them their importance.

Both the NPT and the BWC are of an era now past, with firm roots in the political realities of the Cold War. The CWC is very much a product of the Cold War, although finished on the cusp of the transition to the present era. Absent the balance of forces and strategic constellation that brought them into force, how will they be sustained politically? Not by inertia alone.

The NPT is the linchpin in the global treaty regime. If the April 1995 conference is bungled, the CWC and BWC will also suffer. In the Clinton administration's first two years it has done little more than conduct straw poll votes in anticipation of the April conference.[18] If the technically empowered tier is to sustain a meaningful commitment to the NPT, however, the United States must do much more at the extension conference and beyond. As the world's leading nuclear power—and as the only state ever to use nuclear weapons in war (1995 is also the fiftieth anniversary of this event)—the United States has a special responsibility for taking the lead in articulating and pursuing a vision of international politics and of an allocation of nuclear rights and responsibilities that is politically sustainable in the period ahead. Such a vision must seek to link the concept of nuclear obligations by the existing weapon states to the management of new, not cold war vintage, security challenges.[19]

Among the new tier are many who look at the Clinton administration and wonder if it has any interest in attempting this project. In addition to the reactive nature of U.S. foreign policy at this time and the ad hoc nature of arms-control diplomacy, they note the leisurely pace with which the administration completed reviews of its national security and nuclear strategies

(both completed in summer 1994) as well as a tendency to view those seeking weapons of high leverage as dangerous, uncivilized, "backlash" states.

But the debate about a future nuclear control regime is a debate that must be begun. Within the nuclear-capable states are many who wonder whether the United States has the foresight to start this debate and shape it; so too should U.S. voters. It is on this question of nuclear rights and responsibilities that the trust placed by others in the United States—and in the international system it purports to lead—will be relevant. Do they believe that the emperor has no clothes? Do they outwardly honor American leadership while enriching themselves at U.S. expense and garnering resources against the day of a U.S. demise?

In the United States a general complacency prevails that this treaty regime can and will be strengthened. U.S. diplomats privately assert that whatever the shortcomings of U.S. diplomacy, other states will simply conclude that their own national security is better served with these regimes than without them. Indeed, few in the United States seem to notice that the consensus is under duress. What passes for thinking about the new world order agenda often ranges little beyond the laments of policy pundits about renegade or decomposing states immersed in a broadening sea of instability. The United States tends to turn a deaf ear to the concerns of some members of the international community on questions related to its role and power. By friends and allies as well as adversaries, the United States is today sometimes perceived as arrogant in its unwillingness to discuss competing perceptions of how power and authority might be marshaled in these institutions. The essentially reactive posture of the United States at this time, and its apparent unwillingness to invest political capital in renewing these world order institutions, is criticized publicly and privately by many. Some also fear not just a breakdown in the global security structure but also a capricious United States, either unwilling to pay costs associated with larger shared purposes or enjoying its "unipolar moment" in the way that so many dominant powers have in the past—by using force internationally virtually without immediately apparent cost or risk.

The year 1995 is also the occasion of the fiftieth anniversary of the UN, which is certain to precipitate a debate about the UN's role in addressing the post–cold war security agenda, the credibility of the collective security principle, the allocation of rights and responsibilities at the UN, and the role, structure, and rights of the Security Council and its permanent members. The conflicts in Somalia and Bosnia have dashed the hopes of many that collective security would be resurrected as a principle of international security after the end of the Cold War. But dashed hopes should not turn attention away from the important task of making the best possible use of the imperfect instrument of collective security in this new era. Especially for the United States, a country with a strong isolationist impulse and a noteworthy fickleness in its international "entanglements," collective security is an essential tool for managing the security challenges of the 1990s and beyond.

How is collective security important to the management of the proliferation problem? The history of the Western alliance is a reminder that if the major military powers are to derive the deterrence and reassurance benefits of military forces, they must also attend to the credibility of the threat to employ them. Collective security is relevant because it helps generate the domestic support to go to war and the international legitimacy to win the peace. It provides a measure of reassurance to those who fear the capricious use of U.S. power, by tying that power in some ways to common purposes. It also lashes the United States to an international institution and agenda, thereby increasing the likelihood of continued U.S. engagement and thus dampening proliferation pressures among those who would acquire arms as a hedge against the local security consequences of possible U.S. disengagement. Moreover, the Security Council's January 1992 declaration that proliferation is a threat to international peace serves notice of the intention of the permanent members of the Council to stay centrally involved in the proliferation problem.[20]

If the international community is to reap these nonproliferation benefits of a rejuvenated collective security mechanism, more will be required than simply more forceful leadership by the United States in the Security Council. Overemphasizing U.S. prominence on the Security Council would be foolhardy. Many developing countries already view the Security Council as a kangaroo court, falling under the hegemony of five states that happened to win a war half a century ago, or of one, the "sole remaining superpower." More vigorous use of the Security Council for enforcement purposes in instances where there is not broad international consensus may well cause some among the new tier to seek a more independent course as a counterweight to a balance of power they believe to be unjust—or at least unbalanced.[21]

With the pending anniversary, it is increasingly common to hear diplomats from developing countries talk about the UN Charter as representing a political bargain about the distribution of power and authority internationally, a bargain rooted in a historical epoch now well past. Is this bargain sustainable? Indeed, does it even in fact exist? Can disparate states find mutual accommodation in a modified bargain that still provides for an uneven distribution of power? Where does reform of the Security Council membership and voting rights fit into this problem? There are no ready answers to these questions. Quick fixes, such as the addition of new members to the Council, are unlikely to prove effective—what will new members unable to use military power or with deep aversions to intervention and existing treaty modalities do to improve the capacity of the Security Council to discharge its functions of dealing with major threats to the peace and with securing compliance with the global treaty regime?

Unfortunately, few in the United States concern themselves with these issues. The administration is increasingly perceived (accurately or not) as having abandoned its early commitment to multilateralism and, as a bystander in the debate about UN reform, willing to acquiesce to any good ideas put forward by others.[22]

The coming year will also be a year of decision for the international trading system. It will either take firm steps forward or suffer major new difficulties. The laboriously negotiated Uruguay Round of the General Agreement on Tariffs and Trade (GATT) sets out plans for a new world trade organization. The North American Free Trade Agreement (NAFTA) will enter into force in 1995. Implementation of both promises to be difficult, because states must ratify the new GATT agreement in the face of strong domestic opposition in many countries, developed and developing alike, and NAFTA must begin to deal with the tough issues of Mexican integration into the new trade system. Despite the momentum behind both agreements, obstacles to their effective implementation remain. The odds that both will work as well as they might can be increased significantly with a U.S. diplomatic strategy that gives them prominence and importance. Observers overseas will watch the administration to ascertain whether a "new Democrat" takes charge to promote free trade or the old heart of the party resurfaces in a fit of Japan-bashing, jobs promotion, and America-firstism. If the global arms-control treaties and the UN fall prey to a deepening debate about their long-term goals and the quality of U.S. leadership, we can expect these heretofore quite separate trade-related mechanisms to become increasingly prominent in the larger international debate.

Why is the free trade agenda important to management of the proliferation problem? Not just because of what others will learn about the attitude of the United States toward leadership of an international economy largely of its own creation. More important, a strong and healthy global trading system provides an escape from the view of export controls as instruments to force backwardness and insecurity on the poor. In a robust trading system, such controls serve increasingly as "trade enabling regimes"[23] that establish the conditions whereby exchange occurs and economic interdependence deepens. In a global trading system, where lots of goods and services are moving across borders, the set of economic and political interests shared by states expands, as do the incentives to ensure that dual-use technologies are used in ways that do not threaten larger interests.

Thus, for the technically empowered tier, 1995 will be a year in which each of the major elements of the global political framework are evaluated and refashioned. States in the tier will ask not just how well these elements have worked in the past; they will also look to the future. They will weigh the expected functioning of these regimes in terms of their own national interests. They will wonder whether these regimes are led sufficiently well to offer meaningful promise of future efficacy; they will also question whether there is room at the table for a bit of leadership of their own. They will, in essence, look through these regimes to the United States. As the purported leader of the international community, its credentials are under review. As the world's sole remaining superpower, it generates both hope and fear—while harboring some suspicion of those who would check its credentials.

They will hardly need a microscope to detect the broad themes of U.S. foreign policy at this time. Their concerns about export controls and counterproliferation will resonate with recognition that the Clinton administration and its Republican opponents have abandoned multilateralism as a guiding principle. Among the newly empowered tier are many who share the concern of U.S. voters about "the vision thing." Among those who fear a rudderless America are both friends and potential foes—friends because uncertainty about the international role of the United States casts doubts on the credibility of its commitments, and foes because the world's only superpower has tremendous room to use its power to sole advantage.

Of course, some will look beyond the global role and responsibilities of the United States to its regional roles. Appreciation of an essentially benign United States, whose stable commitment, military presence, and security guarantees make a tangible contribution to positive regional dynamics can be found among many states in the Middle East and Far East. The same may be true of many states in Latin America. Yet in South Asia, Central Asia, and Africa, the regional role of the United States may do less to restore luster to its global credentials.

The widely varied strategic orientations of states of the new tier may be brought into rapid convergence if questions about the world role of the United States sufficiently crystalize to act as a lightning rod. If the United States comes to be perceived as a status quo power unable to look after anything but its own narrow self-interests, international institutions will suffer. If the United States cannot craft with others a vision of progress toward a more pacific and prosperous future, opponents of that status quo will surely gain broader currency. If a split between status quo and dissatisfied powers emerges, a North–South political dynamic will coalesce that will interfere with the accomplishment of major shared purposes. In late 1994 it appears unlikely that many states among the new tier want to abandon existing modalities of international order. But others will join their cause if, through a failure to revitalize the consensus about the means and ends of international security, the United States helps to precipitate a confrontation between states resentful of U.S. power and those fearful of change.

Getting to 1996

Failure to achieve a new global political bargain could have the effect of driving the proliferation problem well beyond the capacity of the United States or the Security Council to handle using only existing mechanisms and the military forces likely to be preserved in an era of fiscal restraint and strategic retreat. Dramatic failure, meaning failure to extend the NPT, would certainly doom the other treaties and would probably bring with it gridlock at the UN and major problems in the free trade movement. Not every state among the new tier is likely to move quickly to build weapons; but many would probably decide that it is prudent to hedge their bets by assembling the ingredients of a virtual arsenal. Whether proliferation might also lead to more, and more lethal, wars, is an open question; with greater confidence we might expect that new strategic arsenals will be used to deter intervention or to exert hegemony over regional neighbors. In this context, what new arsenals do emerge should be seen as hedges against uncertainty and thus in some sense symptoms of a deeper malady in the international system, and not just as problems in and of themselves.

A less dramatic form of failure but failure nonetheless would be the continued functioning of these treaties and institutions in form but not substance. If, for example, NPT extension is secured by forcing a majority vote and not working for consensus, the result could well be a decision among some leading members of the new tier to begin to put together a virtual nuclear arsenal while standing in the way of the CWC and a strengthened BWC and developing an arsenal of biological weapons as an interim measure; it would be a tragedy indeed if the nuclear era were to be succeeded by an era dominated by biological weapons.[24] If the process of strengthening the global treaty regime grinds to a stop

but does not also bring about its collapse, the international community will have lost the benefits of the openness and transparency these regimes are creating among long-time adversaries. Enforcement operations by major interested powers are also likely to emerge as sources of sharp acrimony in the international system.

If this happens, the United States will not have lost its place at the head table, but it might well find itself overruled by erstwhile friends or squandering scarce capital to regain its seat at the center. If it cannot define a global role for itself other than that of primary defender of a fragile status quo, domestic tensions between engagement and isolation will only intensify. Domestic repercussions could be substantial, not just in lost jobs but in the political corrosiveness of cynicism born of an image of America not generous but mean-spirited, not cooperative but imperious, not benign but suspect—evoking painful memories of the Vietnam era.

If the coming year brings success in meeting these challenges, credit will be due to many: to those states in the developing and developed world playing key roles in extending the NPT, building up the CWC, and strengthening the BWC; to those international civil servants who keep international mechanisms functioning; and to those national leaders who sustain the commitment to free trade in the face of staunch domestic opposition. A successful 1995 cannot be delivered by the United States alone—even with the most visionary and assertive leadership. In this new era the United States is at best primus inter pares, leading partner to a great many influential states, developed and developing alike.

But the converse is also true: success

cannot be achieved without U.S. leadership. Many will despair that the United States is so impaired at this critical moment when it should exercise such leadership. But the leadership required here is not the leadership for which students of the Cold War plead. The attempted restoration of U.S. dominance of international events would be inappropriate in an era when so many newly empowered states seek to play a larger world role. It would indeed be counterproductive, driving them away from cooperation with the United States. Moreover, such a restoration is beyond the reach of the United States at this time.

Between ennui and hegemony is a middle ground well suited to American characteristics, resources, and competence. On each of the agenda items cited above, rules need to be negotiated, debates need to be led, decisions need to be enforced collectively. The United States is well suited to cooperative engagement on these terms, to offering stewardship of common interests, to serving as a catalyst to generate change, to building on the investments of the past to derive new dividends in the future. This is a notion of leadership born of the idea that for one to lead, others must want to follow. The United States can only lead on arms control, nuclear diplomacy, collective security, and the international economy if it is working from a position accorded it by others to safeguard shared interests; others will want to follow only if they have played a role in defining a basic direction and the rules of the road. The more simple-minded leadership that asserts narrowly defined U.S. interests aggressively and pursues them dogmatically is bound to prove counterproductive in an era when other states no longer need to tolerate a perfidious great power.

Such leadership will coalesce only if new consensus can be built in the United States and overseas about a vision of the emerging global agenda and of the United States in advancing that agenda. If the vision is to be realized, the United States must be able to act with a degree of consistency and firmness that has not always marked its foreign policy—although they were hallmarks of the anti-Communist campaign. But the test awaiting the United States is not whether it can attain new levels of consistency in its foreign policy or new levels of willingness to use force in support of diplomacy often and decisively; on both points, expectations about the ability of the United States are already well formed. Rather, this will be a test of the nation's ability to articulate the national interest and the interests of the global community, to tie the two together as much as possible, and to act consistently *enough* and to use force *when critical* to bring that vision into being. For the United States, this will mean playing the policeman's role only in support of negotiated rules among nations, as in support of the global treaty norms or in maintaining balanced great power relations, as in East Asia. Where such rules are not yet agreed, this will mean expressing the urgency for them and taking the initiative in defining the terms of debate. This is a test of foresight. And if the large political challenges associated with the emerging agenda are also clearly perceived, this will also be a test of U.S. courage.

Unfortunately, in many segments of U.S. society—government, academe, and the media—a sense of fatalism prevails. The view that the new world disorder has indeed replaced George

Bush's new world order is firmly entrenched. These fatalists opine that any successes in 1995 will prove meaningless in a sea of deepening instability and profound doubt about the will or capacity of the United States or other benign powers to act internationally.

This cynicism is nourished by the basic misreading of the proliferation subject itself described above, and the view that in an era of proliferation the only important world order task is replacing cold war–vintage structures of containment with new structures of global deterrence so that overarmed renegades will not go to war. The primary world order task of the 1990s is not deterring the new tier of technically empowered states—it is integrating them deeper into the existing, well-formed patterns and processes of cooperation and assurance. Their engagement will also require engagement by the United States—engagement not solely or even primarily of its military or economic power, but of its political standing, capacity for vision, and reputation as a benign power with a historic willingness to contribute its advantages of power, wealth, and political energy in the service of common global purposes.

For the near term, it would be foolhardy to expect a lot of progress in the United States in meeting these new challenges. Clinton administration shortcomings, described earlier, are an important part of the problem—but only that. No administration could rapidly come to terms with a fundamentally changed world. In an era of growing partisanship in national politics and of growing public disaffection, early achievement of a broad and deep national consensus about the U.S. world role is probably out of the question. But the process must begin—and it will begin only if there is a sense of

urgency about beginning the journey. With the decisions of 1995 looming before us, it is time to move on from the shallow second-guessing of a reactive foreign policy to a better and more thorough debate about the necessary ingredients of a just and secure world order. Unless the United States can begin with itself and others such a debate, others will surely emerge to set its terms.

Conclusion

Since proliferation emerged as a subject of concern in the 1950s and 1960s, it has sat at the margins of public and governmental concern, overshadowed by the East–West conflict, coming center stage only at rare moments. With the end of the Cold War, proliferation has achieved much greater prominence. The widespread tendency to evoke old models to understand its new dynamics is lamentable, for wrapped inside the proliferation subject are many of the technical, military, economic, and political questions around which the successor world order is being built.

Proliferation's primary impact on the international system is the empowerment of a new tier of states capable of building high-leverage military instruments if they have the will to do so. This tier is composed of a motley group of states, most of which aspire to greater regional and global prominence and that look to the international system for economic and security benefits. For this category of states, 1995 will be a pivotal year. The nature of their participation or nonparticipation in a broad array of global institutions and regimes will be determined then. Their decisions will be made on the basis of their expectations about whether those institutions and regimes serve their national interest, whether there is room for them to play a leading role, and whether the established powers also have their best interests at heart. The United States seeks their full participation and even at times seems to take it for granted. But there is little that suggests that the United States understands the unfolding diplomacy or the stakes for its own interests if 1995 goes badly.

For this new tier of technically empowered states, 1995 marks the end of the post–cold war era. A new era will begin, marked by the effects of their own diplomacy and national actions. Either they will embrace the United States as a power deserving of international leadership. Or they will foster the continuation of a leading U.S. role in a frustrated effort to keep the United States engaged. Or they will abandon existing international mechanisms, whether openly or surreptitiously, out of a concern that the United States, too preoccupied with its domestic agenda and too concerned to preserve the status quo, does not have their best interests at heart.

If the United States turns a blind eye to these decisions, it will surely have missed one of the great opportunities to shape future world order. The nation will then spend decades debating not who lost the war, but who lost the peace.

The author has received many thoughtful responses to the arguments advanced here but would like to recognize particularly the contributions of Michael Moodie, Joseph Pilat, and Victor Utgoff.

Notes

1. See Evgenii Primakov, director of the Foreign Intelligence Service of the Russian Federation, "A New Challenge after the Cold War: The Proliferation of Weapons of Mass Destruction," a report prepared by the Foreign Intelligence Service of the Russian Federation, Moscow, 1993, translated by U.S. Foreign Broadcast Informa-

tion Service in February 1993. Summary and excerpts made available by U.S. Committee on Governmental Affairs, U.S. Senate, February 24, 1993, and subsequently published in *Proliferation Threats of the 1990's*, Hearing before the Committee on Governmental Affairs, U.S. Senate, 103d Cong., 1st sess., February 24, 1993 (Washington, D.C.: GPO, 1993).

2. Andrew L. Ross, "Do-It-Yourself Weaponry," *Bulletin of the Atomic Scientists* 46 (May 1990), p. 20. See also Ralph Sanders, *Arms Industries: New Suppliers and Regional Security* (Washington, D.C.: National Defense University, 1990); and U.S. Congress, Office of Technology Assessment, *Global Arms Trade: Commerce in Advanced Military Technology and Weapons*, OTA-ISC-460 (Washington, D.C.: GPO, June 1991).

3. OTA, *Global Arms Trade*, p. 1.

4. Stephanie Neuman, "The Arms Market: Who's on Top?" *Orbis* 33 (Fall 1989), p. 511.

5. *Discriminate Deterrence*, Report of the Commission on Integrated Long-Term Strategy, Fred C. Iklé and Albert Wohlstetter, cochairmen (Washington, D.C.: GPO, 1988).

6. William C. Potter, "The New Nuclear Suppliers," *Orbis* 36 (Spring 1992), pp. 199–200.

7. Benjamin Frankel, *Opaque Nuclear Proliferation: Methodological and Policy Implications* (London: Frank Cass, 1991), p. 3, especially fn. 8.

8. Roger C. Molander and Peter A. Wilson, *The Nuclear Asymptote: On Containing Nuclear Proliferation*, MR-214-CC (Santa Monica, Calif.: RAND/UCLA Center for Soviet Studies, 1993). See also Roger C. Molander and Peter A. Wilson, "On Dealing with the Prospect of Nuclear Chaos," *The Washington Quarterly* 17 (Summer 1994), pp. 19–39.

9. An important exception should be noted in the case of the "bomb in the basement" in the Middle East. Benjamin Frankel offers a thoughtful assessment of the way in which the processes of so-called opaque nuclear proliferation challenge the models developed for understanding nuclearization of the relationship among states. See Frankel, *Opaque Nuclear Proliferation*. His conceptual framework offers useful touch-

stones for speculating about the stability consequences of illicit chemical and biological weapons programs as well as the implications of the emergence of larger numbers of "virtual weapon states."

10. According to one survey, not a single *interstate* armed conflict occurred in 1993. All 47 active armed conflicts were internal. See Peter Wallensteen and Karin Axell, "Conflict Resolution and the End of the Cold War, 1989–93," *Journal of Peace Research* 31 (Summer 1994), pp. 333–349.

11. Paul W. Schroeder, "Rediscovering the New World Order," *The Washington Quarterly* 17 (Spring 1994), pp. 25–43. See also Janne E. Nolan, ed., *Global Engagement: Cooperation and Security in the 21st Century* (Washington, D.C.: Brookings Institution, 1994).

12. See Daniel Hewitt, "Controlling Military Expenditures: Military Expenditures in the Developing World," *Finance & Development* 28 (September 1991), pp. 22–25; and Hewitt, "What Determines Military Expenditures?" *Finance & Development* 28 (December 1991), pp. 22–25.

13. See speech entitled "The Defense Department's New Nuclear Counterproliferation Initiative" by Secretary of Defense Les Aspin to a public meeting of the National Academy of Sciences, Washington, D.C., December 7, 1993.

14. Thomas G. Mahnken, "America's Next War," *The Washington Quarterly* 16 (Summer 1993), pp. 171–184; and Patrick J. Garrity, *Does the Gulf War Still Matter? Foreign Perspectives on the War and the Future of International Security*, CNSS Report no. 16 (Los Alamos, N.M.: Center for National Security Studies, Los Alamos National Laboratory, May 1993).

15. See Shahram Chubin, "Southern Perspectives on World Order," *The Washington Quarterly* 16 (Autumn 1993), pp. 87–107; and Ali E. Hillal Dessouki, "Globalization and the Two Spheres of Security," *The Washington Quarterly* 16 (Autumn 1993), pp. 109–117.

16. Parts of this argument are drawn from Brad Roberts, "NPT Extension, International Security, and the End of the Cold War," in Marianne van Leeuwen, ed., *The Future of the Nuclear Non-Proliferation Treaty* (Dordrecht, The Netherlands: Martinus Nijhoff Publishers with the Netherlands Institute of International Relations, forthcoming).

17. Edward J. Lacey, "Tackling the Biological Weapons Threat: The Next Proliferation Challenge," *The Washington Quarterly* 17 (Autumn 1994), pp. 53–64.

18. Mitchell Reiss, "April 1995: The Last Nuclear Summit?" *The Washington Quarterly* 17 (Summer 1994), pp. 5–15.

19. George H. Quester and Victor A. Utgoff have set down some markers in this debate in their article, "Toward an International Nuclear Security Policy," *The Washington Quarterly* 17 (Autumn 1994), pp. 5–18.

20. Security Council statement of January 31, 1992, United Nations Security Council, S/23500, January 31, 1992, Report no. 92-04224F.

21. Thomas G. Weiss, ed., *Collective Security in a Changing World* (Boulder, Colo.: Lynne Rienner, 1993); and Thomas G. Weiss and Meryl A. Kessler, eds., *Third World Security in the Post–Cold War Era*, A World Peace Foundation Study (Boulder, Colo.: Lynne Rienner, 1991).

22. Donald J. Puchala, "Outsiders, Insiders, and UN Reform," *The Washington Quarterly* 17 (Autumn 1994), pp. 161–173.

23. I am indebted to Terence Taylor for introducing me to this way of thinking about the problem.

24. Many in the security policy community dismiss the possible military and political consequences of the greater diffusion of biological weapons. For the most part, their views were formed in the 1960s, at a time when the relevant technologies were fairly primitive and the nuclear weapon was paramount in U.S. thinking and strategy, and were given little subsequent consideration once the United States ceased producing biological weapons in 1969. But the biotechnology revolution of the last two decades may yet prove to have nearly the same importance for the military applications of biology as the nuclear revolution has had for the military applications of physics. For a discussion of the changing nature of the problem of biological warfare in the 1990s, see Brad Roberts, ed., *Biological Weapons: Weapons of the Future?* Significant Issues Series 15 (Washington, D.C.: CSIS, 1993). For a discussion of the task of addressing simultaneously the

problems of nuclear, biological, and chemical weapons, see Victor A. Utgoff, "Observations on the Long-Term Future of the Chemical Weapons Convention," in Kyle Olson and Benoit Morel, eds., *The Chemical Convention: The Shadow and the Substance* (Boulder, Colo.: Westview Press, 1993), pp. 95–114.